LITERATURE
FOR TODAY'S
YOUNG ADULTS

Third Edition

LITERATURE FOR TODAY'S YOUNG ADULTS

Third Edition

Kenneth L. Donelson
Arizona State University

Alleen Pace Nilsen
Arizona State University

Scott, Foresman and Company
Glenview, Illinois   London

◆ To Bob Carlsen
partly for what he has done in a lifetime of service to young adult literature,
but mostly for what he has done for each of us

Cover and part opener illustrations by Nanette Biers

The authors and publishers would like to thank all sources for the use of their material. The credit lines for copyrighted materials appearing in this work appear in the
Acknowledgments section beginning on page 589. This section is to be considered an
extension of the copyright page.

Library of Congress Cataloging in Publication Data

Donelson, Kenneth L.
    Literature for today's young adults / Kenneth L. Donel-
son, Alleen Pace Nilsen.—3rd ed.
        p. cm.
    Bibliography
    Includes indexes.
    ISBN 0-673-38400-4
    1. Youth—Books and reading. 2. Teenagers—Books and
reading. 3. Young adults—Books and reading. 4. Young
adult literature—Bibliography. 5. Young adult literature—
History and criticism. 6. Bibliography—Best books—Young
adult literature. I. Nilsen, Alleen Pace. II. Title
Z1037.A1D578 1989
011′.62—dc19   88-31250
                                                      CIP

    3 4 5 6 - RRC - 93 92 91 90

Preface

As we said in the preface to the second edition, revising *Literature for Today's Young Adults* is an obligation *and* an opportunity, for the field of young adult books continually changes and develops. Accordingly, changes in this edition were necessary throughout as we tried to balance the need to include the latest books with the need to include the best in the field, no matter what the copyright date.

We added a new chapter on the symbiotic relationship between mass media, big business, and the books that young people read. One of the results of this beneficial relationship made the opening pages of our first and second editions obsolete. We said that no major prizes were given for adolescent literature, but at the 1988 American Library Association annual meeting, S. E. Hinton received a check for $1,000, a plaque, and a citation as the first winner of the *School Library Journal*/Young Adult Services Division YA Author Award. Plans are to give this award every other year. Given the many fine writers whose works are discussed in this book, the future selection committees should have no trouble finding candidates.

Suggestions from users of this text led us to give more attention to the psychology of the adolescent, to add to the sections on short stories and magazines, to expand our treatment of television and movies, and to develop further the ways in which teachers can use adolescent literature as a tool in teaching written and oral communication skills. To allow for the added material, we streamlined our writing and cut some portions of the three historical chapters (Chapters 13, 14, and 15). Alleen Nilsen was mainly responsible for Chapters 1 through 4, 8, and 10, while Kenneth Donelson was responsible for 5 through 7 and 12 through 15. Chapters 9 and 11 were collaborations. Teaching suggestions have been deleted since they will be covered in a separate instructor's manual written by Betsy Gray.

At the end of each genre chapter in this edition (Chapters 3 through 9) are "30 Recommendations for Reading" which should make it easier for teachers to balance the reading and discussion in their classes. With one chapter, teachers might want to pass around a photocopy of the list as a sign-up sheet so that all the books would be read and talked about. With another chapter, teachers might assign small groups to read from one set and then make group presentations. However teachers decide to use the lists, they should remember that the books are recommended, not engraved in mosaic stone.

We had many reasons for wanting to write this book, but chief among them was our belief that it was needed and worth doing. When in the late 1970s we surveyed teachers of YA literature in library science, English, and education departments, an overwhelming majority expressed a need for a scholarly and readable book to provide history and background for the field. One teacher wrote that her major problem "in establishing and promoting the work of the course was the sometimes skeptical view of colleagues about the worth of this literature," and added that she would welcome a book to educate professionals in related fields about the growing body of good YA books. We hope our book answers some of these needs, not just for academic classes in YA literature but also for librarians, teachers, counselors, and others working with young people between the ages of twelve and twenty.

For our purposes, we define "young adult literature" as any book freely chosen for reading by someone in this age group. We use "young adult" rather than "adolescent" because many people, students particularly, find the word "adolescent" condescending. In this text, we do not make the distinction made by many teachers and a few librarians between books distributed by juvenile divisions and adult divisions of publishing houses because young people read and enjoy both.

We organized the book much as we teach our undergraduate courses: first, an introduction to young adults, their psychology, and their literature; then a look at contemporary books; and finally a view of the professional's role in working with books and young readers. We moved the historical chapters to the end of the book in the second edition. We left them there in the third edition because we continue to believe that while they may be interesting, in part, to undergraduates, they are basic for graduate students who are seriously interested in the field.

Throughout the text, we present criteria for evaluating various kinds of books. Evaluation is always difficult and complicated, and one adventure novel or romance, for example, is so different from another adventure novel or romance that any pretense toward definitive criteria would be foolish. These criteria, then, should be taken as tentative starting places. Developing evaluation skills comes only with wide reading and practice in comparing books and matching them to particular needs.

Because so many excellent books appear each year, lists of recommended titles must be supplemented with the help of current reviewing sources and annual lists of best books compiled by the American Library Association's Young Adult Services Division, *School Library Journal, Booklist*, the *New York Times, VOYA,* and the *English Journal.*

Although we know that paperbacks are far more widely read by young people than the original hardbound books, we show the hardback publishers in our book lists. We do this for two reasons. First, we want to give credit to companies who found the authors and did the editorial labor and the first promotions of each book. Second, by relying on the hardback publishers, we were able to be more consistent and more accurate. The paperback publishing industry is fluid, and a title may be published and then go out of print within a few months. For any of the books we have listed, we recommend that readers refer to the most recent issue of *Paperbound Books in Print* published annually (with periodic supplements) by R. R. Bowker Company and purchased by most libraries.

For help in preparing the third edition, we again need to acknowledge the support of the English Department and the Graduate College at Arizona State University. We thank Dorris Moloso and Jane Sanderson for help with word processing and graduate assistant Jenny Donaldson for library research. We thank friends and colleagues whose ideas and words we admire and respect so much that they have probably found their way into our pages more than we realize—particularly *English Journal* YA book review editors Dick Abrahamson and Ben and Beth Nelms. We are grateful to the Mesa, Arizona, Public Library and its YA librarian Diane Tuccillo for serving as models of what we think YA services can be. We are also grateful to the readers of our manuscript who saved us from more errors than we might have made otherwise: Richard Abrahamson, University of Houston; Carolyn Baggett, University of Mississippi; Betsy Gray, National College of Education; Joyce Lackie, University of Northern Colorado; Maia Pank Mertz, Ohio State University; Bob Small, Virginia Polytechnic Institute; and Elizabeth Wahlquist, Brigham Young University. We are also grateful to the YA authors who contributed to the boxed statements which appear throughout the book. Lastly, we thank Scott, Foresman editors Chris Jennison and Anita Portugal for supporting us on this edition and in helping us in a multitude of ways, and we thank Roberta Casey for bringing it to fruition.

Ninety-nine years ago, Edward Salmon justified his work in children's literature by writing:

It is no uncommon thing to hear children's literature condemned as wholly bad, and some people are good enough to commiserate with me on having waded through so much ephemeral matter. It may be my fault or my misfortune not to be able to see my loss. I have spent many pleasant and I may say not unprofitable hours in company with the printed thoughts of Mr. Kingston, Mr. Ballantyne, Mr. Henty, Jules Verne, Miss Alcott, Miss Mead, Miss Molesworth, Miss Doudney, Miss Younge, and a dozen others, and hope to spend as many more in the time to come as a busy life will permit.*

Today, it is heartening to consider how many talented people share Edward Salmon's feelings, and, like us, feel joy in spending their lives working in a field of literature that is always changing, exciting, and alive.

Kenneth L. Donelson
Alleen Pace Nilsen

*"Should Children Have a Special Literature?" *The Parents' Review* 1 (June 1890): 339.

Contents

PART TWO
MODERN YOUNG ADULT READING   *81*

PART THREE
ADULTS AND THE LITERATURE OF YOUNG ADULTS   335

LITERATURE FOR TODAY'S YOUNG ADULTS

Third Edition

UNDERSTANDING YOUNG ADULTS AND BOOKS

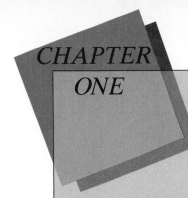

YOUNG ADULTS AND THEIR READING

Until the 1860s when—to the joy of the young and the anguish of the old—dime novels were distributed in the millions, Oliver Optic began publishing his endless series of books, and Louisa May Alcott wrote *Little Women,* there was almost nothing written specifically for adolescents. But still *young adult literature, teenage books,* and *adolescent literature* would have been strange, even meaningless, terms because only within the last half of the twentieth century has literature for young adults developed as a distinct unit of book publishing and promotion. Even today, an optimist might describe the field as *dynamic* while a pessimist would be more apt to say it is *unstable.*

Because of the newness of the concept and practice, there are no longstanding traditions as in children's literature, and opinions vary on whether or not there is even a need for a specialized approach to teenage books. The creation of such books coincided with the developing concept of adolescence as a specific and unique period of life. Puberty is a universal experience, but adolescence is not. Even today, in nontechnological societies the transition from childhood to adulthood may be quite rapid, but in the United States it begins at about age twelve or thirteen and continues through the early twenties. This stretching out of the transition between childhood and adulthood followed the Civil War. Before then, people were simply considered either children or adults. The turning point took place about age fourteen or fifteen when children could go to work and become economic assets to the family and the community. But as the predominantly agricultural society in which children worked with their families gave way to a technological society in which people worked in factories, offices, schools, hospitals, research centers, and think-tanks, available jobs required specialized training. The more complex society became, the longer children had to go to school to prepare for their eventual adulthood. These children, waiting to be accepted as full-fledged members of society, developed their own unique society. They became *teenagers* and *young adults,* or as the psychologists prefer to call them, *adolescents.*

Any change that affects this many people in such a major way demands adjustments and a reshuffling of society's priorities and roles. Such changes do not come automatically and few believe that all the adjustments have been made.

A PLEA FOR THE STUDY OF ADOLESCENT PSYCHOLOGY

We don't need to open a psychology book to realize that working with teenagers is a challenge, but we may feel better about our frustrations when we find that there are understandable reasons for them and that some of the best minds have offered explanations and theories. Linda Nielsen in *Adolescent Psychology: A Contemporary View*[1] divides theoretical perspectives into the organismic theorists and the environmental theorists. Another way of saying this is the nature vs. nurture theorists. Organismic or nature theorists can be further divided into three groups. Those who concentrated on biology, that is, the changes that take place in the teenagers' bodies, include Stanley Hall, Arnold Gesell, Ernst Kretschner, and William Sheldon. The second group concentrated on emotions and offered psychoanalytical views, including Sigmund Freud, Anna Freud, Karen Horney, Erik Erikson, Peter Blos, and James Marcia. The third group concentrated on intellect and offered cognitive and developmental views, including Jean Piaget, David Elkind, Lawrence Kohlberg, and Carol Gilligan.

Environmental theorists fall into two categories. In one group are the observers, those who take a sociological or anthropological view and describe and interpret what they see; people like Ruth Benedict, Kingsley Davis, Robert Havighurst, August Hollingshead, and Margaret Mead. The other group of environmental theorists including B. F. Skinner, Walter Mischel, Albert Bandur, John Dollard, Neal Miller, and J. B. Rotter believe that people's actions are shaped by the rewards and punishments that they get from society.

Because space in this text is too limited to include all that you need to know, a bibliography of new and recommended books on adolescent psychology is appended to this chapter. Some present overviews of typical adolescence, others focus on particular problems, while still others are aimed at adults playing specific roles in the lives of teenagers. We recommend that depending on the depth of your present knowledge as well as on the role you play in relation to young adults, you read one or more of these books.

Implications from Adolescent Psychology for Teachers and Librarians

At the least, teachers and librarians need to be aware of the emotional, intellectual, and physical changes that young adults experience, and they need to give serious thought to how they can best accommodate such changes. Growing bodies need movement and exercise but not just in ways that emphasize competition. Because they are adjusting to their new bodies and a whole host of new intellectual and emotional challenges, teenagers are especially self-conscious and need the reassurance that comes from achieving success and knowing that their accomplishments are admired by others. However, the typical teenage lifestyle is already filled with so much competition that it would be wise to plan activities where there are more winners than losers, for example, publishing newsletters with many student-written book reviews, displaying student artwork, and sponsoring science fiction, fantasy, or other special interest book discussion clubs. A variety of small clubs can provide multiple opportunities for leadership as well as for practice in successful group dynamics. Making friends is extremely important to teenagers, and many shy students need the security of some kind of organization with a supportive adult barely visible in the background.

In these activities, it is important to remember that young teens have short attention spans. A variety of activities should be organized so that participants can remain active as long as they want and then go on to something else without feeling guilty and without letting the other participants down. This does not mean that adults must accept irresponsibility. On the contrary, they can help students acquire a sense of commitment by planning for roles that are within their capabilities and their attention spans and by having clearly stated rules. Teenagers need limitations, but they also need the opportunity to help establish what these limits and expectations will be.

Adults also need to realize that the goal of most adolescents is to leave childhood behind as they move into adulthood. This has implications for whether libraries treat young adult services as a branch of the children's or the adult departments. Few teenagers are going to want to sit on small children's chairs or compete with nine- and ten-year-olds when they pick books off the shelves. Neither are they going to be attracted to books that use the word *children* or picture preteens on the covers.

Young adults want a wide variety of informational books about aspects of their lives that are new, for example, the physical development of their bodies, the new freedom they have to associate mainly with peers instead of family, and the added responsibilities they feel in deciding what kinds of adult roles they will fill.

Cognitive or intellectual development has a tremendous influence on what young people want to read and discuss. Jean Piaget's theory that at about the age of twelve the "formal operational" stage of thinking begins to develop has important implications because it is this stage of thinking that gives young people the power to imagine actions and their results even though there is no way to actually try them out. Having what Boyd McCandless and Richard Coop have labeled "the powers of *if*,"[2] is important not only when reading fantasy and science fiction, but when reading any literature dealing with subjects and viewpoints beyond the reader's actual experience. Even in realistic novels readers are asked to enter into the being and viewpoint of other characters where they must think as if they are someone else. Checking out their interpretations against those of a trusted friend or interested adult is an extension of this intellectual development. Teachers and librarians should provide ample opportunity and encouragement for this kind of discussion.

The more adults know about adolescent psychology, the better relationships they will be able to develop with students. For example, understanding the Rosenthal effect (also talked about as mirror-imaging and as self-fulfilling prophecies in which people become what they see that others expect) may influence what and how adults communicate to youngsters, while an understanding of the gender intensification hypothesis (the increasing pressures during adolescence to behave in sex-appropriate ways) may help them deal more effectively with what looks like blatant sexism on the part of teenagers. And knowing that individuals, especially young women, may suffer from a fear of success almost as often as they suffer from a fear of failure may help adults adapt the approaches they use to involve students in activities.

How Studying Adolescent Psychology Will Make Better Readers and Judges of Young Adult Literature

Specialists in either adolescent literature or adolescent psychology should read widely in the other field because while psychology provides the overall picture, adolescent literature—at least that which is honest—provides the individual portrait. Anyone who reads widely in adolescent literature picks up information about adolescent psychology, but some concentrated study in the field is important because it will provide you with a frame on which to hang the experiences that you read about. There are good books about every conceivable problem (see Chapter 3 for a discussion), but no one can read them all. And those who will succeed in bringing young people and books together will have read far more widely than just problem novels.

Often the difference in the lifespan between two books that are equally well written from a literary standpoint is that the ephemeral book fails to touch kids where they live, while the long-lasting book is one that treats experiences that are psychologically important to young people. It's not that good authors peruse psychology books searching for case histories or symptoms of teenage problems they can envision making into good stories. This would be as unlikely—and as unproductive—as for a writer to study a book on literary devices and make a list: "First, I will use a metaphor, and then a bit of alliteration and some imagery followed by personification."

The psychological aspects of well-written novels are a natural part of the story, and just as being able to recognize the way an author has brought about a particular effect through imagery, metaphor, or allusion will bring you an extra degree of pleasure and understanding, so will being able to recognize the psychological underpinnings of fictional treatments of human problems.

For example, someone familiar with gestalt psychology and its emphases on gaining awareness of moment-to-moment experiences and recognizing that the whole is greater than the elements that compose it will be better able to understand and appreciate two highly acclaimed books, Bruce Brooks' *Midnight Hour Encores* and Bobbie Ann Mason's *In Country*. In both books, young adult protagonists grow curious about a parent they have never known. Mason's *In Country* is the story of seventeen-year-old Sam's attempt to learn all she can about her father who was killed in Vietnam. She reads his journal, looks at old pictures, even runs away and camps in a swamp to see if she can experience his fears and discomforts, and then in the final section of the book makes a kind of pilgrimage to the Vietnam Veterans' Memorial in Washington:

> A group of schoolkids tumble through, noisy as chickens. As they enter, one of the girls says, "Are they piled on top of each other?" They walk a few steps farther and she says, "What are all these names anyway?" Sam feels like punching the girl in the face for being so dumb. How could anybody that age not know? But she realizes that she doesn't know either. She is just beginning to understand. And she will never really know what happened to these men in the war. Some people walk by, talking as though they are on a Sunday picnic, but most are reverent, and some of them are crying.

In Brooks' book, sixteen-year-old Sibilance T. Spooner is a musical prodigy, who has been raised by her father. In retrospect, her mother explains her 1960s hippie-style reaction to Sib's birth:

> I didn't want to give you milk from my body; I wanted my body back for myself, after you had had it from inside for nine months. I wanted to drink brandy again. And coffee. I wanted to sleep until ten, sometimes. I wanted to sleep until ten with a *man* sometimes. When you cried, I didn't give a damn why—I wanted you to shut up.

Sibil's father, himself a bit unconventional, took the day-old baby and headed east not to return to California until Sibil, at the age of sixteen, decides that she wants to leave Juilliard and study cello with a Russian virtuoso teaching in a newly established California conservatory. She figures that:

> I can live with my mother. She'll pretty much have to put me up, the poor old pothead squaw. It might mean she has to clean up her act a little; it might be inconvenient as hell. But it will teach her something she needs to learn: you just don't throw Sibilance T. Spooner away.

Sib's father agrees to take her to California for an audition and a meeting with her mother. His job is editing a weekly publication called *Environmental Impact,* which probably related to his decision to take a gestalt approach in preparing Sibil to meet her mother. He buys an old Volkswagen bus, replaces Sib's "flashy black American Tourister suitcases" with a duffel bag, and takes her to "Lesson One" in an upstairs used-record store where they stock up for the trip on authentic music from the '60s.

Their pilgrimage from Washington, D.C., to California is even more off-brand than Sam's pilgrimage to the Vietnam Memorial, and although what they find is not what they had expected, the happy ending shows that Sib learned more of the gestalt than her father had dared to hope for.

Whether or not young readers are looking for deeper meanings or just enjoying the surface plot of a story, they'll likely be most interested in books whose protagonists face the same kinds of challenges they are experiencing, such as the developmental tasks outlined a generation ago by Robert J. Havighurst:

1. Acquiring more mature social skills.
2. Achieving a masculine or feminine sex role.
3. Accepting the changes in one's body, using the body effectively, and accepting one's physique.
4. Achieving emotional independence from parents and other adults.
5. Preparing for sex, marriage, and parenthood.
6. Selecting and preparing for an occupation.
7. Developing a personal ideology and ethical standards.
8. Assuming membership in the larger community.[3]

Other psychologists gather all of these tasks under the umbrella heading of achieving an identity, which they describe as *the* developmental task of adolescence. In the process of testing the values and ideologies of others, some young people may select a negative identity, one that is obviously undesirable in the eyes of significant others and the community as a whole. Erik H. Erikson and James Marcia have discussed four other stages or types of identity that young people may adopt. One of these, a foreclosed identity, is the result of prematurely internalizing or adopting parents' and society's roles and values without examining them. In order to avoid this, in Hisako Matsubara's *Cranes at Dusk,* Saya's Shinto priest father defends her attendance at the Christian church. When Saya confides to the pastor that her father has read the Bible, he smugly responds, "Your father needs the Bible, doesn't he? Shinto isn't enough for him." When Saya reports this conversation to her father, he:

■ . . . picked out two other heavy books and showed them to her. "Look, this one is the Koran, the sacred book of Islam, and this is the Talmud, the book of laws for the Jews, and that whole row of books up there, those are the Buddhist sutras and everything of Lao-tse's that has come to us."

He explained, "No religion is enough to answer all the questions of mankind. In that sense he is right to say that I need the Bible."

In any year, dozens of young adult books touch on the problem of finding one's identity. The quotes below merely hint at the variety of ways in which the issue is approached:

> ... there are times when I feel like I have this other thing, this something, that's living in me, messing around with me. I'm not trying to make excuses. It's there! Separate but united. Me and not me. D'ya know what I mean, Jerems?
> (from a letter that Rachel writes to her brother in Norma Fox Mazer's *After the Rain*)

> Laura picked up her hair brush, looking into the mirror in her room. . . . She stared at herself intently. . . . Sometimes small alterations are more alarming than big ones. If Laura had been asked how she knew this reflection was not hers she could not have pointed out any alien feature. The hair was hers, and the eyes were hers, hedged around with the sooty lashes of which she was particularly proud. However, for all that, the face was not her face for it knew something that she did not. It looked back at her from some mysterious place alive with fears and pleasures she could not entirely recognize. There was no doubt about it. The future was not only warning her, but enticing her as it did so.
> (from Margaret Mahy's *The Changeover: A Supernatural Romance*)

> I was beginning to develop, at least physically, but nothing seemed to be the right size. Every morning I woke up, I had to check me out to see who was there. Some mornings I was a kid. Some mornings I was a maniac. Some mornings I didn't wake up at all: I just sleepwalked through the day.
> (from Richard Peck's *Remembering the Good Times*)

> "Father, something is bothering me."
> He replied around the meat. "I know. I have seen it."
> "But I don't know what it is."
> "I know that, too. It is part that you are fourteen and have thirteen winters and there are things that happen then which are hard to understand. But the other part that is bothering you I cannot say because I lack knowledge. You must get help from some other place. . . . I think you should go and talk to Oogruk. He is old and sometimes wise and he also tells good stories."
> (from Gary Paulsen's *Dogsong*)

In life the transitions from one stage to another are likely to be continuous rather than discontinuous or abrupt, but because authors are forced by the nature of their craft to select and highlight the bits and pieces that get most quickly to the heart of a story, the transitions in books are likely to appear as specific milestones or as what the psychologists would call discontinuous transitions. Also, there will probably be some outward sign of an initiation or rite-of-passage, and authors need to put into words what may only be a vague feeling or a hunch in real life.

Chris Crutcher's *The Crazy Horse Electric Game* provides a good example of a young man finding his identity. Sixteen-year-old Willie Weaver is the pitcher—and a very good one too—for the Samson Floral team. The game which makes Willie a legend is the one which robs the Crazy Horse Electric team of its fourth straight Eastern Montana American League championship. After this game, Willie is so confident of his identity that he makes jokes with Jenny Blackburn, who on the first day back to school greets him with "Baseball hero, How you doing?" " 'Football hero,' Willie corrects her. 'New season, new image.' "

Willie's father:

▌ . . . was mythic to him; and to most other folks in Coho, Montana, too. Big Will played football for the University of Washington in the early 1960s when the Huskies beat the Michigan Wolverines 19–6 in the Rose Bowl; rushed for more than 150 yards and threw a half-back option touchdown. He was voted Most Valuable Player. . . . And when Big Will finally came back to Coho to settle and raise a family, the town was overjoyed.

Willie is on his way to adopting an identity similar to his father's, but a boating accident robs his body of its smooth and quick coordination and Willie has to start all over to find out who he is and what he can accomplish. He leaves his small Montana town and for nearly two years struggles to find himself—not with the help of family and friends but of strangers. He succeeds, and when he returns home looking "good, much better than anyone would have expected," he is strong enough to accept weaknesses in those he loves and to go forward with his own life.

A fairly subtle aspect of developing an identity relates to an internal vs. an external locus of control. People with an external locus of control believe their lives are controlled from the outside, that is, by luck, chance, or what others do. People with an internal locus of control believe their own actions and characteristics control their lives. As part of this belief, they develop a behavioral and emotional autonomy. E. L. Doctorow's "The Writer in the Family," reprinted in Charlotte Zolotow's *Early Sorrow: Ten Stories of Youth,* revolves around the theme of the development of an internal locus of control. After Jonathan's father dies, his Aunt Frances asks Jonathan to help keep the death from his aged and senile grandmother. She asks him to write letters, supposedly from his father, that would explain why he doesn't visit anymore. Jonathan resents her request, but complies, even putting considerable thought and creativity into them. But then, after a couple of letters, his older brother asks, "What is this ritual? Grandma is almost totally blind, she's half deaf and crippled. . . . Would the old lady know the difference if she was reading the phone book?" Why couldn't Frances write the letters or Frances' sons, who are at Amherst?

> "But they're not Jack's sons," I said.
> "That's exactly the point," my brother said. "The idea is *service*. Dad used to bust his balls getting them things wholesale, getting them deals on things. . . . He was always on the hook for something. . . . They never thought every favor he got was one he had to pay back."

In the midst of this conversation, it dawns upon Jonathan that he is being implicated. When he composes the next letter to his grandmother, he takes a step toward both behavioral and emotional autonomy. The letter begins:

> Dear Mama,
> This will be my final letter to you since I have been told by the doctors that I am dying.
> I have sold my store at a very fine profit and am sending Frances a check for five thousand dollars to be deposited in your account.

Because they are learning to adjust to bodies that look and feel different and because they sense different expectations from their associates, teenagers are extremely self-conscious. Psychologist David Elkind says that many teenagers feel they have an imaginary audience; they think they are continually being surveyed and assessed by other people. Harold Brodkey's story "The State of Grace," which is included in Zolotow's *Early Sorrow,* clarifies Elkind's observation when the thirteen-year-old narrator can't describe a neighborhood man whose son he frequently babysits because "I never looked at men closely in those days but always averted my head in shyness and embarrassment; they might guess how fiercely I wanted to belong to them." Three pages later the boy explains why he is so comfortable playing in the back room with the six-year-old child he is hired to care for. He likes it because he is the chief, but:

> . . . not only that, I was not being seen. There was no one there who could see through me, or think of what I should be or how I should behave; and I have always been terrified of what people thought of me, as if what they thought was a hulking creature that would confront me if I should turn a wrong corner.

Norma Fox Mazer shines a different light on the concept of the imaginary audience in *After the Rain,* which begins:

> "Look down on this scene," Rachel writes in her notebook. "Three people in a kitchen, sitting around a table. A man, a woman, and a girl." She glances up at her parents. "The three people are together but not together. The man and the woman know the girl is there, but they don't really see her. They see her, but they don't really know her."

Throughout this book, which tells the story of Rachel and her grandfather's illness and death, Rachel keeps stepping back to look at herself through the eyes of her imaginary audience. In the midst of interviewing her coach for the school newspaper, she breaks into the middle of a sentence, "My grandfather is dying," and then a few minutes later she responds to an unrelated question from her best friend with, "My grandfather is going to die."

■ . . . all Rachel can think is that she's done it again. First Coach Al, now Helena. Isn't she just using Grandpa Izzy's illness to make herself important? . . . Does she plan to tell everybody? The man behind the counter when she buys a pack of gum? *My grandfather is dying.* Strangers on the street? *My grandfather is dying.* Maybe if she keeps saying it, she will feel it, she will believe it.

When reading about ego-defense mechanisms, most young readers probably do not realize that they are seeing patterns of behavior that have labels. What authors do by focusing attention on such actions is to educate their readers inductively. In Richard Peck's *Remembering the Good Times,* young readers can get the point without learning the term *projection,* when the narrator's divorced mother conjectured that her former husband was probably dating, "but maybe she thought that because *she* was dating." And they don't need to know the term *repression* to understand what happened when after a classroom confrontation, a mentally disturbed student, "just slid out of his desk and loped off. Everybody did. At that age, when there's something you can't explain, you walk away from it." And they don't have to know the term *denial* to understand the feelings of Carson McCullers' thirteen-year-old protagonist in "Like That" when she looks at her broken-hearted older sister whose boyfriend has gone off to college:

■ But when one afternoon the kids all got quiet in the gym basement and then started telling certain things—about being married and all—I got up quick so I wouldn't hear and went up and played basketball. And when some of the kids said they were going to start wearing lipstick and stockings I said I wouldn't for a hundred dollars.

You see I'd never be like Sis is now. I wouldn't. Anybody could know that if they knew me. I just wouldn't, that's all. I don't want to grow up—if it's like that.

Although young students need not know the psychological terminology for the concepts they are reading about, it's helpful if teachers and librarians know not only the terms but also have a full understanding of what they entail. A knowledge of adolescent psychology—something that has only been hinted at here—will help adults:

Judge the soundness of the books they read.

Decide which ones are worthy of promotion.

Predict which ones will last and which won't.

Make better recommendations to individuals.

Discuss books with students from their viewpoints.

Gain more understanding and pleasure from personal reading.

NANCY B. BOND
on Who She Writes for

I don't actually write for young adults. I write *about* them. In my books there are characters who are teenagers; there are also adults and young children. The world I look at and write about is made up of a mixture of people of various ages, trying to live with themselves and each other, struggling with problems and enjoying successes, making friends, fighting, attempting to comfort and love one another, being lonely sometimes, learning to communicate. We all see the world differently, but we also have much in common. The books I like to read best are about these differences and similarities in everyone, no matter how young or old—and they are the books I try to write.

I must confess that one of the things I find a little discouraging is being categorized as a writer for young adults. I know there are good reasons for such categorization—in bookstores, libraries, and schools it is very helpful to know which books are appropriate for each reader. But I don't think that age is necessarily the best key, not once a reader has experience with books. Good books are good books. As a librarian, I often gave "young adult" books to adult readers because I knew they would enjoy the characters and plot; because they were interesting, well-written stories. And I often suggested books published for adults to young adult readers for the same reasons.

I don't much like categorization because it can be very restricting. Readers who don't fit the category often dismiss what's in it without knowing what they are dismissing. Readers who do fit it don't always like being defined in such a way.

Who do I write for? First of all, I write for myself. You've probably heard other writers say this before—it's something of a cliché, but it's true. I write for myself for the most practical of reasons. It takes me a year or more to finish a book (the most recent one has taken over three). In order to spend that long with a story and characters, I have to be really interested; I have to care what happens; as a writer, I have to want to find out and be willing to keep at it stubbornly until I do. If I am involved and interested, then I know there's a good chance that someone else might be, if and when the book is finally published. If I am bored and dissatisfied with what I'm writing, on the other hand, then I know there's something basic wrong with it and I'd better find out what and fix it—if I possibly can, and it isn't always possible. Some stories have to be put away for a while, and some abandoned altogether.

I don't write to teach anyone anything. I write to find out about myself and other people, and to share what I discover with whoever is interested.

Nancy B. Bond's books include *A String in the Harp,* Atheneum, 1976; *The Best of Enemies,* Atheneum, 1978; and *A Place to Come Back To,* Atheneum, 1984.

WHAT IS YOUNG ADULT LITERATURE?

We recently heard young adults defined as "Those who think they're too old to be children but who others think are too young to be adults." In this book we use the term to include students in junior high as well as those who have graduated from high school and are still finding their way into adult reading. However, we should caution that not all educators define young adults in this way. The Educational Resources Information Clearinghouse (ERIC), for example, defines young adults as between the ages of 18 and 22, while the National Assessment of Educational Progress (NAEP) administered by the Educational Testing Service refers to "young adults, ages 21 through 25."

We confess to feeling a bit pretentious when referring to a twelve- or thirteen-year-old as a young adult. However, we shy away from using the term *adolescent literature* because as librarians have told us, "It has the ugly ring of pimples and puberty"; "It's like a conference about young adults with none present"; and "It suggests immature in a derogatory sense." Still, most such college courses offered through English departments are entitled *Adolescent Literature,* and because of our English teaching backgrounds we find ourselves using the term for variety, along with *teenage books.* However, we do not use such terms as *juvenile literature, junior novel, teen novel,* and *juvie.* These terms used to be fairly common, but today they are weighed down with negative connotations. This is unfortunate because there's often a need for communicating that a particular book is more likely to appeal to a thirteen-year-old than to a nineteen-year-old. With adults a six-year age difference may not affect choice of subject matter and intellectual and emotional response, but for teenagers even two or three years can make a tremendous difference.

By *young adult literature,* we mean anything that readers between the approximate ages of twelve and twenty choose to read (as opposed to what they may be coerced to read for class assignments). When we talk about *children's literature,* we refer to books released by the juvenile or junior division of a publisher and intended for children from pre-kindergarten to about sixth grade.

It wasn't until the 1920s and 1930s that most publishers divided their offerings into adult and juvenile categories. And today it is sometimes little more than chance whether an adult or juvenile editor happens to get a manuscript. Robert Cormier had never thought of himself as a writer for young people, but when his agent submitted *The Chocolate War* to Pantheon, the editor convinced Cormier that, as good as the book was, it would be simply one more in a catalog of adult books. On the other hand, if it were published for teenagers, it might sell well, and it certainly would not be one more in a long string of available adolescent novels. The editor's predictions came true, and Cormier later acknowledged that although his initial reaction to becoming a "young adult" author was one of shock followed by a month-long writer's block, he is grateful for the editorial help which led to more attention from reviewers at the juvenile level. Although he had already published several stories and three novels, *The Chocolate War* brought him his first real financial gain. Until recently an author who had a choice of a book coming out as either an adult or a juvenile title probably would have selected the adult division in hopes of receiving greater respect, acclaim, and financial rewards. This is less true today because of several breakthroughs. One is financial. Because we have a youth-oriented society, teenage books are popular choices for general audience movies and television specials (see Chapter 9). And as the book industry discovered that teenagers are willing to spend their own money for paperbacks in shopping mall bookstores (see Chapter 11), the financial base began to change. Developments in the 1970s already brought considerable financial success to the YA book business. Reading came into the high school curriculum as a regular class taken for at least one semester by many students. In such classes students had to read something, and in many cases this was teenage fiction. During the late 1960s, students and teachers turned away from the "classics" and the standard, required four years of English. English departments began offering electives, and courses in modern literature that included both adult and teenage fiction were popular with students. Many teachers who had previously scorned teenage books found themselves being forced to take a new look and to conclude that it was better to teach adolescent literature than no literature at all.

All of the interest has had a circular effect. The more important books for teenagers have become, the more respect the field has gained, and the better talent it has attracted. For example, on the basis of his Pulitzer Prize-winning play, *The Effect of Gamma Rays on Man-in-the-Moon-Marigolds,* Paul Zindel was invited by Harper and Row to try teenage fiction. His first book was the well-received *The Pigman.* Both M. E. Kerr and Robert Cormier, currently two of the most respected YA authors, took positive note of this book as they pondered the effect that writing books for teenagers might have on their own careers.

A Brief Unsettled Heritage

The whole field of young adult literature is one some writers, teachers, and other interested parties have many questions about. It is, after all, a relatively new area. Teenage books have not always enjoyed the best reputation. An article in the *Louisville Courier-Journal* in 1951 indicates no great fondness for adolescent literature:

> The blame for the vulgarity, the dull conformity and the tastelessness of much in American life cannot be laid altogether at the doors of radio, television, and the movies as long as book publishers hawk these books for young people. Flabby in content, mediocre in style, narrowly directed at the most trivial of adolescent interests, they pander to a vast debilitation of tastes, to intolerance for the demanding, rewarding and enabling exercise which serious reading can be. . . . Like a diet of cheap candies, they vitiate the appetite for sturdier food—for that bracing, ennobling and refining experience, immersion in the great stream of the English classics.[4]

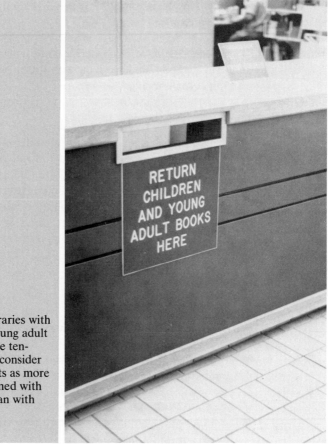

Even in libraries with separate young adult sections, the tendency is to consider young adults as more closely aligned with children than with adults.

Fourteen years later, J. Donald Adams, editor of the "Speaking of Books" page in *The New York Times Book Review,* wrote:

If I were asked for a list of symptoms pointing to what is wrong with American education and American culture, or to the causes for the prolongation of American adolescence, I should place high on the list the multiplication of books designed for readers in their teens. The teen-age book, it seems to me, is a phenomenon which belongs properly only to a society of morons. I have nothing but respect for the writers of good books for children; they perform one of the most admirable functions of which a writer is capable. One proof of their value is the fact that the greatest books which children can enjoy are read with equal delight by their elders. But what person of mature years and reasonable mature understanding (for there is often a wide disparity) can read without impatience a book written for adolescents?[5]

As recently as 1977, John Goldthwaite, writing in *Harper's,* gave as one of his nine suggestions for improving literature for young readers in particular and the world in general:

> *The termination of teen-age fiction.* No one has ever satisfactorily explained why there is or ought to be such a thing as teen-age fiction at all. In the case of science fiction and fantasy, for example, there is little being written for adults that could not be understood by any literate twelve-year-old. Conversely, some prize-winning fantasies for teen-agers have a turgidity of style the worst SF hack would be hard put to achieve. As for all that novelized stuff about alienation, drugs, and pregnancy, the great bulk of it might be more enjoyable presented in comic books. There are any number of very good underground cartoonists on the West Coast who need the money and might be willing to make something halfway real of such material.[6]

Those of us who have more positive attitudes toward teenage books can argue that these critics were writing about books that are far different from good adolescent literature published today. We can also conjecture that they were making observations based on a biased or inadequate sampling. Teenage books were never as hopelessly bad as such statements imply. Criticism of any field, young adult literature or ornithology or submarine designing, begins with firsthand experience of the subject. Critics who decide to do a cursory piece on young adult literature once a year or so seldom have the reading background necessary to choose representative titles. People who make generalizations about an entire field of writing based on reading only five or ten books are not merely unreliable sources, they are intellectual frauds. Wide knowledge surely implies a background of at least several hundred books selected from a variety of types and styles.

Although we have grounds for rejecting the kind of negative criticism quoted above, we need to be aware that it exists. Such a pessimistic view of teenage books is an unfortunate literary heritage that may well influence the attitudes of school boards, library directors, parents, teachers, and anyone else who has had no particular reason to read and examine the best of the new young adult literature. Besides, so many new books for young readers appear each year (approximately 2,000 with about one-fourth of these aimed at teenagers) that people who have already made up their minds about adolescent literature can probably find titles to support their beliefs no matter what they are. In an area as new as young adult literature, we can look at much of the disagreement and the conflicting views as inevitable. They are signs of a lively and interesting field.

The variety on the Honor Sampling contradicts the myths that teenage books are all the same. The honored books include historical fiction, nonfiction, short story collections, humor, new journalism, fantasy, love stories, poetry, and realistic problem novels.

1986

> *All God's Children Need Traveling Shoes.* Maya Angelou. Random House
>
> *A Band of Angels.* Julian Thompson. Scholastic
>
> *Cat, Herself.* Mollie Hunter. Harper & Row
>
> *The Catalogue of the Universe.* Margaret Mahy. Macmillan
>
> *Izzy, Willy-Nilly.* Cynthia Voigt. Atheneum
>
> *Midnight Hour Encores.* Bruce Brooks. Harper & Row

1985

> *Betsey Brown.* Ntozake Shange. St. Martin
>
> *Beyond the Chocolate War.* Robert Cormier. Knopf
>
> *Dogsong.* Gary Paulsen. Bradbury
>
> *In Country.* Bobbie Ann Mason. Harper & Row
>
> *The Moonlight Man.* Paula Fox. Bradbury
>
> *Pocket Poems: Selected for a Journey.* Paul Janeczko, ed. Bradbury
>
> *Remembering the Good Times.* Richard Peck. Delacorte
>
> *Wolf of Shadows.* Whitley Strieber. Knopf

SOME MYTHS ABOUT YOUNG ADULT LITERATURE

Many of the old—and a few new—beliefs about teenagers and books have taken on the characteristics of myths. Some of the myths grew out of attempt to explain apparent contradictions; others are true in certain circumstances but have been overgeneralized and exaggerated; others have been used in such way that they have become self-fulfilling prophecies. It seems appropriate the beginning of a survey of young adult literature to examine these myths and to test them out against what we know about teenage reading and the best young adult literature. Your own wide and continued reading will help you form your own opinions.

We did some research to come up with a body of books that would be representative of what both young adults and professionals working in the field consider the best books. But we should caution that books are selected as "the best" on the basis of many different criteria, and someone else's "best" will not necessarily be yours or that of the young people with whom you work. We hope that you will read many books so that you can recommend them, not because you saw them on a list, but because you enjoyed them and judge them to contain qualities that will appeal to a particular student.

In drawing up our list of "best books," we started with 1967, because looking back this seemed to be a milestone year in which writers and publishers turned in new directions. We went to the Young Adult Services Division of the American Library Association, which each January issues a list containing between 30 and 80 titles considered the best of the previous year, and to sample of approximately 25 young adult librarians and 25 college instructors young adult literature. We also looked at "best book" lists published in *School Library Journal, The New York Times Book Review, English Journal,* and *Booklist.* Although for this edition, we've used our own judgment about delet-ing a few of the older books, we began by putting any book that was named by four out of these six sources on the following list which we refer to as our "Honor Sampling." The strength and value of this list is that it draws upon the judgment of a widely read group of professionals and young adults. The list repeated in Appendix A (page 562) with information about paperback and media versions as well as numbers of pages, genres, and descriptions of the protagonists.

1987

After the Rain. Norma Fox Mazer. Morrow

The Crazy Horse Electric Game. Chris Crutcher. Greenwillow

The Goats. Brock Cole. Farrar, Straus & Giroux

Permanent Connections. Sue Ellen Bridgers. Harper & Row

Princess Ashley. Richard Peck. Delacorte

Sons from Afar. Cynthia Voigt. Atheneum

The Tricksters. Margaret Mahy. Macmillan

1984

The Changeover: A Supernatural Romance. Margaret Mahy. Macmillan

Cold Sassy Tree. Olive Ann Burns. Ticknor & Fields

Downtown. Norma Fox Mazer. Morrow

Interstellar Pig. William Sleator. Dutton

A Little Love. Virginia Hamilton. Putnam

The Moves Make the Man. Bruce Brooks. Harper & Row

One-Eyed Cat. Paula Fox. Bradbury

Sixteen: Short Stories by Outstanding Writers for Young Adults. Donald R. Gallo, ed. Delacorte

1983

Beyond the Divide. Kathryn Lasky. Macmillan

The Bumblebee Flies Anyway. Robert Cormier. Pantheon

A Gathering of Old Men. Ernest J. Gaines. Knopf

Poetspeak: In Their Work, About Their Work. Paul Janeczko, ed. Bradbury

Solitary Blue. Cynthia Voigt. Atheneum

1982

The Blue Sword. Robin McKinley. Greenwillow

Class Dismissed! High School Poems. Mel Glenn. Clarion

The Darkangel. Meredith Ann Pierce. Atlantic

A Formal Feeling. Zibby Oneal. Viking

Homesick: My Own Story. Jean Fritz. Putnam

A Midnight Clear. William Wharton. Knopf

Sweet Whispers, Brother Rush. Virginia Hamilton. Philomel

1981

Let the Circle Be Unbroken. Mildred D. Taylor. Dial

Little, Little. M. E. Kerr. Harper & Row

Notes for Another Life. Sue Ellen Bridgers. Knopf

Rainbow Jordan. Alice Childress. Coward, McCann

Stranger with My Face. Lois Duncan. Little, Brown

Tiger Eyes. Judy Blume. Bradbury

Westmark. Lloyd Alexander. Dutton

1980

The Beginning Place. Ursula K. Le Guin. Harper & Row

Jacob Have I Loved. Katherine Paterson. Crowell

A Matter of Feeling. Janine Boissard. Little, Brown

The Quartzsite Trip. William Hogan. Atheneum

1979

After the First Death. Robert Cormier. Pantheon

All Together Now. Sue Ellen Bridgers. Knopf

Birdy. William Wharton. Knopf

The Disappearance. Rosa Guy. Delacorte

The Last Mission. Harry Mazer. Delacorte

Tex. S. E. Hinton. Delacorte

Words by Heart. Ouida Sebestyen. Little, Brown

1978

Beauty: A Retelling of the Story of Beauty and the Beast. Robin McKinley.
Harper & Row

The Book of the Dun Cow. Walter Wangerin, Jr. Harper & Row

Dreamsnake. Vonda N. McIntyre. Houghton Mifflin

Father Figure. Richard Peck. Viking

Gentlehands. M. E. Kerr. Harper & Row

1977

Hard Feelings. Don Bredes. Atheneum

I Am the Cheese. Robert Cormier. Knopf

I'll Love You When You're More Like Me. M. E. Kerr. Harper & Row

Ludell & Willie. Brenda Wilkinson. Harper & Row

One Fat Summer. Robert Lipsyte. Harper & Row

Trial Valley. Vera and Bill Cleaver. Lippincott

Winning. Robin Brancato. Knopf

1976

Are You in the House Alone? Richard Peck. Viking

Dear Bill, Remember Me? Norma Fox Mazer. Delacorte

The Distant Summer. Sarah Patterson. Simon and Schuster

Home Before Dark. Sue Ellen Bridgers. Knopf

Never to Forget. Milton Meltzer. Harper & Row

Ordinary People. Judith Guest. Viking

1975

Dragonwings. Laurence Yep. Harper & Row

Feral. Berton Roueche. Harper & Row

Is That You Miss Blue? M. E. Kerr. Harper & Row

The Lion's Paw. D. R. Sherman. Doubleday

The Massacre at Fall Creek. Jessamyn West. Harper & Row

Rumble Fish. S. E. Hinton. Delacorte

Z for Zachariah. Robert C. O'Brien. Atheneum

1974

The Chocolate War. Robert Cormier. Pantheon

House of Stairs. William Sleator. Dutton

If Beale Street Could Talk. James Baldwin. Dial

M. C. Higgins, the Great. Virginia Hamilton. Macmillan

1973

A Day No Pigs Would Die. Robert Newton Peck. Knopf

The Friends. Rosa Guy. Holt, Rinehart and Winston

A Hero Ain't Nothin' But a Sandwich. Alice Childress. Coward, McCann

The Slave Dancer. Paula Fox. Bradbury

Summer of My German Soldier. Bette Greene. Dial

1972

Deathwatch. Robb White. Doubleday

Dinky Hocker Shoots Smack. M. E. Kerr. Harper & Row

Dove. Robin L. Graham. Harper & Row

The Man Without a Face. Isabelle Holland. Lippincott

My Name Is Asher Lev. Chaim Potok. Knopf

Soul Catcher. Frank Herbert. Putnam

Sticks and Stones. Lynn Hall. Follett

Teacup Full of Roses. Sharon Bell Mathis. Viking

1971

The Autobiography of Miss Jane Pittman. Ernest Gaines. Dial

The Bell Jar. Sylvia Plath. Harper & Row

Go Ask Alice. Anonymous. Prentice-Hall

His Own Where. June Jordan. Crowell

Wild in the World. John Donovan. Harper & Row

1970

Bless the Beasts and Children. Glendon Swarthout. Doubleday

I Know Why the Caged Bird Sings. Maya Angelou. Random House

Love Story. Erich Segal. Harper & Row

Run Softly, Go Fast. Barbara Wersba. Atheneum

1969

I'll Get There. It Better Be Worth the Trip. John Donovan. Harper & Row

My Darling, My Hamburger. Paul Zindel. Harper & Row

Sounder. William Armstrong. Harper & Row

Where the Lilies Bloom. Vera and Bill Cleaver. Lippincott

1968

The Pigman. Paul Zindel. Harper & Row

Red Sky at Morning. Richard Bradford. Lippincott

Soul on Ice. Eldridge Cleaver. McGraw-Hill

1967

The Chosen. Chaim Potok. Simon and Schuster

The Contender. Robert Lipsyte. Harper & Row

Mr. and Mrs. Bo Jo Jones. Ann Head. Putnam

The Outsiders. S. E. Hinton. Viking

Reflections on a Gift of Watermelon Pickle. Stephen Dunning and others, eds. Scott, Foresman

If a book is included on this honor sampling, then obviously it is in some way an outstanding book, but the reasons might differ considerably. One book may be here because of its originality, another its popularity, and another its literary quality. And we should warn that just because a book has not found its way to this list, it should not be dismissed as mediocre. The list covers 21 years during which there were many more outstanding books published than the 122 included here. Whenever such lists are drawn up, there's a degree of luck involved.

Many of these books will be described in more detail in the following chapters. Here they will simply be cited as the evidence we used to assess the following generalizations or myths as they relate to the best of modern young adult literature. By dispelling some of the myths, we will establish a clearer view of what young adult literature is and can be. But we should caution that we too are using a biased sampling. Whereas some critics use the worst books as examples, we have restricted ourselves to the best. Some of the myths that we reject in relation to the Honor Sampling may very well be true of other books.

Myth No. 1: Teenagers Today Cannot Read

When 1987 was declared "The Year of the Reader," the Ad Council launched such a media blitz that according to their statistics, they increased awareness of functional illiteracy from 21.4 percent to 30 percent of the population (see Chapter 11 for a fuller discussion). However, as Nancy Larrick pointed out, there was little relationship between this statistic and any real effect on illiteracy itself.[7]

It's much more dramatic to talk about the problem than to work to solve it. Ever since 1955, when Rudolf Flesch made such a stir with his book *Why Johnny Can't Read,* journalists, politicians, and general critics have found that as prophets of doom, they can easily gain a large and sympathetic audience. Of course parents want their youngsters to learn to read and are concerned about whether or not schools are succeeding. But few people look for the facts behind the stories of falling test scores and widespread illiteracy. There are seldom enough facts to support the claims.

Miles Myers, writing in the *English Journal* under the title "Shifting Standards of Literacy—the Teacher's *Catch-22*,"[8] explained that while conventional illiteracy—the inability to read a simple message in any language—has virtually disappeared in the United States, functional illiteracy—the inability to read and write at a level required to function in society—appears to be increasing. During World War I only about 45 percent of 17- and 18-year-old recruits could read at what is now identified as a fourth-grade level. By World War II the figure had risen to about 65 percent, while during the Vietnam War it was 80 percent. The problem, as Myers sees it, is that reading at a fourth-grade level is no longer sufficient. When former Defense Secretary Caspar Weinberger said that scientific and technical illiteracy could jeopardize the nation's ability to defend itself, he was talking about a kind of literacy that was never expected in the "good old days," but indeed may be quite necessary for modern life—civilian as well as military. For example, in industry, such trends as automation, shared decision making, and more free time for workers mean that people need to be able to read at higher levels in which they interpret, criticize, and solve problems.

The National Assessment of Educational Progress, administered by the Educational Testing Service in Princeton, published *The Reading Report Card* in September of 1985. This summarized results from four national reading assessments spanning 1971 to 1984. Teenagers in 1984 were reading better than were teenagers in 1971, but what worried the evaluators was that while students had learned to read and comprehend on a literal or basic level, they were unable to use thinking skills to read for understanding, questioning, and evaluating.

What all this means is that as educators, we should not believe everything we read in the newspaper about students not being able to read, but we should recognize that a problem exists, which though not of our making, has nevertheless been given to us to solve. Part of the solution lies in doing whatever we can to encourage students to select reading as one of their leisure-time activities and to guide them to books that not only entertain but will also be thought-provoking.

Myth No. 2: Young Adult Literature is Simplified to Accommodate Low Reading Skills

This myth has more truth to it than some other myths, but it is still overgeneralizing to think, as some people do, that the reason for the rise in popularity of young adult literature over the last few years is that teenagers are incapable of reading regular adult books or "great literature." None of the books on the honor list is of the controlled vocabulary or the easy-to-read variety. However, one of the characteristics of juvenile books as compared to adult books is that they are shorter. When we first made the honor list and counted the pages, we found that the books coming out of juvenile divisions average 192 pages while the adult titles averaged 271. Mildred Taylor's *Let the Circle Be Unbroken* is one of a very few juvenile titles with over 300 pages. It's more common for YA books to be unusually short as with Mel Glenn's *Class Dismissed! High School Poems,* June Jordan's *His Own Where,* and John Donovan's *Wild in the World* with fewer than 100 pages.

In 1964, when the British author, Leon Garfield, submitted his first novel to a publishing house, it was turned down "after three or four agonizing months, when they said they couldn't quite decide whether it was adult or junior." He next submitted it to an editor who was just beginning to develop a juvenile line. Garfield said, "She suggested that, if I would be willing to cut it, then she'd publish it as a juvenile book. And of course, though I'd vowed I'd never alter a word, once the possibility of its being published became real, I cut it in about a week."[9]

We should point out that reading difficulty and level of literary sophistication do not always correlate with length. Teenagers will read longer books. Chaim Potok's *My Name Is Asher Lev* has 369 pages, Jessamyn West's *The Massacre at Fall Creek* 373 pages, Don Bredes' *Hard Feelings* 377 pages, and Olive Ann Burns' *Cold Sassy Tree* 391 pages.

The idea that teenage books are stylistically simple with straightforward plots is not so much a myth as it is an overgeneralization. It is true of the majority of books that teenagers read, but there are certainly exceptions. Gary Paulsen's *Dogsong* blends the past and the future with the present, while none of Robert Cormier's books is simple. In Ernest Gaines' *A Gathering of Old Men,* William Wharton's *Birdy* and Alice Childress' *A Hero Ain't Nothin' But a Sandwich,* readers must draw together and sort out alternating viewpoints and chronologies. And it is obvious from reading Ntozake Shange's *Betsey Brown,* Judith Guest's *Ordinary People,* and Chaim Potok's *My Name Is Asher Lev* that their appeal is based on something other than easy reading.

Myth No. 3: Teenage Books Are All the Same

The existence of this myth says more about the reading patterns of the people who believe it than about the state of young adult literature. There is a tremendous variety of types, subjects, and themes represented in the Honor Sampling. In addition, teenagers read informative nonfiction—trivia, health, history, sports, and how-to books—but because of the way we compiled the Honor Sampling over a 21-year period the popularity of such books is not accurately reflected. See Chapter 8 for a discussion of informative books which by their nature usually have shorter life spans and are aimed at more specific audiences than fiction.

Nevertheless, a few nonfiction books have made it to the list: Maya Angelou's biographical *I Know Why the Caged Bird Sings* and *All God's Children Need Traveling Shoes;* Jean Fritz's *Homesick: My Own Story,* which tells of her

TODD STRASSER
on Kids and Their Reading

I spend about 40 days every year speaking at junior highs and high schools. I do assemblies, writing workshops, and small group gatherings. I talk to students, and I see what they're studying. Obviously, I'm especially interested in their attitude towards reading.

And I can tell you, it isn't good.

Kids today think of reading the way my generation regarded math: as a required subject. Most kids would no sooner read for pleasure than they would do multiplication tables for fun.

If you're a writer, this is depressing news.

Some of you reading this are probably already starting to bristle. "But reading scores have never been higher," you're thinking.

True. This country does a great job of teaching kids to read. But teaching kids to *enjoy* reading is another story.

Why don't kids enjoy reading? Well, one reason is that it's easier to watch TV. Another is that almost all homework involves reading, and thus reading suffers from guilt by association.

But there's a third reason why kids don't enjoy reading—they are given too many unenjoyable books to read. What's an unenjoyable book? I suppose every student has his or her own definition, but in general it's a book written in a ponderous and difficult style about a subject of dubious interest to today's young readers: *The Scarlet Letter* for instance.

Books like *The Scarlet Letter* turn kids off. Kids who write to me actually mention how boring they find that book. After the works of Shakespeare, it is the best-selling study guide in the Cliffs and Monarch series. Why do English departments continue to include it in their curriculums? Is it such a valuable literary work? Shakespeare, yes. Hawthorne, no.

If you want to teach kids to enjoy reading, why not give them something enjoyable to read once in a while? Give them contemporary books written in a contemporary style about issues today's teens will find interesting. There are plenty of well-written, serious YA books around. That's what this textbook is all about.

As long as the average reading curriculum in this country stays heavy on the classics and light to non-existent on contemporary YA literature, schools will continue to produce readers who hate to read. Striking a better balance between the classics and contemporary literature probably wouldn't hurt students one bit, and it might do wonders for their reading.

Todd Strasser's books include *Rock It to the Top,* Delacorte, 1987; *A Very Touchy Subject,* Delacorte, 1985; and *Workin' for Peanuts,* Delacorte, 1983.

childhood in China; and Milton Meltzer's *Never to Forget: The Jews of the Holocaust.* Other historical books include Olive Ann Burns' *Cold Sassy Tree,* Kathryn Lasky's *Beyond the Divide,* and Ernest Gaines' *A Gathering of Old Men.* Several honor books contain elements of fantasy or science fiction. They are as old as the oldest folktales (Walter Wangerin's *The Book of the Dun Cow* and Robin McKinley's *Beauty and the Beast*) and as new as nuclear war and the latest board game (Whitley Strieber's *Wolf of Shadows* and William Sleator's *Interstellar Pig*). They are filled with romance (Virginia Hamilton's *Sweet Whispers, Brother Rush* and Margaret Mahy's *The Changeover*) and with high-tech intrigue (Robert Cormier's *The Bumblebee Flies Anyway* and *I Am the Cheese*).

More than half the books are contemporary realistic fiction, but they are far from being "all the same." They range from tightly plotted suspense stories, including Harry Mazer's *The Last Mission* and Julian Thompson's *A Band of Angels,* to serious introspections, as in Paula Fox's *One-Eyed Cat* and *The Moonlight Man.* M. E. Kerr's novels are in some ways problem novels, but they also make readers smile. And four collections of poems and two collections of short stories have enough variety in them to bring tears as well as laughs.

The theme that most commonly appears in young adult literature regardless of its format is one of change and growth, which suggests either directly or symbolically the gaining of maturity, i.e., the passage from childhood to adulthood. Such stories communicate a sense of time and change, a sense of becoming something and catching glimpses of possibilities—some that are fearful, others that are awesome, odd, funny, perplexing, or wondrous. A related theme is the quest. Realistic quest stories include Cynthia Voigt's *Izzy, Willy-Nilly,* Brock Cole's *The Goats,* Bruce Brooks' *Midnight Hour Encores,* and Bobbie Ann Mason's *In Country.* Quest stories with varying degrees of fantasy include Mollie Hunter's *Cat, Herself,* Gary Paulsen's *Dogsong,* Lloyd Alexander's *Westmark,* and Robin McKinley's *The Blue Sword.*

Other themes emphasize alienation and loneliness as seen in William Wharton's *Birdy,* John Donovan's *Wild in the World,* and Eldridge Cleaver's *Soul on Ice.* The need for a hero is seen in Robert Newton Peck's *A Day No Pigs Would Die* and Glendon Swarthout's *Bless the Beasts and Children.* Threats to the social order are explored in William Sleator's *House of Stairs* and *Interstellar Pig.* A search for values is shown in Richard Bradford's *Red Sky at Morning* and Chris Crutcher's *The Crazy Horse Electric Game.* What it means to care for others is examined in Norma Fox Mazer's *Downtown,* Virginia Hamilton's *A Little Love,* and Isabelle Holland's *The Man Without a Face.*

Myth No. 4: Teenage Books Avoid Taboo Topics and Feature White, Middle-Class Protagonists

In 1959, when Stephen Dunning wrote his dissertation on the adolescent novel, he observed that "junior novels insistently avoid taboo concerns," and that "junior novels are typically concerned with socially and economically fortunate families."[10] This was undoubtedly true then, when the popular books were

Going on Sixteen, Practically Seventeen, Class Ring, and *Prom Trouble.* Anyone familiar with bookselling trends in the 1980s (see Chapter 4 for a discussion of romances) will recognize the similarity between these titles and those of currently popular mass-market romances. The contents are similar, and some of the observations that Dunning made in his dissertation about 1950s "junior novels" are applicable for many of the mass-market romances now in bookstores. But they are not true for the books on the Honor Sampling. The mid-1960s witnessed a striking change in attitudes. One by one, taboos on profanity, divorce, sexuality, drinking, racial unrest, abortion, pregnancy, and drugs disappeared. Books became painfully honest about the reality of young people and the frequently cold and cruel world they face. Some critics suggested, in fact, that modern young adult literature is exclusively pessimistic or cynical, as much of an overgeneralization as the counterclaim that teenage books present a romanticized and frivolous view of life. What has happened in recent years is that restrictions have been lifted so that writers can explore a variety of topics and concerns. For example, it's no longer necessary that a book about a "sensitive" topic such as the pregnancy in Ann Head's *Mr. and Mrs. Bo Jo Jones* come from the adult division of a publishing house.

The Honor Sampling strongly refutes the idea that the protagonists in young adult literature are mainly white and middle class. Probably because there was such a void in good books about non-middle-class protagonists and also because this is where some very interesting things were happening, many writers during the 1970s focused their attention in this direction. With the conservative swing that the country took in the '80s, not as much attention has been paid to minority experiences, but still ten of the books with post-1980 copyrights feature black protagonists, and it's encouraging that they are among the most appealing of the new books and so will be read by large numbers of teenagers of all races. Unfortunately, other minorities are not represented nearly as well, although Judy Blume's *Tiger Eyes* and Richard Bradford's *Red Sky at Morning* have New Mexico Hispanic settings and Frank Herbert's *Soul Catcher* is about a young Native American.

There is also some hope that Americans are becoming less parochial. Mollie Hunter's *Cat, Herself* is the story of a Scottish gypsy, Gary Paulsen's *Dogsong* is about a young Eskimo, and Margaret Mahy's *The Changeover* and *The Tricksters* are set in New Zealand, while Janine Boissard's *A Matter of Feeling* is translated from the French.

Myth No. 5: Teenage Books Are Didactic or Preachy

In this list of myths, this is the one that comes closest to being true. Of course adults want to teach young people what they have learned about life, so when they set out to write a book they probably want to share with their readers some kind of insight, an understanding, or a lesson. This might be said of everyone who writes for readers of any age, but writers for young people have often had more confidence in doing this because of the greater distance between the experience of writer and reader. The major difference between the books on the Honor Sampling and those published in earlier years is the subtlety with which the messages are presented. In earlier books there was a direct hard sell, but today's writers tell stories that point the reader in specific directions and then let the reader arrive at a conclusion.

Writing in 1977 about British young adult literature and a smattering of American young adult novels, Sheila Ray observed that "despite their outspoken coverage of a wide range of controversial topics, the majority of teenage novels tend to reinforce conventional and establishment attitudes."[11] Books on the Honor Sampling support her observation. They are clearly on the side of the angels. Even when the subject is sexuality, alcoholism, divorce, or drugs, the books support conventional middle-class standards. This is to be expected because many writers came from the middle class or aspired to it when young. Also, it is the middle-class value system that supports schools and libraries. But in reality this is not so different from adult books, most of which promote the same attitudes and values.

Myth No. 6: Teenage Books Are Anti-Adult, Especially Anti-Parent

Another common belief is that as part of their desire to achieve independence from their parents, teenagers are resentful of adults, and, at least in fiction, could easily do without them. But such books as Bruce Brooks' *The Moves Make the Man,* Mollie Hunter's *Cat, Herself,* William Armstrong's *Sounder,* Alice Childress' *A Hero Ain't Nothin' But a Sandwich,* Kathryn Lasky's *Beyond the Divide,* and Virginia Hamilton's *M. C. Higgins, the Great* do not support this view. In each book at least one parent is presented as a strong, positive character who plays an important role in the teenage protagonist's development. In Robert Newton Peck's *A Day No Pigs Would Die* the boy loves his father, and the importance that young people attach to finding out about an unknown parent is the main point of Bobbie Ann Mason's *In Country,* Bruce Brooks' *Midnight Hour Encores,* and Virginia Hamilton's *A Little Love.*

However, it is true that young readers want the protagonists in their stories to be young. An interesting thing about the adult books on the Honor Sampling is that, except for three or four, protagonists are under thirty and do not have children of their own. Apparently in the eyes of teenagers, the big dividing line—the final rite of passage—between youth and adulthood is becoming a parent. Teenagers identify with adults and think of them as just slightly older than themselves as long as little or no mention is made of family responsibilities as in Berton Roueche's suspenseful *Feral,* William Wharton's *Birdy* and *A Midnight Clear,* and Jessamyn West's *The Massacre at Fall Creek.*

Myth No. 7: Girls Read About Girls and Boys; Boys Read Only About Boys

Of all the myths, this has the most potential of becoming a self-fulfilling prophecy, at least prior to the consciousness-raising of the 1970s. Studies done in the early 1950s indicated that starting with fourth or fifth grade, boys showed a slight preference for reading stories about males. This kind of information was widely publicized, especially in the education explosion that surrounded the launching of Russia's Sputnick. During this period, there was great emphasis on teaching boys to read and encouraging them in academic endeavors in the hope that they would grow up and become the engineers and the scientists who would help Americans compete successfully against the Russians. Teachers, librarians, publishers, and authors often heard or read statements to the effect that whereas girls will read books about both boys and girls, boys will read only those books that feature males. This led publishers to concentrate on stories about males because they naturally wanted the largest possible market for their books. For example, Scott O'Dell has told how his 1961 Newbery Award winner, *Island of the Blue Dolphins,* was rejected by a publisher who wanted him to change Karana, the heroine, to a boy so it would be read by more people. O'Dell refused because it was a true story, and much of its value rested on the fact that Karana was a female who had to break her tribal male/female restrictions to survive.

O'Dell's experience was typical of a publishing world that considered males to be the reading audience to be wooed. Then, as now, young girls read more than boys, so there was always a market for so-called girls' books. But the kind of books produced with females as the intended audience were lopsided romances that even today boys won't read, although authors M. E. Kerr and Paul Zindel have proven that boys will read well-written romances if the authors have included male and female viewpoints. Bobbie Ann Mason's *In Country,* William Sleator's *House of Stairs,* Robert C. O'Brien's *Z for Zacharia,* Richard Peck's *Remembering the Good Times,* Ursula Le Guin's *The Beginning Place,* and Julian Thompson's *A Band of Angels* also show that boys have no qualms about reading books that have female protagonists filling challenging roles.

Perhaps the literary level at which these books are written has something to do with their contradiction of this myth about "sex appeal." After all, they were chosen as "best" books by many knowledgeable people. The segregation of books by sex may occur more with poorly written, exaggerated romances, adventure stories, and pornography. The implication here seems to be that the topic and the theme have just as much to do with reader choice as the sex of the protagonist.

Myth No. 8: If Teenagers See the Movie, They Won't Read the Book

This is a myth that time has proved unfounded. Although people used to worry about it, today most educators agree that the existence of a well-done media piece increases the number of readers that a book has. If they've enjoyed the film version, young adults are likely to want their pleasure reinforced by encountering the familiar characters and situations again in the book.

In the Honor Sampling, a large percentage of the early books have probably been keep alive both in libraries and on teachers' reading lists because interest is renewed each time a movie is re-released or shown on television: for example the 1967 *Mr. and Mrs. Bo Jo Jones* and *The Chosen,* 1968 *Red Sky at Morning,*

1969 *Sounder* and *Where the Lilies Bloom,* 1970 *Love Story* and *Bless the Beasts and Children,* and 1971 *Go Ask Alice* and *The Autobiography of Miss Jane Pittman.* More recently several books including *Summer of My German Soldier* and *Dinky Hocker Shoots Smack* have been ABC After School Specials, while William Wharton's *Birdy* and all of S. E. Hinton's books have been made into full-length movies.

Throughout the industry, media and book people usually work together so that when books are adapted for television, either the opening or closing credits encourage viewers to read the book. But sometimes producers will use a different title for their media production as when Robb White's *Deathwatch* was given the television name *Savages.* The change, necessary because two other movies already had similar-sounding titles, worked against boosting the book's readership.

Myth No. 9: Young Adult Literature Is Less Enduring— There Are No Classics

All of us who struggle to read each year's new crop of books have probably wondered at one time or another if our jobs wouldn't be easier if only the best twenty or thirty books were published each year or if we had a group of proven classics we could offer. Where's the *Charlotte's Web,* the *Winnie the Pooh,* and the *Alice in Wonderland* of YA lit? Or for that matter, the *Moby Dick* or *Crime and Punishment?*

A great work by definition is individual and rare. Considering how new the phenomenon of young adult literature is, it would be astonishing indeed if there were a teenage book with the stature and enduring quality of *Moby Dick.* Books for young adults range from truly fine and imaginative works to outright trash. And although young adult literature includes books of widely varying quality, certainly the field has no monopoly on mediocrity or hack writing, which can be found in any area. It probably is fair to say, though, that as more freedom has been given to the writers and publishers of teenage books, good writers have used the freedom to produce better books, but poor writers have used it to hang themselves on every social ill they could find. The result has been a widening of the gap between the talented and the hack.

Although young adult literature may not yet have what could undeniably be labeled a classic, it does have some truly outstanding writers. All the authors with four or more books on the Honor Sampling—Robert Cormier, M. E. Kerr, Sue Ellen Bridgers, and Richard Peck—surely deserve to be called stars whether or not they have produced any classics. "Stars" with three honored books include Norma Fox Mazer, Virginia Hamilton, S. E. Hinton, Cynthia Voigt, Margaret Mahy, and Paula Fox. Other good authors may not have as many books on our list but that's only because their writing is more varied with much of it being aimed at adults, for example, William Wharton, Maya Angelou, Chaim Potok, Judy Blume, Alice Childress, and Ernest J. Gaines.

ROSEMARY SUTCLIFF
on Exploration and Increase

I have a very earnest wish, and this is it: that the High-and-Mighty ones of the young people's book world could get rid of their dreary and ultimately dangerous idea that their readers should never (save in the case of Science Fiction) be asked to use their imagination. It used not to be like that. At one time we used to read for the joys of adventure and high romance, for the entrance into a world beyond the confines of our own experience, which was to be found between the covers of a book. This was not mere escapism. Something of escape was in it, of course, but also exploration and increase, the widening of our horizons as by the opening of a window. Now, it seems that the window is to remain closed, and the young must not be expected to reach out to experience anything not actually in the same room with themselves. Admittedly the closed room of actual experience includes plenty of material for the makeup of a dramatic story: divorce, suicide, drug addiction and the like all seem, alas!, to be part of life now for the young as for the fully adult, as well as what used to be known in the theatre world as "kitchen sink." Of course there must be stories dealing with all these matters; there always have been, and the best among them opened windows of their own, though it does not seem to be always the best which are now encouraged. But surely there is still space for a few giants and dragons to be fought, a few heroes to fight them, for laughter and magic and ideals, for the historical or adventure story of quality, which will call its readers, mostly without their being aware of it, to reach out and up, to grapple with ideas still beyond their effortless and immediate comprehension!

Do we really want to become, ultimately, inhabitants of a world in which people have forgotten how to spread the wings of the mind?

Rosemary Sutcliff's books include *The Eagle of the Ninth,* Walck, 1954; *Song for a Dark Queen,* Crowell, 1978; and *Frontier Wolf,* Dutton, 1981.

 WHAT THE BEST YOUNG ADULT LITERATURE PROVIDES

The rejection either in whole or in part of these nine myths has shown what the best of young adult literature is not, but it seems appropriate to turn these statements around and end with a positive statement about what the best young adult literature is. First, it is written in a natural, flowing language much like that which young adults use orally. Although it is not simplified for easy reading, writers avoid long, drawn-out descriptions, the kind of pedantic or overblown language sometimes found in writing for adults, and usually the interweaving of multiple, complex plots.

Writers treat a wide variety of subject matter and themes, including many controversial ideas. And they choose protagonists from minority groups as well as from the white middle-class majority. Like most adult and children's books, young adult literature usually supports the middle-class value system. And though recent books may push the boundaries out a little, they still point young readers toward the moral values and the behaviors deemed desirable by middle-class society. The protagonists, either male or female, are relatively young (in their teens or early twenties) and are virtually free from family responsibilities. The production of a well-done media piece seems to promote the popularity of the book on which it is based. And, finally, in the Honor Sampling, the quality of the writing varies from good to excellent, but in young adult literature as a whole, it varies from poor to excellent, just as it does in writing aimed at any other audience.

Has contemporary young adult literature anything to offer teachers, librarians, or—most of all—students? Is young adult literature worth studying, given the multitudinous responsibilities we all have?

We believe the answer to both questions is an unqualified yes. Young adult literature was never intended to replace other forms of literature. It provides enjoyment, satisfaction, and literary quality while it brings life and hope and reality to young people. Some students may find it beyond their abilities, unfortunately, while other young people will have passed beyond it. Pigeonholing has always been tempting for teachers and librarians. It would be so easy if we could place students in neat categories but reality doesn't work that way. Teachers or librarians who force-feed a steady diet of either great literature or teenage books, or any other particular kind of book, down the gullets of young readers prove that they know nothing about them and care as little about finding out. Susan Sontag reported in an interview in the *New York Times* on January 30, 1978, that she remembered all too well attending a "dreadful high school" where she was reprimanded for reading Immanuel Kant's *Critique of Pure Reason* instead of the assigned portion of the *Reader's Digest*. Responsible teachers and librarians individualize their work, recommending particular books to students, not because they are classics or because everyone else has liked them, but because the student's own personality and interests are respected.

To fill this leadership role, adults must first understand what and who and where young adults are, and second they must know the books. There's only one way to know the books and that is to read them in their entirety, not just the dust jackets or the reviews.

Young adult literature is not the whole of literature, but it is an increasingly important part. The future teacher or librarian unfamiliar with young adult literature begins disadvantaged and, given the flow of the presses, is likely to remain so. To remain ignorant is to be professionally irresponsible with the result being a disaster for students who will miss out on being introduced to the delights of reading for pleasure.

NOTES

[1] Linda Nielsen, *Adolescent Psychology: A Contemporary View* (New York: Holt, 1987).

[2] Boyd R. McCandless and Richard H. Coop, *Adolescents: Behavior and Development,* 2nd ed. (New York: Holt, Rinehart and Winston, 1979), p. 160.

[3] Robert Havighurst, *Developmental Tasks and Education* (New York: McKay, 1972).

[4] "Trash for Teen-Agers: Or Escape from Thackeray, the Brontës, and the Incomparable Jane," *Louisville Courier-Journal,* June 17, 1951, quoted in Stephen Dunning, "Junior Book Roundup," *English Journal* 53 (December 1964): 702–3.

[5] J. Donald Adams, *Speaking of Books—and Life* (New York: Holt, Rinehart and Winston, 1965), pp. 250–52.

[6] John Goldthwaite, "Notes on the Children's Book Trade," *Harper's* 254 (January 1977): 76, 78, 80, 84–86.

[7] Nancy Larrick, "Illiteracy Starts Too Soon," *Phi Delta Kappan* 69 (November 1987): 184–89.

[8] Miles Myers, *English Journal* 73 (April 1984): 26–32.

[9] Justin Wintle and Emma Fisher, eds., *The Pied Pipers: Interviews with the Influential Creators of Children's Literature* (New York: Paddington Press, 1974), p. 194.

[10] Stephen Dunning, "A Definition of the Role of the Junior Novel Based on Analyses of Thirty Selected Novels" (Ph.D. diss., Florida State University, 1959), pp. 317–18.

[11] Sheila Ray, "The Development of the Teenage Novel," in *Reluctant to Read?* ed. John L. Foster (London: Ward Lock Educational Publishers, 1977), p. 63.

RECOMMENDED BOOKS ON ADOLESCENT PSYCHOLOGY

Arnold, L. Eugene. *Preventing Adolescent Alienation.* Lexington, Massachusetts: D. C. Heath, 1983.
Designed for school and other institutional workers as well as family members, Arnold's book focuses on sexual development, child abuse, truancy, dropping out of school, substance abuse, and moral and spiritual confusion.

Csikszentimahalyi, Mihaly, and Reed Larson. *Being Adolescent.* New York: Basic, 1984.
Based on a study of teenagers from one high school, this book clearly identifies the patterns of adolescent life. The research format is a bit difficult and there is some overgeneralizing; nevertheless the book does a good job of revealing how adolescents view reality.

Davis, Inger D. *Adolescents: Theoretical and Helping Perspectives.* Norwell, Massachusetts: Kluwer-Nijhoff, 1985.
Davis' book is especially good on the needs of young people in remarried, adoptive, or single-parent families, as well as in foster family care, community group residence, and institutions.

Fairchild, Thomas. ed. *Crisis Intervention Strategies for School Based Helpers.* Springfield, Illinois: Charles C. Thomas, 1986.
Crises that are discussed include parental separation and/or divorce, problems in stepfamilies, death and grief, violence, suicide, eating disorders, unwanted pregnancy, abuse, neglect, and stress. Included is a helpful list of curricular materials, films, suggested readings, and names of resource agencies and organizations.

Fuhrman, Barbara Schneider. *Adolescence. Adolescents.* Boston: Little, Brown, 1986.
Part 1 treats adolescent development from historical, societal, family, peer, and school

contexts, Part 2 looks at normal adolescent development, and Part 3 looks at problematic responses to the pressures of adolescence.

Kaplan, Louise. *Adolescence: A Farewell to Childhood.* New York: Simon and Schuster, 1984.
Based on the theories of Freud, this book treats biological/sexual development and the tendency for adolescents to pursue perfection in often maladaptive ways.

Newman, Barbara, and Phillip R. Newman. *Adolescent Development.* Columbus, Ohio: Charles E. Merrill, 1986.
The Newmans treat adolescence as a period with an integrity of its own rather than as a transitional period between childhood and adulthood. They emphasize theory and research and make special notes on gender differences in the contexts of work, high school, and college.

Nielsen, Linda. *Adolescent Psychology: A Contemporary View.* New York: Holt, Rinehart and Winston, 1987.
Its readable style makes this 750-page compendium a welcome resource book. The initial overview of theories and research is especially well done.

Offer, Daniel, Eric Ostrove, and Kenneth I. Howard. *The Adolescent: A Psychological Self-Portrait.* New York: Basic, 1981.
The basis of this book was questionnaires through which young people described themselves in psychological, social, sexual, familial, and coping terms.

Rice, F. Phillip. *The Adolescent: Development, Relationships, and Culture* 4th edition. Boston: Allyn and Bacon, 1984.
With a mixture of data and convincing examples, Rice draws on sociology, anthropology, education, and family studies to write about

normal and atypical adolescent behavior and group life. Included are chapters on early marriage, nonmarital cohabitation, adolescent culture and subcultures, and participation in religion and cults.

Sebald, Hans. *Adolescence: A Social Psychological Analysis* 3rd edition. Englewood Cliffs, New Jersey: Prentice-Hall, 1984.
Sebald has especially good chapters on social change and the intergenerational conflict, conditions of postindustrial life, American culture influences, and teen subcultures.

Sugar, Max. *Responding to Adolescent Needs.* New York: Spectrum, 1980.
Suggestions for improving the relevance of secondary education to adolescent development tasks are explored. The influences of family, schools, law, health, sex, and work are covered. The book helps distinguish between the normal working-through of the identity crisis and more severe problems that need help from outside.

Walsh, William M. *Childhood and Adolescence: Counseling Theory and Technique.* Berkeley, California: McCutchan Publishers, 1985.
Walsh explains and applies to the school setting the major tenets of rational-emotive, play, and reality therapy, and discusses behavioral, Adlerian, gestalt, client-centered, existential, and eclectic counseling.

Waterman, Alan S. *Identity in Adolescence: Process and Contents.* San Francisco: Jossey-Bass, 1985.
Waterman discusses the development of identity in relation to thinking about vocations, religion, political socialization, and choice of social roles. Especially insightful is the chapter on religious thinking and moral development.

◧ TITLES MENTIONED IN CHAPTER ONE IN ADDITION TO THE HONOR SAMPLING

Flesch, Rudolf. *Why Johnny Can't Read and What You Can Do About It.* Harper & Row, 1966.

Kant, Immanuel. *Critique of Pure Reason.* St. Martin, 1919 (written in 1781).

McCullers, Carson. "Like That." In *The Mortgaged Heart,* copyright, 1941, reprinted in *Early Sorrow: Ten Stories of Youth,* Charlotte Zolotow, ed. Harper & Row, 1986.

Matsubara, Hisako, tr. Leila Vennewitz. *Cranes at Dusk.* Doubleday, 1985.

O'Dell, Scott. *Island of the Blue Dolphins.* Houghton Mifflin, 1960.

Zindel, Paul. *The Effect of Gamma Rays on Man-in-the-Moon-Marigolds.* Dramatists, 1970.

Zolotow, Charlotte, ed. *Early Sorrow: Ten Stories of Youth.* Harper & Row, 1986.

For information on the availability of paperback editions of these titles, please consult the most recent edition of *Paperbound Books in Print,* published annually by R. R. Bowker Company.

LITERARY ASPECTS OF YOUNG ADULT BOOKS

In beginning the systematic study of young adult literature, we quickly discover many of the same questions and considerations we face in studying any body of literature. Writers of books for young readers work in much the same way as writers of other sorts of books. They have the same tools and largely the same intent: to evoke a response in a reader through words on a page. And young adult readers read with the same range of responses as any other group of readers.

STAGES OF LITERARY APPRECIATION

One of the reasons that within any group of readers there may be many different responses to the same piece of literature is that individuals develop reading skills and their appreciation of literature in different stages, which they reach at different times. Rather than *going through* these stages of reading development, they *add on*. With each additional level they have all that they had before, plus a new way to gain pleasure and understanding. The first stage is the simple realization that words coming from a printed page can bring enjoyment.

Lucky children who have bedtime stories and frequent visits to the library for storyhour and checking out books and also have songs, nursery rhymes, and jingles woven into the fabric of everyday life are fortunate enough to develop this first stage of appreciation before they enter school. Jim Trelease in his highly acclaimed *Read-Aloud Handbook* explained that he was not writing a book to help parents teach their children to read but to help them teach their children to *want to read.* His interest was in building a firm foundation for the development to follow.

The challenge for teachers and librarians is to find where a particular reader is and then provide the kind of support that will be most beneficial. For example, a child who has been introduced to literature in the loving arms of parents or others has an advantage over the child who first meets the printed page under the stress of school. Teachers need to concentrate on providing the kind of pleasure and fun that will show children what they have to gain from learning to read. If children see no benefit, they can hardly be expected to put forth the tremendous intellectual effort needed to learn to read.

For most children, the obvious benefit is enjoyment, but in today's increasingly print-oriented society, preschool children may also develop an awareness of concrete benefits. For example, there's hardly a four-year-old in United States metropolitan areas who doesn't recognize the golden arches of a McDonald's restaurant. And toddlers too young to walk around grocery stores reach out from their seats in grocery carts to grab favorite brands of cereal. We know one child who by the time he entered first grade had taught himself to read from *TV Guide.* The format of *TV Guide* breaks almost every rule any good textbook writer would follow in designing a primer for clear and easy reading, but it did have one overpowering advantage. The child could get immediate feedback. If he made a correct guess he was rewarded by getting to watch the program he wanted. If he made a mistake, he knew immediately that he had to return to the printed page to try again.

This first stage of development, called "reading readiness," used to be the goal of most kindergarten teachers. But now with increased worry over declining reading interest and ability, there is widespread pressure to push children ahead. Many school districts expect children to come to kindergarten knowing the letters of the alphabet, and many ambitious parents are caught up with the "Super Baby" syndrome teaching their two- and three-year-olds the names and sounds of the letters of the alphabet. Bright children able to learn early do so for the reward of their parent's approval. The time and energy would be better spent in reading stories to the children so that they would begin to understand and develop an appreciation of the value of the printed word.

Learning to read, which is the second stage of development, gets maximum attention during the primary grades where as much as 70 percent of the school day is devoted to the language arts. But developing literacy is a never-ending task for anyone who is intellectually active. Even at a mundane level, adults continue working to develop their reading skills. The owner of a new VCR trying to tape a television program, the person trying to get a new printer to "handshake" with the computer, or the person who rereads several tax guides in preparation for an audit, all exhibit the same symptoms of concentrated effort as do children first learning to read: they point with their fingers, move their lips, return to reread difficult parts, and perhaps in frustration slam the offending booklet to the floor. But in each case, they are motivated by a vision of some benefit to be gained and so they increase their efforts.

It's been so long since most of us learned the basic skills of decoding that we have probably forgotten the work involved. And since we are among those who have chosen literature as our lifetime work, it probably came easily to us. This means we may lack empathy for those children who must struggle to read. In our impatience as we wait for them to master reading skills, we may forget to help them find pleasure and enjoyment.

Children who learn to read easily—the girl who sits in the backseat of the car and reads all through the family vacation and the boy who reads a book while delivering the neighborhood newspapers—find their own rewards for reading. For these children, the years between seven and twelve are golden. They can read the great body of literature that the world has saved for them: *Charlotte's Web, The Little House* books, *The Borrowers, The Chronicles of Narnia, The Wizard of Oz, Where the Red Fern Grows,* and books by Beverly Cleary, Judy Blume, John Fitzgerald, and hundreds of other good writers.

At this stage children are undemanding. They are in what Margaret Early has described as a stage of unconscious enjoyment.[1] With help, they may enjoy such classics as *Alice in Wonderland, The Wind in the Willows, Treasure Island,* and *Little Women,* but by themselves they are far more likely to turn to less challenging material. This is the age when children have traditionally gobbled up series books such as *The Hardy Boys, The Bobbsey Twins, Nancy Drew,* and *Tom Swift.*

Parents, who are more aware than are children of how brief childhood is, worry that their children are wasting time reading what some people label subliterature. These parents take seriously the often quoted "Only the rarest kind of best is good enough for children." This is a noble sentiment, but there's a problem in interpretation. *Best* from whose viewpoint? Children will most likely tell you that the book that is the best is the one that is the funniest (or the most gross or the most extreme) while adults are more likely to judge on the basis of subtlety, the lesson taught, the literary skill displayed, or the author's reputation.

When parents consult us about their children reading "trash," the only comfort we can give is that when our college students write their reading histories, nearly 100 percent of the ones who say they love to read went through childhood stages of being addicted for months to one particular kind of book. Today it may be *Encyclopedia Brown* stories or *Choose Your Own Adventure* paperbacks or "everything" by a particular author. Apparently readers find comfort in knowing the characters in a book and what to expect. They develop speed and skill which stand them in good stead when they tire of a particular kind of book—they always do sooner or later—and go on to reading some of the books parents and teachers wished they had been reading all along.

It's during middle childhood that differences in reading abilities stretch out across the wide spectrum that high school teachers are accustomed to meeting. Children who love to read may check out a book a day from their school library or go once a week to a public library where they take out the maximum allowed. They may spend a couple of hours a night reading at home. In contrast, those who don't like to read do it only for the assigned time in school, perhaps a half-hour or an hour, much of which may be devoted to "skills development," the filling in of worksheets rather than reading.

The difference, of course, is going to be noticeable. Many of these school-only readers will never lose themselves in a book, the third stage of reading development. And if they do, it is likely to happen much later than in second, third, or fourth grade, more typical of good readers. In this segment from *The Car Thief* by Theodore Weesner, Alex Housman, who is being kept in a detention home, is seventeen years old when he first has the experience of losing himself in a story.

■   After breakfast they did not return immediately upstairs but followed Mr. Kelly to his office. There on the floor was a long wooden crate filled with books, and Mr. Kelly was saying that someone had donated them to the home and they could have them upstairs if they liked, as long as the books were not mistreated, were not torn or mutilated. No one said much of anything. They carried the box upstairs, Red Eye taking one end, Billy Noname the other. Placing it on the picnic table, they waited without touching for Mr. Kelly to leave, to see what they had.

Their disappointment was calm. They expected little. There were no photographs, no drawings, nothing but words packed on each fanned page as thickly as leaves on a tree. The first book grabbed—it had the only dust jacket, the only color—was called *The Egyptian*. It was dropped at once, by Leonard, and picked up by Thomas, who said, "The *what*?" Red Eye said, "Oh, man, *The Egyptian*, mummy stuff—man, you so dumb!"

The other books were old novels, books with pale and faded covers by authors named A. J. Cronin, Hans Hellmut Kirst, Virgil Scott, Jan Struther, Vincent Carr.

Alex was the only one who read, perhaps the only one who could read, although Thomas sat with *The Egyptian* for a while before he pitched it back into the box.

Alex started to read a book called *Gunner Asch,* starting it mainly because he knew how to read, although he was intimidated by the mass of words. He had never read anything but the lessons in schoolbooks—assignments in history or science spaced with water colors of Washington crossing the Delaware or Thomas Edison working under candlelight. But the novel was simply written and fairly easy to understand, and he soon became interested enough in what was happening to stop reminding himself page after page that he was reading a book, to turn the pages to see what was going to happen next.

He sat on the floor reading until he grew sleepy. When his eyelids began to slide down and his head began to cloud, he lay over on his side on the floor to sleep awhile, pulling up his knees, resting his head on his arm. When he woke he got up and carried the book with him to the bathroom . . . reading the book again, he became so involved in the story that his legs fell asleep. He kept reading, intending to get up at the end of this page, then at the end of this page, if only because he would feel more comfortable with his pants up and buttoned, but he read on. He rose finally at the end of a chapter, although he read a little into the next chapter before he made himself stop. His legs were buoyant with saws and needles as he buttoned up, and he had to hold a hand against the wall not to sway from balance. Then he checked the thickness of pages he had read between his fingers, and experienced something he had never experienced before. Some of it was pride—he was reading a book—and some of it was a preciousness the book had assumed. Feeling relaxed, unthreatened, he wanted to keep the book in his hands for what it offered. He did not want to turn the pages, for then they would be gone and spent; nor did he want to do anything but turn the pages.

He stepped over legs again and sat down to read, as far from anyone as he could get, some fifteen feet, to be alone with the book. He read on. Something was happening to him, something as pleasantly strange as the feeling he had had for Irene Sheaffer. By now, if he knew a way, he would prolong the book the distance his mind could see, and he rose again, quietly, to sustain the pleasant sensation, the escape he seemed already to have made from the scarred and unlighted corridor. Within this shadowed space there were now other things—war and food and a worry over cigarettes and rations, leaving and returning, dying and escaping. The corridor itself, and his own life, was less present.[2]

The more experience children have with reading, the more discriminating they become. The rest of their lives they will be on the lookout for "a good read" and will anticipate the kind of pleasure in a book that surprised Alex in *The Car Thief,* but to receive pleasure they have to respect the book. In reminiscing about his childhood fondness for both *The Hardy Boys* and motorcycles, the late John Gardner remarked that his development as a literary critic took a step forward when he lost patience with the leisurely conversations that the Hardy boys were supposed to have as they roared down country roads, side-by-side on their motorcycles.

Good readers begin developing this critical sense in literature at about the same time they develop it in real life—at the end of childhood and the beginning of their teen years. They move away from a simple interest in what happened in a story to ask *why.* They want logical development. They are no longer satisfied with stereotypes. They want characters controlled by believable human motives. They are more demanding in what they read because now their reading has a real purpose to it. They read to find out about themselves, not simply to escape into someone else's experiences for a few pleasurable hours.

The egocentric way that some teenagers read was shown by an incident at our local high school. A fifteen-year-old girl went to her counselor and asked that she please inform the librarian she was not "that kind of a girl." When the counselor questioned why she was to deliver this message, she found that the girl had been going to the librarian all year for reading suggestions. The girl read and identified strongly with everything the librarian gave her. She apparently used the reading suggestions much the way some people use the news-paper horoscopes. But now she was upset because the librarian had handed her Ann Head's *Mr. and Mrs. Bo Jo Jones,* which is about a young couple who have to get married when the girl becomes pregnant.

Fortunately this kind of egocentric reading is not an end in itself, but a basis from which teachers and librarians can help young readers go beyond their narrow concerns to think about society as a whole. As they anticipate leaving their parents' homes and protection, teenagers are understandably curious about the world and may read dozens of contemporary, teenage novels looking for lives as much like their own as possible. On the other hand, they are curious about other sides of life too and so they seek out books which present lives totally different from their own. They look for anything bizarre, unbelievable, weird, or grotesque: stories of occult happenings, trivia books, and horror stories. Whatever it is they read, the purpose is largely one of finding themselves and their places in society.

The next stage in reading development comes when people go beyond their egocentrism and look at the larger circle of society. Senior high school English teachers have some of their best teaching experiences with books by such writers as Ernest Hemingway, John Steinbeck, Harper Lee, F. Scott Fitzgerald, Carson McCullers, William Faulkner, Arthur Miller, and Flannery O'Connor. Students respond to the way these books raise questions about conformity, social pressures, justice, and all the other aspects of human frailties as well as strengths. It is at this level that students are ready to begin looking at shades of gray rather than black and white. Book discussions can have real meat to them because readers make different interpretations as they bring their own experiences into play against those in the books.

Obviously, getting to this level of literary appreciation is more than a matter of developing an advanced set of decoding skills. It is closely tied in with intellectual, physical, and emotional development. Teenagers face the tremendous responsibility of assessing the world around them and deciding where they might best fit in. Reading at this level allows teenagers to focus on their own psychological needs in relation to society. The more directly they can do this the more efficient they feel, which probably explains the popularity of contemporary problem novels featuring young protagonists as in the books by Bruce Brooks, M. E. Kerr, Robert Cormier, Alice Childress, Sue Ellen Bridgers, and Richard Peck.

While many people read fantasy and science fiction at the level of losing themselves in a good story, others may read such books as William Sleator's *House of Stairs,* Virginia Hamilton's *Sweet Whispers, Brother Rush,* and Robin McKinley's *The Blue Sword* at a higher level of reflection. They come back from spending a few hours in the imagined society with new ideas about their own society.

When people have developed the skills and attitudes that are necessary to read at all of the levels described so far, then they are ready to read for literary or aesthetic appreciation. This is the level at which authors, critics, and literary scholars concentrate their efforts. But even they don't work at this level all of

PAULA FOX
on the Life of the Imagination

Often, the letters I receive from young people about my novels are written as class assignments. They urge me to reply at once so they can get their reports done in time for a grade. Some of their questions seem to have been devised for interviewing criminals. "What was your motivation in writing the book?" they ask. "How long have you been doing this?" "What made you start?" "Are you ever going to stop?"

Of course, many questions are not real questions. They are part of a young person's struggle to get something down on paper that will evoke a response from that unknown person who has some mysterious connection with the book they were assigned to read. I would guess that readers have as much difficulty imagining the writer as the writer has in imagining the reader. Some of that difficulty may arise from what we think a story is—what its relationship to daily life is.

The two most frequently asked questions are: "Is this a true story?" and "Where do you get your ideas from?" I can't recall a letter in which the word *imagination* appeared. "Did you make up the story?" is the closest to it. I get the sense that making up a story means to these young readers that the story is untrue. Yet it is imagination that is the source of the power and endurance of a good story. Goethe wrote "Great imagining is the imagining of truth, the effort to grasp truth through the imagination."

As to whether a story is "real" or not, E. B. White gave this response: "But real life is only one kind of life—there is also the life of the imagination."

Perhaps young people could be helped to grasp more about "real life" and the life of imagination, if they were shown that the writer's effort is to awaken their imaginations through stories and so remind them of that real life. At its best, good writing gives readers metaphors which can help us to understand what we have lived through, our pleasures, our sufferings, the mystery of our lives.

Paula Fox's books include *The Slave Dancer,* Bradbury, 1968; *One-Eyed Cat,* Bradbury, 1984; and *The Moonlight Man,* Bradbury, 1986.

the time because it's as demanding as it is rewarding. The professor who teaches Shakespeare goes home at night and loses himself in a televised rerun of "M*A*S*H" or "Cheers," and the author who writes for hours in the morning might read herself to sleep that night with an Agatha Christie mystery.

The reason that reading for aesthetic enjoyment is so demanding is that readers' minds must work at each of the lower levels of finding enjoyment, developing and exercising reading skills, losing and/or finding themselves in the story, relating the story to society, and then adding to all this the conscious awareness and analysis of the literary techniques through which authors perform their magic. In writing about this level of literary appreciation, Margaret Early described a *New Yorker* cartoon in which an aggressive character, with martini in hand and chip on shoulder, accosts a guest at a literary cocktail party and says, "So you write? Well, I read!"

The implication is that at the highest level, reading is an active, rather than a passive, endeavor, and that to get the maximum good out of a piece, readers must do half the work. Reading at that level is becoming a literary critic, a creative act much like being an author.

In a 1983 article entitled, "Finally Only the Love of the Art,"[3] poet Donald Hall wrote about his own development as a reader and writer. Except for the speed befitting his giftedness, the excerpts printed below show that Hall's development progressed in the same order as that described here for more typical readers.

The family lived in a variety of homes until, during Hall's early school years in the 1930s, his family assumed a mortgage on a house that a bank had repossessed because of the Depression.

When I was in my snooty teens I would have denied it, but these houses were bookish. Because the Book-of-the-Month club supplied 13 master-pieces a year, because the Reader's Digest and Collier's lay beside easy chairs, I felt superior. My father read Kenneth Roberts, not Gerard Manley Hopkins, but he read *books*—which means that I grew up un-American. An only child, I lived with people who continually gazed at print. My mother even read poems and read them aloud to me when I was little. My favorite was Vachel Lindsay's "The Moon's the North Wind's Cooky."

My grandfather said poems all day long without repeating himself, recited not Keats or Henry King or Vachel Lindsay but (without ascription) "Casey at the Bat" and "Lawyer Green" and "What the Deacon Said"—long poems, usually narrative, either comic or melodramatic. I sat in the tie-up on a three-legged stool watching him milk his Holsteins as his dear voice kept time with his hands and he crooned wonderful bad poems with the elocutionary zeal of another century.

By the time I was 12 I spent all summer there. I got up at 6 and fed the chicks and read and wrote all morning; in the afternoon I hayed with my grandfather, absorbing his stories and poems. . . . There was also a great-uncle, Luther the retired minister, born in 1856, who had taught himself Greek and who wrote verses mainly devotional; we sat on the porch as he recollected his boyhood during the Civil War. There was my literary Aunt Caroline, English teacher in Massachusetts, who amused herself writing light verse and rhymes for greeting cards; we went on long walks and she told me about a seafaring adventurer trapped by a cruel one-eyed giant.

And in Hamden from September to June I dreamed of returning to the farm. I did not enjoy the company of other children; I wanted to grow up, even to be old, like the people I loved the most. Alone after school I took pleasure in books—in the Bobbsey Twins, in the Hardy Boys, later in Roy Helton's "Jimmy Sharswood," then gradually in grown-up books. And in movies of werewolves and vampires, which when I was 12 prompted a boy next door (bless you, wherever you are) to recommend the works of Edgar Allan Poe.

I swallowed Poe whole. Then I swallowed Hervey Allen's biography of Poe, "Israfel," and discovered for myself the thrilling role of *poete maudit*. . . . From 12 to 14 I wrote poems and short stories. I started novels and five-act tragedies in verse. But I had not yet committed myself wholly to writing. I entertained occasional notions of becoming an actor, or President. ("Nothing is so commonplace," Oliver Wendell Holmes said, "as to wish to be remarkable.")

When he was fourteen, Hall went to a Boy Scout meeting and happened to tell another boy that he had written a poem that day in study hall. The boy confessed that writing poems was "his profession" and he took Hall with him on poetic excursions into New Haven where he introduced him to "Yale freshmen—18-year-olds!—who were literary geniuses."

It was during this "heady time" that Donald Hall first began to get poems accepted by "little" magazines and eventually bigger ones. And now in his fifties, he's still aspiring for the top level of literary appreciation. He concluded his article:

If you continue to write, you go past the place where praise, publication or admiration sustains you. The more praise the better—but it does not sustain you. You arrive at a point where only the possibilities of poetry provide food for your desires, possibilities glimpsed in great poems that you love. What began perhaps as the north wind's cooky—what continued variously as affectation and self-love; what zaps crazily up and down in public recognition—finds repose only in love of the art, and in the desire, if not precisely the hope, that you may make something fit to endure with the old ones.

BECOMING A LITERARY CRITIC

As Hall indicates, the top level is not something a writer reaches effortlessly, or that once reached requires no further effort. Reaching that level as a reader means becoming a literary critic, not necessarily for other people but at least for oneself. The difference between being a critic and a reviewer is that a reviewer evaluates and makes recommendations about who would most like to read which book. Critics do more. Besides evaluating and recommending books, they give guidance. They explain. The good critic makes observations that when shared, help others to read with understanding and insight.

Developing into the kind of reader able to derive nourishment at the highest level of literary response is a lifelong task, one which challenges all of us. The information presented in this chapter is basic to identifying with a story through the eyes of the author as well as through the eyes of the characters. We present it at the beginning of this textbook for three reasons. First, it will help you get more out of the reading you do throughout this course. Second, when you enjoy the books you read in this way and when you sharpen your insights into authors' working methods, you will be able to share your insights with young readers who are ready for them. You will also be better able to evaluate new books and to help young readers move along in developing their abilities to evaluate and to receive pleasure at higher levels of reading appreciation. A third advantage to understanding literary terms and concepts is that they will provide you with handles for discussion. Without terminology, it's almost impossible to carry discussions beyond the "I-like-it" and "I-don't-like-it" stage. It is much easier to appreciate and to understand what an author has done when you are acquainted with techniques and can give them names. Knowing and using literary terms correctly will enable you to get maximum benefits from book discussions with both students and colleagues. It will also help you to read reviews, articles, and other books with greater understanding.

Some people speak of literature with a capital *L* to identify the kind of literature that is set apart from, or has a degree of excellence not found in, the masses of printed material that daily roll from the presses. This literature rewards study, not only because of its content, but because of its style, the techniques used, and the universality, permanence, and congeniality of the ideas expressed.

It is on the question of universality and permanence that some critics have asked whether stories written specifically for young readers can be considered Literature. Their feeling is that if a story speaks only to readers of a certain age, then it cannot really have the kind of universality required in true literature. However, every adult has lived through an adolescence and continues to experience many of the doubts, leave-takings, embarkings on new roles, and sudden flashes of joy and wonder that can be found in books with protagonists between the ages of twelve and twenty-five. Books that show the uniqueness and at the same time the universality of such experiences—*Adventures of Huckleberry Finn, The Catcher in the Rye, Little Women,* and *Lord of the Flies,* for example, are often referred to as classics. They have proven themselves with different readers across different time periods. And they are the books that readers return to for a second and third reading, each time feeling rewarded.

In contrast to literature with a capital *L,* there is formula literature and escape literature. In truth, all stories consist of variations on a limited number of plots and themes, but the difference between what is referred to simply as literature and what is referred to as formula literature is one of degree. Formula literature is almost entirely predictable. Many of the situation comedies, crime shows, and adventure shows on television are formula pieces. So are many of the books that young people—and adults—enjoy reading.

Because formula literature is highly predictable, the reader can relax and enjoy a story while expending a minimum of intellectual energy. For this reason, formula literature is often used as escape literature—something people read only for entertainment and relaxation with little or no hope of gaining insights or learning new information. Many paperbacks sold in airports and hospital waiting rooms were written as escape literature. Some people prefer to escape for a few hours with a murder mystery, others with a gothic, others with science fiction, and still others with a Harlequin romance. Much television programming meets many of the same needs as escape literature.

A difference between "significant" and "formula" fiction is that while some significant literature will have an exciting enough plot that it can be read at the level of escapism and fun, the reverse isn't true. There simply isn't enough content in formula fiction to make it worthy of the kind of reading done at the upper levels. Because of this, many "literary" people are prone to look down their noses at it. But when viewed in perspective as only part of the world's literature, there is nothing wrong with young people enjoying formula or escape literature either in books or on film.

However, it is understandable that the goal of most educators who work with young readers is to help them develop enough skill that they are not limited only to this kind of reading. We want them to be able to receive pleasure from all kinds of literature, including that which offers much more than escape or amusement.

Authors of the best young adult books use the same literary techniques— though perhaps to a different degree—as the authors of the best books for adults. As will be seen in the following chapters, these literary techniques can be discussed in many different ways. Two approaches that have proven useful include classification by genre and the analysis of such essential literary elements as plot, theme, character, point of view, tone, setting, and style.

PLOT

In examining books that become popular with young adults compared to those that do not, a crucial difference often appears in the plotting. The plot of a story is the sequence of events in which the characters play out their roles in some kind of conflict. Plot is what happens.

Elements of Plot

For most young readers, there needs to be a promise within the first few pages that something exciting is going to happen, that there is going to be a believable conflict. Authors use various techniques to get this message across to their readers, or to "hook" them. S. E. Hinton did it with her first sentence in *Taming the Star Runner,* "His boot felt empty without the knife in it," while Bruce Brooks did it with the first two paragraphs in *The Moves Make the Man:*

▐   Now, Bix Rivers has disappeared, and who do you think is going to tell his story but me? Maybe his stepfather? Man, that dude does not know Bix deep and now he never will, will he? Only thing he could say is he's probably secretly happy Bix ran away and got out of his life, but he won't tell you even that on account of he's busy getting sympathy dumped on him all over town as the poor deserted guardian.

How about Bix's momma? Can she tell you? I reckon not—she is crazy in the hospital. And you can believe, they don't let crazies have anything sharp like a pencil, else she poke out her eye or worse. So she won't be writing any stories for a long time. But me—I have plenty of pencils, number threes all sharp and dark green enamel on the outside, and I have four black and white marble composition books. Plus I can tell you some things, like Bix was thirteen last birthday (same as me), Bix was a shortstop (supreme), Bix gets red spots the size of a quarter on his cheekbones when angry and a splotch looks like a cardinal smack in the middle of his forehead when he is ashamed. I can tell a lot more, besides, . . .

Other authors use catchy titles as narrative hooks, for example, Paula Fox's *The Moonlight Man,* Olive Ann Burns' *Cold Sassy Tree,* and Cynthia Voigt's *Izzy, Willy-Nilly.* Titles that are questions, such as Richard Peck's *Are You in the House Alone?,* M. E. Kerr's *If I Love You, Am I Trapped Forever?,* and Nat Hentoff's *Does This School Have Capital Punishment?* trigger other questions in readers' minds and make them pick up the book to find the answers.

Asking questions like this works much the same as *in media res,* Latin for "in the midst." It's a technique that authors use to bring the reader directly into the middle of the story. This will usually be followed by a flashback to fill in the missing details. Paul Zindel did this in *The Pigman.* Few readers put the book down after they get acquainted with two likable teenagers and then read John's statement:

▐   Now Lorraine can blame all the other things on me, but she was the one who picked out the Pigman's phone number. If you ask me, I think he would have died anyway. Maybe we speeded things up a little, but you really can't say we murdered him.

Not murdered him.

The most exciting plots are the ones in which the action is continually rising, building suspense, and finally leading to some sort of climax. After an exciting climax, readers need to be let down gently. This brief subsiding and wrapping up of details is called the *denouement.*

In Bruce Brooks' *The Moves Make the Man,* the denouement removes any doubt as to whose story was being told. It is the narrator Jerome's as much as it is Bix's. Jerome makes the transition to his own story with "Then it was summer and no sign of Bix and I decided to write this book. Now it is fall and you have the story." The remaining six paragraphs reassure the reader that although Bix is gone Jerome is going to make it and without getting "all soft and mellow and full of good teary jive."

> I got my own fakes to worry about now. I have not played ball since Bix ran away. Are my moves gone? I doubt it. But I will find out tonight. My head is healed up and the nights are getting cooler and everybody is still full of baseball and summer jive, so they won't notice old Jerome slip out in the dark with his lantern and slide across the marsh and vanish into the forest. Then it will be just Jerome and Spin Light and we will see what we can see and there will be nobody else, not for a long time.

In contrast to plots with rising action are those that are episodic. Writers of nonfiction will use many of the literary techniques discussed here so that as they describe incidents and quote dialogue, the paragraphs they write will differ little from fiction. However, rather than developing an overall plot, they are more likely to present a series of episodes as in Theodore Kazimiroff's true account, *The Last Algonquin.* The chapters, for example, "A Clay Pot," "On the Hudson River," "The Red-Haired Woman," and "The Hardest Winter" are all more or less of equal interest. The title of the book, as well as the dust jacket design, removes any vestige of suspense about whether Joe Two Trees will be able to find and join others of his tribe. Although the chapters are related chronologically, they do not build on each other in such a way that the reader's excitement is brought to a peak because everything is falling into place. This is typical of memoirs such as James Herriot's *All Creatures Great and Small,* Maya Angelou's *I Know Why the Caged Bird Sings,* and Milton Meltzer's *The American Revolutionaries: A History in Their Own Words.*

The more unusual a plot is, the greater is the need for the author to drop hints that will prepare readers for what is ahead. This is called foreshadowing. In *Cat, Herself,* Mollie Hunter does it through fortune telling and the vision that Cat sees of herself. In *Dogsong,* Gary Paulsen devotes a whole chapter to "The Dream," which serves as foreshadowing for the boy in the story as well as for the readers.

> There were swirls of fog like steam off the water in the ice leads; thick fog, heavy fog, that would start to clear and close again, then clear a little more until finally he could see, could see, could see . . .
>
> As the man grabbed the long killing-lance and jumped from the ivory and bone sled, the wind blew off his parka hood and Russel saw the man's face and knew it.
>
> The man was him: Russel, with more hair, longer hair, and a small beard and mustache, but he was Russel and Russel knew fear, deep fear, because with the knowledge that he was the man in the dream he knew that he would have to fight the mammoth. He would have to fight it and kill it.
>
> And the mammoth charged.

In fantasy and science fiction, foreshadowing may be what identifies the genre. For example, in William Sleator's *Interstellar Pig,* the foreshadowing starts with the first sentence, "I'm telling you, there's more history to this house than any other place on Indian Neck, and that's the truth." On page 5, the landlord says about the new neighbors, "This here's the place they wanted, but they were too late. Already rented it to you folks. Man, were they ever disappointed. Never heard anybody get so upset about a summer rental."

When the neighbors arrive—two gorgeous young men and an equally gorgeous woman—they use such words as *logement, genante, tinder, frisson,* and *beurre noire.* Barney, the teenage narrator, describes them as having "a casual, animal grace to their movements that attracted the eye simply because it was so unusual. I knew they were just three people—but somehow I felt as though I were watching three lions." There are enough such clues, that by page 12, readers have figured out what Barney's parents never do figure out. The new neighbors are definitely not ordinary humans.

The effect of this foreshadowing is not to give away the ending, but to increase excitement and suspense and prepare the reader for the outcome. If authors fail to prepare readers—at least on a subconscious level—their stories may lack verisimilitude or believability. Readers want interesting and exciting plots, but they don't want to feel manipulated. Authors must therefore keep themselves and their efforts out of sight. They write as omniscient observers recounting events that appear to be under the control of some greater power than that of a poor, working writer.

Traditionally readers have expected to know all the answers by the end of the book, to have the plot come to a tidy close. But with some of the new stories authors feel this is an unrealistic expectation and so they leave it up to the reader to imagine the ending. In *A Hero Ain't Nothin' But a Sandwich,* Alice Childress didn't think it fair to predict either that Benjie would become a confirmed drug addict or that he would go straight. Boys in his situation turn either way and Childress wanted readers to think about this. Although stories with open-ended plots are sometimes frustrating, they are interesting to read and discuss as a group because they force readers to ponder the story and come to conclusions.

Another modern trend that is frustrating to some readers and critics is that as authors strive for realism, they forget about plot. Instead of writing stories, some critics say, they write case histories. Such books often have to do with a young person's struggle with drug or alcohol addiction, mental or physical illness, conflict with parents, sexual problems, or problems with the law. When an author has not planned an exciting plot, it seems that the temptation is greater to rely on unsavory details. These are the books that are often criticized for their sensationalism.

To have an interesting plot, a story must have a problem of some sort. In adult books, several problems may be treated simultaneously, but in most of the books written specifically for young adults, as well as in those that they respond to from the adult list, the focus is generally on one problem. However, authors may include a secondary or minor problem to appeal to specific readers. For example, in most of Paul Zindel's books, the primary problem is one of personal growth and development on the part of either one or two protagonists. But he tucks in an unobtrusive element of love that will bring satisfaction to romantically inclined readers without being bothersome to the rest of his audience.

Types of Plots

Basically the problems around which plots are developed are of four types: protagonist against self, protagonist against society, protagonist against another person, and protagonist against nature.

Protagonist Against Self   A large portion of the rites-of-passage stories popular with young adults are of the protagonist-against-self type. Through the happenings in the book, the protagonist comes to some new understanding or level of maturity. For example, practically the whole story in Paula Fox's *One-Eyed Cat* takes place in the mind of eleven-year-old Ned. An uncle gives him a Daisy air rifle for his birthday, which his father puts in the attic and forbids him to use. But when Ned goes to the attic he finds "it almost at once, as though it had a voice which had called to him." He takes the gun outside and convinces himself that if he tries it just once, he will "be able to do what his father had told him to do—take his mind away from it."

Events do not turn out as Ned anticipated. It's true that after he fires the gun, he no longer has an interest in shooting, but this is because he is tortured by his memory:

> As he blinked and opened his right eye wide, he saw a dark shadow against the stones which the moon's light had turned the color of ashes. For a split second, it looked alive. Before he could think, his finger had pressed the trigger.
>
> There was a quick *whoosh,* the sound a bobwhite makes when it bursts out of underbrush, then silence. He was sure there hadn't been any loud report that would have waked anyone in the house, yet he had heard something, a kind of thin disturbance in the air. He walked over to the barn. There was no shadow now. There was nothing. He might have only dreamed that he had fired the rifle.

But within a few days when Ned is visiting the old man who lives next door, he sees a gaunt-looking cat and then he notices that the cat has dried blood on its face and a little hole where its left eye should be. "A thought was buzzing and circling inside his head, a thought that stung like a wasp could sting. . . . He had disobeyed his father and he had shot at something that was alive. He knew it was that cat."

The rest of the book is the story of Ned's internal anguish, his keeping the terrible secret to himself at the same time he attempts to make up for his action, and finally his coming to terms with the event and his sharing of it with his mother.

Protagonist Against Society   Protagonist-against-self stories are often, in part, protagonist-against-society stories. For example, in Sylvia Plath's *The Bell Jar,* Esther Greenwood is struggling to understand herself, but the depression and the fears and doubts that she feels are brought on by her experience in New York as a college intern on a fashion magazine. Getting accepted for this position had been an important goal of hers, and she is disappointed because, when she achieves this goal, she finds that the work and the life that go with it seem frivolous and hollow.

Sue Ellen Bridgers' *Home Before Dark* is another book in which the protagonist struggles both against herself and against society. Fourteen-year-old Stella has lived most of the life she can remember in the old white station wagon which her family used for traveling from one crop to the next. When finally Stella's father returns to the family farm that he had abandoned years before, Stella does not want to leave—ever. She refuses to leave even after her mother dies and her father remarries. And she explains:

> None of us ever owned anything until we came back to Daddy's home and Newton gave us the little house. But somehow, I felt like it had always been ours. That land out there belonged to us no matter what anyone said. Daddy was born to it, and I was born to Daddy; so the land and the house were mine. They truly belonged to me, and I belonged to them, like I had known the house and land long before and had somehow forgotten about them for a while.

Finally Stella accepts the little house and the farm as being only one part of her life. They will always be there and she can come back to them, but she must go from them too, unless she wants to be trapped at a standstill while the rest of her family moves forward.

Several books that feature characters from "disadvantaged" homes or neighborhoods are also combinations of the protagonist-against-self and protagonist-against-society patterns. In these, the individuals' self-concepts as well as the problems they face are directly related to the society around them as in Danny Santiago's *Famous All Over Town,* Joyce Carol Thomas' *Marked by Fire,* Rosa Guy's *The Friends,* and Sharon Bell Mathis' *Teacup Full of Roses.* Chaim Potok's *My Name Is Asher Lev* and *The Chosen* show boys who are trying to reach understandings of themselves, but these understandings are greatly affected by the Hasidic Jewish societies in which the boys were born and raised.

Robert Cormier's *The Chocolate War, I Am the Cheese, After the First Death, The Bumblebee Flies Anyway,* and *Beyond the Chocolate War* all come close to being pure examples of plots in which the protagonists are in conflict with society. In *The Chocolate War* and its sequel, almost everyone in the school—

faculty and students alike—goes along with the evil plans of Archie and the Vigils. The denouement of *Beyond the Chocolate War* shows that the conflict was more than a personal one between Archie and Obie. There will always be a Bunting, a Janza, and a Harley to take the place of an Archie.

In *I Am the Cheese*, Adam is left friendless and vulnerable in an institution as the result of organized crime combined with government corruption. In *After the First Death*, one young boy is betrayed by his father who is a military psychologist, while another is kept by his father in a terrible state of innocence in which he is trained as a terrorist and never allowed to experience human feelings of compassion, love, or fear. But the blame for the tragic consequences cannot be laid on the fathers' shoulders because each of them is a victim in his own way of the society to which he belongs. *The Bumblebee Flies Anyway* is in some ways a person-against-nature story in that the boys are fighting against their terminal illnesses. But that they have been placed in an experimental hospital where they are at the mercy of "the Handyman" is the fault of society, not just the one doctor.

Protagonist Against Another   Sometimes there is a combination in which the protagonist struggles with self, and also with another person or persons. For example, in Judith Guest's *Ordinary People*, Conrad is struggling to gain his mental health after he attempts suicide, but this struggle is tied to the sibling rivalry that he felt with his older brother who was killed accidentally. And the sibling rivalry is tied to the relationship that exists between him and his parents. Because nearly everyone has experienced conflicts with family members, they can identify with the sibling rivalry in Katherine Paterson's *Jacob Have I Loved*, the tenuousness of the father/daughter relationship in Paula Fox's *The Moonlight Man*, and the family/foster child conflict in Rosa Guy's *The Disappearance*.

Adventure stories, for example, the *Rambo* movies based on David Morrell's *First Blood*, epitomize the person-against-person plot. Other examples include Julian Thompson's *A Band of Angels*, in which five young teens are unaware that they are being pursued by government agents, and Robb White's *Deathwatch*, in which the hunting guide becomes the hunting target.

Fantasy and science fiction will often have person- (or creature-) against-person plots because it is easier to personify evil when the subjects are not real people as with the aliens in William Sleator's *Interstellar Pig*, the twin in Lois Duncan's occult *Stranger with My Face*, and the evil Arawn in Lloyd Alexander's *The Black Cauldron*.

Protagonist Against Nature   Among the most exciting of the protagonist-against-nature stories are accounts of true adventures, such as Piers Paul Read's *Alive: The Story of the Andes Survivors*, Thor Heyerdahl's *The "RA" Expeditions*, and Dougal Robertson's *Survive the Savage Sea*. The stories of contemporary young adults challenging the seas include Steven Callahan's *Adrift: Seventy-six Days Lost at Sea* and Robin Graham's *Dove*.

Within recent years, several authors have done a reverse twist on the person-against-nature plot and have made nature the protagonist and people the antagonists. This is the beginning situation in Richard Adams' *Watership Down* and throughout *The Plague Dogs*. It is also what underlies the story in John Donovan's *Family* and in Robert C. O'Brien's *Z for Zachariah.*

THEME AND MODE

Closely related to plot is theme. Theme in a book is what ties it all together and answers the questions: What does the story mean? What is it about? Theme should not be confused with a didactic moral tagged on at the end of a story, nor should it be confused with plot. Instead it is something that pervades the story and stays with the reader long after details of plot, setting, and even character have faded. Linguistic scholars talk about the deep structure of a sentence as compared to its surface structure. The surface structure is the exact words that are used, whereas the deep structure is the underlying meaning. Dozens of different surface structures could communicate the same idea, a message of love, for example. Plot and theme are related in the same way. A plot relates to a single story, whereas a theme is applicable to hundreds of stories.

Sometimes an author will be very explicit in developing a theme, even expressing part of it in the title as with Maya Angelou's *All God's Children Need Traveling Shoes,* John Knowles' *A Separate Peace,* and S. E. Hinton's *The Outsiders.* At other times the theme is almost hidden so that young readers need help in finding it through discussion of the book with others who have read it. A book can have more than one theme, but usually the secondary themes will be less important to the story. However, because of the experiences that a reader brings to a book, it may be a secondary theme that happens to impress a particular reader. A theme must be discovered by the reader. It can't simply be told or else it is reduced to a moral.

The kinds of themes treated in stories are closely correlated with the mode in which they are written. Mode is most commonly divided into comedy, romance, irony/satire, and tragedy. Together these make up the story of everyone's life, and in literature as in life they are interrelated, flowing one into the other. Comedy might be compared to spring, childhood, innocence, and happiness. Romance also connotes happiness and is often associated with summer, the teen years, young love, and growth. Irony and satire correlate symbolically with fall, middle-age, the existence of problems, and unhappiness. Tragedy is correlated with winter, old-age, suffering, and sadness.[4]

Books for children and young people have most often been written in the comic and romantic modes because as Annie Gottlieb pointed out in "A New Cycle in 'YA' Books," "An unwritten commandment of YA fiction had always been, 'Thou shalt leave the young reader with hope.' " She credited Robert Cormier with shattering this rule in 1974 when he published *The Chocolate War,* and "The American Library Association's *Booklist* gave it a black-bordered review, suggesting an obituary for youthful optimism."[5] Throughout the 1970s the books that got the most attention from teachers, librarians, reviewers, and young readers were books in the darker modes of irony/satire and even tragedy. These included such books as the anonymous (really Beatrice Sparks')[6] *Go Ask Alice,* John Donovan's *Wild in the World,* and Jean Renvoize's *A Wild Thing.* The protagonists in these books are helpless to change the forces of the world that gather against them.

Some critics would argue that such books are tragedies rather than ironies. The reader of a tragedy is usually filled with pity and fear—pity for the hero and fear for oneself that the same thing might happen. The intensity of this involvement causes the reader to undergo an emotional release or catharsis which drains away subconscious fears leaving the reader filled with pride in what the human spirit is able to undergo and still survive.

Robert Cormier's books, including his more recent *After the First Death* and *The Bumblebee Flies Anyway,* stand out as being among a very small number of YA books that come close to being tragedies. However, as shown in Chapter 3, "The New Realism" numerous books are written in the ironic mode.

In the late-1980s, it is easy to find examples of books written in the happier modes, those of comedy and romance. In these optimistic books, there are challenges to be met, but the stories have happy endings. Chapter 4, "The Old Romanticism" explores the romantic mode in two senses, that of a love story and that of an adventure/accomplishment story. Romances are characterized not only by happy endings, but also by exaggeration and wish-fulfillment.

In popular culture, the term *comedy* is most often used in reference to something funny, something that makes people laugh. But in literary criticism, *comedy* or *the comic mode* are terms that can be used as descriptors for stories that are mostly serious, or even grim. What is necessary is that the events in the story move from ironic chaos to a renewal of human hope and spirit. An example is Felice Holman's *The Wild Children* set in the post-revolutionary Russia of the 1920s. Twelve-year-old Alex comes downstairs from his attic bedroom to find that his family has been taken away. He is alone in the world, as are thousands of young Russians who make up the *bezprizorni*—the unsheltered ones. Most of the story is about Alex's terrible fear, his loneliness, and the hardships endured by these children of war. He becomes part of a gang who aid each other in the hard business of survival and at the end of the book escape to Finland. The closing line is a brief sentence which is almost a literal fulfillment of the definition of the comic mode, "Once again, life began." But it is important to the symbolic nature of the story that it wasn't only Alex's life, but also the lives of the other ten children who escaped with him, that could begin again. And hope for the future is made even bigger by the decision of the gang's leader, fourteen-year-old Peter, to stay behind as a helper in the underground bringing more of the orphans to freedom.

CHARACTER

The popularity of many books that do not have exciting or even interesting plots is a testament to the power of good characterization. When, through a writer's skill, readers identify closely with the protagonist, they feel as if they are living the experience. They become more interested in what is going on in the character's mind than they may be in what is happening to the character from the outside. Young adult authors who do an especially good job of developing memorable characters include Virginia Hamilton, Sue Ellen Bridgers, Katherine Paterson, Robert Cormier, Laurence Yep, and Rosa Guy.

Character Development and Types

Because of the shorter length of most adolescent books, the author does not have space to develop fully more than a small cast of characters. There is usually a protagonist, an antagonist, and various supporting characters. The protagonist is usually the central character, the one with whom the reader identifies. Most commonly, this will be a young adult, perhaps a bit older than the reader, but not always. After reading a book with a fully developed protagonist, readers should know the character so well that if a situation outside of the book were described, they could predict how this character would feel and act in the new situation. The reason they would be able to do this is that the author has developed a round character. Many sides—many different aspects—of the character have been shown. A major character can undergo changes in personality in ways a minor character cannot. Such changes are often the heart of the story, but unless the character is well developed, the changes have no meaning. Readers cannot rejoice in the arrival of a character unless they know where the character started.

A character who undergoes changes is said to be dynamic, while a character who stays basically the same is static. Chances are that if the focus of a story is characterization, then the protagonist will be dynamic. Readers will be led to understand how and why the protagonist has changed. Background characters may change too, but in a YA book the author probably won't have the space to develop these changes and so most background characters remain static. And in many books where the focus is on an exciting plot or the protagonist is telling someone else's story, then the main character may also be static, having much the same goals and attitudes at the end as at the beginning.

Many of the static characters found in literature are flat or stereotyped. As books (not just books for teenagers but for all ages) have gotten shorter and shorter, the literary element most affected has been characterization. For the sake of efficiency, authors have begun to rely more heavily on character types than on unique individuals.

Of course this is not entirely new. Since the beginning of literature, there have been archetypes that appear again and again. Archetypal characters include the wise and helpful older person who befriends and teaches a young protagonist, the villain or enemy, and the wicked or unsympathetic parent or stepparent. Archetypes differ from stereotypes in that they are usually main characters and they fill a symbolic as well as an active role. Stereotyped characters will be in the background with very little attention given to their development. The absent-minded professor, the nagging mother, and the "jock" are stereotypes. The hero who leaves home on a danger-fraught mission and returns as a stronger and better person is an archetype seen in stories as divergent as the biblical story of Joseph, Steven Callahan's nonfiction *Adrift: Seventy-Six Days Lost at Sea,* Robin McKinley's fantasy *The Blue Sword,* and Sue Ellen Bridgers' realistic *Home Before Dark.* It is because this particular archetype is a part of most readers' backgrounds that they have a good feeling at the end of Robert C. O'Brien's *Z for Zachariah.* As Ann Burden leaves the "safety" of Hidden Valley and ventures out into the radioactive world, readers feel confident that she will safely complete her quest and find other people with whom she can live and build a new society.

A reviewer is probably making a negative comment in saying that an author's characters are stereotypes, but, in reality, the conventions of writing make it necessary that at least some characters in nearly every story be stereotyped. The word "stereotyped" comes from the printer's world where it used to mean the process by which an image is created over and over again. It would be impossible for an author to have to build a unique personality for every background character. And it would be too demanding for a reader to respond to a large number of fully developed characters. For example, the Newbery Award Winner, *The Westing Game* by Ellen Raskin, is too difficult for many junior high school readers because they can't keep the thirteen characters straight.

The use of stock characters was always accepted as part of the act of storytelling, but in the late 1960s and 1970s, as people's social consciousness grew, so did their dislike for stereotyping. Minority groups complained that their members were stereotyped in menial roles, feminists complained that women and girls always took a back seat to men and boys, and parents complained that they were presented as unimportant or even damaging to their children's lives. Justified as these complaints were (or are), it doesn't mean that writers can get along without relying on stock characters or stereotypes. But they can feature as main characters members of those groups who have previously been ignored or relegated to stereotypes. Doing this well is always a challenge, especially when the character is someone that most young readers are not accustomed to identifying with, for example, a boy with cerebral palsy as in Jan Slepian's *The Alfred Summer,* a lesbian as in Nancy Garden's *Annie on My Mind,* and a despondent Vietnam veteran as in Bobbie Ann Mason's *In Country.*

When an author succeeds in developing the characters in a book, readers get the feeling that the characters are real. They identify with them as friends and find it hard to believe that these "friends" live only between the covers of a book. Because of this involvement, readers often write to authors and request more information. This, along with financial success, sometimes inspires authors to write one or more sequels about the same characters.

Bette Greene said that she hated sequels and would never write one, but every time she sat down to write she found herself thinking about Patty and Ruth from *Summer of My German Soldier*. So five years later she published *Morning Is a Long Time Coming*. Robert Cormier said something similar about being haunted by memories of Obie from *The Chocolate War*. Eleven years after the publication of that ground-breaking book, he told Obie's story in *Beyond the Chocolate War*.

Sequels differ from trilogies or other preconceived sets such as sagas in that they are usually not planned when the original book is written. When a set is preplanned as with Susan Cooper's *The Dark Is Rising* and Anne McCaffrey's *Dragon* books, the authors will have plotted out the whole set. The same is probably true of a saga. The original saga was a heroic prose narrative of twelfth- and thirteenth-century Iceland, but today the term is used for any long and detailed account that covers several years, for example, Cynthia Voigt's various books about the Tillerman family, *Dicey's Song, Homecoming,* and *Sons from Afar*. Series books are more like sequels in being based on favorite characters, for example, M. E. Kerr's new *Fell* books.

Communicating Character

We will focus on Katherine Paterson's 1940s story set on Rass Island in the Chesapeake Bay, *Jacob Have I Loved,* to illustrate techniques authors use to help readers know and understand their characters. Characterization is crucial in this book because the problem in the story—that of sibling rivalry between the competent and practical Sara Louise and her beautiful and talented twin sister Caroline—takes place inside Sara Louise's mind. If readers don't have empathy for Sara Louise, they won't identify with her or appreciate the story.

Paterson explained in her Newbery Award acceptance speech that the conflict at the core of the book:

> ... began east of Eden, in the earliest stories of my heritage. "Cain was jealous of his brother and slew him." If, in our Freudian orientation, we speak of the basic conflict as that between parent and child, the Bible—which is the earth from which I spring—is much more concerned with the relationships among brothers and sisters. "A friend loveth at all times," says the writer of Proverbs, "but a brother is born for adversity." They never taught us the second half of that verse in Sunday School.[7]

She went on to cite the numerous fairy tales in which the youngest brother or sister must surpass the supposedly more clever elders or outwit the wicked ones, and she argued with Bruno Bettelheim's suggestion that the rivalry between brothers and sisters is actually an Oedipal conflict or is about the split self. "I do not think," she said, "we can avoid the most obvious meaning of the stories, which is that among children who grow up together in a family there run depths of feeling that will permeate their souls for both good and ill as long as they live.''

Authors develop characters by telling readers what the characters do, what they say, what others say about them, what they think, and how they feel. *Jacob Have I Loved* is written in the first-person so it's easy and natural for Sara Louise to describe herself and her feelings, but notice how efficiently in this brief quote Paterson introduces Sara Louise and the secondary character McCall Purnell, and also through the dialogue presents some foreshadowing and gives readers a peek at how others relate to Sara.

Call and I made quite a pair. At thirteen I was tall and large boned, with delusions of beauty and romance. He, at fourteen, was pudgy, bespectacled, and totally unsentimental.

"Call," I would say, watching dawn break crimson over the Chesapeake Bay, "I hope I have a sky like this the day I get married."

"Who would marry you?" Call would ask, not meanly, just facing facts.

Readers learn more about Sara Louise a few pages later when she tells Call a joke about a "p-sychiatrist," who gets into heaven because as St. Peter explains, "We got this problem. God thinks he's Franklin D. Roosevelt." Call questions Sara's use of the word "p-sychiatrist," and she explains in hindsight:

I was an avid reader of *Time* magazine, which, besides the day-old Baltimore *Sun,* was our porthole on the world in those days, so although psychiatry was not yet a popular pastime, I was quite aware of the word, if not the fact that the p was silent.

His response to the actual joke is, "How can it be a joke? There ain't neither funny about it."

Paterson's inclusion of these two grammatical "mistakes" was an efficient way to show not only how isolated these children were but also to show how Call looks inward at the Island identifying with the watermen while Sara Louise looks outward at the world.

In the story, Call and Sara are both dynamic characters, who undergo change. Sara's sister, Caroline, is a static character remaining much the same from beginning to end. She's almost a stereotype of the beautiful and adored child, "the kind of person other people sacrifice for as a matter of course" and the kind of person who tells other people's stories, snatching their "rights without even thinking." But Caroline sings so beautifully that on the Saturday night before Christmas, Sara Louise felt surely that she would shatter when Caroline "went up effortlessly, sweetly, and oh, so softly, to the high G, holding it just a few seconds longer than humanly possible and then returning to the last few notes and to silence."

Paterson walked a fine line in creating Caroline, who had to be irritating enough to make Sara's resentment credible, but at the same time typical enough that readers would understand the problem as representative rather than unique. One of the ways that Paterson did this was to filter everything through Sara's eyes as on the summer day that Sara had earned extra money, and as a result her mother was making her and her father's favorite dinner. Sara was relaxed:

> [bathing her] sister and grandmother in kindly feelings that neither deserved, when Caroline said, "I haven't got anything to do but practice this summer, so I've decided to write a book about my life. Once you're known," she explained carefully as though some of us were dim-witted, "once you're famous information like that is very valuable. If I don't get it down now, I may forget."

The worst thing about this statement is that Caroline said it "in that voice of hers that made me feel slightly nauseated."

On balance, readers are also made privy to Sara's daydreams which include catching a German spy and being honored by President Roosevelt.

> There was a final touch with which I closed the award ceremony.
> "Here, Mr. President," I would say, handing back the medal, "use this for our boys at the front. . . . "

She's brought back to reality when she enlists the help of Call to spy on the newcomer to Rass Island. They sneak up on his house through the marsh because "The old man would never expect people from that direction," but one of Call's shoes gets stuck in the mud so that he's left standing "on one leg like an overweight egret." He's sure that his grandmother will beat him for losing his shoe but Sara retrieves it and holds her peace about the ridiculousness of "Call's tubby little grandmother taking a switch to a large fifteen-year-old boy."

> I had a greater problem than that. What would Franklin D. Roosevelt say about a spy who lost his shoe in the salt marsh and worried aloud that his grandma would beat him?

By the latter quarter of the book, readers know Sara so well that they suffer along with her when the Captain shares his idea of sending Caroline to music school and ironically announces that "I have Sara Louise to thank for the idea." And they react right along with Sara Louise's body when after the war Call returns home and before announcing his engagement remarks that he stopped in New York to see Caroline. "My body understood long before my mind did. First it chilled, then it began to burn, with my heart thumping overtime in alarm."

One of the advantages of books over movies and plays is that an author can more easily get inside the characters' minds and tell what they are thinking.

Paterson often uses this technique, having Sara Louise carry on a continual interior monologue. In one of them she acknowledges her lack of generosity in not wanting to share Call with the Captain. "He didn't remember his own father, and if any boy needed a father, it was Call." But "Call was my only friend. If I gave him up to the Captain, I'd have no one."

Authors commonly use physical attributes as a concrete substitute for less easily described abstractions. Throughout *Jacob Have I Loved,* Paterson uses descriptions of hands in this way.

> Caroline would remark mildly that my fingernails were dirty. How could they be anything else but dirty? But instead of simply acknowledging the fact, I would fly into a wounded rage. . . . It wasn't my fingernails she was concerned with, that I was sure of. She was using my fingernails to indict my soul.

Midway in the book when the Captain's house is washed out to sea, Sara Louise hugs him and suddenly hears voices inside her head, one saying "Let go, stupid," while the other urges her to hold him tighter. She is terribly embarrassed and dares to look only at his hands.

> I had never noticed how long his fingers were. His nails were large, rounded at the bottom and blunt and neat at the tips. He had the cleanest fingernails of any man I'd ever seen—it was the male hand in the ad reaching to put the diamond on the Ponds-caressed female hand. Why had I never noticed before how beautiful his hands were?

In another incident, Sara Louise overreacts when Caroline borrows her hand lotion, and that fall Sara Louise studies all the hands in the classroom. "It was my current theory that hands were the most revealing part of the human body— far more significant than eyes."

Names can also be used as clues. Throughout most of the book, Sara Louise is called Wheeze because the two-year-old Caroline couldn't pronounce Sara Louise. One of the ways that Paterson shows the importance of the Captain to Sara Louise is that without appearing to give the matter much thought, he calls her by her full name: "Strange how much that meant to me."

Sara's mother and father are important background characters, but because they act much like readers expect good parents to act, Paterson did not have to devote extensive space to their development but instead relied on a few crucial details. For example, Sara's mother came to Rass Island as the school teacher and stayed on after falling in love with a waterman. After spending the winter on her father's boat, Sara does not want to go back to school and asks her mother to teach her at home. Her mother, who isn't good with math, says that they would have to ask the Captain to teach the math because "There is no one else with the—with the time." Sara explains that her mother "was always very careful not to seem to sneer at the rest of the islanders for their lack of education."

This brief paragraph lets readers know that Mrs. Bradshaw is not the kind of mother who would have fostered unhappiness between her daughters. She is not to blame for Sara's feelings.

The Captain and Sara's grandmother are almost archetypes. The Captain is the foolish young man who left home on a quest only to return many years later kinder and wiser than anyone dared to hope for. The grandmother is the wicked old witch, who mumbles incantations and makes wicked predictions. She's the one who, when Sara's heart is already broken because Caroline is going to be sent to the wonderful music academy in Baltimore, stands close behind her and whispers, "Romans nine thirteen, 'As it is written, Jacob have I loved, but Esau have I hated.' "

Some readers and critics have objected to these contrasting archetypes, the positive portrayal of the elderly man and the negative portrayal of the elderly woman. But, the archetypes are as old as the world's literature and at least Paterson makes a point of revealing some of the reasons behind the grandmother's bad behavior.

At the very end of the book, actually in the denouement, new characters appear, including the man that Sara Louise marries and the twins whose birth she attends. These characters are foils. They are there as background for the simple purpose of making Sara Louise shine. There was no need for Paterson to develop them any further than to give readers a vaguely positive feeling toward them.

This discussion has pointed out several techniques that Paterson used to develop the full range of characters in *Jacob Have I Loved*. She had the narrator describe minor characters, while major characters were not only described but also shown in action. Readers were allowed to listen in on their conversations and to hear what they said as well as how they said it and how others responded to them and talked about them. With the protagonist, readers were privy to her thoughts and her daydreams. Other techniques that Paterson used in developing her characters included the use of Biblical allusion, foreshadowing, descriptions of physical attributes as symbols for abstract ideas, and a change in names to reflect changing attitudes. Examples of each technique were given, but careful readers could find equally interesting additional examples which space does not allow us to include.

POINT OF VIEW

Point of view is expressed largely through the person who tells the story. A story has to be told from a consistent viewpoint. The storyteller has to decide just how far from the characters to stand, from which direction to illuminate their actions with sympathy, and when and if it is time to speak from inside one of them. The viewpoint that gives the storyteller the most freedom is the one called omniscient or "all knowing." With this viewpoint it is as if the writer is present in all the characters, knowing what is inside their minds. This was the viewpoint that Joanne Greenberg, writing under the pseudonym of Hannah Green, used when she wrote *I Never Promised You a Rose Garden.* It would hardly have been believable for the girl Deborah to tell the story since throughout most of the book she is psychotic. Yet it is necessary that the readers be told what she is thinking since the real story takes place in her mind. Also, by using the third person omniscient viewpoint, Green could share the thoughts of the other patients, Deborah's psychiatrist, and her parents.

Writers have much less freedom if they decide to enter into the mind and body of one of the characters and stay there, that is, to write the book in the first person. It takes real skill on the writer's part to tell the story without slipping in facts or attitudes that would be unknown to the character whose voice is being used. First person narrators can describe other characters in an objective manner; that is, they can tell about whatever can be seen from the outside, but they cannot tell what is going on inside the minds of the other characters. One way to get around the limitation of having a first person book come all from the same viewpoint is to have the first person chapters coming alternately from different people. M. E. Kerr used this technique in *I'll Love You When You're More Like Me* and so did Alice Childress in *A Hero Ain't Nothin' But a Sandwich.* William Wharton began *Birdy* by having Birdy's friend Al visit him in a veterans' hospital where he alternates between talking to the unresponsive Birdy and thinking his own thoughts. Birdy's thoughts— at first just fragments and pieces—are given in a slightly different style of type. By the end of the book, Birdy's thoughts have grown to whole chapters.

This technique was satisfying to readers because it put them in a better position to understand Birdy than either his friend or his psychiatrist. It also let them know things about Birdy's childhood and his family that Birdy would never have told, for example:

> Birdy's old lady'd keep any baseballs that went over the fence into their yard. Ball players didn't even try anymore. Semi-pros, everybody, gave up. Hit a homer over that fence, into Birdy's yard; good-bye, ball. Nothing to do but throw in a new one. It got to be expensive playing in that ball park if you were a long-ball-hitting right-hander.
>
> What the hell could she've done with all those baseballs? Birdy and I used to look for those baseballs everywhere around his place. Maybe she buried them, or she could've sold them; big black market source for used baseballs.

In a similar way to how William Wharton told most of Birdy's story through the eyes of his best friend, authors may look around for a relatively minor character to tell the story. Richard Peck has explained that he chooses to do this because the interesting stories are at the extreme ends of the normal curve. The exciting things are happening to the brilliant and successful students such as the girl that Bruce Brooks wrote about in *Midnight Hour Encores.* Or they are happening to the kids at the other end of the scale as in Fran Arrick's

Steffie Can't Come Out to Play and S. E. Hinton's *That Was Then, This Is Now.* Peck says that these extreme characters are wonderful to write about, but they aren't the ones who will read his books. The kids at one end probably don't have the reading skill and at the other end they are too busy, too involved in their own lives. Readers are most likely to come from the large group of students in between whose lives aren't full of such highs and lows. Peck therefore chooses a narrator from the middle group with whom readers can identify. He then tells the story through that person's eyes.

He was clever in *Remembering the Good Times* to establish the story as a reminiscence so that some of his narrator's adultlike observations would be more credible, for example, "If I hadn't been twelve, I'd have seen how great-looking she was going to be," and in reference to a disturbed student "This didn't get a thing out of his system. He'd upped his ante."

◼ TONE

The tone of a book is determined by the author's attitude toward subject, characters, and readers. It is difficult to pick out the exact elements that contribute to the tone of a book because many times the author is not even aware of them. Some people think that the most distinctive thing about young adult literature is its tone. They say they can pick up two books treating protagonists of the same age who are faced with similar problems, and, by reading a few pages, can tell that one has been written for a general adult audience while the other has been written for teenagers. If an author were speaking directly to you, tone would simply be communicated through the lilt of the voice, the lifting of an eyebrow, a twinkle in the eye, or a crease in the forehead. But when tone has to be communicated exclusively through the written word, then it is more complex.

Sometimes language reminiscent of church hymns or the Bible is used to lend weight and dignity to a book as in the titles *All Creatures Great and Small* by James Herriot, *The People Therein,* by Mildred Lee, *Jacob Have I Loved* by Katherine Paterson, and *Manchild in the Promised Land* by Claude Brown.

The tone in these books contrasts sharply with the humorous and irreverent tone that appears in many popular new books. Americans have always been fond of exaggeration or hyperbole and its use is one way of establishing a light, humorous tone. When writers use hyperbole, readers know that what they say is not true, but they nevertheless enjoy the far-fetched overstatement as in Ellen Conford's title, *If This Is Love, I'll Take Spaghetti* and Ron Koertge's *Where the Kissing Never Stops.*

Another literary technique that authors rely on when they are establishing the tone they desire is euphemistic wording. Euphemisms are words or phrases carefully chosen to avoid harsh or unpleasant concepts. In general, modern writers think it better to speak directly than to make the vague kinds of circumlocutions that used to be fashionable in writing. But still there are euphemisms that have literary impact. For example, Margaret Craven's title *I Heard the Owl Call My Name* is more intriguing than a bald statement such as "I knew I was going to die." And Hemingway's title *For Whom the Bell Tolls* is both more euphemistic and euphonious than "the one who has died."

Euphemisms can be created because there are so many ways to denote or communicate the same basic information, but each variation will have a different connotation and will trigger a different emotional response in the reader. In establishing tone, a skilled writer will take advantage of the connotations of words, but because connotations are somewhat vague and will probably be interpreted differently by different readers, the author may not always be in total control of the message that reaches the readers. For example, some, but not all, readers who see the titles of R. R. Knudson's books, *Zanballer, Zanbanger, Zanboomer,* and *Fox Running* will think that sexual connotations were intended. Perhaps they were, but the books do not fulfill the promise as many readers would interpret it.

For certain kinds of books a reverent tone is appropriate, as for example, a memoir about someone who has died. They are usually written in a loving tone but to be successful the tone cannot be so worshipful that it becomes too sentimental. John Gunther's *Death Be Not Proud: A Memoir* telling about Gunther's teenage son's struggle against a fatal brain tumor has remained popular for four decades. Doris Lund's *Eric,* which tells about her seventeen-year-old son's four-year battle with leukemia, is, like Gunther's book, a sad but inspiring memoir.

The tone of a biography is equally important in attracting an audience. Part of the appeal of *Geri,* the autobiography of Geri Jewell, the young actress/comedienne who has cerebral palsy, is its upbeat approach and the candor with which the author discusses her disability. But if throughout the book the tone had been one of feeling sorry for herself, then readers could never have forgotten about the disability and gotten to know the woman behind it. It would have defeated the purpose of the book, which Jewell summed up as being "to show the hardness and usefulness of the disabled."

Another pitfall that young adult authors must try to avoid is an overly didactic tone. Certainly it is the goal—conscious or unconscious—of most adults to teach worthwhile values to young people. Nevertheless, in literary criticism, calling a work "didactic" usually implies that the tone comes across as preachy. The story has been created around a message instead of having a message or a theme grow naturally out of the story. For example, Gertrude Samuels' *Run, Shelley, Run!* appears to have been written for the didactic purpose of bringing the plight of homeless girls to the public's attention, and Gloria D. Miklowitz' *Close to the Edge* is a plea for involvement and service to others as a key to good mental health.

Great literature always leaves the reader with something to think about. Lessons are taught, but they are subtle lessons, and the reader is left with the responsibility of analyzing what the writer has presented and of coming to a conclusion. *Lord of the Flies* is a book from which people learn a great deal, but it is not usually considered a didactic book because the author, William Golding, does not spell out the lesson for the reader. We might contrast Golding's nondidactic tone with the didactic message that appears in an introduction written by E. M. Forster to a 1962 edition of the same book:

> It is certainly not a comforting book. But it may help a few grownups to be less complacent and more compassionate, to support Ralph, respect Piggy, control Jack, and lighten a little the darkness of man's heart. At the present moment (if I may speak personally) it is respect for Piggy that seems needed most. I do not find it in our leaders.

Forster's comments could also be described as editorializing. Notice how he asked permission to express his personal opinion. Sometimes authors will editorialize, or give their own opinions, through the voice of a character as S. E. Hinton did in *The Outsiders* when Ponyboy explains why he wrote his story:

> I could see boys going down under street lights because they were mean and tough and hated the world, and it was too late to tell them that there was still good in it, and they wouldn't believe you if you did. It was too vast a problem to be just a personal thing. There should be some help. Someone should tell their side of the story, and maybe people would understand then and wouldn't be so quick to judge a boy by the amount of hair oil he wore.

In reality, it is probably not so much that we dislike a didactic tone as it is that we dislike that tone when the message is something with which we do not agree. If the message is reaffirming one of our beliefs, we identify with it and enjoy the feeling that other people are going to be convinced of the "truth." It is partly because it is their message that teenagers respond so warmly to Hinton's books.

A nostalgic tone is a potential problem in much young adult literature. Nearly all books with teenage protagonists are of potential interest to young adult readers. But one of the things that keeps some of them from reaching a large YA audience is that the authors have looked back at their own adolescence and have romanticized it. Guarding against such nostalgia was one of the challenges that Charlotte Zolotow had when she collected stories about youthful protagonists for her two books *Early Sorrow* and *An Overpraised Season*. Because the intended audience of the stories by such writers as E. L. Doctorow, Carson McCullers, James Purdy, and Katherine Mansfield was the general population of adults, a few of the stories come close to being nostalgic about the good old days. Most sixteen-year-olds interpret such a tone as condescension, which is unappealing to readers of any age.

■ *SETTING*

Setting—the context of time and place—is more important in some genres than in others. For example, it is often the setting, a time in the future or the far past or some place where people now living on this earth have never actually been, that lets readers know they are embarking on reading a fantasy. The special quality in J. R. R. Tolkien's *The Lord of the Rings* would not be possible were it not set in the mythical world of Middle Earth. Nor would many popular pieces of science fiction be possible without their outer space or futuristic settings.

Historical fiction is another genre in which the setting is important to the story. Bette Greene's *Summer of My German Soldier* could not have happened at any time other than during World War II. Without the war, there would not have been German prisoners in this country, nor would there have been the peculiar combination of public and private hysteria that worked on Patty Bergan's southern Christian community and her Jewish family. All of this makes it easy to think of *Summer of My German Soldier* as a historical novel. In contrast, Maureen Daly's *Seventeenth Summer* was set in approximately the same time period, but the crux of the story does not center around the war. It centers around a young girl's feelings toward the adult role that she is growing into and toward her first experience with love. Many girls who read *Seventeenth Summer* come away with the feeling that they are reading a slightly old-fashioned, but still contemporary, novel.

For our purposes, we have rather arbitrarily chosen to label any book that is set during or prior to World War II as historical fiction. Often-read books whose settings make them fall clearly into the category of historical fiction are Jack Schaefer's *Shane,* Mark Twain's *Adventures of Huckleberry Finn,* and Fred Gipson's *Old Yeller.* Of recent pieces of popular young adult fiction, good examples of how a story is controlled by its historical setting are Robert Newton Peck's *A Day No Pigs Would Die,* a 1920s family story set in a rural Vermont community of Shakers, and Jean Fritz's *Homesick: My Own Story,* the true account of Fritz's growing up in China with her American parents and then coming "home" to the United States in 1927.

Kinds of Settings

There are basically two kinds of settings in stories: one is integral and the other is backdrop. When the setting is a part of the plot, then obviously it is integral, as in the historical books and fantasies mentioned earlier. It is also integral in stories—whether fictional or true—in which the plot or problem is person against nature. In accounts of mountain climbing, survival, exploring, and other sorts of adventuring, the setting is actually the antagonist. It is interesting in and of itself just as a character would be.

Another kind of story in which the setting is integral is the regional story. For example, after reading James Michener's *Hawaii,* we want to visit Hawaii, or, if we live there, we want to learn more about it; and after reading *Caravans,* we have a new interest in Afghanistan. This is similar to the way we develop feelings for particular characters and want to get to know them better in a sequel or in a movie taken from the book. In some degree, nearly all realistic fiction is regional since the setting influences the story, but the term is usually applied to stories where the setting plays an unusually important part. For example, Hal Borland's *When the Legends Die* and Frank Herbert's *Soul Catcher* are both regional stories about young Native American men whose searches for their own identities cannot be separated from the regions in which they grew up. Vera and Bill Cleaver's *Where the Lilies Bloom* is set in back-woods Appalachia while their *Dust of the Earth* is set in the Dakotas during the Depression.

Traditionally most regional stories have had rural settings in which the protagonists are close to nature, but as the United States has changed to an urban society and realism has become more fashionable, cities appear as important background settings as in Nicholasa Mohr's *El Bronx Remembered* and *In Nueva York.* These are both collections of short stories that are held together by their common setting. Mohr communicates the Puerto Rican background of her stories through the touch of Spanish in the titles.

In contrast to stories with integral settings are those with backdrop settings. Stories of this type are set in a small town, an inner-city neighborhood, a modern suburb, or a high school. When authors establish this kind of setting, they are not particularly anxious to make it so clearcut that it would be identifiable as only one place. They want to give enough details so that it comes

Traditionally most regional stories have had rural settings in which the protagonists are close to nature, but as the United States has changed to an urban society and realism has become more fashionable, cities also appear as important background settings as in Nicholasa Mohr's *El Bronx Remembered* and *In Nueva York.*

alive, but to leave it vague enough that readers can imagine the story happening, for example, in their own town or at least in one they know.

The most common backdrop setting in young adult literature is that of a high school because school is the business—the everyday life—of teenagers. The fact that there are only so many ways to describe stairways, restrooms, lockers, cafeterias, classrooms, and parking lots is one of the things that gives a sameness to books for this age group.

How Setting Works

Sue Ellen Bridgers' *Permanent Connections* is a contemporary, realistic novel set in rural North Carolina, up along the ridges of the Appalachians. Casual readers probably take little notice of the setting, but that's because Bridgers has worked it in so skillfully that readers aren't aware of its effect. The book begins with seventeen-year-old Rob waking from a nightmare in his suburban New Jersey home. He's having a "foggy dream of being trapped somewhere, a steeply rising place tangled with rhododendron and blackberry briars." He's "disgusted with his stumbling, backsliding climb" and his mind fights to "tug him out of the nightmare, away from the rumbling sound of a storm he heard moving toward him. . . . "

When he's finally awake, he realizes that what he thought was a storm was "the grumbling thunder" of his Dad complaining about a son whose only summer job was mowing three lawns.

Five pages after this foreshadowing, Chapter 2 begins with another description:

> ▉ They broke through the clouds, and there were the mountains beneath them. August green undulating, here and there open flinty shelves of yellow rock, narrow twisting ribbons of road and river splitting the valleys. Rob studied the terrain searching for landmarks, some sign that would distinguish it from other ranges in the southern Appalachians.

Rob and his father are flying to his father's childhood home because Uncle Fairlee has broken his leg and Rob's father is coming to see what needs to be done to take care of Grandpa, who is partly senile, and Aunt Coralee, who suffers from agoraphobia and has not been out of the house in the past three years.

The change in setting is crucial to the plot of *Permanent Connections* because Rob's father decides to leave him in North Carolina to help the family until Uncle Fairlee recovers, probably around Thanksgiving time. Rob resents being left "in that old falling-down excuse for a house. . . . He pushed up a window but there was no breeze. He was locked in."

His only comfort is Ellery, a neighbor girl who as a student is everything Rob isn't. What they have in common is that they both resent living in the mountains and going to the local high school. Ellery's parents have recently divorced, and her artist mother, Ginny, comes to the area and builds a house halfway up the mountain. Rob spends wakeful nights thinking about Ellery sleeping "on the edge of the mountain above him, out of reach but waiting. . . . "

All through the book, Bridgers uses descriptions of settings to reveal information about her characters. For example, she shows personality differences between Rob and Ellery when she has them argue over which music would be most appropriate in the setting of their mountain picnic. And Ellery explains her frustration about the divorce by saying that the reason she can't go back and visit her "real friends" is that she couldn't stay with her father "all cramped up in his little apartment" and that she knows "just what happens when somebody leaves the group. It closes up and that space is never there again."

Rob's following Ellery on a long-distance run across the top of the ridge is a metaphor for the mental and emotional chase that takes up the larger part of the book but is much harder to describe. In a similar way, Aunt Coralee's struggle with agoraphobia, her fear of open space and her inability to go outside, is comparable to the emotional and mental struggles of Ginny, who whispers in the dark:

> I am afraid too. Hear me, Coralee Dickson, while you are curled like an animal in a hole away from sky and wind and sun. The demons that devour women are all the same.

When Uncle Fairlee tells Rob how Coralee's phobia developed, Bridgers' description of the setting is as important to an understanding as is Fairlee's explanation:

> "In a way it was a gradual thing," Fairlee said to Rob.
> They were on the front porch watching the creeping darkness that came from inside out—first the house and porch lost color, then the field lay in shadows and the woods blurred into solid black mounds. Now only the dense mountains themselves were separate from the pale sky, as if the dark were slowly rising out of them.

When Rob is frustrated, he runs to the barn where he leans "against the splintery wall, relishing the dark. He remembered that sudden calm in his gut when, in a game of hide and seek, he knew he'd discovered the perfect place, somewhere he couldn't be found."

His cousin's boyfriend confides to Rob that his family raises marijuana, "This land up here might not be good for much, but it's perfect for grass. On top of that, it's easier to hide than most places." Rob "cuts a deal" for two joints, which he smokes after school and then tries to drive home in the rain.

He spins out on "the curve he had been warned against" and is arrested and charged with possession. On the morning he was to appear in court, "They crept through the fog, the car lights casting a narrow downward beam on the faded yellow line." But after the charge is dismissed, and Rob finds himself outside, "The sun had pierced the fog, and he blinked in the bright light," no longer feeling trapped. Uncle Fairlee is well enough now so that Rob is free to decide whether to go back to Monmouth or stay in the mountains. That night he runs the ridge using the trail that Ellery had made:

> Surefooted although the gravel tossed and rumbled beneath him, he started down, making his own path toward the hidden farmhouse below where his family waited with supper. His lungs and heart found that magic rhythm that put new spring in his legs, released his tight shoulders so his arms lifted like wings. Finally he could see the lights in brilliant, solid squares. Only he moved. There was no sound except his drumming heart and heavy breath, the dry rustle of leaf and stone beneath his feet. The world was still, waiting for him. And it seemed to him that for the first time in his life he knew where he was going.

Comparing this positive closing scene with the nightmare scene that opened the book shows how far Rob progressed during the late summer and fall. It also shows how a skilled writer uses setting to accomplish various purposes. Bridgers' descriptions make the story come alive for readers. They also serve as foreshadowing while establishing tone and mood. They allow her to be efficient in communicating the time of year, and they reveal information about the personalities of her various protagonists. The mountain setting is integral to the plot when Rob and Ellery both blame their unhappiness on being forced to move and when Rob gets the homegrown marijuana from his friend and wrecks his uncle's truck.

But probably the most important role that setting plays in *Permanent Connections* is the way it serves as a metaphor and a symbol for what is happening in people's minds. Being able to establish settings so that they accomplish multiple purposes is one of the most important skills a writer can develop. Something similar could be said for readers, who will get much more from both fiction and nonfiction if they are sensitive to the way authors incorporate setting in plot, characterization, theme, tone, and mode.

STYLE

Style is the way a story is written as contrasted to what the story is about. It is the result or effect of combining the literary aspects we have already talked about.

An Individual Matter

No two authors have exactly the same style because with writing, just as with appearance, behavior, and personal belongings, style consists of the unique blending of all the choices each individual makes. From situation to situation, these choices may differ, but they are enough alike that the styles of particular authors such as Kurt Vonnegut, Jr., Richard Brautigan, and E. L. Doctorow will be recognizable from book to book. But style is also influenced by the nature of the story being told. For example, Ursula K. Le Guin used a different style when she wrote the realistic *Very Far Away from Anywhere Else* from the one she used when she wrote her science fiction *A Wizard of Earthsea.* Nevertheless, in both books she relied on the particular writing techniques that she likes and is skilled at using.

Virginia Hamilton is another author whose sense of style is evident throughout her writing which ranges from the realistic *M. C. Higgins, the Great* to the romantic *A Little Love,* the occult *Sweet Whispers, Brother Rush,* and the science fiction Justice trilogy beginning with *Justice and Her Brothers.*

Author's styles are influenced by such factors as their intended audience and their purpose in writing. For example, a nonfiction informative book will have a different style from that of an informative book that is written to persuade readers to a belief or an action. And, even after an author has made the decision to write a persuasive book, the style will be affected by whether the author chooses to persuade through humor, dramatic fiction, or a logical display of evidence.

Probably the book that has had the greatest influence on the style of writing about young protagonists is J. D. Salinger's *The Catcher in the Rye.* Nearly every year, promotional materials or reviews compare five or six new young adult books to *Catcher.* Some of these comparisons are made on the basis of the subject matter, but the theme of a boy wavering between the innocence of childhood and the acceptance of the adult world—imperfect as it is—is not all that unusual. It is the style of the writing that makes Salinger's book so memorable, indeed such a milestone, and has inspired other authors to imitate the colloquial speech, the candid revelations of feelings, the short snappy dialogues, the instant judgments, and the emotional extremes ranging from hostility to great tenderness.

One of the most memorable scenes in the book is the one in which the young prostitute comes to Holden's hotel room, and he is so touched by her youth and innocence that he gives up the whole idea:

> She was very nervous, for a prostitute. She really was. I think it was because she was young as hell. She was around my age. I sat down in the big chair, next to her, and offered her a cigarette. "I don't smoke," she said. She had a tiny little wheeny-whiny voice. You could hardly hear her. She never said thank you, either, when you offered her something. She just didn't know any better.

"Allow me to introduce myself. My name is Jim Steele," I said.

"Ya got a watch on ya?" she said. She didn't care what the hell my name was, naturally. "Hey how old are you, anyways?"

"Me? Twenty-two."

"Like fun you are."

It was a funny thing to say. It sounded like a real kid. You'd think a prostitute and all would say, "Like hell you are" or "Cut the crap" instead of "Like fun you are."

As the girl gets ready to leave, Holden observes, "If she'd been a big old prostitute, with a lot of makeup on her face and all, she wouldn't have been half as spooky."

Teenage readers are more likely than adults to appreciate certain kinds of style. One is the hyperbole and exaggeration in Paul Zindel's books as shown through such titles as *Pardon Me, You're Stepping on My Eyeball!* and *The Amazing and Death-Defying Diary of Eugene Dingman*. Sprinkled all through this latter book are such intriguing newspaper headlines as "GRANDFATHER, 87, MAKES DEATHBED WISH TO BE BURIED IN PINK PARTY DRESS," "NUN BATTLES KILLER ANTS TO SAVE RADAR INSTALLATION," and "MARILYN MONROE'S GHOST APPEARS TO SENATE PAGE."

Teenagers who may have shorter attention spans than adult readers are also especially appreciative of succinctness as when the two protagonists in M. E. Kerr's *Night Kites* are swimming and Erick writes, "Somehow we got down to the shallow end, where we could touch, and that was what we did. We touched." Richard Peck was equally succinct in communicating the living situation of his protagonist, Buck Mendenhall, in *Remembering the Good Times*. Buck explains that what his father got out of the divorce was "a full-time trailer and a part-time kid."

Writing in dialect is an effective stylistic device to set a character apart as different from mainstream speakers, but difficulties in spelling, printing, and reading mean that most authors will use this device sparingly, and for the benefit of young readers may offer an explanation as Gary Paulsen did in *Dogsong*. The Eskimo boy, Russel, is camping in a snow-covered wilderness and he finds an ancient lamp.

"See what a man has been given," he said. "By the dogs who brought me. By the night. See what a man has been given." He had dropped into the third person usage without thinking, though it was no longer used very much. He had heard the old people talk that way sometimes out of politeness.

No explanation is needed if the usage is easy to understand as in Hal Borland's *When the Legends Die*, "The Ute people have lived many generations, many grandmothers, in that land." The same can be said for most uses of black dialect which is commonly included in the writings of June Jordan, Brenda

Wilkinson, Maya Angelou, Ntozake Shange, Walter Dean Myers, and others. They use it not only for characterization but also to communicate black pride.

It is possible to describe the literary devices that are the basic ingredients of an author's style. But there is more to literary style than these various devices. Before a writer can be said to have a distinctive style, something has to click so that the devices blend together into a unified whole.

Figurative Language

Much of what determines writers' styles is how they use figurative language. This is language that is interesting and important above and beyond the literal information it communicates. Writers use figurative language to set a mood, to surprise the reader, to create imagery, to make a passage memorable, and sometimes to show off their skill. Words used figuratively have different, or at least additional, meanings from those they have in standard usage. One type of figurative language—metaphors, symbols, allegories, and similes—stimulates the reader's mind to make comparisons. A second type appeals to the sense of sight or hearing. Examples include alliteration, assonance, rhyme, euphony, rhythm, and cadence. In the following sentence from Harold Brodkey's story, "Sentimental Education," both kinds of figurative language occur:

> Dimitri had a car, which Elgin borrowed—an old, weak-lunged Ford— and they could wheeze up to Marblehead and rent a dinghy and be blown around the bay, with the sunlight bright on Caroline's hair and the salt air making them hungry and the wind whipping up small whitecaps to make the day exciting.

The personification of the "weak-lunged Ford" that "wheezes" up to Marblehead helps the reader visualize the old car while the alliteration in "be blown around the bay" and "wind whipping up small whitecaps" and the rhyme in "sunlight bright" and "Caroline's hair and the salt air" affect the reader more subtly in establishing mood. The word "wheeze" is also an example of onomatopoeia in which the sound of a word gives a hint of its meaning.

Poetry, of course, is filled with figurative language because poets have so little space that they have to make their words do double duty. But as Maya Angelou shows in her autobiographical writing, figurative language is not limited to any one genre. She begins her *All God's Children Need Traveling Shoes* with euphonious personification:

> The breezes of the West African night were intimate and shy, licking the hair, sweeping through cotton dresses with unseemly intimacy, then disappearing into the utter blackness. Daylight was equally insistent, but much more bold and thoughtless.

NORMA FOX MAZER
on Respect

I doubt there is a children's book writer extant who hasn't been asked when s/he is going to write a "real" book. A "real" book is, of course, a book for adults. Presumably a grownup book, certainly a book read by people whose hormones have settled down. The question implies that any "adult" book carries more status and is "realer" and therefore worthier than any book written for children.

Why is this so? Isn't it because anything associated with children is diminished, discounted, depreciated? Children are seen as lesser, less than. Children are considered not quite "real." We Americans may love our children, but it's quite clear we don't respect them. They are not seen as completed or finished; this makes them "kids" but not people. Children don't have rights, as other citizens do. They "belong" to their parents. "Cute," "adorable," and "silly" are words used often for kids. We constantly tell them to shut up, grow up, remind them that they're "almost thirteen" or "almost sixteen," thereby letting them know that being a child is something like having a disease. The only cure is to outlive it and become healthy: i.e., older, an adult.

As a society, we don't put our children first. Our maternal death rate is the highest in the Western World. Twenty percent of our children live in poverty. We mouth the idea that our children are our most valuable resource, but as a nation we don't act on it. Too many children are beaten and abused, are torn between their fighting parents, kidnapped as though they were packages rather than people.

But let's not even talk about that kind of stuff, that dangerous, deranged, bizarre, clouded area of life. Let's talk about a couple of "normal" things. That those who stay home with their small children, who "don't work" (that's the way we say it, despite the evidence in front of our eyes) are neither given much respect nor paid. That those who work with children are overworked, underpaid, and undervalued. (In Syracuse, New York, pay for preschool teachers is less than that for garbagemen.)

Reading over what I've written, I see it's depressing. What's worse, I don't know how to end it. No upbeat moral. So let me tell you about a letter I received today. It began, "Hi. My name is Lene Mapp. I live in Abilene Texas. . . . " She talked to me for two pages, asked if Harry would send her a book, and enclosed a picture and three poems. "My life," she wrote, "is just like I, Trissy, except I went off into a (sic) all white section of town. . . . You don't know how relieved (sic) I was to know someone knew what I was going through."

There, of course, is my ending. My reminder that what I do *is* serious stuff and that writing for kids—the hell with the grownup, "adult" world—is very serious stuff not only to those of us who do it, but to those we do it for—the kids, themselves.

Norma Fox Mazer's books include *Taking Terri Mueller,* Morrow, 1983; *Downtown,* Morrow, 1984; and *Three Sisters,* Scholastic, 1986.

And a page later:

> July and August of 1962 stretched out like fat men yawning after a sumptuous dinner. They had every right to gloat, for they had eaten me up. Gobbled me down. Consumed my spirit, not in a wild rush, but slowly, with the obscene patience of certain victors.

Metaphors are among the most common kinds of figurative language. In a metaphor, basically dissimilar things are likened to one another so that the reader gets a new insight. A fresh metaphor can be an effective device for making readers active instead of passive participants. Readers have to become mentally involved in order to make associations that they have not thought of before.

A metaphor can be very simple consisting of only a word or a phrase or it can be a series of interwoven ideas running through an entire book. In at least fourteen places in the Vietnam War story *Fallen Angels,* author Walter Dean Myers makes comparisons to movies or television. One of the soldiers whose uncle is a Hollywood director keeps up a running commentary on how to make "unnatural things look *almost* natural" and on what part they should each play—whether to be Lee Marvin, one of the bad guys riding into town in a cowboy movie, "the good black guy who everybody thinks is a coward and then gets killed saving everybody else," or "the baby-faced virgin who gets killed and all you see is a pan shot of him near the end of the flick."

Seventeen-year-old Richie Perry worries about composing his letters home "right." He doesn't want his little brother "to think about it like you do when you go to the movies." And at night, he can't sleep because of all the short movies that crowd into his mind:

> A few seconds of a medic putting a tag on a wounded soldier. A few seconds of a chopper taking off over the trees. A guy cradling his rifle. A body bag.

Later Richie observes that the stopping and starting of firing in a jungle battle "was as if somebody had changed channels and then switched back to the war." Ten pages later:

> The shadows moved, Peewee moved. He was getting up. I didn't want to get up. I wanted to sit there forever. Where the hell was the popcorn machine? Couldn't I just watch the rest of this f—— war? Couldn't I just be out of it for a few hours, a few minutes?

The fact that the Vietnam War was in many ways the first war fought in front of television cameras makes Myers' metaphor especially appropriate.

A technical distinction is sometimes made between metaphors and similes. Similes, like metaphors, make comparisons between basically dissimilar things, but they are literally true, while metaphors are true only figuratively. The creator of a simile hedges by putting in such words as *like, as, similar,* or *resembles* to indicate that a comparison is being made. In Bruce Brooks' *Midnight Hour Encores,* Sib was glad when her father told her she could choose a new name, because "I had been thrashing around inside that name like it was a wet wool coat worn inside out against my skin." A more fully developed simile appears in Zibby Oneal's *A Formal Feeling.* Sixteen-year-old Anne Cameron must let go of the dream of perfection in which she had wrapped the memories of her deceased mother. Near the end of the book, she was able at least to form the question that had bothered her since she was eight years old and her mother temporarily left the family, "If she loved me, why did she leave me?"

That was one of the questions, but it was only one. Beneath it there was another. It had been swimming at the edges of her mind for days, darting away as a fish does, startled by a movement that comes too close. She thought she could not avoid it any more, and so she pushed herself down one more time, like a diver. She knew the question had always been there, unspeakable, at the bottom of all she remembered and had chosen to forget. And she made herself ask: Did I ever love my mother at all?

Being able to ask this question is in effect the climax of the book, but without the interesting simile readers would have been less likely to recognize its importance. Also, since it was something that occurred in Anne's mind, the only way to make readers visualize it was through some sort of figurative language.

Allegories are extended comparisons or metaphors. They can be enjoyed on at least two levels. One is the literal or surface level on which the story is enjoyed simply for itself. On the second or deeper level, we can interpret and extend the meaning of the story, and it thereby becomes more interesting. It is in part the challenge of interpreting the allegory in William Golding's *Lord of the Flies* that makes it a good piece to read and discuss in a group.

An allegorical device that authors sometimes use is giving their characters symbolic names as Robert C. O'Brien did in *Z for Zachariah.* The title is taken from a Bible ABC book in which the first letter of the alphabet stands for Adam and the last for Zachariah. The symbolism suggests that if Adam were the first man on earth, Zachariah must be the last. The girl in the book who carries a tremendous responsibility and at the end is left with the task of rebuilding a civilization is symbolically named Ann Burden. These names may influence readers' attitudes and enhance their pleasure without their being aware of it. In a similar way, many young readers of Paula Fox's *One-Eyed Cat* probably didn't notice that when Ned confessed to shooting the cat he and his mother were sitting on the front porch of the Makepeace mansion.

Allusions work in the same way. They are an efficient way to communicate a great deal of information because one reference in a word or a phrase triggers the readers' minds to think of the whole story or idea behind the allusion. Robert Cormier's title *I Am the Cheese* is an allusion to the old nursery song and game, "The Farmer in the Dell." Besides being efficient, allusions, like metaphors, are effective in forcing readers to become actively involved in making connections. A lazy or uninterested reader might not see any allusion in Cormier's title. Someone else, especially when discovering that the family's name is Farmer, would connect the title to the nursery rhyme and perhaps think of the last line, "And the cheese stands alone!" An even more thoughtful reader might carry it back one more step and think of the next to last line, "The rat takes the cheese." It is this type of reader who may discover the most in Cormier's writing.

Although in literature, symbols are communicated through words, they are more than words, which is why their meanings cannot be looked up in dictionaries. Also, they are more complex than metaphors. For example, the semantic feature or meaning common to the word *thunder* and the metaphorical phrase *thunderous applause* is that of a big noise. But in Mildred Taylor's title *Roll of Thunder, Hear My Cry* there is no such simple explanation. The idea of noise is still there, but added to it is the idea of size and relativity. It is the power of all nature contrasted to the smallness of one human voice. Additionally, there's the negativeness, the ominous feeling that is communicated through the mention of a storm and the word *cry* which has a negative or at least a serious connotation as compared, for example, with *shout* or *yell*. Yet, in spite of this, the title has an optimistic ring to it, probably because the reader intuitively recognizes the strength of the voice behind the *my*. Weak characters hide under the bedcovers during a thunderstorm. Only the strong stand in the storm and yell back.

Symbolism can be a good subject for discussion because what one reader will miss, another might find. It is almost like hunting for clues in a game. When all the clues are filled in, the total picture is much more meaningful than the separate pieces.

This chapter has been little more than an introduction to—or perhaps for some of you simply a review of—the basics of literary criticism and appreciation. The concepts and the terminology will reappear throughout the rest of this textbook as well as in much of whatever else you read about books written for any age of reader.

We placed this discussion early in the text for two reasons. First, we wanted to make it clear that authors for young adults make use of the same literary techniques as used by all good writers. And second, we wanted to lay a foundation for the way you approach the reading you will do throughout this course. We want you to lose yourselves—and also find yourselves—in some very good stories. But at the same time we want to encourage you to keep a part of your mind open for looking at literature from the pleasure-giving viewpoint of the literary critic.

■ NOTES

[1]Margaret Early, "Stages of Growth in Literary Appreciation," *English Journal* 49 (March 1960): 163–66.

[2]First cited by G. Robert Carlsen in an article exploring stages of reading development, "Literature Is," *English Journal* 63 (February 1974): 23–27.

[3]Donald Hall, "Finally Only the Love of the Art," *New York Times Book Review,* January 16, 1983, pp. 7, 25.

[4]Glenna Davis Sloan, *The Child as Critic* (New York: Teachers College Press, 1975).

[5]Annie Gottlieb, "A New Cycle in 'YA' Books," *New York Times Book Review,* June 17, 1984, pp. 24–25.

[6]Alleen Pace Nilsen, "The House that Alice Built: An Interview with the Author Who Brought You *Go Ask Alice,*" *School Library Journal* 26 (October 1979): 109–12.

[7]Katherine Paterson, "Newbery Medal Acceptance," *Horn Book Magazine* 57 (August 1981): 385–93.

■ TITLES MENTIONED IN CHAPTER TWO

Adams, Richard. *The Plague Dogs.* Knopf, 1978.

—————— . *Watership Down.* Macmillan, 1974.

Alexander, Lloyd. *The Black Cauldron.* Holt, Rinehart and Winston, 1965.

Angelou, Maya. *All God's Children Need Traveling Shoes.* Random House, 1986.

—————— . *I Know Why the Caged Bird Sings.* Random House, 1970.

Anonymous. *Go Ask Alice.* Prentice-Hall, 1969.

Arrick, Fran. *Steffie Can't Come Out to Play.* Bradbury, 1978.

Borland, Hal. *When the Legends Die.* Harper & Row, 1963.

Bridgers, Sue Ellen. *Home Before Dark.* Knopf, 1976.

—————— . *Permanent Connections.* Harper & Row, 1987.

Brodkey, H. "Sentimental Education." In *First Love and Other Sorrows.* Dial Press, 1957.

Brooks, Bruce. *Midnight Hour Encores.* Harper & Row, 1986.

—————— . *The Moves Make the Man.* Harper & Row, 1984.

Brown, Claude. *Manchild in the Promised Land.* Macmillan, 1965.

Burns, Olive Ann. *Cold Sassy Tree.* Ticknor & Fields, 1984.

Callahan, Steven. *Adrift: Seventy-Six Days Lost at Sea.* Houghton Mifflin, 1986.

Childress, Alice. *A Hero Ain't Nothin' But a Sandwich.* Coward, McCann, 1973.

Cleaver, Vera and Bill. *Dust of the Earth.* Harper & Row, 1975.

—————— . *Where the Lilies Bloom.* Harper & Row, 1969.

Conford, Ellen. *If This Is Love, I'll Take Spaghetti.* Four Winds, 1983.

Cooper, Susan. *The Dark Is Rising.* Atheneum, 1973.

Cormier, Robert. *After the First Death.* Pantheon, 1979.

—————— . *Beyond the Chocolate War.* Pantheon, 1985.

—————— . *The Bumblebee Flies Anyway.* Pantheon, 1983.

—————— . *The Chocolate War.* Pantheon, 1974.

—————— . *I Am the Cheese.* Pantheon, 1977.

Craven, Margaret. *I Heard the Owl Call My Name.* Doubleday, 1973.

Daly, Maureen. *Seventeenth Summer.* Dodd, 1942.

Donovan, John. *Family.* Harper & Row, 1976.

—————— . *Wild in the World.* Harper & Row, 1971.

Duncan, Lois. *Stranger with My Face*. Little, Brown, 1981.

Fox, Paula. *One-Eyed Cat*. Bradbury, 1985.

_____ . *The Moonlight Man*. Bradbury, 1985.

Fritz, Jean. *Homesick: My Own Story*. Putnam, 1982.

Garden, Nancy. *Annie on My Mind*. Farrar, Straus & Giroux, 1982.

Gipson, Fred. *Old Yeller*. Harper & Row, 1976.

Golding, William. *Lord of the Flies*. Coward, McCann & Geoghegan, 1955.

Graham, Robin. *Dove*. Harper & Row, 1972.

Green, Hannah. *I Never Promised You a Rose Garden*. Holt, Rinehart and Winston, 1964.

Greene, Bette. *Morning Is a Long Time Coming*. Dial, 1978.

_____ . *Summer of My German Soldier*. Dial, 1973.

Guest, Judith. *Ordinary People*. Viking, 1976.

Gunther, John. *Death Be Not Proud: A Memoir*. Modern Library, 1953.

Guy, Rosa. *The Disappearance*. Delacorte, 1979.

Hamilton, Virginia. *Justice and Her Brothers*. Greenwillow, 1978.

_____ . *A Little Love*. Philomel, 1984.

_____ . *M. C. Higgins, the Great*. Macmillan, 1974.

_____ . *Sweet Whispers, Brother Rush*. Philomel, 1982.

Head, Ann. *Mr. and Mrs. Bo Jo Jones*. Putnam, 1967.

Hemingway, Ernest. *For Whom the Bell Tolls*. Scribner, 1940.

Hentoff, Nat. *Does This School Have Capital Punishment?* Delacorte, 1981.

Herbert, Frank. *Soul Catcher*. Putnam, 1972.

Herriot, James. *All Creatures Great and Small*. St. Martin, 1972.

Heyerdahl, Thor. *The "RA" Expeditions*. New American Library, 1972.

Hinton, S. E. *The Outsiders*. Viking, 1967.

_____ . *Taming the Star Runner*. Delacorte, 1988.

_____ . *That Was Then, This Is Now*. Viking, 1971.

Holman, Felice. *The Wild Children*. Scribner, 1983.

Hunter, Mollie. *Cat Herself*. Harper & Row, 1986.

Jewell, Geri with Stewart Winer. *Geri*. Morrow, 1984.

Kazimiriff, Theodore. *The Last Algonquin*. Walker, 1982.

Kerr, M. E. *Fell*. Harper & Row; series beginning in 1987.

_____ . *If I Love You, Am I Trapped Forever?* Harper & Row, 1973.

_____ . *I'll Love You When You're More Like Me*. Harper & Row, 1977.

_____ . *Night Kites*. Harper & Row, 1986.

Knowles, John. *A Separate Peace*. Macmillan, 1960.

Knudson, R. R. *Fox Running*. Harper & Row, 1975.

_____ . *Zanballer*. Delacorte, 1972.

_____ . *Zanbanger*. Harper & Row, 1977.

_____ . *Zanboomer*. Harper & Row, 1978.

Koertge, Ron. *Where the Kissing Never Stops*. Little, Brown, 1987.

Lee, Mildred. *The People Therein*. Houghton Mifflin, 1980.

Le Guin, Ursula. *Very Far Away from Anywhere Else*. Atheneum, 1976.

_____ . *A Wizard of Earthsea*. Parnassus, 1968.

Lund, Doris. *Eric*. Harper & Row, 1974.

Mason, Bobbie Ann. *In Country*. Harper & Row, 1985.

Mathis, Sharon Bell. *Teacup Full of Roses*. Viking, 1972.

McCaffrey, Anne. *Dragonsong*. Atheneum, 1976; series beginning in 1976.

McKinley, Robin. *The Blue Sword*. Greenwillow, 1982.

Meltzer, Milton. *The American Revolutionaries: A History in Their Own Words*. Crowell, 1987.

Michener, James. *Caravans*. Random House, 1963.

_____ . *Hawaii*. Random House, 1959.

Miklowitz, Gloria D. *Close to the Edge*. Delacorte, 1983.

Mohr, Nicholasa. *El Bronx Remembered*. Harper & Row, 1975.

_____ . *In Nueva York*. Dial, 1977.

Morrell, David. *First Blood*. M. Evans, 1972.

Myers, Walter Dean. *Fallen Angels*. Scholastic, 1988.

O'Brien, Robert C. *Z for Zachariah*. Atheneum, 1975.

Oneal, Zibby. *A Formal Feeling*. Viking, 1982.

Paterson, Katherine. *Jacob Have I Loved*. Harper & Row, 1980.

Paulsen, Gary. *Dogsong*. Bradbury, 1985.

Peck, Richard. *Remembering the Good Times*. Delacorte, 1985.

Peck, Robert Newton. *A Day No Pigs Would Die*. Knopf, 1972.

Plath, Sylvia. *The Bell Jar*. Harper & Row, 1971.

Potok, Chaim. *The Chosen*. Simon & Schuster, 1967.

_____ . *My Name is Asher Lev*. Knopf, 1972.

Raskin, Ellen. *The Westing Game*. Dutton, 1978.

Read, Piers Paul. *Alive: The Story of the Andes Survivors*. Harper & Row, 1974.

Renvoize, Jean. *A Wild Thing*. Little, Brown, 1971.

Robertson, Dougal. *Survive the Savage Sea*. G. K. Hall, 1974.

Salinger, J. D. *The Catcher in the Rye*. Little, Brown, 1951.

Samuels, Gertrude. *Run, Shelley, Run!* Harper & Row, 1974.

Santiago, Danny. *Famous All Over Town*. Simon & Schuster, 1983.

Schaefer, Jack. *Shane*. Houghton Mifflin, 1949.

Sleator, William. *House of Stairs*. Dutton, 1974.

_____ . *Interstellar Pig*. Dutton, 1984.

Slepian, Jan. *The Alfred Summer*. Macmillan, 1980.

Taylor, Mildred. *Roll of Thunder, Hear My Cry*. Dial, 1976.

Thomas, Joyce Carol. *Marked by Fire*. Avon, 1982.

Thompson, Julian. *A Band of Angels*. Scholastic, 1986.

Tolkien, J. R. R. *The Lord of the Rings*. Houghton Mifflin, 1974.

Trelease, Jim. *Read-Aloud Handbook,* Penguin, 1982.

Twain, Mark. *Adventures of Huckleberry Finn*. 1884.

Voigt, Cynthia. *Dicey's Song*. Atheneum, 1982.

_____ . *Homecoming*. Atheneum, 1981.

_____ . *Izzy, Willy-Nilly*. Atheneum, 1986.

_____ . *Sons from Afar*. Atheneum, 1987.

Weesner, Theodore. *The Car Thief*. Random House, 1972.

Wharton, William. *Birdy*. Knopf, 1978.

White, Robb. *Deathwatch*. Doubleday, 1972.

Zindel, Paul. *The Pigman*. Harper & Row, 1968.

_____ . *Pardon Me, You're Stepping on My Eyeball!* Harper & Row, 1976.

_____ . *The Amazing and Death-Defying Diary of Eugene Dingman*. Harper & Row, 1987.

Zolotow, Charlotte, ed. *Early Sorrow: Ten Stories of Youth*. Harper & Row, 1986.

_____ , ed. *An Overpraised Season*. Harper & Row, 1987.

For information on the availability of paperback editions of these titles, please consult the most recent edition of *Paperbound Books in Print,* published annually by R. R. Bowker Company.

THE NEW REALISM
Of Life and Other Sad Songs

When critic Northrop Frye used the term *realism* in his *Anatomy of Criticism,* he put it in quotation marks because with literature the term doesn't—or shouldn't—mean the same thing that it does in other contexts. Frye argues that expecting literature to simply portray real life is a mistaken notion. The artist who can paint grapes so realistically that a bird will fly up and peck at the canvas is not the most highly acclaimed artist. Nor would people want to listen to a symphony in which all the instruments imitated "real" sounds from nature—the cooing of doves, the rushing of a waterfall, a clap of thunder, and the wind whistling through trees.

In arguing this point, G. Robert Carlsen wrote:

> ■ . . . a painting, a sculpture, a drama, a piece of literature is never real. It is an object created out of the imagination from the inner life of the artist. . . . Art is part of the mind set that we term intellectualism, that interest in manipulating ideas rather than things. Literature, as with all art, considers and clothes concepts in symbolic patterns that produce aesthetic satisfaction.

Carlsen went on to say that a piece of literature first exists in the mind of its creator and then in the minds of its readers. And because it was never anything "real," it cannot be tested against an external reality as can the plans for a building, chemical formulas, case studies, etc.

> ■ If we evaluate literature by its realism alone, we should be forced to abandon most of the truly great literature of the world: certainly most of tragedy, much of comedy, and all of romance. We would be forced to discard

the Greek plays, the great epics, Shakespeare, Molière. They succeed because they go beyond the externals of living and instead reach out and touch that imaginative life deep down inside where we live.[1]

When two highly respected critics both argue against "realism" as a literary concept, we owe at least an explanation of why we are using the term in our chapter title. The main reason is that we can't think of a better word. Besides, so many people use it to describe the kinds of books that are being discussed in this chapter that we would be at a communication disadvantage if we tried to invent a new term. Some people call the books *problem novels,* but every novel includes a "problem." If it didn't, there wouldn't be a plot. And so even though we can't give a foolproof definition of "the new realism," and we're not even sure that it's the best term, that's what this chapter is about. By the end of the chapter, you should have a good idea of what such books have in common, but for now we will start by saying that realism is experientially true. It is an author's honest attempt to depict people in ordinary situations without sentimentalizing or glossing over anything.

Good YA authors treat candidly and with respect problems that belong specifically to young adults in today's world. As we pointed out in Chapter 1, adolescence as a unique period of life is a fairly recent development coinciding with the development of complex industrial societies. The problems that go along with modern adolescence did not exist in the nineteenth century, so, of course, they were not written about. At least in this one area, there is ample justification for books directed specifically to a young adult audience because there is a difference in the kinds of real-life problems that concern children, teenagers, and adults.

WHAT ARE THE PROBLEMS?

What are some of the problems faced by today's youth? A look at any newspaper can provide clues, but if all we knew of teenagers came from newspapers, we might well think that all young people drink heavily, have been sexually abused, run away from home, expect contraceptives on demand, commit crimes, and kill themselves. We know this isn't true, but it is true that young people today find themselves having to make decisions regarding their own values and behavior in a bewilderingly complex society. Choices exist that didn't exist even a few years ago: psychoactive drugs are readily available; abortions are legal under many circumstances; a college education is no longer considered the panacea it once was; the traditional structure of marriage and family is being challenged as never before. This is not to say that these are the first teenagers in history with difficult decisions to make, just that every generation of young people has a special set of problems unique to the age. The teenagers of this decade are no exception.

A rather common observation about adolescent reading has been that young people are looking for mirror images of themselves. In relation to realistic fiction, this may be only partially true. A more accurate analogy could be made to the wedding custom in traditional Afghanistan where the bride and groom said their vows in front of a large mirror. Girls began wearing *chaderis* at age twelve, and because marriages were arranged, the new husband and wife remained a mystery to each other until the wedding was performed in front of the two families and the girl would remove her facial covering. Instead of looking at each other, the bride and groom satisfied their curiosity by staring intensely in the mirror. Of course they saw themselves, but what they were really examining was the other person as they asked such questions as, "What is this person like?" "How do I look in relation to this person?" "How should I act toward him (or her)?" and "How will my life be affected?"

Staring face-to-face would not have been culturally acceptable, so the mirror, which was given to the couple as their first piece of household furniture, served a purpose similar to that of books in the lives of adolescent readers. It put a frame around someone who, in relation to the viewer, was of intense interest, and it made it acceptable to stare.

Young readers use books as the Afghans used their wedding mirrors. The author acts as the mirror, absorbing directly from life what is of importance and then reflecting this information back to the viewer so that it can be openly examined as true life never could be. Teenagers examine through this mirroring of life those people and forces that stand between them and the finding of their own identities.

This sounds like a relatively simple task, but a discussion of the books and the various alternatives that they explore will illustrate that the matter is not so simple after all, nor is it easy to write high quality books that can serve this purpose. In order to understand the nature of the problem novel, it is necessary to look not only at the subject matter, but also at how the subject matter influences writing styles and at how one book lays the groundwork for others. Suggestions for evaluating the problem novel are listed in Table 3.1.

THE GROUND-BREAKING BOOKS

If we were to pinpoint the birth of the new realism, the year would probably be 1967, when S. E. Hinton's *The Outsiders,* Robert Lipsyte's *The Contender,* Ann Head's *Mr. and Mrs. Bo Jo Jones,* and Jean Thompson's *House of Tomorrow* appeared. These were followed in 1968 by Paul Zindel's *The Pigman* and Richard Bradford's *Red Sky at Morning.* In the next year came William Armstrong's *Sounder,* Vera and Bill Cleaver's *Where the Lilies Bloom,* and John Donovan's *I'll Get There. It Better Be Worth the Trip.*

These books had a new candor to them. Unlike in previous books for young readers, the protagonists came mostly from lower-class families. Instead of living in idyllic and pleasant suburban homes, the characters had harsh and

Table 3.1   **SUGGESTIONS FOR EVALUATING THE PROBLEM NOVEL**

A good problem novel usually has:	A poor problem novel may have:
A strong, interesting, and believable plot centering around a problem that a young person might really have.	A totally predictable plot with nothing new and interesting to entice the reader.
The power to transport the reader into another person's thoughts and feelings.	Characters that are cardboardlike exaggerations of people who are too good or too bad to be believed.
Rich characterization. The characters "come alive" as believable with a balance of good and negative qualities.	More characters than the reader can keep straight comfortably. Many stereotypes.
A setting that enhances the story and is described so that the reader can get the intended picture.	Lengthy chapters or descriptive paragraphs that add bulk but not substance to the book.
A worthwhile theme. The reader is left with something to think about.	A preachy message. The author spells out the attitudes and conclusions with which he or she wants each reader to leave the book.
A smoothness of style that flows steadily and easily, carrying the reader along.	Nothing that stays with the reader after the book has been put down.
A universal appeal so that it speaks to more than a single group of readers.	A subject that is of interest only because it is topical or trendy.
A subtlety that stimulates the reader to think about the various aspects of the story.	Inconsistent points of view. The author's sympathies change with no justification. Dialogue that sounds forced and/or inappropriate to the characters.
A way of dealing with the problems so that the reader is left with insights into either society or individuals or both.	"Facts" that do not jibe with those of the real world. Unlikely coincidences or changes in characters' personalities for the sake of the plot. Exaggerations which result in sensationalism.

difficult lives. In *The Outsiders,* Hinton wrote about the Socs and the Greasers, and it was the Greasers whose story she told. In *The Contender,* Lipsyte wrote about a black boy hoping to use boxing as his ticket out of the slums. Both Head and Thompson wrote about unmarried girls who are pregnant. In Head's *Mr. and Mrs. Bo Jo Jones,* the girl marries the father, but in Thompson's *House of Tomorrow* the father is already married and the girl goes to a home for unwed mothers.

In Zindel's *The Pigman,* an alienated boy and girl make friends with a lonely old man who can't admit that his wife has died. The three of them share true feelings of love and carefree playfulness, but in the end the old man dies tragically, and the boy and girl are left to ponder their role in his death and what it all means. In Bradford's *Red Sky at Morning,* southerner Josh Arnold and his mother go to a little town in New Mexico where they are to wait out the Second World War. While living there, Josh gains at least a partial understanding not only of his Mexican American neighbors but also of himself. Some people—mostly adults—were shocked by the language in this book.

The next three books continued the trend of pushing away from safe, middle-class settings. Armstrong's *Sounder* is a grim historical piece about a poverty-stricken black family of tenant farmers. In the Cleavers' *Where the Lilies Bloom,* which is set in the Tennessee mountains, fourteen-year-old Mary Call struggles to keep her orphaned brothers and sisters together after they secretly bury their father. And in Donovan's *I'll Get There. It Better Be Worth the Trip,* Davy, who has been raised by his grandmother, has to move to New York to live with an alcoholic mother that he hardly knows and certainly does not understand.

These nine books of the late 1960s exemplify several of the characteristics that during the 1970s came to be associated with the realistic problem novel for young adults. There are basically four ways, besides the subject matter, in which these books differ from earlier books. First, there is the choice of *characters*. Unlike previous books for young people, the protagonists come mostly from lower-class families. This ties in with the second major difference, which is that of *setting*. Whereas most earlier books are set in idyllic and pleasant suburban homes, the settings in these books are often portrayed as harsh, difficult places to live. In order to get the point across about the characters and where and how they live, authors used colloquial *language,* which is the third major difference. Authors began to write the way people really talked. For example, in dialogue, they used profanity and ungrammatical constructions. That the general public allowed this change in language shows that people were drawing away from the idea that the main purpose of fictional books for young readers is to set an example of proper, middle-class behavior.

The fourth difference also relates to this change in attitude, and that is the change in *mode.* As people began to think that the educational value of fiction is to provide readers with more vicarious experiences than would be either desirable or possible in real life, the mode of stories for young adults changed. In the old days most of the books—at least most of the books approved of by parents and educators—were written in the comic and romantic modes. These were the books with upbeat, happy endings. As long as people believed that children would model their lives after what they read, then of course they wanted young people to read happy stories because a happy life is what all of us want for our children. But the problem novel is based on a different philosophy, which is that young people will have a better chance to be happy if they have realistic expectations, if they know both the bad and the good about the society in which they live. This changed attitude opened the door to writers of irony and even tragedy for young people.

Irony differs from tragedy in that it may be less intense, and instead of having heroic qualities, the protagonist is an ordinary person, much like the reader. One definition of irony is "a tennis serve that you can't return." You can admire its perfection, its appropriateness, and even the inevitability of the outcome, but you just can't cope with it.

THE PEOPLE BEHIND THE BOOKS

MARION DANE BAUER
on Windows and Mirrors

My most important goal in writing is to touch that place in a reader of any age which is most hidden, most private, that part of ourselves in which we feel most alone. The more uniquely individual an experience or a feeling is, the more universal I believe it to be. So as a writer I am always writing toward that moment when a reader will say, "But I thought I was the only one who ever thought that, felt that, wanted that. I thought I was alone, and I see now that I am connected with other human beings . . . at least with this one on the page, and if with this one, then why not with others?"

We all read fiction for a multiplicity of reasons, for entertainment, for escape, for information, for meaning. (Life doesn't come equipped with built-in meaning, stories do.) But I think the deepest reason for readers to turn to fiction is that we are searching for connection with other human beings, an understanding of ourselves through the unique glimpse fiction can allow into another. Fiction can provide access inside the skin, inside the soul of another human being (if only an imagined one), which no life experience can accomplish so fully. Even when we choose to reveal ourselves to one another completely, we are always holding bits back, always blind ourselves to bits we might have revealed. The fictional character, with or without the author's choice, reveals the blindest bits of the author, the deepest parts of the author's understanding of self and others.

And story, itself, becomes a vehicle through which the encounter between reader and character can happen with feeling but in complete safety. (How ready I am to meet a murderer on the page, how reluctant in life!) Because I as a reader can always shut the book, can always choose to disbelieve the story, I discover the connections without invasion or threat. Because I as a writer use these paper people to come to know myself, they form a mirror through which others can discover themselves as well as a window through which they and I reach to touch one another.

Marion Dane Bauer's books include *Tangled Butterfly,* Houghton Mifflin, 1980; *Shelter from the Wind,* Houghton Mifflin, 1976; and *Foster Child,* Houghton Mifflin, 1977.

There's a refreshing honesty to stories that show readers they aren't the only ones who get served that kind of ball and that the human spirit, though totally devastated in this particular set, may rise again to play another match. Chris Crutcher's *The Crazy Horse Electric Game,* Richard Peck's *Remembering the Good Times,* and M. E. Kerr's *Night Kites* are books of this sort.

Robert Cormier's books come closer to being tragedies. In traditional literary criticism, tragedies have three distinct elements. First, there is a noble character who, no matter what happens, maintains the qualities that the society considers praiseworthy; second, there is an inevitable force that works against the character; and, third, there is a struggle and an outcome. In Cormier's *I Am the Cheese,* the boy being interrogated throughout the book is the tragic hero. The inevitable force is corruption and government duplicity. And the outcome—in which the best that the boy can hope for is to live his life in a drugged and incoherent state—is indeed a tragedy. Yet the reader is left with some satisfaction and pride because there is a resiliency in the boy that keeps him, even when he is drugged, from totally surrendering to his highly skilled interrogators.

Another tradition sometimes considered essential in tragedy holds that the hero—worthy and admirable as he or she may be—has nevertheless contributed to the unfolding of the terrible events through some tragic flaw of character. With Cormier's book, the reader has the nagging feeling that maybe if the boy had not been so bright and so inquisitive (which were the characteristics that first brought trouble to his father) and had not found out his family's history, then maybe life could have gone on as before and Mr. Grey wouldn't have bothered with him. But at the same time, it is this brightness and persistence that keeps him from surrendering at the end.

The reader of a tragedy is usually filled with pity and fear—pity for the hero and fear for oneself that the same thing might happen. The intensity of this involvement causes the reader to undergo an emotional release as the outcome of the story unfolds. This release is known as catharsis, which has the effect of draining away dangerous human emotions and filling the reader with a sense of exaltation or amazed pride in what the human spirit is called upon to undergo.[2]

THE CHOCOLATE WAR *AS A PROBLEM NOVEL*

The book that we have chosen as an example of the best of modern realism for young adults is Cormier's *The Chocolate War* (1974). It contains the kind of realism that many other books had been leading up to. Its message about conformity and human manipulation is all the more powerful because the young protagonist is so vulnerable. The religious symbolism that pervades the book serves as a contrasting backdrop to the terrible evil that pervades Trinity High School where the protagonist is a freshman. The opening paragraph is the simple line: "They murdered him." Readers, who at first might think the reference is to Jesus, soon find that it is to fourteen-year-old Jerry Renault who is being "tested" to see if he has enough guts to get on the football team.

The story begins and ends on the athletic field where the shadows of the goal posts resemble "a network of crosses, empty crucifixes." On Jerry's third play at Trinity High he is "hit simultaneously by three of them." He blinks himself back to consciousness and jumps to his feet:

◼ . . . intact, bobbing like one of those toy novelties dangling from car windows, but erect.

"For Christ's sake," the coach bellowed, his voice juicy with contempt. A spurt of saliva hit Jerry's cheek.

Hey coach, you spit on me, Jerry protested. Stop the spitting, coach. What he said aloud was, "I'm all right, coach," because he was a coward about stuff like that, thinking one thing and saying another, planning one thing and doing another—he had been Peter a thousand times and a thousand cocks had crowed in his lifetime.

Over the course of the book Jerry gets the courage to think and do the same thing. He refuses to sell fifty boxes of chocolates that the corrupt teacher, Brother Leon, has assigned to each student. For the first ten days of the candy campaign, he simply follows the orders of the Vigils, a gang who in the words of their head man, Archie Costello, "were the school." But when the ten days are up and the Vigils order Jerry to do a reversal and to participate in the selling campaign, he dares to say no.

At first Jerry is a hero, but because this threatens the power of the Vigils, Archie uses his full potential in people management to turn the student body against Jerry. When all the chocolates except Jerry's are sold, Archie arranges a boxing match between Jerry and a bully who is trying to work his way into the Vigils. It is supposed to be set up "with rules. Fair and square," but what Archie really masterminds is a physical and psychological battering much worse than anything Jerry underwent at football practice.

The last chapter of the book could have begun with the same line as the first chapter—"They murdered him"—only this time it would have been more than a metaphor. Although Jerry is probably going to recover physically from a fractured jaw and internal injuries, his spirit has been murdered. In the midst of the fight:

◼ a new sickness invaded Jerry, the sickness of knowing what he had become, another animal, another beast, another violent person in a violent world, inflicting damage, not disturbing the universe but damaging it. He had allowed Archie to do this to him.

And after the fight when the pain—"Jesus, the pain"—brings Jerry back to consciousness, the reader sees how changed he is because of what he tries to tell his friend Goober:

◼ They don't want you to do your thing, not unless it happens to be their thing, too. It's a laugh, Goober, a fake. Don't disturb the universe, Goober, no matter what the posters say.

In selecting *The Chocolate War* as a touchstone example, we asked ourselves several questions about the book. These same or similar questions could be asked when evaluating almost any problem novel. First, does the book make a

Through his own writing as well as what was written about him, Robert Cormier brought adolescent literature a step closer to literary respectability.

distinctive contribution? Does it say something new or does it convey something old in a new way? And if so, is it something of value?

Robert Cormier was praised by *The Kirkus Reviews* because he dared to "disturb the upbeat universe of juvenile books" with *The Chocolate War.* He did not compromise by providing a falsely hopeful conclusion, nor did he sidestep the issue by leaving it open for readers to imagine their own happy ending. Until Cormier, most writers for young readers had chosen one of these two approaches. Yet Cormier was not being "difficult" just for the sake of being different. When he was questioned at a National Council of Teachers of English convention about his motives in writing such a pessimistic book for young readers, he answered that he had written three other novels and numerous short stories all with upbeat endings and that in *The Chocolate War* he was simply providing a balance. He then went on to say that today's young readers are a television generation. They have grown up thinking that every problem can be solved within a half-hour or an hour at the most, with time out for commercials. It's important for people to realize that all problems are not that easily solved. In real life there are some problems that may never be solved and others whose solutions will demand the utmost efforts of the most capable people in the world.

The plot of a book must be examined to see how closely it grows out of the characters' actions and attitudes. Is it an idea that could easily have been dropped into another setting or onto other characters? With Cormier's book, there wouldn't have been a story without the unique but believable personalities of both Jerry and Archie, as well as of Brother Leon. The problem was not so bizarre or unusual that it overshadowed the characters, nor were the characters such unusual people that readers could not identify with them or imagine themselves having to deal with people like them. It is because the characters at first appear to be such ordinary people that readers are drawn into the story. The theme is similar to that in Golding's *Lord of the Flies,* but because Golding's book is set on a deserted island in the midst of a war it could be dismissed as unrealistic. Cormier's book has an immediacy that is hard to deny. The problem is a real one that teenagers can identify with on the first or literal level, yet it has implications far beyond one beaten-up fourteen-year-old and 20,000 boxes of stale Mother's Day candy.

In looking at the setting, we might ask, is it just there or does it contribute something to the mood or the action or to revealing characterization? In *The Chocolate War* the story would not have been nearly so chilling without the religious setting which provided contrast. In some ways the evil in Archie is less hideous than that in Brother Leon, the corrupt teacher who enlists Archie's help in making his unauthorized investment pay off. The Brother hides behind his clerical collar and his role of teacher and assistant headmaster, whereas Archie only identifies himself as a nonbeliever in the so-called "Christian ethic." For example, when his stooge Obie asks him how he can do the things he does and still take communion, he responds, "When you march down to the rail, you're receiving the Body, man. Me, I'm just chewing a wafer they buy by the pound in Worcester."

Another relevant question is the respect the author has for the intended audience. Cormier showed a great deal of respect for his readers: nowhere did he write down to them. The proof of his respect for them is in some of the subtle symbolization that he worked into the story and the care with which he developed his style. For example, the irony of the whole situation is exemplified in the gang's name the *Vigils.* He chose the name as a shortened form of *vigilante,* an accurate description of the way the gang worked. But in response to an interview question about whether or not the name was an ironic reference to vigil lights, the candles placed devotionally before a shrine or image, he agreed that the religious connotation, the image of the boys in the gang standing like vigil lights before Archie, who basked in the glow of their admiration, "was also very much a part of my choice."[3] Another example of Cormier's subtlety is the fact that Archie's name has such meanings as "principal or chief" as in archvillain, "cleverly sly and alert," and "at the extreme, that is, someone or something most fully embodying the qualities of its kind."

The question that has to be asked somewhere in the evaluation process is how many people a particular book attracts as readers. *The Chocolate War* has gone through innumerable reprintings so obviously it's being read, but many of those who read it are doing it as a class assignment either in a college young adult literature class or in a high school English class. It's ideal for class reading and discussion because there's more in the book than any one student sees at a first reading.

Nearly all writers for teenagers make certain adjustments to attract a reading audience. Some authors will say that they write strictly for themselves and it's immaterial to them whether or not anyone reads their books. This is probably either an exaggeration or an ego-defense mechanism. The physical act of typing up a manuscript and mailing it off to an editor is so demanding that someone writing only for personal fulfillment would not be likely to go through the effort. Besides, literature consists of a two-way process in which the reader brings thoughts and feelings to be intertwined with those of the author. If no one is reading a book, then only half the process is taking place.

HOW THE PROBLEM NOVEL HAS CHANGED

When *The Outsiders* and *The Pigman* were written, Americans had not yet sent a man to the moon, nor had they lost a war or had a President resign. It would be strange indeed, for such momentous events and changes in cultural attitudes to have occurred while realistic books for young adults stayed exactly the same.

Because it was new and different and because it explored themes which intrigued and concerned adults *and* young adults, publishers, authors, librarians, teachers and critics treated the problem novel genre as a favored child all during the 1970s. Then in the early 1980s, changes in marketing practices and reading tastes (see Chapter 11 for a fuller discussion) made paperback romances and other mass-produced series (horror stories, science fiction, mysteries) the favorites of young readers. Sweet Dreams and Sweet Valley High were not only checked out of libraries but purchased by the bagfuls from bookstores in shopping malls. That may have delighted some publishers—or at least marketing people—but librarians and English teachers who had welcomed the new YA problem novel were horrified.

They worried and wondered if serious writing for young adults was an endangered species, perhaps even close to extinction. A panel of editors touched on this at the November 1987 National Council of Teachers of English meeting in Los Angeles. Harper and Row editor Marilyn Kriney answered the question "Is the problem novel dead?" with another question, "What's a novel without a problem?" And she warned about the dangers of labeling books, particularly problem novels, when she said, "By pigeonholing, we're denying what makes these books great—their universality."

We agree that the YA realistic problem novel is alive and well, and for us it's still the most intriguing YA reading. We also think that some but not all of the changes that have occurred within the last 25 years have made for better books. One such change is that the modern problem novel is no longer so shocking to young adults. In her 1979 May Hill Arbuthnot lecture, Sheila Egoff listed several reasons that problem novels were popular with young readers— the books featured the unknown and exotic, they flattered readers by making the audience feel grown-up, they appealed to prurient interests, and they were promoted through peer pressure: "Not to have read Judy Blume seems as socially unacceptable as not being familiar with the latest 'in' television show."[4]

Ignoring for the moment that all these reasons were also applicable to selling the hottest "in" best-sellers to adults, most of Egoff's comments seem dated. Perhaps the books have changed; society certainly has. In 1971, *Go Ask Alice* shocked many adults and some adolescents because they had no idea that "nice, middle-class, white girls did such things" (the *things* meaning sex and drugs). Readers were virtuously allowed, or encouraged, to relish all those gorgeous, salacious details because the author was preaching a moral message. Today's television documentaries and magazines and newspapers leave little in the "unknown and exotic" category. In the late 1980s, Marshall McLuhan's idea of the global village took on added meaning as the world listened to insider accounts of political intrigues in the Iran-Contra hearings and gossiped over backyard fences about Gary Hart's and Jim Bakker's libidos, Baby M's mixed-up parentage, and Bernard Goetz's acquittal. The AIDS epidemic was scary enough to bring sex education out into the open, and when a demonstration was given on national television of how to put on a condom the only loud protest came from banana growers who objected to their merchandise being used as a model.

All of this has had a numbing effect. Almost daily we see bumper stickers, T-shirt messages, and tabloid headlines that a few years ago would have been considered so off-color that they would have been whispered among close friends, not put on public display. And if pornographic books and magazines, sexually explicit cable television or videos, and telephone scoop lines devoted to sexual talk are available to adults in a community, they are also available to young adults. Obviously, whether we like it or not, young people today have been exposed to information and opinions about all sorts of things, precisely the kinds of sensitive issues treated in YA problem novels. This means that today's books have to offer more than titillation, which the best ones always did.

Today's problem novels are also likely to contain more excitement, romance, and optimism. Being forced to compete with the unrealistic wish fulfillment of paperback romances, as well as with the equally unrealistic chills of occult and horror tales, has made authors less likely to write starkly grim stories. This was brought forcefully home to us when we looked for a new touchstone example of modern tragedy and then decided to keep Robert Cormier's 1974 *The Chocolate War.* We couldn't find a new book we liked that was a pure example of a tragedy. Authors today tend to soften their stories with wish-fulfilling motifs. For example, young readers can easily be enticed into identifying with the problems faced by the protagonist in Sandy Asher's *Everything Is Not Enough,* in which wealthy Michael Paeglis goes against his father's wishes and takes a summer job as a busboy, or in Robin Brancato's *Uneasy Money,* in which a high school senior wins the New Jersey Lottery.

Another trend is for authors to cram more and more into each book. For example, Julian F. Thompson's 1986 *A Band of Angels* begins with an orphaned boy caught in a political situation somewhat like Cormier's 1977 *I Am the Cheese.* But in Thompson's novel, the boy and the warm and supportive friends that he picks up are largely unaware and untouched by any danger. They camp in the woods and hatch plans to have every kid sign a petition against nuclear war. Al Muller in *The ALAN Review* for Fall 1986 criticized the fact that on the way to the happy ending, readers meet not only the main characters, but also a hippie college professor who takes advantage of teenage runaways, a jailed teenager's suicide, Vietnam veterans hiding in a wilderness, materialistic and capitalistic adults and parents, industrial strength profanity, and historical and literary allusions to Bob Dylan, *Shane,* the Children's Crusade, Descartes, *The Sun Also Rises,* and Marlin Perkins.

Joan Kaywell criticized Isabelle Holland's *The Island* for much the same reason in the Spring 1985 *ALAN Review:* "a heart attack here, a murder there," then some "drugs and an arranged marriage." Kaywell argued that the elements didn't work well together, "especially when the characters are so bland."[5] She compared her disappointment to what she would have felt had she gone to Julia Child's house and been served "chicken cordon bleu a la TV dinner."

The result of both of these trends is a blurring of the dividers between problem novels and other types of stories such as romances, historical fiction, and adventure stories. This has forced us to make some arbitrary decisions because many of the books which we discuss here could also be discussed in other sections.

A positive result from authors' attempts to give their readers more is that there is less stereotyping of characters as well as plots and settings. The kinds of problems that contemporary teenagers face are being written about in a variety of settings. Family problems and strengths are shown in places as far away as World War II Japan (Hisako Matsubara's *Cranes at Dusk*), contemporary Greece (Paula Fox's *Lily and the Lost Boy*), and almost contemporary Cauley's Creek, Kentucky (Jenny Davis's *Goodbye and Keep Cold*). These books also illustrate another change, which is that YA authors are focusing more attention on characters of different ages. Davis' book, although told through the eyes of eighteen-year-old Edda Combs, is really the story of Edda's mother, who was left a widow when Edda's father was killed ten years earlier in a mining accident. And in Matsubara's and Fox's books, the protagonists are really children, but the stories are full enough that teenagers will probably not be put off by reading the thoughts of people a few years younger than they are. In the early problem novels, it was an unrealistic convention that the parents were dead or absent, or as Hazel Rochman recently wrote, they were "hopelessly inadequate dummies or monsters."[6] Although it's still fairly common to have absent or imperfect parents, fuller stories are allowing authors to develop parents who are not quite as one-sided as they used to be.

Sexual stereotyping is also less apparent in the new books. For example, in 1967 when teenager S. E. Hinton wrote the autobiographical *The Outsiders,* her publishers suggested that she go by her initials rather than by her name of Susan Eloise. They feared that readers wouldn't respect a "macho" story if they knew it was written by a woman. These strict male/female expectations are not so much a part of today's books as they were in the '60s. For example, in 1985 when Cin Forshay-Lunsford published the autobiographical *Walk*

Through Cold Fire, a book with a plot and characters that several reviewers compared to *The Outsiders,* no one suggested that the author take a masculine sounding pen name or that the main character in the book be changed from a girl to a boy.

And of course we would expect changes in books focusing on issues related to racial and ethnic differences. Among the most powerful books of the 1960s and early 1970s that young adults responded to were Eldridge Cleaver's *Soul on Ice,* William H. Armstrong's *Sounder,* Maya Angelou's *I Know Why the Caged Bird Sings,* Sharon Bell Mathis' *Teacup Full of Roses,* Alice Childress' *A Hero Ain't Nothin' But a Sandwich,* and Rosa Guy's *The Friends.* As powerful as these books were, they had a grimness and a sameness to them, and it's refreshing today to have them supplemented by books in which a variety of characters from different backgrounds face problems, sometimes separately but often together.

Many of today's authors and publishers grew up in the 1960s and they look back—somewhat idealistically—to this period of their own coming-of-age. As they prepare books for today's young readers, they want to communicate the sense of commitment and excitement they felt, hence we see 1960s settings or related themes in many good new books. Among the best are Alice McDermott's *That Night,* the story of the loss that results from a night of violence when a group of teenagers gather at the home of one of their girl-friends; Walter Dean Myers' *Fallen Angels,* the story of seventeen-year-old Richie Perry's year as a Vietnam soldier; and Bobbie Ann Mason's *In Country,* the story of a teenage girl's efforts to understand the war in Vietnam and the time and place that left her father dead and her beloved uncle emotionally and physically damaged.

These changes affect to varying degrees the different kinds of realistic problem novels discussed below. Of course there will be exceptions, but in general realistic problem novels of today as compared to those of the 1970s will have:

- Less reliance for interest on shock and titillation.
- More excitement, romance, and optimism.
- More variety and less stereotyping of characters, plots, and settings.
- A more balanced and convincing view of parents.
- More sophisticated and varied approaches to problems connected with racism and ethnic identification.

◼ *CATEGORIES OF CONCERN IN PROBLEM NOVELS*

One of the identifying characteristics of YA literature is that the problems that authors choose to write about are those most likely to be met by contemporary teenagers. Because today's society is so different from what it was two or three generations ago, young readers aren't likely to find their kinds of problems in many of the classics. Nor are they likely to find their kinds of problems in contemporary problem novels written for adults because these books are likely

HARRY MAZER
on Surrendering Ourselves

I write novels, yet, inevitably, I find my books listed as useful for various kinds of readers. For instance, my book *The Island Keeper* was described in a single review as useful for "overweight teens, teens with parental or guardian conflicts, teens experiencing the death of a sibling, teens interested in the running away theme, and teens interested in camping or nature."

Somehow this misses by a mile what I had in mind when I wrote this book. I had in mind to write a novel that captured the reader, engaged her, involved her, moved her to tears or laughter or exaltation. Usefulness was low on the list.

I try not to write useful books. There are enough of them in the world. Textbooks, handbooks, manuals, travel guides, stories of great men—and lately great women. I have no argument with them, and they are indeed useful.

But what is the use of fiction, that peculiar long narrative story we call a novel? As a book, a novel can be used to build a wall, hold a door open, balance a rickety table, or throw in anger or defense.

Dogs sometimes will accept a book as a substitute for a bone, and cats have been known to dig into a novel. Kids are notorious unless corrected for turning novels into coloring books.

To spend our time in useless pursuits makes adults uneasy. This is how you distinguish the kids from the grown-ups. Grown-ups work, raise families, have activities and hobbies, useful pursuits that justify their existence. Travel is educational, climbing rocks increases your cardiovascular capacity and white water canoeing stretches your psychic limits. But what does lying in a hammock reading a novel do for you? It's too easy, too much fun, too enjoyable. What can be the use of it? It won't put money in your pocket, it won't advance your career or make you a measurably better or healthier or handsomer person.

For what is the use of a story, but in itself? In the telling . . . and in the listening, in the reading and losing oneself in the unexpected. The novel puts us into a world we can't alter, a world more interesting, intense, and moving than the real world. A world where nothing useful is expected of us, where things happen that we need only observe, wonder at, and think about.

When we read a novel, when we surrender ourselves to the story, our guard drops, and we abandon our slit-eyed purposefulness. We don't have to pretend, we don't have to put on masks, we don't have to posture and behave usefully. We are released.

There we have it—the true use of a novel—it gives us back our purest selves.

Harry Mazer's books include *City Light,* Scholastic, 1988; *The Girl of His Dreams,* Crowell, 1987; and *Cave under the City,* Crowell, 1986.

to focus on marital problems, mature sexual relationships, disappointments in careers, and adjustments to growing old. Teenagers are more interested in how they relate to their parents, siblings, and friends; in how they are going to adjust to society; and in the kinds of sexual experiences and relationships they might expect to have.

Family Relationships

A look at mythology, folklore, and classical and religious literature shows that the subject of parent/child relationships is not what's new about the new realism. One could find virtually thousands of stories touching on the theme. And although in Chapter 1 we identified the idea that books for teenagers are anti-parent or anti-adult as a "myth," it's true that in many YA books teenagers solve all problems without any help from parents. John and Lorraine in Zindel's *The Pigman* may find love and respect from an adult but certainly not from either of their parents. Similarly, in M. E. Kerr's *Dinky Hocker Shoots Smack* or S. E. Hinton's *The Outsiders* or Rosa Guy's *Ruby,* parents were either unable or unwilling to help their children.

Inadequate or absent parents appeal to young adult readers who are desperately involved with changing from someone's child to an individual with rights. As author Richard Peck has observed, young readers don't honestly want realism. Instead they want romance masked as realism. They want to identify with teenage protagonists who accomplish something that in real life teenagers probably couldn't do on their own.

Relative newcomers to YA books are parents who are or have been hippies. Sharon Leezer, one of our graduate students who is a teacher and librarian in Phoenix, wrote a paper asking, "Have the Flower Children Sprouted Weeds in the Garden of Motherhood?" She became interested in the ways parents were portrayed when she noticed how many "older" men and women came to parent/teacher conferences in her suburban, middle-class school. To her surprise, she learned that these were usually grandparents raising offspring left behind as their flower children turned into hardcore, absent hippies. She set out to see if this new reality had found its way into contemporary fiction, and if so, how such parents would be portrayed.

She found that a common way for authors to indicate the flower-child background of parents was to have their children address them by first names: Melody, Taxi, Courtney, Saffron. These parents in turn gave their children unusual names: Galadrial, Pax, Joshua Fortune, Sara Sunshine, and Esalen Starness Blue. It was also common for one or both parents to be away for long periods of time; to send postcards, usually with no return address; to raise false hopes by professing love and a desire to see the child, and to make children wait for calls by public telephones. For example, in Betsy Byars' *The Two-Thousand-Pound Goldfish,* Weezie stands in the designated phone booth at the designated time for 156 weeks but receives only five calls. In Cynthia Voigt's *A Solitary Blue,* when Melody leaves her son, seven-year-old Jeff, she explains in a note that she is needed by hungry people and little hunted-down animals. Years later when Jeff visits his mother at her grandmother's house, she exchanges his plane ticket home for a bus ticket explaining that the extra money could be better spent on poor, starving children. Since she leaves him no money for meals, he becomes one of the starving children she professes to be so concerned about.

However, not all hippie parents were presented negatively. In Sue Ellen Bridgers' *Permanent Connections,* artist Ginny has divorced her husband and moved to the North Carolina mountains to "find herself." She's nevertheless a concerned and competent mother both for her daughter Ellery and for Ellery's boyfriend, Rob. In *The Great Gilly Hopkins,* Katherine Paterson portrayed Courtney Rutherford Hopkins as "a flower child gone to seed," but in *Bridge to Terabithia* she portrayed Leslie's parents, Bill and Judy Burke, as an intelligent, creative couple, who came in their "little Italian car . . . to reassess their value structure" by living in a rundown farm house with lots of books and no television set. They wore old jeans, wrote instead of "worked," and ate clabber.

In Norma Fox Mazer's *Downtown,* Hal and Laura Connors are fugitives from the F.B.I. because they were leaders of an anti-war protest that went awry and killed two people. Their son, named Pax but now called Pete, is left with a bachelor uncle and in general has a good life—except for when he's awakened by what he calls the White Terror or when he's followed by government agents or when he can't tell his girlfriend about his family. Then his mother turns herself in and sends for him to visit her in jail. At first he's exuberantly happy, but as he and his uncle get closer to New York he's overcome with doubts and realizes that he no longer knows where home is, "I finally understand that there is no ending for my story . . . no perfect ending . . . no little-Pax-happy-at-last ending."

In Bruce Brooks' *Midnight Hour Encores,* sixteen-year-old Sib asks her unorthodox father, Taxi, to take her to California to visit Sib's flower-child mother, who gave her away on the day she was born. To Sib's surprise, her mother is now a successful businesswoman, open and warm and at least willing to try being a mother. But in the end, Sib decides to return to Washington, D.C., with Taxi. This refreshing change from the unrealistic child-centeredness of the old problem novels is possible because Sib, along with readers, realizes that contrary to what she would like to think, she did not raise herself with only a little help from Taxi.

Sib is a world-class cellist, and her story is tied together by allusions and metaphors relating to music. In a similar way, Zibby Oneal's *In Summer Light* is strengthened by allusions and metaphors relating to color and light. Kate, the protagonist, is an artist, but unlike Sib, who has a wonderful relationship with her father, Kate is embittered and resentful of her artist father. But in the story, which *School Library Journal* editor Trev Jones described as, "A coming-of-age novel that is light-years above most others,"[7] Kate makes progress in understanding both her father and, more importantly, herself.

In Sonia Levitin's *A Season for Unicorns,* 14-year-old Ingrid is embittered when she learns that her father casually engages in extramarital sex. Learning something similar is even more traumatic for 17-year-old Alan in John Rowe Townsend's *Downstream.* Alan is in love with his 23-year-old tutor and is devastated when he learns that she is having an affair with his father.

In Paula Fox's *The Moonlight Man,* Catherine learns to love the alcoholic father she has hardly known, but at the same time she also becomes aware of his weaknesses. In Richard Peck's *Remembering the Good Times,* readers meet three sets of parents, none of them perfect. In the old problem novels, this would have been enough to send the teenagers out on their own. But here, they talk about it. Kate tells Buck that "I have really got to deal with myself. . . . About my mother. I'm ashamed of her, and it's really immature." She goes on to observe how their best friend also resents his parents:

Because he's exactly like them. . . . When you're as uncomfortable with yourself as Trav is and you see the very same traits in your parents, then you just turn on them. You want to shift the blame onto them and get out from under it yourself.

YA authors have not developed the mother/daughter relationship as fully as they have father/son and father/daughter relationships. However Jamaica Kincaid's *Annie John,* set on the Caribbean Island of Antigua, is a powerful new exploration of a daughter's painful gaining of emotional independence from her mother. And authors Norma Klein, Norma Fox Mazer, and Judy Blume often write about mothers and daughters.

In Paula Fox's *A Place Apart* and in Judy Blume's *Tiger Eyes,* the father in each family dies unexpectedly (a heart attack and a shooting, respectively) and the mothers and daughters move to new locales, almost as if they are embarking on dual quests in search of a way to put their lives back together. In neither book is it easy, as shown by the climax of *Tiger Eyes,* when Davey's mother invites her out to a special dinner:

"This is nice," I say. What I mean is that it is nice to be alone with my mother. This is the first time since we came to Los Alamos that it is just the two of us.

"Yes," Mom says. "It's very nice."

"It's been a long time."

"Yes," Mom says. "And I've wanted to explain that to you Davey." She is arranging and rearranging her silverware, moving the spoon into the fork's place, then the fork into the spoon's. "Up until now, I've been afraid to be alone with you."

"Afraid?"

"Yes."

"But why?"

"I was afraid you'd ask me questions and I wouldn't have any answers. I've been afraid you'd want to talk about Daddy . . . and the night he was killed . . . and the pain would be too much for me."

"I did want to talk about it," I tell her. "For a long time . . . and it hurt me that you wouldn't."

"I know," she says, reaching across the table and touching my hand. "But I had to come to terms with it myself, first. Now I think I'm ready . . . now I can talk about it with you."

"But now I don't need to," I say.

The absence of a fulfilling relationship between a parent and child sometimes opens the way for the young protagonist to establish a friendship with a surrogate parent. In Alice Childress' *Rainbow Jordan,* 14-year-old Rainbow is periodically abandoned by her 29-year-old mother who leaves to live with new boyfriends or to find work as a go-go dancer. One of the strongest parts of the book is the role played by 57-year-old Josephine, a dressmaker who serves as an "interim guardian," and takes Rainbow in even when her own heart is breaking. In Katherine Paterson's *The Great Gilly Hopkins,* readers feel little for Gilly's flower-child mother, but they can't forget Trotter, the foster-mother that even Katherine Paterson describes as "bigger than real life."

Sometimes the surrogate parent friendship will skip over a generation so that it's a surrogate grandparent who is found. In Lois Lowry's *A Summer to Die,* 13-year-old Meg, who has wonderful parents, nevertheless benefits greatly from the friendship of 70-year-old landlord, handyman, and photographer, Will Banks. The family needs all the help it can get the year that Meg's older sister, Molly, develops leukemia.

With extended families no longer living in close proximity of each other, true grandparent/grandchild relationships may develop almost as between strangers. This is the situation in Robin Brancato's *Sweet Bells Jangled Out of Tune* and M. E. Kerr's *Gentlehands.* In both books, the grandparents are far removed from the Norman Rockwell type of "Home, Sweet Home" family members. In Brancato's book, 15-year-old Ellen is drawn to the eccentric old lady that she used to know as her wealthy and elegant grandmother. Now the woman scrounges through trash containers and picks up leftovers (including money) from restaurant tables. In the end, Ellen realizes that her grandmother needs psychiatric help.

In Kerr's book, Grandpa Trenker is the model of elegance, sophistication, and culture—all the upper-class things that Buddy Boyle's middle-class parents are not. He "uses" his grandfather to help him impress Skye Pennington, a wealthy girl that he's courting. But in the end, it backfires when mounting evidence shows Grandpa Trenker to be a Nazi war criminal.

Authors sometimes use aging and dying grandparents as the vehicle through which young protagonists can develop their strengths. In Hadley Irwin's *What About Grandma?,* three generations of women learn much about each other during the summer that 16-year-old Rhys and her mother Eve learn that Grandmother Wyn is dying. In Richard Graber's *Doc,* a beloved grandfather suffers from Alzheimer's disease, and in Norma Fox Mazer's *After the Rain,* Rachel achieves her own maturity as she helps first to entertain and then to care for her demanding and cranky grandfather, who is dying from cancer.

Grandparents have often been presented as irritating or eccentric, but it's unusual to have truly evil grandparents as are the ones in Robbie Branscum's *The Girl.* These grandparents are sharecroppers who take in the girl and her four brothers so they can collect their welfare checks at the same time they use the children as physical laborers.

When the adults in children's lives are so flawed, space is cleared for fully developed sibling relationships. For example, Cynthia Voigt's Newbery Award-winning *Dicey's Song* begins with:

■ AND THEY LIVED HAPPILY EVER AFTER
Not the Tillermans, Dicey thought. That wasn't the way things went for the Tillermans, ever. She wasn't about to let that get her down. She couldn't let it get her down—that was what had happened to Momma.

Dicey's attitude that when parents are weak the children have to be that much stronger is a theme often illustrated through the way brothers and sisters pull together to close gaps in the family circle. This is the way it is in *Dicey's Song* as well as in Voigt's earlier *Homecoming,* where 13-year-old Dicey and her younger sister and two brothers are abandoned by their mother in a shopping mall parking lot. Their father had left six years earlier. They eventually learn that their mother has lost touch with reality and is in a mental hospital. By this time they have set out on a determined quest to find a home where they can stay together as a family. They make it to the rundown farm that their eccentric grandmother owns on the Chesapeake Bay. *Dicey's Song,* as well as later books *The Runner* and *Sons from Afar,* chronicles what it takes to make a family.

Dicey reminds readers of Vera and Bill Cleaver's Mary Call Luther who, in *Where the Lilies Bloom* and its sequel *Trial Valley,* works with the same kind of ingenuity and dedication to keep her family together. Harry Mazer's *When the Phone Rang* is a more contemporary or mainstream exploration of three young people's (ages 12, 16, and 21) struggle to keep their family together after their parents are killed in a plane crash.

One of the best parts of S. E. Hinton's *Tex* is the relationship between the two brothers who are left to fend for themselves when "Pop" forgets to come home or to send money from the rodeo circuit. And although Virginia Hamilton's *Sweet Whispers, Brother Rush* contains a wonderful fantasy element, what many readers will remember the longest is the devotion that 14-year-old Teresa, or Tree, had for her older brother, Dab. Dab is retarded, but their relationship is not one-sided, and when at the end of the book he dies from porphyria, a rare genetic abnormality, Tree is truly devastated. But because of the strength she has developed while she and Dab took care of each other in the absence of their mother, she is able to take tentative steps toward a life without Dab.

The main problem in Richard Peck's *Father Figure* is that 17-year-old Jim has developed a close relationship thinking of himself as a substitute father for his little brother, and when circumstances change bringing the two boys back in touch with their father, Jim feels competitive. He is jealous and hurt when his little brother chooses the real father over the "father figure."

Writers who consistently show strong family relationships include Mildred Taylor with her historical *Roll of Thunder, Hear My Cry* and its sequel *Let the Circle Be Unbroken;* Ouida Sebestyen with *Words by Heart, Far from Home,* and *IOU's;* and Sue Ellen Bridgers with *Home Before Dark, All Together Now, Notes for Another Life,* and *Permanent Connections.*

Friends and Society

Peer groups become increasingly important to teenagers as they move beyond a social and emotional dependence on their parents. By becoming part of a group, clique, or gang which they can rely on for decisions about such social conventions as clothing, language, and entertainment, teenagers take a step toward emotional independence because even though they aren't making such decisions for themselves, it's no longer their parents who are deciding on and enforcing their behavior. As part of a group, teenagers try out various roles ranging from conformist to nonconformist, from follower to leader. These roles can be acted out by individuals within the group or they can be acted out by the group as a whole, as, for example, when one gang challenges another gang. Group members in such a situation are caught up in a kind of emotional commitment that they would seldom feel as individuals.

But it isn't automatic that all teenagers find groups to belong to, and even if they do, they are still curious about other groups. This is where young adult literature comes in. It extends the peer group, giving teenagers a chance to participate vicariously in many more personal relationships than are possible for most kids in the relatively short time that they spend in high school. By reading about other individuals trying to find places for themselves, teenagers begin answering such questions as: Who is making "the right" decisions? What values and attitudes are "best?" How will I be judged by other groups and by other individuals? What are the possible results of certain choices? And what are attractive and reasonable alternatives?

The whole area of making friends is a challenge to teenagers. When they were very young, it was a simple matter of playing with whoever happened to be nearby. Parents were responsible for locating in the "right" neighborhood near "good schools," so that children had no reason to give particular thought to differences in social and economic classes or ethnic backgrounds. But the older children get, the more they own the responsibility for making their friends. Quite suddenly their environments are expanded not only through larger, more diverse schools, but also through jobs, extracurricular activities, public entertainment programs, and just plain living.

Throughout elementary school, young people are taught that America is a democracy and that we do not have a "caste" system. Any boy—and maybe today, any girl—can grow up to be President. But real-life observations don't support this, and that may be why books exploring differences in social classes are especially popular with young adults, who as they emerge from childhood are in a position to begin making observations about social class structures.

One of the most perceptive and at the same time humorous explorations of the topic is E. L. Konigsburg's *Journey to an 800 Number.* When Maximillian Stubbs' divorced mother remarries and leaves for a long honeymoon, he takes his prep school jacket and fifty dollars and heads off to spend time with his father. Woody, the father, makes a living by traveling around to tourist and convention centers where he sells rides on the camel he keeps. Max is horrified at what he perceives as a difference in class between his father and himself, but in the words of *English Journal* reviewers, he gradually learns "to separate the outward, lavish trappings of class from the simple meaning of the word."[8]

Naturally school is a common topic for teenage books since this is what young people are involved in on a daily basis. Gloria Miklowitz is one of the most prolific, though not the most skilled, of the writers whose problem novels are set in rather typical American high schools. For example, *The Day the Senior Class Got Married* and *The War Between the Classes* are both centered on class-sponsored social studies exercises. *The Year of the Gopher* by Phyllis Reynolds Naylor explores the dilemma faced by a bright and successful senior who doesn't want to go to an Ivy League college just to please his parents. Richard Peck's *Princess Ashley* is about Chelsea Olinger's sophomore year at Crestwood High and her hopes of fitting in through being a friend to the rich and confident Ashley Packard.

There are some compassionate teachers in books, for example, Ann Treer in Robin Brancato's *Winning,* Nigeria Green and Bernard Cohen in Alice Childress' *A Hero Ain't Nothin' But a Sandwich,* Miss Stevenson and Miss Widmer in Nancy Garden's *Annie on My Mind,* P. J. Cooper in William Hogan's *The Quartzsite Trip,* and the school nurse in Phyllis Reynolds Naylor's *The Keeper,* but these are the exceptions. Society forces young people to treat authority figures—teachers, librarians, ministers, housemothers, coaches, parole officers, etc.—with respect. Because young people aren't allowed to discuss differences of opinion or "quarrel" with these adults as they might with their parents, hostilities undoubtedly build up. It's therefore fairly common for authors to tap into this reservoir of resentment to bring smiles to young readers as in Paul Zindel's *Confessions of a Teenage Baboon,* when fatherless Chris relates his conversation with a solicitous police officer:

> "What you need is the PAL or a Big Brother," he advised, squeezing my shoulder. "If you were my kid you'd be playing football." "If I were your kid I'd be playing horse," I said. "Horse?" he asked, looking a little puzzled as he opened the patrol-car door. "You know," I clarified. "I'd be the front end—and you could just be yourself."

Although this kind of humor is both unfair and irritating to adults, it serves as a respite and a refreshing change of pace which is necessary to keep some problem novels from becoming too depressing.

The problem of group identification is a part of all of S. E. Hinton's books, especially *The Outsiders,* where the *greasers,* i.e., *the dirt heads,* are in conflict with the *socs,* i.e., *the society kids.* Myron Levoy's *A Shadow Like a Leopard* is the grim, but at the same time upbeat, story of fourteen-year-old Ramon Santiago who makes friends with an old man who is a painter. Ramon is a Puerto Rican living in the slums of New York, and in one scene when people stare at him as he walks through a hotel lobby, he feels ashamed of "his clothing, of his face, of his very bones. Ashamed to be Puerto Rican." In Glendon Swarthout's *Bless the Beasts and Children,* the outsiders are five leftover boys at a summer camp in Arizona. They are known as "the bedwetters," and end up aligning with a herd of mistreated buffaloes.

It's a mark of maturity in the field of young adult literature that it's no longer just the big group distinctions that are being made. In *Tiger Eyes,* Judy Blume includes many subtle observations, which lead readers to inductively see and judge various status symbols in the high tech, scientific community of Los Alamos, for example, Bathtub Row, gunracks in pickup trucks, and tell-tale comments about Native Americans and Chicanos. In *Remembering the Good Times,* Richard Peck's narrator has fun describing the various groups in his new school:

> There were suburbanites still maintaining their position and their Izod-and-L.L. Bean image. . . . a few authentic Slos, the polyester people . . . punk . . . funk . . . New Wave . . . Spaces . . . people at the top of the line looked a lot like the Pine Hill Slos down at the bottom who'd been having to wear this type gear all along except with different labels.

In *Friends,* Rosa Guy does a masterful job in leading her readers to see how Phyllisia is taught that she's too good for the neighborhood. Her family has immigrated to Harlem from the West Indies, and her overly strict, restaurant-owner father constantly instills in her a feeling of superiority. He is horrified when Phyllisia brings home poor "ragamuffin" Edith with her ragged coat, holey socks, turned-over shoes, and matted hair. In *The Disappearance,* Guy explores the mistrust between a "respectable" middle-class black family and 16-year-old Imamu, a street kid from Harlem that they take in as a foster child.

Adolescence is commonly thought to end when a young person marries, becomes a parent, or gains financial independence, which usually means having full-time employment. The children of affluent parents can take longer to choose and prepare for their life's work which gives them alternatives not open to the youngster who must be self-supporting at age sixteen, eighteen, or even twenty. Also, if a middle-class teenager gets into some kind of trouble, chances are that the parents will be able to cushion the blow and provide a second chance, while youngsters without an adult support system may prematurely brand themselves as losers.

By gaining vicarious experiences through reading, young people can, in effect, lengthen the time, or at least make better use of what they have, before they commit themselves to lifelong decisions. This is one of the reasons for encouraging wide reading, including reading about lifestyles far different from that of the reader. For example, it's probably not juvenile delinquents who get the most out of reading such books as Robert Cormier's *The Chocolate War* and *Beyond the Chocolate War,* Theodore Weesner's *The Car Thief,* or S. E. Hinton's *The Outsiders* and *Rumble Fish.* Instead it's more "typical" students who are curious about, and perhaps afraid of, kids like Emmett Sunback in Fran Arrick's *Chernowitz!* Emmett is a high school bully who over a two-year period torments Bob Cherno because he's Jewish. A number of events lead to a showdown and an all-school assembly where anti-Semitism is treated openly and movies of the Holocaust are shown. Most of the students are stunned, but Emmett is not like the others. As Bob observes, " . . . nothing happened on Emmett's insides, nothing. Emmett would go on and on . . . ."

He's the same kind of character as is Urek, the antagonist in Sol Stein's *The Magician.* In this book, the protagonist is 16-year-old Ed Japhet who "could be fairly called an accomplished magician." But after he provides the intermission entertainment at a school dance, Urek and his followers beat him severely because Urek is jealous of Ed's success. The close of the book is ironic because Ed ends up killing Urek and Ed's schoolteacher father phones the same unethical lawyer who had gotten Urek off in the beginning.

In a slightly different kind of book about delinquency, authors lead readers to identify with the lawbreaker, not as an encouragement toward imitation, but toward understanding. In Todd Strasser's *Angel Dust Blues,* readers see how a lonely high school student with well-to-do parents can end up getting busted for selling drugs to an undercover agent. And in Robert McKay's *The Running Back,* readers are on the side of 18-year-old Jack Delaney, who after being released from reform school, works to find acceptance on the football team at Holbrook High School.

A less disturbing aspect of fitting into society is that of gaining financial independence. For young people this is a two-pronged issue. First, they must get enough money to achieve the degree of independence that in their peer groups is considered appropriate. It may be only enough money to buy soda pop and an occasional ticket to the movies, or with other kids the goal may be to acquire enough money to pay for clothing, entertainment, and transportation, or even to take themselves away from parental control by moving out. Achieving this kind of immediate financial independence usually means having a job. Books that touch on this aspect of teenagers' lives include Todd Strasser's *Rock 'n' Roll Nights* and *Workin' for Peanuts,* Robert Lipsyte's *Summer Rules* and *The Summerboy,* and Lynn Hall's *The Leaving.*

The second and probably more significant aspect of gaining financial independence has to do with the future. Young adults must choose and prepare for the way they will earn their living in years to come. Making this choice can bring conflicts and problems as, for example, in Chaim Potok's *My Name Is Asher Lev* in which a young Jewish boy persists in his dream to be an artist in spite of the great disappointment this brings to his traditional father who views art as superfluous. Jan Slepian's *Something Beyond Paradise* is about 16-year-old Franny Simone's struggles with the decision of whether she should leave home and friends in Honolulu and go to New York City to study dance. Lynn Hall's *The Solitary* is the story of 17-year-old Jane Cahill's return to the Arkansas mountain home where twelve years earlier her mother had murdered her father. Jane's goal is to raise rabbits commercially and for the first time be her own independent person.

Jane Resh Thomas' *Fox in a Trap* uses only 57 pages to tell the story of Daniel's fascination and subsequent disillusionment with his Uncle Pete's job of trapping foxes. Gillian Cross's *Chartbreaker* is a British story of 17-year-old Finch, who becomes the lead singer in a successful rock group. Readers who would usually be turned off by British references will probably find them intriguing in this book because of the importance of British rock musicians.

Another powerful British story treating economic issues, but from a broader perspective, is Janni Howker's *The Nature of the Beast*. It won't reach such a wide audience, but thoughtful readers will find much to think about in this story of a small town in England that suffers when the local mill closes. Another "different" book focusing on the question of success is Joyce Carol Thomas' *Marked by Fire*, which one reviewer compared to Maya Angelou's *I Know Why the Caged Bird Sings* and said: " . . . many will be moved by the story of a girl who achieves recognition not through individual career or relationship with a man, but as leader and healer of her community."[9]

Interrelationships between the responsibilities of individuals and the social problems around them are explored for young readers in James Lincoln Collier's *When the Stars Begin to Fall*. When 14-year-old Harry tries to reveal the local carpet factory's part in polluting a river, he learns that not all adults are as honest or as committed as he expected. Stephen Tchudi's *The Green Machine and the Frog Crusade* has a slightly happier ending when David Morgan and his friends go up against the developers of a new shopping mall that will wipe out a town's swampland and destroy much of the existing town. They don't totally win, but they manage to get a commitment for at least a small nature preserve and better traffic routing.

In Joan Phipson's *Hit and Run,* a 16-year-old Australian boy comes of age through his acceptance of social responsibility. He was driving carelessly and hit a baby carriage. He flees in panic sure that his wealthy and unethical father will solve the problem for him. But by the end of the book, the boy is ready to begin relying on his own judgment and strength.

Several recent books are set outside the United States so that readers get the bonus of learning about other cultures too. David Klass' *Breakaway Run,* the story of an American boy spending five months as an exchange student in Japan, is especially good at presenting Japanese customs and living styles. Peter Carter's *Bury the Dead,* the story of a 16-year-old high jumper who may be good enough for the Olympics, is set in East Germany. Paula Fox's *Lily and the Lost Boy* is set on the Greek island of Thasos where an American family is staying while the father finishes a book about the Children's Crusade.

Racial and Ethnic Relationships

According to a United Press International story of January 23, 1988, Judge Thomas Demakos sentenced an 18-year-old white youth to a 31-year prison term for his role in chasing a young black man to his death on a Howard Beach freeway and for savagely beating his companion. Judge Demakos noted that the defendant showed "no remorse, no sense of guilt and, in his mind, depraved indifference to human life." Even more disturbing was the judge's statement that he had been inundated with nearly 2,000 form letters asking for leniency toward the defendants. Only one letter, that from New York Mayor Edward Koch, called for a stiff sentence. The Judge was also distressed by the refusal of individuals—including a state senator and a city councilman—to acknowledge that the matter was a racial assult.[10]

This is only one of several disturbing incidents of the 1980s that showed a scary rise of racism among young adults. Anti-Semitism combined with sexism appeared on college campuses where fraternity men peddled "Slap a JAP" (Jewish American Princess) T-shirts. In January of 1988, the National Council of Churches warned that racist violence had reached "epidemic proportions." Between 1980 and 1986 there were 121 murders, 302 assults, and 301 cross burnings. Under the heading "A Chilling Wave of Racism," *Time* magazine wrote about the thousand or so teenaged skinheads who can be recognized across the nation by their shaved heads, black work boots, flight jackets, and garish tatoos. The editors concluded:

> more than anything else, the skin heads are a frightening, pathetic reminder that the U.S. has not solved its racial problems—and that it is time the subject once more take a prominent place on the national agenda.[11]

Faced with problems of this magnitude, it seems overly optimistic and even naive to suggest that teenage books can be a help. Even the best of teachers isn't likely to change a skinhead into a library groupie or a kid who would rather sit home and read books. But for the large majority of young readers teenage books can be one way of focusing needed attention on the matter of racism.

In the 1960s, when civil rights activists inspired authors, publishers, librarians, teachers, and critics to look at the racial makeup of books presented to young readers, what was found was very disturbing. Rather than enriching and extending young readers' views of the world and the people around them, many of the books reinforced prejudices and relied heavily on negative stereotypes. This was more apparent in juvenile than in adult books for several reasons. First, books for young people are often illustrated with either drawings or photographs, and, when nearly all of the people in the illustrations are white, it makes it more difficult for nonwhite readers to identify with the characters and to imagine that the books are about them and their friends. Second, juvenile books tend to be condensed. With less space in which to develop characters, authors are forced to develop background characters as efficiently as possible. One way to be efficient is to use stereotypes that people already recognize, for example, the stoic Indian, the happy black, the dumb blonde, the insensitive jock, and so forth, down the line through many other demeaning and offensive overgeneralizations. When positive portrayals were made of blacks, Indians, Asians, and other minority group members, the stories were most often historical or in some faraway place. The characters were written about as "foreigners," not as Americans.

A third contributing factor is that much of what young people read is from the popular culture which is even less likely than school materials to have been created with care and thought being given to the presentation of minority members. As Australian writer Ivan Southall said in the 1974 May Hill Arbuthnot Honor Lecture at the University of Washington:

> From our English comics we learned the fundamental truths of life: for instance, people with yellow skins were inscrutable and cunning, people with brown skins were childlike and apt to run amok, people with black skins were savages, but, if tamed, made useful carriers of heavy loads on great expeditions of discovery by Englishmen. It was in order for black people to be pictured without clothes, after all, they didn't know what clothes were and didn't count, somehow.[12]

A difference in the YA book world of today and that of the 1960s is that today there is a visible cadre of stars writing consistently fine books featuring characters from different ethnic groups. Not all of the books are problem novels—thank goodness—but nearly all of them help to break down the old, negative stereotypes.

Black authors of star status include Virginia Hamilton, Alice Childress, Mildred Taylor, Rosa Guy, Walter Dean Myers, Brenda Wilkinson, James Haskins, and Ntozage Shange. Nicholasa Mohr and Myron Levoy write about Puerto Ricans living in the States; Jamake Highwater writes about American Indians, Laurence Yep about Chinese Americans, and Danny Santiago and T. Ernesto Bethancourt about Chicanos. And although their books are not directly about ethnic differences, Judy Blume, Norma Klein, and Robert Lipsyte often include details that increase readers' awareness of what it means to be Jewish.

In this section, we are not including descriptions of all the books that we think do a good job of exploring racial and ethnic differences. Instead such books are scattered throughout all the other chapters. We have both philosophical and pedagogical reasons for not wanting to lump together all the books about minorities. While some of them, such as Toeckey Jones' *Skindeep,* an especially well-done South African love story, are centered on interracial relationships, there's a welcome trend for "differentness" to be treated not just as a matter of black and white. Good authors explore the issue in a variety of

LAURENCE YEP
on Being an Outsider

Probably the reason that much of my writing has found its way to a teenage audience is that I'm always pursuing the theme of being an outsider—an alien—and many teenagers feel they're aliens. As a Chinese child growing up in a black neighborhood, I served as the all-purpose Asian. When we played war, I was the Japanese who got killed; then when the Korean War came along, I was a North Korean communist. This sense of being the odd-one-out, is probably what made me relate to the Narnia and Oz books. They were about loneliness and kids in alien societies learning to adjust to foreign cultures. I could understand these a lot better than the stories in our readers where every house had a front lawn and no one's front door was ever locked. When I went to high school, I really began to feel like an outsider. I lost my grammar school friends because they all went into basketball while I went into science fiction. Then every morning I would get on a bus and ride into Chinatown where I attended Catholic school. My family didn't speak Chinese so I was put in the dumbbell Chinese class. I resented that, but what I resented more was that all the dirty jokes and the snide remarks were told in Chinese so the Sisters wouldn't understand them. I couldn't understand them either.

At first it was only through science fiction that I could treat the theme of the outsider, but then I began to do historical fiction and finally contemporary fiction. *Sea Glass* is my most autobiographical novel, but I can't always write that close to home because it requires me to take a razor blade and cut through my defenses. I'm bleeding when I finish, and I have to take time off by writing fantasy or something only marginally related to my Chinese heritage such as *The Mark Twain Murders*.

Laurence Yep's books include *Mountain Light,* Harper & Row, 1985; *Liar, Liar,* Harper & Row, 1983; *Sea Glass*, Harper & Row, 1979; and *Dragonwings,* Harper & Row, 1975.

ways and with a variety of groups. For example, Kevin Major's *Far from Shore* is set in Newfoundland and one Canadian reviewer praised it because:

> His picture of life in Newfoundland is bright and sharp, not, thank God, that salty picaresque pastich we mainlanders so often get to chuckle indulgently over.[13]

In 1978, Al Muller made the point that at that time novels about blacks were stereotyped negatively to the same degree that young adult novels in general used to be stereotyped positively:

▉   The majority of black Americans are not pushers, pimps, or prostitutes. Not all black Americans live in ghettos. But, to a large extent, a composite of the above statements is the new "black image" presented (constructed?) by the popular media and, to an extent, adopted by the YA novel.[14]

By having characters from different groups involved in the same activities, then much of the stereotyping falls away. Early in his career, Walter Dean Myers was one of the few black writers who wrote upbeat, positive stories about "good, lovable kids." His *Fast Sam, Cool Clyde, and Stuff, It Ain't All for Nothin', The Young Landlords,* and *Motown and Didi* are among the warmest and most enjoyable of those stories about black kids living in inner cities. But just as white authors are getting braver about extending their stories to include blacks, so is Myers to include whites. His *Crystal* is the story of a black model whose biggest worry is not what color she is but what kinds of pictures she should pose for. His *Fallen Angels* is about an integrated group of Vietnam soldiers whose biggest challenge is pulling together for their mutual survival.

Something that probably wouldn't have been in a YA book 25 years ago is the line from Barbara Ann Porte's *I Only Made Up the Roses,* "Like everybody else in the room of relatives, except mother and me, Perley is black. . . . " This line is indicative of one of the biggest changes that has occurred in YA books treating ethnic minorities. The early books were clearly segregated. Characters came from a single race. And when authors chose to write about characters from outside their own groups, they were met with hostility. Fortunately, that kind of parochialism has mostly disappeared and the result has been more books that include characters from different groups interacting with each other in a variety of ways.

Cynthia Voigt has taken black characters with minor roles in her books about the Tillermans *(Homecoming, Dicey's Song,* and *Sons from Afar)* and given them major roles in other books. In *Come a Stranger,* 15-year-old Mina wins a scholarship to summer dance camp. She's the only black and by the end of her second summer is forced to think about what being black means. Tamer Shipp, a young black minister who in Voigt's book *The Runner* was Bullet's friend, helps Mina face up to her feelings.

Bruce Brooks' *The Moves Make the Man* is basically a quest story of accomplishment and it almost doesn't matter that with the two best friends, one is black and the other is white. But when white Bix comes to dinner at black Jerome's house, big brother and future psychologist Maurice is disappointed that they are going to have a white guest because he had hoped for some "in-house observation." The rest of Jerome's family laughs at Maurice's disappointment and his pretentious pronouncement that "Counseling across the color line is notoriously fruitless, due to preconditions of mistrust." But when Bix arrives, Jerome is surprised to see that his old friend has equally strange expectations. When he is introduced to younger brother Henri, he gives Henri an awkward high-five and says "Dig it."

Now, dig it is a very stupid thing to say when being introduced. Henri did not notice, but I did, and I thought it was queer. But when Maurice was there and I introduced him and he peered at Bix like to see if there was any chance of busting the color line with a little counseling anyway, and Bix grinned right into his stare and held out his hand and said, What be happening, Maurice my man?

Maurice, who does not know jive talk from bird song, just looked confused and said Fine thank you and shook hands, but I was nearabout flipped. What be happening, Maurice my man? Where did Bix get this jive talking junk? It was ridiculous.

This light-hearted counterbalancing of stereotypes is possible because today's young readers are more sophisticated about ethnic and racial differences. A generation ago, many white, middle-class readers had been so isolated from other racial groups that learning the generalities—what some would call the stereotypes—was a kind of progress. Today, most teenagers are ready to go beyond those stereotypes.

For example, in Chris Crutcher's *The Crazy Horse Electric Game,* white Willie is rescued by Lacey Casteel, a black pimp, who also happens to be a city bus driver in Oakland, California. Readers, along with Willie, get to know Lacey as much more than a stereotype. He gives Willie a place to live and arranges for him to go to an alternative school. At the end when Willie leaves Lacey and goes back home, the note that Lacey writes to Willie's dad is in stereotypical black English, but it's nevertheless touching to readers who know Lacey's background:

Dear Mr. Will Weaver

Here you boy back. He fix. Be careful how you treet him, he specal. If you don't want him, send him back.

Sinserly,
Lacey Casteel

In her novels about white, middle-class kids, M. E. Kerr often includes shrewd observations about prejudice. For example, in *If I Love You, Am I Trapped Forever?* Alan's grandfather teaches him not to call anyone a Jew. Instead he is to describe people as being "of the Jewish persuasion." Once a year in Cayuta, Rabbi Goldman gives the Sunday sermon at the Second Presbyterian Church while Reverend Gosnell speaks to the Saturday congregation at Temple Emmanuel. Still Jews do not belong to the Cayuta North Country Club and "No one's exactly pushing for intermarriage. . . . "

In *Little Little,* black Calpurnia Dove and white Little Little are in the same English class where they compete as writers. When Miss Grossman reads aloud one of Calpurnia's essays, Little Little thinks that the teacher is only being nice to Calpurnia because she's black. In her heart, Little Little recognizes the ridiculousness of her assumption and conjectures that Calpurnia probably "decides Miss Grossman is only being nice to me because I'm a dwarf." Little

Little goes on to explain that most of the black teenagers in town go to Commercial High to learn business skills or trades. Of the few who do go to her high school, "one is always elected to some office, unanimously. But that high honor rarely gets one of them a seat saved at noon in the cafeteria among the whites, or even a particularly warm hello."

One of the advantages of authors including racism as a secondary, as opposed to a primary theme, is that more readers will meet the issue and be triggered to think about it. Both adults and young readers tend to color-code books thinking that books about blacks or Hispanics, for example, are only for black or Hispanic readers, respectively. Walter Dean Myers has pointed out the ridiculousness of such a notion by asking why those librarians in white, middle-class neighborhoods who refuse to buy books about minority characters keep purchasing Dickens' novels even though they have no nineteenth-century English children in their schools.

Another damaging tendency is for teachers, librarians, and reviewers to present books and discuss them as if they represent THE black point of view or THE Asian-American point of view. It's important that adults look for ways to help young readers realize that people are first individuals and secondly members of particular groups. In John Patrick's play *The Teahouse of the August Moon,* one of the lines that gets a big laugh from the white middle-class American audience is about all Americans looking alike. The audience laughs because the tables are turned on an old joke, and they get a glimpse of how ridiculous it is to think of any group of individuals being carbon copies of one another.

Helping students to realize this and to apply it in their thoughts and their dealings with other people is not quite so simple. People may be grouped together on such bases as their sex, their age, their color, the origin of their last names, the neighborhood they live in, the language or dialect they speak, or the religion to which they subscribe, but there is constant shifting among people and the groups to which they belong. Naturally there are some similarities among group members, but the correlation is far from perfect. For example, Native Americans are often treated as one group, but when Europeans first landed on the American continent there were more than thirty distinct nations speaking perhaps a thousand different languages. During the past 400 years these people have had certain common experiences—losing their lands, being forced to move to reservations, and having to adapt their beliefs and lifestyles to a technological society. These experiences may have affected their attitudes in similar ways, but still it is a gross overgeneralization to write about American Indians as though they were one people holding the same religious and cultural values.

Perhaps for the sake of efficiency, history and social studies textbooks have to lump people together and talk about them according to the characteristics of the majority in the group, but good literature can counterbalance these generalizations and show individual perspectives. When students have read enough to go beyond the stereotypes with at least one group, then they will be more aware that the study of people as groups needs to be filled in with individual portrayals.

Body and Self

Books that treat problems related to accepting and effectively using one's physical body will be treated in several sections of this text. When the physical problem is relatively minor, or is at least one that can be solved, then it might be treated as an accomplishment-romance, as in Robert Lipsyte's *One Fat Summer.* Many pieces of informative nonfiction as well as stories about sports heroes deal with physical problems. And in many pieces of modern realistic fiction, physical problems are a secondary part of the plot. Their real purpose is to serve as a concrete or visible symbol for mental growth, which is harder to show. It has almost become an obligatory element in realistic fiction for young protagonists to express dissatisfaction with their appearance. Part of this is because hardly anyone has a perfect body or hasn't envied others for their appearance or physical skill. A bigger part is that adolescent bodies are changing so fast that their owners have not yet had time to adjust. The reason they spend so much time looking in mirrors is to reassure themselves that, "Yes, this is me!"

In 1970, Judy Blume surprised the world of juvenile fiction by writing a book that gave major attention to physical aspects of growing up. Margaret Simon in *Are You There God? It's Me, Margaret* worries because her breasts are small and because she's afraid she will be the last one in her crowd to begin menstruating. A later Blume book, *Then Again, Maybe I Won't* features Tony Miglione and his newly affluent family. He too worries about his developing body. In fact, he carries a jacket even on the warmest days so that he will have something to hide behind in case he has an erection. These books are read mostly by younger adolescents. But Blume's *Deenie* is read by both junior and senior high students. It is about a pretty teenager whose mother wants her to be a model, but then it's discovered that she has scoliosis and must wear an unsightly back brace. A minor point which goes unnoticed by some readers (but not by censors), is that Deenie worries that her back problem might be related to the fact that she masturbates.

What has made Blume's books so popular is their refreshing candor about worries that young people have. Another plus is that physical development is not treated separately from emotional and social development. This is why Blume's books are more fun to read (and more controversial) than are factual books about the development of the human body.

But the problem novel does not stop with treating the more or less typical problems of growing up. It has gone on to explore such problems as epilepsy in Barbara Girion's *A Handful of Stars,* cerebral palsy in Jan Slepian's *The Alfred Summer,* learning disabilities in Lynn Hall's *Just One Friend,* drug abuse in Sharon Bell Mathis' *Teacup Full of Roses* and Alice Childress' *A Hero Ain't Nothin' But a Sandwich,* anorexia nervosa in Steven Levenkron's *The Best Little Girl in the World* and Margaret Willey's *The Bigger Book of Lydia,* suicide in Fran Arrick's *Tunnel Vision* and Richard Peck's *Remembering the Good Times,* severe handicaps as in Susan Sallis' *Only Love* and *Secret Places of the Stairs,* and the emotional as well as physical pain that is part of recovering from serious accidents as in Cynthia Voigt's *Izzy, Willy-Nilly* and Chris Crutcher's *The Crazy Horse Electric Game.*

The openness with which such a subject as death is discussed is shown in Gunnel Beckman's *Admission to the Feast*. In it, 19-year-old Annika Hallin accidentally learns from a substitute doctor that she has leukemia. She flees by herself to her family's summer cottage where she tries to sort out her reactions:

> I don't think I understood it until last night . . . that I, Annika, . . . will just be put away, wiped out, obliterated. . . . And here on earth everything will just go on. . . . I shall never have more than this little scrap of life.

Zibby Oneal's *A Formal Feeling* is about 16-year-old Anne Cameron's adjustment to the death of her mother and the remarriage of her father. It was refreshing for a contemporary author to find some other way to write about an adjustment to death than simply doing a fictionalized version of the stages of acceptance described by Elisabeth Kübler-Ross. Oneal's title is taken from the beginning line of an Emily Dickinson poem, "After great pain, a formal feeling comes—."

One of the strengths of Alden Carter's *Sheila's Dying* is its description of what happens to those who are caring for a terminally ill friend, especially one portrayed as realistically as is Sheila. In Norma Fox Mazer's *After the Rain,* teenager Rachel establishes a grudging friendship with the cantankerous and dying grandfather that she helps to care for. In *The Keeper* by Phyllis Reynolds Naylor, Nick helps his mother in her futile efforts to care for and shield her mentally ill husband. Bettie Cannon's *A Bellsong for Sarah Raines* is about a 14-year-old's anger and grief over her alcoholic father's suicide, while Jocelyn Riley's *Crazy Quilt,* the sequel to *Only My Mouth Is Smiling,* is the story of Merle Carlson and the responsibilities that she faces with her younger brother and sister when their mentally ill mother is hospitalized.

Although Katherine Paterson's *Bridge to Terabithia* is considered a children's book because it's about two fifth-graders, we know several young adults who have read it and wept, just as have many adults. Jean Ferris' *Invincible Summer* is a restrained but sad love story about two teenagers with leukemia. The boy, Rick, dies, but the book ends with readers and the girl, Robin, still uncertain about her prognosis and her future. Of course she wants to live, but if the treatments are unsuccessful as Rick's were, then she consoles herself by thinking that if it were truly going to be "lights out, the end, eternal sleep, then what was there to worry about?" And, on the other hand, if she were going to be someplace, then Rick would be there too.

The value of such fictional treatments as the ones cited in this section is that they involve readers in the problem from many different viewpoints and they show relationships between physical and emotional problems. For example, one of the strong points of Robin Brancato's *Winning,* the story of a football player paralyzed in a game, is that it shows the ripple effect of Gary's accident: how it changes his friends, his parents, his girlfriend, and his teacher. In one brief moment their definition of winning is forever changed. In the new situation, surviving—just wanting to survive—means winning, and readers cheer with Gary when he makes it through the depression that causes some of his hospital mates to commit suicide.

Sexual Relationships

Here we will give some examples of different kinds of sexual relationships which might be treated in problem novels, but lest we leave the impression that we look at sex only as a problem, we will hasten to add that discussions of the matter also appear in Chapter 4 ("The Love Romances") and in Chapter 8 ("Nonfiction Books").

In trying to satisfy their curiosity, teenagers seek out and read the vivid descriptions of sexual activity in such books as Scott Spencer's *Endless Love* and William Hogan's *The Quartzsite Trip,* both published for adults but featuring young protagonists. Male and female readers have also been intrigued by Don Bredes' *Hard Feelings,* Terry Davis' *Vision Quest,* Jay Daly's *Walls,* and Aidan Chambers' *Breaktime,* all coming-of-age stories which focus on young men's sexual desires. "Equivalent" books featuring young women are much more likely to have sexual desires, if they are included at all, blanketed between the covers of a romance.

In the last edition of this textbook, we wrote that the three issues treated in YA problem novels were rape, homosexuality, and premarital sex resulting in pregnancy. Today we need to add disease, incest, and child abuse. Among the best of several books exploring this latter theme is Hadley Irwin's *Abby, My Love.* The story is told from the viewpoint of college student Chip, who at age 13 fell in love with Abby. She was only 12, but in Chip's words she "sounded so much older, like she was an adult and I was the kid. She wasn't condescending or anything. She was just different." Over their high school years, they develop a close friendship, but her overprotective, dentist father won't allow a normal kind of dating. Chip is frequently puzzled by Abby's behavior, and then one day she confides in him about her father's sexual abuse. Through the help of Chip's mother, steps are taken to help Abby's family face up to the problem and begin a healing process.

Reviewers used such terms as "admirable restraint and sensitivity," "tender, moving love story," "humor, wit, courage and compassion," "well drawn, plausible, and likable characters," and "a credible, optimistic resolution." The only hint of a negative comment came in a *Booklist* review where the writer questioned Chip's long-term obsession with the changeable Abby.[15] Having a desirable young man fall unreasonably in love with the female protagonist of a problem novel is a common literary device. Authors use the wish-fulfillment nature of the romantic element to soften the awfulness of the problem. See, for example, Norma Fox Mazer's *After the Rain* and Jean Ferris' *Invincible Summer.*

Gloria D. Miklowitz's *Secrets Not Meant to Be Kept* explores child abuse at a preschool, while Michael Borich's *A Different Kind of Love* is about a 14-

year-old girl's ambivalence toward the affection she feels for the 25-year-old rock star uncle who has come to live with her and her mother. Fran Arrick's *Steffie Can't Come Out to Play* is a sympathetic portrayal of a teenage prostitute while Richard Peck's *Are You in the House Alone?* and Patricia Dizenzo's *Why Me?* treat the physical, emotional, and societal aspects of rape.

One of the early criticisms of the new realism was that the whole area of sexuality was treated so negatively. For example, in 1975 when W. Keith Kraus analyzed several books about premarital pregnancy, including Ann Head's *Mr. and Mrs. Bo Jo Jones,* Zoa Sherburne's *Too Bad About the Haines Girl,* Jean Thompson's *House of Tomorrow,* Margaret Maze Craig's *It Could Happen to Anyone,* Nora Stirling's *You Would if You Loved Me,* Jeannette Eyerly's *A Girl Like Me,* Paul Zindel's *My Darling, My Hamburger,* and John Neufeld's *For All the Wrong Reasons,* he concluded that "the old double standard is reinforced by the so-called new realism." He compared the wish-fulfilling nature of the stories to the old romances in which the girl is at the beginning an outsider who is discovered by a popular athlete. As she begins to date, a whole new social world opens up to her. But the dating leads to petting, and then to sex, and finally pregnancy and unhappiness. He lamented that "the sexual act itself is never depicted as joyful, and any show of intimacy carries a warning of future danger."[16] Many of the authors whose books will be treated in the next chapter under "The Love Romances" purposely set out to counterbalance the negative images that Kraus and other critics noted.

In the problem novel, the emphasis is usually on the physical aspect of the problem, but it's really the emotional aspects that most readers are interested in. When Paul Zindel was speaking in Arizona in the late 1970s, he commented on the fact that next to *The Pigman,* his most popular book was *My Darling, My Hamburger,* which is about pregnancy and abortion. Soon after the book was published in 1969, a Supreme Court decision made most abortions legal, and Zindel thought that would be the end of all sales because his book would seem terribly old fashioned. However, this didn't turn out to be the case because rather than settling the issue, the legalization of abortions served to increase interest in the moral and psychological aspects of the problem. Decision making was passed from the courts to every female with an unwanted pregnancy. And it isn't just the woman herself who is involved. For example, Jeannette Eyerly wrote about a teenage father who wanted to keep the baby in *He's My Baby Now* while Blossom Elfman showed an entire support system in *A House for Jonnie O.*

In Rosa Guy's *Edith Jackson,* Edith has grown up from the ragamuffin child readers first met when Phyllisia brought her home in *The Friends.* She is now looking forward to her eighteenth birthday in hopes of being free of foster homes and the Institution so that she can try again to set up a home for her younger sisters. But, by the end of the book, the girls are scattered, and Edith realizes that it is her own life she must plan. She has had a brief love affair with a handsome Harlem playboy almost twice her age and is excited at finding herself pregnant. But in the end of the book, she decides that the mature thing to do is to have an abortion.

Even in books where the main focus is not on whether someone is going to have an abortion, it may be mentioned as a possibility. For example in Judy Blume's *Forever,* one of Katherine's friends has an abortion. In *Love Is One of the Choices,* Norma Klein tells the story of two close friends and their first sexual loves. One of them chooses to marry and become pregnant right away while the other one gets pregnant, refuses to marry, and has an abortion.

Three landmark books opened the door to the treatment of homosexuality in books for young readers. They were John Donovan's *I'll Get There. It Better Be Worth the Trip* in 1969, Isabelle Holland's *The Man Without a Face,* and Lynn Hall's *Sticks and Stones,* both in 1972. The protagonists are male and in all three books an important character dies. In none of them can a direct cause-and-effect relationship be charted between the death and the homosexual behavior, but possibilities for blame are there. And because of the coincidence of the three books appearing relatively close in time, critics were quick to object to the cumulative implications that homosexual behavior will be punished with some dreadful event. In spite of this criticism, Sandra Scoppettone's *Trying Hard to Hear You* published in 1974 was surprisingly similar, ending in an automobile accident which killed one of the teenage male lovers.

Books featuring female homosexuals were almost a decade behind the ones about males. In 1976, Rosa Guy published *Ruby,* which was a sequel to *The Friends.* Ruby is Phyllisia's older sister and in the book she had a lesbian relationship with a beautiful classmate. *Publishers Weekly* described the homosexuality in the book as "perhaps just a way-step toward maturity." This relaxed attitude toward female homosexuality was reflected in Deborah Hautzig's 1978 *Hey Dollface* and in Nancy Garden's 1982 *Annie on My Mind,* which was praised for its strong characterization and tender love story. In more recent books, the matter of sexual preference is likely to appear as a secondary rather than a primary theme as in Myron Levoy's *Three Friends* when Lori's bisexuality is acknowledged and in Hila Colman's *Happily Ever After* when Melanie and Paul's friendship survives his confession that he is gay. M. E. Kerr's well-written *Night Kites* starts out as a romance between 17-year-old Erick and a Madonna lookalike. But what readers are going to remember from the book is Erick's relationship with his older brother Pete, who midway through the story is diagnosed as having AIDS. The family has to absorb simultaneously the news of his impending death and the fact that for years this favored son has been hiding his gay lifestyle from them.

In actuality, the big sex-related problems—rape, abuse, illness, homosexuality, and unwanted pregnancy—are experienced by few teenagers while nearly all young people wonder about the moral and social implications of experimenting with sexual activity whether or not it leads to intercourse. Todd Strasser's *A Very Touchy Subject* and Norma Fox Mazer's *Up in Seth's Room* do a good job of showing the magnitude of teenagers' concerns. As Jean Fritz said when she reviewed Mazer's book for the *New York Times Book Review:*

The questions we follow relentlessly from beginning to end are the perennial ones of adolescence: Will she or won't she? And what's it like?. . . . Everyone should be pleased with the outcome. Finn sticks to her guns, although the fact that she "doesn't" is hardly more than a technicality. There are enough explicit scenes to give young readers, who don't know, a good idea of "what it's like."[17]

Mazer said she wrote the book as an antidote to all the "realistic" books implying that having sexual relationships is the norm for high school kids. Half of the kids in high school are not sexually intimate, and even the half that are have dozens of unanswered questions and worries.

To get direct answers to their questions, young readers can turn to the informational books discussed in Chapter 8. But because the questions they are the most concerned with are about moral, emotional, and psychological issues, the fuller kinds of fictional treatments described here will continue to be popular.

NOTES

[1] G. Robert Carlsen, "Bait/Rebait: Literature Isn't Supposed to Be Realistic," *English Journal* 70 (January 1981): 8–12.

[2] Glenna Davis Sloan, *The Child as Critic* (New York: Teachers College Press, 1975), pp. 19–21.

[3] Alleen Pace Nilsen, "The Poetry of Naming in Young Adult Books," *ALAN Review* 7 (Spring 1980): 3–4, 31.

[4] Sheila Egoff, "May Hill Arbuthnot Honor Lecture: Beyond the Garden Wall," *Top of the News* 35 (Spring 1979): 257–71.

[5] Joan F. Kaywell, Review of *The Island, ALAN Review* 12 (Spring 1985): 29.

[6] Hazel Rochman, "The YA Connection: Choosing to Stay Home," *Booklist* 83 (February 1, 1987): 837.

[7] Trev Jones, Review of *In Summer Light, School Library Journal* 31 (October 1985): 186.

[8] Dick Abrahamson and Betty Carter, "Positive Young Adult Novels," *English Journal* 71 (December 1982): 66–68.

[9] Hazel Rochman, Review of *Marked by Fire, School Library Journal* 28 (March 1982): 162.

[10] "18-Year-Old White Given 31-Year Term for NY Racial Attack," *Arizona Republic* (January 23, 1988), p. A4.

[11] "A Chilling Wave of Racism," *Time* 131:4 (January 25, 1988): 57.

[12] Ivan Southall, "Real Adventure Belongs to Us," in *A Journey of Discovery on Writing for Children* (New York: Macmillan, 1976), p. 69.

[13] Janet Lunn, *Books in Canada* 9 (December 1980): 21.

[14] Al Muller, "Some Thoughts on the Black Y.A. Novel," *ALAN Newsletter* 5 (Winter 1978): 13.

[15] Review of *Abby, My Love, Booklist* 81 (March 1, 1985): 944.

[16] W. Keith Kraus, "Cinderella in Trouble: Still Dreaming and Losing," *School Library Journal* 21 (January 1975): 18–22.

[17] Jean Fritz, Review of *Up in Seth's Room, New York Times Book Review* (January 20, 1980), p. 30.

30 RECOMMENDATIONS FOR READING

Family Relationships

Bridgers, Sue Ellen. *Home Before Dark*. Knopf, 1976. Having lived most of her life in the back of a station wagon, 14-year-old Stella Willis isn't about to leave her family's first real home.

Brooks, Bruce. *Midnight Hour Encores*. Harper & Row, 1987. World-class cellist Sib is happily surprised when she meets the mother she has never known.

Childress, Alice. *Rainbow Jordan*. Putnam, 1981. Although Rainbow's mother fails in playing her role, readers still learn something about what "family" means.

Hinton, S. E. *Tex*. Delacorte, 1979. Tex and his older brother Mason prove that two can be a family.

Paterson, Katherine. *The Great Gilly Hopkins*. Crowell, 1979. Up until Gilly gets Trotter as a foster mother, she's been able to manipulate her caregivers. But when Gilly's attempt to find her flower-child mother backfires, not even capable Trotter can help her.

Pfeffer, Susan Beth. *The Year Without Michael*. Bantam, 1987. The effect on a family of a brother's disappearance—it's not known whether he ran away or met foul play—is the heart of this story.

Taylor, Mildred. *Roll of Thunder, Hear My Cry*. Dial, 1976. Along with its sequel, *Let the Circle Be Unbroken,* Taylor's story of the Logan family shows what it was like to be the only black family who owned land when the Great Depression was squeezing all the good feelings right out of folks.

Friends and Society

Blume, Judy. *Tiger Eyes*. Bradbury, 1981. Davey's father is killed in a holdup and the family moves west to Los Alamos, New Mexico, to stay with an uncle and aunt.

Cormier, Richard. *I Am the Cheese*. Pantheon, 1977. Seldom has there been such a powerful story of a young innocent facing incredible odds from organized crime and the U.S. Secret Service. *The Chocolate War* and *Beyond the Chocolate War* look at evil closer to home in a church-sponsored high school.

Hinton, S. E. *The Outsiders*. Viking, 1967. This landmark story about the Socs and the Greasers has probably been read by more teenagers than any other book listed in these bibliographies.

Kerr, M. E. *Gentlehands*. Harper & Row, 1978. Buddy Boyle is forced to think about more than Skye Pennington when his grandfather turns out to be guilty of crimes during World War II.

Mazer, Norma Fox. *Downtown*. Morrow, 1984. Society's ideals of justice clash with its ideals of family life in this story about a boy whose parents are on the run from the F.B.I. because of an antiwar protest that went awry.

Peck, Richard. *Remembering the Good Times*. Delacorte, 1985. Trav, Kate, and Buck are in junior high. Trav's suicide reveals an ugly side to some of the adult "caregivers."

Racial and Ethnic Relationships

Armstrong, William. *Sounder*. Harper & Row, 1969. There's a hint of hope in this stark historical piece in that the old teacher who tells the story was apparently the black boy who had such a terrible childhood.

Brooks, Bruce. *The Moves Make the Man*. Harper & Row, 1986. Jerome, who is black, tells his white friend's story and only part of the interest is that the two friends are different colors.

Hamilton, Virginia. *Arilla Sun Down*. Greenwillow, 1976. Twelve-year-old Arilla is interracial, part black and part Indian, and in the course of this book she forges an identity of her own.

Highwater, Jamake. *The Ceremony of Innocence*. Harper & Row, 1985. In this second book of the Ghost Horse Cycle beginning in the last century, Amana, a Northern Plains Indian, suffers at the hands of white settlers. Companion books are *Legend Days* and *I Wear the Morning Star*.

Mohr, Nicholasa. *Going Home*. Dial, 1986. Along with *Nilda*, *El Bronx Remembered*, and *In Nueva York*, *Going Home* shows what it's like to be a Puerto Rican and a New Yorker.

Yep, Laurence. *Dragonwings*. Harper & Row, 1975. Based on a little known but documented incident, *Dragonwings* tells the story of an early 1900s Chinese immigrant in San Francisco who built an airplane and flew it for a few minutes about the same time as the Wright brothers did.

Body and Self

Blume, Judy. *Are You There, God? It's Me Margaret*. Bradbury, 1970. Growing up means physical changes as well as making decisions about whether to go to the Jewish Community Center or the YWCA.

Childress, Alice. *A Hero Ain't Nothin' But a Sandwich*. Putnam's, 1973. Benjie is hooked on drugs, and in spite of the support he gets, it's not at all clear that he's going to make it.

Ferris, Jean. *Invincible Summer*. Farrar, Straus & Giroux, 1987. Robin and Rick both have leukemia. They meet in the hospital and over the course of a year learn about living as well as dying.

Mazer, Norma Fox. *After the Rain*. Morrow, 1987. Getting to know and love a cantankerous old man just before he dies is hard, especially when he happens to be your grandfather.

Naylor, Phyllis Reynolds. *The Keeper*. Macmillan, 1986. Caring for a father and husband who is mentally ill is more than Nick and his mother bargained for.

Slepian, Jan. *The Alfred Summer*. Macmillan, 1980. After reading Slepian's book, readers will think differently about people with cerebral palsy.

Sexual Relationships

Chambers, Aidan. *Breaktime*. Harper & Row, 1979. A British setting and a slightly wacko format make Ditto's coming-of-age story something out of the ordinary.

Garden, Nancy. *Annie on My Mind*. Farrar, Straus, & Giroux, 1982. Garden's book was praised for its sensitive portrayal of love and romance as integral parts of a lesbian relationship.

Kerr, M. E. *Night Kites*. Harper & Row, 1986. Erick's family is shocked and devastated to learn that older brother Pete has AIDS.

Townsend, John Rowe. *Downstream*. Lippincott, 1987. The summer that he and his dad both fall in love with a 23-year-old German tutor, 17-year-old Alan Dollis learns that sexual feelings are interwoven into wider aspects of life than he thought.

Zindel, Paul. *My Darling, My Hamburger*. Harper & Row, 1969. The problems of an unexpected pregnancy are treated in this book, which gets its title from a home economics teacher's lecture on how girls can avoid getting pregnant. They should suggest going out for a hamburger.

OTHER TITLES MENTIONED IN CHAPTER THREE

Angelou, Maya. *I Know Why the Caged Bird Sings*. Random House, 1976.

Anonymous. *Go Ask Alice*. Prentice-Hall, 1971.

Arrick, Fran. *Chernowitz!* Bradbury. 1981.

_____ . *Steffie Can't Come Out to Play*. Bradbury, 1978.

_____ . *Tunnel Vision*. Bradbury, 1980.

Asher, Sandy. *Everything Is Not Enough*. Delacorte, 1987.

Beckman, Gunnel. *Admission to the Feast*. Holt, Rinehart and Winston, 1972.

Blume, Judy. *Deenie*. Bradbury, 1973.

_____ . *Forever*. Bradbury, 1975.

_____ . *Then Again, Maybe I Won't*. Bradbury, 1971.

Borich, Michael. *A Different Kind of Love*. Henry Holt, 1985.

Bradford, Richard. *Red Sky at Morning*. Lippincott, 1968.

Brancato, Robin. *Sweet Bells Jangled Out of Tune*. Knopf, 1982.

_____ . *Uneasy Money*. Knopf, 1986.

_____ . *Winning*. Knopf, 1977.

Branscum, Robbie. *The Girl*. Harper & Row, 1986.

Bredes, Don. *Hard Feelings*. Atheneum, 1977.

Bridgers, Sue Ellen. *All Together Now*. Knopf, 1979.

_____ . *Notes for Another Life*. Knopf, 1981.

_____ . *Permanent Connections*. Harper & Row, 1987.

Byars, Betsy. *The Two-Thousand-Pound Goldfish*. Harper & Row, 1982.

Cannon, Bettie. *A Bellsong for Sarah Raines*. Macmillan, 1987.

Carter, Alden, *Sheila's Dying*. Putnam, 1987.

Carter, Peter. *Bury the Dead*. Farrar, Straus & Giroux, 1988.

Cleaver, Eldridge. *Soul on Ice*. McGraw-Hill, 1968.

Cleaver, Vera and Bill. *Where the Lilies Bloom*. Harper & Row, 1969.

_____ . *Trial Valley*. Lippincott, 1977.

Collier, James Lincoln. *When the Stars Begin to Fall*. Delacorte, 1986.

Colman, Hila. *Happily Ever After*. Scholastic, 1984.

Cormier, Robert. *Beyond the Chocolate War*. Knopf, 1984.

_____ . *The Chocolate War*. Pantheon, 1974.

Craig, Margaret Maze. *It Could Happen to Anyone*. Berkley, 1970.

Cross, Gillian. *Chartbreaker*. Holiday, 1987.

Crutcher, Chris. *The Crazy Horse Electric Game*. Greenwillow, 1987.

Daly, Jay. *Walls*. Harper & Row, 1980.

Davis, Jenny. *Good-bye and Keep Cold*. Orchard Books/Watts, 1987.

Davis, Terry. *Vision Quest*. Viking, 1979.

Dizenzo, Patricia. *Why Me? The Story of Jenny*. Avon, 1976.

Donovan, John. *I'll Get There. It Better Be Worth the Trip*. Harper & Row, 1969.

Elfman, Blossom. *A House for Jonnie O*. Houghton Mifflin, 1977.

Eyerly, Jeannette. *A Girl Like Me*. Lippincott, 1966.

_____ . *He's My Baby Now*. Archway, 1978.

Forshay-Lunsford, Lin. *Walk Through Cold Fire*. Dell, 1986.

Fox, Paula. *A Place Apart*. Farrar, Straus & Giroux, 1980.

_____ . *Lily and the Lost Boy*. Orchard Books/Watts, 1987.

_____ . *The Moonlight Man*. Bradbury, 1986.

Frye, Northrop. *Anatomy of Criticism*. Princeton Univ. Press, 1957.

Girion, Barbara. *A Handful of Stars*. Scribner, 1981. ,

Golding, William. *Lord of the Flies*. Putnam, 1955.

Guy Rosa. *Edith Jackson*. Viking, 1978.

_____ . *Ruby*. Viking, 1976.

_____ . *The Disappearance*. Delacorte, 1979.

_____ . *The Friends*. Holt, Rinehart and Winston, 1973.

Hall, Lynn. *Just One Friend*. Macmillan, 1985.

_____ . *Sticks and Stones*. Follett, 1972.

_____ . *The Leaving*. Scribner, 1980.

_____ . *The Solitary*. Macmillan, 1986.

Hamilton, Virginia. *Sweet Whispers, Brother Rush*. Putnam, 1982.

Hautzig, Deborah. *Hey Dollface*. Morrow, 1978.

Head, Ann. *Mr. and Mrs. Bo Jo Jones*. Putnam, 1967.

Hinton, S. E. *Rumble Fish*. Delacorte, 1979.

Hogan, William. *The Quartzsite Trip*. Atheneum, 1980.

Holland, Isabelle. *The Island*. Little, Brown, 1984.

_____ . *The Man Without a Face*. Lippincott, 1972.

Howker, Janni. *The Nature of the Beast*. Greenwillow, 1985.

Irwin, Hadley. *Abby, My Love*. Macmillan, 1985.

_____ . *What about Grandma?* NAL Penguin Inc., 1987.

Jones, Toeckey. *Skindeep*. Harper & Row, 1986.

Kerr, M. E. *Dinky Hocker Shoots Smack*. Harper & Row, 1972.

_____ . *If I Love You, Am I Trapped Forever?* Harper & Row, 1973.

_____ . *Little Little*. Harper & Row, 1981.

Kincaid, Jamaica. *Annie John*. Farrar, Straus & Giroux, 1985.

Klass, David. *Breakaway Run*. Lodestart, 1987.

Klein, Norma. *Love Is One of the Choices*. Dial, 1979.

Konigsburg, E. L. *Journey to an 800 Number*. Atheneum, 1982.

Levenkron, Steven. *The Best Little Girl in the World*. Contemporary, 1978.

Levitin, Sonia. *A Shadow Like a Leopard*. Harper & Row, 1981.

_____ . *Three Friends*. Harper & Row, 1984.

Lipsyte, Robert. *One Fat Summer*. Harper & Row, 1977.

_____ . *Summer Rules*. Harper & Row, 1981.

_____ . *The Contender,* Harper & Row, 1967.

_____ . *The Summer Boy*. Harper & Row, 1982.

Lowry, Lois. *A Summer to Die*. Houghton Mifflin, 1977.

Major, Kevin, *Far from Shore*. Delacorte, 1981.

Mason, Bobbie Ann. *In Country*. Harper & Row, 1985.

Mathis, Sharon Bell. *Teacup Full of Roses*. Viking, 1975.

Matsubara, Hisako. *Cranes at Dusk*. Doubleday, 1985.

Mazer, Harry. *When the Phone Rang*. Scholastic, 1985.

Mazer, Norma Fox. *Up in Seth's Room*. Delacorte, 1979.

McDermott, Alice. *That Night*. Farrar, Straus & Giroux, 1987.

McKay, Robert. *The Running Back*. Harcourt Brace Jovanovich, 1979.

Miklowitz, Gloria. *Secrets Not Meant to Be Kept*. Delacorte, 1987.

_____ . *The Day the Senior Class Got Married*. Delacorte, 1983.

_____ . *The War Between the Classes*. Delacorte, 1985.

Myers, Walter Dean. *Crystal*. Viking, 1987.

_____ . *Fallen Angels*. Scholastic, 1988.

_____ . *Fast Sam, Cool Clyde, and Stuff*. Viking, 1975.

_____ . *It Ain't All for Nothin'*. Viking, 1978.

_____ . *Motown and Didi: A Love Story*. Viking, 1984.

_____ . *The Young Landlords*. Viking, 1979.

Naylor, Phyllis Reynolds. *The Year of the Gopher*. Macmillan, 1987.

Neufeld, John. *For All the Wrong Reasons*. NAL Penguin, 1980.

Oneal, Zibby. *A Formal Feeling*. Viking, 1982.

_____ . *In Summer Light*. Viking, 1985.

Paterson, Katherine. *Bridge to Terabithia*. Crowell, 1977.

Patrick, John. *The Teahouse of the August Moon*. Dramatists, 1953.

Peck, Richard. *Are You in the House Alone?* Viking, 1976.

_____ . *Father Figure*. Viking, 1978.

_____ . *Princess Ashley*. Delacorte, 1987.

_____ . *Remembering the Good Times*. Delacorte, 1985.

Phipson, Joan. *Hit and Run*. Macmillan, 1985.

Porte, Barbara Ann. *I Only Made Up the Roses*. Greenwillow, 1987.

Potok, Chaim. *My Name Is Asher Lev*. Knopf, 1972.

Riley, Jocelyn. *Crazy Quilt*. Morrow, 1983.

_____ . *Only My Mouth Is Smiling*. Morrow, 1982.

Sallis, Susan. *Secret Places of the Stairs*. Harper & Row, 1984.

_____ . *Only Love*. Harper & Row, 1980.

Scoppettone, Sandra. *Trying Hard to Hear You*. Harper & Row, 1974.

Sebestyen, Ouida. *Far From Home*. Little, Brown, 1980.

_____ . *IOU's*. Little, Brown, 1982.

_____ . *Words by Heart*. Little, Brown, 1979.

Sherburne, Zoa. *Too Bad about the Haines Girl*. Morrow, 1967.

Slepian, Jan. *Something Beyond Paradise*. Philomel, 1987.

Spencer, Scott. *Endless Love*. Knopf, 1979.

Stein, Sol. *The Magician*. Delacorte, 1971.

Stirling, Nora. *You Would if You Loved Me*. Evans, 1969.

Strasser, Todd. *Angel Dust Blues*. Putnam, 1979.

_____ . *Rock 'n' Roll Nights*. Delacorte, 1982.

_____ . *A Very Touchy Subject*. Delacorte, 1985.

_____ . *Workin' for Peanuts*. Delacorte, 1983.

Swarthout, Glendon. *Bless the Beasts and Children*. Doubleday, 1970.

Taylor, Mildred. *Let the Circle Be Unbroken*. Dial, 1981.

Tchudi, Stephen. *The Green Machine and the Frog Crusade*. Delacorte, 1987.

Thomas, Joyce Carol. *Marked by Fire.* Avon, 1982.

Thomas, Jane Resh. *Fox in a Trap.* Houghton Mifflin, 1987.

Thompson, Jean. *House of Tomorrow.* Harper & Row, 1967.

Thompson, Julian F. *A Band of Angels.* Scholastic, 1986.

Voigt, Cynthia. *Come a Stranger.* Atheneum, 1986.

_____ . *Dicey's Song.* Atheneum, 1982.

_____ . *Izzy, Willy-Nilly.* Atheneum, 1986.

_____ . *A Solitary Blue.* Atheneum, 1983.

_____ . *Sons from Afar.* Atheneum, 1981.

_____ . *Homecoming.* Atheneum, 1981.

_____ . *The Runner.* Atheneum, 1985.

Weesner, Theodore. *The Car Thief.* Random House, 1972.

Willey, Margaret. *The Bigger Book of Lydia.* Harper & Row, 1983.

Zindel, Paul. *Confessions of a Teenage Baboon.* Harper & Row, 1977.

_____ . *The Pigman.* Harper & Row, 1968.

For information on the availability of paperback editions of these titles, please consult the most recent edition of *Paperbound Books in Print,* published annually by R. R. Bowker Company.

CHAPTER FOUR

THE OLD ROMANTICISM
Of Wishing and Winning

A kind of story that serves as a counterbalance to the depressing realism of the problem novel is the romance. Romances were among the first stories to be told. People like to hear them because they have happy endings, and the tellers of romances are willing to exaggerate just enough to make the stories more interesting than real life. A basic part of the romance is a quest of some sort. In the course of the quest, the protagonist will experience doubts and will undergo severe trials, but he or she will be successful in the end. This success will be all the more appreciated because of the difficulties that the protagonist has suffered. The extremes of suffering and succeeding are characteristic of the romance. In good moments, it is like a happy daydream, but in bad moments it resembles a nightmare.

The word *romance* comes from the Latin adverb *romanice* which means "in the Latin manner." It is with this meaning that Latin, Italian, Spanish, and French are described as romance languages. The literary meaning of *romance* grew out of its use by English speakers to refer to French dialects, which were much closer to Latin than was their own Germanic language of English. Later it was used to refer to Old French and finally to anything written in French.

Many of the French stories that were read by English speakers were tales about knights who set out on such bold adventures as slaying dragons, rescuing princesses from ogres, and defeating the wicked enemies of a righteous king. Love was often an element in these stories, for the knight was striving to win the hand of a beloved maiden. So, today, when a literary piece is referred to as a romance, it usually contains either adventure or love or both.

The romance is appealing to teenagers because it is matched in several ways to their roles in life. The symbols that are used often relate to youthfulness and hope, and, in keeping with this, many of the protagonists, even in the traditional and classic tales, are in their teens. Modern young adults are at an age when they leave home or anticipate leaving to embark on a new way of life. It is more likely to be called "moving out" than "going on a romantic quest," but the results are much the same. And seeking and securing a "true love" usually—but not always—takes up a greater proportion of the time and energy of the young than of middle-aged adults. And the exaggeration that is part of the romantic mode is quite honestly felt by young people. Never at any other stage of life do people feel their emotions quite so intensely. Robert Cormier has said that he began writing about young protagonists when he observed that in one afternoon at the beach his own children could go through what to an adult would be a whole month of emotional experiences.

Another teenage characteristic particularly appropriate to the romantic mode is the optimism of youth. Whether or not young people, either as a group or as individuals, are really more optimistic than their elders, they are presumed to be so, and a writer doing the same story for adults might be more tempted to present it as irony than as romance.

THE ADVENTURE/ACCOMPLISHMENT ROMANCE

The great satisfaction of the adventure or the accomplishment romance lies in its wish fulfillment, as when David slays Goliath, when Cinderella is united with the noble prince and given the fitting role of queen, and when Dorothy and Toto find their way back to Kansas. In every culture there are legends, myths, and folk and fairy tales which follow the pattern of the adventure/ accomplishment romance. In the Judeo-Christian culture, the biblical story of Joseph is a prime example. Early in life, Joseph was chosen and marked as a special person. When his brothers sold him as a slave to the Egyptian traders, he embarked on his quest for wisdom and knowledge. Just when all seemed lost, he received divine help in being blessed with the ability to interpret dreams. This got him out of prison and into Pharaoh's court. The climax of the story came years later during the famine that brought his brothers to Egypt and the royal palace. Without recognizing Joseph, they begged for food. His forgiveness and his generosity was final proof of his worthiness.

It is a distinguishing feature of such romances that the happy ending is achieved only after the hero's worth is proven through a crisis or an ordeal. Usually as part of the ordeal the hero must make a sacrifice, be wounded, or leave some part of his or her body, even if it is only sweat or tears. The real loss is that of innocence, but it is usually symbolized by a physical loss as in Norse mythology when Odin gives one of his eyes to pay for gaining knowledge, or in J. R. R. Tolkien's *The Lord of the Rings* when Frodo, who has already suffered many wounds, finds that he cannot throw the ring back and so must let Gollum take his finger along with the ring. What is purchased with the suffering of the hero is nearly always some kind of wisdom, even though wisdom is not what the hero sets out to find.

The adventure/accomplishment romance has elements applicable to the task of entering the adult world, which all young people anticipate. The story pattern includes the three stages of formal initiation as practiced in many cultures. First, the young and innocent person is separated both physically and spiritually from the nurturing love of friends and family. Then, during this separation, the hero, who embodies noble qualities, undergoes a test of courage and stamina that may be either mental, psychological, or physical. In the final stage the young person is reunited with former friends and family in a new role of increased status.

Izzy, Willy-Nilly *and* One Fat Summer *as Adventure/Accomplishment Romances*

Cynthia Voigt's *Izzy, Willy-Nilly* and Robert Lipsyte's *One Fat Summer* are good illustrations of how traditional archetypal initiation rites can be translated into modern and appealing stories for young adults. Voigt's *Izzy, Willy-Nilly* begins:

> "Isobel? I'm afraid we're going to have to take it off."
> "Take it off, take it off," I sang, like a vamp song; but I don't think I actually did, and I know my laughter stayed locked inside my head. I think my voice did too.
> "Isobel. Can you hear me?" I didn't know. I didn't think so. *It* was my leg. I went to sleep.

Izzy wakes up enough to tell the doctor "My name's Izzy," and then she falls back to sleep thinking that by correcting the name he called her, she has also corrected "the disturbing, frightening feeling that something was wrong."

Tenth-grader-cheerleader-nice-girl Izzy has been in a serious automobile accident, and before she is really conscious, her leg is being amputated. Chapter Two is a flashback to before the accident. The author uses this chapter to set the background and to show readers that Izzy Lingard is a special person worthy of the challenge she will face. Izzy is the first of her group to be asked out by a senior and she is strong enough not to succumb to the boy's teasing about asking her parents' permission before she can accept.

Since a romance is essentially the story of one person's achievement and development, everything else is a condensation. For the sake of efficiency, the personalities of the supporting characters are shown through symbols, metaphors, and significant details, all of which highlight the qualities that are important to the story. It is not really the villain whom the hero has ultimately to defeat, but the villain stands in the way of the real accomplishment and gives the hero an enemy upon whom to focus. Without some scary, nightmarish, and usually life-threatening incident, the happy ending could not be appreciated.

JANET QUIN-HARKIN
on the Emancipation of Young Readers

For me, the most exciting development in young adult literature has been the advent of the paperback book. Not only has this made books affordable for anyone who wants to buy them, it has also meant that, for the first time, the buyer is the ultimate reader. Until a few years ago, books for children were chosen by others: by parents, doting aunts, or librarians. All of these people chose books they felt young people should want to read. These were not always the books they *did* want to read. When young people were finally able to purchase their own books, publishers discovered that young people did not really want to read true "problem novels," the sort of YA books that had been appearing in hardback in great profusion towards the end of the seventies which dealt with such heavy subjects as suicide or drug addiction. The message young readers were giving very clearly to publishers and writers

was that they wanted to read about themselves and their own problems, also that their own problems were not as overwhelming as most of those portrayed in books. What concerned them and what they wanted to read about was belonging—belonging to a family, to a peer group, to an ethnic group. They also worried about adjusting—adjusting to a new environment, a new family situation, a new school, or a new relationship. They wanted books that promised hope for the future. They wanted to know what a first date would be like, what high school and college would be like. In other words, they wanted to be reassured rather than scared.

When I am writing, I am always very conscious of my audience and what they expect from a book. I try to make all my stories well within the bounds of possibility. If I am writing a romance, for example, my shy, ordinary heroine will never get the football hero to fall for her, because in real life that sort of thing doesn't happen.

I am always amazed when librarians criticize paperbacks, teenage romances in particular, and refuse to keep the books on their shelves. This is, to me, a very short-sighted viewpoint. Of course the books are not *Jane Eyre,* and maybe it would be more desirable if everyone read *Jane Eyre,* but not everyone would. The sort of books I write keep kids reading when they would otherwise read nothing. At least half of my fan mail is from poor students, some of whom had never read a whole book before. That they should now want to read more of my work is, for me, the ultimate success.

Janet Quin-Harkin's books include the *Sugar and Spice* series from Ballantine, and the *On Our Own* series from Bantam, as well as *Wanted, Date for Saturday Night,* Berkley, 1986, and *My Secret Love,* Bantam, 1986.

The boy who asked Izzy for a date is the villain of the story. He is a "notorious flirt," who at the party gets so drunk that although he isn't hurt when he plows his car into a tree, he does nothing to help Izzy. Then he lies to the police about Izzy doing the driving, and instead of apologizing for what happened, he manipulates Izzy's friend hoping to influence what Izzy will tell the police.

Izzy faces the physical loss of her leg and the challenge of learning to walk with a prosthesis, but the real challenge is the emotional one of acceptance. In the daytime, at least in front of other people, Izzy is cheerful. The first day that she dares to look down at the blanket covering her "leg-and-a-half" she begins her quest for emotional peace. Heroes in traditional romances often had visions or visits from divine beings. Izzie's "vision" comes through her mental image of a tiny little Izzy doll:

> My brain wasn't working. It was as if the little Izzy was running around and around in circles, some frantic wind-up Izzy, screeching *No, no, no*.
> But it was *Yes, yes, yes*.
> And I knew it.
> I knew it, but I couldn't believe it.

Izzy lays her head on the formica hospital table over her bed and although she is not asleep she has a nightmare:

> I felt as if a huge long slide was slipping up past me, and I was going down it. I couldn't stop myself, and I didn't even want to. . . . Something heavy and wet and cold and gray was making me go down, pushing at the back of my bent neck and at my shoulders. At the bottom, wherever that was, something heavy and wet and cold and gray waited for me. It was softer than the ground when I hit it. I went flying off the end of the slide and fell into the gray. The gray reached up around me and closed itself over me and swallowed me up.

When a nurse comes in, Izzy wishes she would leave because she is afraid she might cry, and "We didn't cry, not the Lingards. We were brave and made jokes about things hurting. . . ." The nurse is a physical therapist who gives Izzy painful massages to toughen up her skin and muscles so she will be ready for the prosthesis. Izzy is hurt that the woman concentrates on her work and doesn't look at Izzy's face or talk with her. In her depressed mood, Izzy decides that it is because she is no longer a whole person. "I guessed if you'd finished working on the pizza dough, you wouldn't bend over and say goodbye to it. You don't talk to *things* and that's what I was, a thing, a messed-up body."

The worst times for Izzy are at night when she wakes up alone and can't keep her "mind from going down that slide thinking of all the things that I managed not to think about during the days." She never knew until then, never even suspected how it felt to be depressed.

> I'd been miserable. I'd been blue. But depressed, no, I hadn't been that. I never knew how it felt to sigh out a breath so sad you could almost see tears in it. I never knew the way tears would ooze and ooze out of your eyes. I never knew the way something could hang like a gray cloud over all of your mind and you could never get away from it, never forget it.

Help comes to Izzy from an unexpected source. Occasionally, her old friends come to visit, but they are too involved in their own lives and too uncomfortable with her misfortune to stay long. But then, strange, misfit, Rosamunde—"not at all like Lisa and the rest"—arrives to decorate Izzy's hospital room and to play Yahtze and bring fruit and good conversation and homemade turnovers and piroshki.

When Izzy is released from the hospital she doesn't go back to her old room because it is upstairs. Instead she is given her parents' bedroom on the first floor, and it is here in the middle of the nights that Izzy, isolated from her family and in a strange and lonely place, undergoes the suffering that will make her eventual victory that much sweeter. On the outside, Izzy's victory is shown through her return to school and her eventual confrontation of the boy who caused her to lose her leg. But her more important challenge is an internal one. Voigt uses a conversation between Izzy and Rosamunde to help readers understand:

> "I used to really like watching you move around, because you always seemed so comfortable in your own body, and it wasn't anything you thought about, or even noticed; it was just the way you were, that was what was so great about it."
>
> "You're talking in the past tense," I said, carefully keeping my eyes on the ribbon I was tying, thinking how much I'd changed.
>
> "No, that's not true. I mean, I *was*. I mean, it was the past tense, but you still have that way of being—comfortable to be with. Only it used to show, anybody who saw you saw it, just looking at you. Because it wasn't just being comfortable with your body that made you so nice. But I really mind that."
>
> Then I did look at her. "I mind it too," I said.

Once during a particular bad time, Izzy sees the little doll in her head "standing there waving her detached leg at a crowd of people, like a safety monitor waving her stop sign." In contrast, the first day that someone at school forgets about Izzy's crutches, the little doll "gathered herself up and did an impossible backflip, and then another and another." The book ends with Izzy seeing the little doll:

█ . . . standing alone, without crutches. . . . Her arms were spread out slightly. She looked like she was about to dance, but really her arms were out for balance. . . . The little Izzy balanced there briefly and then took a hesitant step forward—ready to fall, ready not to fall.

Robert Lipsyte's *One Fat Summer* is a story about an overweight boy's quest for self-respect. It begins on the Fourth of July with fourteen-year-old Bobby Marks feeling sorry for himself because that is when his family moves out to Rumson Lake where everyone goes around in a swimming suit so the other kids can see "your thick legs and your wobbly backside and your big belly and your soft arms. And they laugh." Bobby takes a job as an underpaid and overworked yard boy so that he won't have to be a camp counselor or a mother's helper on the beach where he would have to wear a swimming suit. As befits the mode of romance, the place where Bobby works is both idyllic and far removed from his family. He works on the other side of the island taking care of the green velvet lawn that surrounds Dr. Kahn's great white house making it look "like a proud clipper ship riding the crest of the ocean."

Maintaining the hillside lawn is indeed a challenge, and as often happens in a romance, Bobby is almost unaware of what is happening to him as he meets the challenge. Because of the hard work and the fact that he is often too tired to eat when he gets home, pounds melt away.

Another reason he hardly notices his weight loss is that he is so worried about the villain in the story, ex-Marine Willie Rumson, who wants Bobby's job. At first, Willie and his friends just tease Bobby, calling him "The Crisco Kid" because he is "fat in the can," and asking him if he has a license to drag that trailer behind him. But then when Bobby refuses to quit his job, Willie and his buddies grow mean. They take Bobby out onto an island in the middle of the lake, strip him of his clothes, and row away. Symbolically, the peaceful setting of the lake has changed into something fearsome. The night "exploded with thunder and lightning and the wind drove nails of rain" into his naked body. He is lying face-down in the mud, but then he hears a voice encouraging him to get up, telling him he can win. To his surprise he finds that it is his own voice, "Captain Marks, Commander Marks, Big Bob Marks."

He listens and stands up, thereby showing that he is worthy of outside help. It comes in the form of Willie's cousin who arrives in a canoe and takes Bobby back to Rumson Beach. All that Bobby loses in the ordeal is a sock. What he finds is a new kind of confidence, which prepares him for a final confrontation with Willie Rumson and eventually with his boss, Dr. Kahn, who hasn't been paying Bobby what his ad had promised. When Bobby asks Dr. Kahn for fair pay, Dr. Kahn tells him, "You should pay me for this summer. I've watched you change from a miserable fat boy into a fairly presentable young man. On my lawn. On my time." Bobby's response of "You didn't do it, Dr. Kahn. I did it," sums up a prime requisite for a modern young adult romance. The hero has to accomplish the task and it has to be one that readers can respect and at the same time imagine themselves accomplishing.

Other Quest Stories of Accomplishment

The motif of a worthy young hero embarking on a quest of wisdom will appear in many more good books than those mentioned in this chapter because it is a motif that fits well in biographies, adventure stories, historical fiction, fantasy, science fiction, and problem novels. And even when the quest is not the main part of a story, motifs that fit with the quest romance will be incorporated. For example, in traditional romances, the protagonist usually receives the vision or insight "in a high or isolated place like a mountain top, an island, or a tower."[1] In Virginia Hamilton's *M. C. Higgins, the Great,* the boy, M. C., came to his realizations about his family and his role while he contemplated the surrounding countryside from the special bicycle seat affixed to the top of the tall steel pole standing in the yard of his mountain home. The pole was unique and intriguing and M. C. earned it through his own physical efforts. His father gave it to him as a reward for swimming across the Ohio River.

Literal quests appear in several excellent new books in which girls set out to find out about their fathers but end up finding out about themselves, for example, Bobbie Ann Mason's *In Country,* Margaret Mahy's *Catalogue of the Universe,* Virginia Hamilton's *A Little Love,* Bruce Brooks' *Midnight Hour Encores,* and Paul Fleischman's *Rear View Mirrors.* In this latter book, 17-year-old Olivia Tate sets out on a one-day, 70-mile bicycle trip in memory of her late father. Her parents divorced when she was eight months old, and she has not known her father until the previous summer when he summoned her to spend the summer with him in rural New Hampshire. Over the summer, Olivia's reluctance and resentment changes to affection and understanding even though she realizes that she can never be the replacement of himself that her father is hoping for. In Cynthia Voigt's *Sons from Afar,* the two Tillerman brothers, James and Sammy, go looking for the father they never knew. Although they don't find him, they come close enough to realize that they must look to themselves for strength.

Some critics worry about the way authors use such physical changes as Bobby Marks' loss of weight and Willie Weaver's almost miraculous recovery in Chris Crutcher's *The Crazy Horse Electric Game* (described in Chapter 3) as tangible or metaphorical ways to communicate that the young person has made an emotional or mental accomplishment. They fear that young readers will interpret the physical achievement literally rather than figuratively. Teenagers are already overly concerned about their physical bodies and any defects that they might have. Most physical defects—even many cases of obesity—cannot be changed. They would therefore prefer stories in which the protagonist comes to terms with the problem as did Izzy in *Izzy, Willy-Nilly.*

In Anne Eliot Crompton's historical *The Sorcerer,* the young protagonist compensated for, rather than overcame, a disability. The boy was named Lefthand because he was injured by a bear so that he could not hunt. In his tribe, this was a serious problem because hunting was what the men did. There was no miraculous cure for his disability, but he gained both his own and his tribe's respect when he developed enough skill as an artist to draw the pictures of animals needed for the tribe's hunting rituals.

Authors dramatize mental accomplishments as physical ones because it is extremely hard to show something occurring inside someone's head. And if the physical problem were not in some way solved, then the story would be irony or tragedy rather than romance. The tone an author uses might also change a story from romance to irony or tragedy. Although romance has its share of somber moments, the overall tone must be relatively light and optimistic. For example, Holden Caulfield set out on a quest, but J. D. Salinger's *The Catcher in the Rye* does not qualify as a romance. It is too grim. The same could be said for Hannah Green's *I Never Promised You a Rose Garden* and Judith Guest's *Ordinary People.* These three books contain many of the elements of the traditional romance including worthy young heroes who set out to find wisdom and understanding. In the course of the stories, they make physical sacrifices, but these are real rather than symbolic, for example, the suicide attempts in the latter two titles. The wise and kindly psychiatrists are modern realistic counterparts to the white witches, the wizards, and the helpful gods and goddesses who in the traditional romances have been there to aid and instruct worthy young heroes much as Merlin did the young Arthur. The difference between the traditional helpers in romances and the modern ones in realistic stories is that the realistic ones lack magic; they must rely on hard painstaking work. This is what is communicated by the title *I Never Promised You a Rose Garden.* Deborah Blau's psychiatrist said to her, as a warning, that even when she is "cured" and has left the mental institution, life will still be full of problems. If Green's book had been a romance, then there would have been no mention of this fact. Readers could have pictured Deborah leaving the institution and living "happily ever after."

Because of the important role of physical effort and danger in the romantic mode, it used to be hard to find adventure stories with female protagonists. That isn't as true today even though most of the stories with females will have other elements as well. Pam Conrad's *What I Did for Roman* is a family story and a love story as well as a quest. At the book's climax, 16-year-old Darcie frees herself from the emotional bonds of the young zookeeper that she thought she loved. His name is Roman and he holds such power over her that at his request she dares death by entering a lion's cage with him.

A more typical plot for an adventure-romance, but featuring a female, is Deborah Savage's *A Rumour of Otters.* Fourteen-year-old Alexa lives on a New Zealand sheep ranch, and when her father picks her 16-year-old brother to go on the sheep roundup even though he is less interested and less skilled than Alexa, she sets off on her own adventure. She goes to look for otters which most people think are nonexistent in New Zealand. Alexa had her information from Billy, an old Maori tribesman who remembered the otters from the lakes high in the mountains. She succeeds in discovering the otters as well as her own identity and self-respect, but not without risk and suffering.

Sue Ellen Bridgers' *Permanent Connections,* discussed earlier as an example of the importance of setting, is a story where a young man is forced into a situation that leads him into a quest. In contrast, Russel Susskit in Gary Paulsen's *Dogsong* goes to his Eskimo tribe's oldest and wisest man to seek wisdom and instruction in the old ways. He purposely sets out on a quest. The lonely isolation of an Eskimo teenager fighting for survival against snow, ice, and starvation is a powerful image, the same one that Jean George evoked in *Julie of the Wolves,* read mostly by younger adolescents. George's story is a classic example of the romantic quest ending in a compromised dream. Julie's separation from her Eskimo family and friends is the result of her running away from the retarded Daniel, who was planning to make her his wife in fact as well as in name. She sets out with the vague and unrealistic goal of finding her pen pal in San Francisco. As she gains wisdom, she decides to live in the old ways. Amaroq, the great wolf, lends "miraculous" help to her struggle for survival on the Arctic tundra. The climax comes when she learns that her father still lives and she has arrived at his village. When she finds that he has married a "gussack" and now pilots planes for hunters, the disillusioned Julie slips away to return to the tundra. The temperature falls far below zero and "the ice thundered and boomed, roaring like drumbeats across the Arctic." Tornait, Julie's golden plover who has been her faithful companion, dies in spite of all that Julie does to save him. Tornait is the last symbol of Julie's innocence and as she mourns his death, she comes to accept the fact that the life of both the wolf and the Eskimo is changing and she points her boots toward her father and the life that he now leads.

Through her quest, she gains the understanding that her life must change, but she also gains something unexpected. She learns a great deal about her native land and the animals who live there. Readers are optimistic that Julie will not forget what she has experienced and that she will have some part in protecting the land and the animals, though perhaps not to the degree that she desires.

The acceptance of the compromised dream is an element of the romance pattern that is particularly meaningful to young adults. Many of them are just beginning to achieve some of their lifelong goals, and they are finding that the end of the rainbow, which is a symbolic way of saying such things as "When I graduate," "When we get married," "When I'm eighteen," or "When I have my own apartment," is illusory. Like the characters in the romances, young people are not sorry that they have ventured for they have indeed found something worthwhile, but it is seldom the pot of gold that they have imagined.

Since the pattern of the romance has been so clearly outlined by critics, and since its popularity has passed the test of time with honors, it would seem to be a very easy story to write. The plot has already been worked out. An author needs only to develop a likable protagonist, figure out a quest, fill in the supporting roles with stock characters, and then supply a few interesting details. But it is far from being this simple. Sometimes, as in dance, the things that look the simplest are in fact the hardest to execute. The plot must not be so obvious that a reader will recognize it as "the same old thing." The really good author will develop a unique situation that on the surface will appear to be simply a good story. Its appeal as a romantic quest should be at a deep almost subconscious level, with readers experiencing a sense of *déjà vu.* It is as if their own life story is being told because the romantic quest is everyone's story. We are all searching for answers to the great questions of life.

Characterization is especially important in relation to the protagonist in an accomplishment- or adventure-romance. Readers must be able to identify with the hero. As *Dogsong* and *Julie of the Wolves* prove, this does not mean that the hero has to live in the same lifestyle or even have the same conflicts as the reader. But it does mean that the emotions must be ones that the reader can understand, and the author has to present them in such a way as to create empathy.

ACCOMPLISHMENT STORIES WITH RELIGIOUS THEMES

Cynthia Rylant's *A Fine White Dust* exemplifies a subgenre of the accomplishment romance, one in which religion plays a major role. The book's title comes from the chalklike dust that gets on Pete's fingers when he handles the "little bitty pieces of broken ceramic" that used to be a cross he had painted in Vacation Bible School—back before he got so old that it wasn't cool to go anymore. His best friend is a confirmed atheist and he has "half-washed Christians for parents." Nevertheless the summer that the Preacher Man comes to town, "something religious" begins itching Pete, something that going to church couldn't cure.

Rylant's skill in developing Pete's character and revealing the depths of his emotions when he is saved and wooed and then betrayed by the Preacher Man won for her a well-deserved Newbery Honor Award. The book is short and the succinct titles of its twelve chapters could almost be used as a prototypical description of the accomplishment romance. It opens with "Dust" and a sense of the ennui and ends with the unnumbered "Amen" when Pete finally decides that "The Preacher Man is behind me. But God is still right there, in front." At last Pete can throw away the cross that broke when he kicked his duffel bag in rage at learning that Preacher Man wasn't coming for him. In between are the chapters, "The Hitchhiker," "The Saviour," "The Joy," "The Change," "The Telling," "The Invitation," "The Leaving," "The Wait," "Hell," "The Messenger," and "The Light."

Books that do what *A Fine White Dust* does, that is, unabashedly explore religious themes, are relatively rare partly because schools and libraries fear mixing church and state through spending tax dollars for religious books. Also, mainstream publishers fear cutting into potential sales by printing books about protagonists whose religious beliefs may offend some readers and make others uncomfortable. It's been easier for schools to include religious books with historical settings such as Lloyd Douglas' *The Robe,* Scott O'Dell's *The Hawk That Dare Not Hunt by Day,* Elizabeth George Speare's *Bronze Bow,* and Jessamyn West's *Friendly Persuasion.* Also accepted are books with contemporary settings that have "proven themselves" with adult readers, for example, Margaret Craven's *I Heard the Owl Call My Name,* Catherine Marshall's *A Man Called Peter,* and William Barrett's *Lilies of the Field.* These books, along with Chaim Potok's coming-of-age stories in a community of Hasidic Jews, *The*

Chosen, In the Beginning, and *My Name Is Asher Lev,* are almost classical in the popular culture sense.

However, there is a growing body of good authors who include religion as one of the ways for contemporary young protagonists to find help much as Rob did when he went to the little country church in Sue Ellen Bridgers' *Permanent Connections.* YA author Dean Hughes, in encouraging other authors to "confront religion directly as an important, integral part of maturation," wrote:

> We need to be careful that, in effect, we do not say to young people that they *should* be most concerned about pimples and clothes and dates and football games—or even sex. Part of being human is addressing oneself to questions about justice, creation, morality, and the existence of divinity.[2]

Katherine Paterson, who has attended theological school and served as a missionary in China, includes both implicit and explicit religious references in her books, most directly in *Jacob Have I Loved* and *Bridge to Terabithia.* The main problem in Judy Blume's best-selling *Are You There, God? It's Me, Margaret* is Margaret's decision of whether to go to a Christian church like her mother's parents or to a Jewish temple like her father's parents. In Fran Arrick's *Tunnel Vision,* religion comes into the picture as Anthony Hamil's friends and family try to console themselves over his suicide. Arrick's *God's Radar* is about Roxie Cable and her family's adjustments to the religious elements of the small southern town to which they have moved. Gloria D. Miklowitz's *The Love Bombers* and Robin Brancato's *Blinded by the Light* are fictional explorations of cults and what they offer young people.

Robert Cormier's *The Chocolate War* (see Chapter 3) is heavily influenced by religion, while Alice Childress' *Rainbow Jordan* has several references to religious people and beliefs. One of Phyllis Reynolds Naylor's most powerful books is *A String of Chances.* Sixteen-year-old Evie Hutchins' first experience away from home is going to help her cousin care for a new baby. Evie's father is a minister and she has always believed in God and the tenets of her religion, but the sudden death of the baby forces her to rethink her religious beliefs.

In Norma Howe's *God, the Universe, and Hot Fudge Sundaes,* Alfie asks some tough questions about God. Her parents are separating and her younger sister is dying. Alfie wants God to make her sister well, but at the same time she finds it hard to believe in a God who would allow people to suffer so much. Alfie's wit and her friendship with a handsome college student keep the book from being too grim.

M. E. Kerr is one of the few popular YA authors who has consistently included religious experiences as stepping stones for her protagonists. *Is That You, Miss Blue?* is the story of Flanders Brown and what she learns from observing the ironic situation of a religious teacher being asked to resign from a church-sponsored school because her faith made teachers and students uncomfortable. Little Little, in the book of the same name, is being courted by another dwarf, Lionel Knox, who under his slogan of "scheme" has become a successful evangelist preacher. Little Little makes a wise decision when she chooses instead the physically crooked, but morally straight, Sydney Cinnamon.

In Kerr's *What I Really Think of You,* 16-year-old Opal Ringer never leaves the small town of Seaville, but she nevertheless goes on a quest. She is the daughter of a struggling pentecostal preacher, and she goes looking for acceptance by the teenagers in her affluent high school. But in the course of her quest, she develops as her own person in such as way that she could never be "one of them."

Kerr wrote this book a decade before the Jim Bakker and Jimmy Swaggart scandals and before Oral Roberts went into his prayer tower seeking a million dollars in donations lest he "be called home." It was simultaneously criticized for "copping out" with a "spiritual" ending and for "taking cheap shots at religion." Other readers interpreted the "cheap shots" as "healthy skepticism" which illustrates some of the difficulties inherent in writing about and discussing religious topics.

Teachers and librarians may find some useful books produced through religious publishing houses. However, as Kathy Piehl explained, many of these publishers have a built-in market and are affiliated with a single group of churches and its teachings. "Consequently, the books contain assumptions about faith and life that may be unfamiliar to the general public."[3] Also, some of the books are aggressively aimed at converting readers and may contain offensive polemics against other groups competing for the same potential converts.

In relation to the accomplishment-romance, an especially troublesome group are the many books in which a misguided life is set right by an end-of-the-book conversion. An extreme example of such books are those written by John Benton and sold in Christian bookstores. The books have girls' names (*Debbie, Patti, Sheila, Carmen,* etc.) and are sold to give financial support to the Walter Hoving Home for delinquent girls. Patty Campbell described her reaction to *Carmen* as one of astonishment:

Here from the people who gave us such shocked opposition to *Steffie Can't Come Out to Play,* was a book that surpassed in sordid detail any realistic Young Adult novel I had ever read. A young girl runs away from her brutal, alcoholic father to a life as a junkie and prostitute. True, there is no explicit sex, only hints and suggestions for the imagination to fill in. Also, there are no four-letter words. But there *are* lingering, loving descriptions of the joys of shooting up with heroin; there are enthusiastic scenes of beatings, muggings, knife fights, razor slashings. . . . The life of the hooker is made to seem attractive and exciting with hard drugs the ecstatic reward for a night's work. In the very last chapter, Carmen gets saved by David Wilkerson's Teen Challenge, but this is tame stuff compared to what went before.[4]

Teachers and librarians would do well to visit local religious bookstores to see what is offered because some students may prefer to fill their independent reading assignments with books from these sources. The variety of the offerings and the slick covers and sophisticated marketing techniques may be a surprise. Buyers can choose from biblical romances by Marjorie Holmes, western romances and adventures by Janette Oke, self-help and inspirational stories by Lorraine Peterson and Phyllis Reynolds Naylor, diet and exercise books by Marie Chapin, persuasive nonfiction such as books against rock music, and inspirational biographies including *Never Quit* by Glen Cunningham, *Debby Boone So Far* by Debby Boone with Dennis Baker, and *Joni* by Joni Eareckson.

When selecting books with religious themes, teachers and librarians need to seek out and support those authors and publishers who treat religious motifs with honesty and respect and at the same time demand high literary quality. They also need to help parents and other critics realize that religious doubts are part of the maturation process and that reading about the doubts that others have or about imperfections in organized religion will not necessarily destroy one's own faith. Adults working with young readers also need to be careful in their book discussions to distinguish between criticizing the subject matter of a book and criticizing the way the author handles that subject matter. Probably one of the reasons that books in which young people achieve maturity through some kind of religious experience have not received their fair share of attention is that teachers fear that in the process of building up literary sophistication they may be tearing down religious faith.

THE LOVE-ROMANCE

The love-romance is of a slightly different nature, but it shares many characteristics with the accomplishment- or adventure-romance. Love stories are symbolically associated with youth and with springtime. There is an ordeal or a problem to be overcome followed by a happy ending. The "problem" is invariably the successful pairing of a likable young couple. An old definition of the love-romance patterns is, "Boy meets girl, boy loses girl, boy wins girl." This is a fairly accurate summary except that with teenage literature it is often the other way around. Most of the romances are told from the girl's point of view. She is the one who meets, loses, and finally wins a boy.

The tone of the love-romance is lighter than that of the adventure-romance. In a love story the protagonist neither risks nor gains as much as in an adventure. Notwithstanding *Romeo and Juliet,* people seldom die, emotionally or physically, because of young love. For this reason, the love-romance tends to be less serious in its message. Its power lies in its wish fulfillment.

Women of all ages enjoy reading romances for the same reasons that people have always enjoyed either hearing or reading wish-fulfilling fantasies. The "Open Sesame" door to prosperity and the transformation of a cindermaid into a queen, a frog into a prince, and a Scrooge into a kindly old man are all examples of the same satisfying theme that is the key to the appeal of love-romances. In the teen romances an ugly duckling girl is transformed by the love of a boy into a swan. In her new role as swan she is not only popular and successful; she is happy.

Characteristics of Successful Love Stories

For the writer of a love story, there is probably no talent more important than the ability to create believable characters. If readers do not feel that they know the boy and girl or the man and woman as individuals, then they can't identify with them and consequently won't care whether they make it or not. It's the effective characterization that makes the following books stand out in readers' memories: Joyce Carol Thomas' *Bright Shadow*, Ursula K. Le Guin's *Very Far Away from Anywhere Else*, James Baldwin's *If Beale Street Could Talk*, Katie Letcher Lyle's *Fair Day and Another Step Begun*, and Katherine Paterson's *Rebels of the Heavenly Kingdom*.

The better love stories will not be so lopsided that only one sex will read them. In 1977, Robert Unsworth, writing in *School Library Journal*, decried the dearth of books giving an unbiased treatment to the part that male sexuality plays in the growing-up process of all boys. He wrote, "We do not need explicit sex in teenage fiction any more than we need the head-in-the-sand approach to sexuality that seems to be the current norm. There is middle ground."[5] Books he commended for including at least some honest mention of male sexual development were Judy Blume's *Then Again, Maybe I Won't*, Robert Cormier's *The Chocolate War*, Mildred Lee's *Fog*, and Don Moser's *A Heart to the Hawks*.

Today Unsworth's list could be much longer because of the development of a new type of "boys' book" far different from the sports, adventure, and mystery stories traditionally thought of as "boys' books." Hazel Rochman described such books as "domestic novels about boys in which heroes stay home and struggle with their feelings and their conscience rather than with tumultuous external events." Many such books are love stories, and as Rochman observed:

> The theme of so many girls' books—finding that you love the boy next door after all—has a new vitality from the male perspective, as in [Harry] Mazer's *I Love You, Stupid!* Sex is treated with honesty: in [Chris] Crutcher's *Running Loose*, after a long romantic buildup in which the couple drive and then ski to an isolated cabin for a weekend of lovemaking, the jock hero finds that he cannot perform. In [Richard] Peck's *Father Figure* and [Katie Letcher] Lyle's *Dark But Full of Diamonds*, the love for an older woman, in rivalry with the boy's own father is movingly handled . . . in *The Course of True Love Never Did Run Smooth*, [Marilyn] Singer's heroine finds strong and sexy a boy who is short, funny, and vulnerable.[6]

ROBERT KAPLOW
on Journeys

Most of adolescence—as most of adolescent fiction—seems to be a journey out of aloneness—at least a temporary journey out of aloneness. The trip has been made one hundred times before, but the spirit in the best of these books is so startling, brave, vulnerable, and fragile that we're forced again to care. This is an old magic. We begin reading with the certainty that our heart is closed—and suddenly, like falling in love after years of solitude, the panic returns: the phone calls and letters and dates and dinners hold promise, vitality, uncertainty. We're awkward again. And what a miraculous nightmare life seems.

Robert Kaplow's books include *Two in the City,* Houghton Mifflin, 1979; *Alex Icicle,* Houghton Mifflin, 1984; and *Alessandra* (in press).

The most obvious difference between these "boy" books and the larger body of love stories written from a girl's point of view is that their authors, who are mostly males, tend to put less emphasis on courtship and romance and more on sexuality. Rather than relying on discreet fadeouts, they allow their readers to remain for the grand finale. For the most part, the descriptions are neither pornographic nor lovingly romantic, but in such books as Robert Lipsyte's *Jock and Jill,* Todd Strasser's *Workin' for Peanuts,* Chris Crutcher's *Running Loose,* Robert Lehrman's *Juggling,* Terry Davis' *Vision Quest,* and Thomas Rogers' *At the Shores* there is little doubt about the abundance of sexual feelings that the characters experience.

As an antidote to the lopsidedness of books that are either overly romantic or sexy, some adult critics suggest offering books where boys and girls are as much friends as lovers. Friendship stories differ from the more traditional romances in several ways. First, there is something more to the story than the relationship, which despite its emotional importance is only part of a bigger story. Second, the story is not told exclusively from the girl's point of view. As a ploy to attract male readers, since authors already feel confident that girls will read love stories, the narrator may be the boy, or there may be a mix with alternate chapters coming from the boy and the girl as in Paul Zindel's *The Pigman* and M. E. Kerr's *I'll Love You When You're More Like Me.* A third difference is that there is no indication of either partner exploiting or manipulating the other as often happens in exaggerated romances or in pornographic or sex-oriented stories. In the friendship stories that appeal to both sexes, no one is out to "make a catch." Instead the couple works together to solve some kind of mutual problem or to achieve a goal of some sort.

An example is Harry Mazer's *The Girl of His Dreams.* Willis Pierce, the boy Mazer wrote about in his first book *The War on Villa Street,* has graduated from high school and is living by himself. He is a runner but too shy to compete or to make friends, but on his long solitary runs he dreams about the girl he is sure to meet one day. When he meets Sophie, who takes care of the newsstand by the factory where he works, she doesn't look or act like the girl of his dreams. Nevertheless, Mazer has done such a good job of character development, that readers understand why the two are attracted to each other and they end the book feeling like Sophie does: "She's happy, but the little bit of worry is always there, the little bit of uncertainty." Other good books of the boy/girl friendship type include: Laurence Yep's *Sea Glass,* Katherine Paterson's *Bridge to Terabithia,* Myron Levoy's *Alan and Naomi,* and Jan Slepian's *The Alfred Summer.*

Interesting historical details or glimpses into social issues will not save a weak story, but they will add interest to a strong one as with Jessamyn West's *The Massacre at Fall Creek.* It illustrates how a love story that is integrated into a larger story can be better because of the dual plot. Readers get to know the young couple through the part they play in the first American court case (Fall Creek, Indiana, 1824) in which white men were tried, convicted, and executed for killing Indians. Mildred Lee's *The People Therein* also has a frontier, or pioneer, setting. But what stays in the mind after reading the book is not the setting as much as the characterization of the physically lame Lanthy and her lover, a traveling botanist and scholar who comes to the backwoods from Boston in hopes of curing his own lameness, an addiction to alcohol. Other recommended love stories with interesting historical settings are Mollie Hunter's *Hold On to Love,* the romantic sequel to *A Sound of Chariots,* and Ilse Koehn's *Tilla,* which is set in postwar Germany.

The best books include the happy and the sad and even the plain old boring parts of love and commitment. Barbara Robinson tried to do this for young teens in *Temporary Times, Temporary Places.* It's the dual story of Janet whose summer crush is foiled by a case of poison ivy and Janet's Aunt May who comes home to recover from a broken heart. Robinson does a good job of presenting revealing details showing how relationships change but how what they have meant to individuals remains a part of their total life experience. Carolyn Cooney's *I'm Not Your Other Half* shows that while having a boyfriend is nice, it isn't all there is to life.

The Formula Romance

The runaway popularity of formula love-romances written especially for teenagers and published as original paperbacks was the big marketing surprise of the 1980s. In the late 1970s, Scholastic Book Club editors noticed that their best-selling books, especially in junior high, were those that treated boy/girl relationships. They decided to launch a clearly identifiable line of "squeaky clean" young love stories. They called the line Wildfire, and within the first year sold 1.8 million titles. Bantam soon followed with Sweet Dreams and Simon and Schuster with Silhouette First Love. Dell combed through its Yearling and Laurel Leaf reprints to pull out romances which could be packaged under a Young Love insignia. They then went on to create the Sorority Sisters series. Berkley came in with a Confidentially Yours Series and Archway with a Dream Girls and a Dawn of Love Series. The Harlequin company in Canada—the publishers who perhaps started the whole thing by selling paperback romances to the mothers of teenagers—created its own line of romances specifically for teenagers. And many of the American books are being sold to publishers in foreign countries for translation and distribution. Today there are probably fifty different series for teenagers.

These paperback formula romances are marketed through traditional school book clubs as well as through the mail and in bookstores, supermarkets, and drugstores. (See Chapter 11 for a fuller discussion.) Prices are less than the cost of a movie or about the same as that of a magazine, which makes them eligible for impulse buying. In some stores, potential readers literally stumble over the display racks which are set on the floor and clearly labeled "Young Adult." The covers grab attention with their appealing photos of the same models that appear in *Seventeen Magazine*. Pamela Pollack described them as "nineteen-year-olds who are a thirteen-year-old's ideal image of a sixteen-year-old."[7]

Told from the girl's point of view, formula romances most often feature girls 15, 16, or 17 years old with boyfriends who are slightly older. The target audience is supposedly girls between the ages of twelve and sixteen although some ten- and eleven-year-olds are also finding them. The typical setting is a small town or suburb. There is no explicit sex or profanity. As one editor told us, "If there are problems, they have to be normal ones—no drugs, no sex, no alcohol, no bad parents, etc."

The kinds of problems featured are wish-fulfilling ones that most girls dream of coping with. For example, in Jill Ross Klevin's *That's My Girl,* ice skater Becky has to fight off getting ulcers while worrying about the upcoming Nationals, her chance at making the Olympics. Her biggest worry is whether she will lose her boyfriend who feels ignored. Janet Quin-Harkin's *California Girl* has an almost identical plot except that Jennie is competing for the Olympics as a swimmer. In Rosemary Vernon's *The Popularity Plan,* Frannie is too shy to talk to boys but her friends draw up a plan in which she is assigned certain ways to relate to a boy each day. Sure enough, she is soon asked for so many dates she has to buy a wall calendar to keep from getting mixed up. But by the end of the story she is happy to "give it all up" and settle for Ronnie, the boy she really liked all along.

Formula romances have many of the same qualities that publishers have developed for high interest/low vocabulary books. They are short books divided into short chapters. They have quick beginnings, more action than description, considerable use of dialogue, a straightforward point of view, and a reading level not much above fifth grade. And perhaps most important of all, the books are clearly labeled so that readers know what they will be getting. As shown by the popularity of movie sequels, television serials and reruns, and continuing columns in newspapers, although viewers and readers do not want to see or read the exact same thing over and over again, they are nevertheless comforted by knowing that a particular piece is going to be very similar to something they have previously enjoyed.

In recent years, *School Library Journal,* which prides itself on reviewing every book published for young readers, was swamped with so many romances that it set up a new section, "Paperback Romance Series Roundup" in which a single reviewer would be sent all the books published over several months. The reviews consisted mostly of plot summaries, but to save space and also relieve the boredom of making the same kinds of evaluative statements over and over, the editors used a set of metaphors to communicate good, medium, and bad. One month the best books appeared under the heading "Prime Rib." The middle set was labeled "Hamburger," and the poorly done ones "Turkey Franks." In other months it was "Nikon, Sure Shot, and Instamatic"; "Grape-nuts, Oatmeal, and Gruel"; "Pure-Bred Afghan, Cock-a-Poo, and Mongrel"; "Fireworks, Sparks, and Duds"; and "100 Watts, 60 Watts, and Refrigerator Bulbs." The editors could probably go on forever making up such metaphors, but let's hope that the popularity of the romances has peaked and reviewers as well as librarians and teachers can go back to evaluating books one at a time instead of by the basketful.

Some adults worry that teenage readers take the books seriously, that they fail to recognize them as fantasy, and that they therefore model their behavior and attitudes—and, more importantly, their expectations—after those portrayed in the romances. As one of our students wrote in her reading autobiography:

> Today when I read a romance, I just shake my head. Men do not ever act that way or say those things. I think teens should be exposed to some reading that is more realistic so they have some idea what to expect. I never knew what quite to expect. That was why I was so hurt by my first boyfriends and why I hurt them so bad.

A sampling of published quotations from critics illustrates a wider range of concern:

> The real power of the Wildfire books is that they purport to depict the real lives and problems of U.S. teenagers. Playing on the insecurities and self-doubt which plague most teenaged girls, the Wildfire romances come just close enough to real life to be convincing to young readers. But implicit in these hygienic stories are the old, damaging and limiting stereotypes from which we've struggled so hard to free ourselves and our children: that the real world is white and middle-class; that motherhood is women's only work; that a man is the ultimate prize and a woman is incomplete without one;

and that in the battle for that prize, the weapons are good looks and charm, intelligence is a liability, and the enemy is other women.[8]

■   Absence is, in fact, at the heart of the criticism of these books. Third World people are absent, disabled people are absent, lesbians and gay men are absent, poor people are absent, elderly people are absent. . . .[9]

■   There is an eternal paradox here. We read such romantic stories as an escape from reality and yet they form our ideals of what reality should be. Hence that frustration, that vague sense of failure and disappointment when a night out at the disco doesn't turn out the way it does in the magazines.[10]

Although the formula romances have been promoted as "squeaky clean" and as an antidote to depressing problem novels, in reality many of them rely for their appeal on sexual titillation. A few years back when we asked an editor about the white, see-through leotard that showed the skater's nipples on the cover of Jill Ross Klevin's *That's My Girl,* she blamed "the accident" on the bright lights necessary for a good photo. But a year later, the paperback cover of Bonnie and Paul Zindel's *A Star for the Latecomer* featured a young dancer whose nipples were also showing through a white leotard. Since this almost identical cover was a painting instead of a photograph, it could hardly have been an oversight. And we don't need Wilson Bryan Key, author of *Subliminal Seduction,* to identify the forbidden nature of such titles as *On Thin Ice, Against the Rules, Coming on Strong, Stolen Kisses, Playing House,* and *Anything to Win* all reviewed in a single *SLJ* column.[11]

Defenders of the romances most often focus on their popularity and the fact that they are recreational reading freely chosen by young girls who would most likely be watching TV. Vermont Royster, writing in the *Wall Street Journal,* compared the romances to the reading of books his mother considered trash— Tom Swift, the Rover Boys, Detective Nick Carter, and Wild Bill Hickok. He acknowledged that the plotting was banal and monotonous and that writers could probably turn them out wholesale, but at least, "The spelling is correct and they do manage mostly to abide by the rules of English grammar." He welcomed the books as an aid in helping a generation of television-oriented kids acquire the habit of reading. Once they are hooked, "Call it an addiction if you will . . . young people can be led by good teachers to enlarge their reach."[12]

Teachers and librarians need to be especially careful in criticizing students' enjoyment of romances because young readers are as sensitive as anyone else to hints that they are gullible and lacking in taste and sophistication. So rather than making fun of love romances, it is better to approach them from a positive angle, offering readers a wide variety of books including ones that treat boy/ girl relationships not as the only thing of importance, but as part of a bigger picture.

The Cyclical Effects of the Success of the Formula Romances

During the 1980s, the financial success of the teenage formula romances undoubtedly influenced not only marketing practices, but also the decisions made by editors, authors, and publishers. *Love* became a popular word in book titles, even in books by authors well established prior to the popularity of the romances, for example, *A Little Love* by Virginia Hamilton, *Him, She Loves?* by M. E. Kerr, *Fat: A Love Story* by Barbara Wersba, *Love & Kisses* (a poetry collection) by Lee Bennett Hopkins, *Risking Love* by Doris Orgel, and *Motown and Didi: A Love Story* by Walter Dean Myers. Mollie Hunter's sequel to *A Sound of Chariots* was entitled *The Dragonfly Years* when it was published in England, but in the United States it was given the more romantic title *Hold On to Love*.

Writers of romances whose names hadn't appeared with new books for decades were brought back in hopes that they could repeat the success they had enjoyed years ago. The most notable example was Maureen Daly, author

Even when the same company publishes both the hardcover and the paperback editions of a title, as when Harper & Row did Sue Ellen Bridgers' *Permanent Connections*, the paperback cover will more likely focus on the story's boy-girl relationship.

of the 1942 *Seventeenth Summer* (see Chapter 15). Scholastic published her *Acts of Love* in 1986. In reviewing the book, Marjorie Kaiser wrote that in the new book, Daly was presenting "essentially the same story and themes she did more than 40 years ago. . . . Sadly, we're not the same readers we were then, adolescent girls hungry for stories which featured characters our own age who yearned for love and romance and believed that everything was possible if only we found the right man."[13]

Forty-one years after Betty Cavanna published *Going on Sixteen,* Morrow published Cavanna's *Banner Year.* In reviewing it, Virginia Monseau described Cavanna's story as "in many ways a typical love-romance." However, in keeping up with changing times Cavanna attempted to "cast Cindy in a liberated light." Cindy and Tad are racing down the beach, and "not because it was expected of her, but because Tad's legs were longer and faster, Cindy lost."[14]

A convention borrowed from the romances and now appearing in a much wider range of books is the glossing over of the part that sex plays in male/female relationships. In the romances, it's love at first sight, which must imply a physical attraction, that is, a sexual attraction, yet the boys in many of the stories are portrayed as being almost platonically interested in the girl's thoughts and feelings rather than her body. When Rainbow Jordan, the protagonist in Alice Childress' realistic book of the same name, learned that this wasn't the way it was in real life, she complained:

True love is mostly featured in fairy tales. Sleepin' Beauty put off sex for a hundred years. When a prince finally did find her . . . he kiss her gently, then they gallop off on a pretty horse so they could enjoy the happy-ever-after. They never mentioned sex.

In their pseudo-attempt to be "squeaky clean," many of the formula romances encourage a kind of wish fulfillment that relates to the psychological ambivalence that many young females feel about sexuality. On the one hand, they want to be loved, not just because of the glamour and excitement of dating and courtship. But on the other hand, many of them are not yet ready for a sexual relationship and would be happy to have the dating and the cuddling without the complications of sex.

Barbara Wersba's *Fat: A Love Story* is a perfect illustration of how this kind of wish-fulfillment has found its way into mainstream YA literature. (We are defining "mainstream" as a well-designed and publicized hardback book written by a noted author and released by a prestige publisher.) In Wersba's book, 16-year-old overweight Rita gets a part-time job delivering cheesecakes for 32-year-old Arnold Bromberg. She is a virgin; he isn't. She thinks she's in love with the wealthy and handsome Robert and that her friend Nicole is going to help her catch Robert. But instead, Nicole and Robert run off together, and in the last 20 pages of the book Rita is left to fall in love with Mr. Bromberg.

When she tells him that she loves him "as a man," he is astonished because he loves her too, "passionately and deeply":

> I caught my breath with surprise, and then Arnold was kneeling by my chair. He took my face in his hands and kissed me—and I realized that a miracle was happening. Because the kiss that Arnold was giving me was a totally new thing. It was gentle and caring, with an element of restraint in it, but underneath there was a volcano raging.

Rita sleeps on Mr. Bromberg's couch, he teaches her to drive his car, they adopt two kittens, he buys her new clothes, he consoles her about her best friend's betrayal, counsels her about why she overeats, and plans and cooks their food so that she loses two pounds a week. During all of this, he insists that he won't have sex with her until she is eighteen.

> Oh, we made love at every possible opportunity, but it never ended in the bedroom. It ended in the kitchen—with us having a cup of tea. We loved each other, we were committed to each other, but Arnold would not take that final step.

Of course there is a happy ending. On Christmas Eve Rita gets Arnold to the church where she performs a pretend wedding ceremony complete with dime-store rings so that at last they can sleep together. On Christmas morning, Rita wakes up and looks at Arnold and sees her present and her past and also her future. She sees herself thin and grown up and married to Arnold for the rest of her life.

In the old days when realism was the undisputed king of YA books, such an unlikely plot would never have gotten past the desk of a literary agent, much less an editor, and on into the bookstores with two sequels: *Love Is the Crooked Thing* and *Beautiful Losers*.

In spite of the reservations that we have expressed about the popularity of the formula romances overwhelming and changing the rest of young adult literature, we will conclude by saying that both the accomplishment and adventure-romance and the love-romance are psychologically satisfying stories. More than any other genre, these stories are matched to the particular stage of life that is young adulthood. They are optimistic and wish-fulfilling, and their basic pattern resembles the real-life activities of young people who are moving from childhood into adulthood. Romances incorporate the successful completion of a quest in which the protagonist is elevated in status. But usually more important than the respect earned from others is the feeling of self-respect and self-confidence that the young hero gains in the course of the story. All of these things work together to ensure that the books treated in this chapter will be among the most popular in the young adult section of any library.

■ NOTES

[1]Glenna Davis Sloan, *The Child as Critic* (New York: Teachers College Press, 1975), p. 33.

[2]Dean Hughes, "Bait/Rebait: Books with Religious Themes," *English Journal* 70 (December 1981): 14–17.

[3]Kathy Piehl, "Bait/Rebait: Books with Religious Themes," *English Journal* 70 (December 1981): 14–17.

[4]Patty Campbell, "The Young Adult Perplex," *Wilson Library Bulletin* 56 (April 1982): 612–13, 638.

[5]Robert Unsworth, "Holden Caulfield, Where Are You?" *School Library Journal* 23 (January 1977): 40–41.

[6]Hazel Rochman, "Bringing Boys' Books Home," *School Library Journal* 29 (August 1983): 26–27.

[7]Pamela D. Pollack, "The Business of Popularity: The Surge of Teenage Paperbacks," *School Library Journal* 28 (November 1981): 28.

[8]Brett Harvey, "Wildfire: Tame but Deadly," *Interracial Books for Children Bulletin* 12 (1981).

[9]Sharon Wigutoff, "First Love: Morality Tales Thinly Veiled," *Interracial Books for Children Bulletin* 12:4 and 12:5 (1981): 17.

[10]Mary Harron, "Oh Boy! My Guy," (London) *Times Educational Supplement* (July 1, 1983), p. 22.

[11]Kathy Fritts, "Paperback Romance Series Roundup," *School Library Journal* 33 (January 1987): 86–88.

[12]Vermont Royster, "Thinking Things Over: The Reading Addiction," *Wall Street Journal* (June 24, 1981), p. 30.

[13]Marjorie Kaiser, Review of *Acts of Love, The ALAN Review* 14 (Fall 1986).

[14]Virginia Monseau, Review of *Banner Year, The ALAN Review* 15 (Fall 1987).

■ 30 RECOMMENDATIONS FOR READING

Accomplishment/Adventure Romances

Bridgers, Sue Ellen. *Permanent Connections.* Harper & Row, 1987. Rob and Ellery are both someplace they don't want to be, but by the end of the book they have a new respect for each other as well as for the little town in southern Appalachia where their families have brought them.

Crompton, Anne Eliot. *The Sorcerer.* Second Chance, 1982. As Crompton's book shows, healing is mental as much as physical.

Crutcher, Chris. *The Crazy Horse Electric Game.* Greenwillow, 1987. All those things that aren't supposed to happen to a nice, normal family do, and the misfortunes leave Willie Weaver to work out his own manner of healing.

Fleischman, Paul. *Rear-View Mirrors.* Harper, 1986. Seventeen-year-old Olivia Tate sets out on a commemorative bike trip in remembrance of the father she learned to love only a few months before his death.

George, Jean. *Julie of the Wolves.* Harper & Row, 1972. This Newbery Award-winning book is a plea for ecology as well as a story of wilderness survival by a young Eskimo girl.

Hall, Lynn. *The Solitary.* Scribners, 1986. At 17, Jane Cahill leaves the home of relatives where she feels like an intruder and sets out to become independent by raising rabbits.

Hamilton, Virginia. *M. C. Higgins, the Great.* Macmillan, 1974. M. C. doesn't leave his mountain home, but he nevertheless travels a road to maturity.

Lipsyte, Robert. *One Fat Summer.* Harper & Row, 1977. Bobby's story continues as he grows and develops in two sequels, *Summer Boy* and *Summer Rules.*

Mason, Bobbie Ann. *In Country.* Harper & Row, 1985. Sam's acceptance and partial understanding of her father's death comes through a trip that she takes with her uncle and her grandmother to the Vietnam War Memorial in Washington.

Mahy, Margaret. *The Catalogue of the Universe.* Macmillan, 1986. Angela's falling in love turns out to be more of a success than meeting her father for the first time.

Paulsen, Gary. *Dogsong.* Bradbury, 1985. Dreams and real life swirl together like heavy fog and steam rising from the ocean as Russel, an Eskimo boy, gets ready for his future.

Savage, Deborah. *A Rumour of Otters.* Houghton Mifflin, 1986. A brother and sister each come of age in this New Zealand story of wilderness survival and family relationships.

Voigt, Cynthia. *Izzy, Willy-Nilly.* Atheneum, 1986. Isobel learns a new kind of balance after she loses her leg as a result of an automobile accident.

——————. *Sons from Afar.* Atheneum, 1987. In this continuation of the story of the Tillermans from *Homecoming* and *Dicey's Song,* brothers James and Sammy go looking for the father they never knew.

Accomplishment Stories with Religious Themes

Arrick, Fran. *God's Radar.* Bradbury, 1983. Roxie Cable and her family move to a small southern town and are faced with taking a new look at religion.

Craven, Margaret. *I Heard the Owl Call My Name.* Doubleday, 1973. A young vicar who is dying but doesn't know it serves his last two years with a remote Indian tribe in British Columbia.

Howe, Norma. *God, the Universe, and Hot Fudge Sundaes.* Houghton Mifflin, 1984. Alfie learns that it's easier to face family problems and sadness when you have someone to love.

Kerr, M. E. *Is That You, Miss Blue?* Harper & Row, 1975. Girls at a church-sponsored boarding school conspire to soften the blow for a teacher who is fired because her faith is unsettling to other faculty members.

——————. *What I Really Think of You.* Harper & Row, 1982. The daughter of a small-town pentecostal preacher and the son of a big-time television evangelist explore what they have in common.

Naylor, Phyllis Reynolds. *A String of Chances.* Atheneum, 1982. When a new baby dies, 16-year-old Evie faces some tough questions.

Potok, Chaim. *The Chosen.* Simon and Schuster, 1967. Potok's books including *My Name Is Asher Lev, In the Beginning,* and *Davita's Harp* explore what it means to be Jewish.

Rylant, Cynthia. *A Fine White Dust.* Bradbury, 1986. Pete's religious, his best friend isn't, but that doesn't stop them from helping each other out.

Love and Friendship Romances

Baldwin, James. *If Beale Street Could Talk.* Doubleday, 1974. In this mature story told in frank, black English, pregnant Tish loves Fonny who has been jailed on a false charge.

Blume, Judy. *Forever.* Bradbury, 1975. Katherine and Michael have sexual intercourse, and while nobody gets punished their love does not last forever.

Cooney, Caroline B. *I'm Not Your Other Half.* Pacer/Putnam, 1984. In this original paperback romance, the heroine decides she has to do something to keep her personality from being totally absorbed into that of her boyfriend's.

Cormier, Robert. *The Bumblebee Flies Anyway.* Pantheon, 1974. The grim setting of an experimental hospital treating young adults with terminal illnesses is made more bearable by the tender love story that provides a secondary theme.

Daly, Maureen. *Seventeenth Summer.* Dodd, Mead, 1942. Daly's book, a classic in the popular culture sense of being read by generations, makes for interesting comparisons with contemporary teenage romances.

✓ Hamilton, Virginia. *A Little Love.* Philomel, 1984. In this combination love story and romantic quest, Sheena and her boyfriend Forrest set out to look for Sheena's father.

Mazer, Harry. *Hey, Kid! Does She Love Me?* Crowell, 1984. Eighteen-year-old Jeff finds that when the girl he had a crush on in high school comes back to town with a baby, he's still infatuated.

Peck, Richard. *Close Enough to Touch.* Delacorte, 1981. Matt is devastated when his first girlfriend dies but then he meets someone who shows him that life goes on.

■ OTHER TITLES MENTIONED IN CHAPTER FOUR

Arrick, Fran. *Tunnel Vision.* Bradbury, 1980.
——————. *Steffie Can't Come Out to Play.* Bradbury, 1978.

Barrett, William. *Lilies of the Field.* Doubleday, 1962.

Benton, John. *Carmen.* Revell, 1974.
——————. *Debbie.* Revell, 1980.
——————. *Sheila.* Revell, 1982.

Blume, Judy. *Are You There God? It's Me, Margaret.* Bradbury, 1973.
——————. *Then Again Maybe I Won't.* Bradbury, 1971.

Boone, Debby, with Dennis Baker. *Debby Boone So Far.* Jove, 1982.

Brancato, Robin. *Blinded by the Light.* Knopf, 1978.

Brooks, Bruce. *Midnight Hour Encores.* Harper & Row, 1986.
——————. *The Moves Make the Man.* Harper & Row, 1984.

Cavanna, Betty. *Banner Year.* Morrow, 1987.
——————. *Going on Sixteen.* Ryerson, 1946.

Childress, Alice. *Rainbow Jordan.* Putnam, 1981.

Conrad, Pam. *What I Did for Roman.* Harper & Row, 1987.

Cooper, M. E. *Coming on Strong.* Scholastic, 1986.

Cormier, Robert. *The Chocolate War.* Pantheon, 1974.

Crutcher, Chris. *Running Loose.* Greenwillow, 1983.

Cunningham, Glen. *Never Quit.* Chosen Books/ Zondervan, 1981.

Daly, Maureen. *Acts of Love.* Scholastic, 1986.

Davis, Terry. *Vision Quest.* Viking, 1979.

Douglas, Lloyd. *The Robe.* Houghton Mifflin, 1942.

Eareckson, Joni, and Joe Musser. *Joni.* Zondervan, 1976.

Goudge, Eileen. *Against the Rules.* Dell, 1986.

Green, Hannah. *I Never Promised You a Rose Garden.* Holt, Rinehart and Winston, 1964.

Guest, Judith. *Ordinary People.* Viking, 1976.

Hopkins, Lee Bennett, comp. *Love & Kisses.* Houghton Mifflin, 1984.

Hunter, Mollie. *A Sound of Chariots.* Harper & Row, 1982.
——————. *Hold On to Love.* Harper & Row, 1984.

Jacobs, Barbara. *Stolen Kisses.* Dell, 1986.

Joyce, Rosemary. *Anything to Win.* Archway, 1986.

Kerr, M. E. *Him She Loves?* Harper & Row, 1984.
——————. *I'll Love You When You're More Like Me.* Harper & Row, 1977.

Key, Wilson Bryan. *Subliminal Seduction.* NAL Penguin, 1974.

Klevin, Jill Ross. *That's My Girl.* Scholastic, 1981.

Koehn, Ilse. *Tilla.* Greenwillow, 1981.

Le Guin, Ursula K. *Very Far Away from Anywhere Else.* Atheneum, 1976.

Lee, Mildred. *Fog*. Houghton Mifflin, 1972.
_____ . *The People Therein*. Houghton Mifflin, 1980.
Lehrman, Robert. *Juggling*. Harper & Row, 1982.
Levoy, Myron. *Alan and Naomi*. Harper & Row, 1977.
Lipsyte, Robert. *Jock & Jill*. Harper & Row, 1982.
Lyle, Katie Letcher. *Dark But Full of Diamonds*. Putnam, 1981.
_____ . *Fair Day and Another Step Begun*. Lippincott, 1974.
Marshall, Catherine. *A Man Called Peter*. McGraw-Hill, 1951.
Mazer, Harry. *I Love You Stupid!* Harper & Row, 1981.
_____ . *The Girl of His Dreams*. Harper & Row, 1987.
_____ . *The War on Villa Street*. Delacorte, 1978.
Miklowitz, Gloria. *The Love Bombers*. Delacorte, 1980.
Moser, Don. *A Heart to the Hawks*. Atheneum, 1975.
Myers, Walter Dean. *Motown and Didi: A Love Story*. Viking, 1984.
O'Dell, Scott. *The Hawk That Dare Not Hunt by Day*. Houghton Mifflin, 1975.
Orgel, Doris. *Risking Love*. Dial, 1984.
Paterson, Katherine. *Bridge to Terabithia*. Crowell, 1977.
_____ . *Jacob Have I Loved*. Crowell, 1980.
_____ . *Rebels of the Heavenly Kingdom*. Lodestar, 1983.
Peck, Richard. *Father Figure*. Viking, 1978.
Potok, Chaim. *In the Beginning*. Knopf, 1975.

Quin-Harkin, Janet. *California Girl*. Bantam, 1981.
Robinson, Barbara. *Temporary Times, Temporary Places*. Harper & Row, 1982.
Saal, Jocelyn, and Margaret Burman. *On Thin Ice*. Bantam, 1983.
Salinger, J. D. *The Catcher in the Rye*. Little, Brown, 1951.
Simon, Jean. *Playing House*. Silhouette, 1986.
Singer, Marilyn. *The Course of True Love Never Did Run Smooth*. Harper & Row, 1983.
Slepian, Jan. *The Alfred Summer*. Macmillan, 1980.
Speare, Elizabeth George. *Bronze Bow*. Houghton Mifflin, 1973.
Strasser, Todd. *Workin' for Peanuts*. Delacorte, 1983.
Thomas, Joyce Carol. *Bright Shadow*. Avon, 1983.
Tolkien, J. R. R. *The Lord of the Rings*. Houghton Mifflin, 1974.
Vernon, Rosemary. *The Popularity Plan*. Bantam, 1981.
Wersba, Barbara. *Beautiful Losers*. Harper & Row, 1988.
_____ . *Love Is the Crooked Thing*. Harper & Row, 1987.
_____ . *Fat: A Love Story*. Harper & Row, 1987.
West, Jessamyn. *Friendly Persuasion*. Harcourt Brace Jovanovich, 1956.
_____ . *The Massacre at Fall Creek*. Harcourt Brace Jovanovich, 1975.
Yep, Laurence. *Sea Glass*. Harper & Row, 1979.
Zindel, Paul & Bonnie. *A Star for the Latecomer*. Harper & Row, 1980.
Zindel, Paul. *The Pigman*. Harper & Row, 1968.

For information on the availability of paperback editions of these titles, please consult the most recent edition of *Paperbound Books in Print,* published annually by R. R. Bowker Company.

EXCITEMENT AND SUSPENSE
Of Sudden Shadows

Something within us does not love our quiet lives. Something within us demands vicarious thrills, suspense, danger, the unknown. When we are young, we love to frighten others with stories of bogeymen, murderers, and spooks, anything to make friends' blood chill and hands sweat. Tales of horror, danger, and mystery allow us the delicious luxury of knowing fear without living it.

As we grow older, our need for vicarious danger hardly lessens, though we pretend that it becomes more sophisticated. Instead of simple tales, we read the latest thriller by Stephen King to learn again the eternal fear of the unknown. We read a historical novel by Rosemary Sutcliff to learn the dangers of living in Roman Britain. We read a new mystery by P. D. James to remind us that in the midst of life there is death.

We go to amusement parks, not to sit sedately on a merry-go-round but to head for the latest thrill-a-minute, guaranteed-to-cause-a-heart-attack ride. We go to car races knowing that danger and death are always present. We stay up till the wee hours to watch a favorite old horror film and feel cheated if nothing terrifies us. We watch reruns of old movies like Charles Laughton's *The Night of the Hunter* (1955), Jules Dassin's *Topkapi,* and almost anything by the master of suspense, Alfred Hitchcock: *The Thirty-Nine Steps* (1935), *The Lady Vanishes* (1938), *Strangers on a Train* (1951), or *North by Northwest* (1959). And if we needed proof that contemporary Americans love to feel danger, the popularity of the 1978 film *Halloween* and its ilk and that finest of modern pure adventure films, the 1981 *Raiders of the Lost Ark,* should dispel doubts.

Why are we so eager to be in the midst of danger? Why do we need to feel fear? Perhaps it is because our lives are so mundane and uneventful and dull that vicarious danger is all we will ever know. Perhaps we fear death so much that we need to tempt and cheat it for the moment. Certainly, every culture has its folktales and stories well-calculated to make goosebumps rise and bad children behave—tales embodying terror, mystery, death, the unknown, the impossible, the deadly—in short, all that we fear. Perhaps adventure stories allow us a catharsis, if not an Aristotelian purging of emotions, at least a purging of primeval fears, of monsters and enemies we might eons ago have faced in bloody battle. Denied those outlets today, we gladly pay others to provide them for our reading and viewing pleasure.

In tales of adventure and stories from the past, we can revel in times and places when evil was evil, good was good, and each was easily distinguishable. Such stories allow us to believe that humanity will not merely survive but that our courage makes us worthy of surviving.

ADVENTURE STORIES

"Once upon a time" are magic words. Stated directly or implied, they open every adventure tale and suggest action and excitement to follow. We may care about the people, but the action and violence are all-important. And the greatest of these is implied violence, things we fear may happen. Pace and tempo force action to move faster and faster and speed us into the tale.

The most common of all stories of pure adventure, largely devoid of characterization, pits one human against another. Richard Connell's "The Most Dangerous Game," perhaps *the* classic adventure short story, reduces the cast of characters to two people, the big game hunter Sanger Rainsford and General Zaroff, in a simple setting, an apparently deserted island with an evil reputation. Before he is accidently cast ashore on the island, Rainsford and a friend talk about the nature of hunting and debate whether an animal can feel fear and impending death. Rainsford says, "Be a realist. The world is made up of two classes—the hunter and the huntee," words he will soon regret. When he meets the apparently highly civilized Zaroff, Rainsford soon learns that Zaroff is a hunter gone sour and mad through lack of game worth hunting. He lives only "for danger." Once Zaroff implies that only one animal—a human—is worth hunting, few readers can stop reading.

The better adventure stories demand more than mere excitement and action (see Table 5.1). Writers must provide believable characters, at the very least a likable and imperfect (and young) protagonist and a wily and dangerous antagonist (or villain). But because we are primarily interested in action, we are likely to be irritated by the intrusion of long descriptive or meditative passages. Writers must reveal characterization through the plot—what could happen, what might happen, and how do all these tie together?

We want surprises and turns of the screw. Heroes become entrapped, and the way to safety lies only through greater jeopardy. Of the three basic conflicts, adventure tales will usually center on person against person, though person against nature and person against self will often become important as the tale unfolds and the protagonist faces frustration and possible failure.

Table 5.1   **SUGGESTIONS FOR EVALUATING ADVENTURE STORIES**

A good adventure story has most of the positive qualities generally associated with good fiction. In addition it usually has:	**A poor adventure story may have the negative qualities generally associated with poor fiction. It is particularly prone to have:**
A likable protagonist with whom young readers can identify.	A protagonist who is too exaggerated or too stereotyped to be believable.
An adventure that readers can imagine happening to themselves.	Nothing really exciting about the adventure.
Efficient characterization.	Only stereotyped characters.
An interesting setting that enhances the story without getting in the way of the plot.	A long drawn-out conclusion after the climax has been reached.
Action that draws readers into the plot within the first page or so of the story.	

The most significant literary device found in adventure stories is verisimilitude. With so much emphasis on danger, writers must provide realistic details galore to reassure us, despite our inner misgivings, that the tale is possible. We want to believe that the hero's frustrations and the cliffhanging episodes really could have happened. Without that, the story is a cheat, and that we cannot tolerate, no matter how we try.

A love interest is possible but unlikely. Perhaps there is a love left behind, but none during the tribulations. A girl and boy may flee together, and sex is possible—some writers would have us believe that sex is inevitable—but only as a momentary diversion.

Robb White's *Deathwatch* epitomizes the elements of adventure novels—person versus person, person versus nature, person versus self, conflicts, tension, thrills, chills, a hero frustrated at every turn by an inventive, devious, and cruel villain.

The first paragraph forces us into the action and introduces the two actors:

> "There he is!" Madec whispered. "Keep still!" There had been a movement up on the ridge of the mountain. For a moment something had appeared between the two rock outcrops.
> "I didn't see any horns," Ben said.
> "Keep quiet!" Madec whispered fiercely.

We know from those few words that *Deathwatch* has something to do with hunting, though we have no reason yet to believe that hunting will become an ominous metaphor. We recognize that the name *Madec* has a harsh sound and that it seems vaguely related to the word *mad,* again without recognizing how prescient we are. Within the next few pages, we learn how carefully White has placed the clues before us. Ben crouches with his little .22 Hornet and watches

Madec with his "beautifully made .358 Magnum Mauser action on a Winchester 70 stock with enough power to knock down an elephant—or turn a sleeping Gila monster into a splatter" and remembers that Madec had been willing to shoot anything that moved.

> Madec huddled over his gun. There was an intensity in his eyes far beyond that of just hunting a sheep. It was the look of murder.

And murder is there. Before long, Madec takes a shot at a bighorn sheep, which turns out to be an old desert prospector—now quite dead—and he asks Ben to quash the incident and forget it ever happened. Ben refuses, and the book is off and running. So is Ben, running for his life, without gun, water, or food, amid hostile desert mountains and sand and a killing gun.

Madec personifies the maddened but crafty villain, able to read Ben's mind and forestall his attempts to get clothes or weapons or water. We are almost certain Ben will win but we wonder, for Madec is a worthy opponent. And at each of Madec's devious turns to stop Ben from escape, we doubt that sanity and the right will win, just as we should in a good adventure novel. Ben changes from a calm and rational young man to a frightened, desperate animal and then to a cold and dangerous person who must think as Madec thinks to win out over the villain. Madec begins with all the power on his side—guns, water, food, and wealth. Given reality, we know what Madec must win, but given our sense of rightness and justice, he cannot be allowed to win. Ben has little interest in right or wrong after the first few pages. His interest is more elemental and believable, simple survival until he can escape.

Many adventure stories focus on person versus nature. Harry Mazer's *Snow Bound* shows us two young people caught in a blizzard who survive despite cold, wild dogs, and no food. How they change makes a fine story despite poor characterization.

Far better is Mazer's *The Island Keeper;* Cleo Murphy is an overweight sixteen-year-old who wilfully decides to run away from her unhappy home and return to her father's isolated island in Canada. She discovers that the cabin she had assumed would shelter her has burned down, and when the lovely weather turns miserable, Cleo learns that she must find shelter and she must learn to kill if she is to survive:

> "What do I do now?" she cried out. Then she listened, as if someone would answer. She heard the wind and water—nothing else. The island didn't care. It wouldn't cheer if she struggled. It wouldn't cry if she lost. The island was indifferent to her tears and cries. It had always been indifferent to her, to her self-pity and self-loathing, to the masks and disguises she hid behind; indifferent, too, to her conceit that she was herself at last, one with nature. All vanity, foolishness, stupidity. She was alone, isolated, and forgotten, with no expectations except the one nature forced on her.

She knows that the doe she had so admired must die if she is to live. And she learns how to live.

█   The deer was standing directly over the snare. Cleo leaned forward. The sapling whipped into the air. The deer recoiled, one of its hind legs caught by the rope. Cleo darted forward. The deer leaped up. A hoof caught Cleo in the shoulder as she drove the knife into its body. The animal cried out. She drove the knife in again. The deer grunted, sighed quietly, died. Cleo looked around. She was acutely aware of every single thing, of the silence, of her aloneness. The two other deer had disappeared. She shuddered. A black smear spread across the velvet fur.

One of the most intriguing adventure stories of recent years is Julian F. Thompson's *The Grounding of Group Six*. A group of admittedly misfit teenagers, despised by their parents who have paid to have them killed, survive this very special school. Thompson's novel works because he makes us care about these young people, because the novel is genuinely thrilling, and mostly because Thompson has a delightful, and sometimes morbid, sense of humor and the book is often extraordinarily funny.

Also recent but quite different in most ways—save that both are often funny—is Philip Pullman's *The Ruby in the Smoke*. In late Victorian London, orphaned but spunky Sally Lockhart searches for clues to her father's death and a mysterious lost ruby while evil old women and pirates and opium dealers thwart Sally at every turn. Pullman promises more than he can deliver in one novel, but the excitement and the good humor deliver more than most first novels. Sally reappears in *Shadow in the North*.

Spy thrillers have, for years, been among the most popular adventure books. John Buchan's *The Thirty-Nine Steps* and *Greenmantle* are still readable, if more than a bit exaggerated, the first particularly because of Alfred Hitchcock's screen version. The realistic novels of John le Carré (whose real name is David John Moore Cornwell) may move believably, sometimes too slowly so, but his spies move and act and think the way real spies do—or should do. The world of George Smiley, le Carré's chief spy who binds a number of books together, is rarely happy or settled, but it is a world in which people rarely are what they seem to be and betrayal and danger are facts of life.

Most amusing, if possibly a bit less believable, are William F. Buckley's Blackford Oates spy thrillers. *Operation Mongoose, R.I.P.* is the most recent Oates vehicle, the eighth in the series, and this tale of treachery and Fidel Castro and President Kennedy mixes Buckley's gentle (and not so gentle) spoofing of the political left-wing. Whatever one thinks of Buckley's politics, he can spin a tale with the best of them.

For those who really care about spy thrillers, nonfiction has had special appeal in the last few years. The British version of the FBI, the MI-5, has had problems keeping secrets secret, what with the departure of Kim Philby and Guy Burgess and Donald Maclean over the years, but even more embarrassment came with the publication in 1987 of Peter Wright's *Spycatcher: The*

Candid Autobiography of a Senior Intelligence Officer. The British government prevented its publication in Great Britain and tried desperately, and unsuccessfully, to prevent publication in Australia and the United States. In the same way that Wright irritated officials in Great Britain, the publication of Howard Blum's *I Pledge Allegiance . . . The True Story of the Walkers* humiliated and worried U.S. officials. Blum's account of a family led by a retired Navy chief warrant officer (and followed by three others) who passed on vital secrets to the Russians is no great literary gem, but it is disturbing and it is about reality, and that may depress a great many readers.

Mountains have figured in a number of adventure stories, real and fictional. The abiding fascination with mountains has been part of our lives for centuries, and William Blake's lines from "Gnomic Verses" aptly describes their appeal:

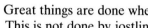
   Great things are done when men and mountains meet;
   This is not done by jostling in the street.

True accounts of mountain climbing differ slightly from the usual person versus nature story. People go forth to seek adventure, to challenge nature, and to find themselves. Few acts of courage (or foolhardiness) appeal more to young adults. Why does the climber go on against snow, ice, rocks, cold, uncertainty, and loneliness? The classic answer, "Because it's there," is enough for most climbers, though they might add, somewhat self-consciously, "Because I am there, too, the real me."

While Maurice Herzog's *Annapurna: First Conquest of an 8000 Meter Peak* was, for many readers, their first book on mountain climbing, even better books are easily found today, good as Herzog's book still is. Chris Bonington's several books about adventure and the world of mountains and snow and danger are superb. And if the writing is distinguished, the many excellent photographs that accompany *The Everest Years: A Climber's Life, Everest: The Unclimbed Ridge,* and *Quest for Adventure* make the books even better. Most of us may never tackle the impossible world that faces Bonington or his peers, but we can live some of that world with books like these.

In *Clouds from Both Sides: An Autobiography,* Julie Tullis tried to explain why she climbed, why—with a husband and two children at home constantly worrying about her—she took on a world that threatened at every turn and every moment to send her to her death. This is how she answered that question:

   People are always asking why I climb. There is no short easy answer. It is a love, a great desire, a passion to be with the mountains, like a sailor feels for the sea. Mountains are all individuals, like people. Each one has its own character, shape, composition of terrain, vegetation, animal life, type of rock, steepness and mood. Every side of a mountain is different as well, and again, like people their moods can vary, particularly with the weather.

   There are many comparisons to be made between mountains and the human race. You often love them but you do not always have to like them, and I often have a love/hate relationship, particularly when struggling for survival. There are times when you are sad to leave them, but others when you are relieved, glad to be away from the inevitable sheer hard work of achieving the closeness necessary to get to know them. But in a short while, you long to be back and start dreaming, hoping, planning, scheming to make it possible.

Other books that try to answer that question in action but not words include Galen Rowell's *In the Throne Room of the Mountain Gods* and *Mountain Light: In Search of the Dynamic Landscape,* Arlene Blum's *Annapurna—A Woman's Place,* Tom Holzel and Audrey Salkeld's *First on Everest: The Mystery of Mallory and Irvine,* and Elaine Brook and Julie Donnelly's *The Windhorse.* The latter is genuinely different since Julie Donnelly has been blind since she was eight, and she convinced a friend, experienced mountaineer Elaine Brook who had climbed in the Himalayas, to teach her first how to rock climb in England and then to take on an 18,000-foot mountain in Nepal.

However, the best of the survival stories isn't about mountains at all. It's Steve Callahan's *Adrift: Seventy-Six Days Lost at Sea.* Callahan set out to sail, but instead watched his boat sink and then spent 76 days of hardship on a five-foot raft.

MYSTERIES

Daniel's detection of the guilty Elders in *The Story of Susanna* in the *Apocrypha* may be the world's first detective story, but the modern mystery begins with Edgar Allan Poe's "The Murders in the Rue Morgue," although the tale of detection in his later "The Purloined Letter" is certainly more satisfying. Dime Novel detectives soon appeared, notably Old King Brady, Old Sleuth, Young Sleuth, Cap Collier, and—best known of them all—Nick Carter. Surely the world's first great detective appeared in 1887 when Sherlock Holmes strode out of the pages of Arthur Conan Doyle's *A Study in Scarlet* accompanied by the ever-faithful and always befuddled Dr. Watson.

Holmes was soon followed by some almost as distinctive detectives. Jacques Futrelle's Professor S. F. X. Van Deusen *(The Thinking Machine)* and G. K. Chesterton's Father Brown in several collections of short stories, most notably *The Innocence of Father Brown,* which contains "The Secret Garden" and "The Blue Cross." And after Father Brown came the deluge.

Why are mysteries so popular? Basically they are unrealistic and have almost nothing to do with real-life detection by police or private agents as mystery writers cheerfully admit. They demand deep suspension of our disbelief yet the faithful gladly give it. Mysteries are mere games, but we love games. We hope, or so many of us claim, to beat the detective to the murderer, but we rarely do, and when it does happen, we feel cheated.

JOAN LOWERY NIXON
on the Novel with the Plus: YA Mysteries

I like the attitude the British take toward the mystery novel. In 1975, at the First International Crime Writers Congress in London, one of the speakers stated, "We have the highest respect for our British authors of crime novels. They have not only written good novels, they have been clever enough to put mysteries into them, too."

In the United States the opposite idea is prevalent. Perhaps we were brought up on too many Nancy Drew type stories in which the characters are stereotyped and their actions are often unrealistic, so that we think all mysteries fall into this category.

Or maybe we still have a hang-up left over from colonial days in which we believe that anything that provides a great deal of pleasure must be suspect; because many adults consider young adult mysteries to be fluff, certainly not in the class of "better books" to be read. Even in the adult book field, a mystery sells many more copies when it's marketed as mainstream fiction instead of as part of the mystery genre.

Granted, in the young adult mystery field a few potboilers can certainly be found, but many excellent mystery novels are published, and there are definite criteria which separate them.

In a good mystery novel the characters are handled with depth. I've heard authors speak of the writing process as one that is done with pen and blood; but it's not just our own blood we're using. It's the blood of our characters which blends with ours.

In a well-written mystery novel the storyline has two levels: There is the personal problem the main character faces, and there is the mystery which he, or she, must solve. These two factors are intertwined throughout the story. Some of the problems young people have today are tough ones. They can be presented realistically and with responsibility within the framework of the mystery novel, which is often more appealing to young readers than a straight "problem novel."

Just because mystery novels are consistently at the top of the popularity charts with young readers doesn't mean they should be lightly dismissed as nothing more than "fun reading." They should be thought of as what they are: They're well-written novels with a plus—and the plus is the mystery.

Joan Lowery Nixon's books include *The Other Side of Dark,* Delacorte, 1986; *Caught in the Act,* Bantam, 1988; and *The Dark and Deadly Pool,* Delacorte, 1987.

The characteristics of the traditional murder mystery are well known and relatively fixed. Devotees are more interested in variations on the theme than in violations of the rules, and variations are apparently endless.

There must be a crime. A short story may settle for blackmail or robbery, but a novel demands a murder; whatever lesser crimes the writer chooses to toss in are fine as long as there is at least one murder. The murder normally takes place after a few chapters introduce the characters, including the victim and those who might hope for his or her death. Soon after the murder, perhaps before, a detective enters, though he or she may not be a part of the official police force. Clues are scattered, the investigation proceeds, and the detective solves the case and explains the solution. The plot is an intricate interweaving of suspicion, motives, clues, red herrings, but the characters are often undeveloped stick-figures save in the best of the genre. The average reader of mysteries simply cares more about the puzzle than the people.

The hard-boiled mystery differs in significant ways. The detective is usually male. He is privately employed and has no altruistic motives. He enters the case for pay, not for love of the chase or the intellectual love of a puzzle. The traditional detective/solver of crimes is cheerful and optimistic, sometimes painfully so. Not so the private detective. Working out of a cheerless office and around even less cheerful people, he is tired and cynical, having seen too much of the seamy side of life to feel hope for anything. He often has a quiet dignity that he covers by wisecracks. He believes in justice, but he is not above going outside the law to do the job. He is cynical about the courts, the police, the system, class distinctions, and the establishment in general. The traditional detective is bright and sees what others fail to see. The private eye knows that detective work is hard and routine, and any bright person could find what he will find had he or she the patience. The traditional mystery may have some violence after the murder, but in the private eye's world, violence comes with the territory.

The quite arbitrary rules of the traditional mystery were itemized by Hillary Waugh:

Rule One: All clues discovered by the detective must be made available to the reader.

Rule Two: Early introduction of the murder.

Rule Three: The crime must be significant.

Rule Four: There must be detection.

Rule Five: The number of suspects must be known and the murderer must be among them.

Rule Six: Nothing extraneous must be introduced.[1]

The traditional, sometimes called the golden-age, mysteries flourished in the 1920s to the 1940s, and while some are dated, some still seem fresh and fun. Ellery Queen, who directly challenged readers after he laid out all the clues, was at his best in his 1932 *The Greek Coffin Mystery.* Agatha Christie, who began writing in the 1920s, scattered her best books throughout her life. Her 1939 *And Then There Were None* is her best book without a detective. Others include Christie's 1950 *A Murder Is Announced,* a Miss Marple book, and her 1968 *By the Pricking of My Thumbs* in which the usually tiresome Tommy and Tuppence Beresford stumble into a believable mystery. Some readers, of course, still hunger for the even more traditional tales of Arthur Conan Doyle's Sherlock Holmes or G. K. Chesterton's Father Brown.

Whether mysteries are better today may be open to debate, but the fact that hotels and ships and trains sponsor parties in which a mock murder takes place with actors playing parts and partygoers playing detectives shows that mystery and murder and suspense are still good entertainment. Some writers maintain popularity, year after year. For example, John D. MacDonald's twenty-first Travis McGee book, *The Lonely Silver Rain,* is no exception. P. D. James may be the most literate English writer of mysteries, and *A Taste for Death* shows James' power, though many readers would argue that *An Unsuitable Job for a Woman* is still James' best novel. Her study, with coauthor T. A. Critchley, *The Maul and the Pear Tree: The Ratcliffe Highway Murders 1811,* recreates a real case involving an apparently pointless triple murder. Ruth Rendell's books hold up well, and some have maintained that books like *Death Notes, Speaker of Mandarin, An Unkindness of Ravens,* and *Live Flesh* establish Rendell as the heir apparent to Christie's crown as the Queen of Mystery.

Other and newer writers have gained their share of the mystery-reading crowd. Robert Barnard's *Political Suicide* is a delightful portrait of a Scotland Yard Chief Inspector eager to retire and anything but eager to take on another murder case. Martha Grimes' *I Am the Only Running Footman,* like her other titles, comes from the name of an English pub, and for sheer delight in its setting and characters is hard to equal. Stuart Kaminsky's Toby Peters stories, tough private-eye thrillers set in 1930-40s Hollywood, can be delightful, particularly the first one, *Murder on the Yellow Brick Road,* in which a munchkin has been murdered on the set of *The Wizard of Oz.* Ellis Peters' series of Medieval England mysteries centering on Brother Cadfael can be sampled in the first one, *A Morbid Taste for Bones: The First Chronicle of Brother Cadfael.* Robert Parker's *Pale Kings and Princes* is one of several funny and literate mysteries about Spenser, private eye. R. D. Rosen's *Strike Three, You're Dead* is a wonderful and funny first novel set in major league baseball. And Scott Turow's *Presumed Innocent,* about the death of an ambitious deputy prosecutor and an ex-lover, who in the course of the book changes from investigator to suspect, was so popular that the paperback rights sold for a record $3 million.

Two mystery writers, Tony Hillerman and Dick Francis, deserve more than passing attention. Hillerman's Navajo police novels began in 1970 with *The Blessing Way* and officer Joe Leaphorn's detection while the villain uses Navajo religion to protect himself. The Indian lore and the religious aspects of the book are accurate, just as they are in later Hillerman novels—*The Dance Hall of the Dead, The Listening Woman, People of Darkness, The Dark Wind, The Ghostway,* and *Skinwalkers.* Joe Leaphorn and Jim Chee, Hillerman's detectives, have the best of two worlds, the Anglo and the Indian, just as they are often confused about who and what they are, although they always ultimately find they are Indian at the core. Hillerman respects and obviously admires his Navajo policemen, just as he does his readers. His books are sometimes mysteries, more often police procedurals with a mystery attached, but they always respect people with a particular way of life.

Dick Francis' many mysteries set in the world of horseracing, particularly steeplechase racing, combine the excitement of sports and the grubbiness of the hangers-on of racing with the cold analytical skill of detection. In *Hot Money,* Francis' twenty-sixth book, Ian Pembroke, amateur jockey and son of a rich man, tries to puzzle through who is trying to kill his father—and has already succeeded in killing his wife.

No one writes police procedural novels better than Ed McBain (real name, Evan Hunter). McBain's make-believe but very real world inhabited by police of the 87th precinct often centers on detective Steve Carella, but mostly it's about the plodding and dull grind of work that police officers go through trying to figure out who has done what to whom. *Poison: An 87th Precinct Novel* and *Cinderella,* a Matthew Hope mystery, are just two of McBain's most recent books, but they are all satisfying.

Joseph Wambaugh's *The Onion Field* and *The Glitter Dome* are straightforward and bloody police procedurals. Other writers working the area who deserve attention include James McClure for *The Steam Pig* and *The Artful Egg,* Jerry Oster for *Sweet Justice,* and Thomas Boyle for *Only the Dead Know Brooklyn.*

A few writers have developed such interesting characters that they are worth reading for that alone. Lillian de la Torre's (real name, Lillian Bueno McCue) delight in using Dr. Samuel Johnson, he of dictionary fame in eighteenth-century London, makes any of her short stories about Dr. Sam: Johnson great fun. Maybe more to the point, if some stories stretch the original tales, the stories begin in truth and did once involve Dr. Johnson. Robert Van Gulik's seventh-century Judge Dee did exist once, though doubtless as a somewhat less extraordinary detective, but whatever the truth, novels like *The Chinese Nail Murders* are much prized by many Van Gulik fans. Not historically true, save perhaps in spirit, Arthur W. Upfield's Australian Inspector Napoleon Bonaparte, a brilliant Aborigine tracker and thinker, is delightful to follow in any of his cases, notably *Death of a Lake.*

Two mystery writers have created amusing detectives who, unlike most of the kind, do not become instantaneous bores. Edmund Crispin's Gervase Fen, Oxford don and eccentric, is seen to best advantage in *The Long Divorce,* Crispin's most believable mystery, and *Buried for Pleasure* in which Crispin (real name, Bruce Montgomery) pokes fun at eccentric country characters and English politics. John Mortimer's series of hour-long television movies about a grubby old English lawyer was so popular that Mortimer charitably turned them into short stories, less mysterious generally than studies in English types but mysteries nonetheless. Rumpole is one of the great characters of our time.

In a field that is based on fictionalized fact, nonfiction usually gets little attention. Still, Sidney D. Kirkpatrick's *A Cast of Killers* ought to be fascinating for readers of mysteries or Hollywood scandal. The death of Hollywood director William Desmond Taylor in February 1922 was a major scandal even at a time when scandals were not all that rare, and the case ruined the careers of two actresses, May Miles Minter and Mabel Normand, the latter the most brilliant comedienne of her day. Edna Buchanan's autobiography of her life as a crime reporter, *The Corpse Had a Familiar Face: Covering Miami, America's Hottest*

Beat, may sound melodramatic, and no one could accuse the book of being quiet meditation, but Buchanan is widely respected for her journalism and Miami cops respect her. Besides, the stories she tells may sometimes be bloody but she tells them well.

A Philadelphia murder case in 1979 attracted two writers, Joseph Wambaugh and Loretta Schwartz-Nobel, who presented somewhat different focuses on the case of two educators who murdered a fellow teacher and her two children for sex and money. Wambaugh's *Echoes in the Darkness* and Schwartz-Nobel's *Engaged to Murder: The Inside Story of the Main Line Murders* are, despite their noisy titles, serious efforts to determine why the murders took place and what kind of people the killers were. Vain as the attempt proves to be, both books are readable and deserve reading, Schwartz-Nobel's particularly.

Of mysteries written for young adults, Jay Bennett's novels and Joan Lowery Nixon's novels stand out. Bennett's *Deathman, Do Not Follow Me,* his first book, began as a great, finely tuned, characterization of a loner, but the introduction of a mystery does little to help the book. Bennett's later books are both well-written character studies *and* pleasantly diverse mysteries. Nixon's *The Dark and Deadly Pool* concerns a young girl who discovers a body floating in a pool, a typical ploy for Nixon who usually pushes a young adult into a sudden crisis which leads to involvement in a murder.

T. Ernesto Bethancourt's series about slightly overweight and less than stunning Doris Fein, uncertain detective, is great fun for almost any reader. Teachers and librarians may mistake Doris Fein for Nancy Drew from the titles of books in the two series, but the confusion will end when readers get into any Doris Fein novel. Doris is fun, Nancy is a bore. Doris is possible, Nancy is not. *Doris Fein: Quartz Boyar* and *Doris Fein: Murder Is No Joke* are two exciting and amusing introductions to a delightful detective.

STORIES OF THE SUPERNATURAL

The supernatural has been an important part of our conscious fascination and our subconscious fear ever since humanity learned to communicate. That ambivalence may go back to prehistoric times when cave shadows and lighting and darkness mystified and frightened us. We have demanded answers to the unknown but have rarely found them, and the answers we found have provided myths and legends about superior and unseen beings. Such explanations are satisfying because when fighting the inexplicable, they make winning more pleasing and losing more acceptable.

Amidst all our modern knowledge and sophistication, we hold onto our fascination with the unknowable. We delight in chambers of horrors, tunnels of terror, haunted houses. We claim to be rational beings, yet we read astrology charts. We mock superstitions of others yet hold as pets one or two ourselves, joking all the time that we don't take them seriously when we toss salt over our shoulder, refuse to walk under a ladder, avoid black cats, and knock on wood. We follow customs without wondering why the custom came about. Black is assumed to be the appropriate dress for funerals since it is dark and gloomy and demonstrates solemnity. We may not know that black was worn at some time lost in history because spirits, sometimes malignant or perhaps indignant, were thought to linger near a corpse for a year. Wearing black made it more difficult for these evil spirits to see the living. As long as spirits were around, danger lurked. Hence, long mourning periods.

Greek and Roman literature abounds with supernatural elements. So does Elizabethan literature. Whether Shakespeare believed in ghosts or witches or things that go bump in the night is anyone's guess. Certainly, his audiences often did.

The Gothic novel of unexplained terror began with Horace Walpole's *The Castle of Otranto* in 1764. Success breeds imitators and Clara Reeves' *The Old English Baron* appeared in 1780 and William Beckford's *Vathek* in 1786. The two greatest of the Gothics appeared in the 1790s: Ann Radcliffe's *The Mysteries of Udolpho* and Matthew Gregory Lewis' *The Monk*. Though Jane Austen did much to demolish the fad with *Northanger Abbey* in 1818, that posthumously published novel did not prevent Mary Shelley's *Frankenstein, or the Modern Prometheus,* the apotheosis of the genre, from winning admirers. The Romantic poets and prose writers continued to be half in love with the dark and the unknown as much of Coleridge and Keats and the novels of the Brontë sisters illustrate.

Television never capitalized on the supernatural, perhaps because it is too literal a medium. Radio shows did far better, as anyone old enough to have enjoyed "Inner Sanctum" or "The Whistler" will testify. Horror movies, such as Carl Mayer's *The Cabinet of Dr. Caligari* (1919), F. W. Murnau's *Nosferatu* (1922), Carl Dreyer's *Vampyr* (1932), Val Lewton's *Cat People* (1942), and Robert Wise's *The Haunting* (1963), have sometimes produced masterpieces of our internal struggles against the evil of the unknown. And anyone who saw the episode with Michael Redgrave playing a schizophrenic ventriloquist in *Dead of Night* (1945) knows how intensely powerful such movies can be.

That power has been equally apparent in the best literature in the genre, particularly the short story where brevity allows for intensity without letting up. H. P. Lovecraft, *the* master, wrote much that is still highly readable, but nothing surpasses two stories, "The Rats in the Wall" and "The Dunwich Horror." M. R. James' "The Mezzotint" and "Oh, Whistle, and I'll Come to You, My Lad," Walter de la Mare's "A Recluse" and "What Dreams May Come," Arthur Machen's "The White People," and H. G. Wells' "The Pollock and the Porroh Man" are still read with horror. Saki's "The Open Window" is both a fine story and a send-up of the type. The best collection of such stories is Herbert A. Wise and Phyllis Fraser's *Great Tales of Terror and the Supernatural.* Joan Kahn's four collections, *Some Things Dark and Dangerous, Some*

Things Fierce and Fatal, Some Things Strange and Sinister, and *Ready or Not: Here Come Fourteen Frightening Stories!* ought to be in any library of anyone who loves the creepy and crawly and unknown.

Supernatural novels have well-established ground rules. Settings are usually in some eerie or haunted house or in a place where a mysterious event occurred years ago. Some thrillers are set in more mundane places, perhaps a brownstone in New York City or a hotel shut down for the season, but readers know the mundane will remain calm only for a short time as frightening events begin and strange people come out to play. Darkness is essential, usually but not always physical darkness. The protagonist, male or female, will be oblivious to evil for a time but ultimately will recognize the pervasive power of the darkness of the soul. Sometimes, the wife or husband will sell out to evil and entice the spouse to join in a black mass. Rituals or ceremonies are essential. Family curses or pacts with the Devil have become commonplaces of the genre.

Among YA novelists, Lois Duncan has proved consistently popular. In *Summer of Fear,* Rachael Bryant's family is notified that relatives have died in a car crash leaving a seventeen-year-old daughter, Julia, behind. The girl, who looks surprisingly mature, soon arrives and changes the lives of everyone around her. Rachael, the narrator, knows, without knowing quite how or why, that Julia is different, somehow sinister, particularly because Julia has "the strangest eyes." The family dog Trickel clearly distrusts Julia—according to legend, animals have insight about the forces of evil. Trickel does not last long, but then neither does anyone who gets in Julia's way. A burned wax image, Julia's inability to be photographed, and some more spookiness contribute to her downfall. *Stranger with My Face* and *The Third Eye* were enjoyable but hardly added to Duncan's luster after *Summer of Fear. Locked in Time,* however, is as spooky as *Summer of Fear* and in some ways superior to the earlier book. When Nora Robbins meets her new stepfather in *Locked in Time,* she's immediately attracted to Gabe, but her father's new wife and her children have something distinctly odd about them.

British novelist Robert Westall is the best YA writer in the field, but since his novels have not appeared in paperback in the United States, they have not yet found their audience. Violence in *The Wind Eye* is powerfully implied as three youngsters find an old boat with strange designs, which they learn can take them back to St. Cuthbert's time and place. *The Watch House* carries on the theme of time shifts. A young girl's imagination is captured by an old crumbling watch house on the coast. *The Devil on the Road* is the best of Westall's supernatural tales. A university student on a holiday travels north and finds temporary employment as a caretaker of an old barn, once the home of a witch hanged 300 years before. *Break of Dark* is a fine series of chilling short stories, as is *The Haunting of Chas McGill and Other Stories. Rachel and the Angel and Other Stories* is particularly interesting for young writers since one story, "Urn Burial," was later developed into a full-scale novel under the same title.

ROBERT WESTALL
on Nightmares for Money

I was recently asked to do an anthology of supernatural stories for 11–12 year olds. Doing an anthology is very salutary. With one's own creativity in abeyance, one's critical sense becomes especially sharp. Mine told me I was in some danger of giving children nightmares to turn a quick buck; not a noble posture to find oneself in, especially after a lifetime as a teacher nurturing children.

But then I asked myself if some nightmares weren't worth having. If some fears have not a survival value? Like the fear of napalm, or of all low-flying military aircraft, in certain areas of Southeast Asia.

I found a story by Adele Geras, "Live Music," which concerns a vampire music teacher who sucks not blood, but musical talent from her pupils, leaving them technically brilliant but without inspiration. There seemed a profound life-truth here. Physical vampirism is confined to a few wretched bats lying in the mud of South America, sucking at the heels

of cows they will not kill by six months of sucking. But *I* have had ex-pupils drained of vision by their university lecturers, so that they could paint brilliantly, but had nothing left to say. Emotional vampirism is the rampant danger. Encouraged by Adele, I proceeded.

I soon found that the supernatural broke down quite naturally into horror stories and ghost stories. I soon wearied of the horror stories. They only have one thing to say: that the human organism is a frail thing of flesh subject to an infinity of abuse, and that it is painful and undignified for the human spirit to have to dwell in it. That is true; so I suppose it is worth saying once and getting over with. But to say it over and over again, as the horror-practitioners do, is depressing, demeaning, and in the end, boring. I never read a horror story that did not leave me feeling dirty, disorganized, and depressed. Some practitioners, like Poe and Lovecraft, are extremely ingenious and powerful. But if one is on the way to build the Taj Mahal, or paint the Sistine Chapel ceiling, or even have a happy love affair, they are merely useless baggage to be shrugged off before the true work can be begun. In the end, horror-authors do not mean readers well. They are full of the hate, the envy, and the spite of those old 17th-century English tombstones which read:

As you are now, so once was I
As I am now, soon you will be.

The envy of the dying for the living. Let us leave them and pass on. We have lives to live, before we too die.

On the other hand, the ghost story is about the undying spirit, not the dying flesh. I have only ever had one encounter with what I *think* was a ghost. I saw and heard nothing; but I felt a presence that seemed male, adolescent, malicious, but extremely weak. It wished harm, but could not perform it. A friend, independent of me, felt the same presence in the same place. It annoyed us; it was not interesting in the least; so we banished it with a single

---

Robert Westall's books include *The Scarecrows,* Greenwillow, 1981; *The Haunting of Chas McGill and Others,* Greenwillow, 1977; and *Rachel and the Angel and Other Stories,* Greenwillow, 1986.

prayer and got on with our holiday. It had all the power of one buzzing fly.

But the fact that I cannot prove ghosts exist is neither here nor there. Most people *want* ghosts to exist (though only in places some distance away that they can visit when they feel like it). I set one of my own ghost stories in an old coast guard watch-house. There was certainly no ghost in the place when I got there. I made it up at leisure, some time later, sitting in my own home several hundred miles away. But since the book has been published, nobody living locally will believe me. They say I didn't make it up, I *sensed* it. I feel that, like Doctor Frankenstein, I have created a monster that is no longer under my control. They *want* their ghost, and be damned to the boring guy who first created him, then wants to deny him.

Why do we need ghosts? Of course they add an exciting fifth dimension to the often-boring four dimensions of real life. They make it possible for us to escape into the land of the impossible where, delightfully, anything can happen. They are also a comfort; a reassurance of our own immortality. I would adore to spend my first few years of death as a ghost, drifting round the world painlessly in the company of other friendly ghosts, seeing all the things I never got round to seeing in life because there were other boring earthbound things to be done. Like watching the rabbits come out at dawn on Eggardun Hill, the ancient British hill-fort. Being supremely *nosy* too. Eavesdropping on all the secret moments of history. I wouldn't have the least desire for revenge; I wouldn't want to *scare* anybody. Well, Hitler, maybe? The Ayatollah? Bastards who really deserve it?

Aye, there's the rub. The temptations of infinite power without responsibility. Which is the temptation all competent writers of supernatural stories have. When you ask someone to write a ghost story, you see the real inside man, with all the polite wrappings off. You are infinitely exposed to them; but if you keep a cool head, they are infinitely exposed to you. It is a kind of Day of Judgment for the writer, when the secrets of all his heart are revealed.

Oh, I have met some *sweet* souls, making my anthology. Their stories *sing,* pitched as perfectly as Yehudi Menuhin's violin. They have made me weep with the joy and sadness of love and the passing of time. But others, great names some of them, have filled me with disgust with their release of sadism and masochism, and gone into my wastebasket, only three-quarters read. It has been rather a heady experience, like being God part-time.

True ghost-stories are about love and the passing of time. And we need them, because in terms of love and the passing of time, we are all haunted houses, full of rooms we have shut off because of loss, or fear, or regret. To spend all our time wandering through such rooms would lead to madness. But to wander sometimes can be agonizingly sweet and rich. And never to dare to wander through them can make life a dusty boring hell. As T. S. Eliot said, "See, the dead return, and bring us with them."

I have met ghosts, through my anthology, from all over the world. I have a ghost story from India, "The Barber and the Ghost" that is both truthful and riotously funny. Chinese ghosts are teasing, but handled right, they will cook your meals. French ghosts (like Guy de Maupassant's in "Was it a Dream?") are compelled to rise and write the truth about themselves on their fatuously worded tombstones. English ghosts are shy and sly, often have unfinished business, but seldom hurt the innocent, though they give the heedless many a nasty fright.

Modern American spooks, I must confess, worry me deeply. After a worldwide view of ghosts, Frank de Felliti's "Entity" seems no better than a male chauvinist pig with the power of the U.S. Sixth Fleet, a cosmic brutal rapist that neither church nor state can stop. I suppose there is no way of stopping American children reading him? No English child will hear of him from me.

Margaret Mahy, less well known than Duncan or Westall to many teachers and librarians, is certain to become far better known as readers sample her offbeat fare like *The Tricksters, The Changeover,* and *The Haunting.* Mahy makes her readers care about her characters, no mean achievement given the inherent strangeness of her plots. Mahy may try to accomplish too much too fast in too few pages, but she is worth watching.

Tales of exorcism and devil worship remain popular, and two books, standards by now, are widely read, William Blatty's *The Exorcist* and Ira Levin's *Rosemary's Baby.* V. C. Andrews' books defy rational explanation and their popularity is yet more difficult to explain. Her tales of incest and general family ghoulishness and foolishness in *If There Be Thorns, Flowers in the Attic,* and *My Sweet Audrina* are mawkish and badly written but no one can question their popularity with many readers, young adults among them.

Leading all the writers in the field is Stephen King. *Carrie* appeared in 1974, sold well for a then unknown writer, and from that point on, King maintained his place as *the* writer of the genre. Carrie is a young outsider, the daughter of religious fanatics, and the brunt of cruel jokes. She possesses the power of telekinesis, and she uses it to destroy the school, the students, and the town in a fit of justified rage. *Salem's Lot,* though better characterized, is something of a letdown after *Carrie,* as are *The Stand* and *The Shining,* possibly better known through its film version than as a novel. *Firestarter* is far better with its portrait of an eight-year-old girl with the power to start fires merely by looking at an object. A government agency, "The Shop," learns about the child and launches a search for her while King effectively indicts bureaucracy gone evil. *Firestarter* may not be King's best book, but it is his most penetrating study of character and our country.

King's later books have added to his sales without adding to his reputation. *Different Seasons* is four generally effective novelettes. *Cujo* is a messy and disappointingly obvious horror tale of the loveable St. Bernard dog gone mad. *Christine* is a 1958 Plymouth Fury gone equally mad. Only *Pet Sematary* has some of the old King about it. A variation of W. W. Jacobs' "The Monkey's Paw"—and so acknowledged by King—*Pet Sematary* has a power that cannot be ignored although it remains something of a prolonged ghastly joke. And *Tommyknockers* and *It,* his most recent books, added a chill or two to King's repertoire and little more.

Dixie Tenny's recent *Call the Darkness Down* is an impressive YA first novel about the spirit world in modern Wales. Morfa Owen is anxious to study in Wales, partly because of her Welsh ancestry, partly because her mother has created a family mystery by refusing to tell anyone why she and her sister fled Wales when they were teenagers. Despite some clichés, the feeling that is Wales and the convincing characters make for a fine ghost story.

Because young adults are curious and relatively open about exploring new ideas, the supernatural has a natural appeal to them. Treading on spooky ground is a social experience—one not always approved of by censorious parents—and teenagers delight in rounding up friends to see a scary movie or discussing the possibilities of ghosts and goblins and worse horrors.

◼ *HISTORICAL NOVELS*

Most of us read historical novels because we are curious about other times and other places and other peoples, and most important, because we want adventure and suspense and mystery. Movies as old as *Captain Blood* or *Gone with the Wind* or *The Scarlet Pimpernel* continue to pique our interest, however ignorant we may be of the times and places described.

Certainly, best-selling historical fiction has provided excitement. Adventures galore can be found in historical novels as good and as popular as Sir Walter Scott's *Ivanhoe* (1819), Alexander Dumas' *The Count of Monte Cristo* (1844), Mary Johnston's *To Have and to Hold* (1900), Rafael Sabatini's *Scaramouche* (1921), Helen Waddell's *Peter Abelard* (1933), Elizabeth Goudge's *Green Dolphin Street* (1944), or Margaret Walker's *Jubilee* (1966). Indeed, all these novels remain readable today, a claim impossible to make for novels of the same time written about contemporary issues.

As in any literary form, historical novels have their conventions. They should be historically accurate and steeped in the sense of time and place (see Table 5.2). We should recognize totems and taboos, food, clothing, vocations, leisures, customs, smells, religions, literature, all that goes to make one time and one place unique from another. Enthusiasts will forgive no anachronism, no matter how slight. Historical novels should give a sense of history's continuity, a feeling of the flow of history from one time unto another that will, for good reason, be different from the period before. But as writers allow us to feel that flow of history, they should particularize their portraits of one time and place. Historical novels should tell a lively story with a sense of impending danger, mystery, suspense, or romance. Action aplenty there must be.

Historical novels allow us—at their best they force us—to make connections to realize that despair is as old, and new, as hope, that loyalty and treachery, love and hatred, compassion and cruelty, were and are inherent in humanity whether it be in ancient Greece or Elizabethan England or Post-World War I Germany.

That poses a problem. Interested as we may be in the past, we are always more concerned about the present, and we find ourselves comparing the past with today, perhaps even imposing present-day values on the past. Historians can pretend to be objective, but historical novelists, concerned about people they have created and those they address, may find such objectivity harder to come by. What Henry Seidel Canby wrote in 1927 concerns anyone working with history:

> ◼ Historical fiction, like history, is more likely to register an exact truth about the writer's present than the exact truth of the past.[2]

And sometimes, the historical novelist may be grinding an ax. How hidden the ax may be is for the reader to determine. Christopher Collier, for example, makes no pretense why he and his brother write about the American Revolution in their fine historical novels:

Table 5.2 **SUGGESTIONS FOR EVALUATING HISTORICAL FICTION**

A good historical novel usually has:	A poor historical novel may have:
A setting that is integral to the story.	A story that could have happened any time or any place. The historical setting is for visual appeal and to compensate for a weak story.
An authentic rendition of the time, place, and people being featured.	
An author who is so thoroughly steeped in the history of the period that he or she can be comfortably creative without making mistakes.	Anachronisms in which the author illogically mixes up people, events, speaking styles, social values, or technological developments from different time periods.
Believable characters with whom young readers can identify.	Awkward narration and exposition as the author tries to teach history through the characters' conversations.
Evidence that even across great time spans people share similar emotions.	Oversimplification of the historical issues and a stereotyping of the "bad" and the "good" guys.
References to well-known events or people, or other clues through which the reader can place the happenings in their correct historical framework.	Characters who fail to come alive as individuals who have something in common with the readers. They are just stereotyped representatives of a particular period.
Readers who come away with the feeling that they know a time or place better. It is as if they have lived in it for at least a few hours.	

... the books I write with my brother are written with a didactic purpose—to teach about ideals and values that have been important in shaping the course of American history. This is in no way intended to denigrate the importance of the dramatic and literary elements of historical novels. Nothing will be taught, and certainly nothing learned, if no one reads the books.[3]

But teachers and librarians need to remind themselves that no matter how enthusiastic some young adults feel about *Gone with the Wind* or *Jubilee* or any historical novel, many young adults resist the fascination of this genre. Some voracious readers clearly feel what novelist Penelope Lively feels:

I prefer my own history straight—as debated among historians. And when I want the flavor of the past, I would not go to historical novels but to survivals—to diaries and letters and documents. I don't want the interference of the novelist; the past is quite capable of speaking for itself.[4]

Obviously Lively's words may apply to young adults who love history but who reject historical novels, but it may also apply to young adults who prefer to read about more recent events like the Holocaust or America's internment of the Japanese during World War II straight, rather than fictionalized. There are, after all, some who prefer no sugarcoating to history, no matter how much more palatable that supposedly makes history for the masses.

Among the best YA historical novels have been Norma Farber's *Mercy Short: A Winter Journal, North Boston, 1692–93* and Patricia Clapp's *Witches' Children*. Farber's book is based on fact with young Mercy recently released from Indian captivity forced by Cotton Mather to keep a journal to redeem her soul. Rosemary Sisson's *Will in Love* conveys the spirit of Shakespeare's time, as does Claudia Von Canon's *The Inheritance* and *The Moonclock*.

James Lincoln and Christopher Collier have written several fine, admittedly didactic, novels about the Revolutionary War, any of which would let students see the nature of the cause that led to the war and understand the people behind the cause. The protagonists of *My Brother Sam Is Dead, The Bloody Country,* and *The Winter Hero* are young, and young adults may find a point of contact that may lead them to understand that the war involved everyone, not just the heroes they have read about in schoolbooks. *Jump Ship to Freedom* and *War Comes to Willy Freeman* tell of black former slaves involved in the Revolution, an even more appealing theme.

Rosemary Sutcliff won admirers and readers with her first books. The books that followed further enhanced her reputation as the finest historical novelist for young adults. She is a born storyteller whose tales are intense and fast-moving and poetic. Her novels have ranged in time from the Bronze Age to the Iron Age, as in *Warrior Scarlet* and *Sun Horse, Moon Horse*. She has

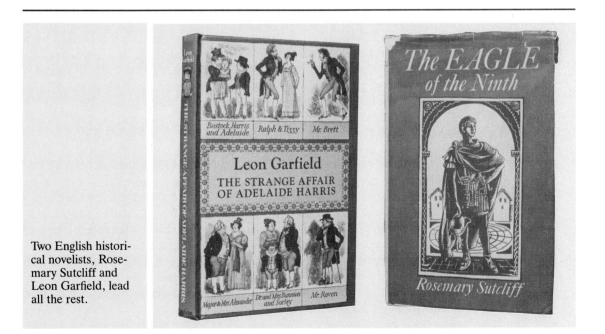

Two English historical novelists, Rosemary Sutcliff and Leon Garfield, lead all the rest.

touched on many periods of English history in *Blood Feud* (tenth century), *The Shield Ring* (Normans and Saxons), *Dawn Wind* (Saxons), *Knight's Fee* (William the Conquerer), and *Simon* (English Civil War).

But Sutcliff is almost certainly best known for her novels set in Roman Britain, particularly *The Mark of the Horse Lord, Outcast, The Capricorn Bracelet, Song for a Dark Queen,* and *Frontier Wolf.* Her favorite novel and probably her best, opens the trilogy completed by *The Silver Branch* and *The Lantern Bearers. The Eagle of the Ninth* is set in Roman Britain, and, as is true in most Sutcliff novels, the protagonist must face up to problems inherent in different kinds of handicaps. Marcus, a young Roman centurion, is forced by a leg wound to leave the legions. The Ninth Legion, the Lost Legion once led by his father who is now presumed dead, may have fallen into the hands of a tribe beyond Hadrian's Wall to the north. Marcus deeply believes in honor— deep convictions typify Sutcliff's books—and along with his British slave, he sets out on this personal quest, for himself, for his father, for Rome, for honor.

Leon Garfield's world is the eighteenth century, with an occasional detour into early nineteenth-century England. Beginning with *Jack Holborn* in 1965, Garfield set a standard for historical writing that few can match.

Garfield's eighteenth century is the world of Fielding and Smollett, lusty and squalid and ugly and bustling and swollen, full of life and adventure and the certainty that being born an orphan may lead you ultimately to fame and fortune. Typically, eighteenth-century novels open with an orphan searching for identity. Garfield does not fear conventions, but his stories also play with reality versus illusion, delight versus dreams, flesh versus fantasy. His ability to sketch out minor characters in a line or two and make them come alive is impressive. Of a man in *The Sound of Coaches,* he writes, "He was one of those gentlemen who affect great gallantry to all the fair sex except their wives." Of a prostitute, he writes, "A face full of beauty spots, with graveyard dust between." And of the protagonist we are told, "although jealousy was ordinarily foreign to Sam's nature, they did, on occasion, talk the same language." Garfield's epigrams are often most effective, for example, "Many a man is made good by being thought so."

Garfield's best book is *The Sound of Coaches* with an opening that catches the sights and sounds and feeling of the time:

> Once upon a winter's night when the wind blew its guts out and a fishy piece of moon scuttled among the clouds, a coach came thundering down the long hill outside of Dorking. Its progress was wild and the coachman and his guard rocked from side to side as if the maddened vehicle was struggling to rid itself of them before going on to hell without the benefit of further advice. Even the passing landscape conspired to increase the terror of the journey, and the fleeting sight of a gibbet—its iron cage swinging desolately against the sky—turned the five passengers' thoughts towards the next world . . . of which destination there'd been no mention in Chichester where they'd booked their passage.

Once the five passengers, the coachman and the guard (who is the coach-man's wife) reach Dorking, a young girl has a baby, dies, and leaves the orphan behind without any identity. The passengers, though at first annoyed by the irregularity of all that has happened, become parents of sorts to the baby, while the coachman and his wife raise the child. When Sam, our hero, grows up, he heads for London searching for his father.

Wit and humor and liveliness permeate Garfield's books. Perhaps the fun-niest are *The Strange Affair of Adelaide Harris* and its sequel *The Night of the Comet.* In *Adelaide,* Bostock and Harris, two nasty pupils in Dr. Bunnion's Academy, become so entranced with stories of Spartan babies abandoned on mountain tops, there to be suckled by wolves, that they borrow Harris' baby sister to determine for themselves the truth of the old tales. Therein begins a wild comedy of errors and an even wilder series of coincidences and near-duels and wild threats which hardly lets up until the last lines.

Scott O'Dell's books lag behind Garfield and Sutcliff but not by much. *The King's Fifth* is probably O'Dell's most convincing work with its picture of sixteenth-century Spaniards and the moral strains put on anyone involved in the search for gold and fame. It is convincing and often disturbing, and like most of O'Dell's historical novels generally worth pursuing.

Some adult writers of historical novels continue to appeal to young adults *if* teachers and librarians provide a bit of assistance. For example, Mary Renault (real name, Mary Challans) consistently provided first-rate fiction with accurate and perceptive history. *The Persian Boy* tells of a dying Alexander the Great, only 35, and the contenders who battle for his place on earth and his place in the sun, a book almost as good as the more famous *The King Must Die.*

The staying power of some historical novels may not yet be clear, but anyone who reads books as good as Marion Zimmer Bradley's *The Firebrand,* a femi-nist rewriting and perspective on Homer's *Iliad,* Elizabeth Marshall Thomas' *Reindeer Moon,* a recreation of hunter clan life 20,000 years ago in Siberia, or Edward Rutherfurd's *Sarum,* a sprawling and huge account of the development of Salisbury and Salisbury Cathedral in southern England, will have hours of enjoyment ahead.

The historical novelist who seems most likely to endure is Gore Vidal, whose brilliance and historical intelligence shines through his epic of the United States. *Burr* recreated a period less known than it should be for many adults and probably even more young readers willing to stick with history that was not over-simplified (and sometimes over-interpreted). Vidal's recent *Empire* is his best yet, moving readers through American history from 1898 to 1906 and acquainting us with people who are more historical than real to the majority of readers—William McKinley, William Randolph Hearst, and Henry Adams for example. Anyone who questions Vidal's talent need only read William Safire's equally recent *Freedom: A Novel of Abraham Lincoln and the Civil War.* Safire is a brilliant political commentator and perhaps an even more brilliant student of the language, but his history remains factual and dead compared to Vidal's recreation of life and people.

◼ *WESTERNS*

The appeal of the American West is as old as the first explorer who saw it and marveled. Dime novelists of the 1870s and 1880s glorified the wildness and vitality of miners and cowboys and mountain men and soldiers and outlaws. Ned Buntline was particularly effective in his tall stories—amidst some out-and-out lies—about Buffalo Bill and his supposed exploits.

If anything else were needed to make the West the heartland of adventure, movies provided rootin'-tootin'-shootin' cowboys and rustlers, good guys and bad guys—always easy to separate depending on who wore white and who wore black. Edwin S. Porter's *The Great Train Robbery* in 1903, although filmed in New Jersey, helped develop the Western myth, but later films like James Cruze's *The Covered Wagon* (1923), John Ford's *Stagecoach* (1939), and Fred Zinnemann's *High Noon* (1952) helped mightily.

Perhaps films were not needed, for Owen Wister's *The Virginian* (1902) had already established the central characters of too many Westerns, the quiet and noble hero, the schoolmarm heroine, the hero's weak friend, the villain, and rustlers; these along with some basic plot devices, cattle drives, the inevitable showdown between good guys and bad guys, violence aplenty, and revenge-revenge-revenge. Andy Adams' *The Log of a Cowboy: A Narrative of the Old Trail Days* (1903) brought a semblance of honesty to the field, and that was heightened by the honest and fine novels of Eugene Manlove Rhodes, for example his wonderful novelette *Pasò Por Aquì* (1927).

For the most part, realism was rare in Westerns; note the romanticized but highly popular novels of Zane Grey and the equally popular and much derided screen series of Hopalong Cassidy westerns.

But a larger number of fine writers than most casual observers have any reason to suspect lived and breathed the real West and wrote accurate, non-romanticized novels. Vardis Fisher's *The Mothers* is a superior story of the Donner Party disaster when people ignorant of the early snows in California mountains died of hunger and bitter cold. Willa Cather's *The Professor's House* is not her greatest novel, but its account of the finding of the Mesa Verde ruins is exciting even today. Will Comfort's *Apache* was widely admired when it was published as a superior story of Apache life and culture. Dorothy Scarborough's now nearly forgotten *The Wind* may be out of fashion but the portrait of a young wife driven mad by the ever-persistent Texas wind and from sheer loneliness stays with readers.

Conventions of the Western are so well established for commercial books that any writer who ignored them would be laughed out of bookstores. The setting is obviously the West, preferably some time between 1880 and 1895, the high point of cowboy life. Excitement pervades the novel—attacks, rustlers, the cavalry, lynchings, bank holdups, jailbreaks, goldfields, ladies of the evening (and night), crooked lawyers, and on and on. Violence is far more likely to be gaudily portrayed rather than implied. Nostalgia permeates everything in this best of all the old times when men were rugged and life was cheap. The hero (a marshal, cowboy, drifter, ex-gunfighter, wagonmaster, mountain man) will be moral, though that may have come after a reformation which he rarely will be willing to talk about with anyone but the heroine in one tender moment. And morality will ultimately triumph as the hero plays Hamlet and puts the world aright.

The villain could be a crooked lawyer (or banker), owner of the biggest spread in the territory, a gunfighter looking to nick one more notch on his gun, or a political boss.

Others in the cast are likely to include the hero's sidekick, a trail boss or ranch owner, a saloon girl or two, one oh-so-decent woman (the heroine), several second-string bad guys, and assorted townspeople or rovers to make all the appropriate crowd noises. Action will come fast on the open range (or in a mine, in a showdown on Front Street or Main Street or some corral or other, or in a saloon).

Fortunately, some good Westerns either ignore these hackneyed conventions or freshen them up. Louis L'Amour was unquestionably the most famous of all recent Western writers. He was also a much better novelist than most teachers and librarians realize, hardly a surprise since all too many ignore L'Amour and practically all of Western literature. L'Amour loved the West, but more important, he knew Western literature and Western history. L'Amour's readers know that details will be true and history will be accurate. Among his books, the one most likely to appeal to beginners in the field is one of his best, *Down the Long Hills.* Seven-year-old Hardy wakes up one morning to find his horse missing. He leaves the wagon train, followed by his little sister, and when he returns he finds everyone massacred. Hardy and his sister head west facing starvation and blizzards and wild animals.

Kathryn Lasky's *Beyond the Divide* is a remarkable novel, a record of the coming of age of a young girl in journal form from April 1, 1849, until June 1, 1850. Meribad Simon and her father question their Amish community and head West after her father is shunned for attending the funeral of a friend who had not strictly observed Amish custom. What they encounter is anything but a storybook delight—cruel emigrants, death everywhere, selfishness and miserliness, rape, and finally the father's death. It is an engrossing book, surehanded throughout, and a strong portrait of a most determined and believable young woman who is a survivor.

If Lasky's book seemed a rare young adult novel foray into new territory, that of the Western, this seems no longer to be the case. Theodore Taylor's beautifully and accurately, if lengthily, titled *Walking up a Rainbow; Being the True Version of the Long and Hazardous Journey of Susan D. Carlisle, Mrs. Myrtle Dessery, Drover Bert Petitt, and Cowboy Clay Carmer and Others* reads as well as it sounds. Joan Lowery Nixon, better known for her YA mysteries, proved a good historian and a fine western spinner of tales in the first two of a proposed quartet of novels about an orphan train.

The clash of cultures, obviously Indian versus Anglo but also new Western versus old Eastern United States, has received attention in many novels. Benjamin Capps' *The Man's Road* and *A Woman of the People,* Will Henry's (real name, Henry Wilson Allen) *From Where the Sun Now Stands,* and James Welch's *Fool's Crow, The Death of Jim Loney,* and *Winter in the Blood* belong to the first class. Alan LeMay's *The Searchers,* Ann Turner's *Third Girl from the Left,* and Edward Abbey's many books, notably *The Brave Cowboy,* belong to the second group.

Inevitably, given the showdowns on Main Street in too many bad cowboy films, some books are about good men gone bad with guns. William Decker's *To Be a Man* and Charles O. Locke's *The Hell Bent Kid* are among the best. The latter doubtlessly sounds melodramatic, but it is not.

Westerns are sometimes so grim in describing the battle for range rights or between cultures that it is pleasant to read a few that are funny, deliberately so. Students either love Rex Benedict's quartet of tall and wild tales about Luke Gore and his horse, Bullet Proof, and Sheriff Sagebrush Sheridan and other equally unlikely people, or they hate them; slapstick isn't for everyone. More sophisticated and one of the funniest books in English is David Wagoner's *The Road to Many a Wonder.* Ike Bender, age twenty, leaves home to find gold and is soon followed by his younger bride-to-be. Their struggles to reach Colorado and find the pot at the end of their rainbow are believable and sometimes charming and always delightful.

Most readers assume that Westerns will, of course, be about the old West, and that's generally true. But a few writers have staked out the modern West as their territory. Edward Abbey, already mentioned, quietly bewails the freedom that the modern world has killed. Larry McMurtry may be equally unhappy about the philosophical state of the west, but his books are more humor than desperation. *The Last Picture Show* is about the death of a small town, but that one-liner in no way conveys the sadness and the wild humor of much of the book. More recently, McMurtry's sequel, *Texasville,* tells us more about *The Last Picture Show*'s characters and adds to it an account of a town trying to find its heritage and the wildest egg fight in history.

ANIMAL STORIES

Anyone who realizes American's fondness for pets or who watched episodes about animals on PBS should hardly be surprised about the number of popular books about animals, surprisingly enough mostly nonsentimentalized. Not all are adventure stories, but many are, involving adventures for the animals themselves or the people around them.

Few readers will wonder at the many dog stories available. *Nop's Trials* by Donald McCaig is a recent best-seller about a Border Collie stolen from his owner and the adventures Nop has in getting back home. William Hallstead's *Tundra* is told from the point of view of a Siberian Husky also trying to find his way home, a superior book to *Nop's Trials* though aimed originally at a younger audience. Best of the three, and one of the superior animal books of recent years, is J. R. Ackerley's *My Dog Tulip: Life with an Alsatian.* Ackerley comes across as a bumbling, typically dog-loving person, unsure of what to do with the object of his love. Tulip is a delight, a dog that readers believe in who has real problems with a vet and her owner. Most important, Tulip is a dog and remains a dog, not an anthropomorphic object.

Among the many books about wolves—and there are many—R. D. Lawrence's books stand out. *The North Runner* is probably the best introduction to Lawrence's work with its picture of Yukon, a half-wolf sled dog who is Lawrence's friend, co-worker, and companion in the Canadian north. *In Praise of Wolves* came out of Lawrence and his wife's observation of a pack of captive, but untamed, wolves in the Upper Peninsula of Michigan. He wanted to compare these wolves with ones he had known and a pair of wolves he had raised earlier, and he wanted to learn about pack selection of leaders and pack hierarchy. Mostly, Lawrence wanted to reaffirm his love of wild things and particularly wolves.

One animal book stands out as something quite different. Chris Freddi's *Pork and Others* appears at first glance to be cutesy little tales about our animal friends. It is not. Rather, it is a collection of nonromanticized stories about animals, most of the tales ending in death.

Best of all the writers about animals is Farley Mowat. *The Dog Who Wouldn't Be* and *Owls in the Family* are warm and funny family novels, distinguished more for their humor than their content. That is not true of *Never Cry Wolf*. Whether all the details Mowat gives in the book are totally accurate, and there is disagreement about that, hardly alters the obvious truth—that Mowat cares about the deprivation humanity is wishing on wild animals who have done little harm to humanity. *A Whale for the Killing* is an even more bitter book. Mowat believed he had found a real home in a small port only to learn that a beached whale brought out the bestial in the villagers, and that grew worse when Mowat published his account of the stupid and pointless slaughter of a whale that had done no one any harm.

Sea of Slaughter and *Woman in the Mists: The Story of Dian Fossey and the Mountain Gorillas of Africa* are among Mowat's angriest books. Mowat did not wholly support Dian Fossey in all she did, but he found her fascinating and her work necessary, and he concluded his book with some ugly words about people and some lovely words about Fossey.

As for the mountain kings of the Virungas, the gorillas, who can say what fate awaits them at our hands. But if they *do* survive, it will be due in no small measure to the dedication of a woman who was in love with life—with *all* of life—a woman who did what great lovers must always do: who gave herself completely to those she loved.

Others have also written good books about the slaughter and poaching of Africa's wild animal heritage, for example, Roger Caras' *Mara Simba: The African Lion,* Jane Goodall's *The Chimpanzees of Gomba,* and Mark and Delia Owens' *Cry of the Kalahari.*

As the books mentioned in this chapter illustrate, adventure and suspense stories provide opportunities for sharing other's lives. Readers feel emotions they can get in few other ways, whether it is the joy of reaching a mountain top, the satisfaction of winning out against great odds, or just the weak-kneed relief that comes from living through a harrowing experience.

With some recent stories, authors offer a bonus, the opportunity to think about something after the story is over. The bonus may be about cultural clashes or ecological concerns. It may be about prejudice and the unfairness of things that seem to strike minorities. Whatever the problem, the mark of success in these stories is the degree to which the authors have involved the reader's emotions.

NOTES

[1]Hillary Waugh, "The Mystery Versus the Novel," in *The Mystery Story,* John Ball, ed. (New York: Penguin, 1978), pp. 71–73.

[2]Henry Seidel Canby, "What Is Truth?" *Saturday Review of Literature* 4 (December 31, 1927): 481.

[3]Christopher Collier, "Criteria for Historical Novels," *School Library Journal* 29 (August 1982): 32.

[4]Penelope Lively, "Bones in the Sand," in *Innocence and Experience: Essays and Conversations on Children's Literature,* Barbara Harrison and Gregory Maguire, eds. (New York: Lothrop, Lee and Shepard, 1987), p. 19.

30 RECOMMENDATIONS FOR READING

Adventure

Bonington, Chris. *The Everest Years: A Climber's Life.* Viking, 1987. The dangers and fascinations of Mount Everest with many splendid illustrations. See also his *Annapurna: South Face* (McGraw-Hill, 1971), *Everest: The Unclimbed Ridge* with Charles Clarke (Norton, 1984), and *Quest for Adventure* (Potter, 1982).

Buckley, William F., Jr. *Operation Mongoose, R.I.P.* Random House, 1987. All about Blackford Oates, spy and bon vivant, and the villainous Cubans from the Bay of Pigs to President Kennedy's assassination. See also earlier and wondrous Oates thrillers in *Who's on First?* (Doubleday, 1980), *The Story of Henri Tod* (Doubleday, 1983), and *See You Later, Alligator* (Doubleday, 1985).

Callahan, Steven. *Adrift: Seventy-Six Days Lost at Sea.* Houghton Mifflin, 1986. Perhaps the consistently most exciting nonfiction adventure tale in years.

le Carré, John. *A Perfect Spy.* Knopf, 1986. The latest spy thriller by *the* master of the genre. See also earlier stories like *The Spy Who Came in From the Cold* (Coward, McCann, 1963), *Tinker, Tailor, Soldier, Spy* (Knopf, 1974), *The Honorable Schoolboy* (Knopf, 1977), *Smiley's People* (Knopf, 1980), *The Quest for Karla* (Knopf, 1982), and *The Little Drummer Girl* (Knopf, 1983).

Thompson, Julian F. *The Grounding of Group Six.* Avon, 1983. A fantastic and bizarre story of unwanted adolescents scheduled for execution by their parents. Exciting and often wildly amusing.

White, Robb. *Deathwatch.* Doubleday, 1972. A young guide for a mad hunter becomes the quarry. Never bettered as a straight adventure story.

Mystery

Christie, Agatha. *And Then There Were None.* Dodd, Mead, 1939. The greatest of the classic mystery writers in her finest story of murder and retribution. But then see her other representative books: *By the Pricking of My Thumbs* (Dodd, Mead, 1968), *A Murder Is Announced* (Dodd, Mead, 1950), and *Miss Marple: The Complete Short Stories* (Dodd, Mead, 1985).

Francis, Dick. *Hot Money.* Putnam, 1988. The latest thriller/mystery from an ex-professional steeplechase rider and author. Who killed a wealthy gold trader's wife and how will Francis involve the world of horse racing? Anything by Francis is a pleasure to read, for example, *Trial Run* (Harper & Row, 1979), *Reflex* (Putnam, 1981), *Twice Shy* (Putnam, 1982), *Banker* (Putnam, 1983), *The Danger* (Putnam, 1984), *Proof* (Putnam, 1985), *Break In* (Putnam, 1986), and *Bolt* (Putnam, 1987).

Hillerman, Tony. *Skinwalkers*. Harper & Row, 1986. Hillerman uses both his detectives, Jim Chee and Joe Leaphorn, in a case involving Shamanism. See also *The Blessing Way* (1970), *The Dance Hall of the Dead* (1973), *Listening Woman* (1978), *People of Darkness* (1980), *The Dark Wind* (1982), *The Ghostway* (1985), all published by Harper & Row.

McBain, Ed. *Cinderella*. Holt, 1986. One of the Matthew Hope mysteries, this one about an operative shot to death while he's investigating two cases—the question is, which case? *Poison: An 87th Precinct Novel* (Arbor House, 1987) is the most recent McBain police procedural. See also *Cop Hater* (Perma-books, 1956), *Lady Killer* (Simon and Schuster, 1950), *'Til Death* (Simon and Schuster, (1958), and *Long Time No See* (Random House, 1977).

Supernatural

Duncan, Lois. *Locked in Time*. Little, Brown, 1985. When Nora Robbins meets her new stepfamily, she senses something odd. See also Duncan's other supernatural thrillers, *Summer of Fear* (Little, Brown, 1976), *Stranger with My Face* (Little, Brown, 1981), and *The Third Eye* (Little, Brown, 1984).

Mahy, Margaret. *The Tricksters*. McElderry, 1987. A seventeen-year-old girl accidentally calls back a ghost to life. See also Mahy's other brilliant books—*The Changeover* (Antheneum, 1984) and *The Haunting* (Atheneum, 1982).

King, Stephen. *Firestarter*. Viking, 1980. A young girl has the power to start fires as she wishes. King's books are so popular that any short list is certain to leave out favorites, but here are a few: *Different Seasons,* four short novels but especially outstanding for *The Body,* filmed as *Stand by Me* (Viking, 1982); *Skeleton Crew,* a collection of poems and stories (Putnam, 1985); *Pet Sematary* (Doubleday, 1983); *The Tommyknockers* (Putnam, 1987); *The Shining* (Doubleday, 1977); *It* (Vi-

king, 1986); *Danse Macabre,* another collection (Everest House, 1981); and *Carrie* (Doubleday, 1974).

Westall, Robert. *The Watch House*. Greenwillow, 1978. For a summer, Anne lives near the Watch House, a museum/storehouse for a lifesaving brigade, and she learns to fear what is in the Watch House and what it represents. Note also several other books by this too-often ignored British writer, all published by Greenwillow—*Break of Dark* (1982), *The Devil on the Road* (1979), *The Wind Eye* (1977), *The Haunting of Chas McGill and Other Stories* (1983), *Rachel and the Angel and Other Stories* (1988), and *Urn Burial* (1987).

Historical Novels

Farber, Norma. *Mercy Short: A Winter Journal, North Boston, 1692–93*. Dutton, 1982. A remarkably accurate and fascinating fictionalized account of a young girl forced by Cotton Mather to keep a journal to save her soul.

Garfield, Leon. *The Sound of Coaches*. Viking, 1974. The finest of contemporary historical novelists writes of a young man in search of his heritage, an old topic, but not at all stale in Garfield's book. Other books worth reading include *Jack Holborn* (Pantheon, 1965), *Smith* (Pantheon, 1967), *Black Jack* (Pantheon, 1969), *The Pleasure Garden* (Viking, 1976), *The Strange Affair of Adelaide Harris* (Pantheon, 1971). *The Night of the Comet* (Delacorte, 1979), *The Prisoners of September* (Viking, 1975), *The Confidence Man* (Viking, 1978), *The Apprentices* (Viking, 1978), and *The December Rose* (Viking, 1978).

O'Dell, Scott. *The Serpent Never Sleeps: A Novel of Jamestown and Pocahontas*. Houghton Mifflin, 1987. Serona sails off for the new world in 1609 and spends two months at sea before being shipwrecked off Bermuda. O'Dell's several other historical novels deserve readers, particularly *The King's Fifth,* probably his finest work (Houghton Mifflin,

1966), *Sarah Bishop* (Houghton Mifflin, 1980), *Sing Down the Moon* (Houghton Mifflin, 1970), *The Hawk That Dare Not Hunt by Day* (Houghton Mifflin, 1975), and *Streams to the River, River to the Sea* (Houghton Mifflin, 1986).

Renault, Mary. *The King Must Die,* Pantheon, 1958. Theseus discovers a sword and a pair of sandals when he is a boy, and when his mother tells him he is the son of a king, Theseus sets out to reclaim his heritage. See anything by this master reteller of Greek stories, for example, *Fire from Heaven* (1969), *The Persian Boy* (1972), *The Funeral Games* (1982), and *The Praise Singer* (1979), all published by Pantheon.

Sutcliff, Rosemary. *The Eagle of the Ninth.* Walck, 1954. A young Roman Centurian learns that the eagle standard of his father's legion may have fallen into the hands of a rebellious tribe in Britain. Sutcliff is without peer in the YA historical novel field, and anything she has touched is worthwhile, especially *The Silver Branch* (Walck, 1957), *The Mark of the Horse Lord* (Walck, 1965), *Blood Feud* (Dutton, 1977), *Song for a Dark Queen* (Crowell, 1978), and *Frontier Wolf* (Dutton, 1981).

Vidal, Gore. *Empire.* Random House, 1987. The United States from 1898 to 1906 seen through the eyes of twenty-year-old Caroline Sanford. Others of Vidal's creations worth reading include *Washington, D.C.* (Random House, 1967), *Burr* (Random House, 1974), *1876* (Random House, 1976), and *Lincoln* (Random House, 1984).

Westerns

Abbey, Edward. *The Brave Cowboy: An Old Tale in a New Time.* Dodd, Mead, 1956. An anachronistic cowboy sets out to break a friend out of jail only to learn that the friend wants no part of the jailbreak. See also Abbey's other iconoclastic works—*Fire on the Mountain* (Dial, 1962), *Desert Solitaire: A Season in the Wilderness* (Simon and Schuster, 1968), and *Beyond the Wall: Essays from the Outside* (Holt, 1984).

Capps, Benjamin. *The White Man's Road.* Harper & Row, 1969. Young Indian males try to find a way to satisfy their need to prove manhood on a sterile Indian reservation. Note also Capps' underrated books like *Sam Chance* (Duell, Sloan, and Pearce, 1965), *Hanging at Comanche Wells* (Ballantine, 1962), *The Track to Ogallala* (Duell, Sloan, and Pearce, 1964), *The True Memoirs of Charlie Blankenship* (Lippincott, 1972), and *A Woman of the People* (Duell, Sloan, and Pearce, 1966).

Clark, Walter Van Tilburg. *The Ox-Bow Incident.* Random House, 1940. The prototypical Western novel about lynching and mob justice.

McMurtry, Larry. *The Last Picture Show.* Dial, 1966. A small Texas town watches itself die. Other McMurtry books worth reading include *Horseman, Pass By* (Harper & Row, 1961), *Leaving Cheyenne* (Harper & Row, 1962), *Lonesome Dove* (Simon and Schuster, 1985), and *Texasville* (Simon and Schuster, 1987).

Wagoner, David. *The Road to Many a Wonder.* Farrar, Straus and Giroux, 1974. In what may well be the funniest Western ever written, a young couple set off to the West and the answer to all their hopes and dreams.

Waters, Frank. *The Man Who Killed the Deer.* Farrar, 1942. A young Indian is caught between two traditions and ways of life. Anything by Waters is worth reading but see especially *Mountain Dialogues* (Ohio University Press, 1982).

Animals

Ackerley, J. R. *My Dog Tulip.* Poseidon Press, 1986. Ackerley's fifteen years with an Alsatian bitch who loved him almost as much as he loved her.

Freddi, Chris. *Pork and Others*. Knopf, 1981. Unsentimentalized stories about forest animals, most of them about life and death.

Lawrence, R. D. *The North Runner*. Holt, 1979. Yukon, the half-wolf sled dog, was for five years Lawrence's closest friend in the Canadian north. Lawrence is both sympathetic and realistic about animals and people, and all his books are worth reading—*Secret Go the Wolves* (Holt, 1980), *The Zoo That Never Was* (Holt, 1981), *Voyage of the Stella* (Holt, 1982), *The Ghost Walker* (Holt, 1983), and *In Praise of Wolves* (Holt, 1986).

Mowat, Farley, *A Whale for the Killing*. Little, Brown, 1972. Mowat thought he had found a fine place to settle down. Then a beached whale arouses the blood lust of the villagers. Mowat's angry prose also typifies *Never Cry Wolf* (Little, Brown, 1963), *Sea of Slaughter* (Atlantic, 1985), and *Woman in the Mists: The Story of Dian Fossey and the Mountain Gorillas of Africa* (Warner, 1987). Mowat is less angry in *The Dog Who Wouldn't Be* (Little, Brown, 1957) and *Owls in the Family* (Little, Brown. 1961).

▊ OTHER TITLES MENTIONED IN CHAPTER FIVE

Adams, Andy. *The Log of a Cowboy*. Houghton Mifflin, 1903.

Andrews, V. C. *Flowers in the Attic*. Simon and Schuster, 1979.

_____ . *If There Be Thorns*. Simon and Schuster, 1981.

_____ . *My Sweet Audrina*. Simon and Schuster, 1982.

Austen, Jane. *Northanger Abbey*. 1818.

Barnard, Robert. *Political Suicide*. Scribner, 1986.

Beckford, William. *Vathek*. 1786.

Bennett, Jay. *Deathman, Do Not Follow Me*. Hawthorne, 1968.

Bethancount, T. Ernesto. *Doris Fein: Murder Is No Joke*. Holiday House, 1982.

_____ . *Doris Fein: Quartz Boyar*. Holiday House, 1980.

Blatty, William. *The Exorcist*. Harper & Row, 1971.

Blum, Arlene. *Annapurna—A Woman's Place*. Sierra Club Books, 1983.

Blum, Howard. *I Pledge Allegiance . . . The True Story of the Walkers: An American Spy Family*. Simon and Schuster, 1987.

Boington, Chris. *Everest: The Unclimbed Ridge*. Norton, 1984.

_____ . *Quest for Adventure*. Crown, 1982.

Boyle, Thomas. *Only the Dead Know Brooklyn*. Godine, 1986.

Bradley, Marion Zimmer. *The Firebrand*. Simon and Schuster, 1987.

Brook, Elaine, and Julie Donnelly. *The Windhorse*. Dodd, Mead, 1987.

Buchan, John. *Greenmantle*. Doran, 1915.

_____ . *The Thirty-Nine Steps*. Doran, 1915.

Buchanan, Edna. *The Corpse Had a Familiar Face*. Random House, 1987.

Caras, Roger. *Mara Simba: The African Lion*. Holt, 1985.

Cather, Willa. *The Professor's House*. Knopf, 1925.

Chesterton, G. K. *The Innocence of Father Brown*. Lane, 1911.

Christie, Agatha. *A Murder Is Announced*. Dodd, Mead, 1935.

Clapp, Patricia. *Witches' Children*. Lothrop, Lee and Shepard, 1982.

Collier, James Lincoln, and Christopher Collier. *Jump Ship to Freedom*. Delacorte, 1981.

_____ . *My Brother Sam Is Dead*. Four Winds, 1974.

_____ . *The Bloody Country*. Four Winds, 1976.

_____ . *The Winter Hero*. Four Winds, 1978.

_____ . *War Comes to Willy Freeman*. Delacorte, 1983.

Comfort, Will. *Apache*. E. P. Dutton, 1931.

Crispin, Edmund. *Buried for Pleasure*. Lippincott, 1949.

_____ . *The Long Divorce*. Dodd, Mead, 1951.

Decker, William. *To Be a Man*. Little, Brown, 1967.

Doyle, Arthur Conan. *A Study in Scarlet*. Penguin, 1982.

Dumas, Alexandre. *The Count of Monte Cristo*. 1844.

Fisher, Vardis. *The Mothers: An American Saga of Courage*. Vanguard, 1943.

Futrelle, Jacques. *Great Cases of the Thinking Machine*. Dover, 1976.

Goodall, Jane. *The Chimpanzees of Gomba*. Harvard University Press, 1986.

Goudge, Elizabeth. *Green Dolphin Street*. Coward, McCann & Geoghegan, 1944.

Grimes, Martha. *I Am the Only Running Footman*. Little, Brown, 1986.

Hallstead, William F. *Tundra*. Crown, 1985.

Henry, Will. *From Where the Sun Now Stands*. Random House, 1960.

Herzog, Maurice. *Annapurna: First Conquests of an 8000 Meter Peak*. E. P. Dutton, 1952.

Holzel, Tom, and Audrey Salkeld. *First on Everest: The Mystery of Mallory and Irvine*. Holt, 1986.

James, P. D. *A Taste for Death*. Knopf, 1986.

_____ . *An Unsuitable Job for a Woman*. Scribner, 1972.

_____ , and T. A. Critchley. *The Maul and the Pear Tree: The Ratcliffe Highway Murders 1811*. Mysterious Press, 1986.

Johnston, Mary. *To Have and to Hold*. 1900.

Kahn, Joan, ed. *Ready or Not: Here Come Fourteen Frightening Stories!* Greenwillow, 1987.

_____ . *Some Things Dark and Dangerous*. Harper & Row, 1970.

_____ . *Some Things Fierce and Fatal*. Harper & Row, 1971.

_____ . *Some Things Strange and Sinister*. Harper & Row, 1973.

Kaminsky, Stuart. *Murder on the Yellow Brick Road*. St Martin's Press, 1977.

King, Stephen. *Christine*. Viking, 1983.

_____ . *Cujo*. Viking, 1981.

_____ . *Salem's Lot*. Doubleday, 1975.

_____ . *The Shining*. Doubleday, 1978.

_____ . *The Stand*. Doubleday, 1978.

Kirkpatrick, Sidney D. *A Cast of Killers*. E. P. Dutton, 1986.

L'Amour, Louis. *Down the Long Hills*. Bantam, 1968.

Lasky, Kathyrn. *Beyond the Divide*. Macmillan, 1983.

LeMan, Alan. *The Searchers*. Harper & Row, 1954.

Levin, Ira. *Rosemary's Baby*. Random House, 1967.

Lewis, Matthew Gregory. *The Monk*. 1796.

Locke, Charles O. *The Hell Bent Kid*. Norton, 1957.

MacDonald, John D. *The Lonely Silver Rain*. Knopf, 1985.

Mazer, Harry. *Snow Bound*. Delacorte, 1973.

_____ . *The Island Keeper,* Delacorte, 1981.

McCaig, Donald. *Nop's Trials*. Crown, 1984.

McClure, James. *The Artful Egg*. Pantheon, 1985.

_____ . *The Steam Pig*. Pantheon, 1972.

Mitchell, Margaret. *Gone with the Wind*. Macmillan, 1936.

Nixon, Joan Lowery. *A Dark and Deadly Pool*. Delacorte, 1987.

Oster, Jerry. *Sweet Justice*. Harper & Row, 1985.

Owens, Mark, and Delia Owens. *Cry of the Kalahari*. Houghton Mifflin, 1984.

Parker, Robert. *Pale Kings and Princes*. Delacorte, 1987.

Peters, Ellis. *A Morbid Taste for Bones: The First Chronicle of Brother Cadfael*. Random House, 1977.

Pullman, Philip. *Shadow in the North.* Knopf, 1988.

————— . *The Ruby in the Smoke.* Knopf, 1987.

Queen, Ellery. *The Greek Coffin Mystery.* Stokes, 1932.

Radcliffe, Ann. *The Mysteries of Udolpho.* 1794.

Reeves, Clara. *The Old English Baron.* 1780.

Rendell, Ruth. *An Unkindness of Ravens.* Pantheon, 1985.

————— . *Death Notes.* Pantheon, 1981.

————— . *Live Flesh.* Pantheon, 1986.

————— . *Speaker of Mandarin.* Pantheon, 1983.

Rhodes, Eugene Manlove. *Pasò Por Aquì.* Houghton Mifflin, 1927.

Rosen, R. D. *Strike Three, You're Dead.* Walker. 1984.

Rowell, Galen. *In the Throne Room of the Mountain Gods.* Sierra Club Books. 1977.

————— . *Mountain Light: In Search of the Dynamic Landscape.* Sierra Club Books, 1986.

Rutherfurd, Edward. *Sarum.* Crown, 1987.

Sabatini, Rafael. *Scaramouche.* Grossett and Dunlap, 1921.

Safire, William. *Freedom: A Novel of Abraham Lincoln and the Civil War.* Doubleday, 1987.

Scarborough, Dorothy. *The Wind.* Harper, 1925.

Schwartz-Nobel, Loretta. *Engaged to Murder: The Inside Story of the Main Line Murders.* Viking, 1987.

Scott, Sir Walter. *Ivanhoe.* 1819.

Shelley, Mary. *Frankenstein; or the Modern Prometheus.* 1818.

Sisson, Rosemary Anne. *Will in Love.* Morrow, 1977.

Sutcliff, Rosemary. *Blood Feud.* E. P. Dutton, 1977.

————— . *Dawn Wind.* Walck, 1961.

————— . *Knight's Fee.* Walck, 1960.

————— . *Outcast.* Oxford University Press, 1955.

————— . *Simon.* Oxford University Press, 1954.

————— . *Sun Horse, Moon Horse.* E. P. Dutton, 1978.

————— . *The Capricorn Bracelet.* Walck, 1973.

————— . *The Lantern Bearers.* Walck, 1959.

————— . *The Mark of the Horse Lord.* Walck, 1959.

————— . *The Shield Ring.* Oxford University Press, 1957.

————— . *The Silver Branch.* Oxford University Press, 1954.

————— . *Warrior Scarlet.* Walck, 1958.

Taylor, Theodore. *Walking up a Rainbow; Being the True Verson of the Long and Hazardous Journey of Susan D. Carlisle, Mrs. Myrtle Dessery, Drover Bert Petitt, and Cowboy Clay Carmer and Others.* Delacorte, 1986.

Tenny, Dixie. *Call the Darkness Down.* Atheneum, 1984.

Thomas, Elizabeth Marshall. *Reindeer Moon.* Houghton Mifflin, 1987.

Tullis, Julie. *Clouds from Both Sides: An Autobiography.* Sierra Club Books, 1987.

Turner, Ann. *Third Girl from the Left.* Macmillan, 1986.

Turow, Scott. *Presumed Innocent.* Farrar, Straus & Giroux, 1987.

Upfield, Arthur W. *Death of a Lake.* Doubleday, 1954.

Van Gulik, Robert. *The Chinese Nail Murders.* Harper & Row, 1961.

Von Canon, Claudia. *The Inheritance.* Houghton Mifflin, 1983.

————— . *The Moonclock.* Houghton Mifflin, 1979.

Waddell, Helen. *Peter Abelard.* 1933.

Walker, Margaret. *Jubilee.* Houghton Mifflin, 1966.

Walpole, Horace. *The Castle of Otranto.* 1764.

Wambaugh, Joseph. *Echoes in the Darkness.* Perigord/Morrow, 1987.

————— . *The Glitter Dome.* Morrow, 1981.

————— . *The Onion Field.* Delacorte, 1973.

Welch, James. *Fool's Crow.* Viking, 1986.
_____ . *The Death of Jim Loney.* Harcourt Brace Jovanovich, 1979.
_____ . *Winter in the Blood.* Harcourt Brace Jovanovich, 1974.
Westall, Robert. *Break of Dark.* Greenwillow, 1982.
_____ . *The Wind Eye.* Greenwillow, 1977.

Wise, Herbert A., and Phillis Fraser, eds. *Great Tales of Terror and the Supernatural.* Modern Library, 1944.
Wister, Owen. *The Virginian: The Horseman of the Plains.* Macmillan, 1922.
Wright, Peter. *Spycatcher: The Candid Autobiography of a Senior Intelligence Officer.* Viking, 1987.

For information on the availability of paperback editions of these titles, please consult the most recent edition of *Paperbound Books in Print,* published annually by R. R. Bowker Company.

CHAPTER SIX

FANTASY, SCIENCE FICTION, AND UTOPIAS
Of Wondrous Worlds

All of us, save the most literal-minded, need occasionally to go outside ourselves, to dream old and new dreams about the strange and impossible and dangerous and exacting, to travel to lands that lie beyond our mundane and limited worlds and exist only in the imaginations of other people. We may even create a new world for ourselves, peopled with creations fashioned in our own image or in the images of people and animals and things we love. The works we create often derive from favorite authors. Thousands of young people have loved *The Wizard of Oz* so much that they borrowed from Frank Baum to create their own Oz books or became wrapped in the wonderful world of Kenneth Grahame's *The Wind in the Willows* and have written amazingly parallel stories.

That need hardly diminishes as we grow older, and that helps to account for the continuing popularity of science fiction, fantasy, and utopian books. Fantasy and science fiction allow us to see the golden worlds of the past and future, and utopias permit us to see a perfect society made attainable. Without dreams, we die. But we worry about becoming too preoccupied with our dreams. To live permanently in science fiction, fantasy, and utopia is to divorce ourselves from the very real concerns of our very real world. On the other hand, to accept the real world we know as the only possible world is to damn ourselves to a stifling and deadly existence. Perhaps because young adults have not yet been hopelessly squelched by society, they often respond openly to the kinds of books presented in this chapter. Many young people are still examining lifestyles and societies around them, and they are keenly interested in looking at the alternatives in fantasy, science fiction, and utopias (see Table 6.1).

Table 6.1   *SUGGESTIONS FOR EVALUATING IMAGINATIVE LITERATURE*

A good piece of imaginative literature has most of the positive qualities generally associated with good fiction. In addition it usually has:	A poor piece of imaginative literature has the negative qualities generally associated with poor fiction. In addition it may have:
A smooth, unhackneyed way of establishing the imaginative world.	An awkward transition between reality and fantasy.
An originality of concept. Without this originality, it cannot accurately be labelled *fantasy*.	A reliance on trite stereotypes already created by other writers of science fiction or fantasy.
Enough relationship to the real world so that the reader is led to look at the world in a new way or from a new viewpoint.	No relationship to the real world or to human nature.
Something that stimulates readers to participate in the author's creative thinking and to carry the story further in their own minds.	Inconsistencies within the story. The author unpredictably changes the behavior of the characters or relies on unexpected magical solutions to solve problems.
A rigorous adherence to the "rules" of the imaginative world so that the story is internally consistent even though it may break with the physical laws of this world as they are now known.	

FANTASY

In the *Saturday Review* of November 4, 1972, Patrick Merla argued that as young readers' literature became more realistic, adult literature grew more fantastic:

> The paradox of "reality" for children versus "fantasy" for adults may be double-edged—children looking for facts to help them cope with an abrasive environment while adults probe a deeper archetypal reality that can transform society altogether. A paradox not merely bemusing or amusing, but one that betokens a renascence of the wish to live humanely: a wealth of profound possibilities for mankind.[1]

What Merla wrote about adult reading remains true. But he overestimated the power of realistic literature and badly underestimated the power of fantasy on young people. Fantasy now is popular with readers of all ages.

Testimony to the therapeutic value of fantasy is easy to find. Folklorist and fantasy writer J. R. R. Tolkien wrote:

> Fantasy is a natural human activity. It certainly does not destroy or even insult Reason; and it does not either blunt the appetite for, nor obscure the perception of, scientific verity. On the contrary, the keener and the

> clearer is the reason, the better fantasy it will make. If men were ever in a state in which they did not want to know or could not perceive truth (facts or evidence) then Fantasy would languish until they were cured.[2]

Theologian Harvey Cox maintains that fantasy is essential and allows humanity to relive and anticipate, to remake the past and create new futures:

> Fantasy is the richest source of human creativity. Theologically speaking, it is the image of the creator God in man. Like God, man in fantasy creates whole worlds *ex nihilo,* out of nothing.
>
> Yet despite its importance, our era has dealt shabbily with fantasy. In many other cultures fantasy has been carefully nurtured and those with unusual abilities in fantasy honored. In ours, we have ignored fantasy, deprecated it, or tried to pretend it wasn't really there. Above all, we pride ourselves on being "realists."[3]

But Ray Bradbury agreed that fantasy is essential to our lives today:

> The ability to "fantasize" is the ability to survive. It's wonderful to speak about this subject because there have been so many wrong-headed people dealing with it. We're going through a terrible period in art, in literature and living, in psychiatry and psychology. The so-called realists are trying to drive us insane, and I refuse to be driven insane. . . . We survive by fantasizing. Take that away from us and the whole damned race goes down the drain.[4]

The appeal of fantasy may come from a simple fact with complex underlyings. The world of fantasy is both greater and seemingly simpler than our mechanistic, technologically absurd, mad world. Most of us are—or will be—bound by making a living, paying taxes, trying desperately to find a bit of satisfaction in our jobs and in our lives. We will never have the opportunity to battle for pure good against total evil, as happens in fantasy, or so we think. But we can fight that battle and journey on fabulous quests in strange lands against frightening beasts by reading Tolkien or Ursula Le Guin or Anne McCaffrey or Walter Wangerin, Jr. What is rational is important, but it is not all of life.

Fantasy allows—or forces—us to become greater than we had hoped we were. Fantasy confronts us with the major ambiguities and dualities of life—evil and good, guilt and innocence, appearance and reality, baseness and nobility, weakness and strength, life and death, negligence and responsibility, the cowardly and the heroic, indolence and hard work, vacillation and determination, affectation and openness, anarchy and order, dark and light, confusion and discipline. And the multitudinous shadings in between these linked pairs must be considered and thought through, by adults and young adults.

Two attacks have been leveled against fantasy. It is sometimes said to be childishly easy reading, but only nonreaders of fantasy could long persist in that nonsense. Fantasies are often very long, and they are almost always more difficult and require closer reading than most other literature, filled as they are with strange beings and mythical overtones and ambiguities.

Fantasy is often labeled escapist literature, and, of course, it is, in several ways. Fantasy allows readers to escape the mundane reality that surrounds all of us and to revel in glorious adventures. For some readers, that is quite enough to ask of books. For other readers, venturing into possibly endless quests (for the books often come in series), discovering incredible obstacles, and facing apparently unbeatable antagonists, all to defend good and defeat evil, transitory though the defeat will prove, leads to more than mere reading. The escape from reality sends them back into their own limited and literal worlds to face many of the same problems they found in fantasy. Fantasy in many ways parallels life. The quest is the long journey we all set out on, seeking the good and fighting the bad, facing obstacles and barriers throughout, and ultimately hoping that we will find satisfaction and meaning during and after the quest. Our emotional and intellectual wrestling with life's dualities and ambiguities may not be as earth-shaking as those of fantasy heroes, but it may shake our own personal worlds.

In the December 1971 *Horn Book Magazine,* Lloyd Alexander drew the parallel between the fantasy hero and the lives of readers:

The fantasy hero is not only a doer of deeds, but he also operates within a framework of morality. His compassion is as great as his courage—greater, in fact. We might consider that his humane qualities, more than any other, are what the hero is really all about. I wonder if this reminds us of the best parts of ourselves?[5]

In his brilliant and often difficult *After Babel: Aspects of Language and Translation,* George Steiner wrote:

Language is the main instrument of man's refusal to accept the world as it is. . . . Ours is the ability, the need, to gainsay or "unsay" the world, to image and speak it otherwise.[6]

Fantasy comes from a Greek word meaning "a making visible." Perhaps more than any other form of literature, fantasy is a way of refusing to "accept the world as it is," a way of making experience visible so readers can see what could have been—and could be—rather than merely what was or must be. Certainly, fantasy gives hope where much literature denies the right to hope.

In an article on teaching science fiction, Ursula Le Guin distinguished fantasy from science fiction:

The basic concept of fantasy, of course, is this: you get to make up the rules, but then you've got to follow them. Science fiction refines the canon: you get to make up the rules, but within limits. A science-fiction story must not flout the evidence of science, must not, as Chip Delaney puts it, deny what is known to be known.[7]

JANE YOLEN
on Reading with the Heart

Whenever I am asked what I do, I say "I am a storyteller" and then add, almost as an afterthought, that I do my storytelling on the page as well as in the mouth. A number of my books have been for the young adult audience, but they were never written for young adults. They were written for the young Jane Yolen who still exists inside my 40+ year-old body, like an antic woodsprite caught inside the bole of a tree. And while I may steal pieces of souls to populate my books and tales from the people I know best—my husband or my three children—the one I write about most is me. *I am the blood and bones, the sinews and heart of all my characters.*

Yet when someone reads my stories, there is a strange exchange, a transfusion. The reader brings him/herself to the book and takes from it the nourishment needed. I always marvel at the way people read my stuff. I heard from a junior high boy that, since he was small and not any good at sports, he felt useless, depressed until he read about Jakkin in *Dragon's Blood* and then understood he could do anything he really wanted to do. Now isn't that strange, since Jakkin is not described as small anywhere in the book? And I heard from a nurse in a hospital that she read my *Girl Who Loved the Wind* to a child dying of cancer, and the story helped the child in her last moments, though the book is not about death or sickness at all. It is about a girl whose overprotective father keeps her walled up in a castle until the wind woos her and takes her out into the everchanging world. I heard from a California storyteller that she had been requested to tell my "Dawn Strider" at a wedding, though it is a tale about a giant who captures the child who brings the sun and releases him only when another child comes and makes friends with them both. A wedding story?

We read with our hearts. The best books infuse us with lifeblood. The worst books make no intrusions at all. I hope that what I write are stories that give life, but when I am creating a story, I don't hold such difficult goals in mind. I simply tell the tale, touch the magic, and pass it on.

Jane Yolen's books include the Pit Dragon Trilogy published by Delacorte, *The Magic Three of Solatio,* Crowell, 1974; *The Gift of Sarah Barker,* Viking, 1981; and *Chaya,* Viking, 1986.

But no matter what the definition, or who propounds it, the boundaries between the two are often fuzzy, witness any Science Fiction Book Club ad. Invariably, the ad mixes science fiction with fantasy books that seem difficult (or impossible) to pigeon-hole into either category. That should surprise few readers since the Club obviously has great appeal to science fiction and fantasy buffs alike. Indeed, many people read both avidly and almost interchangeably.

The conventions of fantasy are well-established though any clever writer is encouraged to create new ones. There must be a quest. Someone, probably a young person, alone or accompanied by friends goes on a quest to protect someone or some country from the powers of evil. The quest may be ordained or required or may, occasionally, be self-determined. Good and evil may be confused briefly by the hero, but the protagonist will ultimately recognize the distinction. The obligatory battle between the powers of good and evil will result in victory for the side of good, though the struggle may be in doubt and may be prolonged. But the victory is always transitory.

John Rowe Townsend, both a fine writer of YA novels and one of the most perceptive and honored critics of the field, maintained that the quest motif was a powerful analogy of life's pattern:

> Life is a long journey, in the course of which one will assuredly have one's adventures, one's sorrows and joys, one's setbacks and triumphs, and perhaps, with luck and effort, the fulfillment of some major purpose.[8]

Heroes must prove worthy of their quest though they may early be fumbling or stumbling or unsure about both themselves and their quests. Heroes in fantasy are young, but the quests hasten maturity, and the striplings we first saw soon prove wise and courageous.

Fantasy is clearly related to mythology, either creating new myths with hobbits or dragons or using old myths many readers will recognize, particularly from Arthurian legend or the Welsh *Mabinogion*. Fantasy is a world of magic. Colors may be important symbols, but light and dark are always symbolic. And to aid readers, the author will usually preface the book with a map which will introduce readers to the new world and aid them in following the hero's quest.

Important Writers of Fantasy

For many fantasy enthusiasts, J. R. R. Tolkien's novels are not merely among the earliest of significant fantasies, Tolkien and his novels are the yardsticks for all fantasy that follows. *The Hobbit, or There and Back Again* began in 1933 as a series of stories Tolkien told his children about the strange little being known as Bilbo, the Hobbit. Even more famous is his trilogy, *The Lord of the Rings*. His love of language led him to create a language, Elfish, for his own amusement and for the book. Appendices to *The Lord of the Rings* are devoted to the history of Middle-Earth, its language, and its geography. An extension of Tolkien's work, *The Silmarillion,* led the *New York Times* bestseller list for several weeks in 1977, amazing for a fantasy, though the work proved disappointing to many Tolkien fans. Tolkien created many of the conventions of fantasy. For that alone, he would be important. But his greatest importance lies in the excellence of *The Hobbit* and *The Lord of the Rings* which can be— and for many people are—read again and again for delight and insight.

Two writers dominate contemporary fantasy—Ursula Le Guin and Anne McCaffrey. Le Guin's early books, *The Left Hand of Darkness* and *The Dispossessed,* were intelligent mixtures of science fiction and fantasy, but her finest three books, "The Earthsea Trilogy," are the purest of fantasies. The setting of *A Wizard of Earthsea,* is of course, Earthsea, a world of vast oceans and multitudinous islands. Duny demonstrates early that he is capable of becoming a wizard, is given his true name, Ged, and learns the names of all things—word magic binds the worlds of fantasy and fairy tales together. Childishly showing off in a forbidden duel of sorcery at his school on Roke Island "where all high arts are taught," he uses his powers to call a woman from the dead and accidentally releases an evil Power, a Shadow that follows him thereafter. That capricious and childish act causes Ged to become deaf, blind, and mute for four weeks in a hot summer. The Archmage Gensher comes to Ged and says:

> You have greater power inborn in you, and you used that power wrongly, not knowing how that spell affects the balance of light and dark, life and death, good and evil. And you were moved to do this by pride and by hate. Is it any wonder the result was ruin?

Ged completes his training and leaves a certified wizard, but with Ged goes the shadow, of what he knows not except that it is evil.

The remaining two-thirds of the novel consists of many adventures, but always, at the center of Ged's existence, is his quest for the meaning of the shadow. Ged ultimately recognizes that his quest is not to undo what he has done but to finish what he has started. On a lonely shore, Ged meets the shadow, and as if they were one—and they are—they speak the shadow's name, "Ged," and "Light and darkness met, and joined, and were one."

Vetch, Ged's friend, believes that Ged has been overcome by his foe, and he runs to help Ged. When Vetch finds Ged safe:

> he began to see the truth, that Ged had neither lost nor won but, naming the shadow of his death with his own name, had made himself a whole: a man who, knowing his whole true self cannot be used or possessed by any other power other than himself, and whose life therefore is lived for life's sake and never in the service of ruin, or pain, or hatred, or the dark.

A short work less than two hundred pages long, *A Wizard of Earthsea* is rich in characters and suspense and meaning. Ged's quest is an initiation rite which leads him to understand the nature of responsibility and who and what he is.

Ged reappears in *The Tombs of Atuan,* but the chief character is Tenar, dedicated from youth to the Powers of the Earth. In the final book of the trilogy, *The Farthest Shore,* Ged, now Archmage and the most powerful of wizards, accompanies a young man on a quest to seek out the evil that threatens to destroy the lands and the powers of the wizards. The evil is Cob, one of the living dead who seeks the peace of death but cannot find it. Ged helps to find death for Cob, but it costs Ged dearly. Even that is not too much, for earlier Ged had told the young man:

■ You will not die. You will not live forever. Nor will any man nor any thing. Nothing is immortal. But only to us is it given to know that we must die. And that is a great gift: the gift of selfhood. For we have only what we know we must lose, what we are willing to lose.

"The Earthsea Trilogy" entertains—above all it is a remarkable and long adventure tale—as it poses unanswerable and eternal questions to readers. What is the purpose of life? Of death? Of balance and equilibrium? What is the nature of evil? Of good? Of humanity? Le Guin's work rarely disappoints and in these three books, she satisfies readers, not by offering easy, pat answers but by respecting her readers and offering truths in all their richness and complexities and frustrations. Her books are not merely based on myths and magic. Her books *are* myths. Her books *are* magic.

Anne McCaffrey's fantasy world is set on Pern. In her trilogy of *Dragonsong, Dragonsinger,* and *Dragondrums,* Pern is threatened every two hundred years by shimmering threadlike spores. Inhabitants protect themselves through the great Pern dragons who destroy the threads as they fall. In *Dragonsong,* Menolly is forced by her father to give up music and her dream of becoming a Harper, though at the book's conclusion she is known to the Master Harper and is well on her way to a life of music. In the lesser second volume, Menolly trains to become a Harper and meets the sweet-voiced young boy, Piemur. In this fantasy version of an old-fashioned school story, Menolly has trouble with envious students and faces demanding teachers. *Dragondrums* gets back on track in an exciting finale to the series. Pern is again threatened by the deadly Threadfall, and Piemur, whose voice has changed and made him doubt his future as a singer, is sent off as a drum apprentice and then is stranded along with a stolen firedragon. A bit rambling, *Dragondrums* is a satisfying portrait of a troubled boy who learns about responsibility and survival.

McCaffrey tells fine stories of adventures of young people in the throes of initiation rites, but rarely does she approach the complexity of thought or the mythic qualities of Le Guin's work, not even in *The White Dragon* or *Moreta: Dragon Lady of Pern,* satisfying fantasies though they are.

A recent German entry into the field of fantasy, Hans Bemmann's *The Stone and the Flute,* is almost a prototype of the genre. Listener, the hero, loves music more than fighting; at seventeen, he receives a magic agent and only a bit later, he inherits a silver flute; and the remainder of his life clearly will be spent trying to understand the significance and power of these two things. There are, as is true with Le Guin's books and other good fantasies, multiple layers of meanings and ideas, riches piled on riches, each time surprising readers convinced that Bemmann could not surpass the last episode, the last insight. Though Bemmann is not young (he was born in 1922), this is a young book with a sense of adventure and power and compassion that sometimes seems reckless but ultimately is wise and reasoned.

While most fantasies will follow the basic conventions, they tend to fall into these categories: those set in new worlds, as with Le Guin and McCaffrey;

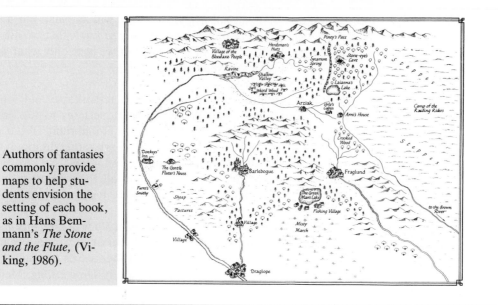

Authors of fantasies commonly provide maps to help students envision the setting of each book, as in Hans Bemmann's *The Stone and the Flute,* (Viking, 1986).

those following myths from the Welsh *Mabinogion*; those celebrating Arthurian legends; those with one foot in contemporary reality and one foot in a fantasy world; those employing animals and often aiming moral barbs at humans; and those using fantasy to amuse. Obviously, some overlapping occurs in many fantasies.

Marion Zimmer Bradley's "Darkover" books are among the most popular of the fantasies set in a new world. Colonists from Earth come to the planet, Darkover, with its one sun and four multicolored moons. Over two thousand years, they lose contact with their home planet and evolve new cultures and new myths alongside the psi-gifted natives. *Darkover Landfall* is a good introduction to the series, although wherever fantasy buffs enter Darkover will likely serve equally well as a starting point. Darkover fans have written so extensively about Bradley's imaginary world that DAW books recently collected some of the best articles under the title, *Red Sun of Darkover* with an introduction by Bradley along with two Bradley articles about Darkover and thirteen contributions by fans elaborating on the magic and power and people of Darkover. For readers getting started on the Darkover books, *Red Sun* is especially helpful since two pages prior to the title page list all the Darkover titles and, more important, briefly describe the Darkover world and the major plot developments.

Katherine Kurtz's Deryni series features a race of extrasensory-powered people in *Deryni Rising, Deryni Checkmate,* and *High Dernyi.* Her Camber series takes place two hundred years before the Deryni books.

Two satisfying writers of other-world fantasies for young adults are Patricia McKillip and Jane Yolen. McKillip creates a land of witches and magic and riddles in *The Forgotten Beasts of Eld* and later books, especially two recent books, *Moon-Flash* and *The Moon and the Face,* which are particularly exciting love stories. Perhaps a bit more traditional are Jane Yolen's trilogy of dragons, a young and unsure young hero, and one of the most intriguing and strongest females in recent fiction in *Dragon's Blood, Heart's Blood,* and *A Sending of Dragons.*

Fantasy and The Mabinogion

The Mabinogion is a collection of medieval Welsh tales, first published in English in 1838–1849 by Lady Charlotte Guest. The eleven stories fall into three parts: the four branches of the Mabinogi (tales to instruct young bards) deal with Celtic legends and myths dealing with (1) Pywll, prince of Dived, (2) Branwen, daughter of Llyr, (3) Manawyddan, son of Llyr, and (4) Math, son of Mathonwy; four independent tales; and four Arthurian romances. Several writers have used the Mabinogi myths and legends as a basis for their books.

Lloyd Alexander's "Prydain Chronicles" consists of five volumes about Taran, the young Assistant Pig-Keeper. The opening book of this rich fantasy, *The Book of Three,* introduces the main characters, especially Taran, and sends him on his quest to save his land, Prydain, from evil. He seeks his own identity as well, for none know his heritage. Taran's early impatience is understandable but vexing to his master, Dalben, who counsels patience "for the time being."

> "For the time being," Taran burst out. "I think it will always be for the time being, and it will be vegetables and horseshoes all my life."
>
> "Tut," said Dalben, "there are worse things. Do you set yourself to be a glorious hero? Do you believe it is all flashing swords and galloping about on horses? As for being glorious . . ."
>
> "What of Prince Gwydion?" cried Taran. "Yes, I wish I might be like him."
>
> "I fear," Dalben said, "that is entirely out of the question."
>
> "But why?" Taran sprang to his feet. "I know if I had the chance . . ."
>
> "Why?" Dalben interrupted. "In some cases," he said, "we learn more by looking for the answer to a question and not finding it than we do from learning the answer itself."

Taran, youthful impetuousness and righteous indignation aglow, is bored by Dalben's thoughts and wants action, and that he finds soon enough.

In *The Black Cauldron,* Taran faces the evil Arawn, and in *The Castle of Llyr,* he and his friends rescue Princess Eilonwy from an evil enchantress. In *Taran Wanderer,* he searches for his heritage and learns something about accepting that most dreadful of events, failure. In the last book, *The High King,* the sword of Dyrnwyn falls into the hands of Arawn, and once more Taran and Prince Gwydion and friends march against evil. Taran learns what all other heroes of fantasy learn, that evil is difficult to conquer even temporarily and impossible to conquer permanently.

Taran's quest allows Alexander to portray a young man stumbling into maturity. From a child who admires heroes for their derring-do, Taran grows into a man who recognizes heroes as symbols of good. From a child who idealizes and then idolizes Princess Eilonwy, he grows into a man who can woo and win her. (One of the appeals of fantasy for young males may be that they can read high adventure stories and real love stories at the same time.) From a child who sees the quest as an adventure leading to heroism, Taran grows into a man who recognizes that heroism requires making choices between good and evil and continuing the quest though it takes a lifetime if necessary. Late in the series when Dalben warns Taran that the tasks he has set for himself are difficult and without certainty of attainment, Taran responds:

> So be it. . . . Long ago I yearned to be a hero without knowing, in truth, what a hero was. Now, perhaps, I understand it a little better. A grower of turnips or a shaper of clay, a common farmer or a king—every man is a hero if he strives more for others than for himself alone. Once . . . you told me that the seeking counts more than the finding. So, too, must the striving count more than the gain.

Far more difficult than Alexander and aimed at an older audience, Alan Garner's earlier books force his young protagonists to face the problem of good versus evil in *The Weirdstone of Brisingamen, The Moon of Gomrath,* and *Elidor.* Though Garner maintains they are less successful than his later work, the three books have proved popular in England while they are less widely used in America. His two best works are *The Owl Service* and *Red Shift,* both complex—perhaps unduly so—and rewarding. *The Owl Service* has been praised by Mary Cadogan and Patricia Craig:

> *The Owl Service* is perhaps the first really adult children's book; the first book, that is, in which childish sensibilities are not deferred to, in which the author has not felt that his audience needs, above all, to be protected.[9]

Based on the legend of Blodenweddin in "Math, son of Mathonwy" in the *Mabinogion, The Owl Service* tells of three young people who find a set of old dishes in an attic and learn that the pattern in the dishes is related to an old Welsh legend involving love and jealousy and hatred. *Red Shift* uses three parallel narratives about love—contemporary, seventeenth century, and second century—intertwining them to make connections about love and about our relationships with the past.

Among other writers who have used the *Mabinogion* as a basis for fantasy, Evangeline Walton (real name, Evangeline Walton Ensely) stands out. Her four-part series, *Prince of Annwn: The First Branch of the Mabinogion, The Children of Llyr: The Second Branch of the Mabinogion, The Song of Rhiannon: The Third Branch of the Mabinogion,* and *The Virgin and the Swine: The*

Fourth Branch of the Mabinogion (the last volume was reprinted in 1970 as *The Island of the Mighty: The Fourth Branch of the Mabinogion*) are among the best of direct retellings of the old Welsh legends. Walton's quartet is both mythology and ecology, for the author makes the earth a divinity which must not be despoiled by humanity. In an afterword to the first book, Walton writes:

> When we were superstitious enough to hold the earth sacred and worship her, we did nothing to endanger our future upon her, as we do now.

King Arthur *and Other Myths in Fantasy*

Arthurian legends have long been staples of fantasy. T. H. White's *The Once and Future King* (a source, for which it can hardly be blamed, for that most dismal of musicals, *Camelot*) is basic to any reading of fantasy. In four books, *The Sword in the Stone, The Witch in the Wood, The Ill-Made Knight,* and *The Candle in the Wind,* White retells the story of Arthur—his boyhood, his prolonged education at the hands of Merlin, his seduction by Queen Morgause, his love for Guinivere and her affair with Lancelot, and Mordred's revenge and Arthur's fall. A later work, *The Book of Merlyn: The Unpublished Conclusion* to *The Once and Future King,* should, like most work left unpublished at an author's death, have been allowed to remain unpublished and largely unknown.

Among the shorter retellings of the legends, no one has surpassed the three-part series by Rosemary Sutcliff. *The Sword and the Circle: King Arthur and the Knights of the Round Table, The Light Beyond the Forest: The Quest for the Holy Grail,* and *The Road to Camlann: The Death of King Arthur* are masterfully written by a writer who loves the legends and has a firm grasp on the materials and the meanings.

Mary Stewart, author of several fine suspense novels, focuses more on Merlin than Arthur in *The Crystal Cave, The Hollow Hills,* and *The Last Enchantment* and on Mordred rather than Arthur in the last book, *The Wicked Day.* Even better are Gillian Bradshaw's three books; *Hawk of May, Kingdom of Summer,* and *In Winter's Shadow* may puzzle a few readers at first—the author writes about Medraut instead of Mordred, Gwynhwyfar rather than Guinivere, Gwalchmai rather than Gawain—but readers who stay with the books will find them readable and most satisfying. Marion Zimmer Bradley's *The Mists of Avalon* takes a different approach, the conflict between the old religion of the Celtics, represented by Morgan Le Fay (here called Morgaine), and the new religion of Christianity, represented by Guinivere (here called Gwenhyfar).

Australian writer Patricia Wrightson has written excellent fiction about mythology of her native land from *The Nargun and the Stars* to *A Little Fear.* A young Aborigine, Wirron, struggles against ice-spirits who plan to cover the continent with a new ice age in *The Ice Is Coming.* He battles other spirits in *The Dark Bright Water* and *Journey Behind the Wind.*

Two exceptional talents handle humanity's obsession with flying in books that go back and forth between reality and fantasy. William Wharton's *Birdy* tells of two boyhood friends, reunited in a World War II psychiatric ward. Always worried about his parents and life generally, Birdy invents another self who can fly away, becomes fascinated by canaries, and tries to dream himself into the soul and body of a bird. Jane Langton's *The Fledgling* is transcendental in tone and setting. Uncle Freddy Hall, founder of the Condord College of Transcendental Knowledge, asks, "Why should we not have been born with wings?" His young niece yearns to fly and, helped by a wild goose, she does, in this warm and delicious novel.

Animal stories aimed at instructing humans are as old as Aesop and almost as recent as yesterday's book review. One of the most beloved is Kenneth Grahame's *The Wind in the Willows* about Toad, Rat, and Mole, just as it is about Toad Hall, fast driving, medieval dungeons, pantheism, and delights fondly remembered by thousands.

The finest of all recent animal fables about humanity's foibles is Walter Wangerin, Jr.'s *The Book of the Dun Cow*, a delightfully funny theological thriller retelling the story of Chauntecleer the Rooster. Nominally the leader of good against evil (the half-snake, half-cock Cockatrice, and the black serpant, Wyrm), Chauntecleer is beset by personal doubts. He is aided by the humble Mundo Cani, the dog, some hilariously pouting turkeys, and other assorted barnyard animals. If the cast sounds cute, Wangerin's novel is not, and the battle scenes are bloody and horrifying. *The Book of Sorrows* is a recent, less successful, sequel.

Writing for young adults, Clare Bell has three almost mythic novels about animals. In *Ratha's Creatures,* Ratha, a cat in a world where cats rule other animals, is a young herder who discovers fire and for that is banned from her kingdom. She fights her way back to power and in the sequel, *Clan Ground,* Ratha is now the established leader who faces her own rebelling subjects. *Tomorrow's Sphinx* is a story of the future when a cheetah tries to survive despite humans' attempts to capture her.

Many readers of fantasy associate the genre with high seriousness, but Peter Beagle stands out for his quiet and witty and amusing *A Fine and Private Place* and *The Last Unicorn.* The titles of *A Fine and Private Place* come from Andrew Marvell's "To His Coy Mistress":

> The Grave's a fine and private place,
> But none, I think, do there embrace.

The grave is also a lively and frequently funny place in Beagle's fantasy. A living human talks to a delightfully tough old raven. In *The Last Unicorn,* a lonely unicorn seeks the company of others of its kind, helped by the magician Schmendrick who is incapable of telling any story without wild elaboration. Stopping at a town early in the quest, Schmendrick tells of his adventures:

> During the meal Schmendrick told stories of his life as an errant enchanter, filling it with kings and dragons and noble ladies. He was not lying, merely organizing events more sensibly.

Robin McKinley deserves special attention for *The Blue Sword* and *The Hero and the Crown*. Her *Beauty* is a retelling of the "Beauty and the Beast" legend, differing from earlier versions in a few significant details. McKinley's Beauty is strong and unafraid and loving. When her father tells her that he has been condemned to death by the Beast for stealing a rose, Beauty gladly agrees to change places with her father:

> "He cannot be so bad if he loves roses so much."
> "But he is a Beast," said Father helplessly.
> I saw that he was weakening, and wishing only to comfort him, I said, "Cannot a Beast be tamed?"

McKinley's version lacks the surrealistic quality of Jean Cocteau's magnificent film, but in most important ways, McKinley's novel compares favorably with any other retelling.

SCIENCE FICTION

Science fiction enjoys tremendous popularity today, but not too many years ago that was hardly the case. A visit to the paperback racks of a bookstore then would likely have revealed no section devoted to science fiction though science fiction books might have been sprinkled here and there in the fiction department. Today's science fiction fan would have no trouble finding a large section given over to the genre, though frequently science fiction is mixed in with fantasy, mostly because borders between the two genres are sometimes extremely blurry. Publishers, hardback and paperback, recognize the size and purchasing power of the market, and several have developed a separate division for science fiction alone.

Science fiction's popularity is well established. If serious science fiction films like *Things to Come* in 1936 were a rarity and most filmgoers still assumed science fiction consisted of speedily tossed together pasteboard scenery and pasteboard characters like the "Flash Gordon" serials, that is certainly not true today. *Invasion of the Body Snatchers* in 1956 (and its inferior remake in 1978), the superb and too little known *Village of the Damned* and *The Time Machine* in 1960, *2001: A Space Odyssey* in 1968, *Close Encounters of the Third Kind* in 1977, and George Lucas' trilogy—*Star Wars* in 1977, *The Empire Strikes Back* in 1980, and *Return of the Jedi* in 1983—are perhaps more watched today in reruns and videotapes than when they were released.

And we cannot ignore the continuing popularity of "Star Trek" on television. No great success when it opened its first season with "The Man Trap" on September 8, 1966, and still largely a cult show when it concluded its third, and final, season with "Turnabout Intruder" on June 3, 1969, the seemingly perpetual TV reruns of "Star Trek" have built an apparently vast group of enthusiasts who do not tire of anything about the series or Captain Kirk or Mr.

Every year science fiction fans gather at conventions to talk about their favorite characters, authors, and books.

Spock or anyone else directly, or tangentially, connected to the show. For snobs who never deigned to read or see anything remotely concerned with science fiction, "Star Trek" was sometimes a revelation. For those who thought science fiction consisted largely of purple prose writing and tired plots straight out of "Off we go to Venus with Buck Rogers," "Star Trek" established that science fiction could be fresh and fun and sometimes even profound or witty. For those who had read science fiction for years, "Star Trek" was great fun, but more so, it established on television what fans had long known about print matter, that science fiction was delightful reading by writers who had something to say and who had considerable talent in saying it—and a few, notably Ray Bradbury, had literary talent beyond that.

"Star Trek" had engaging and sometimes provocative characters involved in matters which often threatened to cause the end of human life (and sometimes the end of a galaxy—or worse). The words we heard at the opening of each show, "To explore strange new worlds . . . to seek out new life and new civilizations . . . to boldly go where no man has gone before," grabbed us and held us. Some episodes had titles that intrigued us—"Tomorrow Is Yesterday," "This Side of Paradise," "Is There in Truth No Beauty?" and two titles that must have pleased English teachers and were appropriate to the scripts, not merely pretentious bones for the cultured, "The Conscience of the King" and "All Our Yesterdays." Some titles struck us as vaguely mystical or poetic—"A City on the Edge of Forever" and "For the World Is Hollow and I Have Touched the Sky." And at least one episode was great fun, proving that the writers could handle comedy—"The Trouble with Tribbles."

Ray Bradbury argues that the appeal of science fiction is understandable because science fiction is important literature, not merely popular stuff. Opening his essay on "Science Fiction: Why Bother?" he compares himself to a fourth-rate George Bernard Shaw who makes an outrageous statement and then tries to prove it. Bradbury's statement is that "Science fiction is the most important fiction being written today." He adds that it is not "part of the Main Stream. It *is* the Main Stream."[10]

Carl Sagan, the Cornell University astronomer-author, has added his testimony, writing that it was science fiction that brought him to science. Kurt Vonnegut, Jr., also applauded science fiction through character Eliot Rosewater in *God Bless You, Mr. Rosewater, or Pearls Before Swine*. Stumbling into a convention of science fiction writers, Rosewater drunkenly tells them that he loves them because they are the only ones who:

> . . . know that life is a space voyage, and not a short one either, but one that'll last for billions of years. You're the only ones with guts enough to really care about the future, who really notice what machines do to us, what wars do to us, what cities do to us, what big, simple ideas do to us, what tremendous misunderstandings, mistakes, accidents and catastrophes do to us.

He goes on to praise them for being "zany enough to agonize over time and distances without limit, over mysteries that will never die, over the fact that we are right now determining whether the space voyage for the next billion years or so is going to be Heaven or Hell."

Science fiction writer and scientist Arthur C. Clarke agrees with Rosewater on the admittedly limited but still impressive power of science fiction to scan the future. In his introduction to *Profiles of the Future,* Clarke writes:

> A critical—the adjective is important—reading of science-fiction is essential training for anyone wishing to look more than ten years ahead. The facts of the future can hardly be imagined *ab initio* by those who are unfamiliar with the fantasies of the past.
>
> This claim may produce indignation, especially among those second-rate scientists who sometimes make fun of science-fiction (I have never known a first-rate one to do so—and I know several who write it). But the simple fact is that anyone with sufficient imagination to assess the future realistically would, inevitably, be attracted to this form of literature. I do not for a moment suggest that more than one percent of science-fiction readers would be reliable prophets; but I do suggest that almost a hundred percent of reliable prophets will be science-fiction readers—or writers.[11]

Why does science fiction appeal to young adults, and to adults? First and probably most important, it is exciting. Science fiction may have begun with the "rah-rah-we're-off-to-Venus-with-Buck-Rogers" kind of book, and while it has gone far beyond that, the thrill of adventure is still there in most science fiction. Science fiction writers refuse to write down to their audience, the highest praise they can give to their readers, and this is recognized and admired. Science fiction allows anyone to read imaginative fiction without feeling the material is kid stuff. Science fiction presents real heroes to readers who find their own world often devoid of anyone worth admiring, heroes doing something brave, going to the ultimate frontiers, even pushing these frontiers further back, particularly important at a time when many young people wonder if any new frontiers exist. Most important, science fiction writers see their readers as intellectually curious, praise of the highest order, and that is repaid by readers who often venerate the best of science fiction writers.

Science fiction has its heritage of fine writers and important books. Some critics maintain that the genre began with Mary Wollstonecraft Shelley's *Frankenstein, or The Modern Prometheus* in 1818. Others argue for Swift's *Gulliver's Travels* in 1726 or the much earlier Lucian's *The True History* in the second century A.D. No matter, for nearly everyone agrees that the first major and widely read writer was Jules Verne whose *Journey to the Center of the Earth* in 1864 and *Twenty Thousand Leagues under the Sea* in 1870 pleased readers on several continents. The first American science fiction came with Edgar Allan Poe's short story, "The Unparalleled Adventures of One Hans Pfaall" which appeared in the June 1835 *Southern Literary Messenger* and was included in *Tales of the Grotesque and Arabesque* in 1840. Hans Pfaall's balloon trip to the moon in a nineteen-day voyage may be a hoax, but the early trappings of science fiction are there. Dime novels occasionally used science fiction, particularly in the "Frank Reade" series, as did some books from the Stratemeyer Literary Syndicate, particularly in the "Tom Swift" and "Great Marvel" series.

The development of modern science fiction began with Hugo H. Gernsback. (The Hugo Awards given each year for science fiction excellence honor his name.) An electrical engineer, in 1908 he began publishing *Modern Electrics,* the first magazine devoted to radio. In 1911, finding a few extra pages in his magazine, he began a serial about inventions and innovations in the future. Because it was successful, Gernsback used similar stories later, and in 1926 he began *Amazing Stories* and in 1929 *Science Wonder Stories.* His insistence on too-literal and sterile scientific accuracy in stories made his work formula-ridden and repetitive, but he did offer a market for a type of science fiction story. Later magazines proved somewhat more liberal and willing to accept what then appeared offbeat, and many of today's major science fiction writers broke into print in those magazines.

Science fiction took great strides toward respectability as literature and prophecy after World War II, partly because science fiction writers had predicted both the atomic age and the computer revolution. Perhaps, because a long and deadly war was now over, people seemed more willing to consider alternatives and to reappraise society and to read literature that did both. The paperback revolution flourished, and science fiction became easily available to many readers.

Sure proof that science fiction had become academically respectable came in December 1959 when the prestigious and stuffy Modern Language Associ-

MONICA HUGHES
on Four Dimensions of Science Fiction

It is a pity that *Science Fiction* is so often wedged between *Romance* and *Western* by virtue of its place in the alphabet, and that not enough attention is paid to its strengths as a genre. As the first mythology helped to explicate the terrifying and apparently irrational prescientific world, so can the new mythology of science fiction explicate the possibilities of the Einsteinian universe in which we find ourselves. It can be a bridge between the world in which we live and the even more bewildering world of tomorrow which, whether we like it or not, is the world with which our young people will have to cope.

Science fiction may also be prophetic: some of the earlier writers were extraordinarily prescient in their understanding of the social problems that might follow the wholesale acceptance of a technological society. It is also an excellent way of presenting social problems in parable form, problems such as prejudice, as in the love between Olwen and Mark in *Keeper of the Isis Light,* doomed because Mark loves the superficial, not the real, Olwen. Or, as I did in *Ring-Rise, Ring-Set,* one can present a modern dilemma in an unthreatening way: the dichotomy between the exponents of new technology at all costs and those of the rights of indigenous peoples.

Recognition of these hidden elements in science fiction for the young adult can lead to very fruitful classroom discussion. Discussion leads readily to writing, out of that marvelous story starters: What would happen if . . . ? Plays, poems, art projects, board games, future fashion shows, and cookery are all possibilities arising from the stimulus of science fiction.

Obviously the teacher or librarian must read science fiction with a discerning eye, as well as an open mind, because there is a lot of poor science fiction around. But if the same criteria are applied as would be for realistic fiction: sound plot, well-researched settings, believable characters and dialogue, then, without prejudice, science fiction can be not only an exciting read, but also a marvelous classroom tool as myth, prophesy, and parable.

Monica Hughes' books include *Devil on My Back,* Macmillan, 1986; *The Isis Peddlar,* Macmillan, 1983; and *Hunter of the Dark,* Macmillan, 1983.

ation began its science fiction journal, *Extrapolation.* Colleges and secondary schools offered courses in the genre. Major publishers and significant magazines recognized and published science fiction.

Robert A. Heinlein, one of science fiction's big four writers, defined science fiction in 1953:

> But what, under rational definition is *science* fiction? There is an easy touchstone; science fiction is speculative fiction in which the author takes as his first postulate the real world as we know it, including all established facts

and natural laws. The result can be extremely fantastic in content, but it is not fantasy; it is legitimate—and often very tightly reasoned—speculation about the possibilities of the real world.[12]

Science fiction must adhere to natural law. A novel can use quite different laws of another planet, but those laws must be scientifically clear and consistent. No dragons need apply for work in science fiction—they are the province of fantasy. The limitation has rarely proved onerous to science fiction writers, many of whom are engineers or scientists or had their early training in the sciences.

There are other conventions though none so important as Heinlein's. Characters voyage into space facing all sorts of dangers—science fiction is, after all, more adventure than philosophy, though the latter is often present. Other planets have intelligent and/or frightening life forms, though they may differ drastically from Earth's humans. Contemporary problems are projected hundreds or thousands of years into the future, and those new views of overpopulation, pollution, religious bickering, political machinations, and sexual disharmony often give readers a quite different perspective of our world and our problems today. Prophecies are not required in science fiction, but some of the richest books of Isaac Asimov and Arthur C. Clarke have been prophetic. Occasionally a scientifically untenable premise may be used. On the August 15, 1983, "Nightcap" talk show on Arts Cable Television, Isaac Asimov said, "The best kind of sci-fi involves science" and then agreed that "Time travel is theoretically impossible but I wouldn't want to give it up as a plot gimmick." Essentially, he was agreeing with Heinlein but adding that the plot and excitement counted even more. The internal consistency and plausibility of a postulated imaginary society creates its own reality.

Four Significant Science Fiction Writers

Ballantine editor Judy Del Rey said, "Defining science fiction is simply saying three names—Isaac Asimov, Robert A. Heinlein, and Arthur C. Clarke, one could almost add Ray Bradbury. The four of them established touchstones for those who are to come."[13]

Bradbury's *The Martian Chronicles* is widely known and taught in secondary schools, though whether the work is science fiction is open to argument. Bradbury has no interest in science, except that humans use science to destroy one another. He certainly pays no attention to the way in which passengers get to Mars. They get on a rocket, and somehow it takes them where they want to go. The novel, really a collection of some good, some excellent, short stories loosely tied together, is an important work, whether science fiction or not. In a prefatory note to Bantam's 1954 paperback edition of *The Martian Chronicles,* Clifton Fadiman perceptively writes that Bradbury:

has caught hold of a simple, obvious but overwhelmingly important moral idea, and quite properly, he will not let it go. That idea . . . is that we are in the grip of a psychosis, a technology-mania, the final consequence of which can only be universal murder and quite conceivably the destruction of our planet.

His colonizers—not all, but the majority—cannot help destroying the magnificent civilization of Mars, any more than they could help destroying their own earth civilization.

And Bradbury has said, "I don't try to predict the future—I try to prevent it."

Bradbury's only true science fiction novel (or novelette) is *Farenheit 451*, a warning about a world to come so anti-intellectual that firemen are trained to burn books, not protect the world from fires.

Arthur C. Clarke is another important science fiction writer, and *Childhood's End* is frequently listed among the great science fiction novels, though more readers begin rather than finish it. The story of aliens who take over the Earth's problems and ultimately the Earth itself is utopian science fiction. Under the guidance of Chief Overlord Karellan, aliens develop what seems to be a perfect society for humans. "For the first time in human history, no one worked at tasks they did not like . . . Ignorance, disease, poverty, and fear had virtually ceased to be." More approachable is *Rendezvous with Rama* set in 2130 as humans investigate a hollow fifty-kilometer long cylindrical alien spaceship called Rama and inhabited by robots.

Isaac Asimov remains one of the most popular writers in the field, more for what he has done in the past than what he has done recently. Author of an incredible number of books, all revealing a curious and perceptive mind, he is best known for his *Foundation* trilogy. *Foundation* prophesies the doom of the Empire. Mathematician Hari Selden establishes two Foundations to survive the coming crisis, one on the planet Terminus for hard science, one on the other end of the galaxy for purposes unclear. *Foundation and Empire* describes the destruction of the imperial planet with much about the first foundation and a genetic mutant, Mule, who hopes to take over the fallen empire. *Second Foundation* tells of the Mule who seeks to destroy the first foundation. The second foundation physically challenges the mutant.

Some Asimov fans believe his stories about robots and their relationship to humanity are among his best work. A recent collection contains his fine short story, "Runaround," along with Asimov's best known contribution to science fiction, the Three Laws of Robotics:

1. A robot may not injure a human being, nor through inaction allow a human being to come to harm.
2. A robot must obey the orders given it by human beings except where such orders would conflict with the First Law.
3. A robot must protect its own existence as long as such protection does not conflict with the First or Second Law.[14]

Asimov's autobiography covering the years before he became a well-known writer, *In Memory Yet Green: The Autobiography of Isaac Asimov, 1920–1954*, tells of his early interest in science fiction, but the book is such that almost anyone curious about an interesting life will enjoy it.

The giant of science fiction writers was Robert A. Heinlein. Prolific and consistently fine, his novels ranged from relatively unsophisticated thrillers for young readers from the 1940s through the early 1960s: *Citizen of the Galaxy, Starman Jones, Farmer in the Sky, Have Space Suit—Will Travel. Podkayne of Mars* was a rarity for its time, for the hero is female. But if Heinlein had done little more than continue to mine the science fiction vein for young readers, he would not be considered important.

Stranger in a Strange Land in 1961 marked the major change in Heinlein's work. One of the most widely read novels during the revolutionary 1960s and 1970s, *Stranger* became something of a bible to many college students and was used to justify everything from total sexual freedom to humanity's eternal need for spiritual love, though most readers seemed to lean more toward the sexual than the spiritual.

Valentine Michael Smith feels and thinks like a Martian, but when he is brought to Earth, he finds human feelings coming out as he meets and travels with Jill. He learns about sex—an un-Martian quality—and religion as he founds his church, "The Church of All Worlds." When his church is destroyed, Smith escapes with Jill, only to be stoned by a crowd who calls Smith a heretic.

The Moon Is a Harsh Mistress appeared five years later and it is a far more satisfying, if simpler, novel than *Stranger.* Three people and a humanized computer lead a revolt in Luna, a penal colony in the twenty-first century. The story parallels our own Revolution against the British—the Declaration of Independence is dated July 4, 2076. *The Number of the Beast* in 1980, Heinlein's first novel in seven years, was more self-indulgent, a fascinating failure but worth reading because it was by Heinlein. Four people zip around the universe finding universe after universe, some of them already familiar to readers— Lewis Carroll's *Wonderland* and Frank Baum's *Oz. Friday,* far more successful, wastes no words getting started:

> As I left the Kenya Beanstalk capsule, he was right on my heels. He followed me through the door leading to Customs, Health, and Immigration. As the door contracted behind him I killed him.

Friday is an A.P. (artificial person) who acts as courier for someone she knows only as Boss. Earth has become some 400 territorial states, and intrigue and death are everywhere. As usual, Heinlein attacks common humanity and praises the military, savages organized religion and praises rugged individualism. And once more, his female characters are weakly developed. But *Friday* is an important book.

Two later works, *Job: A Comedy of Justice* and *The Cat Who Walks through Walls,* are worth reading because they are by Heinlein, though they may as often disappoint as please. More mystical and more concerned with the human failings than almost anything Heinlein has done before, they are almost certain to fade away while standards like *Stranger in a Strange Land* and *The Moon is a Harsh Mistress* are still read.

Other Important Science Fiction Writers

If the Big Four are still the most widely revered, it is apparent that an additional name may soon join them. Orson Scott Card won the Locus Award for the Best Science Fiction Novel in 1987 with *Speaker for the Dead,* but *Wyrms,* his tenth book, is his best thus far. *Wyrms'* hero is a thirteen-year-old girl, Patience, who has been trained by her father as an assassin and a diplomat who feels a mighty urge, or "Cranning Call," to complete her destiny by journeying to a strange and seductive creature. *Wyrms* is a rich book—a quest, a search for the nature of the good, the eternal battle between good and evil (or, in this case, that which appears to be evil fought by that which appears to be good), and far far more.

Certain themes run through much of science fiction—the fear of aliens or the awareness that the aliens are already among us; time travel; strange and wondrous other worlds; dangers of overpopulation; sex and sexism in the future; religion and the future or religion and other worlds; and the potential horrors of technology.

Ever since H. G. Wells' pioneering *The War of the Worlds,* the aliens-are-coming theme has been a science fiction favorite and since then always in danger of being another cliché, another stereotype. But some writers use it intelligently, and it is, obviously, a fascinating idea. As anthropologist Loren Eiseley said, "One does not meet oneself until one catches the reflection from an eye other than human."

Particularly disagreeable aliens can be found in two science fiction classics. John Wyndham's *The Midwich Cuckoos* focuses on one quiet, almost idyllic, English village. During one September night and the daylong blackout that follows, every woman in the village becomes pregnant. Nine months later, sixty children are born, all quiet, all odd, all with strange eyes that bore into other people. It was filmed under the title, *Village of the Damned,* and a fine film it is. In Jack Finney's *The Body Snatchers* (better known under its film title, *Invasion of the Body Snatchers*), alien forces use pods to replace the population of a small town. The novel ends with the main character trying desperately and vainly to convince others that something sinister is afoot. And two novels by Larry Niven and Jerry Pournelle, *The Mote in God's Eye* and *Footfall*, are about aliens who threaten humanity.

Time travel is a constant of early science fiction which soon became a cliché, but occasional later books made excellent use of it without falling into the usual traps. Jack Finney's *Time and Again* is deservedly read and reread. Simon Morely goes on a secret mission back to the New York City of the 1980s, and there in the midst of danger, he falls in love.

Travel forward in time to different planets was a staple of early boys' series books cranked out by the Stratemeyer Literary Syndicate, particularly the "Great Marvel" series written by the Syndicate housename, Roy Rockwood, with garish but grabby titles like *Lost on the Moon, or In Quest of a Field of Diamonds* and *By Air Express to Venus, or Captives of a Strange Planet.* But good writers have used the topic to effect. Katherine Kurtz's *The Legacy of Lehr* is a murder mystery set aboard a luxury spaceship. One of the premier writers of science fiction, Stanislaw Lem, used space travel in his recent *Fiasco.* Earth has proof that life exists on a silent planet called Quinta, and a spaceship is sent to open communication. Only when the ship approaches the planet does it become obvious to the crew that the planet's inhabitants are not quite what Earth has believed.

Both Lester Del Rey's *The Eleventh Commandment* and John Brunner's *Stand on Zanzibar* are about future world overpopulation. Del Rey's book takes the biblical edict to be fruitful and multiply to its logical and horrifying conclusion. Brunner's novel concerns the world of 2010 which has massive overpopulation and ugly consequences.

Ursula K. Le Guin's *The Left Hand of Darkness* describes a race neither male nor female, neither asexual nor bisexual, on the planet Gethen. The Gethenians' sexual cycle is twenty-six days; for four-fifths of the period they are sexually inactive, and then on the twenty-first or twenty-second day, they become sexually active with either female or male hormones dominating. Individuals have neither choice nor interest in which sex they will be at any particular time. It is possible to be pregnant and bear a child, and then father a child at another time. Le Guin's *The Dispossessed* also attacks the conventional-traditional male-female roles. Joanna Russ' *The Female Man* treats the theme of sex and sexism.

Religion has been central to Frank Herbert's science fiction series about the planet Dune. The first, and still far and away the best, is *Dune* about the inhabitants of the planet. *Chapterhouse: Dune* is recent and worth reading by those who have not yet had enough of the Dune world.

Walter H. Miller, Jr.'s *A Canticle for Leibowitz* is a science fiction standard, and a powerful satire on religion and much more. *A Canticle* may be a wise choice for anyone who wishes to sample among the best in science fiction. Indeed, *A Canticle* has been relished by young adults who have no fondness for the genre before or after reading Miller's book.

Technology run mad is a common theme. Walter Tevis' *Mockingbird* shows us a world where humans are subservient to robots, and where robots wish only to die but must await the death of the last human. David Gerrold's *When Harlie Was One* has a hero who is a superhuman computer with the emotional temperament of a dangerous and powerful child. Philip K. Dick's finest novel *Do Androids Dream of Electric Sheep?* is set in a polluted future Earth. Humans have fled the filth, leaving androids behind. Over successive generations, the androids become more and more human, and dangerous, and a bounty hunter is sent to find androids attempting to flee their environment. Yevgeny Zamyatin's *We* was written in 1920 and published in 1924, though never in the author's native Russia. (An Associated Press dispatch for June 25, 1987, announced that Soviet authorities planned to publish *We*, though precisely when was left comfortably vague.) *We* is set in a twenty-sixth century totalitarian society where people are forced to live in glass apartments, to do away with privacy, and people bear numbers, not names.

Satire is a common element in much science fiction and fantasy, but two novels satirizing advertising and Madison Avenue excesses—and published thirty-five years apart—deserve readers. Frederick Pohl and C. M. Kornbluth's *The Space Merchants* is something of a science fiction classic in which Mitchell Courtenay is assigned the job of persuading people to emigrate to Venus. It is predictably delightfully nasty. Brad Strickland's *Moondreams* is not as witty, but the tale of Jeremy Sebastian Moon, ace advertising copywriter, who finds himself in a different world is considerably more than a mere diversion. That's especially true when Moon discovers that his training as an ad man is the salvation of his dilemma.

One recent science fiction novel deserves mention if for nothing more than its originality. Larry Niven, Jerry Pournelle, and Steven Barnes' *The Legacy of Heorot* is a retelling of the legend of Beowulf set on the planet Avalon. A group of space pioneers come to Avalon in the twenty-first century, and the place seems to be idyllic, until the small animals begin to disappear and the inhabitants realize that a monster and his mother are causing the destruction and must be destroyed.

UTOPIAS

Utopias are never likely to be popular with the masses. Utopias lack excitement and fast-moving plots needed for fast reading and easy appeal. Writers of adventure or fantasy or science fiction begin with a story, the more thrilling the better, and later, if at all, add a message. Writers of utopias think first of the message, and then devise a story to carry the weight of the message.

And utopias are usually about dissatisfaction with contemporary society. Many readers have no wish to think seriously about societal issues, much less to read about them. Readers often do not share the anger or irritation of utopian writers, and they will easily miss the allusions needed to follow the story or find the message.

For these reasons, utopian literature is likely to appeal only to more thoughtful and intellectual readers. Young adults may not share all the anger of the writer, but given their idealism, they share the writer's concerns about society and humanity.

The centuries-old fascination with utopias is suggested by the Greek origin of the world which includes two meanings, "no place" and "good place." Most of us, in idle moments, dream of a perfect land, a perfect society, a place that would solve all our personal problems and, if we are altruistic enough, all the world's problems as well. Few of us do more than dream. That may explain why some people are so intrigued with others who take the dream onto the printed page.

In his *Republic* in the fifth century B.C., Plato presented his vision of the ideal world, offering suggestions for educating the ruling class. With wise philosopher-kings, or so Plato maintains, the people would prosper, intellectual joys would flourish (along with censorship for Plato would ban poets and dramatists from his perfect society), and the land would be permanently safe.

Later utopias were geared less to a ruling class and more to a society that would preserve its peace and create harmony and happiness for the people. Sir Thomas More's *Utopia* (1516) argued for mental equality of the sexes, simple laws understandable to all, and common ownership of everything. Whether More intended his book as a practical solution to society's problems is doubtful, but he probably did mean it as a criticism of contemporary English life. Utopias, after all, are personal and reflect an author's enthusiasm for (or abhorrence of) certain ideas. That was clearly true of two other early utopias, Francis Bacon's *The New Atlantis* (1626) and Tommaso Campanella's *City in the Sun* (1623).

During the 1800s, utopias were popular, notably Samuel Butler's *Erewhon* (1872) and *Erewhon Revisited* (1901); William Morris' *News from Nowhere, or an Epoch of Rest* (1891); William Dean Howells' *A Traveler from Altruia* (1894); and the most famous of them all, Edward Bellamy's *Looking Backward* (1888) and its less well-known sequel, *Equality* (1897). In the United States, people sought for better societies through various utopian schemes, rarely more than temporarily satisfactory, in places like Harmony, Pennsylvania; New Harmony, Indiana; Brook Farm, Massachusetts; Fruitlands, Massachusetts; Oneida, New York; Nauvoo, Illinois; and Corning, Iowa.

Twentieth-century writers produced more dystopias (diseased or bad lands) than perfect lands and perfect societies. Dystopias warn us of society's drift toward a particularly horrifying or sick world lying just over the horizon. They are sometimes misinterpreted as prophecies alone, but books like Aldous Huxley's *Brave New World* and George Orwell's *1984* and *Animal Farm* are part prophecy, part warning.

A utopia first serialized in 1915 in an obscure magazine, *The Forerunner,* and seemingly forgotten was reprinted in 1979 and emerged as a book deserving wide attention. Charlotte Perkins Gilman's *Herland* has clear and obvious appeal to feminists. But its importance is broader than merely for that group, for it is about real equality for all people. Three male adventurers stumble onto an all-female society. Sociologist Vandyck Jennings announces, "This is a civilized country! There must be men." Inhabitants of the land frustrate the three men by making clear that the women have no understanding of words such as *lover* or *wife* or *home*:

We are not like the women of your country. We are not Mothers, and we are People, but we have not specialized in this line.

The men learn how very strange it is to be treated as people, not men, and how odd it is that the land has no sexual tension. They recognize that sex is often a practice used by males to subjugate females. They learn that this world is based on love and reason with ideas being "Beauty, Health, Strength, Intellect, and Goodness."

Actual utopian communities have been used in several novels. Elizabeth Howard's *Out of Step with the Dancers* shows a celibate Shaker community in 1853 through the eyes of Damaris as she accompanies her converted father to a strange new life. Religious pacificism facing the Civil War is the subject of Janet Hickman's *Zoar Blue* about the German separatist community of Zoar, Ohio. Lynn Hall's excellent *Too Near the Sun* focuses on sixteen-year-old Armel Dupree and his Icarian community near Corning, Iowa. To the shame of his family, Armel's older brother has sought life in the outside world. Armel now wonders if he should follow his brother as he views an ideal community composed of less than ideal people. The world outside and inside the Oneida, New York, community where love is everywhere and sex is to be shared with all proves something other than a heaven to the Berger family in Blossom Elfman's *The Strawberry Fields of Heaven*.

Two novels set in older utopias stand out. Jane Yolen's *The Gift of Sarah Barker* is set in the Shaker village of New Vale. Taken there by her psychotic mother, Sarah learns that whatever happiness she can find with her beloved Abel, it cannot be in New Vale. Benjamin Capps' *The Brothers of Uterica* deserves far more readers than it has found. Brother Jean Charles Bossereau leads a group into Texas to establish a utopian community predicated on religious freedom, universal suffrage, community-owned land, care of the old, and reward for hard work. The premise of the community is stated in item eleven of the "Goals of Our Common Faith" in the New Socialist Colonization Company. "We seek a life ordered by reason and good will; we expect to find such a life amid the beauties and common virtues of nature." Nature refuses to cooperate, and the people inside and outside the community lack reason and good will as well as common sense, and the venture fails.

Yearnings for the simpler life where we dream of being part of something greater than ourselves is natural. But for some young people the search has led to religious groups less like communes and more like cults. Robert Coover explored the power and madness of a cult in *The Origin of the Brunists*. In that novel, a mining explosion kills 97 people, but one survivor believes that God has saved him to proclaim the approaching end of the world. Two sound nonfiction works give insights about cults and why and how they are often so successful in attracting the most sincere young adults—Willa Appel's *Cults in America: Programmed for Paradise* and David G. Bromley and Anson D. Shupe, Jr.'s *Strange Gods: The Great American Cult Scare*.

If utopias are fantasies of better worlds out there, someplace, dystopias are nightmares of a dreaded world to come. For many young adults, and for some older adults, the most obvious dystopia today is the post-nuclear world some short—or distant—time ahead of us. Robert C. O'Brien's *Z for Zachariah* was an early young adult example of what many readers fear, being alone in a world that has gone mad and that may have no other human survivors or, perhaps worse yet, that has other survivors no longer quite human.

The theme has been common to several recent novels. Robert Swindells' *Brother in the Land* presents a post-nuclear world in which authorities seek to establish a new feudal society, and a resistance group tries to fight back. Even less optimistic is Susan B. Weston's *Children of the Light*. Walter M. Miller and Martin Greenberg's excellent, if depressing, collection of twenty-one short stories about the world after the nuclear holocaust, *Beyond Armageddon*, should be available for readers who can stomach a truth that lies ahead of us *if* we choose not to alter our lives and our world.

Two books on this theme stand out. Louise Lawrence's *Children of the Dust* carries the nuclear holocaust through three generations, and James D. Forman's *Doomsday Plus Twelve* shows the inevitable struggle and war that must come again even after the nuclear holocaust. Neither Lawrence nor Forman are sanguine, but both are honest and both write extremely well.

With a few exceptions, young adults are basically optimistic and imaginative. They have not yet lived long enough to lose their natural curiosity, nor have they yet been weighed down with adult problems such as failing health, heavy family responsibilities, expenses far surpassing income, and dreams gone bankrupt.

The three types of books in this chapter are generally optimistic. Even the visions of a world gone mad or the books about cults gone insane leave readers grateful for the world as it usually is. These books start with life as we know it and attempt to stretch the readers' imaginations.

We need to dream, all of us, not to waste our lives but to enrich them. To dream is to recognize humanity's possibilities. In a world hardly characterized by undue optimism, the three genres treated in this chapter offer us hope, not the sappy sentimentalism of "everything always works out for the best"—for it often does not—but realistic hope based on our noblest dreams of surviving. If we go down, we do it knowing that we have cared and dreamed and found something for which we are willing to struggle.

NOTES

[1]Patrick Merla, " 'What Is Real?' Asked the Rabbit One Day," *Saturday Review* 55 (November 4, 1972): 49.

[2]J. R. R. Tolkien, *The Tolkien Reader* (New York: Ballantine, 1966), pp. 74–75.

[3]Harvey Cox, *The Feast of Fools: A Theological Essay on Gesticity and Fantasy* (Cambridge: Harvard University Press, 1969), p. 59.

[4]Mary Harrington Hall, "A Conversation with Ray Bradbury and Chuck Hall," *Psychology Today* 1 (April 1968): 28–29.

[5]Lloyd Alexander, "High Fantasy and Heroic Romance," *Horn Book Magazine* 47 (December 1971): 483.

[6]George Steiner, *After Babel: Aspects of Language and Translation* (New York: Oxford University Press, 1975): pp. 217–218.

[7]Ursula K. Le Guin, "On Teaching Science Fiction." In Jack Williamson, ed., *Teaching Science Fiction: Education for Tomorrow* (Philadelphia: Oswick Press, 1980), p. 22.

[8]John Rowe Townsend, "Heights of Fantasy." In Gerard J. Senick, ed., *Children's Literature Review,* vol. 5 (Detroit: Gale Research Company, 1983), p. 7.

[9]Mary Cadogan and Patricia Craig, *You're a Brick, Angela! A New Look at Girls' Fiction from 1839 to 1975* (London: Gollancz, 1976), p. 371.

[10]Ray Bradbury, "Science Fiction: Why Bother?" *Teacher's Guide: Science Fiction* (New York: Bantam, n.d.), p. 1.

[11]Arthur Clarke, *Profiles of the Future* (New York: Holt, Rinehart and Winston, 1984), p. 9.

[12]Robert Heinlein, "Ray Guns and Rocket Ships," *Library Journal* 78 (July 1953): 1188.

[13]Aljean Harmetz, "Filming a Ray Bradbury Fantasy," *New York Times,* April 24, 1983, p. 17–H (National Edition).

[14]Introduction to "Runaround," in *Machines That Think: The Best Science Fiction Stories about Robots and Computers,* Isaac Asimov, Patricia S. Warrick, and Martin H. Greenberg, eds. (New York: Holt, Rinehart and Winston, 1984), p. 209.

30 RECOMMENDATIONS FOR READING

Fantasy

Alexander Lloyd. *The Book of Three.* Holt, Rinehart and Winston, 1964. An introduction to Taran, the assistant pigkeeper, and his quest. Continued in *The Black Cauldron* (1965), *The Castle of Llyr* (1966), *Taran Wanderer* (1967), and *The High King* (1968), all published by Holt, Rinehart and Winston.

Beagle, Peter. *The Last Unicorn.* Viking, 1968. Touching and delightful and often funny account of the last unicorn's search for his fellows.

Bemmann, Hans. *The Stone and the Flute,* trans. Anthea Bell. Viking, 1986. First published in Germany in 1983.

Bradley, Marion Zimmer. *The Best of Marion Zimmer Bradley,* DAW Books, 1988. A sample of her "Darkover" books, all published by DAW Books, would include *Darkover Landfall* (1972), *The Spell Sword* (1974), *The Heritage of Hastur* (1975), *The Shattered Chain* (1976), *Two to Conquer* (1980), and *Red Sun of Darkover* (1987).

Garner, Alan. *The Owl Service.* Walck, 1967. Three young people, a set of dishes with a peculiar pattern, and jealousy and hatred in Wales.

Le Guin, Ursula K. *A Wizard of Earthsea.* Parnassus, 1963. The first of the "Earthsea" Trilogy and Ged's search for wisdom and truth.

Continued in *The Tombs of Atuan* (Atheneum, 1972) and *The Farthest Shore* (Atheneum, 1972).

McCaffrey, Anne. *Dragonsong*. Atheneum, 1976. The strange planet, Pern, and threads and dragons. Followed by *Dragonsinger* (1977) and *Dragondrums* (1979), both published by Atheneum.

McKinley, Robin. *Beauty: A Retelling of the Story of Beauty and the Beast*. Harper & Row, 1978.

Sutcliff, Rosemary. *The Light beyond the Forest*. Dutton, 1979. First of three Arthurian stories, continued in *The Sword and the Circle* (1981) and *The Road to Camlann* (1982), all by Dutton.

Tolkien, J. R. R. *The Hobbit, or There and Back Again,* Houghton Mifflin, 1938. Also, Tolkien's greatest book, maybe one of the great books of the century, was *The Lord of the Rings* in three parts—*The Fellowship of the Ring* (1954; rev. ed., 1967), *The Two Towers* (1955; rev. ed., 1967), and *The Return of the King* (1956; rev. ed., 1967), all published by Houghton Mifflin.

Walton, Evangeline. *The Island of the Mighty.* Ballantine, 1970. First printed as *The Virgin and the Swine* (Willett, Clark, 1936). The opening chapter of Walton's *Mabinogion*. Followed by *The Children of Llyr* (1971), *The Song of Rhiannon* (1972), and *The Prince of Annwn* (1974), all published by Ballantine.

Wangerin, Walter, Jr. *The Book of the Dun Cow*. Harper & Row, 1978. An allegory of good vs. evil with Chauntecleer and Pertelote. *The Book of Sorrows* (Harper & Row, 1985) is the sequel.

Wharton, William. *Birdy*. Knopf, 1979. A young man is kept in an army psychiatric hospital while doctors try to learn why he is so attracted to birds and to flight.

White, T. H. *The Once and Future King*. Putnam, 1958. The Arthurian tale brilliantly retold.

Science Fiction

Asimov, Isaac. *Foundation*. Ballantine, 1984. A mathematician establishes two foundations to survive the end of the Empire. Followed by *Foundation and Empire* (Ballantine, 1986) and *Second Foundation* (Ballantine 1983).

Bradbury, Ray. *Farenheit 451*. Ballantine, 1953. Future fireman, who set fires rather than put them out, guard against the dangers of reading and books. Some critics believe that the collection of stories published as *The Martian Chronicles* (Doubleday, 1950) is Bradbury's finest work.

Card, Orson Scott. *Speaker for the Dead*. Tor Books, 1986. Ender Wiggin sets out to get rid of his miserable reputation when colonists on a planet discover a brutal, warlike, but intelligent species. See also *Wyrms* (Arbor House, 1987).

Clarke, Arthur. *Rendezvous with Rama*. Harcourt Brace Jovanovich, 1973. Humans investigate a hollow and long spaceship inhabited by robots. *Childhood's End* (Houghton Mifflin, 1953) is often cited as Clarke's greatest book but it is more often opened than completed.

Dick, Philip K. *Do Androids Dream of Electric Sheep?* Doubleday, 1968. Androids in colonies humans have polluted slowly evolve to become more and more human.

Finney, Jack. *Time and Again*. Simon and Schuster, 1970. For a secret project, Simon Morley goes back to the New York City of the 1880s and falls in love.

Heinlein, Robert A. *Stranger in a Strange Land*. Putnam, 1961. A Martian brought to Earth finds himself feeling human emotions wholly un-Martian. *Stranger* may not be Heinlein's best book, but it is certainly his most widely cited work and it comes close to being a cult book.

Herbert, Frank. *Dune*. Chilton, 1965. An extraordinarily widely read book, almost certainly the most influential science fiction book about religion.

Le Guin, Ursula K. *The Left Hand of Darkness.*
Ace, 1969. The planet Gethen has a race neither exclusively male nor female. A highly influential book, as are two other Le Guin
novels—*The Lathe of Heaven* (Scribner, 1971)
and *The Dispossessed: An Ambiguous Utopia*
(Harper & Row, 1974).

Miller, Walter H., Jr. *A Canticle for Leibowitz.*
Lippincott, 1959. A satirical novel attacking
excesses in religion and tradition.

Pohl, Frederick, and C. M. Kornbluth. *The
Space Merchants.* Ballantine, 1953. A satire
on Madison Avenue and doublespeak way before it became fashionable. Not always amusing but nearly always on the mark. A recent
sequel, *The Merchants' War* (St. Martin's,
1985) is unsuccessful, at least in part because
Kornbluth died in 1958, and Pohl lacks Kornbluth's fine satirical touch.

Zamyatin, Yevgeny. *We.* Dutton, 1924. People in
a totalitarian society in the twenty-sixth century live in glass houses to eliminate privacy.

Utopias and Dystopias

Bellamy, Edward. *Looking Backward, 2000–
1887.* First published in 1888, Bellamy's utopian romance about Julian West falling into a
hypnotic sleep in 1887 and waking in a socialist wonderland of 2000 is no great novel
though it remains a fascinating vision.

Capps, Benjamin. *The Brothers of Uterica.* Meredith Press, 1967. An attempt to found a perfect society in early Texas founders on human
impulses.

Forman, James D. *Doomsday Plus Twelve.*
Scribner, 1984. Twelve years after a nuclear
holocaust, a fascist group begins recruiting a
People's Army and Valerie Tucker leads a
crusade against the Army.

Lawrence, Louise. *Children of the Dust.* Harper
& Row, 1985. The horrors of a nuclear holocaust carried through three generations.

OTHER TITLES MENTIONED IN CHAPTER SIX

Appel, Willa. *Cults in America: Programmed
for Paradise.* Holt, 1983.

Asimov, Isaac. *In Memory Yet Green: The Autobiography of Isaac Asimov.* Doubleday, 1979.

Baum, L. Frank. *The Wizard of Oz.* Reilly,
1900.

Beagle, Peter. *A Fine and Private Place.* Viking,
1960.

Bell, Clare. *Clan Ground.* Atheneum, 1984.

———. *Ratha's Creature.* Atheneum, 1983.

———. *Tomorrow's Sphinx.* McElderry,
1986.

Bradley, Marion Zimmer. *The Mists of Avalon.*
Knopf, 1983.

Bradshaw, Gillian. *Hawk of May.* Simon and
Schuster, 1980.

———. *In Winter's Shadow.* Simon and
Schuster, 1982.

———. *Kingdom of Summer.* Simon and
Schuster, 1981.

Bromley, David G., and Anson D. Shupe, Jr.
*Strange Gods: The Great American Cult
Scare.* Beacon Press, 1982.

Brunner, John. *Stand on Zanzibar.* Doubleday,
1968.

Clarke, Arthur C. *Profiles of the Future.* Holt,
Rinehart and Winston, 1984.

Coover, Robert. *The Origin of the Brunists.* Viking, 1977.

Del Rey, Lester. *The Eleventh Commandment.*
Regency, 1962.

Elfman, Blossom. *The Strawberry Fields of
Heaven.* Crown, 1983.

Finney, Jack. *The Body Snatchers.* Dell, 1955.

Garner, Alan. *Elidor.* London: Collins, 1965.

_____ . *The Moon of Gomrath*. London: Collins, 1963.

_____ . *Red Shift*. Macmillan, 1973.

_____ . *The Weirdstone of Brisingamen*. London: Collins, 1960.

Gerrould, David. *When Harlie Was One*. Ballantine, 1972.

Gilman, Charlotte Perkins. *Herland*. Pantheon, 1979.

Grahame, Kenneth. *The Wind in the Willows*. Scribner, 1908.

Guest, Lady Charlotte. *The Mabinogion*. 1838–1849.

Hall, Lynn. *Too Near the Sun*. Follett, 1970.

Heinlein, Robert A. *The Cat Who Walks Through Walls*. Putnam, 1986.

_____ . *Citizen of the Galaxy*. Scribner, 1957.

_____ . *Farmer in the Sky*. Scribner, 1950.

_____ . *Friday*. Holt, 1982.

_____ . *Have Space Suit—Will Travel*. Scribner, 1958.

_____ . *Job: A Comedy of Justice*. Ballantine, 1984.

_____ . *The Moon Is a Harsh Mistress*. Putnam, 1966.

_____ . *The Number of the Beast*. Fawcett, 1966.

_____ . *Podkayne of Mars: Her Life and Times*. Putnam, 1963.

_____ . *Starman Jones*. Scribner, 1953.

Herbert, Frank. *Chapterhouse: Dune*. Putnam, 1985.

Hickman, Janet. *Zoar Blue*. Macmillan, 1978.

Howard, Elizabeth. *Out of Step with the Dancers*. Morrow, 1978.

Huxley, Aldous. *Brave New World*. Harper & Brothers, 1933.

Kurtz, Katherine. *Deryni Checkmate*. Ballantine, 1972.

_____ . *Deryni Rising*. Ballantine, 1970.

_____ . *High Deryni*. Ballantine, 1973.

_____ . *The Legacy of Lehr*. Walker, 1986.

Langton, Jane. *The Fledgling*. Harper & Row, 1980.

Lem, Stanislaw. *Fiasco*. Harcourt Brace Jovanovich, 1987.

McCaffrey, Anne. *Moreta: Dragon Lady of Pern*. Ballantine, 1983.

_____ . *The White Dragon*. Ballantine, 1978.

McKillip, Patricia. *The Forgotten Beasts of Eld*. Atheneum, 1974.

_____ . *The Moon and the Face*. Atheneum, 1985.

_____ . *Moon-Flash*. Atheneum, 1984.

_____ . *The Riddle Master of Hed*. Atheneum, 1976.

McKinley, Robin. *The Blue Sword*. Greenwillow, 1982.

_____ . *The Hero and the Crown*. Greenwillow, 1984.

Miller, Walter M., Jr., and Martin H. Greenberg. *Beyond Armageddon*. Fine, 1985.

Niven, Larry, and Jerry Pournelle. *Footfall*. Ballantine, 1985.

_____ . *The Mote in God's Eye*. Simon and Schuster, 1974.

Niven, Larry, Jerry Pournelle, and Steven Barnes. *The Legacy of Heorot*. Simon and Schuster, 1987.

O'Brien, Robert. *Z for Zachariah*. Atheneum, 1975.

Orwell, George. *Animal Farm*. Harcourt Brace, 1954.

_____ . *1984*. Harcourt Brace, 1940.

Russ, Joanna. *The Female Man*. Bantam, 1975.

Stewart, Mary. *The Crystal Cave*. Morrow, 1970.

_____ . *The Hollow Hills*. Morrow, 1973.

_____ . *The Last Enchantment*. Morrow, 1979.

_____ . *The Wicked Day*. Morrow, 1984.

Strickland, Brad. *Moondreams*. New American Library, Signet, 1988.

Swindells, Robert. *Brother in the Land*. Holiday House, 1985.

Tevis, Walter. *Mockingbird*. Doubleday, 1980.

Tolkien, J. R. R. *The Silmarillion*. Houghton Mifflin, 1983.

Vonnegut, Kurt, Jr. *God Bless You Mr. Rosewater*. Holt, Rinehart & Winston, 1965.

Weston, Susan B. *Children of the Light*. St. Martin's Press, 1986.

White, T. H. *The Book of Merlyn: The Unpublished Conclusion*. University of Texas Press, 1977.

Wrightson, Patricia. *The Dark Bright Water*. Atheneum, 1979.

——————. *The Ice Is Coming*. Atheneum, 1977.

——————. *Journey Behind the Wind*. Atheneum, 1981.

——————. *A Little Fear*. Atheneum, 1983.

——————. *The Nargun and the Stars*. Atheneum, 1974.

Wyndham, John, *The Midwich Cuckoos*. Random House, 1957.

Yolen, Jane. *Dragon's Blood*. Delacorte, 1982.

——————. *The Gift of Sarah Barker*. Viking, 1981.

——————. *Heart's Blood*. Delacorte, 1984.

——————. *A Sending of Dragons*. Delacorte, 1987.

For information on the availability of paperback editions of these titles, please consult the most recent edition of *Paperbound Books in Print,* published annually by R. R. Bowker Company.

CHAPTER SEVEN

LIFE MODELS
Of Heroes and Hopes

The word *hero* may conjure up a picture of King Arthur and his Knights of the Round Table seeking the Holy Grail or John Wayne charging up a hill ahead of a company of marines. All societies and cultures have had their heroes who embodied the proper virtues and values of that culture. Prior to the beginning of writing, storytellers kept legends of heroes alive—and likely embroidered and magnified heroes and legends with each retelling. As writing and then printing appeared, these tales were permanently recorded so new generations would remember the deeds of great heroes of old. The Greeks gave us their gods and heroes who confronted the gods, Prometheus, Oedipus, and Antigone. Writers provided fictional heroes as different as Shakespeare's Portia, Dostoevsky's Prince Myshkin, Ibsen's Dr. Stockmann, and Shaw's St. Joan. These characters have always competed for readers' attention with historical heroes like Ruth, Muhammad, Galileo, Eleanor of Aquitaine, Thomas Jefferson, Helen Keller, Chief Joseph, Margaret Sanger, John Kennedy, and on and on.

WHO ARE THE HEROES? WHO NEEDS THEM?

Joe McGinnis wrote in *Heroes:*

I had a theory: America no longer had national heroes as it once did because the traditional sources of heroes had dried up. The sources had dried up, I believed, because the values and ideals that traditional heroes once had personified no longer were dominant in American society. My theory was that after a long period of erosion, they had ceased to be dominant in the 1960s.[1]

And he concluded the chapter:

> ■ The truth was, we did not have heroes any more because *there were no heroic acts left to be performed.*[2]

Is McGinnis right? Certainly, we once needed heroes. In 1941, Dixon Wecter argued, "Hero-worship answers an urgent American need."[3] Seventeen years later, Arthur Schlesinger worried that if our need for hero-worship was no longer a national need, "then our instinct for admiration is likely to end by settling on ourselves."[4] And in 1978, Henry Fairlie agreed when he wrote, "A society that has no heroes will soon grow enfeebled."[5]

We need heroes today even more desperately than we did only a few years back. Author Mollie Hunter reflects what many of us believe when she began a *Horn Book Magazine* article, "There is a need for heroes in children's books."[6]

We need to find people worth looking up to, no matter what our ages. We need reassuring that even if we are all mortal, a few of us find ways to transcend earthly mortality and to leave behind a record of noble or brave acts. We need to see people who are pushed to the edge of psychological or physical disaster but who fight back. We need reminders that humans will not merely survive but that we are worth surviving. We need to see that some people are willing to stand up for their beliefs no matter what the pressures.

Henry James said that life is a slow march into enemy territory. Maybe being a hero means marching onward without making peace with the enemy, no matter what or who that is.

To have heroes means that we must accept ourselves, not for what we are but for our potential to become what we could be. If some people seem to have no heroes, or strange heroes, perhaps it is because they find little of the hero in themselves. People who have little but contempt for themselves or their beliefs, who seem to have few roots and no future, who flounder trying to find something and someone to believe in, may resist the heroic impulse in others.

We may all be diverted in our search for heroes and attacted to the merely charismatic entertainer or politician. We may for a time seek someone who talks and acts and thinks as we do. But what we need to seek out—and we *do* in our better moments—are heroes with dignity who rise above the crowd and are admirable, though not necessarily immediately likeable. Looking up to the heroes mentioned in the sections that follow allows us to survive and make that survival worthwhile.

A character in Jerzy Kosinski's *The Devil Tree* sums up the nature of the hero:

Of all mammals, only a human being can say "no." A cow cannot imagine itself apart from the herd. That's why one cow is like any other. To say "yes" is to follow the mass, to do what is commonly expected. To say "no" is to deny the crowd, to be set apart, to reaffirm yourself.

QUIET HEROES

Fiction abounds with quiet heroes worth admiring and emulating. They reassure us that although we are mortal, a few individuals find ways to transcend their mortality to leave behind a record. In these books, attention is paid to character development, especially of the quiet hero. Other characters may reflect or comment on the hero. The works are often episodic, and particular episodes focus on problems confronting the heroes and forcing them into decisions that will clarify their values or beliefs. Heroes are often pushed to physical or psychological precipices to establish their beliefs and their quiet, but obvious, superiority to other people. Quiet heroes carry burdens, but they do so quietly, not dramatically. What the magician Schmendrick said in Peter Beagle's *The Last Unicorn* about great heroes applies almost equally to quiet heroes: "Great heroes need great sorrows and burdens, or half their greatness goes unnoticed." With quiet heroes, greatness often goes unnoticed by friends and neighbors but not by readers.

Papa in Robert Newton Peck's *A Day No Pigs Would Die* has great dignity. Poor in money he may be but rich in spirit he is. The narrator in this novel-autobiography sometimes does not understand his father, but he always respects him, knowing instinctively that Papa has stature and dignity.

Two crucial and bloody scenes establish Papa's humanity, his willingness to admit error, and his dignity. The first is for many readers the ugliest episode in the book. A weasel has been caught and Papa puts the weasel and a dog, Hussy, in a barrel to teach the dog to hate and kill weasels, an age-old if cruel way to educate a dog. Rob protests, but the weasel is killed, the dog nearly so, and Pa knows he was wrong.

The second episode is near the end of the book when Rob and Papa discover that Pinky, Rob's pet pig, is sterile. Given the Depression setting and the sad state of the family's finances, Pinky must die to give the family food for the coming winter. Rob cannot, for a moment, accept the necessity of Pinky's death:

"Oh, Papa. My heart's broke."

"So is mine," said Papa. "But I'm thankful you're a man."

I just broke down, and Papa let me cry it all out. I just sobbed and sobbed with my head up toward the sky and my eyes closed, hoping God would hear it.

"That's what being a man is all about. It's just doing what's got to be done."

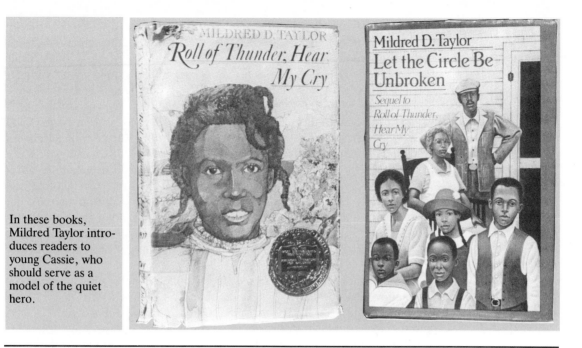

In these books, Mildred Taylor introduces readers to young Cassie, who should serve as a model of the quiet hero.

Alice Childress' *A Hero Ain't Nothin' but a Sandwich* could easily have become a sociological treatise about drugs and drug users, but through Childress' artistry her work becomes a story about people and loneliness and quiet heroism. Benjie is no case study specimen but then neither is Butler Craig, Benjie's would-be stepfather and one of the noblest creations in modern young adult fiction. Butler saves Benjie's life and later, when Benjie admits his mistakes and apologizes, Butler makes clear what the quiet hero is, though Butler would never have admitted he was in any way heroic:

> I say, "I'm sorry, Butler."
> "Look here," he say. "Square your shoulders, admit you been a junkie, but now gonna stay clean and report to daytime center for your followups. If you don't do right, Butler gonna have to knuckle you down, you hear?"
> "I can do it," I say, "long as somebody believe in me."
> "Dammit, Benjie," he say, "you gotta do it even if *nobody* believe in you, gotta be your own man, the supervisor of your veins, the night watchman, and day shift foreman in charge-a your own affairs."

The quiet heroes we admire today include all those civil rights workers who did nothing most of them thought unusual or outstanding or brave. All they did was to change the course of America's attitudes about justice and equality and honor. Juan Williams' *Eyes on the Prize: America's Civil Rights Years, 1954–1965* is the printed version of the PBS television series from the U.S.

Supreme Court decision in *Brown v. Board of Education of Topeka, Kansas* that began the struggle against racism in the schools until the Selma, Alabama, demonstrations and street marches. Margaret Edds' *Free at Last—What Really Happened When Civil Rights Came to Southern Politics* supplements Williams' book. More personal and often more touching is Mary King's *Freedom Song— A Personal Story of the 1960s Civil Rights Movement.*

Americans sometimes tend toward early canonization of their heroes, and William Manchester comes close to that at times in *One Brief Shining Moment: Remembering Kennedy.* Nat Hentoff's *American Heroes: In and Out of School* avoids excessive veneration, mostly because his heroes are generally unremarkable people suddenly tossed into the limelight and forced to act for good or evil. All of Hentoff's heroes fight the good fight on behalf of the First Amendment, and one of them, folk singer and activist Joan Baez, is prominently featured in another book of quiet heroes who talk about their beliefs and visions, Phillip L. Berman's stimulating and insightful *The Courage of Conviction.*

The most impressive collection of portraits of quiet heroes certainly was not designed at all to be that. Charles Kuralt's *On the Road with Charles Kuralt* began when Kuralt was given the opportunity to travel America with his CBS crew to make brief news stories about common people wherever and whenever he found anyone worth talking about. Kuralt found many people worth talking about and writing about, none of them people of national renown, most of them not all that well known in their local communities. One was a doctor in Lincoln, Missouri, who worked virtually for nothing and had been doing that for 48 years. Another was a roadside gardener in Surry, Virginia, who wanted to leave a little loveliness behind that others might enjoy. Another was a bricklayer in Winston-Salem, North Carolina, who took deep pleasure in his simple work. It is tempting to say that Kuralt's book is a sentimental tribute to the essential goodness of people, but Kuralt does not sentimentalize his people. He likes them too much to make them into something phony or quaint. Kuralt's book is about honest, dedicated, tolerant, compassionate people—in other words, quiet heroes—uncommon people no matter how common they might consider themselves to be. And what Kuralt set out to find, he found heroes, as he writes in the last paragraph of the preface to his book:

To read the front pages [of newspapers], you might conclude that Americans are mostly out for themselves, venal, grasping, and mean-spirited. The front pages have room only for defense contractors who cheat and politicians with their hands in the till. But you can't travel the back roads very long without discovering a multitude of gentle people doing good for others with no expectation of gain or recognition. The everyday kindness of the back roads more than makes up for the acts of greed in the headlines. Some people out there spend their whole lives selflessly. You could call them heroes.

And we do. Or we should.

◼ *HEROES IN BIOGRAPHIES AND AUTOBIOGRAPHIES*

Humanity's need for the life stories of important and admirable people is much older than the word *biography* first used by John Dryden in his 1683 edition of Plutarch's *Parallel Lives.* Indeed, Plutarch's first century A.D. account of fifty famous Greeks and Romans, usually paired to make a moral or historical point, has served for fifteen hundred years as a source of heroes and heroic tales.

But other life stories, perhaps less famous today, also served as models. Bishop Asser's *The Life of Alfred the Great* in the late ninth century, William Roper's fine biography of his father-in-law, *Life of Sir Thomas More,* about 1557, and Samuel Clarke's compilation of ecclesiastical biographies, *Collection of the Lives of Ten Eminent Divines,* in 1662, provided many lives worth emulating. Indeed, that presents a problem for those of us today who try to read Clarke's book, for he early declares about his divines:

> ◼ We must eye them, as we look into Glasses, to dress and adorn ourselves thereby. We must eye them for imitation: We must look upon the best, and the best in the best.

As we seek someone admirable, we also seek someone human, someone who might understand us because the hero has suffered the problems of being human and being imperfect. Clarke's figures are divine and glorious but they lack the common touch. We may admire them, but they are too much above us, impossible to emulate.

Pepys' *Diary,* though never intended for publication, is the first life story which lets us see the subject, warts and all. From the first entry on January 1, 1660, until the last on May 31, 1669, we are allowed to see an important man—he was both the Secretary of the Admiralty and President of the Royal Society—who writes about the politics of the time amidst the London Fire of 1666 and the plague of 1665, but who also writes of love and music and life. Pepys celebrates life, all of it, and what makes his autobiography so incredible is his honesty.

James Boswell's *The Life of Samuel Johnson,* published in two volumes in 1791, is usually considered to be the first modern biography. Boswell revered his friend, but the tone is not entirely reverential, and Boswell clearly is writing more than simply the record of deeds done in one man's life. Boswell set out to give an accurate history of Johnson, Johnson's thoughts as best Boswell knew them, the people Johnson had known and what he thought of them, how the times influenced Johnson and how Johnson influenced the times; in short the cultural and historical milieu. The book was not a series of moral lessons nor was it so laudatory that a reader could model a life after Samuel Johnson.

A modern biography aims at catching the spirit of the subject, the passions and fears, the essence that made the subject distinctive and memorable. It attempts to make the subject's time come alive and place the subject within

Table 7.1   SUGGESTIONS FOR EVALUATING BIOGRAPHIES

A good biography usually has:	A poor biography may have:
A subject of interest with whom the author and, therefore, the readers feel intimately acquainted.	A subject who happens to be of current interest but whose life the author has no real commitment to or knowledge of beyond that available in any good public library.
Documentation of sources and suggestions for further reading—both done inconspicuously so as not to interfere with the story.	An adulatory tone which makes the person too good to be true.
New and/or unusual sources of original information.	Sensationalism, that is, a focus on the negative aspects of the subject's life. A debunking of a historically respected character without adequate documentation of the reasons that the author's viewpoint differs from history's perception.
Accurate facts about setting and characters.	
A central theme or a focus point that has been honestly developed from the author's research.	
In-depth development of the character so that readers understand the way in which the subject shaped his or her own life. Things did not just happen to the person.	None of the interesting detail that makes the story of a person's life unique.
Use of language that is appropriate to the historical period and the literary style of the book.	A disproportionate emphasis on the history and the circumstances surrounding this subject's life so that the reader does not get acquainted with the person. E.g., one biography of Golda Meir is really the story of modern Israel using Mrs. Meir as an attention-getting device and a selling point for libraries looking for biographies of strong women.
Information showing how the subject was thought about by contemporaries.	

that time. It attempts to make the subject come alive, not to present a perfect, wholly admirable person without defects. Authenticity and objectivity are the guides to the biographer.

Biographies and autobiographies often remain popular with young adults for several years. One reason is that the genre often fills in details about the past that we recognize, at least vaguely, at the same time letting us in on parts of a life we admire yet know only superficially.

Why do young adults read biography or autobiography?

They may read to find out about people who have led lives so widely and sometimes so wildly different from the commonplace that young adults may wonder how these people survived, physically or psychologically. Christopher Nolan's autobiography, *Under the Eye of the Clock: The Life Story of Christopher Nolan,* brilliantly conveys what it is like to grow up so impaired that it is something of a miracle that he ever learned to communicate with his extraordinarily caring family. Nolan endured a period of asphyxiation during his birth which left him partially brain-damaged, incapable of coordinating his bodily movements, and without speech. He learned to type with the aid of a pointer attached to his head, so well indeed that he wrote publishable poetry and eventually attracted attention, not for merely overcoming his handicaps—

though that might have seemed enough reason—but for his genuine talents as a writer.

Different in almost every way save the human spirit that refuses to accept defeat, Nien Cheng's *Life and Death in Shanghai* is the remarkable record of a woman who not merely survived the Chinese Cultural Revolution with all the horrors that accompanied it but who became stronger because of the Revolution. Mrs. Cheng's husband died in 1957, and when she took over his duties in Shanghai, she assumed that a loyal Chinese follower of Chairman Mao would be able to survive and be quietly accepted. Then in 1966, Mao's Cultural Revolution struck and she was arrested, shut up in a damp cell, and finally put in solitary confinement for more than six years. How she survived and battled pneumonia and her tormentors in jail and then learned that her daughter had been murdered is the story of a woman who found more strength in herself than she could have believed.

And young adults might find equal strength in Haing Ngor's *A Cambodian Odyssey.* Ngor had been a wealthy doctor in Cambodia, almost a playboy among rich friends, when the Khmer Rouge took over his country, and Ngor was enslaved along with his pregnant wife. Ngor was forced to sit silently by and watch his wife die, because if he had performed the caesarean operation his wife needed he would have revealed to authorities that he was an educated man. This would have led to his own death, not just that of his wife and unborn child. Later Ngor was tied to a cross and tortured before escaping to Thailand and a refugee camp. From there Ngor went to America and to fame of sorts for his academy award-winning performance in *The Killing Fields.*

Less spectacular and less bloody but quietly moving, and for some readers equally disturbing, Julius Lester's *Livesong: On Becoming a Jew* reveals the spiritual quest of a fine writer from his black heritage and Christian background—his father was a Methodist minister—through his flirtation with Catholicism and a few other religions to his decision to become a Jew in early 1983.

Young adults can continue their reading of Maya Angelou's fifth in her series of autobiographies. As usual, her *All God's Children Need Traveling Shoes* is engaging and wise and often funny. Her fifth study of herself takes her up to 1966 and includes her work teaching at the University of Ghana and her futile attempts to make her black roots into a palatable home country.

And young adults seeking other interesting lives about public figures can find them in Nat Hentoff's delightful story of his Jewish boyhood in the anti-Semitic world of 1930s Boston, *Boston Boy,* or Joan Baez's anecdotal accounts of folksinging and concert-making in the 1960s in *And a Voice to Sing With: A Memoir.* Less well done, though more touching for obvious reasons, is Robert Hohler's *"I Touch the Future . . . ": The Story of Christa McAuliffe,* about the teacher aboard the doomed Challenger. Unhappily, the writing does not equal the obvious sincerity of either Hohler or McAuliffe.

The world of dance by itself, to choose only one delightful and stressful life, has many biographies and autobiographies to offer any intrigued reader. The

RICHARD PECK
on Landmarks

There are two elements that fuel my books. One is this young generation's need for landmarks. The old landmarks of coming-of-age are pretty much gone now: the diagrammed sentence; the required history, geography, and language; the chaperoned dance; the draft card that told you when your adolescence was over; the high-school diploma that represented a marketable skill for a job in the community; the college degree that led to something apart from graduate school.

The young need landmarks. Adolescence is too painful a period to last as long as it does today and not to lead to anything better. For those who can read them, books provide vicarious landmarks. In all my books young surrogates for the readers have to take steps nearer maturity. The protagonists not only experience new awarenesses, but act upon them. The real-life young aren't liable to see that anywhere else today, not in the permissive home nor in the elective school. Adolescence isn't the search for the challenge; it's the last ditch effort to see if the world

will change to accommodate you. But our books are full of stern realities, and our heroes and heroines are role models who face them and learn that leaving your immaturity behind isn't as perilous as staying where you are.

The other factor that keeps me bent over my typewriter is the present-day power of the peer group. Now that family membership itself is optional for most teenagers, they turn to their peers for a dominating, problem-solving authority. In my day, when you wanted to have a party at home, you checked with your parents to make sure they'd be there. Now, the young check with their parents to be sure they won't be there. That's not a difference in style; it's a difference in substance.

If we'd wanted our children to be honestly questioning, we'd never have delivered them into the hands of each other. For a teenager will question every value an adult holds dear, but few have any mechanism for challenging the rules of their peers. And what are those peer-group commandments?

- that you can drive while drunk
- that you are immune to sexually transmitted diseases
- that adults don't have to be negotiated with
- that no narcotic is addictive
- that your friends are a better family than the one you came from
- that you won't be held responsible for the consequences of your actions.

There are some thoughtful young readers out there who don't believe those lies, and good books give them something better to believe in. In my novels, the steps the protagonists take toward maturity are away from the peer group. Even in real life, nobody ever grows up in a group, and honest novels illustrate that. As a result, we often depict loners; that's good too because some of our best readers are solitary young people. We have the chance to let them know that self-improvement is usually lonely work and that the full-time conformists aren't heading anywhere in particular.

Richard Peck's books include *Princess Ashley,* Delacorte, 1987; *Close Enough to Touch,* Delacorte, 1981; and *Remembering the Good Times,* Delacorte, 1985.

master choreographer of our time, George Balanchine, is the subject of Bernard Taper's *Balanchine: A Biography* and Richard Buckle's *George Balanchine: Ballet Master,* but far more engaging—and probably more honest in the details—are several autobiographies of dancers who worked and suffered under Balanchine's direction. Peter Martins' *Far from Denmark* takes one of the chief male dancers of our time from his home in Denmark to his work as the heir presumptive of Balanchine's New York City Ballet. Merrill Ashley's *Dancing for Balanchine* is pleasant enough and surely more tasteful than the often shocking expose of the ballet world and some dancers' preoccupation with drugs in Gelsey Kirkland's *Dancing on My Grave: An Autobiography.* The best of all the accounts of a dancer's life, particularly when the dancer realizes that the world of the star is forever closed because the talent is almost, but not quite, there, can be found in Toni Bentley's *Winter Season: A Dancer's Journal.*

But anyone curious about ballet, and the incredible work that goes into something so apparently floating and graceful, can find much to admire in Ernestine Stodelle's *Deep Song: The Dance Story of Martha Graham,* James Haskins' *Katherine Dunham,* Robert Maiorano's *Worlds Apart: The Autobiography of a Dancer from Brooklyn,* or Christopher d'Amboise's *Leap Year.*

Readers looking for contrasts in biographies will find that in abundance in four stories of outstanding women, two of them far too little known. Carol Felsenthal's *The Sweetheart of the Silent Majority: The Biography of Phyllis Schlafly* honestly and at times vividly conveys the spirit of the leading conservative of the time. One may not admire Schlafly, and there are those who do not, but readers will admit that she is gutsy and driven. Dorothy Greenbaum's *Lovestrong: A Woman Doctor's True Story of Marriage and Medicine* sounds like something straight out of a soap opera or, perhaps, something from one of those "Can This Marriage Be Saved?" features, but it is not. Instead, it is the quiet story of a woman who had the best of both worlds, marriage and a career, and it is readable and sometimes far better than merely that. Betty Ford's *Betty: A Glad Awakening* probably provides little that hasn't been shown on television or in the newspapers, but the life of a quiet winner who beats alcohol and fame is satisfying. Pauli Murray is probably unknown to most readers, young or old, but *Song in a Weary Throat* is worth any reader's time. Murray, the granddaughter of a slave and the great-granddaughter of a slave-owner, worked her way through school, went to Hunter College during the Depression, worked for the WPA, and became a friend of Eleanor Roosevelt.

To summarize, biographies and autobiographies are popular with many young adults. If the genre once concentrated on the lives of men, and often told didactically as models for readers, many current biographies are about heroic women and minorities. Although most biographies are written about someone who is admired, and often famous, authors present balanced material to give both the positive and the negative sides of the subjects. As with modern fiction, many readers prefer realism over romanticism. And most biographies provide young adults today with models worth emulating, people who are frank and spirited and compassionate.

HEROES IN SPORTS

Adults and young adults alike have been fascinated by sports and sports heroes as far back as the Olympic Games in ancient Greece. Today, spectator and participation sports are highly popular activities across the world. Every day, millions of people go jogging or play tennis or swim or golf. Even more people watch basketball or football or baseball on television. Others play in organized softball or soccer leagues sponsored by churches, city recreation departments, or private clubs. Sports play an incredibly important part in our lives, and in our language, witness the clichés of adults—*play for the team, go for broke, red-dog the opponents, win at all costs,* and on and on. Given our national mania, most of us would be shocked if the current president of Cornell University repeated what his predecessor said in 1873 about a proposed football game with the University of Michigan: "I will not permit 30 men to travel 400 miles merely to agitate a bag of wind."

More than any other important facet of American life, sports are youth oriented. Athletes reach their peak in their teens or their twenties, and that leads to a powerful identification between sports heroes and young adults. Other than in sports, where could young adults dream of the fame and adulation heaped upon Nadia Comaneci or Boris Becker or Tracy Austin so early in their lives? Sports are emphasized so much in the maturation of young adults that it would be an unusual American child who has not been pressured, by parents or peers, to try out for some sort of team.

Parents and schools encourage young people to engage in sports because, in addition to providing good physical exercise, sports are thought to be one way to teach the principles of competition. Sports provide, so people think, an outlet for young adults to play out conflicts within the security of the rules of the game. And the game, so people think, is a microcosm of the great American system of competition.

Sports books, fiction or nonfiction, have common elements. A description of the game itself—rules, training, crowds, thrills, appeal—has increasingly been expanded to include the players and what the game does to them. Rather than being simply an account, as some older books seem to be too much of the time, one inning or one quarter after another, emphasis is now on the toughening, the character-changing aspects of the sport. At the heart of most contemporary sports fiction is an examination of the price of fame, the worth of the game, the transitory nature of glory, and the temptation, always doomed, to make temporary glory permanent.

Early sports writers taught the same kinds of things that they had learned through idealized participation in sports. The purity of sports at the turn of the last century was preached by Ralph Henry Barbour who devoutly believed in hard play, fair play, and the amateur spirit and dedicated his 1900 novel, *For the Honor of the School,* "To That School, Wherever It May Be, Whose Athletics Are Purest." Dated though his fine novel now seems, Barbour was deadly serious in his belief that school spirit was inextricably coupled with athletic *and* academic excellence. He and other writers for young adults preached this doctrine until the 1940s.

Despite the American love affair with sports, surprisingly little serious fiction about sports emerged until recent times. Barring an occasional boxing story by Hemingway, some outlandish and amusing stories by Damon Runyon, and some savagely ironic yet uproarious stories by Ring Lardner, only a few major writers wrote about sports: Bernard Malamud in his mythic and underrated *The Natural;* Mark Harris' touching story of baseball and death, *Bang the Drum Slowly;* or Robert Coover's strange and compelling tale of baseball as the counterpart of American life, *The Universal Baseball Association, Inc., J. Henry Waugh, Prop.*

The traditional sport novels for young adults go unread and largely unwritten. John Tunis' many excellent novels filled with heroes who reek of sweat sit sedately on library shelves, and books of the late 1950s and early 1960s written by John F. Carson and H. D. Francis are going out of print. Perhaps kindly old Pop Dugout, wily with his sports wisdom and remembered for his warm and genial backpatting, was never very real, but somehow sentimental fiction of the past had a charm that we have lost and with it many sports heroes for young readers.

To attract young adults, sports fiction must now provide something not present in either the old sports fiction or in nonfiction stories or current media. It must, essentially, bring a sense of reality about sports, a sense of the joy in sports.

A few recent books have tried to convey the true spirit of sports, what is left when the game is over and the postmortems have grown stale. David Halberstam's *The Amateurs* concerns four young men who row for exercise and aesthetic delight and who train for the 1984 Olympics. Of the four oarsmen, Halberstam clearly is most interested in the oldest, Tiff Wood, the one who has sacrificed the most to stay an amateur in a field which delays entering an occupation and which promises almost nothing in the way of fame, or anything else—only the sheer satisfaction of the sport. Halberstam obviously wants readers to share his joy in competition and sports for their own sake.

Perhaps Donald Hall is less successful in *Fathers Playing Catch with Sons: Essays on Sport (Mostly Baseball),* but if so, it is because Hall is sometimes more determinedly the essayist and less the sportswriter. Still, this collection by a first-rate poet who also clearly loves sports—mostly baseball—is something some young people will thoroughly enjoy.

Of all sports enthusiasts, Roger Angell is the living embodiment of the graceful writer at work. Red Smith may have been the greatest day-by-day writer about sports—and most sportswriters of whatever kind would grant that—but Angell can take the most obvious topic, a hitting streak or the melodrama of a close game or a visit to Baseball's Hall of Fame, and make the obvious memorable. For example, when Angell visited the Hall of Fame, he noticed, as if for the first time, an old photograph of the first inductees in 1939, and he wrote:

Tris Speaker, playing short centerfield as usual, stands directly behind Babe Ruth, and Honus Wagner and Walter Johnson, with their famous country sweetness perfectly visible, occupy the corners. As you study the photograph (never a quick process, no matter how many times you have seen it), your gaze stops at the other men's faces, one by one, as recollection of their deeds and their flair for the game comes flooding back: Eddie Collins, Grover Cleveland Alexander, Nap Lajoie, Cy Young (pipe in hand), and George Sisler—old warriors squinting in the sun, comfortable at last.

Angell's facility in prose and with sports hardly comes as any surprise. Anyone who has been involved with baseball has almost surely read *The Summer Game* or *Season Ticket* or books in between, but the work of Christopher Lehmann-Haupt is less obvious. Lehmann-Haupt has been a book reviewer for the *New York Times* for years, but less apparent, he has also been a baseball nut since he was young. His fascination with baseball's legendary power hitter, Joe DiMaggio, began in 1948 when he heard Mel Allen announce a game between the Yankees and the Indians when DiMaggio hit three home runs. Apparently secretly, Lehmann-Haupt has harbored a desire to meet DiMaggio and discover all he ever wanted to know about baseball, and that is what he sets out to do in *Me and DiMaggio: A Baseball Fan Goes in Search of His Gods*. Lehmann-Haupt makes his share of goofs—some closer to the game may question whether he did not exceed his quota of mistakes—but he serves as the common person's Everyman who goes where many would like to go, into a mystical world where the heroes are tall and graceful and all of them are willing to talk to us about anything we want to know.

The best account of a game, one game play-by-play, in written form is Bob Ryan and Terry Pluto's *Forty-Eight Minutes: A Night in the Life of the NBA,* a deadly sounding title which may well become a sports classic. The authors decided to write up a moment-by-moment account of a pro basketball game between the Cleveland Cavaliers and the Boston Celtics on January 16, 1987. A game which might have been boring turned out to be a thriller which Boston won, 133–128, in overtime.

Two excellent accounts of the transitory nature of fame in sports are Martin Ralbovsky's *Destiny's Darlings: A World Championship Little League Team Twenty Years Later* and Jay Acton's *The Forgettables*. Ralbovsky's portrait of Schenectady's Little League championship team on August 27, 1954, and what happened to the players in the twenty years since, is rarely shocking, which in its own way may suggest how little respect we have for the used-up athlete who becomes a nuisance and a bore by outliving his fame. Acton's portrait of pro football players nearly (but not quite) good enough to make the big time is sometimes funny, sometimes sad, sometimes desperate.

A few writers for young adults have made the game and sometimes the players come alive. Perhaps the best is relatively new to the field—he has published only three novels as of 1987—but Chris Crutcher seems likely to become a staple in sports fiction. Better yet, as most young adults add, his books are not *just* about sports but about people readers care about. *Running Loose,* his first novel, presents readers with Louie Banks who wants to play football but not the way the creep/coach wants to play it. The novel is about football and fair play and running, but it also is about love and death and caring and maturing, more than John Tunis might have included in one of his 1930s–1950s sports novels but not by much. And as Tunis loved sports, so does Crutcher, and as Tunis worried about what some people might do in the name of sports, so Crutcher worries. His two other novels, *Stotan!* and *The Crazy Horse Electric Game,* are less concerned with games and more concerned with people, but both do involve players and what games can do to them—and us.

Richard Blessing's *A Passing Season* was arguably the most promising sport novel written for young adults since John Tunis' books, but Blessing's death before he could follow up the success of his first YA book was a major setback for sports books, and YA books in general. Few writers have done better than Blessing portraying the desperation of young athletes anxious to escape a dying town. Craig Warren is a third-string quarterback with great ability who plays scared and indifferently, as his coach knows all too well. Warren loves books and English class and poetry as well or better than football. Blessing's talent in describing a young man caught between two worlds and trying to find himself and a way out still impresses the sensitive reader as it saddens those aware of Blessing's death.

Other books of particular value would include Walter Dean Myers' studies of a black youth trying to find his way out of poverty through basketball in *Hoops* and *The Outside Shot* and Terry Davis' *Vision Quest,* a rare insight into amateur wrestling and the mysticism that often accompanies it.

The color line that existed so long in baseball has had a steady appeal for writers and readers. William Brashler's novel, *The Bingo Long Traveling All-Stars and Motor Kings,* and Robert Peterson's *Only the Ball Was White: A History of Legendary Black Players* are satisfying and forthright.

The history of baseball continues to attract readers. Jack Lang and Peter Simon's *The New York Mets: Twenty-Five Years of Baseball Magic* is one of the better accounts of one team though inferior to Ken Coleman and Dan Valenti's *The Impossible Dream Remembered: The 1967 Red Sox.* And neither book is as good as Charles C. Alexander's *John McGraw* and Noel Hynd's *Giants of the Polo Grounds: The Glorious Times of Baseball's New York Giants,* both first-class nostalgia and history.

The prize for the oddest—and funniest—sports story in many years surely goes to George Plimpton for *The Curious Case of Sidd Finch.* Plimpton, famous with some for his work with the *Paris Review* and with others for his true sports tales, began *Sidd Finch* as a short story in the April 1, 1985, *Sports Illustrated,* an April Fool's hoax about a wonderful and warm would-be Buddhist monk who also possesses a 168 miles-per-hour fastball and the wisdom to mouth epigrams which sound mystical and wise and make little sense to the baseball players he encounters. When, for example, Sidd is offered a New York Mets contract, he says, "A pair of monkeys are reaching for the moon in the water";

wise to be sure, delightful perhaps, but cloudy to most of those around him. *Sidd Finch* is a parody and a satire, but it is told by a writer who knows and loves sports, particularly baseball.

HEROES IN DEATH

In the mid-1970s when young adults were surveyed about their favorite nonfiction books, the favorites included these books—*Eric, Brian's Song, I Am Third, Death Be Not Proud,* and *Brian Piccolo: A Short Season.*

Those books were hardly surprising. Indeed, they remain popular even today. What seemed surprising to some adults, though to few teachers or librarians, was that these books were all concerned with death. It seemed odd or ironic, to some, that young people, presumably on the threshold of life, were so intrigued by death.

But an interest in death is no oddity. When the electives were all the rage in many schools, the "Education" section of the March 14, 1977, *Newsweek* reported that "death, a topic most people would prefer to ignore, is an increasingly popular subject among U.S. high-school students."

Parents, and some teachers and librarians, are worried about the interest in death. Some argue it is a morbid subject for otherwise healthy young people to be concerned with. Others see the sinister hand of the international Communist party at work. Others thought and remembered that they, too, had been preoccupied with "easeful death" when they were young, not because they were unduly morbid or nigh unto death, but because death is an eternal mystery, as anyone who has read *Hamlet* or Dickinson's poetry or Edgar Lee Masters' *Spoon River Anthology* knows full well.

Young adults sometimes complain bitterly about the "morbid" and "sick" literature adults foist off on the young, *Macbeth,* Romantic poetry, "Thanatopsis," *Death of a Salesman, Oedipus Rex,* and "A Rose for Emily." What is equally clear is that young adults are every bit as preoccupied with death, but they prefer to choose their own literature. Surely reading such literature helps young adults begin to develop their own code of values to hold dear in the dread times to come, to take a closer look at adults and young adults who face death in the midst of life, and to develop an even greater appreciation of the life that flies by so very soon.

For a few young people, that may lead to reading mature books by Elisabeth Kübler-Ross, for example: *On Death and Dying, Questions and Answers on Death and Dying, Death: The Final Stage of Growth,* and *Coping with Death and Dying.* Others will want to examine the moral and legal dilemmas involved in the modern euthanasia movement—James Rachels' *The End of Life: Euthanasia and Morality* and Derek Humphrey and Ann Wickett's *The Right to Die: Understanding Euthanasia.* Others will find satisfaction—and some needed answers, or questions—in novels about the death of a young adult. Alice Bach's

Waiting for Johnny Miracle is set in a cancer ward and a plot summary may make the novel appear somber, or worse. Readers of Bach's book know that is not true. Similarly, Gunnel Beckman's *Admission to the Feast* is ultimately hopeful even though it is about a young girl who learns that she will die soon. Todd Strasser's *Friends Till the End* begins as a sports book and ends as a novel about death, or approaching death, and the maturation of a sports star who learns that some things are more important than games. Barbara Wersba's *Run Softly, Go Fast* nears the classic stage of YA novels, but its portrait of a young man who claims to hate his father but who is deeply troubled by his father's death is brilliant, the best book Wersba has written.

Others will find satisfaction in reading about real people who fought death and who were ultimately beaten, in one sense, but whose lives made more sense because of their fight. Doris Lund's story of her son and his leukemia has long been popular with young adults, and there is little reason to believe that *Eric* will not be read several years from now. The three books about Chicago Bears' running back Brian Piccolo and his battle with cancer continue to be read. The favorite of the three is usually William Blinn's *Brian's Song,* created from the television movie script which many young adults see every year on the late (or early) show. That movie plot came originally from a chapter in Gale Sayers' *I Am Third.* The most complete of the three is Jeannie Morris' *Brian Piccolo: A Short Season.* William Buchanan's *A Shining Season* tells how a twenty-four-year-old runner spent the last eighteen months of his life. It deserves to be more widely recommended.

Two fine books focus on the death of a central character. Mike Rankin in Monica Hughes' *Hunter in the Dark* has reason to be bitter about his parents, for they have kept him in the dark about his illness, preferring to protect him from reality. Knowing that he is ill and getting no better, Mike uses the name of his medicine, vincristine, to discover his disease in a medical book in the local library.

He knows he is going to die, but first he must shoot a white-tail buck deer, to get the antlered head that will prove his manhood. At the close of the novel, Mike has the buck in his rifle sights, a buck "better than his dreams," and then he finds that he cannot pull the trigger, and with that comes his own resignation to his impending death.

When the Bishop in Margaret Craven's *I Heard the Owl Call My Name* learns that twenty-seven-year-old Mark Brian has a terminal illness with less than two years to live, he says to the doctor:

> So short a time to learn so much? It leaves me no choice. I shall send him to my hardest parish. I shall send him to Kingcome on patrol of the Indian Villages.

And off Mark goes, there supposedly to help but actually, as the Bishop knows, to learn how to live and how to die. He approaches the Indians both fearfully and thankfully, fitting his ambivalent view of the world. Craven's book is filled with ambivalence, life and death, success and failure, sympathy and cruelty, pride and resentment, giving and begging, keeping and releasing, destroying and honoring, all there to help readers recognize the ambivalence of life.

And, of course, the greatest ambivalence in the novel is reserved for Mark's death. Sent to an obscure village to prepare for death by learning about life, Mark succeeds in learning about life and death. Then prepared for his end, the end comes suddenly, capriciously, almost like the jest of some maniac gods determined to prove that whatever mortals plan for, even death, the gods will rip asunder. This is a remarkably mature book young adults will admire, just as they will admire the heroism of Mark and others in the book.

And two other books approach classic stature in the field. James Agee's *A Death in the Family* and Katherine Paterson's *Bridge to Terabithia.* After the quiet opening of the prose-poem "Knoxville: Summer 1915" with its affirmation of the dignity of the family and the need for love, Agee's novel reaffirms the love of Jay Follett for his wife Mary and his children Rufus and Catherine. When Jay leaves early of a morning to see Grandfather Follett who has been taken ill, he is too rushed to wake the children to say goodbye. Tragically, he is killed in a car accident, and his wife and children, especially Rufus, try to make sense out of his death and his life.

Although written for younger readers, Katherine Paterson's *Bridge to Terabithia* is a warm and wise book for any reader, child, young adult, or adult. Ten-year-old Jess Aarons runs to impress his father who detests the artistic side of his son. But Jess, to his surprise, is beaten in a race by Leslie Burke, new girl at school. Drawn to each other because both are loners, they create the magic kingdom of Terabithia. While Jess is away, Leslie dies in a tragic accident. Jess's reaction is self-pity, feeling that she has betrayed him by leaving, but as others help to comfort him, he begins to feel a more honest grief and an awareness that he has learned about himself and his needs through Leslie and their mutual love for Terabithia. Jess is, above all else, a survivor.

Among the best books on the topic of death are Mark and Dan Jury's *Gramp,* a photographic portrait of a proud old man who realizes he is slowly losing touch with reality and decides to stop eating and drinking and thus starve himself to death. John Gunther's *Death Be Not Proud* is a classic in its field. At sixteen, Gunther's son developed a cancerous brain tumor, and the book is an account of the boy's death and Gunther's attempt to keep himself sane.

Two recent books by young cancer patients are wise and funny by turns. Though they will certainly bring tears to their readers, that is clearly not their purpose. Matthew Lancaster's *Hang Toughf* is a solid little classic in which a ten-year-old author gives sound advice to other kids who have cancer. As he says, it's not fair, "but it happened, and you and I have to except it." And if your hair falls out, then "if your friends laugh at you, they're not very good friends." Eight-year-old Jason Gaes hated other books about kids with cancer because they always died, and he had cancer and he hadn't died, so he wrote *My Book for Kids with Cansur,* almost as good (and sometimes funnier) than *Hang Toughf.*

For many adults, books about suicide are even more worrisome than other books about death. These adults worry that young adults curious about suicide are doubtless contemplating their own suicides, and that such reading is best ignored by healthy young people. But young adults know the reality of suicide, especially in their own schools. It has been for years the second leading cause of teenage deaths, surpassed only by accidents, and some accidents *may* have been suicides in disguise.

Headlines have bannered the news across the country. The June 17, 1978, *Chicago Tribune* announced "Suicide No. 3 Killer of Teens" as its major headline on the front page. The May 23, 1982, *Los Angeles Times* headlined "Shaken by Teen Suicides, School District Seeks a Cure for the Hidden Epidemic." And *Education Week* for February 26, 1986, announced on page 5, "Suicide Phenomenon Hitting Communities in 2 States." Writing in the June 22, 1987, *New American* (a highly conservative magazine), Samuel L. Blumenfeld worried about "Teen Suicide" and decided that the real causes were drugs, alcohol, values clarification, humanism, death education, and the National Education Association (the latter at least by implication or innuendo).

Perhaps young people sometimes want to read about suicide because it is omnipresent in their world, perhaps because it has an ambivalent appeal to them—many adults when they were young contemplated suicide, not necessarily seriously, wondering what it might be like to end all their problems so easily—perhaps because they are curious as to what would drive another person to want to end life. Nonfiction like Francis Klagsbrun's *Too Young to Die: Youth and Suicide,* John Langone's *Dead End: A Book about Suicide,* and Jane Leder's *Dead Serious* need to be read. All three books are serious and honest and factual.

Sylvia Plath's *The Bell Jar* is a fictionalized autobiography about her own life and her own death-wish. Esther is preoccupied by the execution of the Rosenbergs, and throughout her story she reads constantly about death and suicide. At one point, Esther says, "I am an observer," and later she withdraws more and more from reality:

> I slunk down on the middle of my spine, my nose level with the rim of the window, and watched the houses of outer Boston glide by.
> As the houses grew more familiar, I slunk still lower.

Esther dreams of a wonderful career in exciting and glamorous New York City and a perfect marriage.

> I was supposed to be having the time of my life. I was supposed to be the envy of thousands of other college girls just like me all over America. . . . Look what can happen in this country, they'd say. A girl lives in some out-of-the-way town for nineteen years . . . then gets a scholarship to college and wins a prize here and a prize there and ends up steering New York like her own private car. *Only I wasn't steering anything, not even myself.*

Fran Arrick's *Tunnel Vision* is about the people fifteen-year-old Anthony Hamil left behind when he hanged himself in his bedroom, apparently without reason. Two fine dramas will interest most mature young people. Marsha Norman's *'night, Mother* slowly reveals the plans of a woman to kill herself as she spends a last evening with her mother. She is not seeking pity nor anyone to stop her, but she does want her mother to know so that her mother will not blame herself.

The right to choose one's own way out of life is made by Ken Harrison, an artist now totally paralyzed by a car accident, in Brian Clark's play, *Whose Life Is It, Anyway?* Harrison could hardly have demanded better treatment than that accorded him at the hospital, but the doctors fight to keep him alive when all he wants is to be allowed to die with dignity. His lawyer sues for Harrison's simple right to die. In a moving scene, Harrison explains his reasoning:

> Ken: I choose to acknowledge the fact that I am in fact dead and I find the hospital's persistent effort to maintain this show of life an indignity and it's inhumane.
>
> Judge: But wouldn't you agree that many people with appalling physical handicaps have overcome them and lived essentially creative, dignified lives?
>
> Ken: Yes, I would, but the dignity starts with their choice. If I choose to live, it would be appalling if society killed me. If I choose to die, it is equally appalling if society keeps me alive.
>
> Judge: I cannot accept that it is undignified for society to devote resources to keeping someone alive. Surely it enhances that society.
>
> Ken: It is not undignified if the man wants to stay alive, but I must restate that the dignity starts with his choice. Without it, it is degrading because technology has taken over from human will. My Lord, if I cannot be a man, I do not wish to be a medical achievement.

The moral question is not easily solved in this play, or in life, but the issues and arguments for both sides are well and fairly presented in Clark's play.

HEROES IN WAR

War is a constant in our lives. Old war movies abound on the late show. Newspapers and magazines banner the headlines of this new or that old war. Television news programs barrage us with the latest atrocities.

Why are we so continually preoccupied with war, bloodshed, and death? Perhaps because war is inherently frightening and evil, and in the minds of too many of us, horribly inevitable. The Bible is full of battles, but then so are the *Iliad* and the *Odyssey*. War serves as background for *Antigone* just as it does for *The Red Badge of Courage*. War has influenced artists and musicians, or, perhaps, it would be fairer to say that it has left its indelible mark on them.

JAMES D. FORMAN
on Becoming a Storyteller

Why did I chose to devote my life to writing for young readers, and if given a second chance would I do it again? Tough questions; not to become philosophically entangled, but I wonder to what extent choice had anything to do with it. I grew up an only child in a rather remote house. For amusement I very often had to rely on the fantasies of my own imagination. Along the way such inclinations were encouraged by a series of supportive English teachers who were more concerned with the use of words than how they were spelled. At Princeton I digressed into psychology, with law school following. In retrospect, while neither discipline was directly keyed to creative writing, both have been helpful in that regard. Though an attorney, I have never thought of myself as having the properly combative temperament for the trade and have confined myself to real estate management in a long-time family firm, thus leaving considerable free time for writing.

Once out of school and confronting the realities of the law, my discontents were largely sublimated in a passion for photography. This would impact directly on my later writing, for it led to an assignment for the American Geographic Society, four months in Greece taking pictures and preparing an accompanying text. This was a heady time which encouraged me first to produce a cumbersome manuscript which still abides in the attic, from there to picture books in partnership with my wife, who was a trained fashion illustrator. Nobody wanted these either, and the compromise was young adults, and I was launched and evidently addicted with four such novels set during the period of World War II in Greece, which became more directly the subject of my next several books. Some thirty-five books later I am still at it.

So in a way it simply seems to have happened, yet more positively I might say I like the format, around 200 manageable pages. I like to preach a bit, I hope not too obviously, a rather pacifistic theme hoping that my fervor on behalf of humanity and the preservation of this fragile globe which we share with so many other creatures will rub off on the next generation. There is also the pleasure of pure private creativity, of doing the research and having the time to make discoveries, and of course the hope of giving some pleasure.

Lastly, if given the chance, would I do it again? Probably yes. The only aesthetic discipline which perhaps has greater appeal is painting, and I have struggled sufficiently with a brush to recognize a dearth of talent in this regard. Otherwise I might hope to concentrate sufficient energies to press home a book of adult fiction to publication while continuing to turn out, I trust, valuable books for younger readers.

James Forman's books include *My Enemy, My Brother,* Hawthorn, 1969; *A Fine, Soft Day,* Farrar, 1978; and *Cry Havoc,* Scribners, 1987.

Young adults are painfully aware of the nearness of war, though they may know little about the realities of war and even less about the details of past wars. Reading war literature, fiction or not, serves to acquaint young people with some of war's horrors and how easily people forget, or ignore, their humanity in the midst of war. War novels must, of course, have a war at the center but authors are almost always more interested in what war does to humans than in a mere historic recounting of battles and campaigns and casualties. War books are likely to center on physical and psychological suffering. Death lurks on every doorstep, or it did once, and emotionally it still may for the characters. Often the war seems to happen in slow motion, focusing on one person engaged in one act. Or the reverse may be true, events being telescoped to eliminate the trivial or nonessential to force readers (and sometimes characters) to see the realities and horrors of war even more intensely. At one time, we might have accepted romantic war stories, but a romanticized picture of war today would seem dishonest and offensive to most readers.

Five novelists have written particularly effective war novels.

Harry Mazer's *The Last Mission* is set in the last months of World War II. Jack Raab uses his older brother's identification to lie his way into the Air Force to destroy Hitler and save democracy, all by himself. That dream lasts only a short time before Jack learns that the Air Force is more training and boredom than fighting. When Jack does go to war, his first twenty-four bombing raids go well, but on the last mission, his plane is hit, all his buddies die, and he is captured. When he returns home, the principal at his old school asks him to talk:

> "I'm glad we won," he said. "We couldn't let Hitler keep going. We had to stop him. But most of all, I'm glad it's over." Had he said enough? There was a silence . . . a waiting silence. There was something more he had to say.
>
> "I don't like war. I thought I'd like it before. But war is stupid. War is one stupid thing after another. I saw my best friend killed. His name was Chuckie O'Brien. My whole crew was killed." Now he was talking, it was coming out, all the things he'd thought about for so long. "A lot of people were killed. Millions of people. Ordinary people. Not only by Hitler. Not only on our side. War isn't like the movies. It's not fun and songs. It's not about heroes. It's about awful, sad things, like my friend Chuckie that I'm never going to see again." His voice faltered.
>
> "I hope war never happens again," he said after a moment. "That's all I've got to say."
>
> He sat down. He hardly heard the applause. The floor of the radio room was still slippery with Chuckie's blood. . . . Dave was still fumbling with his chute . . . the plane was still falling through the sky.

Six high-I.Q. soldiers in an intelligence and reconnaissance platoon are sent to find if any Germans are near a French chateau during World War II in *A Midnight Clear* by William Wharton (a pseudonym of a writer who refuses to identify himself publicly). The six play bridge, chess, and word games and refuse to admit they have anything to do with the war. Then the Germans show up, but instead of warfare, both Americans and the supposed enemy engage in a snowball fight. A meeting is arranged, they fraternize, they sing Christmas carols and set up a Christmas tree, and then as peace reigns, war starts up again and the killing begins. Wharton tells a powerful story which is as much about humanity's goals being above its ability as it is about war. This is a powerful story no reader will forget.

English novelist Robert Westall writes about young people who refuse to stay outside the war in *The Machine Gunners* and its sequel, *Fathom Five*. The first novel is set in an English coastal town during 1940–1941. Rumors of a German invasion are rife, and Chas McGill wants to help win the war. Westall is superb at catching some of the humor of the time. Bombs drop, Chas' family heads for the shelter, and his mother remembers insurance policies they must have with them. They turn back toward home.

A body fell through. It was Mrs. Spalding.

"Is she dead?" said Mrs. McGill.

"No, but she's got her knickers round her ankles," said Mr. McGill.

"Aah had tey hop aal the way," gasped Mrs. Spalding. "I was on the outside lav and I couldn't finish. The buggers blew the lav door off, and they've hit the Rex Cinema as well. Is there a spot of brandy?"

"Aah pulled the chain, Mam. It flushed all right." It was Colin, with a self-satisfied smirk on his face.

"You'll get the Victoria Cross for that," said Chas with a wild giggle.

Chas and his friends locate a downed German plane, find the machine gun in working order, and hide it. When his school is hit by another plane a bit later, Chas steals sandbags to create a fortress, a safe place to display the machine gun. Then the rear gunner of the downed plane stumbles onto their fortress and becomes the boys' prisoner. The end of childish innocence comes when adults discover the fortress, the German is shot, and the young people are rounded up by their parents. *Fathom Five* is a rousing spy story set a little later in the war and is a story of Chas' lost love. Westall has amazing ability to portray the ambivalence of young people, the alienation they feel mixed with love and duty.

Howard Fast's *April Morning* with its Revolutionary War setting has sometimes been favorably compared with *The Red Badge of Courage*. Fast's novel focuses on fifteen-year-old Adam Cooper, no hero but only a frightened mortal. He knows the rightness of war until he is thrust into the midst of it, and then he wonders more about the carnage and stupidity than the heroism. In eight sections which take readers from the afternoon of April 18, 1775, through the evening of April 19, *April Morning* explodes the family relationships of Adam and his father, his mother, his beloved Granny, and the girl he loves.

It would be unfair and inaccurate to call Adam a hero in the usual sense. But Adam is a hero in other important ways. He survives, he does what has to be done, and he tries to make sense out of the horror, to understand what the war is all about. It is about him, whether he wants it to be or not.

James Forman's finest work, too little known, is *Ceremony of Innocence.* Hans and Sophie Scholl, brother and sister in Nazi Germany, print and distribute literature attacking Hitler. Arrested by the Gestapo, they are urged to escape by friends and to plead insanity by a lawyer Hans suspects is a Nazi. They refuse, endure the mock trial, are found guilty, and are taken away to be executed. Hans is the last to die by the guillotine.

> Hans heard the sound of rollers, and at last there burst from his throat a cry, uttered in a great voice, a voice that combined anger, reproof, and an overwhelming conviction for which he was willing to die.
>
> "Long live freedom!"
>
> Then the greased blade fell. His teeth met through his tongue, and it was over.

Forman's novel is powerful, terrifying, and heroic, but no more so than the true story of Hans and Sophie—and their work as members of the "White Rose," an underground group of Munich University teachers and students opposed to Hitler—in Annette E. Dumbach and Jud Newborn's *Shattering the German Night: The Story of the White Rose,* Inge Jens' *At the Heart of the White Rose: Letters and Diaries of Hans and Sophie Scholl,* or Hermann Vinke's *The Short Life of Sophie Scholl.*

Nonfiction about war, if anything, is often superior to fiction in recreating the stupidity and folly and bloodiness and, sometimes, the valor. Two books parallel recent PBS televised series and serve as ample introductions to any study of war, Gwynne Dyer's *War,* covering the history of humanity's military duplicities, and John Keegan's *Soldiers,* covering soldiers from the foot soldiers of 2500 B.C. Mesopotamia to sophisticated foot soldiers today.

World War II is well documented. Studs Terkel's *"The Good War": An Oral History of World War Two* tells about the last of the holy, good vs. evil, wars, through the eyes of all sorts of people who watched it or fought it. Annette Tapert's *Lines of Battle: Letters from American Servicemen, 1941–1945* succeeds in making the war a personal problem for human beings, as does the most famous account of a major World War II battle, Richard Tregaskis' *Guadalcanal Diary.*

Ernie Pyle was probably the American soldiers' favorite war correspondent, mostly because he took a genuine interest in people and demanded no special favors for being shot at. *Ernie's War: The Best of Ernie Pyle's World War II Dispatches* (edited by David Nichols) collects some of the work Pyle did in Great Britain, North Africa, Sicily, France, and the Pacific from 1940 until his death in 1945. Pyle wrote honestly without the trite theatrics of too many newspaper writers. Writing about the death of Captain Henry T. Waskow, one of the most "beloved" men Pyle ever found in war, he told of Waskow's men coming in, gently, to see and honor the body, and Pyle ended the account this way:

■ Then a soldier came and stood beside the officer, and bent over, and he spoke to his dead captain, not in a whisper but awfully tenderly, and he said:

"I sure am sorry, sir."

Then the first man squatted down, and he reached down and took the dead hand, and he sat there for a full five minutes, holding the dead hand in his own and looking intently into the dead face, and he never uttered a sound all the time he sat there.

And finally he put the hand down, and then reached up and gently straightened the points of the captain's shirt collar, and then he sort of rearranged the tattered edges of his uniform around the wound. And then he got up and walked away down the road in the moonlight, all alone.

After that the rest of us went back into the cowshed, leaving the five dead men lying in a line, end to end, in the shadow of the low stone wall. We lay down on the straw in the cowshed, and pretty soon we were all asleep.

Few books about World War II, or any other war, succeed so well in creating a revulsion to the blood and messiness as does Farley Mowat in *And No Birds Sang*. After Mowat's company encountered and killed six truckloads of German soldiers, Mowat said:

■ It was not the dead that distressed me most—it was the German wounded. There were a great many of these, and most seemed to have been hard hit. . . .

One ghastly vignette from that shambles haunts me still: the driver of a truck hanging over his steering wheel and hiccuping great gouts of cherry-pink foam through a smashed windscreen, to the accompaniment of a sound like a slush pump sucking air as his perforated lungs labored to expel his own heart's blood . . . in which he was slowly drowning.

Mowat's book is hardly the only honest account but it reeks of death and lost dreams and anyone wanting to know what war is like should not miss it.

The most shameful American action during World War II began in February 1942 when President Roosevelt ordered the forced evacuation of anyone of Japanese ancestry on the West Coast into detention camps scattered in desolate places inland. More than 120,000 people were deported for the remainder of the war. Jeanne Wakatsuki Houston and James D. Houston's *Farewell to Manzanar* describes the first author's life in a camp ringed by barbed wire and guard towers and open latrines. That three-year ordeal destroyed the family's unity and left them a heritage of personal self-inadequacy that took years to remove. Florence Crannell Means' *The Moved-Outers,* an impassioned YA novel in 1945, suggested some of the problems in living in those detention camps, but later books reveal far more of the misery inmates faced. Daniel S. Davis' *Behind Barbed Wire: The Imprisonment of Japanese Americans During World War II,* Peter Irons' *Justice at War,* John Tateishi's *And Justice for All: An Oral History of the Japanese American Camps,* and Deborah Gesensway and Mindy

Roseman's *Beyond Words: Images from America's Concentration Camps* need to be read and remembered. In 1988, Congress provided a token reimbursement for the survivors of the camps.

Retribution for Pearl Harbor finally came in the form of the atomic bomb dropped on Hiroshima. John Hersey's book celebrating/lamenting that horror first appeared in the *New Yorker* in 1946. If anything, it is more important today than it was then. Rodney Barker's *The Hiroshima Maidens* is a follow-up to Hersey's *Hiroshima,* an account of the "Maidens Project" which helped to bring twenty-five disfigured women victims to the United States for treatment.

The war in Vietnam seemed for years to be the one war that would be ignored in print, and then a few years ago the dam broke and the deluge followed. Novels like Philip Caputo's *A Rumor of War* appeared later, followed by his *Indian Country* about Vietnam memories. Then two brothers, R. Lanny Hunter and Victor L. Hunter, shared their different perceptions of the war in *Living Dogs and Dead Lions,* and a recent view of the war came from the perspectives of an American major and a North Vietnamese general in Chris Bunch and Allan Cole's *A Reckoning for Kings: A Novel of the Tet Offensive.*

Nonfiction poured forth; overviews of the war like Thomas D. Boettcher's *Vietnam, the Valor and the Sorrow: From the Home Front to the Front Lines in Words and Pictures* and Peter Goldman and Tony Fuller's *Charlie Company: What Vietnam Did to Us*; oral histories and interviews and personal accounts like Terry Wallace's *Bloods: An Oral History of the Vietnam War by Black Veterans* and Al Santoli's *Everything We Had: An Oral History of the Vietnam War by Thirty-Three American Soldiers Who Fought It*; photos like Mark Jury's *The Vietnam Photo Book*; letters home like Bernard Edelman's *Dear America: Letters Home from Vietnam*; stories from those who survived and were bitter like John Nichols' *American Blood* and Joel Osler Brende and Erwin Randolph Parson's *Vietnam Veterans: The Road to Recovery*; and books about women who served in the war like Linda Van Devanter's *Home Before Morning,* Keith Walker's *A Piece of My Heart: The Stories of 26 American Women Who Served in Vietnam,* and Kathryn Marshall's *In the Combat Zone: An Oral History of American Women in Vietnam, 1966–1975.*

Most touching of all, Laura Palmer's *Shrapnel in the Heart: Letters and Remembrances from the Vietnam Veterans Memorial* conveys the spirit and sadness and loss and wonderment that was the Vietnam experience for so many young people. This record of the 58,132 Americans whose names are inscribed on the black granite memorial in Washington, D.C., does not equal a trip to the memorial, best seen on a gusty and bleak December day, but it comes decently close.

Of all the many books on war, there is no greater indictment of the absurdity and cruelty of war than Roger Rosenblatt's *Children of War.* Rosenblatt circled the globe seeking out children in Belfast, Ireland, in Israel, in Cambodia, in Hong Kong, and in Lebanon and asking them about themselves and what war had done to them. A nine-year-old girl in Cambodia made a drawing, and after a year of help by an American psychologist, she was able to explain how the instrument in the drawing worked. Rosenblatt writes:

■   The children harvesting rice include Peov. She is the largest of the three. Whenever a child refused to work, he was punished with the circular device. The soldiers would place it over the child's head. Three people would hold it steady by means of ropes. . . . A fourth would grab hold of the ring at the end of the other rope. . . . When the rope with the ring was pulled . . . the child would be decapitated. A portable guillotine.

But it wasn't the soldiers who worked the device. It was the children.[7]

■ *HEROES OF THE HOLOCAUST*

Only a few years back, anyone wishing to read about the Holocaust would read Anne Frank's *Diary of a Young Girl.* Advanced students might find a few other sources, mostly historical, and the most mature students might view Alain Resnais' powerful short film, "Night and Fog."

Today an outpouring of books about the Holocaust means that, fortunately, no one can pretend not to know about the happenings and the evils that went with it. Roselle Chartok and Jack Spencer's *The Holocaust Years: Society on Trial* presents the documents; Miriam Chaikin's *A Nightmare in History: The Holocaust 1933–1945* presents the case for younger readers; Milton Meltzer's *Never to Forget: The Jews of the Holocaust* and *Rescue: The Story of How Gentiles Saved Jews in the Holocaust* tells of events involving young adults; and Lucy Dawidowicz's *The War Against the Jews, 1933–1945,* Paul Hilberg's *The Destruction of the European Jews,* and Martin Gilbert's *The Holocaust: A History of the Jews of Europe during the Second World War* present facts and interpretations for adults and young adults. The role of the United States in the Holocaust, and none too proud a role at that, can be read in Deborah Lipstadt's *Beyond Belief: The American Press and the Camps of the Holocaust 1933–1945* and David S. Wyman's *The Abandonment of the Jews: America and the Holocaust, 1941–1945.*

But history pales alongside accounts by those who lived through the terror of the concentration camps. Sylvia Rothchild's *Voices from the Holocaust* is arguably the best brief series of personal histories, but anyone who cares about humanity ought to read David Adler's *We Remember the Holocaust* and the script of a powerful film, Claude Lanzmann's *Shoah: An Oral History of the Holocaust.* Longer individual testimonies can be found in Isabella Leitner's *Fragments of Isabella: A Memoir of Auschwitz,* Fania Fenelon's *Playing for Time,* Joza Karas' *Music in Terezin,* and Ruth Sender's *The Cage,* the latter particularly appealing and disturbing because of the youth of the main character. character.

Most young adults will seek out books about young people caught in the Holocaust because they are better able to identify with people their own age or slightly older. Anne Frank's *Diary of a Young Girl* is, as noted above, still one of the best starting points, and recently more material about Anne Frank has been published. Anne Frank's *Tales from the Secret Annex* is a collection of personal essays and stories and fables she wrote during her time hiding from the Germans. She writes about elves and flower girls and dreams and fears and happiness, all youthful, all saddened by what we know will happen to Anne all too soon. Miep Gies' *Anne Frank Remembered: The Story of the Woman Who Helped to Hide the Frank Family* will also prove worth reading by anyone who cares about Anne.

For those seeking similar accounts, Etty Hillesum's *An Interrupted Life: The Diaries of Etty Hillesum, 1941–1943* is the answer. Hillesum's record is not better or worse than Anne Frank's; it is the product of a twenty-seven-year-old woman who knows precisely what her fate is certain to be. She begins her first entry, "Here goes, then," and she writes of her love affairs, her graduate study at the University of Amsterdam, and her friends and ideas. She seems to have had little interest in politics until Jews were required to wear the yellow star. That jolted her, but she never sought to escape. In her last days, she volunteered to go with a group of condemned Jews to Westerbork Camp. She must have known that Westerbork was the usual first step before Auschwitz. Her journal complements Anne's *Diary*; Etty's irony and sophistication neatly counterpointing Anne's simplicity and innocence. *An Interrupted Life* is completed in *Letters from Westerbork*.

Horrible as the camp killings were as described in Robert Lifton's *The Nazi Doctors: Medical Killing and the Psychology of Genocide*, Miklos Nyiszli's *Auschwitz: A Doctor's Eyewitness Account of Mengele's Death Camp*, Sara Nomberg-Prztyk's *Auschwitz: True Tales from a Grotesque Land*, and Yitzhak Arad's *Belzec, Sobibor, Treblinka: The Operation Reinhard Death Camps*, more painful by far are the records of the death of the young victims. Hana Volavkova's *I Never Saw Another Butterfly: Children's Drawings and Poems from Terezin Concentration Camp, 1942–1944* and Chana Byers Abells' *The Children We Remember* make for painful but necessary reading if we and young adults, and children, are to remember the lesson of the Holocaust.

The postwar aspects of the Holocaust seem less painful at first reading. Hanna and Walter Kohner's *Hanna and Walter: A Love Story* tells us of two teenagers in Czechoslovakia who fall in love and are separated by the war when the Nazis march in. Hanna later married, survived the Holocaust, and later, widowed, found Walter again, and married. Kitty Hart's *Return to Auschwitz: The Remarkable Story of a Girl Who Survived the Holocaust* reminds readers that horrible events are not easily forgotten and may not be forgotten at all.

Heroes exist in real life and in fiction. We read about quiet heroes, sports heroes, war heroes, heroes in death, heroes of the Holocaust. They do not parade forth their heroism, except to the sound of their own drummers.

In Sam Peckinpah's film, *Ride the High Country,* two aging former U.S. Marshals down on their luck are hired to bring a gold shipment down from a mountain mining town. Gil Westrum wants to take the money and run. Steve Judd refuses to go along with his old friend, and when Westrum asks him why, Judd answers simply, "All I want is to enter my house justified."

That is all any hero could ask, to live a life of integrity, humanity, and dignity based upon what she or he believes in. That's all, but it is everything. To our eternal gratitude, heroes do exist, heroes willing to die for what they believe in, but more important, willing to live to fight for their beliefs. We all need heroes to help us stumble through the darkness of our lives to help us find the light, as they have, to falter and fail and fight and maybe even win sometimes. We do not need those grandiose heroes of old so much as we need heroes like ourselves who achieve an immortality within a family or a community. As teachers and librarians, we have both the responsibility and the opportunity to bring books to young adults that tell them about heroes and the possibility of becoming heroes.

NOTES

[1]Joe McGinnis, *Heroes* (New York: Viking, 1976), p. 16.

[2]McGinnis, p. 21.

[3]Dixon Wector, *The Hero in America: A Chronicle of Hero-Worship* (New York: Charles Scribner's Sons, 1941), p. 1.

[4]Arthur Schlesinger, Jr., "The Decline of Greatness," *Saturday Evening Post* 231 (November 1, 1958): 70.

[5]Henry Fairlie, "Too Rich for Heroes," *Harpers Magazine* 257 (November 1978): 33.

[6]Mollie Hunter, "A Need for Heroes," *Horn Book Magazine* 59 (April 1983): 146.

[7]Robert Rosenblatt, *Children of War* (Garden City, NY: Anchor Press/Doubleday, 1983), p. 148.

30 RECOMMENDATIONS FOR READING

Quiet Heroes

Childress, Alice. *A Hero Ain't Nothin' But a Sandwich.* Coward, McCann, 1973. A middle-aged black man tries to save a young boy from drugs and the man becomes one of the most heroic characters in modern fiction.

Kuralt, Charles. *On the Road with Charles Kuralt.* Putnam, 1985. Kuralt's travels around America for CBS News leads him to some curious people and to some quiet heroes.

Peck, Robert Newton. *A Day No Pigs Would Die.* Knopf, 1973. A simple hog butcher during the Depression teaches decency and honor through example.

Williams, Juan. *Eyes on the Prize: America's Civil Rights Years, 1954–1965.* Viking, 1987. The print version of the PBS TV series about people seeking justice.

Biography

Cheng, Nien. *Life and Death in Shanghai.* Grove Press, 1987. Mrs. Cheng survives the Cultural Revolution in China and ultimately comes to America.

Lester, Julius. *Livesong: On Becoming a Jew.* Holt, 1988. A black man recounts his racial and Christian heritage and his decision to become a Jew.

Ngor, Haing, with Roger Warner. *A Cambodian Odyssey.* Macmillan, 1988. A wealthy Cambodian doctor's life goes downhill during the Khmer Rouge regime.

Nolan, Christopher. *Under the Eye of the Clock: The Life Story of Christopher Nolan.* St. Martin's Press, 1988. A young man of 22, born brain damaged, has written two widely acclaimed books, this and a volume of poetry.

Heroes in Sports

Angell, Roger. *The Summer Game.* Simon and Schuster, 1972. The finest living sportswriter conveys what sports are all about. Angell's magic prose is also in *Five Seasons: A Baseball Companion* (Simon and Schuster, 1977), *Late Innings: A Baseball Companion* (Simon and Schuster, 1982), and *Season Ticket: A Baseball Companion* (Houghton Mifflin, 1988).

Halberstam, David. *The Amateurs.* Morrow, 1985. Through examining the lives and hopes of the U.S. Olympic rowing team, Halberstam defines what amateurism and personal commitment are all about.

Hall, Donald. *Fathers Playing Catch with Sons: Essays on Sport (Mostly Baseball).* North Point, 1985. Seven essays and two poems about baseball and other sports by a poet who clearly loves sports.

Smith, Red. *The Red Smith Reader,* Dave Anderson, ed. Random House, 1982. America's finest sportswriter is celebrated after his death through reprinting selected columns. Other collections of Smith's columns appear in *Strawberries in Winter: The Sporting World of Red Smith* (Quadrangle, 1974) and *To Absent Friends from Red Smith* (Atheneum, 1982). Ira Berkow's biography, *Red: A Biography of Red Smith* (Times Books, 1986) is great fun.

Ryan, Bob, and Terry Pluto. *Forty-Eight Minutes: A Night in the Life of the NBA.* Macmillan, 1988. Superb play-by-play of a game between the Cleveland Cavaliers and the Boston Celtics on January 16, 1987.

Heroes in Death

Agee, James. *A Death in the Family.* McDowell, Obolensky, 1956. A father dies in a car crash and leaves a son and a wife to understand his death.

Craven, Margaret. *I Heard the Owl Call My Name.* Doubleday, 1973. A young priest is sent to live in an Indian village to prepare for his death, though he does not know that he has only two years to live.

Enright, J. D., ed. *The Oxford Book of Death.* Oxford University Press, 1983. An anthology of poems, essays, and excerpts from fiction.

Gunther, John. *Death Be Not Proud.* Harper & Row, 1949. A father watches his son die slowly. A classic in the field.

Langone, John. *Dead End: A Book about Suicide.* Little, Brown, 1986. A general history of suicide and what causes young people to consider taking their lives.

Paterson, Katherine. *Bridge to Terabithia.* Crowell, 1977. A children's book which has become a standard. An unlikely friendship leads to an imaginary land and a death and desolation.

Heroes in War

Forman, James. *Ceremony of Innocence.* Hawthorne, 1970. A brother and sister in Nazi Germany are part of the "White Rose," dedicated to overthrowing Hitler.

Hersey, John. *Hiroshima.* Knopf, 1946. Hersey's piece, first printed in the *New Yorker,* recounts the bombing of Hiroshima and Nagasaki.

Houston, Jeanne Wakatsuki, and James D. Houston. *Farewell to Manzanar.* Houghton Mifflin, 1973. With her husband, Jeanne Wakatsuki tells the story of her Japanese family's internment in an Idaho relocation center.

Mowat, Farley. *And No Birds Sang.* Little, Brown, 1980. The Canadian writer's account of his service in World War II.

Palmer, Laura. *Shrapnel in the Heart: Letters and Remembrances from the Vietnam Veterans Memorial.* Random House, 1987. Palmer's book is fashioned around materials the author discovered left at the memorial.

Terkel, Studs. *"The Good War": An Oral History of World War Two.* Pantheon, 1984. Terkel interviewed people who served in the Armed Forces as well as those who supported the effort from home.

Heroes of the Holocaust

Chartok, Roselle, and Jack Spencer, eds. *The Holocaust Years: Society on Trial.* Bantam, 1978. Nearly 300 pages of documents and excerpts on the Holocaust.

Frank, Anne. *The Diary of a Young Girl,* Trans. B. M. Mooyaart. Doubleday, 1952. Recent supplements to the classic diary include *Anne Frank's Tales from the Secret Annex* (Doubleday, 1984) and Miep Gies' (with Alison Leslie Gold) *Anne Frank Remembered: The Story of the Woman Who Helped To Hide the Frank Family* (Simon & Schuster, 1987).

Gilbert, Martin. *The Holocaust: A History of the Jews of Europe During the Second World*

War. Holt, Rinehart and Winston, 1985. The most complete and well organized of the histories of this period.

Lanzmann, Claude. *Shoah: An Oral History of the Holocaust, The Complete Text of the Film.* Pantheon, 1985. The text of the nine-hour film based mostly on interviews.

Rothchild, Sylvia, ed. *Voices from the Holocaust.* New American Library, 1981. Life before and during and after the Holocaust described by survivors.

◾ OTHER TITLES MENTIONED IN CHAPTER SEVEN

Abells, Chana Byers. *The Children We Remember.* Greenwillow, 1986.

Acton, Jay. *The Forgettables.* Crowell, 1973.

Adler, David. *We Remember the Holocaust.* Holt, 1987.

Alexander, Charles C. *John McGraw.* Viking, 1988.

Angelou, Maya. *All God's Children Need Traveling Shoes.* Random House, 1986.

Arad, Yitzhak. *Belzec, Sobibor, Treblinka: The Operation Reinhard Death Camps.* Indiana University Press, 1987.

Arrick, Fran. *Tunnel Vision.* Bradbury, 1980.

Ashley, Merrill. *Dancing for Balanchine.* Dutton, 1985.

Bach, Alice. *Waiting for Johnny Miracle.* Harper & Row, 1980.

Baez, Joan. *And a Voice to Sing With: A Memoir.* Summit, 1987.

Barker, Rodney. *The Hiroshima Maidens.* Viking, 1985.

Beagle, Peter. *The Last Unicorn.* Viking, 1968.

Beckman, Gunnel. *Admission to the Feast.* Holt, 1972.

Bentley, Toni. *Winter Season: A Dancer's Journal.* Random House, 1982.

Berman, Phillip L., ed. *The Courage of Conviction.* Dodd, Mead, 1985.

Blessing, Richard. *A Passing Season.* Little, Brown, 1982.

Blinn, William. *Brian's Song.* Bantam, 1972.

Boettcher, Thomas D. *Vietnam, The Valor and the Sorrow: From the Home Front to the Front Lines in Words and Pictures.* Little, Brown, 1985.

Brashler, William. *The Bingo Long Traveling All-Stars and Motor Kings.* Harper & Row, 1973.

Brende, Joel Osler, and Erwin Randolph Parson. *Vietnam Veterans: The Road to Recovery.* Plenum Press, 1985.

Buchanan, William. *A Shining Season.* Coward, McCann, 1978.

Buckle, Richard, with John Taras. *George Balanchine: Ballet Master.* Random House, 1988.

Bunch, Chris, and Allan Cole. *A Reckoning for Kings: A Novel of the Tet Offensive.* Atheneum, 1987.

Caputo, Philip. *Indian Country.* Bantam, 1987.

_____ . *A Rumor of War.* Holt, 1977.

Chaikin, Miriam. *A Nightmare in History: The Holocaust 1933–1945.* Clarion, 1987.

Clark, Brian. *Whose Life Is It Anyway?* Dodd, Mead, 1979. First televised on Granada (British) television on March 12, 1972. First staged in London on March 6, 1978. First staged in New York City, April 17, 1979.

Coleman, Ken, and Dan Valenti. *The Impossible Dream Remembered: The 1967 Red Sox.* Stephen Greene Press, 1987.

Coover, Robert. *The Universal Baseball Association, P. Henry Waugh, Prop.* Random House, 1968.

Crutcher, Chris. *The Crazy Horse Electric Game.* Greenwillow, 1987.

_____ . *Running Loose.* Greenwillow, 1983.

_____ . *Stotan!* Greenwillow, 1986.

d'Amboise, Christopher. *Leap Year.* Doubleday, 1983.

Davis, Daniel S. *Behind Barbed Wire: The Imprisonment of Japanese Americans During World War II.* Dutton, 1982.

Davis, Terry. *Vision Quest.* Viking, 1979.

Dawidowicz, Lucy S. *The War Against the Jews, 1933–1945,* 10th Anniversary edition. Free Press, 1986.

Dumbach, Annette E., and Jud Newborn. *Shattering the German Night: The Story of the White Rose.* Little, Brown, 1986.

Dyer, Gwynne. *War.* Crown, 1985.

Edds, Margaret. *Free at Last—What Really Happened When Civil Rights Came to Southern Politics.* Adler and Adler, 1987.

Edelman, Bernard, ed. *Dear America: Letters Home from Vietnam.* Norton, 1985.

Fast, Howard. *April Morning.* Crown, 1961.

Felsenthal, Carol. *The Sweetheart of the Silent Majority: The Biography of Phyllis Schafly.* Doubleday, 1981.

Fenelon, Fania. *Playing for Time.* Atheneum, 1977.

Ford, Betty, with Chris Chase. *Betty: A Glad Awakening.* Doubleday, 1987.

Gaes, Jason. *My Book for Kids with Cansur.* Melius and Peterson, 1987.

Gesensway, Deborah, and Mindy Roseman. *Beyond Words: Images from America's Concentration Camps.* Cornell University Press, 1987.

Goldman, Peter, and Tony Fuller. *Charlie Company: What Vietnam Did to Us.* Morrow, 1983.

Greenbaum, Dorothy M.S., and Deidre S. Laiken. *Lovestrong: A Woman Doctor's True Story of Marriage and Medicine.* Times Books, 1984.

Harris, Mark. *Bang the Drum Slowly.* Knopf, 1956.

Hart, Kitty. *Return to Auschwitz: The Remarkable Story of a Girl Who Survived the Holocaust.* Atheneum, 1982.

Haskins, James. *Katherine Dunham.* Coward, McCann, 1982.

Hentoff, Nat. *American Heroes: In and Out of School.* Delacorte, 1987.

——————. *Boston Boy.* Knopf, 1986.

Hilberg, Paul. *The Destruction of the European Jews,* rev. ed. Holmes and Meier, 1985.

Hillesum, Etty. *An Interrupted Life: The Diaries of Etty Hillesum, 1941–1943.* Pantheon, 1984.

——————. *Letters from Westerbork.* Pantheon, 1986.

Hohler, Robert T. *"I Touch the Future . . . ": The Story of Christa McAuliffe.* Random House, 1986.

Hughes, Monica. *Hunter in the Dark.* Atheneum, 1983.

Humphry, Derek, and Ann Wickett. *The Right to Die: Understanding Euthanasia.* Harper & Row, 1986.

Hunter, R. Lanny, and Victor L. Hunter. *Living Dogs and Dead Lions.* Viking, 1986.

Hynd, Noel. *Giants of the Polo Grounds: The Glorious Times of Baseball's New York Giants.* McGraw-Hill, 1988.

Irons, Peter. *Justice at War.* Oxford University Press, 1984.

Jens, Inge, ed. *At the Heart of the White Rose: Letters and Diaries of Hans and Sophie Scholl.* Harper & Row, 1987.

Jury, Mark. *The Vietnam Photo Book.* Grossman, 1971.

——————, and Dan Jury. *Gramp.* Grossman, 1976.

Karas, Joza. *Music in Terezin, 1941–1945.* Beaufort, 1985.

Keegan, John. *Soldiers.* Viking, 1986.

King, Mary. *Freedom Song—A Personal Story of the 1960s Civil Rights Movement.* Morrow, 1987.

Kirkland, Gelsey, with Greg Lawrence. *Dancing on My Grave: An Autobiography.* Doubleday, 1986.

Klagsbrun, Francine. *Too Young to Die: Youth and Suicide,* 3rd ed. Houghton Mifflin, 1984.

Kohner, Hanna, and Walter Kohner with Frederick Kohner. *Hanna and Walter: A Love Story.* Random House, 1984.

Kozinski, Jerzy. *The Devil Tree.* Harcourt Brace Jovanovich, 1973.

Kübler-Ross, Elisabeth. *Coping with Death and Dying*. Macmillan, 1981.

————— . *Death: The Final Stage of Growth*. Prentice-Hall, 1975.

————— . *On Death and Dying*. Macmillan, 1969.

————— . *Questions and Answers on Death and Dying*. Macmillan, 1974.

Lancaster, Matthew. *Hang Toughf.* Paulist, 1985.

Lang, Jack and Peter Simon. *The New York Mets: Twenty-Five Years of Baseball Magic*, rev. ed. Holt, 1987.

Leder, Jane. *Dead Serious*. Macmillan, 1987.

Lehmann-Haupt, Christopher. *Me and Di-Maggio: A Baseball Fan Goes in Search of His Gods*. Simon and Schuster, 1986.

Leitner, Isabella. *Fragments of Isabella: A Memoir of Auschwitz*. Crowell, 1978.

Lifton, Robert. *The Nazi Doctors: Medical Killing and the Psychology of Genocide*. Basic Books, 1986.

Lipstadt, Deborah. *Beyond Belief: The American Press and the Camps of the Holocaust 1933–1945*. Free Press, 1986.

Lund, Doris. *Eric*. Lippincott, 1974.

Maiorano, Robert. *Worlds Apart: The Autobiography of a Dancer from Brooklyn*. Coward, McCann, 1980.

Malamud, Bernard. *The Natural*. Farrar, Straus, 1952.

Manchester, William. *One Brief Shining Moment: Remembering Kennedy*. Little, Brown, 1984.

Marshall, Kathryn, ed. *In the Combat Zone: An Oral History of American Women in Vietnam, 1966–1975*. Little, Brown, 1987.

Martins, Peter, with Robert Cornfield. *Far from Denmark*. Little, Brown, 1983.

Mazer, Harry. *The Last Mission*. Delacorte, 1979.

Means, Florence Crannell. *The Moved Outers*. Houghton Mifflin, 1945.

Meltzer, Milton. *Never to Forget: The Jews of the Holocaust*. Harper & Row, 1976.

————— , *Rescue: The Story of How Gentiles Saved Jews in the Holocaust*. Harper & Row, 1988.

Morris, Jeannie. *Brian Piccolo: A Short Season*. Rand McNally, 1971.

Murray, Pauli. *Song in a Weary Throat*. Harper & Row, 1987.

Myers, Walter Dean. *Hoops*. Delacorte, 1981.

————— . *The Outside Shot*. Delacorte, 1984.

Nichols, John. *American Blood*. Holt, 1987.

Nomberg-Prztyk, Sara. *Auschwitz: True Tales from a Grotesque Land*. University of North Carolina Press, 1985.

Norman, Marsha. *'night, Mother*. Hill and Wang, 1983.

Nyiszli, Miklos. *Auschwitz: A Doctor's Eyewitness Account of Mengele's Death Camp*. Seaver, 1986.

Peterson, Robert. *Only the Ball Was White. A History of Legendary Black Players and All-Black Professional Teams*. Prentice-Hall, 1970.

Plath, Sylvia. *The Bell Jar*. Harper & Row, 1971.

Plimpton, George. *The Curious Case of Sid Finch*. Macmillan, 1987.

Pyle, Ernie. *Ernie's War: The Best of Ernie Pyle's World War II Dispatches,* David Nichols, ed. Random House, 1986.

Rachels, James. *The End of Life: Euthanasia and Morality*. Oxford University Press, 1986.

Ralbovsky, Martin. *Destiny's Darlings: A World Championship Little League Team Twenty Years Later*. Hawthorne, 1974.

Rosenblatt, Roger. *Children of War*. Doubleday, 1983.

Santoli, Al, ed. *Everything We Had: An Oral History of the Vietnam War by Thirty-Three American Soldiers Who Fought It*. Random House, 1981.

Sayers, Gale. *I Am Third*. Viking, 1970.

Sender, Ruth. *The Cage*. Macmillan, 1986.

Stodelle, Ernestine. *Deep Song: The Dance Story of Martha Graham*. Macmillan, 1984.

Strasser, Todd. *Friends Till the End*. Delacorte, 1981.

Taper, Bernard. *Balanchine: A Biography,* 3rd ed. Times Books, 1984.

Tapert, Annette. *Lines of Battle: Letters from American Servicemen, 1941–1945*. Times Books, 1987.

Tateishi, John. *And Justice for All: An Oral History of the Japanese American Detention Camps.* Random House, 1984.

Tregaskis, Richard. *Guadalcanal Diary.* Random House, 1943.

Van Devanter, Linda. *Home Before Morning.* Beaufort, 1983.

Vinke, Hermann. *The Short Life of Sophie Scholl.* Harper & Row, 1984.

Volavkova, Hanna, ed. *I Never Saw Another Butterfly: Children's Drawings and Poems from Terezin Concentration Camp, 1942–1944.* Schocken, 1978.

Walker, Keith. *A Piece of My Heart: The Stories of 26 American Women Who Served in Vietnam.* Presidio, 1986.

Wallace, Terry, ed. *Bloods: An Oral History of the Vietnam War by Black Veterans.* Random House, 1984.

Wersba, Barbara. *Run Softly, Go Fast.* Greenwillow, 1979.

Westall, Robert. *Fathom Five.* Greenwillow, 1979.

————— . *The Machine Gunners.* Greenwillow, 1976.

Wharton, William. *A Midnight Clear.* Knopf, 1982.

Wyman, David S. *The Abandonment of the Jews: America and the Holocaust, 1941–1945.* Pantheon, 1984.

For information on the availability of paperback editions of these titles, please consult the most recent edition of *Paperbound Books in Print,* published annually by R. R. Bowker Company.

NONFICTION BOOKS
Of Interesting Information

When E. L. Doctorow, the author of *Ragtime,* accepted the National Book Critics Circle Award, he said, "There is no more fiction or nonfiction—only narrative." Some critics think that the blending of fiction and nonfiction which Doctorow alluded to may be the most significant literary development of the century. Certainly today it is harder than it was seventy-five or a hundred years ago to make a clearcut distinction between novels and informational books that are based on real events. How closely fiction and nonfiction have blended together in the minds of teachers was shown by a survey in which 300 English teachers responded to a request to list ten adolescent novels and ten adult novels worthy of recommending to teenagers for reading. Among 20 nonfiction titles recommended as novels were Piers Paul Read's *Alive,* James Herriot's *All Creatures Great and Small,* Robin Graham's *Dove,* Peter Maas' *Serpico,* Doris Lund's *Eric,* Alvin Toffler's *Future Shock,* Maya Angelou's *I Know Why the Caged Bird Sings,* Dee Brown's *Bury My Heart at Wounded Knee,* Claude Brown's *Manchild in the Promised Land,* Eldridge Cleaver's *Soul on Ice,* and John H. Griffin's *Black Like Me.*

The blending has occurred from both directions. On one side are all the nonfiction writers who use the techniques of fiction including suspense, careful plotting and characterization, and literary devices such as symbolism and metaphor. Nonfiction pieces are also being gathered and printed in anthologies much like short story collections, for example, *Grass Roots & Schoolyards: A High School Basketball Anthology* edited by Nelson Campbell. On the other side are the novelists who collect data as an investigative reporter would. Here at Arizona State University, our faculty members are currently waging a campaign to convince the administration that they need to be provided with research assistants just as much as do faculty members in history or chemistry. In *Midnight Hour Encores* Bruce Brooks acknowledged 32 individuals for talking to him "about music in relentless detail," and at the beginning of *Izzy, Willy-Nilly* Cynthia Voigt acknowledged help from medical personnel who taught her about physical and mental aspects of amputation. When Richard Peck wrote *Are You in the House Alone?* he gathered current statistics on rape and then fashioned his story around the most typical case, that is, a young girl in a familiar setting being raped by someone she knows who is not prosecuted for the crime.

These books are fiction in the sense that fictional names are used and also that they combine bits and pieces of many individual stories. Nevertheless, in another sense, these stories are more real and actually present a more honest portrayal than some pieces labeled nonfiction that are true accounts of bizarre or strange happenings. See Table 8.1 for help in evaluating journalistic fiction.

The question of what is true (nonfiction) and what is untrue (fiction) might be compared to the question of what we mean by "real" that Margery Williams asks in her children's classic *The Velveteen Rabbit*. She answers that when something has lived a long time and is well loved and well worn through use, then it becomes real. According to this definition, Louisa May Alcott's *Little Women* is real. A mental image of the warm supportive family portrayed in the book is a real part of the psyches of literally millions of readers around the world who believe that the book is a true presentation of the Alcott family. Actually, the genteel poverty that Alcott wrote about is a far cry from the facts. It was not so much a question of the girls' not having matching gloves on their

Table 8.1   *SUGGESTIONS FOR EVALUATING JOURNALISTIC FICTION*

A good piece of journalistic fiction usually has:
An authentic story that is individual and unique but also representative of human experience as a whole.

Information that is accurate and carefully researched. This is extremely important because, with most of these stories, readers will have heard news accounts and will lose faith in the story if there are inconsistencies.

A central thesis that has grown out of the author's research.

Enough development to show the relationship between the characters' actions and what happens. People's motives are explored, and cause and effect are tied together.

An author with all the writing skills of a good novelist so that, for example, the characters reveal themselves through their speech and actions, rather than through the author's descriptions.

A dramatic style of writing that draws readers into the story.

A poor piece of journalistic fiction may have:
A stacking of the evidence to prove a sensational idea. The author set out not to find the truth but to collect evidence on only one side of an issue.

A trite or worn subject that is not worthy of booklength attention from either writer or reader.

Evidence of sloppy research and little or no documentation of sources.

Conversations and other accessory literary devices that contradict straight news accounts.

Inclusion of extraneous information that does not help the story build toward a central idea or thesis.

A pedestrian style of writing that lacks drama.

hands as it was a question of their not having food on the table. We can say, then that the "reality" of *Little Women* exists quite apart from verifiable facts.

Literature—fiction and nonfiction—is more than a simple recounting or replaying of the life that surrounds the writer. It is a distillation and a crystallization. Only when an author skillfully chooses descriptive details and develops believable dialogue does an account of an actual event become "real" to the reader. Certainly Alex Haley's *Roots* became real to millions of television viewers as well as to millions of readers, yet the book contains many fictional elements in both subject matter and presentation. It is these elements that make the book stand out as "literature," whereas the histories of other families are little more than dreary records read on special occasions by dutiful family members. Although dozens of reasons could be given for the success of Haley's book, many of them would probably relate to the matter of choice. Alex Haley was a master at selecting the incidents and the details he wanted to include. Good writers of nonfiction do not simply record everything they know or can uncover. For example, with Haley's book, people's imaginations were captured by the fact that on September 29, 1967, he "stood on the dock in Annapolis where his great-great-great-great-great-grandfather was taken ashore on September 29, 1767," and sold as a slave to a Virginia plantation owner. From this point, Haley set out to trace backwards the six generations that connected him to a sixteen-year-old "prince" newly arrived from Africa.

What the public might not stop to consider as they read about this dramatic incident is that it is setting the stage for only a small portion of Haley's "roots." In the generation in which Haley started his story with the young couple Omoro and Binta Kinte and the birth of their first son, Kunta, there were 256 parents giving birth to 128 children, each one of whom is also a great-great-great-great-great-grandfather or grandmother to Alex Haley. Even though Haley was writing nonfiction, he had an almost unlimited range of possibilities from which to choose. With the instincts of a good storyteller he chose to trace the family line that could be presented in the most dramatic fashion. At each stage of the writing, he made similar choices. Part of the reason that his book is literature, rather than only a family record, is that he made the choices as a storyteller instead of as a clerk.

Because of the mass media, today's readers are so accustomed to strange facts and hard-to-believe stories that they have begun consistently to ask such questions as "Is it true?" "Is that for real?" and "Honestly?" This emphasis on "truth" has put some writers of fiction in a peculiar situation, witness the strange case of Clifford Irving, the novelist who in the 1970s served a jail term for claiming that his story about an eccentric billionaire was a biography of Howard Hughes.

Alfred Slote, an author of sports stories, reported a less dramatic case to the fourth annual conference of the Children's Literature Association. He told how his publishers decided to illustrate his books with photographs rather than drawings in an attempt to make his fiction look like sports nonfiction which sells better. Slote is a photographer as well as a writer, so he offered to take the pictures, and he was surprised at how his writing became influenced by whether or not he would be able to get an actual photograph. He concluded by asking whether he could build castles in the sky if he had to produce a photograph of each one.

Several authors are probably asking themselves similar questions. The public wants "true" stories, yet expects them to be as well crafted and as exciting as the best of fiction. Beatrice Sparks, who seven years after the publication of the "anonymous" *Go Ask Alice,* came forward and announced herself on the covers of two other books (*Voices* and *Jay's Journal*) as "the author who brought you *Go Ask Alice,*" said that the reason she published the story, which was "based on" a girl's actual diary, anonymously, was to make it seem more authentic. She thought that having the story appear to come directly from a young girl who died of an overdose would make its anti-drug message more acceptable to the target audience.[1] Also, when a book comes out as nonfiction, it will be reviewed differently. For example, adult critics who questioned the likelihood of so many drug-related misfortunes happening to the same girl in such a short period of time did not criticize the book in the same way they might have if they had known it was fiction.

THE NEW JOURNALISM

Several factors have contributed to the development of what Truman Capote called, "the most avant-garde form of writing existent today." He was the one who coined the term "nonfiction novel" for *In Cold Blood,* an account of an especially brutal murder and the subsequent trial. Tom Wolfe prefers the term "new journalism" and wrote a book by that name in which he proposes that it is the dominant form of writing in contemporary America. Other terms that are used include "creative nonfiction," "literary journalism," "journalistic fiction," and "advocacy journalism." Although its roots were growing right along with journalism in general, it did not really begin to flower until the 1950s and 1960s. Part of the reason for its development is the increased educational level of the American public. Newspaper readers and television viewers, including young adults, are no longer satisfied with simplistic explanations in which people and issues are either all good or bad. Readers recognize not just black and white but many shades of gray, which they are curious to read about.

Our affluence, combined with modern technology, helps make the new journalism possible. Compare similar incidents that happened 126 years apart. In 1846 a group of travelers who came to be known as the Donner party were trapped in the high Sierras by an early snow. They had to stay there all winter without food except for the flesh of their dead companions. After they were rescued, word of their ordeal gradually trickled back East so that for years afterward sensationalized accounts were being made up by newspaper reporters who had no chance to actually come to the scene or interview the survivors.

Nonfiction books usually have shorter life spans and are aimed at more specific audiences than are fiction titles. Nevertheless, over the last two decades, nonfiction sales have increased continuously for leisure reading.

Contrast that with what happened in 1972 when a planeload of Uruguayan travelers crashed in the Andes mountains. Just as in the Donner party, some of the people knew each other before the trip but others were strangers. During the terrible weeks of waiting they all got to know each other and to develop intense relationships revolving around leadership roles and roles of rebellion and/or giving up. They endured unspeakable hardships. Many died; those who lived did so because they ate the flesh of those who died. But in this situation, the people were rescued by helicopters after two of the men made their way out of the mountains. Word of their two-and-a-half month ordeal was flashed around the world and by the time the sixteen men, mostly members of a rugby team, had been flown back to Uruguay, reporters from many nations were there. A press conference was held, and the journalists were told about the cannibalism.

This was the second surprise in the story. The first had been their survival. The drama of the situation naturally fired imaginations all around the world. Lippincott suggested to author Piers Paul Read that this was the kind of story that would make a good book. He went to Uruguay where he stayed for several months interviewing survivors, rescuers, family, and friends of both the deceased and the survivors, and government officials who had been in charge of the search. More than a year later, Lippincott published *Alive: The Story of the Andes Survivors,* which was on the *New York Times* best-seller list for seven months, and which will probably continue to be read by young adults for the next several years both in their English classes and in their free time.

The fact that the survivors were in their early twenties undoubtedly helps teenagers to identify with the story, but so do the literary techniques that Read used. He focused on certain individuals, presenting miniature character sketches of some and fully developed portraits of others. The setting was crucial to the story and he described it vividly. He was also careful to write in such a way that the natural suspense of the situation came through. His tone was consistent throughout the book. He respected and admired the survivors but he did not shy away from showing the negative aspects of human nature when it is sorely tried. In a foreword he said that the only liberty he allowed himself was the creation of dialogue between the characters, although, whenever possible, he relied on diaries and on remembered comments and quarrels as well as on his acquaintance with the speaking styles of the survivors.

The influence of the new journalism is seen in many aspects of books promoted for young readers. William Norris' *The Man Who Fell from the Sky,* for example, is described as a "true-life mystery," and Theodore Taylor's *Battle in the Arctic Seas* is described as a "re-creation . . . drawn from naval records and a personal diary." An unusual combination is Nadine Gordimer and David Goldblatt's *Lifetimes Under Apartheid.* Excerpts from Gordimer's fiction are presented alongside 60 of Goldblatt's dramatic photographs of life in South Africa. M. E. Kerr's *Me, Me, Me, Me, Me, Not a Novel* has too much truth in it to be a novel, but it also has too much creative exaggeration in it to be accurately classed as an autobiography. Likewise Jean Fritz hesitated to claim that *Homesick: My Own Story* was an autobiography. In the foreword she explained:

> When I started to write about my childhood in China, I found that my memory came out in lumps. Although I could for the most part arrange them in the proper sequence, I discovered that my preoccupation with time and literal accuracy was squeezing the life out of what I had to say. So I decided to forget about sequence and just get on with it. . . . letting the events fall as they would into the shape of a story, lacing them together with fictional bits, adding a piece here and there when memory didn't give me all I needed. . . . So although this book takes place within two years—from October 1925 to September 1927—the events are drawn from the entire period of my childhood, but they are all, except in minor details, basically true. The people are real people; the places are dear to me. But most important the form I have used has given me the freedom to recreate the emotions that I remember so vividly. Strictly speaking, I have to call this book *fiction,* but it does not feel like fiction to me. It is my story, told as truly as I can tell it.[2]

Many books of the type treated in Chapter 7 on heroes are written by authors using the techniques of the new journalism, for example, Tom Wolfe's

The Right Stuff, the story of the astronauts; Elaine Ipswitch's *Scott Was Here,* the story of her fifteen-year-old son's losing battle with Hodgkin's disease; and Steven Callahan's *Adrift: Seventy-Six Days Lost at Sea.*

What these books have in common is a combination of factual information and emotional appeal. They are stories of real people with whom readers can identify. Technically they might be classified under many different genres: biography, history, drama, essay, and personal philosophy. But regardless of classification, they are among those books that are likely to serve young adults as a bridge between childhood and adult reading. They have this power because of the straightforward, noncondescending manner of writing which is a characteristic of good journalism.

THE EVALUATION OF NONFICTION

Nonfiction best-sellers often outsell fiction best-sellers, and on television, producers know they can add millions of viewers if they advertise a program as "a documentary" rather than "a drama." And some of the most popular movies are done in "nonfiction" style, for example, *Ghandi, Silkwood, Mask,* and *The Last Emperor.* But in young adult literature, we sometimes treat informational books as unwelcome or at least unrecognized cousins of "real" literature. Milton Meltzer has written a sterling defense of nonfiction, "Where Do All the Prizes Go?: The Case for Nonfiction" in which he stated:

> Librarians, teachers, reviewers—the three groups who usually administer the awards or serve as judges—seem confident that only fiction can be considered literature. But what is Henry David Thoreau's *Walden*? What is James Boswell's *Life of Samuel Johnson*? What is Tom Paine's *Common Sense*? Not one of them literature? All merely nonfiction?

He took to task several critics and writers about children's literature who ignored nonfiction and then argued:

> But I say that the best writers of nonfiction put their hearts and minds into their work. Their concern is not only with what they have to say but with how they say it. Lillian Smith, like so many others, is guilty of bearing in mind only the finest writers of fiction when she discusses children's literature and thinking only of run-of-the-mill writers when she discusses information books.[3]

As we prepared this chapter, Meltzer's implied question of why nonfiction is less honored than fiction kept coming back to us and giving us the feeling that if we could answer his question we would learn something important about a kind of book that is moving up in the literary hierarchy. And also, if teachers and librarians understand the problems involved in evaluating nonfiction, they

MILTON MELTZER
on Fiction and Nonfiction

During many years of writing nonfiction about social issues, I've often used the devices of fiction to mul-

tiply the power of facts by evoking from readers their sense of concern, even of constructive anger. I've wanted to help them to see the weaknesses of our world, its inequality, its injustice, that leave so many poor, so many ignored, abused, betrayed. To obtain any betterment of such lives people need to care, need to respect these "others," and to respect themselves and their own ability to bring about social change by making democracy work to its fullest capacity. So I investigate thoroughly whatever interests me—it could be poverty, crime, terrorism, racism, slavery, war, politics, the Holocaust—and with the facts gathered from the greatest variety of sources I can unearth, try to make the issue real to the reader. I think I've used almost every technique fiction writers call on (except to invent the facts) in order to draw the readers in, deepen their feeling for people whose lives may be remote from their own, and enrich their understanding of forces that shape the outcome of all our lives. In the end, I believe it is not a question of what is fiction and what is fact, but what is true and what is false. Fiction can lie about reality; so can nonfiction. And both can tell the truth.

Milton Meltzer's books include *The American Revolutionaries: A History in Their Own Words,* Crowell, 1987; *The Landscape of Memory,* Viking Kestrel, 1987; and *Ain't Gonna Study War No More: The Story of America's Peace Seekers,* Harper & Row, 1985.

may be less likely to think of nonfiction as "nonliterature." There are at least four complicating factors in the evaluation of fiction.

1. People select information books primarily on the basis of the subject matter, and since there is such incredible variety in subjects, people's choices vary and there is less agreement on what is "the best."
2. Nonfiction books become dated more quickly than do fiction books, and their transitory nature discourages teachers from giving them serious consideration as instructional materials. Out of 85 books on ALA's Young Adult Services Division "The Best of the Best Books 1970–1983," only 15 were nonfiction, and these were mostly personal adventures. On the yearly lists between one-third and one-half of the titles have been nonfiction, but books on such topics as computers and car repair rapidly become obsolete. And if someone wants to prepare for taking the SAT tests or to read advice on handling money, selecting a college, or planning for a career, recent information will be best.

3. Reviewers and prize givers may not feel competent to judge the technical or other specialized information presented in many informative books. Also, many reviewers, especially those working with educational journals, come from an English-teaching tradition, and they naturally tend to focus their attention on books that would be used in conjunction with literature rather than biology, home economics, social studies, industrial arts, history, or business classes.

4. In evaluating nonfiction, there is no generally agreed-upon theory of criticism or criteria for judgment.

We suggest that the evaluation situation can be improved by readers looking at fiction and nonfiction in similar ways. Replace the idea of looking at plot and characterization with looking at the intended audience and the content of the book (What is it about? What information does it present?), then look at the appropriateness and success with which each of the following is established. The ideas in Table 8.2 may also be helpful.

Setting

Informative books have settings or scopes. For example, they may be historical as is Trudy J. Hanmer's *The Advancing Frontier.* They may be restricted to regional interests as is S. Allen Chambers' *Discovering Historical America: Mid-Atlantic States,* or they may be limited in scope as is Penelope and Raymond McPhee's *Your Future in Space: The U.S. Space Camp Training Program,* which is about the camp in Huntsville, Alabama, for fifth to tenth graders. In evaluating the setting and/or the scope of a book, one needs to ask whether the author set realistic goals considering the reading level of the intended audience and the amount of space and back-up graphics available.

Theme

Informational books also have themes or purposes which are closely tied to the author's point of view. Authors may write in hopes of persuading someone to a particular belief as did Hope Ryden when she wrote *God's Dog* as a defense of the coyote. Or the purpose may be to inspire thoughtfulness as Albert Marrin did in *Hitler* and Milton Meltzer did in *Ain't Gonna Study War No More: The Story of America's Peace Seekers.* Some authors shout out their themes so no potential reader can miss the point, for example, Melvyn Bernard Zerman's *Taking on the Press: Constitutional Rights in Conflict* and Diane A. Wallace and Philip L. Hershey's *How to Master Science Labs.*

Tone

The manner in which an author goes about achieving a desired goal, whether it is to persuade, inform, inspire, or amuse, sets the tone of a book. Is it hard-sell, strident, one-sided, humorous, loving, sympathetic, adulatory, scholarly, pedantic, energetic, or leisurely? Authors of informative books for children used to take a leisurely approach because they were thinking of children as empty vessels waiting to be filled with information. They considered it their task to trick children into becoming interested in their subject and so they tried to be as entertaining as possible. But today's young readers are just as busy as their parents and most likely go to informative books, not for leisure-time

Table 8.2   **SUGGESTIONS FOR EVALUATING INFORMATIVE NONFICTION**

A good piece of informative writing usually has:
A subject of interest to young readers, written about with zest. Information that is up-to-date and accurate.

New information, or information organized in such a way as to present a different point of view than in previously available books.

A reading level, vocabulary, and tone of writing that are at a consistent level appropriate to the intended audience.

An organization in which basic information is presented first so that chapters and sections build on each other.

An index and other aids to help readers look up facts if they want to return to the book for specific information or to glean ideas and facts without reading the entire book.

Adequate documentation of the sources of information, including some original sources.

Information to help interested students locate further readings on the subject.

In how-to books, clear and accurate directions including complete lists of the equipment and supplies needed in a project.

Illustrations that add interest as well as clarity to the text.

A competent author with expertise in the subject matter.

A poor piece of informative writing may have:
Obsolete or inaccurate information and/or illustrations. Even one such occurrence causes the reader to lose faith in the rest of the book.

Evidence of cutting-and-pasting in which the author merely reorganized previously prepared material without developing anything new in content or viewpoint.

Inconsistencies in style or content, for example, college level vocabulary but a childish or cute style of writing.

An awkward mix of fiction and nonfiction techniques through which the author unsuccessfully tries to slip information in as an unnoticed part of the story.

A reflection of out-of-date or socially unfair attitudes, for example, a history book that presents only the history of white upper-class males with a title and introduction that give the impression that it is a comprehensive history of the time period being covered.

A biased presentation in which only one side of a controversial issue is presented with little or no acknowledgement that many people hold different viewpoints.

In how-to books, frustrating directions, that oversimplify and/or set up unrealistic expectations so that the reader is disappointed in the result.

---

entertainment but to get quick information. A boy who wants to repair a bicycle doesn't want to start out by reading about the Wright brothers and their bicycle shop before getting to the part on how gears and brakes work.

Style

The best informative books also have style. They "exude some kind of passion or love or caring and they have the potential for leaving a mark on the readers, changing them in some way.[4] George A. Woods, former children's book review editor of the *New York Times Book Review* said that he selected the informational books to be featured in his reviews mostly on his own "gut-level" reactions of what was "new or far better than what we have had before." He looked for a majesty of language and uniqueness and for books that would add to children's understanding by making them eyewitnesses to history.[5] A problem in examining an author's style is that each book must be judged according to the purpose that the author had in mind. From book to book, purposes are so different that it is like the old problem of comparing apples and oranges. Some books will be successful simply because they are different—more like a mango than either an apple or an orange.

David Macaulay's *Unbuilding* is such a book. Technically it should probably be classed as fiction because it's the make-believe story of an Arab oil magnate who purchases the Empire State Building and has it dismantled and crated up for shipment to his Arab desert to be reconstructed as his company's office building. In the fictional part of the book, Macaulay makes snide jokes about big money, historical preservationists, and people's gullibility. The nonfiction, informative part of the book is the accuracy of the detailed architectural drawings which show how the building was created.

Cutaways and double-page spreads emphasize the building's beauty as well as the magnificent accomplishment of its 1930s construction. From a purely informational stand, Macaulay could have used the same drawings and entitled the book something like *Construction of the Empire State Building.* That's really what readers learn, but the effect of the clever reversal—turning the book into what one reviewer called "an urban fairy-tale"—was to take it out of the "ordinary" category and to make it a book that, in Jane Langton's words, exudes "some kind of passion or love or caring."

CONTEMPORARY INFLUENCES ON THE PUBLISHING OF INFORMATIONAL BOOKS

Prior to the 1950s what was published for young readers was in the main either fiction (novels or short stories), poetry, or textbook material to be used in school. No one thought that young readers would be interested in factual books unless they were forced to study them as part of their schoolwork. But then the Russians launched Sputnik, and Americans were sincerely frightened that Russia was scientifically and technologically ahead. In 1961, Congress passed the National Defense Education Act, which gave millions of dollars to school libraries initially earmarked for the purchase of science and math books. These books were to be supplements to the curriculum, which students would read independently. Publishers competed to create informative books that would qualify for purchase under the Act and would attract young readers.

The rise in the popularity of nonfiction has paralleled the information explosion and the rise in the power and influence of the mass media. Today there is simply more information to be shared between reader and writer. Television, radio, movies, newspapers, and magazines all communicate the same kinds of information as do books, but people expect more from books because the other media are limited in the amount of space and time that they devote to any one topic. And whatever is produced by the mass media must be of interest to a *mass* audience while individual readers select books. Of course publishers want masses of individual readers to select their books, but still there is more room for experimentation and for controversial ideas in books than in the kinds of media which are supported by advertisers and therefore must aim to attract the largest possible audience.

At the 1988 meeting of the Conference on College Composition and Communication in St. Louis, science writer Jon Franklin spoke on a panel entitled "Nonfiction: The Genre of a Technological Age." Formerly a science writer for the *Evening Sun* in Baltimore and now a teacher of journalism at the University of Maryland in College Park, Franklin's topic was "Literary Structure: A Growing Force in Science Journalism." He pointed out how in the past decade, more than half the winners of the Pulitzer Prize in nonfiction had been science books, and how the increasingly important role of scientific writing in newspapers and magazines is changing basic concepts of journalism. The upside-down pyramid, in which the important facts are stated first and the details filled in later so that an editor can cut the story whenever the available space is filled, does not work for science writing. This kind of traditional journalistic organization does a disservice to science because it results in oversimplification. Science stories have to be written inductively building from the small to the large points because most of the scientific developments and concepts that are in the news are too complex for readers to understand unless they get the supporting details first.

Just as journalists are having to learn new ways to write, Franklin says that readers are going to have to learn new ways to read. He made a persuasive plea for teachers to focus more attention on helping students learn to read and feel comfortable with scientific writing. If people feel uncomfortable with scientific writing, they are likely to resent and reject scientific concepts, witness the controversy over creationism and evolution.

Franklin worries about the development of a new kind of elitism based on scientific literacy. He gave examples of science stories that were acceptable as books but not as newspaper features because only a few hundred people in any metropolitan area were prepared to read and understand the concepts. Book publishers face the challenge of finding this relatively small number of scientifically literate people across the nation and marketing their books to them. Franklin's proposal to keep the gap from widening between the scientifically literate and those who reject all science is two-pronged. On the one hand, science writers have to work harder to find organizational patterns and literary techniques that will make their material understandable and interesting. On the other hand, schools must bring the reading of technological and scientific information into the curriculum with the goal of preparing students to balance their lifetime reading.

As the most pervasive of the media, television has tremendous potential for enticing readers into science reading, for example, Carl Sagan's *Cosmos* based on his television series. Less obvious TV tie-ins include books about those current events which are discussed enough on television that authors are inspired to do research to answer the questions that cursory news reports don't have time or space to probe, for example, Gail Kay Haines' *The Great Nuclear Power Debate,* and Robert D. Ballard's *The Discovery of the Titanic.* Less technological but equally interesting TV tie-ins include Robert McCrum's *The Story of English* and Jim Arnosky's *Drawing from Nature*, both written as companion pieces to PBS series of the same names.

The influence of television on format and design is hard to prove, but there's an obvious difference between the majority of informative books coming out today and those that were published twenty years ago. More of the current books are illustrated with numerous photographs, many in color, and they are organized and laid out in chunks of information so that readers can browse, skim, and take rest breaks—comparable to taking time out for commercials.

Three very personal books by photographer Jill Krementz, *How It Feels When a Parent Dies, How It Feels When Parents Divorce,* and *How It Feels to Be Adopted* feature personal interviews with several young people. Krementz chose to present the accounts as if the young people are speaking directly to the reader. The well-done photographic portraits—which is what Krementz was famous for long before she became an author—give readers the feeling that they are watching television and listening while nearly twenty unique stories are told. In the adoption book, for example, Joey, age fourteen, was adopted by a Chicago priest when he was twelve. Joey explains:

Father Clements thought it would be nice to invite me to his house for Christmas dinner, but when he asked me I said I had to think about it because I had a lot of other invitations from family and friends. I was lying because I had too much pride to let him think I didn't have any place to go. And it was my pride which actually impressed this priest and made him come back to see me again and again.[6]

BOOKS TO SUPPORT AND EXTEND THE SCHOOL CURRICULUM

Informational books purchased by school libraries are usually referred to as "books to support the curriculum," but a more accurate term would probably be "books to extend the curriculum." For the most part, these books do not help students who are doing poorly in class. Instead, such science books as A. Zee's *Fearful Symmetry*, Jon Franklin's *Molecules of the Mind*, and Frank H. Wilcox's *DNA: The Thread of Life* provide challenges for successful students to go further than their classmates. Alexander Kohn's *False Prophets*, a detailed account of intentional as well as accidental incidents of scientific fraud, is an intriguing but challenging book as is Niles Eldredge's *Life Pulse*, an enthusiastic introduction to paleontology. Easier science books include Vicki Cobb's *Chemically Active! Experiments You Can Do at Home*, Alvin and Virginia Silverstein's *World of the Brain*, and Brent Filson's *Exploring with Lasers*.

The good language student, the one who may go into linguistics as a career, will be fascinated to read Francine Patterson and Eugene Linden's *The Edu-*

cation of Koko, the story of a lowland gorilla's acquisition of sign language. The same student will probably enjoy Alvin and Virginia Silverstein's *Wonders of Speech,* John Ciardi's *Good Words to You,* and Willard R. Espy's *O, Thou Improper, Thou Uncommon Noun.*

Students assigned to write a research paper may be inspired by the exemplary research of James Cross Giblin's *The Truth about Santa Claus* or by Jay Daly's *Presenting S. E. Hinton,* which *Booklist* described as "a model for teen's own research." David S. Broder's *Behind the Front Page* is good for advanced journalism students, while Robert E. Dunbar's *How to Debate* is good for speech students. Shirley Glubock's art books are highly recommended, including *The Art of Egypt under the Pharaohs, The Art of the Plains Indians,* and *The Art of the Old West.*

Good history students will want to read the following books which present information that is too complicated, too detailed, too obscure, or too controversial to be included in their regular textbooks: Milton Meltzer's *The Jewish Americans: A History in Their Own Words, The American Revolutionaries: A History in Their Own Words 1750–1800,* and *Poverty in America*; Brent and Melissa Ashabranner's *Into a Strange Land: Unaccompanied Refugee Youth in America;* and Russell Freedman's *Indian Chiefs* and *Cowboys of the Wild West.*

Recent books about World War II go beyond the obvious historical facts; for example, Daniel S. Davis' *Behind Barbed Wire: The Imprisonment of Japanese Americans during World War II* traces political, economic, and social factors that resulted in a shameful chapter in American history. Hasso G. Stachow's *If This Be Glory,* translated from German by J. Maxwell Brownjohn, raises questions about patriotism and courage through interviews with a former Nazi soldier. Robert Goldston's *Sinister Touches: The Secret War Against Hitler* shows how underground spies influenced the outcome of the war and A. J. P. Taylor's *The Origins of the Second World War* shows that the responsibility for the war must be shared by both the Germans and the Allies.

A legitimate complaint often voiced about history books is that they focus on war and violence and leave out life as lived by the majority of people. As a counterbalance, authors have done several good books on women's history, including Joanna L. Stratton's *Pioneer Women: Voices from the Kansas Frontier,* Robert McHenry's *Famous American Women: A Biographical Dictionary from Colonial Times to Present,* Charlotte Streifer Rubenstein's *American Women Artists: from Early Indian Times to the Present,* Bernice Selden's *The Mill Girls,* Linda Peavy and Ursula Smith's *Women Who Changed Things: Nine Lives that Made a Difference,* and Diana C. Gleasner's *Breakthrough: Women in Science.* Arlene Hirschfelder's *Happily May I Walk: American Indians and Alaskan Natives Today* received a starred review in *School Library Journal* where Karen Zimmerman said that even if readers "never get beyond Hirschfelder's four-page introduction, they will have read enough to challenge many stereotypes."[7]

An illustration of how quickly informative books change is the fact that in the first edition of this text we did not list a single book on computers. Today there are probably over a hundred that we could recommend for teenagers, including computer dictionaries as well as guides to specific kinds of hardware or software. These practical how-to types of books for young readers will most likely be about personal computers because that is what teenagers have access to, but that doesn't mean that they aren't interested in learning about larger computers and about the theoretical bases of such. Roger Ford and Oliver Strimpel's *Computers: An Introduction* is one of the best general books because of its clear writing and full-color photographs. Margaret O. Hyde's *Computers That Think?: The Search for Artificial Intelligence* and Stan Augarten's *State of the Art: A Photographic History of the Integrated Circuit* are also good for taking computer "whiz kids" beyond the basics. Michael Crichton, already known to young readers as the author of *The Andromeda Strain* and *The Great Train Robbery,* wrote the excellent *Electronic Life: How to Think about Computers.* See "Computer Books for Young Adults" by Betty Carter in *English Journal* (November 1984) for a discussion of Crichton's book as well as guides to use in selecting other types of computer books.

There's no way in this chapter to provide anything other than a sampling of the many books available as companion reading, or even replacement reading, for typical textbooks. In selecting academically oriented books, librarians should remember that teenagers most often pick up such books to find specific information. They want the material to be streamlined and to the point. They also want it to be indexed and organized in such a way that they can easily refer back to something or can look up facts without reading the whole book. And since young readers lack the kind of background knowledge that most adults have, it is especially important that the basic information comes first so they won't be confused by unclear references.

Preparing for College

In an *English Journal* article, Richard F. Abrahamson and Betty Carter noted that for academic teenagers books about college are the number one nonfiction choice. They recommended Clifford J. Caine's *How to Get Into College,* "not a guaranteed formula for success but rather a step-by-step three-year planning manual . . . a surrogate guidance counselor."[8] Richard Moll's *The Public Ivys* is written on the assumption that some state universities provide education equivalent to that of the best Ivy League schools. The book chronicles visits to eighteen such schools. The author combines hard facts with anecdotes and the kind of trivia that made *Lisa Birnbach's College Book* fun to read. Similar books include Edward B. Fiske's yearly *The Best Buys in College Education* and *Selective Guide to Colleges.* Fiske's qualifications include being education editor of the *New York Times.*

For really serious students—or more likely, their parents—Ernest Boyer's *College: The Undergraduate Experience in America* presents an overview of American higher education. Sixteen observers visited 29 U.S. colleges and universities. More specific books with self-explanatory titles include Boykin Curry and Brian Kasbar's *Essays that Worked: 50 Essays from Successful*

Applications to the Nation's Top Colleges and Sarah McGinty's *Writing Your College Application Essay.* Harlow G. Unger, a former admissions officer at Yale, aimed *A Student's Guide to College Admissions: Everything Your Guidance Counselor Has No Time to Tell You* at highly motivated students. Besides doing a good job of explaining that students must take the responsibility for getting into the school of their choice, Unger warns that the actual application process takes eighteen months and that its success or failure may depend on what classes one took in the freshman year of high school.

Other good recent books about specialized schools include Judith Kogan's *Nothing But the Best,* a profile of the Juilliard School of music, and Perri Elizabeth Klass's *A Not Entirely Benign Procedure,* the story of the author's four years at Harvard Medical School. Kenneth Klein's *Getting Better* and Melvin Konner's *Becoming a Doctor* are also about medical school.

Preparing for Careers

The work ethic may be more important to Americans than to some other cultures because of our frontier heritage and the value that was put on hard work. Folklorists point out that only frontier cultures such as those of the United States, Canada, and Australia have stories about work heroes like John Henry, Paul Bunyan, Pecos Bill, and Old Stormalong. In other cultures, it is common for folk heroes to be tricky individuals who manage to get out of work, but in the United States people are accorded social standing in relation to the jobs they hold, rather than their ancestry, religion, or wealth. Even the

College and career books are among the most popular in high school libraries.

children of very wealthy parents prepare for and usually pursue a career because work is considered an essential part of a meaningful life.

The work heroes of today are individuals whose jobs may be quite ordinary but who have found personal fulfillment through what they do. Readers are interested first in the person as a whole and second in the job as it relates to the person. Artist Peter Parnall's *The Daywatchers* is excellent in showing that an artist does not work only with his hands. Parnall shares his experiences and the respect that he feels for the thirteen birds of prey that he draws in this oversized and beautiful book.

Today's readers want real people, not the old-fashioned Cherry Ames kind of career book. The success of Studs Terkel's *Working: People Talk About What They Do All Day and How They Feel About What They Do* is largely due to Terkel's skill in communicating the emotional side of people's jobs and how their work affects every aspect of their lives. Some parents have objected to use of the book in high school English classes ostensibly because of the language, but part of their discomfort may actually be due to the ambivalent or even negative feelings that some of the interviewees expressed about work. Terkel's *American Dreams Lost and Found* is in some ways a better book for high school students because it includes interviews with teenagers and its focus is on the whole of life, including work and what it means to dream.

Young readers want a here-and-now immediacy in career books so they like to read financial success stories about teenagers. However, adults need to help young readers be realistic about the wish-fulfillment inherent in such a book as Gloria D. Miklowitz and Madeleine Yates' *The Young Tycoons: Ten Success Stories.* Some books make things look so easy that readers will think that with a little effort they too can become rich overnight. If it doesn't happen they are likely to lose faith in the printed word, and more importantly in themselves.

James Herriot's four books introduce young people to a world they hardly know exists, a veterinarian's life in northern England. More important, the books are warm and funny stories about strange people, and sometimes even stranger animals. The first in the series, *All Creatures Great and Small,* may be the most appealing, but once young readers are caught by that, they will probably go on to *All Things Bright and Beautiful, All Things Wise and Wonderful,* and *The Lord God Made Them All.*

Naturalist Farley Mowat worked for the Canadian Wildlife Service where he was assigned to study the problem of wolves killing the caribou on the northern Tundra. He went to live among the wolves, and to everyone's surprise found that they were not destroying the caribou. Mowat's *Never Cry Wolf* recounting his experience is both an intriguing account of a naturalist at work and a stirring defense of wolves. Readers become aware of the many myths surrounding this animal, most of them unpleasant and untrue. Joy Adamson's *Born Free: A Lioness in Two Worlds, Living Free, Forever Free, The Spotted Sphinx,* and *Pippa's Challenge* are similar in being excellent studies of animals as well as of a naturalist's work. Frank C. Craighead, Jr.'s *Track of the Grizzly* shows two naturalists studying three thousand square miles of Yellowstone National Park, the home of the American grizzly bear.

Career-related books are extremely important to young adults because they must make decisions that will strongly influence not only how they will earn a living but also what lifestyles they will have. Teachers and librarians should make a special effort to bring books of this type to the attention of all students. The more knowledge they have the better position they will be in to make the kinds of far-reaching decisions that society demands of its young adults.

NONFICTION TO HELP TEENAGERS LEARN WHO THEY ARE AND WHERE THEY FIT

When young adult librarian and critic Patty Campbell spoke at the 1983 American Library Association annual meeting, she pointed out that teenagers are so wrapped up in what the psychologists have labelled the "adolescent identity crisis" that they simply do not have the time for, nor the interest in, sitting down and reading about the world in general. What they are looking for are books that will help them decide on who they are and where they fit into the scheme of things. Informative books they judge to be helpful include sex education books, some physical and mental health books of the *I'm Okay, You're Okay* type, selected how-to-books, and biographies or true accounts of experiences teenagers can imagine themselves or their acquaintances having. Nearly all of the other information books published for teenagers are read under duress—only because teachers assign reports and research papers.

In this section, we will discuss some of the books that Campbell said teenagers read to help them figure where they fit in. Noticeably absent are the true accounts of experiences that teenagers imagine themselves as having because many of these are in Chapter 7 under "Heroes."

From the very beginning of life, babies are testing their limits. They want to know how much they can eat, how far they can reach, how loudly they can scream, and how much their parents will let them get away with. As the years go by and children grow into teenagers, they become more subtle and more sophisticated, but they are still interested in testing limits. The difference is that with young adults, their sphere of interest is now so much broader that it includes the whole world and even beyond. There is no way that they can personally test all the limits in which they are interested. Some would be too dangerous, some are mutually exclusive, some would take too long, and some cannot be entered into voluntarily. Because of these and other considerations, teenagers (as well as many adults) turn to books that present the extremes of life's experiences.

Whatever is the biggest, the best, or the most bizarre is of interest. That is the basis of the *Ripley's Believe It or Not* series, as well as the *Guinness Book of World Records*. An additional appeal of such trivia books is that they are instant entertainment. Someone with only a minute or two can open David Wallechinsky and Irving Wallace's *The People's Almanac,* for example, and read a complete discourse.

T. ERNESTO BETHANCOURT
on Facts as Fun

There are times when I find it hard to think of myself as an author, at all. I spent the first forty years of my life as a professional entertainer, jazz musician, and song writer. I didn't write my first novel for young people until I was forty-one years old. Even then, it was intended as a memoir-cum-biography for my then-newborn daughter, Kimi. It's now thirteen years, and twenty hardcover titles later. Maybe I am an author, after all. As Prosper Merimée has Don José say: "You are what you do. . . . "

For me to hold forth on what's wrong and right with Juvenile Fiction is, I feel, a bit pretentious. I can tell you freely that I know what's wrong or right with the novels I have written for Young Adults. But they're in print now, and it's somewhat after the fact. But here goes:

I don't care for "problem novels," about kids dying of "the disease of the week," according to what's in the headlines of the AMA Journal. I feel there's nothing wrong with a kid being able to read for sheer entertainment values. I try to write the sort of book *I* wanted to read as a young adult, but never could find. Happily, it seems many kids of today share my enthusiasms and taste for Adventure, Fantasy, Detective Tales, Science Fiction, and Humor.

If, along the way, a kid gets some good, solid information, properly researched, I feel it's a bonus, but not essential. Many of my books contain factual and historical material, and I always do exhaustive research on the topics or historical periods covered. The information is there, and can be trusted, if one takes the time to read it carefully.

My novels are all structured like parfait desserts. The material is in layers. You can eat off the top, or dig down to the bottom. I'm rather proud that years before the Congressional investigations, I treated in my *Doris Fein* novels the Japanese-American internment during World War II. In other books, I have explored interracial relations, and depicted Blacks, Asians, and Latinos in nonstereotypical roles.

I hope I may have created some positive role models for young people of minority descent. I also hope that I haven't been didactic in the process. My primary motive is to entertain, and to involve young people in the reading process, for life.

A number of years ago, there was a national slogan that said to young people: "Reading Is Fun." It was later modified to "Reading Is Fundamental." I don't see why both statements can't be true. This attitude may never result in my writing a "serious" book of the sort that wins "serious" national book awards. Then again, nobody took Mark Twain seriously until after he died. Now that people do, I think it would make him laugh. That's fine, with me. Turn on your TV news, or read the newspapers. You'll see a good laugh is hard to come by, these days.

T. Ernesto Bethancourt's books include several Doris Fein stories published by Holiday House, *The Dog Days of Arthur Cane,* Holiday House, 1976, and *Tune in Yesterday,* Holiday House, 1978.

More serious than the trivia books but with a similar appeal based on learning about extremes are such books as Frederick Drimmer's *The Elephant Man,* the true story of the terribly deformed John Merrick who lived in England between 1862 and 1890, and Herma Silverstein and Caroline Arnold's *Hoaxes that Made Headlines.* Don L. Wulffson's *Incredible True Adventures,* Jennifer Westwood's *The Atlas of Mysterious Places,* and Jack Sullivan's *The Penguin Encyclopedia of Horror and the Supernatural* also show people, places, and events that have tested human limits.

How-To Books

Part of understanding where one fits into the world comes through the challenge of learning how to do things. Few how-to books ever find their way to best-book lists simply because they appeal to such specific interests, for example, Elaine MacGregor's *Cake Decorating,* Erik Fair's *Right Stuff for New Hang Glider Pilots,* Fred Puhn's *Brake Handbook,* and Vivian Dubrovin's *Creative Word Processing.* The more specific such a book is the more it will appeal to a specialized—and therefore limited—audience.

Authors of how-to books need to be extremely good writers. Even one ambiguous sentence can cause a project to fail. Directions that are hard to understand, failure to list all the supplies and tools that will be needed, and come-on statements that make projects look easier than they are set the stage for frustration. If there is no index to aid readers in finding what they need to know, or if the illustrations are inaccurate, then readers are apt to lose interest in the project and also to lose faith in such books.

Some libraries have given up stocking books on automobile and motorcycle repair because readers find them so useful that they don't bring them back. Readers aren't so tempted to keep for reference the more general books such as Jim Mateja's guide to buying, *Used Cars,* and Vic and Barbara Goulter's *How to Keep Your Car Mechanic Honest.*

Recent recommended how-to books include Gerald Durrell and Lee Durrell's *The Amateur Naturalist,* John Gardner's *The Art of Fiction: Notes on Craft for Young Writers,* and Elaine Costello's *Signing: How to Speak with Your Hands.* One of the few how-to books to make it to several best book lists is Jean Young's *Woodstock Craftsman's Manual.* It comes in two volumes and includes directions for such crafts as quilting, wood carving, and making stained-glass windows. Eliot Wigginton's *The Foxfire Books* show such varied skills as slaughtering hogs, reading weather signs, recording snake lore, and building log cabins. Wigginton is a teacher who began working with his students to investigate and record the everyday life around Rabun Gap, Georgia. Wigginton is the editor of over a half-dozen books dating from 1972, but the pieces are written by the students.

The topics for how-to books are almost unlimited. They range from something as simple as how to embroider your jeans to the moderately complex task of making your own shoes to the very complex task of building your own solar energy house.

In some cases, how-to books may open the door for high-school students who have never really gotten into books. The challenge for the teacher or librarian is to let students know about the range of how-to books that are available. For example the babysitter needs to know about Phil Wiswell's *Kid's Games,* the loner student who escapes through solitary running needs to know about Allan Lawrence and Mark Scheid's *The Self-Coached Runner II,* and the student hoping for a trip to Europe needs to know about the Council on International Educational Exchange's *The Teenager's Guide to Study, Travel, and Adventure Abroad.* Once students learn of a book about one of their interests, perhaps through a display, a booktalk, a school newspaper article, a giveaway bibliography, or a recommendation from a friend, they are likely to find their way into a library. If they find what they want, they will most likely return. And if motivated by a desire to accomplish something, they may read above their school-tested reading levels. One reason is that how-to books incorporate principles of programmed learning by immediately rewarding good readers by helping them succeed.

With sports books, obviously the first thing a reader looks for is the particular sport and so authors choose titles that practically shout to potential readers, for example, *The Skater's Handbook* by John Misha Petkevich, *The Official Pompon Girl's Handbook* by Randy Neil, and *Football Rules in Pictures* by Don Schiffler and Lud Duroska.

The sports books that stand out from the crowd usually have a believable and likeable personality behind them. They are inspirational as much as instructive, but one thing to watch for in how-to sports books is whether there is any mention of the costs involved. It is almost cruel of an author to write a glowing account of a child star in tennis, gymnastics, skating, swimming, or dancing and leave young readers with the impression that all it takes is hard work. Those readers whose parents do not have time or money for transportation, lessons, entry fees, equipment, and clothes should be let in on the secret that there's more to how you play the game than meets the eye.

Self-Help Books

A kind of how-to book deserving its own category is that of self-help, i.e., managing one's own life so as to be successful right now as well as in the future. This includes taking care of one's physical body. When young people go to the shelves of libraries in search of books about health it is most often in search of an answer to a specific problem, for example:

>   Am I pregnant? Do I have diabetes? What's mononucleosis? How serious is scoliosis? Is being fat "really" unhealthy? What causes pimples? What happens if someone has Hodgkin's disease? My mother has breast cancer; is she going to die? Is anorexia nervosa just in a person's head? Why does my grandfather say such strange things? Will I be like that when I'm old? What will happen if I have V.D. and don't go to the doctor?

Saul Levine and Kathleen Wilcox's *Dear Doctor* is a well-indexed book that can answer many such questions. The authors are Canadian physicians who have a "Youth Clinic" column in the *Toronto Star.* The letters are taken from this column.

If a book on the physical body is to attract readers who aren't looking for specific answers, the book needs to have some distinctive quality. It might be an especially attractive format or it might be a specialized approach as in Richard Mangi, Peter Jokl, and O. William Dayton's *Sports Fitness and Training.* Or it might be that the book is specifically aimed at teenagers as is Kathy McCoy's *The Teenage Body Book.* The amazing photographs in the books of Lennart Nilsson, including *Behold Man* and *A Child Is Born,* make them appealing to readers of all ages. Fitness books that appeal to teenagers' desire to look their best include the best-selling *Jane Fonda's Workout Book* and Joey Mills' *New Classic Beauty.*

Going Vegetarian: A Guide for Teen-Agers by Sada Fretz is the kind of sensible well-written book that any age reader could profit from. The reason the author chose to aim her book toward teenagers is that because their growing bodies have certain nutritional needs, they may be in more danger than adults if they do not understand the intricacies of balancing their diets.

A decade ago, dozens of books on drugs were being published, but the flood has slowed to a trickle probably because there's not much left to say. A recent book that does a good job of being interesting and objective is Andrew Weil and Winifred Rosen's *Chocolate to Morphine: Understanding Mind-Active Drugs.* Another recommended book is the most recent edition of Margaret O. Hyde's *Mind Drugs* in which six experts discuss with the author particular drugs, patterns of behavior, alternatives to drug abuse, and the extent of the drug culture. In selecting books on drugs, adults should remember that most teenagers think and know more about drugs than do teachers and librarians and this results in a credibility gap. We therefore need to be extra careful to provide realistic books. Back in the 1970s, Peter G. Hammond, writing in *School Library Journal,* said that after the National Coordinating Council on Drug Education, of which he was executive director, had studied some 1,000 books and pamphlets and 300 drug abuse education films, they reached this conclusion:

> You can trust most contemporary pieces of drug information to be valid and relevant about as much as you can trust the drug sold by your friendly street pusher to be potent, safe, and unadulterated. In both cases vested interests abound: scientists and drug educators can be just as irrational about the dangers and benefits of drugs as can those who promote these chemicals to the youth culture.[9]

In the late 1960s and early 1970s there was a blitz of information on drugs, but Hammond says that information and education are not the same thing. One of the problems has been that everyone wants a pat answer, a quick and easy solution to a very complex problem. Sociologists and anthropologists know it is a temptation when studying any new culture to want to simplify matters by lumping everything together in one clear-cut picture. Such a one-dimensional presentation would make the drug culture so much easier to comprehend, but in reality it isn't that simple.

Richie by Thomas Thompson is a true story of the George Diener family and what happens when their teenage son begins taking puffs of his friends' marijuana cigarettes and then goes on to barbiturates. When Richie is on drugs, he becomes aggressive, and earns himself a police record as well as his father's hatred. In the midst of one bitter quarrel after Richie had had two automobile accidents in the same afternoon, George Diener shoots and kills his son. At the trial he is acquitted. The concluding pages of the book make a vivid statement about both drugs and the generation gap.

Audrey Conant described Eric E. Rofes' *The Kids' Book About Death and Dying: By and For Kids* as "unique and valuable" because it blends "the best aspects of student authorship, case histories, handbooks, cultural anthropology, bibliographies, advice books and almanacs."[10] Karen Gravelle and Bertram A. John's *Teenagers Face to Face with Cancer* also includes contributions from young people, cancer patients between the ages of 13 and 21. Elizabeth Richter's *Losing Someone You Love: When a Brother or Sister Dies* is based on interviews with 15 young people who have suffered such losses. Graham Hancock and Enver Carim's *AIDS: The Deadly Epidemic* is frightening but it's information that we all need to know and it's presented in a readable and well organized style.

Books designed to help teenagers manage their mental health range from Andrea Boroff Eagan's *Why Am I So Miserable If These Are the Best Years of My Life?* also available in Spanish, to *Step Kids: A Survival Guide for Teenagers in Stepfamilies* by Ann Getzoff and Carolyn McClenahan. *The Teenage Survival Guide* by Kathy McCoy is filled with solid advice on a myriad of problems— school, family, health, etc. Claudine Wirths and Mary Bowman-Kruhm's *I Hate School: How to Hang in and When to Drop Out* has a nonpreachy tone but still gives good suggestions for improving academic performance, while Lorraine Peterson's *If God Loves Me Why Can't I Get My Locker Open?* combines spiritual with psychological advice. Diana Shaw starts from an optimistic viewpoint in *Make the Most of a Good Thing: You!* while Helen Benedict's *Safe, Strong, and Streetwise* starts from the assumption that the world is basically a dangerous place. It addresses sexual assault and harassment, date-rape, molestation, obscene phone calls, and self-defense.

Some of the teen books focus on specific problems at home, for example, *The Kids' Book of Divorce: By, For and About Kids* was edited by Eric Rofes and based on the experiences of twenty kids between the ages of 11 and 14 who were part of a class at the Fayerweather Street School in Cambridge, Massachusetts. Richard Gardner's *A Boys' and Girls' Book About Divorce* has good information in it, but some librarians report that the size and the format make it seem too difficult for junior high readers while the words "Boys' and Girls' " keep high school students from approaching it. Eric W. Johnson has put together some common sense advice for younger teens in *How to Live with Parents and Teachers,* while Joyce L. Vedral has taken a more assertive tone in *My Parents Are Driving Me Crazy.* The dust jacket of Judith S. Seixas' *Living with a Parent Who Drinks Too Much* states that perhaps as many as "20 million children live in homes where there is an alcoholic parent." The book gives advice on coping and includes names and addresses of places to go for help.

Probably the mental health book most appreciated by young adults is Robert M. Pirsig's *Zen and the Art of Motorcycle Maintenance: An Inquiry into Values.* In this the author writes a gently persuasive book about the Zen approach to working on "the motorcycle that is yourself." The narrative that holds it all together is an account of a cross-country motorcycle trip that Pirsig took with his eleven-year-old son.

Sex Education Books

The exploration of sexual matters in books for young readers is an especially sensitive area for the following reasons:

1. Young adults are physically mature, but they probably have had little intellectual and emotional preparation for making sex-related decisions.
2. Parents are anxious to protect their children from making sex-related decisions that might prove harmful.
3. Old restraints and patterns of behavior and attitudes are being questioned so that there is no one clearcut model to follow.
4. Sex is such an important part of American culture and the mass media that young people are forced to think about and take stands on such controversial issues as homosexuality, premarital sex, violence in relation to sex, and the role of sex in love and family relationships.
5. Talking about sexual attitudes and beliefs with their teenage children may make parents uncomfortable especially if the father and the mother have different feelings and opinions. This means that many young people must get their information outside of the home.

With all categories of books, but especially with sex education, no one book can satisfy all readers. An entire eollection must be evaluated and books provided for a wide range of interests, attitudes, beliefs, and lifestyles. Those who criticize libraries for including books that present teenage sexual activitiy as the norm have a justified complaint if the library does not also have sex education books that present, or even promote, abstinence as a normal route for young people. Teachers as well as librarians should see the American Library Association's video *The Facts of Love in the Library: Making Sexuality Information Relevant and Accessible to Young People.* Dr. Ruth Westheimer introduces the tape, which features Patty Campbell, author of *Sex Guides,* published in 1986 by Garland.

Certainly the authors of sex education books do not intend to promote promiscuity, but the fact that topics are being treated "nonjudgmentally" may give some readers that impression. It is similar to the quandary that the authors of one sex education book found themselves in when they did a chapter on abortion. They felt compelled to explain that simply because they were including a chapter on abortion, they were not advocating it as the "right" or "best" or "most-liberated" decision to make. Instead, they chose to give it considerable space because it was information which had been unavailable in past years.

Among the most highly recommended sex education books are the 1988 updated and revised version of Ruth Bell's *Changing Bodies, Changing Lives,* Lynda Madaras' *What's Happening to My Body? A Growing Up Guide for Mothers and Daughters,* Sol Gordon and Roger Conant's *You! The Teenage Survival Book,* and Gary F. Kelly's *Learning About Sex: The Contemporary Guide for Young Adults.*

Materials dealing with sex are judged quite differently from books on less controversial topics. For example, in most subject areas, books are given plus marks if they succeed in getting the reader emotionally involved, but with books about sex, many readers feel more comfortable with straightforward, "plumbing manuals"—the less emotional involvement the better. Other readers argue that it's the emotional part that young people need to learn.

Another example of how differently teachers, librarians, and critics treat sex-related materials is the way in which we ignore pornography as a reading interest of teenagers, especially boys. Most of us pretend not to know about pornography so that we won't have to analyze and evaluate it or talk with students about it. One of the few mentions of this kind of reading that has appeared in professional literature was a mid-1970s survey made by Julie Alm of the spare-time reading interests of high school students in Hawaii. In this survey, fourteen students listed *The Sensuous Woman* by "J" as their favorite book. This was the same number as listed John Steinbeck's *The Pearl,* John Knowles' *A Separate Peace,* and the *Bible.*

Tone seems extra important in books about sex because people come to them with their own ideas about appropriateness. Peter Mayle's books give a light, even humorous touch to the whole matter of sex. A surprised graduate student, when he looked at them, exclaimed, "Why, I'd rather make fun of the flag than of sex." Mayle's book for children, *Where Did I Come From?* is read by teenagers because of the humor and cartoonlike drawings. The two specifically for teenagers are *What's Happening to Me?* and *Will I Like It?*

When selecting sex education books, one of the things to watch for is whether or not sex is portrayed from only one viewpoint, either male or female. For example in *Where Did I Come From?* sexual intercourse is described from the traditional active man/passive woman stance:

> The man loves the woman. So he gives her a kiss. And she gives him a kiss. And they hug each other very tight. And after a while, the man's penis becomes stiff and hard, and much bigger than it usually is. It gets bigger because it has lots of work to do.
>
> By this time, the man wants to get as close to the woman as he can, because he's feeling very loving to her. And to get really close the best thing he can do is lie on top of her and put his penis inside her, into her vagina.[11]

While defenders will point out that Mayle's book is simplified so as to be readable by very young children, critics argue that because young children are so impressionable it's more important than ever that readers do not come away with the impression that sex is something done *to* women *by* men.

The design and format of all books, but especially of books about such a sensitive subject as sex, send out their own messages. For example, the cover of *Changing Bodies, Changing Lives* has five snapshots on it, only one of which is a boy and girl, and instead of looking "romantic," they look playful. The other shots are of group activities with teens not necessarily paired off but obviously enjoying each other's company. The effect is to make sexuality seem like a normal, pleasant part of growing up.

The dust jackets to Wardell B. Pomeroy's two books on the same subject provide a stark contrast and show how an entirely different message can be sent out. The first big difference is that Pomeroy's books are segregated. He has *Boys and Sex: A Revised Edition of the Classic Book on Adolescent Sexuality* and *Girls and Sex: A Revised Edition of the Classic Book on Adolescent Female Sexuality.* Pomeroy tried to aim his books at both parents and their children, but the clinical sounding subtitles will do little to attract teenagers. If they should find the books in their home libraries, they might read them, but the boldface print, the blatant titles, and the colors of the dust jackets (bright

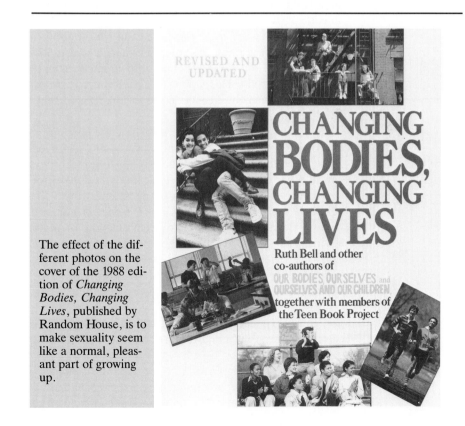

The effect of the different photos on the cover of the 1988 edition of *Changing Bodies, Changing Lives*, published by Random House, is to make sexuality seem like a normal, pleasant part of growing up.

purple and orange) will practically ensure that no self-conscious teenager is going to check these books out of a library, unless the librarian has been perceptive enough to provide a plain brown wrapper.

The fact that Pomeroy treats boys in a separate book from girls is itself a controversial issue. And notice the difference in the titles which imply that male sexuality is the norm. In no other area, except perhaps athletics, is there such purposeful separation between boys and girls. Starting in the fourth grade, girls are taken off to see their first movie on menstruation and boys are left in the room to be given a talk by the coach. Some people believe that this kind of separation is quite appropriate, and in fact, has advantages similar to the check-and-balance system practiced by the separate branches of the federal government. However, others believe that since sex is something participated in by males and females together, they should be taught the same set of rules. If they understood each other a bit better, perhaps men and women wouldn't have so much trouble communicating and establishing fulfilling lifelong relationships.

Although a few new books focus specifically on AIDS, for example, Margaret O. Hyde and Elizabeth H. Forsyth's *AIDS: What Does It Mean to You?* and Alvin and Virginia Silverstein's *AIDS: Deadly Threat,* most information about STD (sexually transmitted diseases) is incorporated into overall treatments that cover emotional as well as physical aspects of sexual activity. Jacqueline Voss and Jay Gale's *A Young Woman's Guide to Sex* and Jay Gale's *A Young Man's Guide to Sex* are especially good about including emotional as well as physical aspects of sexuality. *What Teenagers Want to Know About Sex,* questions and answers organized into nineteen chapters by the staff of the Boston Children's Hospital with Dr. Robert P. Masland, Jr., is especially efficient because the questions are in boldface so that skimmers can quickly find their areas of interest.

If a teenager becomes pregnant, there are so many aspects of the matter to be considered that it takes a whole book—or even several—to satisfy her need to collect information before she is ready to ponder and make a decision about her and her baby's future. A book that was chosen for the 1983 YASD Best Books for Young Adults list is Arlene Kramer Richards and Irene Willis' *What To Do If You or Someone You Know Is Under 18 and Pregnant.* This is definitely written for teenagers, although it isn't cloying or written-down. The authors say such things as "If you are able to afford real maternity clothes, one of the most useful items is a pair of maternity pants in a dark color." Then it goes on to give advice about getting hand-me-down clothes or buying a winter coat from a thrift shop since it will be worn only one season. Such common-sense suggestions are surprising only when contrasted to those in more typical books for newly expectant mothers. They advise buying so many things that one suspects the publishers are more interested in boosting the economy than in launching a new life.

In Paula McGuire's *It Won't Happen to Me: Teenagers Talk About Pregnancy,* fifteen girls from an assortment of social levels and ethnic groups tell how their lives have been changed by unplanned pregnancies. Sean Gresh's *Becoming a*

Father is a welcome balance to all the attention that goes to the mother. It presents information on childbirth methods, care of the newborn, and the emotional changes that fathers are likely to undergo.

The mother who is thinking of giving up her baby for adoption should have access to Laurie Wishard and William Wishard's *Adoption: The Grafted Tree,* which besides providing basic information, includes state-by-state adoption laws. Young people planning to raise their child would profit from Linda McDonald's *Everything You Need to Know About Babies,* Jeanne Warren Lindsay's *Teens Parenting,* Tracy Hotchner's *Pregnancy and Childbirth: The Complete Guide for a New Life,* and Sol Gordon and Myra Wollin's *Parenting: A Guide for Young People.*

Maria Corsaro and Carole Korzeniowsky have written *A Woman's Guide to Safe Abortion* which promises to provide "Everything you need to know about tests, costs, procedures, facilities, physical and emotional complications, and birth control." The abortion issue is also discussed as part of several of the already mentioned books.

Because there are relatively few books on the subject of homosexuality and because students hesitate to read what there is, each book takes on a disproportionate level of importance. Morton Hunt, who wrote the well-received *Young Person's Guide to Love,* was criticized by John Cunningham for his *Gay: What You Should Know about Homosexuality.* Cunningham pointed out that although it is common for sex education books to have a conversational style using the second person pronoun "you," Hunt consistently used the third person pronoun "them," showing that he did not intend "to put the gay reader at ease or to suggest that the book might be directed to gays."[12]

Because he was dissatisfied with Hunt's book, as well as with others on the topic, Cunningham worked with Frances Hanckel to write *A Way of Love, A Way of Life: A Young Person's Introduction to What It Means to Be Gay.* Some of the chapter titles give the flavor of the book: "Sticks and Stones: Understanding Names and Terms about Homosexuality," "How to Tell If You're Gay," "Feeling Bad about It; Feeling Good about It," "Sex Isn't All Good News," and "A Dozen Gay Lives." Hanckel and Cunningham's book solved some of the problems that Cunningham had with Hunt's book, but because people have such different ideas about the topic of homosexuality, not all readers were pleased with it. David E. Wilson wrote an article, "The Open Library: YA Books for Gay Teens" published in the November 1984 *English Journal.* Among the nonfiction that he recommended were *Young, Gay and Proud* edited by Sasha Alyson, *Reflections of a Rock Lobster* by Aaron Fricke, and *One Teenager in Ten* edited by Ann Heron.

Students may also be reticent to read about child abuse, but they can hardly avoid being aware of the issue because of the way it is discussed on television and radio and in newspapers and magazines. A decade ago, the topic was seldom mentioned either in public or private. For example, it's likely that if Beverly Cleary had published her autobiography *A Girl from Yamhill* in 1980 instead of 1988, the sexual encounter with her Uncle Joe would probably have been left out. But it's probably healthy for such an incident to be included as part of a larger story. Those readers looking specifically for information on the topic can choose from several new books including Margaret O. Hyde's *Sexual Abuse: Let's Talk About It* and Elaine Landau's *Child Abuse: An American Epidemic.* Lynn B. Daugherty's *Why Me? Help for Victims of Child Sexual Abuse (Even If They Are Adults Now)* was a *Booklist* "Editors' Choice" for 1985.

When helping young adults make reading decisions in this area, we need to consider the reader's purpose. If the reader wants basic information, then nonfiction is far superior because it can present a wider range of information in a clear and unambiguous way. But if it is an understanding of the emotional and physical aspects of one particular relationship, an honest piece of fiction usually does a better job. The important thing for adults to remember is that they should provide both kinds of material in conjunction with a listening ear and a willingness to discuss questions.

Because the area of sex is such a sensitive and personal one, this is probably the one area most in need of open discussion and exchanges of ideas. Schools and libraries need to seek community help in developing policies. Family values must be respected, but honest and accurate information must also be available for those who are seeking it. Charting a course along this delicate line is more than any one individual should be expected to do. People need to get together to work out the philosophy and policy that best fits their particular situation. But this cannot be done in ignorance. The general public may get away with objecting to or endorsing ideas and books that they have never really explored or read, but a professional working with books is obligated to find and study the latest, most authentic information and to bring that information to those who are helping to shape policies and practices. Such policies and practices will differ from group to group and from person to person. The more you understand about such differences the better able you will be to participate in book selection, discussion, and sometimes, defense.

◼ NOTES

[1] Alleen Pace Nilsen, "The House That Alice Built: An Interview with the Author Who Brought You *Go Ask Alice*," *School Library Journal* 25 (October 1979): 109–12.

[2] Jean Fritz, *Homesick: My Own Story* (New York: Putnam, 1982), p. 9.

[3] Milton Meltzer, "Where Do All the Prizes Go? The Case for Nonfiction," *Horn Book Magazine* 52 (February 1975): 17–23.

[4] Meltzer, p. 23.

[5] George A. Woods, Personal correspondence to Alleen Pace Nilsen (Summer 1978).

[6] Jill Krementz, *How It Feels to Be Adopted* (New York: Knopf, 1982), pp. 103–4.

[7] Karen Zimmerman, review of *Happily May I Walk, School Library Journal,* 33 (January 1987): 82–83.

[8] Richard F. Abrahamson and Betty Carter, "Of Survival, School, Wars, and Dreams: Nonfiction that Belongs in English Classes," *English Journal* 76 (February 1987): 104–9.

[9] Peter G. Hammond, "Turning Off: The Abuse of Drug Information," *School Library Journal* 19 (April 1973): 17–21.

[10] Audrey K. Conant, review of *The Kids' Book about Death and Dying: By and For Kids, School Library Journal* 31 (August 1985): 81.

[11] Peter Mayle, *Where Did I Come From?* (Secaucus, NJ: Lyle Stuart, 1973), pp. 14, 16.

[12] John Cunningham, "Growing Up Gay Male," *Voice of Youth Advocates* 1 (June 1978): 11–16.

◼ 30 RECOMMENDATIONS FOR READING

The New Journalism (See also Chapter 7, "Heroes")

Berman, Phillip L., ed. *The Courage of Conviction.* Dodd, Mead, 1985. Well-known individuals defend their beliefs and actions in this anthology of personal essays.

Finnegan, William. *Crossing the Line: A Year in the Land of Apartheid.* Harper & Row, 1986. A young American teacher recounts his experience in a South African mixed-race high school.

Fritz, Jean. *Homesick: My Own Story.* Putnam, 1982. Younger teens can easily read this interesting autobiography of a young American's childhood in pre-revolution China.

Hersey, John. *Hiroshima.* Knopf, 1946. Only 100 pages long, Hersey's powerful book tells the personal stories of six people in Hiroshima when the bomb was dropped.

Mowat, Farley. *Never Cry Wolf.* Little, Brown, 1963. It's a toss-up whether the animal or the human part of this story is the most interesting.

Read, Piers Paul. *Alive: The Story of the Andes Survivors.* Lippincott, 1974. Part of the fascination of this book is that we have all imagined being in a plane that crashes.

Steinbeck, John. *Travels with Charley.* Viking, 1962. Steinbeck and his dog went all over America in his Rocinante truck, and the writings he did along the way are all the more interesting now that the 1960s are history.

Books to Support/Extend the School Curriculum/College/Careers

Adamson, Joy. *Born Free: A Lioness in Two Worlds.* Pantheon, 1960. All of Adamson's books are good for learning about an interesting career as well as nature.

Ballard, Robert D. *The Discovery of the Titanic.* Random House, 1987. Savoring the "then" and "now" close-up photos is only one of the pleasures of this oversized book which illustrates the way books present fuller information than is possible on television.

Broder, David S. *Behind the Front Page.* Simon & Schuster, 1988. This introduction to political journalism will be appreciated by students with ambitions to become another Woodward or Bernstein.

Brown, Dee. *Bury My Heart at Wounded Knee: An Indian History of the American West.* Holt, Rinehart and Winston, 1971. Readers will learn not only something about history but also about point of view.

Crichton, Michael. *Electronic Life: How to Think about Computers.* Knopf, 1983. Crichton's ability as a writer and his feeling for the subject make this more than a how-to manual.

Fiske, Edward B. *The Best Buys in College Education 1988.* Times Books, 1988. The education editor of *The New York Times* gives up-to-date basic statistics plus a couple of pages of informal information on over 200 colleges that "offer high quality education at reasonable cost."

Haley, Alex. *Roots.* Doubleday, 1976. *Roots* is recommended not only for the history it tells, but also for what it shows about the development of a writing style.

Meltzer, Milton. *The American Revolutionaries: A History in Their Own Words 1750–1800.* Crowell, 1987. Similar in structure to his books on black Americans and Jewish Americans, this is a well-researched and well-introduced compilation of original writings.

Morrow, Lance. *America: A Rediscovery.* Henry Holt, 1987. Teenagers are going to look at the photographs rather than read this picture book for grownups, but that's fine because they're truly a magnificent collection.

Parnall, Peter. *The Daywatchers.* Macmillan, 1984. The thirteen chapters focus on thirteen birds of prey drawn by this well-known illustrator who shares the firsthand experiences he's had in observing these birds.

Tchudi, Stephen. *The Young Learner's Handbook: A Guide to Solving Problems, Mastering Skills, Thinking Creatively.* Scribner, 1987. Tchudi teaches the skills from Bloom's *Taxonomy* in language that teenagers can understand and work with.

Terkel, Studs. *The Good War: An Oral History of World War Two.* Pantheon, 1984. This can be not only a history book but an introduction to collecting and recording oral histories.

Nonfiction to Help Teenagers Learn Who They Are and Where They Fit: How-to/Self-Help/Sex Education

Bell, Ruth, and others. *Changing Bodies, Changing Lives,* 2nd ed. Random House, 1987. The people who put together *Our Bodies, Ourselves* worked on this successful book which is now in its second edition and is aimed at males and females from a variety of backgrounds.

Benedict, Helen. *Safe, Strong, and Streetwise.* Little, Brown, 1987. The worldview presented in this guide to self-protection is a far cry from that presented in teen romances.

Drimmer, Frederick. *The Elephant Man.* Putnam, 1985. There are two heroes here, the terribly deformed John Merrick and the surgeon Frederick Treves who tried to help him.

Eagan, Andrea Boroff. *Why Am I So Miserable If These Are the Best Years of My Life?* Harcourt Brace Jovanovich, 1976. Several successful editions of this book, including paperbacks and a Spanish translation, prove that it speaks directly to young women.

Fonda, Jane. *Jane Fonda's Workout Book.* Simon and Schuster, 1981. When even Raisa Gorbachev does exercises to a Jane Fonda videotape, it's not surprising that American teenagers still rely on Fonda's workout book for inspiration as well as direction.

Fowler, Elizabeth M. *The New York Times Career Planner.* Times Books, 1987. Mature teens will browse through this book which is mostly taken from the author's newspaper "Careers" column.

Gale, Jay. *A Young Man's Guide to Sex.* Henry Holt, 1984. Informative, sensitive, and even gently humorous, Gale's book made it to several "best book" lists.

Gravelle, Karen, and Bertram A. John. *Teenagers Face to Face with Cancer.* Messner, 1986. Emotions and facts are woven together in these stories of sixteen teenage cancer patients.

Krementz, Jill. *How It Feels to Be Adopted.* Knopf, 1982. Along with *How It Feels When a Parent Dies* (Knopf, 1981) and *How It Feels When Parents Divorce* (Knopf, 1984), these interviews with young people from a variety of backgrounds touch on the obvious as well as more subtle aspects of human relationships.

Pirsig, Robert M. *Zen and the Art of Motorcycle Maintenance: An Inquiry into Values.* Morrow, 1974. The quality of the writing makes this more than a book on mental well-being.

Voss, Jacqueline, and Jay Gale. *A Young Woman's Guide to Sex.* Henry Holt, 1986. It's a mark of the times that this well-written book includes a chapter on sexual exploitation as well as an extensive appendix on places to get help for all kinds of sex-related problems.

OTHER TITLES MENTIONED IN CHAPTER EIGHT

Adamson, Joy. *Forever Free.* Harcourt Brace Jovanovich, 1963.

—————. *Living Free.* Harcourt Brace Jovanovich, 1961.

—————. *Pippa's Challenge.* Harcourt Brace Jovanovich, 1972.

—————. *The Spotted Sphinx.* Harcourt Brace Jovanovich, 1969.

Alcott, Louisa May. *Little Women.* 1868.

Alyson, Sasha, ed. *Young, Gay and Proud.* Alyson Publications, 1980.

Angelou, Maya. *I Know Why The Caged Bird Sings.* Random House, 1970.

Anonymous. *Go Ask Alice.* Prentice-Hall, 1971.

Arnosky, Jim. *Drawing from Nature.* Lothrop, 1982.

Ashabranner, Brent and Melissa. *Into a Strange Land: Unaccompanied Refugee Youth in America.* Dodd, 1987.

Augarten, Stan. *State of the Art: A Photographic History of the Integrated Circuit.* Ticknor and Fields, 1983.

Birnbach, Lisa. *Lisa Birnbach's College Book.* Ballantine, 1986.

Boyer, Ernest. *College: The Undergraduate Experience in America.* Harper & Row, 1988.

Brooks, Bruce. *Midnight Hour Encores.* Harper & Row, 1986.

Brown, Claude. *Manchild in the Promised Land.* Macmillan, 1965.

Caine, Clifford J. *How to Get Into College: A Step-by-Step Manual.* Greene, 1985.

Callahan, Steven. *Adrift: Seventy-Six Days Lost at Sea.* Thorndike, 1986.

Campbell, Nelson, ed. *Grass Roots & Schoolyards: A High School Basketball Anthology.* Stephen Greene, 1988.

Campbell, Patty. *Sex Guides.* Garland, 1986.

Capote, Truman. *In Cold Blood.* Random House, 1966.

Chambers, Allen. *Discovering Historical America: Mid-Atlantic States.* E. P. Dutton, 1983.

Ciardi, John. *Good Words to You: An All-New Browsers' Dictionary & Native Guide to the Unknown American Language.* Harper & Row, 1987.

Cleary, Beverly. *A Girl from Yamhill: A Memoir.* Morrow, 1988.

Cleaver, Eldridge. *Soul on Ice.* McGraw-Hill, 1968.

Cobb, Vicki. *Chemically Active! Experiments You Can Do at Home.* Harper & Row, 1985.

Corsaro, Maria, and Carole Korzeniowsky. *A Woman's Guide to Safe Abortion.* Holt, Rinehart and Winston, 1983.

Costello, Elaine. *Signing: How to Speak with Your Hands.* Bantam, 1983.

Council on International Educational Exchange. *The Teenager's Guide to Study, Travel, and Adventure Abroad, 1987–1988.* St. Martin's, 1986.

Craighead Jr., Frank C. *Track of the Grizzly.* Sierra, 1982.

Crichton, Michael. *The Andromeda Strain.* Knopf, 1969.

_____ . *The Great Train Robbery.* Knopf, 1975.

Curry, Boykin, and Brian Kasbar. *Essays that Worked: 50 Essays from Successful Applications to the Nation's Top Colleges.* Mustang, 1986.

Daly, Jay. *Presenting S. E. Hinton.* G. K. Hall, 1987.

Daugherty, Lynn B. *Why Me? Help for Victims of Child Sexual Abuse (Even If They Are Adults Now).* Mother Courage, 1985.

Davis, Daniel S. *Behind Barbed Wire: The Imprisonment of Japanese Americans during World War II.* E. P. Dutton, 1982.

Doctorow, E. L. *Ragtime.* Random House, 1975.

Dubrovin, Vivian. *Creative Word Processing.* Watts, 1987.

Dunbar, Robert E. *How to Debate.* Watts, 1987.

Durrell, Gerald, and Lee Durrell. *The Amateur Naturalist.* Knopf, 1983.

Eldredge, Niles. *Life Pulse.* Facts on File, 1987.

Espy, Willard R. *O Thou Improper, Thou Uncommon Noun.* Clarkson N. Potter, 1978.

Fair, Erik. *Right Stuff for New Hang Glider Pilots.* Publitec, 1987.

Filson, Brent. *Exploring with Lasers.* Messner, 1984.

Fiske, Edward B. *Selective Guide to Colleges.* Times Books, 1983.

Ford, Roger, and Oliver Strimpel. *Computers: An Introduction.* Facts on File, 1985.

Franklin, Jon. *Molecules of the Mind: The Brave New Science of Molecular Psychology.* Atheneum, 1987.

Freedman, Russell. *Cowboys of the Wild West.* Ticknor & Fields, 1985.

_____ . *Indian Chiefs.* Holiday, 1987.

Fretz, Sada. *Going Vegetarian: A Guide for Teenagers,* Morrow, 1983.

Fricke, Aaron. *Reflections of a Rock Lobster.* Alyson Publications, 1981.

Gardner, John. *The Art of Fiction: Notes on Craft for Young Writers.* Knopf, 1984.

Gardner, Richard. *A Boys' and Girls' Book About Divorce.* Bantam, 1971.

Getzoff, Ann, and Carolyn McClenahan. *Stepkids: A Survival Guide for Teenagers in Stepfamilies.* Walker, 1984.

Giblin, James Cross. *The Truth about Santa Claus.* Harper & Row, 1985.

Gleasner, Diana C. *Breakthrough: Women in Science.* Walker, 1983.

Glubok, Shirley. *The Art of Egypt Under the Pharoahs.* Macmillan, 1980.

_____ . *The Art of the Old West.* Macmillan, 1971.

_____ . *The Art of the Plains Indians.* Macmillan, 1975.

Goldston, Robert. *Sinister Touches: The Secret War Against Hitler.* Dial, 1982.

Gordimer, Nadine, and David Goldblatt. *Lifetimes Under Apartheid.* Knopf, 1986.

Gordon, Sol, and Myra Wollin. *Parenting: A Guide for Young People.* Oxford Press, 1975.

_____ , and Roger Conant. *You! The Teenage Survival Book.* Times Books, 1981.

Goulter, Vic, and Barbara Goulter. *How to Keep Your Car Mechanic Honest.* Stein & Day, 1987.

Graham, Robin. *Dove.* Harper & Row, 1972.

Gresh, Sean. *Becoming a Father.* New Century, 1980.

Griffin, John H. *Black Like Me.* Houghton Mifflin, 1977.

Haines, Gail Kay. *The Great Nuclear Power Debate.* Dodd, Mead, 1985.

Hanckel, Frances, and John Cuningham. *A Way of Love, A Way of Life: A Young Person's Introduction to What It Means to Be Gay.* Lothrop, Lee and Shepard, 1979.

Hancock, Graham, and Enver Carim. *AIDS: The Deadly Epidemic.* David & Charles, 1987.

Hanmer, Trudy. *The Advancing Frontier.* Watts, 1986.

Heron, Ann, ed. *One Teenager in Ten.* Alyson Publications, 1983.

Herriot, James. *All Creatures Great and Small.* St. Martin's, 1972.

————— . *All Things Bright and Beautiful.* St. Martin's, 1974.

————— . *All Things Wise and Wonderful.* St. Martin's, 1977.

————— . *The Lord God Made Them All.* St. Martin's, 1981.

Hirschfelder, Arlene. *Happily May I Walk: American Indians and Alaskan Natives Today.* Macmillan, 1986.

Hotchner, Tracy. *Pregnancy and Childbirth: The Complete Guide for a New Life.* Avon, 1979.

Hunt, Morton. *Gay: What You Should Know About Homosexuality.* Farrar, Straus & Giroux, 1977.

————— . *Young Person's Guide to Love.* Farrar, Straus & Giroux, 1977.

Hyde, Margaret O. *Computers That Think?: The Search for Artificial Intelligence.* Enslow Publishers, 1982.

————— . *Mind Drugs.* Dodd, 1986.

————— . *Sexual Abuse: Let's Talk About It.* Westminster, 1987.

Hyde, Margaret O., and Elizabeth H. Forsyth. *AIDS: What Does It Mean to You?* Walker Education, 1986.

Ipswitch, Elaine. *Scott Was Here.* Delacorte, 1979.

"J." *The Sensuous Woman.* Lyle Stuart, 1970.

Johnson, Eric W. *How to Live with Parents and Teachers.* Westminster, 1986.

Kelly, Gary F. *Learning About Sex: The Contemporary Guide for Young Adults.* Barron, 1986.

Kerr, M. E. *Me, Me, Me, Me, Me, Not a Novel.* Harper & Row, 1983.

Klass, Perri Elizabeth. *A Not Entirely Benign Procedure: Four Years as a Medical Student.* Putnam, 1987.

Klein, Kenneth. *Getting Better: A Medical Student's Story.* Little, Brown, 1981.

Knowles, John. *A Separate Peace.* Macmillan, 1960.

Kogan, Judith. *Nothing but the Best: The Struggle for Perfection at the Juilliard School.* Random House, 1987.

Kohn, Alexander. *False Prophets: Fraud, Error & Misdemeanour in Science & Medicine.* Blackwell, 1987.

Konner, Melvin. *Becoming a Doctor: A Journey of Initiation in Medical School.* Viking, 1987.

Landau, Elaine. *Child Abuse: An American Epidemic.* Messner, 1985.

Lawrence, Allan, and Mark Scheid. *The Self-Coached Runner II: Cross Country and the Shorter Distances.* Little, Brown, 1987.

Levine, Saul, and Kathleen Wilcox. *Dear Doctor.* Lothrop, Lee and Shepard, 1987.

Lindsay, Jeanne Warren. *Teens Parenting.* Morning Glory Press, 1981.

Lund Doris, *Eric.* Harper & Row, 1974.

Maas, Peter. *Serpico.* Viking, 1973.

Macaulay, David. *Unbuilding.* Houghton Mifflin, 1980.

MacGregor, Elaine. *Cake Decorating: A Step-by-Step Guide to Making Traditional & Fancy Cakes.* HP Books, 1986.

Madaras, Lynda. *What's Happening to My Body? A Growing Guide for Mothers and Daughters.* Newmarket, 1983.

Mangi, Richard, Peter Jokl, and O. William Dayton. *Sports Fitness and Training.* Pantheon, 1987.

Marrin, Albert. *Hitler: A Portrait of a Tyrant.* Viking, 1987.

Masland, Robert P. Jr., ed. *What Teenagers Want to Know About Sex: Questions and Answers by Boston Children's Hospital.* Little, Brown, 1988.

Mateja, Jim. *Used Cars: Finding the Best Buy.* Bonus Books, 1987.

Mayle, Peter. *What's Happening to Me?* Lyle Stuart, 1975.

————— . *Where Did I Come From?* Lyle Stuart, 1973.

————— . *Will I Like It?* Corwin, 1977.

McCoy, Kathy. *The Teenage Survival Guide.* Simon and Schuster, 1981.

McCoy, Kathy. *The Teenager Body Book.* Wallaby, 1979.

McCrum, Robert, et al. *The Story of English.* Viking, 1986.

McDonald, Linda. *Everything You Need to Know About Babies.* Oaklawn Press, 1978.

McGinty, Sarah. *Writing Your College Application Essay.* College Board, 1986.

McGuire, Paula. *It Won't Happen to Me: Teenagers Talk About Pregnancy.* Delacorte, 1983.

McHenry, Robert, ed. *Famous American Women: A Biographical Dictionary from Colonial Times to Present.* Dover, 1983.

McPhee, Penelope, and Raymond McPhee. *Your Future in Space: The U. S. Space Camp Training Program.* Crown, 1986.

Meltzer, Milton. *Ain't Gonna Study War No More: The Story of America's Peace Seekers.* Harper & Row, 1985.

————— . *Poverty in America.* Morrow, 1986.

————— . *The Jewish Americans: A History in Their Own Words.* Crowell, 1982.

Miklowitz, Gloria D., and Madeleine Yates. *The Young Tycoons: Ten Success Stories.* Harcourt Brace Jovanovich, 1981.

Mills, Joey, *New Classic Beauty: A Step-by-Step Guide to Naturally Glamorous Makeup.* Random House, 1987.

Moll, Richard. *The Public Ivys: A Guide to America's Best Public Undergraduate Colleges and Universities.* Viking, 1985.

Neil, Randy. *The Official Pompon Girl's Handbook.* St. Martin's, 1983.

Nilsson, Lennart. *A Child Is Born.* La Leche, 1983.

————— . *Behold Man.* Little, Brown, 1974.

Norris, William. *The Man Who Fell from the Sky.* Viking, 1987.

Patterson, Francine, and Eugene Linden. *The Education of Koko.* Holt, Rinehart and Winston, 1981.

Peavy, Linda, and Ursula Smith. *Women Who Changed Things: Nine Lives that Made a Difference.* Scribner, 1983.

Peck, Richard. *Are You in the House Alone?* Viking, 1976.

Peterson, Lorraine. *If God Loves Me Why Can't I Get My Locker Open?* Bethany House, 1980.

Petkevich, John Misha. *The Skater's Handbook.* Scribner, 1984.

Pomeroy, Wardell B. *Boys and Sex: A Revised Edition of the Classic Book on Adolescent Sexuality.* Delacorte, 1981.

————— . *Girls and Sex: A Revised Edition of the Classic Book on Adolescent Female Sexuality.* Delacorte, 1981.

Puhn, Fred. *Brake Handbook.* HP Books, 1985.

Read, Piers Paul. *Alive.* Lippincott, 1974.

Richards, Arlene Kramer, and Irene Willis. *What To Do If You or Someone You Know Is Under 18 and Pregnant.* Lothrop, Lee and Shepard, 1983.

Richter, Elizabeth. *Losing Someone You Love: When a Brother or Sister Dies.* Putnam, 1986.

Ripley, Robert. *Ripley's Believe It or Not.* Warner, 1976.

Rofes, Eric, ed. *The Kids Book About Death and Dying: By and For Kids.* Little, Brown, 1985.

————— . *The Kids Book of Divorce: By, For and About Kids.* Random House, 1982.

Rubenstein, Charlotte Streifer. *American Women Artists: From Early Indian Times to the Present.* G. K. Hall, 1982.

Russell, Alan, ed. *Guinness Book of World Records.* Sterling, 1988.

Ryden, Hope. *God's Dog.* Viking, 1979.

Sagan, Carl. *Cosmos.* Random House, 1983.

Schiffler, Don, and Lud Duroska. *Football Rules in Pictures.* Putnam, 1983.

Seixas, Judith. *Living with a Parent Who Drinks Too Much.* Greenwillow, 1979.

Selden, Bernice. *The Mill Girls.* Atheneum, 1983.

Shaw, Diana. *Make the Most of a Good Thing: You!* Little, Brown, 1987.

Silverstein, Alvin, and Virginia Silverstein. *AIDS: Deadly Threat.* Enslow, 1986.

————— . *Wonders of Speech.* Morrow, 1988.

————— . *World of the Brain.* Morrow, 1986.

Silverstein, Herma, and Caroline Arnold. *Hoaxes That Made Headlines.* Messner, 1987.

Sparks, Beatrice. *Jay's Journal.* Times Books, 1979.

_____ . *Voices.* Times Books, 1978.

Stachow, Hasso G. *If This Be Glory.* Doubleday, 1982.

Steinbeck, John. *The Pearl.* Viking, 1947.

Stratton, Joanna L. *Pioneer Women: Voices from the Kansas Frontier.* Simon and Schuster, 1981.

Sullivan, Jack. *The Penguin Encyclopedia of Horror and the Supernatural.* Penguin, 1986.

Taylor, A. J. P. *The Origins of the Second World War.* Atheneum, 1983.

Taylor, Theodore. *Battle in the Arctic Seas.* Harper & Row, 1976.

Terkel, Studs. *American Dreams Lost and Found.* Pantheon, 1980.

_____ . *Working: People Talk about What They Do All Day and How They Feel about What They Do.* Pantheon, 1974.

Thompson, Thomas. *Richie.* Saturday Review Press, 1973.

Unger, Harlow G. *A Student's Guide to College Admissions: Everything Your Guidance Counselor Has No Time to Tell You.* Facts on File, 1986.

Vedral, Joyce L. *My Parents Are Driving Me Crazy.* Ballantine, 1986.

Voigt, Cynthia. *Izzy, Willy-Nilly.* Macmillan, 1986.

Wallace, Diane A., and Philip L. Hershey. *How to Master Science Labs.* Watts, 1987.

Wallechinsky, David, and Irving Wallace. *The People's Almanac.* Doubleday, 1975.

Weil, Andrew, and Winifred Rosen. *Chocolate to Morphine: Understanding Mind-Active Drugs.* Houghton Mifflin, 1983.

Westwood, Jennifer, ed. *The Atlas of Mysterious Places.* Weidenfield, 1987.

Wigginton, Eliot, ed. *The Foxfire Book: Hog Dressing, Log Cabin Building, Mt. Crafts, Foods Planting by the Signs, Snake Lore, Hunting Tales, Faith Healing, Moonshining & Other Affairs of Plain Living.* Doubleday, 1972. (Followed by *Foxfire Two . . . ,* all from Doubleday.)

Wilcox, Frank H. *DNA:The Thread of Life.* Lerner, 1988.

Williams, Margery. *The Velveteen Rabbit.* Doubleday, 1958 (written in 1922).

Wirths, Claudine, and Mary Bowman-Kruhm. *I Hate School: How to Hang In and When to Drop Out.* Harper & Row, 1986.

Wishard, Laurie, and William Wishard. *Adoption: The Grafted Tree.* Cragmont, 1980.

Wiswell, Phil. *Kids Games: Traditional Indoor & Outdoor Activities for Children of All Ages.* Doubleday, 1987

Wolfe, Tom. *The Right Stuff.* Farrar, Straus and Giroux, 1979.

Wulffson, Don L. *Incredible True Adventures.* Dodd, Mead, 1986.

Young, Jean. *Woodstock Craftsman's Manual.* Praeger, 1972.

Zee, Anthony. *Fearful Symmetry: The Search for Beauty in Modern Physics.* Macmillan, 1986.

Zerman, Melvyn Bernard. *Taking on the Press: Constitutional Rights in Conflict.* Harper & Row, 1986.

For information on the availability of paperback editions of these titles, please consult the most recent edition of *Paperbound Books in Print,* published annually by R. R. Bowker Company.

CHAPTER NINE

POETRY, SHORT STORIES, DRAMA, AND HUMOR
Of Lines and Laughs

The poetry, drama, humor, and to a lesser extent, the short stories that young adults enjoy belong less exclusively to them than do their reading choices in other genres. If one examines the anthologies studied in high school literature classes, the plays that students read will have been produced for general adult audiences and the short stories they read will have been published in the *New Yorker* or the *Saturday Evening Post*. And with humor, teenagers often find themselves laughing at the same jokes that make their parents laugh. The lyrics of popular songs, which are one form of poetry, are sung by people of all ages, and when we examined the card catalogues of three different libraries to see how the books on the Honor Sampling were purchased and shelved, the only book we found in three different areas of the same library—children's, young adult, and adult—was a poetry collection, *Reflections on a Gift of Watermelon Pickle*.

Perhaps one of the reasons that these genres tend to transcend age divisions is that they are social. Rather than being enjoyed in solitude as is a good mystery or a sad problem novel, poetry is better when it's read aloud—note the popularity of poetry readings. With humor, normal people laugh more when they are with others than they do when they are alone. And when someone is watching a dramatic presentation, it's noticeably different to be part of a large, enthusiastic audience than to be by oneself listening to a cassette tape or watching a televised production. (See Chapter 11 for more about television.) And in the days before mass media magazines turned away from fiction to feature information instead, regular family entertainment consisted of reading the short stories that arrived in weekly or monthly magazines.

■ *POETRY*

If poets are as honorable as Humpty Dumpty, who explained to Alice in *Through the Looking Glass,* "When I make a word do a lot of work like that, I always pay it extra," then they too will pay words extra because of the demands they place on them. Poets use words not only for their literal meanings, but also for figurative meanings, and they select and place them in their poems according to their sounds and the patterns that they make.

Almost everything we've said about literature in general could also be said about poetry. Poets use the same literary devices discussed in Chapter 2, only they do it more succinctly. One of the characteristics of poetry is its compactness. Poets do with words something similar to what manufacturers do with dehydrated food. They shrink bulky thoughts down to packageable sizes which they expect consumers to fluff back up. With dried food the consumer usually adds water. With poetry, the consumers have to add their own thoughts, ideas, memories, and images. This is why reading poetry is harder work than reading prose, but it can also be more rewarding because the reader is more involved.

Readers' appreciation for poetry develops in much the same way as their appreciation for prose. They begin with an unconscious delight in sounds—the repetition and rhythm of nursery rhymes, songs, and television commercials. Then they go on to the fun of riddles, puns, playground chants, and autograph rhymes. Researchers into child language development have found that many times children do not understand the dual meanings of the words that are keys to particular jokes or riddles, yet they take pleasure in hearing themselves recite joke patterns, and then when they learn enough about the world to catch onto the double meanings of what they are saying, their pleasure is increased.

In a study where children were asked to select from a long list those words that went well together, the younger children—those in the primary grades—matched *monsoon,* with *baboon* and *cocoon.* In contrast, the older children used meaning as their basis for selection. To go with *cocoon,* they chose the words *moth* and *butterfly.* This doesn't mean that the sounds of words were no longer important; it simply means that as the children matured and knew more about the world they could rely on more than sound.

Something similar can be observed in children's appreciation of poetry. Although it may be the sounds of the nursery rhymes which first appeal to them, very soon they get involved in such simple plots as those found in "This Little Piggie Went to Market," "Ring Around the Rosie," and "Pat-a-Cake, Pat-a-Cake." By the time children are in the middle grades, their favorite poems are those that tell stories, for example, Robert Browning's "The Pied Piper of Hamelin," Henry Wadsworth Longfellow's "Hiawatha's Childhood" and "The Midnight Ride of Paul Revere," Robert Service's "The Cremation of Sam McGee," Alfred Noyes' "The Highwayman," Ernest L. Thayer's "Casey at the Bat," James Whitcomb Riley's "The Gobble-Uns'll Get You If You Don't Watch Out," and Edgar Allan Poe's "The Raven."

The next stage in development is taking pleasure in recognizing a kinship with a poet, finding someone who expresses a feeling or makes an observation that the reader has come close to but hasn't quite been able to put into words. Much of the "pop" poetry that English teachers consider trite or overdone is appreciated by young readers in this stage. We know a creative writing teacher who criticized a student-written poem as being overly sentimental by writing on the paper, "This sounds like Rod McKuen." The student was thrilled at being compared to McKuen, and the teacher didn't have the heart to explain that she had not intended the remark as a compliment.

Progressing from this stage, readers begin to identify with the poet as a writer. They understand and appreciate the skill with which the poet has achieved the desired effect. This understanding brings extra pleasure, which is why English teachers are interested in helping students arrive at this level of poetic appreciation, but the teacher who tries to get there too fast runs the risk of leaving students behind.

Poet Eve Merriam believes that something like this has happened to most of the upper-grade students who are turned off to poetry. They were made to feel dumb because they didn't catch on to every nuance of meaning or sound that their teacher saw, hence the experience was a negative one and they don't wish to repeat it. But fortunately, more teachers are realizing the damage that can be done by too early and too intensive a concentration on "literary" aspects of poetry. They are providing students with a variety of poems and encouraging them to read first for pleasure and secondarily for literary analysis. They let students start where they are in their appreciation of poetry, whether it's with the humorous poems of Shel Silverstein in his *Where the Sidewalk Ends* and *A Light in the Attic,* the religious poems selected by Nancy Larrick in her *Tambourines! Tambourines to Glory! Prayers and Poems,* the wordplay poems of Eve Merriam in her *Rainbow Writing* and *Out Loud,* the almost militant poems in Maya Angelou's *And Still I Rise,* or the almost classic poems in Edna St. Vincent Millay's *Poems Selected for Young People.*

Poetry Written or Collected Specifically for Young Adults

We did not include poetry in the first edition of this book because we were convinced that people do not write poetry specifically for teenagers. There are such poets as David McCord and Aileen Fisher who search for topics especially appealing to and appropriate for children, but we didn't know anyone who did this for young adults. Then in 1982, Mel Glenn published *Class Dismissed! High School Poems,* which was chosen for several best-book lists. So was its 1986 sequel, *Class Dismissed II: More High School Poems.* Here is poetry with all the characteristics of the modern YA problem novel. Young protagonists from a variety of racial and socioeconomic backgrounds use candid, first-person speech to discuss intense situations ranging from having a crush on a teacher, to quitting school, to getting caught shoplifting, and to getting stabbed. The titles of the poems are kids' names and each poem is illustrated with a photo-

The informal format of *Postcard Poems* by Paul B. Janeczko, published by Bradbury House, makes it accessible to students.

graph. Although Glenn wrote the poems himself, the design of the book gives the impression that the kids in the photographs are the poets. The publishers probably wanted to capitalize on the current popularity of "folk poetry," that is, the writing and sharing of original poems.

Although writing poetry specifically for a young adult audience is a recent development, collecting poems with special appeal to teenagers and packaging them for the high school market has a much longer history. A book that twenty-five years ago proved the potential success of this kind of venture was *Reflections on a Gift of Watermelon Pickle,* published first by Scott, Foresman in 1966 and later reprinted in various formats and issued on a record. Editors Steve Dunning, Edward Lueders, and Hugh L. Smith selected the poems by getting the reactions of teenagers to both well known and new poems gleaned from hundreds of poetry magazines. But there was more to their success than just the individual poems. The title, taken from the concluding poem (see "Reflections on a Gift of Watermelon Pickle" and "Further Reflections on 'A Gift of Watermelon Pickle' " *English Journal,* April and September, 1983) was intriguing. The spacious design of the book with its watermelon green cover and reddish-pink endpapers highlighted the title poem, making the book memorable.

Dunning, Lueders, and Smith combined efforts to do a second book, *Some Haystacks Don't Even Have Any Needle and Other Complete Modern Poems.* Reviewers praised the book as highly, or even more highly than *Watermelon Pickle,* but probably only because they were now alert to the names of the anthologists. Lueders went on to do a third collection with the help of Primus St. John, *Zero Makes Me Hungry: A Collection of Poems for Today.* The books are both highly recommended, but neither one was quite as successful as *Watermelon Pickle,* which leads one to suspect that the anthologists used the first-place winners in their initial book and then came back to the second and third choices for the later books.

Paul Janeczko, a high school English teacher in Auburn, Maine, is the newest anthologist to achieve a success comparable to that of the *Watermelon Pickle* book. Janeczko says that "Today I read poetry the way some people watch soap operas, work in their gardens, or follow the Red Sox: irrationally, compulsively, endlessly."[1] Out of this compulsion has come six anthologies including *Pocket Poems,* which is small enough to fit into a jeans pocket, and *Going Over to Your Place: Poems for Each Other.*

His first collection, *Postcard Poems,* is filled with poems short enough to send to a friend on a postcard, for example, W. S. Merwin's "Separation":

Your absence has gone through me
Like thread through a needle.
Everything I do is stitched with its color.[2]

and Ralph Waldo Emerson's "Poet":

To clothe the fiery thought
In simple words succeeds,
For still the draft of genius is
To mask a King in weeds.

Most of Janeczko's books have a cyclical organization with between two and five poems on similar subjects. For example, in *Don't forget to fly,* Constance Sharp's "I show the Daffodils to the Retarded Kids," is grouped with Joyce Carol Oates' "Children Not Kept at Home," and Theodore Roethke's "My Dim-Wit Cousin." In all, there are forty groupings with subjects ranging from suicide to dressmaker's dummies, swimming, and Sunday. In *Strings: A Gathering of Family Poems,* Janeczko uses a similar kind of organization only going through members of the family: wives, husbands, grandparents, etc. and through places with special meanings for families such as kitchens—with a "slice of sun and a song," as well as one where a 1940s child playing under the table hears the radio announcer, "We interrupt this broadcast . . . " and has his head filled with thoughts of Hitler, Roosevelt, and Joe Louis.

Janeczko does not put in divider pages or subject headings because he does not want "to limit the reader's response. I don't want a reader to see a poem in the flower section and think only of flowers." Nor does he make study questions for teachers. He doesn't want to encourage the idea that poetry is inaccessible. Instead of thinking of poems as puzzles, he wants teachers to think of them as language experiences. Once teachers have found a few poems that they like, then they can share them as a pleasurable experience with students.[3]

Janeczko's favorite, and the one which will probably be used in the most English classes, is *Poetspeak: In Their Work, About Their Work.* Probably because of the success of his earlier anthologies, Janeczko was able to convince

MEL GLENN
on Remembering

I write because I remember.

In one sense I never left home because I teach in the same high school I went to as a kid. I teach in some of the same rooms I sat in when I went to Lincoln High School in Brooklyn.

I write to open up the lines of communication, to explain my past to myself and others. On a certain level we are all emotionally 14. Good writing can put us in touch with who we were and who we are.

No matter who you are, where you came from, there is a little piece of high school still in you. It attaches to your subconscious, but every so often it leaps out at you and screams, "I'm back!"

I write because I want to remember how it felt not making the basketball team, worrying about my finals, thinking about the future.

If high school is the universal experience, one that everyone has gone through, I am still part of that universe because of my teaching and writing. If my adolescence was scarred by the usual slings and arrows, it is not very different from the experiences teenagers go through today. Although times and fashions change, certain things always ring true, certain questions are still paramount: Am I pretty or handsome enough, smart or athletic enough? Will people like me? Will I be a success? Will my parents stay together?

The fundamental things still apply. Beneath all the acting out, the bravado, and the silences are the turbulent feelings and haunting questions of every generation.

Adolescence is the time when feelings are at war with everything and everyone. It is sometimes one long ache with fragmentary sparkles of firework joy, often a lonely time spent lurching between a sullen funk and outrageous behavior making adults worry about the future of western civilization.

I write because we have lost touch with the kids we teach, are going to teach, or the kid within ourselves. Sometimes we fail as teachers and/or writers when measured against the real world of friends, movies, basketball, love, and hanging out. But I feel the challenge to teach and write, especially when student horizons are limited by the parameters of their neighborhoods and the durability of their VCRs.

Teachers have a difficult job. They may feel like academic Rodney Dangerfields or educational equivalents of M*A*S*H surgeons dealing with too many walking wounded. Students have it rough too trying to find the pieces when they are the puzzle, looking for the answers that seem to just elude their grasp.

Mark Twain said that all writing is autobiographical, and so it is when my literary characters are imaginative extensions of my own feelings and experiences, close to the mind, heart, and memory.

I write because I remember.

Mel Glenn's books include poetry collections, *Class Dismissed*, Houghton Mifflin, 1982; and *Class Dismissed II*, Houghton Mifflin, 1986; and a novel, *One Order to Go*, Houghton Mifflin, 1984.

several poets to contribute more than their poems. Forty-four contributed their photographs, and more importantly, over sixty contributed notes ranging from a few sentences to a few pages telling how they happened to write the included poem, what it means to them, or some other interesting details about the writing of poetry. If all of the poems were accompanied by such an essay, it might be tedious, but as it is there is a good balance between prose and poetry. What makes *Poetspeak* ideal for either class or individual young adult reading is that the poems are dramatic enough to demand the reader's involvement. Also, the statements from the poets are reassuring in helping students and their teachers look at poetry as the sharing of an experience rather than the creating of a secret code to be unlocked.

Stanley Kunitz's poem "The Portrait," published in *Poetspeak* on page 73, with the author's statement following on pages 74 and 75, is a good example of a poem that tells a story. Kunitz wrote:

> . . . a poem demands of its readers that they must come out to meet it, at least as far as it comes out to meet them, so that *their* meaning may be added to its. A common fallacy is to think that a poem begins with a meaning which then gets dressed up in words. On the contrary, a poem is language surprised in the act of changing into meaning.

The story is more subtle than the kinds students relate to when they're in the middle grades. High school students are beginning to enjoy the stories of the inner self, to see the intensity of the feelings of the two characters in this poem.

The Portrait
by Stanley Kunitz
My mother never forgave my father
for killing himself,
especially at such an awkward time
and in a public park,
that spring
when I was waiting to be born.
She locked his name
in her deepest cabinet
and would not let him out,
though I could hear him thumping.
When I came down from the attic
with the pastel portrait in my hand
of a long-lipped stranger
with a brave moustache
and deep brown level eyes,
she ripped it into shreds
without a single word
and slapped me hard.
In my sixty-fourth year
I can feel my cheek
still burning.[4]

As the conclusion to his comments, Kunitz wrote:

> ■   I have nothing left to say except that more years than I want to count have passed, according to the relentless calendar, since my widowed mother and I acted out our wordless drama in the house on Providence Street in Worcester; and it might as well be yesterday. Memory is each man's poet-in-residence.

The biggest controlling influence on the format and design of most poetry books is the theme that the collector has decided to pursue. The current trend in anthologizing is to select a topic and then find either a goodly number of poems or a number of good poems (depending on the standards of the anthologist) on a similar topic. Limiting themselves to either a particular topic or a particular poet gives anthologists a way to get a handle on what could be an overwhelming job of selection. It also makes designing and naming a book easier, but at the same time it handicaps the anthologist by restricting the raw material from which selections can be made. Some of the best poems are those that treat unique experiences or that explore hidden sides of life. These poems are appealing simply because they are on topics that are usually ignored.

Poetry appeals to the senses—sight as well as sound—and because of this its reading shouldn't be rushed. Books of poems need to be designed to give readers room to breathe. A book jam-packed with poems exudes a sense of urgency, a need to speedread. Such books are good reference tools for someone wanting to find a particular poem, but they aren't books that readers—teenage or adult—are likely to pick up for pleasure time browsing.

Current interests and trends are just as likely to influence the reception of poetry as the reception of fiction. Considering the popularity of Vietnam fiction, we shouldn't be surprised at the appearance of Steve Mason's *Johnny's Song: Poetry of a Vietnam Veteran.* We see America's increased interest in native American culture reflected in the publication of John Bierhorst's *In the Trail of the Wind: American Indian Poems and Ritual Orations.* On another plane, but still relating to current interests, we see poets and publishers producing collections of love poems to capitalize on the popularity of the romances. Lee Bennett Hopkins came out with the simplest and most obvious *Love & Kisses* in 1983. This was followed by Eve Merriam's *If Only I Could Tell You: Poems for Young Lovers and Dreamers* also in 1983, Frances McCullough's *Love Is Like the Lion's Tooth* in 1984, and Ruth Gordon's *Under All Silences: Shades of Love* in 1987. A *School Library Journal* reviewer praised Gordon's skill in bringing together the thoughts of ancient Egyptian, Chinese, Japanese, Persian and modern poets into "one wonderful volume." The poems in Gordon's book range from a 1500 B.C. Egyptian hieroglyphic text:

> *I wish to paint my eyes,*
> *so if I see you, my eye will glisten.*

to modern lines by Tuvia Ruebner:

> *Among iron fragments and rusty dreams*
> *I found you*
> *lost in my astonished hands.*[5]

Because readers come to poetry not so much for gathering information as for seeking a change of pace, a bit of pleasure through word play, a sudden recognition or insight, a recollection from childhood, or a time of emotional intensity, the design of the book needs to invite readers in. Book designer Jane Halverson did a good job for Random House in creating covers showing the relationship between Maya Angelou's autobiographies *I Know Why the Caged Bird Sings, Singin' and Swingin' and Gettin' Merry Like Christmas,* and *The Heart of a Woman* and her poetry collections *Just Give Me a Cool Drink of Water 'fore I Die, Oh Pray My Wings Are Gonna Fit Me Well,* and *And Still I Rise.* Halverson used the same bright colors to create variations on a basic rainbowlike design. But even more pleasing is Angelou's latest book, *Now Sheba Sings the Song,* in which her poems are accompanied by Tom Feelings' unusually perceptive portraits of black women.

Even though poetry can usually be read and enjoyed by a much wider age range than prose, there is still a subtle dividing line between children's and young adult poetry. Teenagers will be amused by the humorous poetry in Jack Prelutsky's *Nightmares: Poems to Trouble Your Sleep,* Alvin Schwartz's *Tomfoolery: Trickery and Foolery with Words,* William Cole's collection *Beastly Boys and Ghastly Girls,* and some of the poems from Lewis Carroll's *Alice in Wonderland* and *Through the Looking Glass,* but they will be slightly insulted if offered serious children's poetry. It's the same old thing about their being offended if they should be taken to the children's department of a store to buy their clothes, but by themselves, they might wander into a children's department to buy a stuffed animal. Two poetry books that are clearly made for children but that teenagers might like in the same way that they like stuffed animals (probably because of a combination of nostalgia and basic attractiveness) are Susan Jeffers' picture book interpretations of Longfellow's *Hiawatha* and Robert Frost's *Stopping By Woods on a Snowy Evening.* Another beautifully illustrated book that teenagers will probably like is a new Greenwillow edition of Robert W. Service's *The Cremation of Sam McGee.*

The freedom of choice is what's at issue, and the thing for book people to realize is that if a collection of poems is going to be marketed basically to high schools the designers should be aware of their audience's feeling that they have passed through childhood and are now young adults.

Helen Plotz is a good anthologist who has put together several collections for Crowell, Macmillan, and Greenwillow. These books, for example, *Imagination's Other Place: Poems of Science and Mathematics* and *Eye's Delight: Poems of Art and Architecture,* find their way into many young adult collections. However, it seems to us that some of the titles stand between the poems and a young adult audience. One example is the title *Saturday's Children: Poems of Work.* It makes an appropriate allusion to the old nursery rhyme about Monday's child being fair of face, Tuesday's child full of grace, etc., but without encouragement from a forceful teacher or librarian, not many young adults are going to pick up a book whose five-word title includes three words that for most teenagers have negative connotations: *children, poems,* and *work.* Another example is *Gladly Learn and Gladly Teach: Poems of the School Experience,* which seems to exude a sort of middle-aged, schoolmarm fussiness.

Poetry for Sophisticated Readers

Well-read sophisticated young adults are ready to read and enjoy the same poetry that educated adults enjoy, but a few guiding principles might help teachers and librarians smooth the path to what they consider appropriate appreciation of the best poetry.

1. Young adults, who simply haven't been around as long as adults and therefore haven't had time to pick up as much background information, will be more likely to understand the allusions made by contemporary as opposed to historical poets. We are not recommending that anyone try to limit the poetry that young adults are exposed to, but we do think that they should first be offered the works of modern poets such as:

Maya Angelou	Eve Merriam
John Berryman	Robert Morgan
James Dickey	Joyce Carol Oates
Nikki Giovanni	Linda Pastan
Donald Hall	Marge Piercey
Judith Hemschemeyer	Adrienne Rich
Ted Hughes	Theodore Roethke
Randall Jarrell	William Stafford
Donald Justice	Anne Sexton
X. J. Kennedy	Karl Shapiro
Ted Koozer	May Swenson
Maxine Kumin	John Updike
Denise Levertov	Robert Penn Warren
Joan LaBombard	Paul Zimmer

2. Young adults will be better able to relate to poets who are presenting their own cultures. Certainly we are not asking for segregation of poetry by race, country, or ethnic background of the poet. But it stands to reason that an American teenager is going to be able to picture the Boston that Anne Sexton wrote about in "The Wedding Night" and the allusions both to Walt Whitman and to American lifestyles that Allen Ginsberg wrote about in "A Supermarket in California" better than is an Australian or British teenager. Likewise, a Native American teenager might be more ready to appreciate poetic renditions of ceremonial chants than will be a child from white, middle-class suburbia. And the minority child who has grown up being forced to think about racial differences is in a better position than other readers to relate to Imamu Amiri Baraka's (LeRoi Jones) "Poem for Half White College Students" and Nikki Giovanni's "Ego Tripping." The power of literature is that it helps people transcend the circumstances that they happened to be born into, and so we highly recommend that students be offered poetry representing cultures and times different from their own, but

adults who work with young readers need to realize that they will probably need to make a conscious effort to help even bright and sophisticated students transcend cultural barriers.

3. It helps to ease students into literary criticism through a biographical approach. Successful high school students are accustomed to reading biographies, but they probably haven't had much experience with literary criticism. Fortunately most biographies of poets, whether they are book length as is Neil Baldwin's *To All Gentleness, William Carlos Williams: The Doctor Poet,* chapter length as in Jean Gould's *American Women Poets: Pioneers of Modern Poetry,* or only a few paragraphs in length as in Paul Janeczko's *Poetspeak,* include substantial doses of *explication de texte* which can serve as an introduction to literary criticism.

4. Since prose is much more like everyday language than poetry is, young people usually find it easier to read prose than poetry. Adults can help students bridge this gap by bringing to their attention poetry written by authors whose prose works they already feel comfortable with. For example, someone who has read Alice Walker's *The Color Purple* will probably be ready to appreciate the poems in her *Good Night Willie Lee, I'll See You in the Morning.* In a similar way, Ray Bradbury's science fiction fans may want to read his fifty-plus poems in *When Elephants Last in the Dooryard Bloomed* and students who have read Richard Brautigan's books may relate to his poetry, for example *June Thirtieth, June Thirtieth,* or *The Pill Versus the Springhill Mine Disaster.* On a less sophisticated level, students familiar with the work of YA writers Lois Duncan, Richard Peck, and R. R. Knudson may be interested in their collections of poetry.

The Writing and Reading Connection

Today there are hundreds of small poetry magazines published in the United States, and many of these include poems written by high school and college students. A class assignment that we have given for several years is to ask our college students to collect examples they like of ten different kinds of poems, for example, a narrative or storytelling poem, a nonsense poem, a poem set to music, a humorous poem, a poem that describes an everyday happening, a concrete or visual poem, a haiku or cinquain, etc. One of the categories is an original, unpublished poem written by either the student or a roommate, friend, or family member. No student has ever complained about not being able to find a friendly poet willing to share.

Poets are looking for audiences. After a poetry reading on our campus by a nationally known poet, a man in the audience stood up to complain that he had been told by the editor of the local newspaper, who kept rejecting his poems, that there were too many people writing poems today. The poet looked thoughtful for a moment and then responded, "No, there just aren't enough people reading poems."

Poetry lovers all over are working to change this state of affairs. Don Mainprize, who teaches English at Houghton Lake High School in Michigan, made the following suggestions on increasing the writing, and indirectly the reading, of poetry in an article entitled "Ouchless Poetry":

- Have in-class readings by students.
- Read poetry to other classes or hold full, voluntary, or selective assembly readings.
- Make classroom displays of poems and art. Volunteer to do the hallway or a library display with creative writing.
- Choose or have students choose ten poems of the week for display (with names displayed or not, as the poet wishes).
- Hold a poetry open house for the public.
- Put a poem a day in the office bulletin.
- Have a poem chosen for each edition of the school paper.
- Get your radio station to air poems on its weekly school program.
- Send poems to the local newspaper if you can arrange for a regular feature.
- Enter poems in state and national contests.
- Publish a book of student poems.
- Early on announce these end-of-the-year awards for the Honors Banquet: Poet Laureate, Most Improved Poet, Most Prolific Poet, Best-Anything-You-Can-Come-Up-With Poet. These awards mean a lot more to kids than you think.[6]

Another good article worth looking up and reading is Jesse Hise's "Writing Poetry: More than a Frill" in the November 1980 *English Journal.* He begins with poetry patterns guaranteed to bring feelings of success and then goes on to show ways of breaking out of the patterns. Kenneth Koch's *Wishes, Lies, and Dreams,* and *Rose, Where Did You Get That Red?* are excellent in presenting poetry ideas or patterns and also some very enjoyable poetry written by students in the New York Public schools where Koch was a poet-in-residence. Alberta Turner, who teaches at Cleveland State University, advises making poetry writing spontaneous:

Surprise the class. Don't call it poetry. Don't assign it ahead of time. Don't discuss the poetry in the literature book first. Trick them into letting their subconscious minds present them with concerns, feelings they haven't yet had time to formulate into verbal clichés. For instance, have them dump out their pockets and purses and list the things contained in order of increasing importance to themselves. Students may discover they're very cautious, others that they're dreamers, still others that they're light travelers.

I would discourage some of the time-honored ways of writing poetry in the classroom, the poems that fill traditional literary forms, such as limericks or haiku. Feeling doesn't occur first in such forms, and to force feeling into forms before it has expressed itself in unconscious impulse—chiefly images and emotional rhythms—may make the poems mechanical and/or trite. However, natural forms like questions and answers or counting-out chants or game tunes don't have that disadvantage. I'd discourage assigning first drafts of poems for homework. The poem, unlike the essay, doesn't benefit from being planned. It needs to surprise the poet. It's the final editing that can be done at home.[7]

What these teachers have in mind is making young people comfortable with poetry so that their pleasure can be increased in reading as well as writing "throughout the year . . . not something we do to be 'creative' or to separate us from the normal writing [and reading] process."[8] Anyone who wants to accomplish this goal should have an ample supply of poetry books for readers to pick up and browse through whenever there's extra time as well as when class attention is specifically focused on poetry. These should include small magazines, local literary publications of your own and neighboring schools, and poetry anthologies from national presses.

Poetry is a medium that lends itself to brief but intense encounters with strong emotions, hence when young people write poetry they are apt to write about things that upset or worry them—unfairnesses, hostilities, sexuality, disagreements with adults, etc. During the 1970s, two books that frequently found their way to lists of censored books were *the me nobody knows: children's voices from the ghetto* edited by Stephen M. Joseph and *Male and Female Under Eighteen* edited by Eve Merriam and Nancy Larrick. Both books contained poetry as well as short prose statements by young writers. They were criticized for "objectionable" words as well as for expressions of ideas thought to be inappropriate for young readers.

Another poetry book that during the 1970s was so controversial that it virtually disappeared from library shelves was Eve Merriam's parody *Inner City Mother Goose*. It was reissued by Bantam in 1984 and may serve as an inspiration for students to write parodies. Myra Cohn Livingston's less controversial collection of parodies *Speak Roughly to Your Little Boy* would also be good for this because it includes the original pieces along with parodies of them.

As a final note, we should point out that what we have presented in this section has been little more than a sampling of available poetry. Young readers are fortunate in having practically the whole world of poetry from which to choose. They are also fortunate in that poetry-loving adults are anxious to recruit young readers as poetry lovers and so they make an extra effort to design books that are particularly inviting because of their spaciousness and high-quality design and layout.

SHORT STORIES

Short stories fit into today's penchant for hurry-up ideas, condensations, and instant gratification. But a short story is more than a *Readers' Digest* version of a novel because from the beginning it is planned to fit into less space. Short stories are uniquely appropriate to young readers for the following reasons:

1. Short stories have a limited number of characters.
2. Their plots are usually straightforward.
3. The development is most often direct and to the point.
4. In a classroom, students can read 15 short stories in the time it takes to read one or two novels. Through reading the larger number of short stories, they can meet a greater variety of viewpoints and representatives of different ethnic groups and cultures.
5. The best of modern American authors have written short stories, which means that students can experience high quality writing in pieces that are short enough for comfortable reading.

Because of these advantages, short stories have always had a place in high school English classes. But even though many of the stories had young protagonists, they were generally written and published for adults and then selected for inclusion in anthologies or literature textbooks. But today, some of the best YA authors are writing short stories aimed directly at a teenage audience, and these are being published in original collections marketed for leisure time as well as classroom reading.

Most notable is Don Gallo's *Sixteen,* which Delacorte published in 1984, and his *Visions,* published in 1987. Gallo invited well-known YA authors, including Sue Ellen Bridgers, Richard Peck, Bette Greene, Robert Lipsyte, Kevin Major, Ouida Sebestyen, and Rosa Guy to contribute unpublished short stories. It was a good idea to ask these authors for short stories because short stories and YA novels have many similarities. M. E. Kerr began her career writing short stories about teenagers for *Compact* and *Ladies Home Journal,* and at least two other contributors had already published their own collections

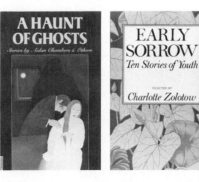

These books, published by Harper & Row, are examples of short stories that publishers are promoting directly to students.

of short stories. Norma Fox Mazer's 1976 *Dear Bill, Remember Me? & Other Stories* is on the Honor List (see Chapter 1), and her 1982 *Summer Girls, Love Boys* was almost as well received. Robert Cormier has published dozens of short stories, and in 1980 published *Eight Plus One,* an anthology of his stories judged most appealing to the young adults who liked his novels. He added background information about how each story developed.

In recommending Gallo's *Visions,* Richard Abrahamson and Kylene Beers showed how in a single day's reading, a teacher could present a mini-unit on cultures, customs, and "fitting in." They suggested using Lensey Namioka's "The All-American Slurp," a story about the efforts of a modern Chinese immigrant family to fit into their new culture as viewed through the critical eyes of a teenager, along with two children's books, Ina Friedman's *How My Parents Learned to Eat* and Tomie dePaola's *Watch out for the Chicken Feet in Your Soup.*

They also recommended M. E. Kerr's contribution in *Visions.* It's a science-fiction story entitled "The Sweet Perfume of Good-bye," about a 17-year-old girl doing scientific research on another planet. The only smell on that planet is a pleasant odor which a person develops one hour before death. Kerr's realistic novel *Night Kites* ends with a reference to just such a story, which the big brother who has AIDS is trying to write, but can't seem to finish. Seeing an author step in and write a story for one of her fictional characters could be the basis for an interesting discussion on creative thinking and the art of writing.[9]

At a session on "The Resurgence of the Short Story" at the 1987 National Council of Teachers of English convention, teacher Bob Seney from Houston, Texas, recommended more than two dozen collections of short stories and showed how they represent realistic fiction, science fiction, fantasy, humor, folklore, and myth. He recommended Ellen Conford's *If This Is Love, I'll Take Spaghetti* and Barbara Girion's *A Very Brief Season* as good transitions from the Sweet Valley High romances, Elizabeth Segel's *Short Takes* as an all-around good collection, Diana Wynne Jones' *Warlock at the Wheel* as a humorous spoof on horror stories, and Alvin Schwartz's *Scary Stories to Tell in the Dark* and *More Scary Stories to Tell in the Dark* as funny collections of contemporary folklore. Students will remember having told many of the Schwartz stories at slumber parties and summer camp.

While advising teachers not to overanalyze short stories, he suggested using them for reading aloud in class to introduce a topic for discussion or writing, to illustrate a point, or to fill out a thematic unit. Short stories are also good for readers' theatre and dramatization, and they can be used to give students enough experience with literary concepts so that they can learn the meanings of literary terms from actual experience rather than from memorization.

Collections of short stories come in various types. For example, everyone expects myths and folktales to be in story form, but they might be pleasantly surprised at how beautifully Virginia Hamilton retells black folktales in *The People Could Fly.* Animal stories are another expected genre as in *James Herriot's Dog Stories* and *Roger Caras' Treasury of Great Cat Stories* and *Roger Caras' Treasury of Great Dog Stories.*

also can serve as guides when predicting the potential of other scripts for in-class reading.

- It calls for twelve continual parts, enough to satisfy all students who like to read aloud.
- It teaches practical lessons of value to students' lives.
- It may serve as a springboard for research and further discussion on how the judicial system works.
- It creates a forum for students to probe the psychology of group dynamics and peer behavior.
- It sparks student excitement from the beginning and sustains it throughout.
- It can be read in two-and-a-half class sessions.
- The "business" is minimal and can be easily carried out as students read from scripts.
- Pertinent questions can be asked when the jury recesses after Acts I and II.
- The setting is a hot, stuffy jury room—just like our classrooms in June.
- Students are attracted to the realism and they can relate to a motherless, slum youth of nineteen.
- The excellent characterization allows students to discover a kaleidoscope of lifelike personalities.

The influence of the mass media was seen in several teachers' explanations of why other plays worked in their classes. For example, one teacher explained that he goes back to the days of radio for Lucille Fletcher's *Sorry, Wrong Number.* Since "it was written to be heard and not seen, it is ideal for reading aloud." Another teacher said that because Gore Vidal's *Visit to a Small Planet* was written for television, "the action was easy to visualize and the stage directions were simple enough to discuss as an important aspect of the drama itself." Television writer Rod Serling's *A Storm in Summer* was recommended for the way it relates an encounter between a ten-year-old Harlem boy and a bitter, sarcastic, Jewish delicatessen owner in upstate New York.

Suggested plays from the more standard lists included Thornton Wilder's *Our Town,* to be taught along with Edgar Lee Masters' *Spoon River Anthology.* Robert Bolt's *A Man for All Seasons* was recommended for its portrayal of one of the most famous periods of English history and also for its exploration of a hero. Comparisons can be drawn to works treating heroes of noble birth as in *Antigone* and *Hamlet* and heroes of ordinary birth as in *Death of a Salesman* and *The Stranger.* Oliver Goldsmith's *She Stoops to Conquer* was recommended for seniors of average as well as superior ability levels. "Despite its eighteenth-century origins, the dialogue is surprisingly modern, with very few words needing explanation. . . . The characters are warm, human, and lovable; the humor, easygoing and readily accessible." Robinson Jeffers' translation of Euripedes' *Medea* was recommended as more accessible to average students than other Greek plays such as *Oedipus* and *Antigone.* Students readily understand jealousy and the desire for revenge. And the idea that Medea kills her children

A genre all of its own are the anthologies marketed for study in literature classes such as *The Signet Classic Book of American Short Stories* edited by Burton Raffel, *Great American Short Stories* edited by Wallace Stegner, and *Point of Departure* edited by Robert S. Gold. There are so many of these—we counted 47 in one distributor's catalog—that we can't evaluate them individually. The main differences are whether they are restricted to a specified time period, one particular author (Twain, Poe, London, Salinger, O. Henry, etc.), or to a particular theme.

Anthologies marketed to libraries for young people's independent reading are more apt to center around a theme, as in Charlotte Zolotow's *An Overpraised Season,* which gets its title from Samuel Butler's "Youth is like spring, an overpraised season." Under such a broad title, it was possible to include almost any story about youth, but her second collection *Early Sorrow: Ten Stories of Youth* was restricted to such painful experiences as the disillusionment of finding oneself unloved, the fear of growing up, the challenge of asserting one's independence, and the sadness of unwise behavior that cannot be relived. All of the stories were written for adults by such authors as E. L. Doctorow, Reynolds Price, John Updike, Kurt Vonnegut, Jessamyn West, James Purdy, and Harold Brodkey.

Other recent collections that have received starred reviews in either *Booklist* or *School Library Journal* include *The Oxford Book of English Ghost Stories,* edited by Michael Cox and R. A. Gilbert, and *Stories We Listened To,* outdoor survival stories from the Alaskan wilderness, edited by John Haines. Janni Howker is the British author of the five stories in *Badger on the Barge and Other Stories,* which feature teenagers undergoing periods of uncertainty and doubt but being helped by eccentric and elderly people that they befriend.

Other excellent authors who have written several stories to be published together include Cynthia Rylant with her book *Every Living Thing,* twelve stories in which human lives are changed through close dealings with animals, and for slightly younger readers, *Children of Christmas: Stories for the Season.* Joan Aiken has done several books of short stories including *A Whisper in the Night,* while Aidan Chambers has done *Out of Time* and *Shades of Dark.* Peter Cameron's *One Way or Another* includes fourteen stories, some humorous, about contemporary teenagers. Paul Fleischman's *Graven Images,* a Newbery Honor Book, features three early American stories centered around a carved sailor, a marble statue, and a weathervane. The four 1800 stories in his *Coming-And-Going Men* are tied together by the setting of New Canaan, Vermont, a town which leaves its mark on those traders and craftsmen who pass through.

Robert Westall wrote some wonderfully scary stories in *The Haunting of Chas McGill & Other Stories* and *Rachel & the Angel & Other Stories.* And as with other good writers who enjoy reading, he also edits collections (see his statement on page 166). While fantasy writer Robin McKinley was riding the Staten Island ferry and watching the skyline of New York disappear on the horizon, she got the inspiration for her collection of stories, *Imaginary Lands.* She went looking for stories which start with real-life settings but as the fantasy element in each story takes over the settings draw farther and farther away until they exist only in the realm of imagination.

Isaac Asimov with the help of others has edited *Young Monsters,* a collection of the macabre created by authors as varied as Ray Bradbury, Stephen King, and Jane Yolen. A *School Library Journal* reviewer wrote that "The editors have done a masterful job of arranging the stories to alleviate tension. For example, the grisly 'Disturb Not My Slumbering Fair' by Chelsea Quinn Yarbro, which features Diedre, a zombie who feasts on the dead ('It would be so good to sip the marrow from his bones, to nibble the butter-soft convolutions of his brain') is followed by Richard Parker's 'The Wheelbarrow Boy,' a humorous study of a teacher who changes an unruly student into a wheelbarrow—and then can't change him back."[10] Other titles in the series include *Young Ghosts, Young Extraterrestrials, Young Star Travelers,* and *Young Mutants.*

In conclusion, short stories are as varied in style and subject matter as are novels, and because of their brevity they are especially appealing to young readers. We are fortunate that today's publishers have recognized the appeal of short stories to teenagers and are marketing collections for independent reading as well as for class use.

■ DRAMA

In a 1984 *English Journal* article, Anthony L. Manna complained that for English teachers and librarians, drama was the "hidden genre." He examined several recent best-of-the-year lists compiled by such publications as *Booklist, School Library Journal,* and the *New York Times Book Review* and found only one play, Paul Zindel's *Let Me Hear You Whisper.* To prove that the exclusion wasn't because good drama isn't being written, he went on to recommend more than a dozen contemporary plays that would be excellent for reading in either junior or senior high school classrooms.[11]

In pondering Manna's point and trying to figure out why drama has been the "hidden genre" for young adults, we came up with the following reasons:

1. Teenagers are not the ones buying the tickets to Broadway plays nor flying to London on theater tours. Therefore not many playwrights purposely set out to write plays that will appeal exclusively to a young adult audience.
2. Scripts are harder for teachers to obtain than are books of poetry, information, and fiction. A much smaller number of plays are published by mass market or school-oriented publishers. Occasionally a play will prove to be such good reading that it will be published in book form as was Ossie Davis' *Langston,* Joan Aiken's *Street,* and Paul Zindel's *The Effect of Gamma Rays on Man-in-the-Moon Marigolds,* but usually the plays that are published for general consumption are the classics that are used as college textbooks, for example, Pocket Book's *Four Tragedies,* which includes *Romeo and Juliet, Macbeth, Julius Caesar,* and

Hamlet, or they are collections of either excerpted scenes or short pl[a] as with Paul Kozelka's *Fifteen American One-Act Plays.* Teachers m[a] not want to buy whole collections when they only want students to re one play. And since those companies specializing in publishing scrip[do not advertise directly to schools, teachers may not realize that th[e can order reading scripts for about the same price as a quality paper back book. Teenagers miss out on the heritage of children's theater which encourages playwrights, producers, and actors to work with [drama. In even moderately sized communities there are usually co[r munity theater groups or college or university sponsored groups w[produce plays for children. Parents either bring their children or th[plays are brought directly to elementary or junior high schools. In[trast, high school students are more likely to select their own live e tainment of athletic events or musical performances. Of course ma[high school students attend school-produced plays, but the discou[r news on this front is that fewer schools can afford the time and the money to produce such plays, and an ever increasing percentage o[dents leave school early in the day because of part-time employme and so are unable to participate in drama as an extracurricular ac[

3. In 1939 when Dora V. Smith began the first adolescent literature for future teachers at the University of Minnesota, she excluded [from consideration, and as might be expected so did most of her dents who went forth to spread the word about adolescent literat[u

4. Neither English teachers nor librarians have been trained in dra[m They therefore are not likely to pick up plays for their own leisu[r reading and hence find it more comfortable to leave the whole m plays to the drama teacher.

5. Plays are written to be seen, not read. To translate words on a p into the imaginative experiences that the playwright had in mind quires a kind of active involvement that demands a great deal fr reader. Young people may not be ready to bring this much to th[reading and hence are not inclined to pick up plays for leisure t[

In spite of these factors—or maybe because of the last one—some are bringing plays into their English classrooms. For a feature in *Englis* (see "Our Readers Write," October 1984), we invited teachers to plays they had successfully used for classroom reading. That tw teachers responded surprised us. A further surprise was that fou[r suggested the same play, Reginald Rose's three-act television play *Tw Men.* It is the story of a jury making a decision on the future of a year-old boy who is charged with murdering his father. Three out [teachers made some comment to the effect that they and their stud tionately called the play "Twelve Angry People" since girls as well as assigned to read the parts. The following excerpts taken from th descriptions not only show why this particular play is successful i

A genre all of its own are the anthologies marketed for study in literature classes such as *The Signet Classic Book of American Short Stories* edited by Burton Raffel, *Great American Short Stories* edited by Wallace Stegner, and *Point of Departure* edited by Robert S. Gold. There are so many of these—we counted 47 in one distributor's catalog—that we can't evaluate them individually. The main differences are whether they are restricted to a specified time period, one particular author (Twain, Poe, London, Salinger, O. Henry, etc.), or to a particular theme.

Anthologies marketed to libraries for young people's independent reading are more apt to center around a theme, as in Charlotte Zolotow's *An Over-praised Season,* which gets its title from Samuel Butler's "Youth is like spring, an overpraised season." Under such a broad title, it was possible to include almost any story about youth, but her second collection *Early Sorrow: Ten Stories of Youth* was restricted to such painful experiences as the disillusionment of finding oneself unloved, the fear of growing up, the challenge of asserting one's independence, and the sadness of unwise behavior that cannot be relived. All of the stories were written for adults by such authors as E. L. Doctorow, Reynolds Price, John Updike, Kurt Vonnegut, Jessamyn West, James Purdy, and Harold Brodkey.

Other recent collections that have received starred reviews in either *Booklist* or *School Library Journal* include *The Oxford Book of English Ghost Stories,* edited by Michael Cox and R. A. Gilbert, and *Stories We Listened To,* outdoor survival stories from the Alaskan wilderness, edited by John Haines. Janni Howker is the British author of the five stories in *Badger on the Barge and Other Stories,* which feature teenagers undergoing periods of uncertainty and doubt but being helped by eccentric and elderly people that they befriend.

Other excellent authors who have written several stories to be published together include Cynthia Rylant with her book *Every Living Thing,* twelve stories in which human lives are changed through close dealings with animals, and for slightly younger readers, *Children of Christmas: Stories for the Season.* Joan Aiken has done several books of short stories including *A Whisper in the Night,* while Aidan Chambers has done *Out of Time* and *Shades of Dark.* Peter Cameron's *One Way or Another* includes fourteen stories, some humorous, about contemporary teenagers. Paul Fleischman's *Graven Images,* a Newbery Honor Book, features three early American stories centered around a carved sailor, a marble statue, and a weathervane. The four 1800 stories in his *Coming-And-Going Men* are tied together by the setting of New Canaan, Vermont, a town which leaves its mark on those traders and craftsmen who pass through.

Robert Westall wrote some wonderfully scary stories in *The Haunting of Chas McGill & Other Stories* and *Rachel & the Angel & Other Stories.* And as with other good writers who enjoy reading, he also edits collections (see his statement on page 166). While fantasy writer Robin McKinley was riding the Staten Island ferry and watching the skyline of New York disappear on the horizon, she got the inspiration for her collection of stories, *Imaginary Lands.* She went looking for stories which start with real-life settings but as the fantasy element in each story takes over the settings draw farther and farther away until they exist only in the realm of imagination.

Isaac Asimov with the help of others has edited *Young Monsters,* a collection of the macabre created by authors as varied as Ray Bradbury, Stephen King, and Jane Yolen. A *School Library Journal* reviewer wrote that "The editors have done a masterful job of arranging the stories to alleviate tension. For example, the grisly 'Disturb Not My Slumbering Fair' by Chelsea Quinn Yarbro, which features Diedre, a zombie who feasts on the dead ('It would be so good to sip the marrow from his bones, to nibble the butter-soft convolutions of his brain') is followed by Richard Parker's 'The Wheelbarrow Boy,' a humorous study of a teacher who changes an unruly student into a wheelbarrow—and then can't change him back."[10] Other titles in the series include *Young Ghosts, Young Extraterrestrials, Young Star Travelers,* and *Young Mutants.*

In conclusion, short stories are as varied in style and subject matter as are novels, and because of their brevity they are especially appealing to young readers. We are fortunate that today's publishers have recognized the appeal of short stories to teenagers and are marketing collections for independent reading as well as for class use.

DRAMA

In a 1984 *English Journal* article, Anthony L. Manna complained that for English teachers and librarians, drama was the "hidden genre." He examined several recent best-of-the-year lists compiled by such publications as *Booklist, School Library Journal,* and the *New York Times Book Review* and found only one play, Paul Zindel's *Let Me Hear You Whisper.* To prove that the exclusion wasn't because good drama isn't being written, he went on to recommend more than a dozen contemporary plays that would be excellent for reading in either junior or senior high school classrooms.[11]

In pondering Manna's point and trying to figure out why drama has been the "hidden genre" for young adults, we came up with the following reasons:

1. Teenagers are not the ones buying the tickets to Broadway plays nor flying to London on theater tours. Therefore not many playwrights purposely set out to write plays that will appeal exclusively to a young adult audience.

2. Scripts are harder for teachers to obtain than are books of poetry, information, and fiction. A much smaller number of plays are published by mass market or school-oriented publishers. Occasionally a play will prove to be such good reading that it will be published in book form as was Ossie Davis' *Langston,* Joan Aiken's *Street,* and Paul Zindel's *The Effect of Gamma Rays on Man-in-the-Moon Marigolds,* but usually the plays that are published for general consumption are the classics that are used as college textbooks, for example, Pocket Book's *Four Tragedies,* which includes *Romeo and Juliet, Macbeth, Julius Caesar,* and

Hamlet, or they are collections of either excerpted scenes or short plays as with Paul Kozelka's *Fifteen American One-Act Plays.* Teachers may not want to buy whole collections when they only want students to read one play. And since those companies specializing in publishing scripts do not advertise directly to schools, teachers may not realize that they can order reading scripts for about the same price as a quality paperback book. Teenagers miss out on the heritage of children's theater which encourages playwrights, producers, and actors to work with child drama. In even moderately sized communities there are usually community theater groups or college or university sponsored groups which produce plays for children. Parents either bring their children or the plays are brought directly to elementary or junior high schools. In contrast, high school students are more likely to select their own live entertainment of athletic events or musical performances. Of course many high school students attend school-produced plays, but the discouraging news on this front is that fewer schools can afford the time and the money to produce such plays, and an ever increasing percentage of students leave school early in the day because of part-time employment and so are unable to participate in drama as an extracurricular activity.

3. In 1939 when Dora V. Smith began the first adolescent literature class for future teachers at the University of Minnesota, she excluded drama from consideration, and as might be expected so did most of her students who went forth to spread the word about adolescent literature.

4. Neither English teachers nor librarians have been trained in drama. They therefore are not likely to pick up plays for their own leisure-time reading and hence find it more comfortable to leave the whole matter of plays to the drama teacher.

5. Plays are written to be seen, not read. To translate words on a page into the imaginative experiences that the playwright had in mind requires a kind of active involvement that demands a great deal from the reader. Young people may not be ready to bring this much to their reading and hence are not inclined to pick up plays for leisure time reading.

In spite of these factors—or maybe because of the last one—some teachers are bringing plays into their English classrooms. For a feature in *English Journal* (see "Our Readers Write," October 1984), we invited teachers to report on plays they had successfully used for classroom reading. That twenty-four teachers responded surprised us. A further surprise was that four of them suggested the same play, Reginald Rose's three-act television play *Twelve Angry Men.* It is the story of a jury making a decision on the future of a nineteen-year-old boy who is charged with murdering his father. Three out of the four teachers made some comment to the effect that they and their students affectionately called the play "Twelve Angry People" since girls as well as boys were assigned to read the parts. The following excerpts taken from the teachers' descriptions not only show why this particular play is successful in class but also can serve as guides when predicting the potential of other scripts for in-class reading.

- It calls for twelve continual parts, enough to satisfy all students who like to read aloud.
- It teaches practical lessons of value to students' lives.
- It may serve as a springboard for research and further discussion on how the judicial system works.
- It creates a forum for students to probe the psychology of group dynamics and peer behavior.
- It sparks student excitement from the beginning and sustains it throughout.
- It can be read in two-and-a-half class sessions.
- The "business" is minimal and can be easily carried out as students read from scripts.
- Pertinent questions can be asked when the jury recesses after Acts I and II.
- The setting is a hot, stuffy jury room—just like our classrooms in June.
- Students are attracted to the realism and they can relate to a motherless, slum youth of nineteen.
- The excellent characterization allows students to discover a kaleidoscope of lifelike personalities.

The influence of the mass media was seen in several teachers' explanations of why other plays worked in their classes. For example, one teacher explained that he goes back to the days of radio for Lucille Fletcher's *Sorry, Wrong Number*. Since "it was written to be heard and not seen, it is ideal for reading aloud." Another teacher said that because Gore Vidal's *Visit to a Small Planet* was written for television, "the action was easy to visualize and the stage directions were simple enough to discuss as an important aspect of the drama itself." Television writer Rod Serling's *A Storm in Summer* was recommended for the way it relates an encounter between a ten-year-old Harlem boy and a bitter, sarcastic, Jewish delicatessen owner in upstate New York.

Suggested plays from the more standard lists included Thornton Wilder's *Our Town,* to be taught along with Edgar Lee Masters' *Spoon River Anthology.* Robert Bolt's *A Man for All Seasons* was recommended for its portrayal of one of the most famous periods of English history and also for its exploration of a hero. Comparisons can be drawn to works treating heroes of noble birth as in *Antigone* and *Hamlet* and heroes of ordinary birth as in *Death of a Salesman* and *The Stranger.* Oliver Goldsmith's *She Stoops to Conquer* was recommended for seniors of average as well as superior ability levels. "Despite its eighteenth-century origins, the dialogue is surprisingly modern, with very few words needing explanation. . . . The characters are warm, human, and lovable; the humor, easygoing and readily accessible." Robinson Jeffers' translation of Euripedes' *Medea* was recommended as more accessible to average students than other Greek plays such as *Oedipus* and *Antigone.* Students readily understand jealousy and the desire for revenge. And the idea that Medea kills her children

repels yet intrigues them, but by the end of the play they develop understanding and sympathy for her. George Bernard Shaw's *Arms and the Man* may help students view the almost daily news accounts about war from a different slant. A lighter, more frivolous play that also helps students gain a new perspective is John Patrick's *The Teahouse of the August Moon,* which was recommended for the lighthearted way that it pokes fun at American customs and values.

Jerome Lawrence and Robert E. Lee's *Inherit the Wind,* which is based on the Scopes trial, was recommended because of its relevance to the current controversy over creationism versus evolution and also because the lines are easy to read aloud and there is enough balance between sharp wit and high drama "to allow would-be actors the chance to step out as much as they wish." William Gibson's *The Miracle Worker* was recommended not only for the poignancy of the story of Helen Keller and Annie Sullivan, but also for its illustration of such dramatic devices as flashbacks, foreshadowing, symbolism, and dramatic license—when compared to such biographies as Nella Braddy's *Anne Sullivan Macy* and Helen Keller's *The Story of My Life.*

Junior high students can understand the lesson of faith in William Saroyan's short play, *The Oyster and the Pearl.* It's a good one-day reading to use as a companion piece to Ring Lardner's short story "Haircut" or Moss Hart and George S. Kaufman's play *You Can't Take It With You. Pygmalion* was recommended as a "turn-on" for students in basic skills English classes who "have reading, writing, and sometimes attitude problems about school." They have empathy for Eliza Doolittle because "she speaks the same way they do, and, as one student commented, 'Eliza probably don't spell too hot, either!' " *The Diary of a Young Girl,* "a roller coaster of emotions," is appreciated because "Anne Frank is someone who has lived, who has shared her experiences, and who has described them *while* she was a teenager and knew most about them."

The plays mentioned above are only a sampling which show the variety of drama that is being read and studied in English classes. Probably the key point about these plays is that most of them wouldn't have been picked up for leisure-time reading. A teacher's encouragement was needed to help students make the conceptual leap from reading words on a page to seeing images on the stage in the mind.

New books that might make it easier to bring plays into classrooms include Wendy Lamb's *Meeting the Winter Bike Rider and Other Prize Winning Plays,* a collection of eight plays written by teenagers and performed off-Broadway at the Young Playwrights Festival. *The Actor's Book of Contemporary Stage Monologues* edited by Nina Shengold includes 150 monologues written by over 70 playwrights. For further recommendations of plays that are good for classroom reading, refer to Anthony Manna's article in the October 1984 *English Journal* "Curtains Up on Contemporary Plays." You might also write the Young Adult Services Division of the American Library Association, 50 E. Huron Street, Chicago, IL 60611 and ask for the most recent edition of *Outstanding Books for the College Bound.* It's a compilation of the brochures which the division used to publish under the categories of fiction, nonfiction, biography, theater, and other performing arts.

HUMOR

Rafael Sabatini began his finest novel, *Scaramouche,* with a one-sentence characterization of his hero, "He was born with a gift of laughter and a sense that the world was mad." The ability to laugh at ourselves and the madness of the world is nature's kindest, most needed, gift to a perpetually beleaguered humanity. The need seems even more desperate today, though probably every previous generation could have made the same claim, so we laugh at almost everything and anything. At a time when taxes and death and sex are serious matters indeed, they are the staples of humor. We laugh at taxes because they are plagues, and we must laugh at things that threaten us. We laugh at death because it is inevitable, and we must laugh at things that terrify us. We laugh at sex because it is an enigma, and we must laugh at things that bewilder us.

We are pleased when we find something, anything, to laugh at. We are even more pleased when we discover someone who consistently makes us laugh. As Steve Allen reminds us:

> Without laughter, life on our planet would be intolerable. So important is laughter to us that humanity highly rewards members of one of the most unusual professions on earth, those who make a living by inducing laughter in others. This is very strange if you stop to think of it; that otherwise sane and responsible citizens should devote their professional energies to causing others to make sharp, explosive barking-like exhalations.[12]

Given their enforced world of school and an ever-demanding society, young people need laughter every bit as much as adults, maybe even more so.

What do young people find funny? Lance M. Gentile and Merna M. McMillan's article, "Humor and the Reading Program," offers a starting point. Their stages of children's and young adult's interests in humor, somewhat supplemented, are:

- Ages 10–11: literal humor, slapstick (e.g., "The Three Stooges"), laughing at accidents (banana-peel humor) and misbehavior, sometimes mildly lewd jokes (usually called "dirty jokes"), and grossness.
- Ages 12–13: practical jokes, teasing, goofs, sarcasm, more lewd jokes, joke-riddles, sick jokes, elephant jokes, grape jokes, tongue-twisters, knock-knock jokes, moron jokes, TV blooper shows, and grossness piled upon grossness.
- Ages 14–15: more and more lewd jokes (some approaching a mature recognition of the humor inherent in sex), humor aimed at schools and parents and adults in authority, "Mork and Mindy" and their ilk, and grossness piled upon even greater grossness. Young adults may still prefer their own humor to their parents' humor but they are increasingly catching on to adult humor and may prefer it to their own.
- Ages 16–up: more subtle humor, satire and parody now acceptable and maybe even preferable, witticisms (rather than last year's half-witticisms

which they now detest in their younger brothers and sisters). Adult humor is increasingly part of their repertoire, partly because they are anxious to appear sophisticated, partly because they *are* growing up.[13]

During the summer of 1986 about sixty undergraduate and graduate students in an adolescent literature course at Arizona State University conducted an unscientific poll on what young adults found funny. Each student talked to two young adults and asked what made them laugh. The results were hardly surprising.

The most popular personalities were Eddie Murphy and Robin Williams, way out in front of anyone else though several youngsters liked Richard Pryor (mostly for his films a few years ago, nothing recent) and a few mentioned Chevy Chase, David Letterman, and Johnny Carson. The funniest TV show by far, mentioned by more than half the young adults, was the "Cosby Show," but there were enough mentions of "Family Ties" and reruns of "The Brady Bunch" to assume they were popular. "Star Trek" and "M*A*S*H" and Saturday morning cartoons were also mentioned more than once. Funny films were scattered across the sample, no film standing out as being popular and funny though *Down and Out in Beverly Hills, Beverly Hills Cop, Nightmare on Elm Street, The Breakfast Club, Back to the Future, Airplane,* and *Rambo* (?) were mentioned more than once. Comics went virtually unmentioned; one young man liked "Garfield," "Peanuts," "Wizard of Id," "B.C." and a young woman enjoyed "Family Circus." That was that.

These young adults seemed to consider books or literature generally outside the pale of humor. One boy mentioned *Huck Finn,* another *A Light in the Attic* and *Where the Sidewalk Ends,* but except for a mention of Judy Blume books written for young grade school students, that, again, was that. One student was quoted as saying when he was asked if he's ever read anything funny.

> Funny? I guess. If you consider M. E. Kerr or Richard Peck funny. But they're pretty grim also. I don't think books are very funny; they're usually about serious things. At least the books our teacher says are okay to read for our book reports.

Apparently, some teachers have forgotten what Charles B. Shaw said whimsically but yet seriously in 1923.

> In this present-day, topsy-turvy, all-too-mirthless world, smiles and chuckles are well worth broadcasting.[14]

Despite what must seem obvious truth to good teachers and librarians, that a sense of humor is essential for survival of educators and students, some deadly serious people wonder if this (or any other time, presumably) is the time for levity. The answer is, of course, yes—this is the time (and so is any other time).

Ellen Conford apparently ran into one of those humorless individuals at a librarians' meeting. During a question-answer session, Conford was asked if there was any subject she felt she couldn't treat humorously. She answered, "Cancer and abortion. Other than those two, I can make jokes about almost anything." Another person, a man, asked about the nuclear holocaust, specifically what was Conford doing about it.

> "Don't you think," he went on, "that it's your responsibility as a writer for young people to alert them about the dangers of the arms race?"
>
> "No!" I said, horrified.
>
> "But if their own authors don't tell them, who will?"
>
> "Dan Rather," I said. "Peter Jennings. Tom Brokaw. Any kid with ears already knows about the possibility of being incinerated in three seconds. And they know they have no power to do anything to save themselves. You want me to scare them some more?"
>
> *"Not me!"*[15]

Conford added that there are already talented YA authors who can treat the world seriously, but there are all too few who can make young people laugh. She's right.

Maybe English teachers assume that life is too serious to be treated any other way in school. They may assume that since there's next to no humor in literary anthologies, especially those used in secondary school, literature is too sacred for humor. That would have seemed odd to Mark Twain, who—an oversight?—is in American literature anthologies. Maybe the problem is that high school English teachers got their training in oh-so-serious-literature classes in college and those high school teachers don't know where to turn to for humor. The comic strips might be one place—Jeff McNelly's "Shoe" or Berke Breathed's "Bloom County" or Bill Watterson's "Calvin and Hobbes" are imaginative and often satiric and often extremely funny (if comics have to be justified, the insecure teacher could point out that McNelly won a Pulitzer Prize for editorial cartooning so he's not merely funny). Old-time radio, particularly the work of Paul Rhymer and "Vic and Sade," might be worth considering, especially when James Thurber thought Rhymer was a genius, but then so do Jean Shepherd and Ray Bradbury.

Anyone who has worked with young people knows how important humor is to them. Shel Silverstein's witty children's poetry that any age would love, Leonard Wibberley's genial satire, *The Mouse That Roared,* Joseph Heller's biting *Catch-22* and even wiser *God Knows,* Paula Danziger's YA novels, Dr. Seuss' *Horton Hatches the Egg,* and Sue Townsend's Adrian Mole books amuse people, though what will amuse whom is something teachers and librarians will need to discover. In this, and in some other important ways, young adults are the authorities.

Print material isn't all that's funny, and for many students, nonprint material may seem far more amusing. TV shows like "M*A*S*H" or "Happy Days" or "Facts of Life" may be the ultimate in humor. For others more sophisticated,

"Rocky and His Friends" or "Taxi" or "Cheers" may be the answers. And in films, some young people find humor in the *Porky* or *Police Academy* films while others will find pleasure in *The Gold Rush* or Laurel and Hardy films.

YA Novels and Humor

Librarians and teachers who have kept up-to-date with the best of YA fiction may wonder if much quality YA humor can be found. Certainly, few readers would associate humor with the compelling dramas of Robert Cormier, the historical novels of Rosemary Sutcliff or Scott O'Dell, the realism of Alice Childress, or the fantasies of Alan Garner. The high seriousness of these writers may have won them richly deserved applause by adult critics. Inadvertently, that may have cost them some young adult readers who prefer the light to the serious.

Few critics would place Paula Danziger's novels in the pantheon of YA fiction, yet Danziger is among the most popular writers for young adults. Her novels are, admittedly, loaded with puns and jokes and one-liners and visual humor, but they are far more than mere collections of laughs. *Can You Sue Your Parents for Malpractice?* and *The Divorce Express* remain favorites with junior high school students because they do not talk down to their readers and because they do not pretend that there are easy answers to any problems. Danziger's inability to develop characters, particularly adults, and her willingness to toss glib comments around as if they were profound, may annoy adults, but her humor is exactly what her readers want.

More successful by far for a slightly older audience is T. Ernesto Bethancourt's *The Dog Days of Arthur Cane.* Reduced to the simple plot of a young man who irritates an African student and is thereafter turned into a mongrel dog, the novel sounds simple-minded, but it is not. Arthur wakes up one morning, finds that he is a quite different self, and tries to resolve the immediate problems (and eventually must solve some long-range problems or die).

And he grows thirsty:

Thinking that a drink of water would help, I went back into the bathroom. I looked up at a sink that seemed ten feet high. I could see my glass up there, but no way to reach it. But being a good sized dog, I could get up on my hind legs and get my head into the sink. After falling down a few times, I got my front paws hooked over the edge of the sink and my hind feet braced. The only problem was that the water wasn't running, and I couldn't turn it on.

And later, still unsatisfied:

My thirst was worse now, if that was possible. And there was the john, with cool water in it. But I still couldn't bring myself to drink any.

And even later, even more unsatisfied:

> I won't lie to you about what I ended up doing. By the way, that blue stuff doesn't taste bad at all. Kind of like raunchy Kool-Aid.

And all this in the first chapter.

M. E. Kerr is consistently funny though all her novels are essentially serious studies of young people caught up in emotional quandaries. If Kerr looks wryly at her young characters, she never lacks compassion for them or her readers.

Dinky Hocker Shoots Smack, her first novel and the only one not told in first person, is filtered through the consciousness of fifteen-year-old library habitué Tucker Woolf, whose sketches remind his mother of a "depressing Bosch." In advertising for a home for his cat Nader (named after Ralph Nader), Tucker meets Dinky, whose mother suffers for the ills of the world and ignores Dinky; Dinky's cousin Natalia, who is emotionally troubled and talks in rhymes; and P. John Knight, whose left-wing father has made P. John become right wing with a vengeance. Kerr's humor in this book, as in later ones, does not arise from one-liners or obvious jokes but from the characters themselves. She does not write down to her readers, dropping references to Nader, Bosch, Dostoevsky, and the Bible, among others, in her books. She assumes young adults can think and feel and laugh.

Kerr's best and funniest book is *If I Love You, Am I Trapped Forever?* Alan Bennett, the narrator, lives in upstate New York with a grandfather and a mother deserted by Alan's father years before. Alan describes himself early in the book as "The most popular boy at Cayuta High. Very handsome. Very cool. Dynamite." His life and his love life with Leah are perfect in every way until Duncan Stein moves to town, and slowly Alan's life and world crumble. Whatever else Doomed (Alan's nickname for Duncan) is, he is untypical. No basketball, no school clubs, no going steady, nothing that makes him identifiable to Alan. But Doomed does gain notoriety with his underground newspaper, *Remote,* and creates a dating fad at Cayuta High—going steady is out and one-time-only dates become the in-thing.

Alan's puzzlement is obvious and understandable. Doomed plays by no rules Alan knows, nor is Doomed interested in Alan's friendship. When Alan and Doomed walk together from homeroom to English class, they have a short pointed conversation:

> We were studying Alfred, Lord Tennyson's poem "In Memoriam" that week. The poem was a tribute to his friend, Arthur Hallam, who died suddenly of influenza when he was just twenty-two.
>
> I said something to Doomed then about trying to make friends with him, and then I said, "Well, I guess we'll never be known as Tennyson and Hallam, will we, Stein?"
>
> Stein said, "Croak and find out, why don't you?"
>
> How hostile can you get?

M. E. KERR
on Cover Art

Sometimes I feel sick when a new paperback edition of one of my books arrives. This happened when Dell first published *Is That You Miss Blue?* There taking up the whole cover was a grim, gray-haired octogenarian in black, sitting in an armchair reading the Bible. Never mind that Miss Blue was supposed to be only around forty; what made the artist think this picture would appeal to kids? I wrote letter after letter to Dell asking them to change the cover, but they never would. When the term was up on the book and Harper & Row took it over for their Key-point series, I was shocked to see the very same apparition in black on the new cover, surrounded by young men and women straight out of the 1950s.

If there is a reading problem today, I sometimes think the covers on paperbacks are contributing to it. Here we have a generation of kids, who grew up with dazzling and sophisticated visual concepts on shows like "Sesame Street," still being treated to exciting and innovative art on MTV, on record cov-

ers, in fashion ads, in movies, etcetera, and they are expected to grab for paperbacks with artwork still in the time tunnel of ten and twenty years ago. No preceding generation has ever been so visually oriented, yet publishers dismiss cover art as a primary factor in sales.

It is the greatest arrogance, to my way of thinking, to merchandise with no studied concern about the package. No product is that unexpendable. Nothing written inside a book can withstand an outside that is dull, unimaginative, unattractive, and unprovocative.

Few readers of *Seventeen* are probably seventeen—they're twelve and thirteen, reading for information about the best they can become and addressing problems seventeen-year-olds have already solved. The YA audience, too, has little interest in these cartoon renditions of ditzy-looking kids their own age (or, on the other extreme of octogenarians in black). But put attractive kids in their late teens on the cover of a YA book, suggest some tension, have the title in legible script, bother to make the ambience fetching, and with luck you'll have a winning cover, such as Harper & Row's Keypoint edition of *Night Kites.*

If authors are bright enough to know what kids like to read, why should they leave it up to the publisher to decide how their "babies" should be dressed? The cover is too important to the sale of the book for the author to be left out of this part of the decision-making in the partnership. Paperback publishers need input and we authors have to insist on the right to okay how they're going to present us to our readers.

M. E. Kerr's books include *Dinky Hocker Shoots Smack!* Harper & Row, 1972; *Gentlehands*, Harper & Row, 1978; *Me, Me, Me, Me, Me, Not A Novel*, Harper & Row, 1983; and *Night Kites*, Harper & Row, 1987.

Even if Kerr's later books have not lived up to the promise of her first two, they are all enjoyable.

The funniest American YA novel and one of the finest parodies of Poe's style is Robert Kaplow's *Alex Icicle: A Romance in Ten Torrid Chapters.* Alex adores Amy who quietly hardly knows that Alex exists. He endures, beating his breast against the imagined slights of the world and he matures, slightly.

The funniest YA novels are two English imports, Sue Townsend's *The Secret Diary of Adrian Mole, Aged 13 3/4* and *The Growing Pains of Adrian Mole.* Both are about young Adrian who tells his diary of the horrors of growing up in a family where the mother does not love the father, where no one (especially the BBC) fully appreciates the value of his sensitive writings, where his beloved Pandora does not long for his caresses as much as Adrian longs to caress her, and where things almost never go right and almost always go wrong.

Townsend understands Adrian and young people generally. Adrian often sounds naive, sometimes he sounds foolish, but he is never ridiculed, though he may look ridiculous, sometimes even in his own eyes. Adrian tells all—or what he thinks is all—in his diary, but he has almost no objectivity about his world and often the readers can be far more objective about Adrian's life and world. Above all, Adrian is honest. He does not lie to himself or us, the readers of his diary. He may be misguided or dead wrong or hopelessly unaware of adult duplicities at times but his honesty is fixed and admirable. Late in *The Secret Diary* Adrian's form (school class) is preparing for a trip to the British Museum.

> Wednesday, September 16th—Our form is going to the British Museum on Friday. Pandora and I are going to sit together on the coach. She is bringing her *Guardian* from home so that we can have some privacy.
>
> Thursday, September 17th—Had a lecture on the British Museum from Ms. Fosington-Gore. She said it was a "fascinating treasure house of personkind's achievements." Nobody listened to the lecture. Everyone was watching the way she felt her left breast whenever she got excited.

Others do not always understand or appreciate Adrian's wish to crowd in all of life's experiences into a few months. When Adrian asks Pandora to show him one of her nipples, she writes him this letter:

> Adrian
> I am writing to terminate our relationship. Our love was once a spiritual thing. We were united in our appreciation of art and literature, but Adrian you have changed. You have become morbidly fixated with my body. Your request to look at my left nipple last night finally convinced me that we must part.
>
> Do not contact me.
>
> Pandora Braithwaite
> P.S. If I were you I would seek professional psychiatric help for your hypochondria and your sex mania. Anthony Perkins, who played the maniac in *Psycho,* was in analysis for ten years, so there is no need to be ashamed.

Later, we see Adrian at his most incisive.

> My mother has decided that sugar is the cause of all the evil in the world, and has banned it from the house.
> She smoked two cigarettes while she informed me of her decision.

Richard Peck's *The Ghost Belonged to Me* and other novels about Blossom Culp and ghosts and funny things that may go bump in the night are all fine as is Benjamin Lee's *It Can't Be Helped,* a delightful English novel about an inept but charming young would-be radical.

Humor and Poetry

Too many young adults, hardly enamored of poetry to begin with, assume that poetry and humor are mutually exclusive terms. Librarians and teachers can, of course, remind youngsters of the joys of the poetry in Lewis Carroll's *Alice in Wonderland* and *Through the Looking Glass,* remembering all the time that virtually all these poems are parodies of poetry doomed to nonexistence through the success of Carroll's work, or of the wonderful wit available by reading Gilbert and Sullivan's *The Pirates of Penzance* or *The Mikado* or *Iolanthe,* but the fun of reading Carroll or Gilbert and Sullivan are largely reserved for adults. Ernest Lawrence Thayer's "Casey at the Bat" and much of Ogden Nash will remain unfunny to many young adults.

Far funnier is Don Marquis' *archy and mehitabel.* Marquis' archy is a gigantic cockroach with guts, a born writer who had a desperate drive to write. He approached the typewriter and then:

> . . . would climb painfully upon the framework of the machine and cast himself with all his force upon a key, head downward, and his weight and the impact of the blow were just sufficient to operate the machine, one slow letter after another. He could not work the capital letters, and he had a great deal of difficulty operating the mechanism that shifts the paper so that a fresh line may be started. We never saw a cockroach work so hard or perspire so freely in all our lives before. After about an hour of this frightfully difficult literary labor he fell to the floor exhausted, and we saw him creep feebly into a nest of the poems which are always there in profusion.

So Marquis discovers archy's first literary effort, and he follows with other poems, all of them funny, though they are well over fifty years old: "the song of mehitabel," "the cockroach who had been to hell," "aesop revised by archy," "pete the parrot and shakespeare," and "freddy the rat perished."

Dutch poet and wit Piet Hein calls his poetry *grooks,*[16] aphoristic verses accompanied by simple line drawings. Two grooks from his first collection illustrate the form:

Living is
  a thing you do
now or never—
  which do you?

Man's a kind
  of Missing Link,
fondly thinking
  he can think.

Other grooks are widely quoted by fans, and there are many:

To make a name for learning
when other roads are barred,
take something very easy
and make it very hard.

Wisdom is
the booby prize
given when you've been unwise.

Those who always
know what's best
are
a universal pest.

Limericks, often assumed to be the funniest of poems and rarely so, can be found in abundance in Ray Allen Billington's *Limericks Historical and Hysterical, Plagiarized, Arranged, Annotated, and Some Written by Ray Allen Billington.* The collection is excellent and, surprisingly enough, often funny and sometimes even witty, but teachers and librarians are warned that the limericks are often bawdy and coarse and, of course, delightful.

Gentle, Almost Nostalgic Humor

In the last fifteen years, several books of humor have appeared that are mildly mocking but clearly do not mean to hurt anyone, unless it is the authors as they reminisce on their ill-spent youth. Librarians and teachers will recognize that the type derives from Stephen Leacock, as in "My Financial Career," and Paul Rhymer who wrote so many warm and funny scripts for "Vic and Sade."

Garrison Keillor's "A Prairie Home Companion" on National Public Radio is consistently funny and warm about the people in the fictitious town of Lake Wobegon, Minnesota. The advertisements are amusing (Ralph's Pretty Good Grocery store and Powdermilk Biscuits, "made from the whole wheat that gives shy persons the strength to do what needs to be done") and Keillor's quiet charm make Lake Wobegon ("the town that time forgot and the decades cannot improve") come alive.

Keillor's humor comes across in the pages of *Happy To Be Here,* especially in a brief plea, "Shy Rights: Why Not Pretty Soon," which gently spoofs the noisier arguments advanced by other minority groups for their rights.

Better known, and for some young adults one of their peak reading experiences, is the work of Jean Shepherd. While Shepherd enthusiasts are fond of *In God We Trust, All Others Pay Cash, A Fistful of Fig Newtons,* and *The Ferrari in the Bedroom,* most readers agree that his funniest book is *Wanda Hickey's Night of Golden Memories and Other Disasters.*

Shepherd is clearly fond of his characters. While he certainly uncovers some of life's absurdities, there is no bitterness in his work. Shepherd relishes the golden memories, slightly painful and slightly exaggerated, of his own youth and his own youthful dreams.

The title story in *Wanda Hickey's Night . . .* begins as Shepherd remembers back on his junior prom, renting a white jacket formal, polishing up the old Ford V-8 convertible, and vainly pushing himself to ask Daphne Bigelow for the big date. ("Each time, I broke out in a fevered sweat and chickened out at the last instant.") In desperation, he asks the ever-present, ever-available Wanda Hickey to double-date with a friend.

Off to the Cherrywood Country Club to dance to Mickey Isley and his Magic Music Makers, our hero discovers that he soon develops a bad case of the sweats which soon leads to an even worse case of rash. Outside and ready for the big drink at the Red Rooster Roadhouse, he discovers that he has left the convertible top down and rain has poured, and the foursome, miserable and wet, drive off.

But the roadhouse proves no oasis of sanity. Proving his masculinity and sophistication, he orders triple shots of bourbon on the rocks and drinks up:

> Down it went—a screaming 90 proof rocket searing savagely down my gullet. For an instant, I sat stunned, unable to comprehend what had happened. Eyes watering copiously, I had the brief urge to sneeze, but my throat seemed to be paralyzed.

All during this, Wanda coos into his ear, "Isn't this romantic? Isn't this the most wonderful night in all our lives?"

Our hero, sure that the liquor had done its worst, proceeds to eat a meal of lamb chops, turnips, mashed potatoes, cole slaw, and strawberry shortcake, almost immediately followed by a trip to the restroom where he sees his meal a second time. Later he takes Wanda home, but he cannot bring himself to kiss her when he smells sauerkraut on her breath. He returns home to a sardonic, if mildly sympathetic, father who reassures his son that his head will "stop banging" in a couple of days, and an exhausted and strangely satisfied young man falls into bed.

Nora Ephron's *Crazy Salad* is stronger fare than either Keillor's or Shepherd's book, but many young women will laugh as they read "A Few Words about Breasts" and "On Never Having Been a Prom Queen."

Some Gentle Satires

One of the more widely used handbooks of literature opens its definition of satire this way:

> A literary manner which blends a critical attitude with humor and wit to the end that human institutions of humanity itself may be improved. The true satirist is conscious of the frailty of institutions of man's devising and attempts through laughter not so much to tear them down as to inspire a remodeling.[17]

Some teachers and librarians assume that satire must be vicious or biting in tone and content, but some effective satires are gentle, even loving.

Jean Merrill's *The Pushcart War* is a classic among children's and young adult books, a gentle and most effective satire of war and human cupidity. Supposedly written in 1996, ten years after the end of the brief "Pushcart War," the novel is presented as straight, factual history, allowing the reader to see the humor and nobility and nastiness of humans as the war unfolds. The war begins as a truckdriver drives over and demolishes a pushcart while the pushcart owner is propelled into a pickle barrel. Soon the pushcart owners band together to fight back and the war is on. Noble figures like General Anna (formerly Old Anna), Maxie Hammerman, Morris the Florist, and Frank the Flower walk across history as do bad guys like Albert P. Mack (usually known as Mack, the truckdriver), Big Moe, Louis Livergreen, and Mayor Emmett P. Cudd. *The Pushcart War* is funny and wise and learned and utterly delightful for almost any reader, young adult or adult.

More Sophisticated Satire

Several writers, all of whom have written for the *New Yorker,* offer young adults the chance to sample somewhat more sophisticated, though still reasonably gentle, satire.

James Thurber's gentleness may be more apparent then real, but many of his short sketches and short stories have proved popular to the young. Nostalgic pieces like "The Night the Bed Fell" and "University Days" are accessible to young people, and "Fables for Our Time," especially "The Shrike and the Chipmunk," "The Owl Who Thought He Was God," and "The Unicorn in the Garden," are popular with many teenagers. His rewriting of history, "If Grant Had Been Drinking at Appomattox," is funny *if* readers know history just as "The Macbeth Murder Mystery" is funny *if* readers know the play. Thurber's three best short stories are, unhappily, often beyond the emotional understanding of young adults, but if readers can handle them, "The Secret Life of Walter Mitty," "The Catbird Seat," and "The Greatest Man in the World" are among the finest, most sophisticated, and least gentle satires.

E. B. White is far more gentle and likeable than Thurber, although his adult material has less immediate appeal to the young. *The Second Tree from the Corner* is, simply put, one of the great works in American literature and why it goes largely unknown among so many teachers and librarians is one of life's great mysteries. White's poetry in that book is clever and amusing, especially "The Red Cow Is Dead" and "Song of the Queen Bee," and "The Retort Transcendental" is a wonderful parody of Thoreau taken too far. The finest short stories are "The Decline of Sport," a relatively funny satire on the inevitable decline in sports, and "The Morning of the Day They Did It," a less than amusing satire on the end of the world.

Two wonderfully witty men are probably doomed never to have wide appeal to young people, though some adults revere them and their work. Frank Sullivan's wit is most apparent in *The Night the Old Nostalgia Burned Down,* a collection of columns, largely from the *New Yorker,* about the Cliché Expert who appears as a witness at court trials and spouts clichés of every profession. A bit more accessible and less dated is the sketch on "Dr. Arbuthnot's Academy" where people come to see if clichés are literally possible (a woman learns to tickle people pink, others learn how to rub people the wrong way, a woman in a kettle on a stove learns how to stew in her own juice, and an accountant learns how to add insult to injury). S. J. Perelman was once a writer for the Marx Brothers, and titles for several of his sketches in *The Most of S. J. Perelman* and *The Last Laugh* suggest the wackiness of Marx Brothers comedies: "Waiting for Santy," "Farewell, My Lovely Appetizer," "Rancors Aweigh," and "To Yearn Is Subhuman, to Forestall Divine." Young people fascinated by comic wordplay will love Perelman. Others are hereby warned.

Woody Allen is a favorite of young people, though many probably have trouble following his verbal play. His movies, especially *Annie Hall* and *Take the Money and Run,* are filled with wackiness and wisdom, more often than not strangely mixed, but Allen's books are far wittier and have far better one-liners than his films. *Getting Even* is typical Allen wit which assumes readers will know Freud and the Hasidic Jews and what college catalogues read like and more. *Without Feathers* and *Side Effects* assumes intelligent and sophisticated readers. Allen is fascinated by God and death, and his books have wisdom and some wacky wit about both.

Black Humor and Satire

So-called Black Humor uses irony and fantasy to ridicule the absurdities and bleakness of the human situation. Often savagely satirical, Black Humor virtually forces readers to laugh at the despair they feel when they are confronted by war, bureaucracies, social control, obsessive love—and obsessiveness generally—illogical political talk and propaganda, television, advertising, *the* bomb, and psychiatrists. If Black Humor has an obvious weakness, which goes largely happily ignored by most readers, it is an obsession with the theme which arises out of situations to illustrate the theme, rather than the more traditional method of beginning with a human situation involving believable characters and letting theme emerge.

Of the many writers plowing this field, two have proved popular with young people who enjoy iconoclastic literature. Ken Kesey's *One Flew Over the Cuckoo's Nest* concerns Randal Patrick McMurphy's confinement to a mental hospital because he refuses to knuckle under to authority. He changes the lives of and brings hope to other patients despite the attempts of Nurse Ratchet to bring peace and conformity to the ward.

Perhaps even more popular is Joseph Heller's savage attack on war and wartime stupidity in *Catch-22*. Captain John Yossarian, bombardier in the 25th squadron based on a Mediterranean island near the end of World War II, wants no part of any more missions. He believes that if he can convince everyone that he is crazy, he will be freed of all combat duty. But Doc Daneeka points out a catch:

> "You mean there's a catch?"
> "Sure there's a catch," Doc Daneeka replied. "Catch-22. Anyone who wants to get out of combat duty isn't really crazy."
> There was only one catch and that was Catch-22, which specified that a concern for one's own safety in the face of dangers that were real and immediate was the process of a rational mind. Orr was crazy and could be grounded. All he had to do was ask; and as soon as he did, he would no longer be crazy and would have to fly more missions. Orr would be crazy to fly more missions and sane if he didn't but if he was sane he had to fly them. If he flew them he was crazy and didn't have to; but if he didn't want to he was sane and had to. Yossarian was moved very deeply by the absolute simplicity of this clause of Catch-22 and let out a respectful whistle.
> "That's some catch, that Catch-22," he observed.
> "It's the best there is," Doc Daneeka agreed.

Heller's novel preceded the Vietnam War and the peace movement by several years, but because the book so perfectly pointed out the absurdity of a pointless war, *Catch-22* became something of a rallying point for protesters, just as it still rallies those who wonder about the military mind and bureaucracies gone mad in wartime.

Parodies

Because parody assumes readers' awareness of the work being satirized, gently or otherwise, some teachers and librarians conclude that young adults would find parody difficult if not impossible. That may be true for the more esoteric sort of parody, usually of poetry, to be found in anthologies of parody, but some parodies are not merely within the grasp of young people, they are works young people would very much enjoy.

Two young adult novels are excellent parodies, although whether they will be read as parodies (or in the case of the first book, read at all) is uncertain. John Rowe Townsend's *Kate and the Revolution* is set in the fictitious country of Essenheim. Heroine Kate and George, an English reporter, become entangled in a palace coup to overthrow Rudi, Crown Prince of Essenheim. Other characters in the Graustarkian tale of intrigue and derring-do are Dr. Stockhausen, a reactionary, Herman Schweiner, leader of the first coup, and Konrad Finken, leader of the second coup. When Kate and George visit Essenheim's national university, they find strange things going on as they talk to Klaus Klappdorf, Dean of the Faculty of Arts, Sciences, and Other Studies:

> A clutch of young people in dirty jeans, most with uncombed hair, emerged from a doorway they were passing. Beside the doorway was a placard that read PASSIVE RESISTANCE 102.
>
> "Is passive resistance taught as a course for credit?" asked George, startled.
>
> "To be sure!" Klaus replied happily. "As you may know, this university was founded only twelve years ago, when Herr Finkel decided that pickles were no longer a profitable business. When the university opened, we felt that we ought to have our own specialty, something this university could become known for. Something that wasn't done elsewhere. And we hit upon Studentship Studies."
>
> George looked up at Klaus with a dubious expression. Klaus, unaware of it, went on. "The young people who come to the University of Essenheim are students for four of the most formative years of their lives. What ought they be studying? The answer is obvious, isn't it? They should be studying the thing that most concerns them, namely being a student. So"—he cleared his throat—"so we have established Studentship Studies, in the context of the interpersonal and transsocietal relationship structure that we seek to encourage through a meaningful, ongoing dialogue between the new generation and the world that surrounds it. The world of today."

Judie Angell's *Suds: A New Daytime Drama Brought to You* features Sue Sudley, orphaned when her parents, flying in separate planes, collided in mid-air. She comes to live with her aunt and uncle in Pallantine, Ohio. Readers who wonder about the likelihood of such a strange airplane accident will wonder even more as they meet the cast of stereotypes straight out of soap-operaland. Sue meets Storm Ryder, former football star but now paralyzed in a wheelchair; Dinah Deenie, video junkie; Joe Coffee, English teacher at Pallantine High and frustrated novelist; Joanna Coffee, Joe's wife and schoolbus driver and soon-to-be amnesia victim; Roger Gurney, Jr., Pallantine High's school newspaper editor; and assorted other dingalings. Sue saves the soul and cash of Dinah Deenie. And Sue prays that Storm will recover from his bout with paralysis, and he does. Near the end of the book as Sue has wrapped up most of the problems of the town and the universe, Storm has an accident. Dr. Proctor comes out of the hospital room:

■ "It's going to be all right," Dr. Proctor said. He was smiling faintly. "He's recovered consciousness and—"

"And what," Will Ryder said, almost whispering.

"And his left foot—*twitched.*"

Anyone who watches soap operas—and that covers a major portion of young adults—and can still see the silliness in much of what passes for soap opera drama should love this book. So should adults.

Equally funny are two books about Miss Piggy. Jim Henson's *Miss Piggy's Guide to Life* is 113 pages of undiluted wisdom. Miss Piggy's eclectic diet (choose carefully from each diet whatever goodies are there and ignore the rest) and her advice to the lovelorn are particularly good. Asked what a woman should do if the man still wishes to see other women, Miss Piggy sensibly replies that she would "calmly, reasonably, and maturely explain to him that if he values his life, he should change his behavior." Henry Beard's *Miss Piggy's Treasury of Art Masterpieces from the Kermitage Collection* will likely appeal to fewer readers, but Muppet fans are insatiable.

Douglas Adams' quartet, *The Hitchhiker's Guide to the Galaxy, The Restaurant at the End of the Universe, Life, The Universe, and Everything,* and *So Long, and Thanks for All the Fish,* began as BBC radio scripts, progressed to television scripts, and ultimately became highly successful novels. The first, far and away the best of the lot, begins as Arthur Dent's house is due for demolishment to make way for a highway. He finds Ford Prefect, a somewhat strange friend and an apparently out-of-work actor, anxiously seeking a drink at a nearby pub. Ford seems hopelessly indifferent to Arthur's plight, mostly, as Ford tells Arthur, because the world will be destroyed in a few minutes to make way for a new galactic freeway. Soon, the pair are safe aboard a Vogon Construction Fleet Battleship only to find danger awaiting as the Vogon Commander of the ship orders them tossed out into space. Death appears likely, but they are picked up by a ship powered by Infinite Improbability Drive piloted by Zaphod Bettlebrox, a two-headed and three-armed ex-president of the Galaxy.

Improbabilities arise out of more improbabilities, but by this time, readers are caught up in the wild, and utterly unbelievable, adventures and the wildness of the tale and the characters, and the improbabilities are less important than the sheer enjoyment and humor of Adams' novel. In what other book, recent or old, can readers learn that the answer "to life, the universe, and everything" is "forty-two."

Readers who have wondered about the apparent superhuman efforts of scientists to unravel the secrets of everything and anything will find David Macaulay's *Motel of the Mysteries* a wonderful spoof of scientific arrogance unmasked as wild guessing games. The book begins with the ominous description of the burial of the North American continent under tons of third- and fourth-class mail (caused by an accidental reduction in postal rates). Since 3850, scholars have wondered about the lost civilization, but it is left to forty-

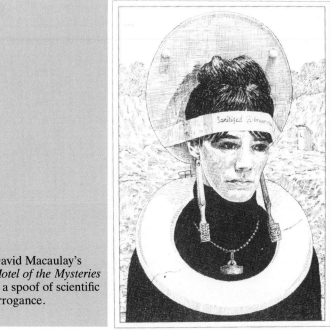

David Macaulay's
Motel of the Mysteries
is a spoof of scientific
arrogance.

two-year old Howard Carson to stumble and fall into a secret chamber. There he discovers "a gleaming secret seal" (DO NOT DISTURB) and "a plant that would not die." He enters the chamber and finds a body atop a "ceremonial platform" near a statue of the "deity WATT" and a container, "ICE," designed to "preserve, at least symbolically, the major internal organs of the deceased for eternity." Later he enters the inner chamber and there finds another body "in a highly polished white sarcophagus" behind translucent curtains. Near this body is a "sacred urn" and a "sacred parchment" holder and the "sacred collar" with a headband bearing a ceremonial chant, "Sanitized for Your Protection."

Macaulay's spoof should have wide appeal, and his drawings of Howard Carson playing savant and the many artifacts recovered from the two chambers add to the fun. Adults who have been to museums will particularly enjoy the concluding section of the book devoted to "Souvenirs and Quality Reproductions" from the Carson excavations now for sale.

The Humor of Death

Of all catastrophes, death is perhaps most feared. Perhaps for that reason, death is often the subject of humor. Charles Addams' macabre cartoons in the *New Yorker* have always been popular, and discovering humorous epitaphs on gravestones is almost an American industry. Fritz Spiegl's *A Small Book of Grave Humor*[18] has several examples that are funny to many readers and at least strange to those few who cannot regard anything about death as amusing:

HERE LIES	*HERE LIES*
Poor Charlotte	*Lester Moore*
Who dies no harlot—	*Four slugs*
But in her Virginity	*From a 44*
Of the age of nineteen	*No Les*
In this vicinity	*No More*
Rare to be found	
or seen	

Humor about death goes back to the Greeks. In the mammoth collection of odds-and-ends verses called *The Greek Anthology*[19] can be found tributes to fallen heroes and conventional poems and some that seem strikingly unconventional. Dudley Fitts translates them in the following manner. A few are bitter:

"Epitaph of Dionysius of Tarsos"
At Sixty I, Dionysius of Tarsos, lie here,
Never having married:
*   And I wish my father had not.*

A few are satiric and amusing to us if not the object of scorn.

"On Marcus the Physician"
Yesterday Dr. Marcus went to see a statue of Zeus.
Though Zeus,
*   and though marble,*
We're burying the statue today.

"On Envious Diophon"
Diophon was crucified:
But seeing beside him another on a loftier cross,
He died of envy.

Mark Twain makes great fun of bad poetry about death in *Adventures of Huckleberry Finn,* and he may have been inspired by Julia Moore, "The Sweet Singer of Michigan," who never lost an opportunity to write about the dead and the bereaved. Granted that she wrote in dead seriousness, her poetry can now be read only as amusing, or odd, verse. One of her major works concerned a little girl named Libbie:

One morning in April, a short time ago,
*   Libbie was alive and gay;*
Her Savior called her, she had to go,
*   Ere the close of that pleasant day,*

While eating dinner, this dear little child
    Was choked on a piece of beef.
Doctors came, tried their skill awhile,
    But none could give relief.

A contemporary of Julia Moore, Howard Heber Clark, who tilled the same poetic field, possibly helped to kill obituary verse with this tribute to little Willie:

Willie had a purple monkey climbing on a yellow stick,
And when he sucked the paint all off it made him deathly sick,
And in his latest hours he clasped that monkey in his hand,
And bade good-bye to earth and went into a better land.

Oh! no more he'll shoot his sister with his little wooden gun;
And no more he'll twist the pussy's tail and make her yowl, for fun.
The pussy's tail now stands out straight; the gun is laid aside;
The monkey doesn't jump around since little Willie died.[20]

If Clark's little Willie was presumably not meant for our laughter, a series of poems about another little Willie deliberately provoked laughter. Harry Graham, an English soldier in the Coldstream Guard who wrote under the penname Col. D. Streamer, produced an enduring and much quoted masterpiece in 1902 with his *Ruthless Rhymes for Heartless Homes*[21] with poems like these:

Billy, in one of his nice, new sashes,
Fell in the fire and was burned to ashes.
Now, although the room grows chilly,
I haven't the heart to poke poor Billy.

Making toast at the fireside,
Nurse fell in the grate and died;
And what makes it ten times worse,
All the toast was burnt with nurse.

Father heard his children scream,
So he threw them in the stream,
Saying, as he drowned the third,
"Children should be seen, not heard."

So popular were these sadistic poems that papers printed new catastrophes by imitators, most—but not all—about Little Willie and his latest nastiness, and the form of poetry became known as "Little Willie" poems.[22] A few of the most popular imitations were these:

Willie poisoned Auntie's tea.
Auntie died in agony.
Uncle came and looked quite vexed.
"Really, Will," he said, "what next?"

Willie fell down the elevator—
Wasn't found till six days later.
Then the neighbors sniffed, "Gee Whiz!
What a spoiled child Willie is."

Dr. Jones fell in the well,
And died with a moan.
He should have tended to the sick
And left the well alone.

Little Willie, mean as hell,
Drowned his sister in the well.
Mother said, while drawing water,
"Gee, it's hard to raise a daughter."

In 1944, an article by Dorothy Wynn Downes asked, "Do You Remember Little Willie?" in the *Saturday Review of Literature*. Downes' many examples sparked something of a "Little Willie" revival and the magazine's "Letters to the Editor" section for weeks was full of more examples. A brief updating of these poems followed Dorothy Rickard's "The Further Adventures of Little Willie" in the *Saturday Review* in 1952.[23] There's apparently still a lot of life in "Little Willie."

The classic satiric novel about death is, of course, Evelyn Waugh's *The Loved One,* a delightfully nasty assault on American tastes in general and our death customs particularly. Dennis Barlow, English expatriate, failed poet, and now a Hollywood hanger-on, must arrange the funeral of an old friend. Dennis goes to Whispering Glades to see about arrangements and there meets cosmetician Aimee Thanatogenous and funeral person Mr. Joyboy, the man who puts smiles on the faces of all the "loved ones."

The Ultimate in Humor

For some young adults, and for far more adults, the finest of all humorists was and still is P. G. Wodehouse. This English writer of nearly one hundred novels created a fantasy world permanently locked somewhere vaguely in the 1920s and 1930s and featuring some highly unbelievable characters. But other writers as different politically and socially as Evelyn Waugh and George Orwell and Rudyard Kipling ardently admired Wodehouse and thought him a genius. So he is.

Wodehouse's best-known creations are the feeble-brain Bertie Wooster and his brilliant and snobbish butler, Jeeves. Readers who begin with some of the Jeeves short stories in *Very Good, Jeeves* (especially "Jeeves and the Song of Songs," "The Love That Purifies," and "Jeeves and the Impending Doom") or *Carry On, Jeeves* (particularly "Without the Option," "Jeeves and the Hard-Boiled Egg," and "Jeeves Takes Charge") may be puzzled by the comic opera world they find, but they will discover wit and charm and fun in abundance.

Readers may then be prepared to move on to the Jeeves novels, for example, *The Inimitable Jeeves, The Mating Season, Jeeves and the Feudal Spirit, Stiff Upper Lip, Jeeves,* and *Much Obliged, Jeeves.*

Wodehouse enthusiasts may differ on the stories or novels they consider the funniest (some would vote for "Mulliner's Buck-U-Uppo" in *Meet Mr. Mulliner* while others would argue for "Uncle Fred Flits By" in *Young Men in Spats*), but almost anyone who has sampled Wodehouse will stay for other items on the menu.

The range of humor available to young adults is incredible. Mockery, hero-ism, naivete, cynicism, stupidity, cruelty, mayhem, death, the quest, madness, nastiness, sexuality, insults, viciousness, innocence, tears, the macabre, bitter-ness, and laughter, laughter, laughter in abundance are easily found to meet the tastes of any reader. There is almost nothing we cannot and will not laugh at. Librarians and teachers who wonder if any humor for young adults deserves their attention need only read works as different as Dr. Seuss' *Horton Hatches the Egg,* Douglas Adams' *The Hitchhiker's Guide to the Galaxy,* Robert Kap-low's *Alex Icicle: A Romance in Ten Torrid Chapters,* David Macaulay's *Motel of the Mysteries,* Sue Townsend's Adrian Mole masterworks, C. S. Lewis' *The Screwtape Letters,* Morris Udall's *Too Funny To Be President,* "Little Willie" poems, or anything—anything at all—by P. G. Wodehouse to know better.

NOTES

[1] Paul Janeczko, "Facets: Successful Authors Talk about Connections between Teaching and Writing," *English Journal* 73 (November 1984: 25.

[2] "Separation" by W. S. Merwin, from *The Moving Target* by W. S. Merwin (New York: Atheneum, 1963).

[3] Richard F. Abrahamson, "Books for Adolescents: Of Poetry and Teenagers: An Interview with Poetry Anthologist Paul Janeczko," *Journal of Reading* 30 (March 1987): 562–66.

[4] Stanley Kunitz in *Poetspeak: In Their Work, About Their Work,* edited by Paul B. Janeczko (New York: Bradbury Press, 1983), p. 74.

[5] Kathleen Whalin, "Review of *Under All Silences: Shades of Love,*" *School Library Journal* 34 (October 1987): 144.

[6] Don Mainprize, "Ouchless Poetry," *English Journal* 71 (February 1982): 31–33.

[7] Alberta Turner, "Teaching Poetry Writing in Secondary School," *English Journal* (September 1982): 53–56.

[8] Jesse Hise, "Writing Poetry: More Than a Frill," *English Journal* 69 (November 1980): 19–22.

[9] Richard F. Abrahamson and Kylene Beers, "Books for Adolescents: From Short Stories to Social Activism," *Journal of Reading* 31 (January 1988): 386–90.

[10] Carolyn Gabbard Fugate, "Review of *Young Monsters,*" *School Library Journal* 31 (May 1985): 98.

[11] Anthony L. Manna, "Curtains Up on Contemporary Plays," *English Journal* 73 (October 1984): 51–54.

[12] Steve Allen, *Funny People* (New York: Stein and Day, 1981), p. 1.

[13] Lance M. Gentile and Merna M. McMillan, "Humor and the Reading Program," *Journal of Reading* 21 (January 1978): 343–50.

[14] Charles B. Shaw, "Good Light Fiction," *Public Libraries* 28 (January 1923): 21.

[15] Ellen Conford, "I Want to Make Them Laugh," *ALAN Review* 14 (Fall 1986): 21.

[16] Grook Poems by Piet Hein from *Grooks, Grooks 2, Grooks 3,* and *Grooks 5* by Piet Hein (New York: Doubleday, 1969–1973).

[17] Willard Flint Thrall and Addison Hibbard, *A Handbook to Literature,* revised by C. Hugh Holman (New York: Odyssey, 1960), p. 436.

[18] Epitaphs by Fritz Spiegl from *A Small Book of Grave Humor* by Fritz Spiegl (New York: Arco, 1973).

[19] Epitaphs from *Poems from the Greek Anthology,* translated by Dudley Fitts (New York: New Directions, 1956).

[20] Walter Blair's edition of *The Sweet Singer of Michigan* (New York: Pascal Covici, 1928) is excellent on Clark and Moore. A deliciously funny article by Bradley Hayden, "In Memoriam Humor: Julia Moore and the Western Michigan Poets," *English Journal* 72 (September 1983): 22–28, is a fine introduction to these wonderful nonpoets.

[21] From *Ruthless Rhymes for Heartless Homes* by Harry Graham (Col. D. Streamer), 1902.

[22] More anonymous "Little Willie" poems from *Poet's Handbook* by Clement Wood (Greenberg, 1940).

[23] Dorothy Wynn Downes, "Do You Remember Little Willie?" *Saturday Review of Literature* 27 (March 25, 1944): 18, 20. See the letters to the editor for April 8, 1944, p. 15; April 15, 1944, p. 31; April 22, 1944, p. 20; May 20, 1944, p. 17; June 10, 1944, p. 21; and June 17, 1944, p. 24. Dorothy Rickard, "The Further Adventures of Little Willie," *Saturday Review* 35 (March 15, 1952): 15 and letters to the editor for April 19, 1952, p. 29.

30 RECOMMENDATIONS FOR READING

Poetry

Angelou, Maya. *Now Sheba Sings the Song.* Dial, 1987. Angelou is at her best with this sensual poem which is accompanied by beautifully done portraits of black women. Her other books are equally recommended.

Dunning, Stephen, and others, eds. *Reflections on a Gift of Watermelon Pickle and Other Modern Verse.* Scott, Foresman, 1966. After more than 20 years this collection is still a favorite along with its sequel, *Some Haystacks Don't Even Have Any Needle: And Other Complete Modern Poems* (Lothrop, Lee & Shepard, 1969).

Glenn, Mel. *Class Dismissed: High School Poems.* Clarion Books, 1982. Along with its 1986 sequel, *Class Dismissed II: More High School Poems* (also Clarion), Glenn's books inspire students to think and write about their own experiences.

Gordon, Ruth, sel. *Under All Silences: Shades of Love.* Harper & Row, 1987. The 66 poems in this book were so carefully chosen that the book was selected for several best-book lists.

Janeczko, Paul, ed. *Poetspeak: In Their Words, About Their Work.* Bradbury, 1983. Over 60 of the poets whose work is here wrote explanatory notes on the writing of poetry and/or on how they wrote the particular poem chosen for the collection. Janeczko's other anthologies are also highly recommended.

Lueders, Ed, and Primus St. John, eds. *Zero Makes Me Hungry: A Collection of Poems for Today.* Scott, Foresman, 1976. A spacious layout with bright splashes of color make the format as attractive as the well-chosen poems are appealing.

Merriam, Eve. *Rainbow Writing.* Atheneum, 1976. In this and other books, Merriam uses a lively and accessible style that dispels the idea that poems are puzzles.

Silverstein, Shel. *Where the Sidewalk Ends.* Harper & Row, 1974. Although this hilarious book and its 1983 sequel *The Light in the Attic* (Harper & Row) are "children's books" they have both been on many adult bestseller lists.

Short Stories

Asimov, Isaac, ed. with others. *Young Monsters.* Harper & Row, 1985. Part of a well-done series on the occult, each story in this book features a child-ghoul.

Gallo, Don, ed. *Sixteen.* Delacorte, 1984. Both *Sixteen* and *Visions* (Delacorte, 1987) are made up of newly published stories written by the best of current YA authors.

Mazer, Norma Fox. *Dear Bill, Remember Me? & Other Stories.* Delacorte, 1976. Several of the stories in this and in Mazer's other book, *Summer Girls, Love Boys* (Delacorte, 1982), have romantic elements, but they also have much more.

Schwartz, Alvin. *Scary Stories to Tell in the Dark.* Harper & Row, 1981. Along with its sequel, *More Scary Stories to Tell in the Dark* (Harper & Row, 1984) Schwartz's collection of kids' folklore is just plain fun.

Zolotow, Charlotte, ed. *Early Sorrow: Ten Stories of Youth.* Harper & Row, 1986. These stories by some of today's "best" writers could easily support class study by serious students.

Drama

The Bad Seed by Maxwell Anderson. Dramatists, 1954. Stephen King would be proud of this thriller about a very naughty little girl.

Becket by Jean Anouilh. French, 1959. This story of the British King Henry and his friend Thomas à Becket, whom he made Archbishop of Canterbury, explores the nature of friendship vs. duty.

Children of a Lesser God by Mark Medoff. Dramatists, 1980. Especially since the success of the movie, students will appreciate this Tony Award-winning play about a deaf young woman and her relationship with a hearing teacher.

The Crucible by Arthur Miller. Dramatists, 1952. This historical drama comments on the nature of humanity as it probes the background of the Salem Witch Hunt.

The Effect of Gamma Rays on Man-in-the-Moon Marigolds by Paul Zindel. Dramatists, 1970. A moving story of the damaging forms that love can take, this Pulitzer Prize-winning play brought Paul Zindel to the attention of the literary world.

Inherit the Wind by Jerome Lawrence and Robert E. Lee. Dramatists, 1955. Based on the famous Scopes Monkey Trial, this play explores commitment to an ideal and the responsibilities and possible consequences of that commitment.

Our Town by Thornton Wilder. French, 1938. This classic drama is a tribute to life in pre-WWII rural America.

Humor

Adams, Douglas. *The Hitchhiker's Guide to the Galaxy.* Harmony, 1979. The life of Arthur Dent from the time he learns his English home lies in the path of a freeway to his space travels and his discovery of the answer to the meaning of life. Continued in the less funny sequels—*The Restaurant at the End of the Universe* (Harmony, 1980), *Life, the Universe, and Everything* (Harmony, 1982), and *So Long, and Thanks for All the Fish* (Harmony, 1985).

Bethancourt, T. Ernesto. *The Dog Days of Arthur Cane.* Holiday House, 1976. An often funny (and sometimes hysterical) story of a young man turned into a mutt. *Cane* is short for *Canine.*

Breathed, Berke. *Bloom County Babylon: Five Years of Basic Naughtiness.* Little, Brown, 1986. The most inspired satire and sometimes sheer lunacy on the comic pages today. Bill the Cat, Opus (the penguin), Oliver Wendell Jones, Milo Bloom, and other weird people.

Keillor, Garrison. *Happy to Be Here.* Atheneum, 1982. Sketches and stories, sometimes funny, sometimes somber, but mostly witty and clever. Followed by *Lake Woebegon Days* (Viking, 1985), often funny but not to be read at one sitting but spread out over several days (better during several weeks).

Kaplow, Robert. *Alex Icicle: A Romance in Ten Torrid Chapters.* Houghton Mifflin, 1984. Still the funniest adolescent novel around a spoof of books and styles, all without a moment's condescension.

Lewis, C. S. *The Screwtape Letters.* Macmillan, 1943. Hardly new, but one of the finest modern satires. An older devil, Screwtape, writes letters to his young nephew Wormwood about Christianity and tempting Christians. Witty and profound.

Macaulay, David. *Motel of the Mysteries.* Houghton Mifflin, 1979. An archeologist of the future excavates a twentieth-century motel and comes to all sorts of fallacious conclusions. Wonderfully illustrated by Macaulay as well.

Merrill, Jean. *The Pushcart War.* W. R. Scott, 1964. The finest satire yet for children or adolescents. A few years in the future, a war breaks out in New York City between pushcart owners and truck drivers.

Townsend, Sue. *The Secret Diary of Adrian Mole, Aged 13 3/4.* Grove Press, 1986 (first published in England in 1982); and *The Growing Pains of Adrian Mole* (Grove Press, 1986, first published in England, 1982). The diary of a young man who takes himself deadly seriously, who is a genius by his own admission, but who fails to see clearly most of what is going on around him.

Udall, Morris. *Too Funny to Be President.* Holt, 1987. Politics, occasionally serious, but mostly taken lightly by a former presidential candidate who could never have been taken seriously by voters because he never took himself all that seriously.

◼ OTHER TITLES MENTIONED IN CHAPTER NINE

Aiken, Joan. *A Whisper in the Night: Tales of Terror & Suspense.* Delacorte, 1984.

_____ . *Street.* Viking, 1978.

Allen, Woody. *Getting Even.* Random House, 1971.

_____ . *Side Effects.* Random House, 1980.

_____ . *Without Feathers.* Random House, 1975.

Angell, Judie. *Suds: A New Daytime Drama Brought to You.* Bradbury, 1983.

Angelou, Maya. *And Still I Rise.* Random House, 1978.

_____ . *I Know Why the Caged Bird Sings.* Random House, 1970.

_____ . *Just Give Me a Cool Drink of Water 'fore I Die.* Random House, 1971.

_____ . *Oh Pray My Wings Are Gonna Fit Me Well.* Random House, 1975.

_____ . *Singin' and Swingin' and Gettin' Merry Like Christmas.* Random House, 1976.

_____ . *The Heart of a Woman.* Random House, 1981.

Asimov, Isaac et al., ed. *Young Extraterrestrials.* Harper & Row, 1984.

_____ . *Young Ghosts.* Harper & Row, 1985.

_____ . *Young Mutants.* Harper & Row, 1984.

_____ . *Young Star Travelers.* Harper & Row, 1986.

Baldwin, Neil. *To All Gentleness, William Carlos Williams: The Doctor Poet.* Atheneum, 1984.

Beard, Henry, ed. *Miss Piggy's Treasury of Art Masterpieces from the Kermitage Collection.* Holt, Rinehart and Winston, 1984.

Bierhorst, John, ed. *In the Trail of the Wind: American Indian Poems and Ritual Orations.* Farrar, Straus & Giroux, 1987.

Billington, Ray Allen, ed. *Limericks Historical and Hysterical, Plagiarized, Arranged, Annotated, and Some Written by Ray Allen Billington.* Norton, 1981.

Bolt, Robert. *A Man for All Seasons.* Baker (also French), 1960.

Bradbury, Ray. *When Elephants Last in the Dooryard Bloomed.* Knopf, 1973.

Braddy, Nella. *Anne Sullivan Macy.* Doubleday, 1933.

Brautigan, Richard. *June Thirtieth, June Thirtieth.* Delacorte, 1977.

_____ . *The Pill Versus the Springhill Mine Disaster.* Dell, 1969.

Cameron, Peter. *One Way or Another.* Harper & Row, 1986.

Caras, Roger. *Roger Caras' Treasury of Great Cat Stories.* Dutton, 1987.

_____ . *Roger Caras' Treasury of Great Dog Stories.* Dutton, 1987.

Carroll, Lewis. *Alice in Wonderland,* 1865.

_____ . *Through the Looking Glass,* 1872.

Chambers, Aidan. *Out of Time.* Harper & Row, 1985.

_____ . *Shades of Dark.* Harper & Row, 1986.

Cole, William, ed. *Beastly Boys and Ghastly Girls.* Collins/World, 1964.

Conford, Ellen. *If This Is Love, I'll Take Spaghetti.* Four Winds, 1983.

Cormier, Robert. *Eight Plus One.* Pantheon, 1980.

Cox, Michael, and R. A. Gilbert, ed. *The Oxford Book of English Ghost Stories,* Oxford University Press, 1987.

Danziger, Paula. *Can You Sue Your Parents for Malpractice?* Delacorte, 1979.

_____ . *The Divorce Express.* Delacorte, 1982.

Davis, Ossie. *Langston.* Delacorte, 1982.

DePaola, Tomie. *Watch Out for the Chicken Feet in Your Soup.* Treehouse, 1974.

Dunning, Steve, and Hugh L. Smith, eds. *Some Haystacks Don't Even Have Any Needle and Other Complete Modern Poems.* Lothrop, Lee & Shepard, 1969.

Ephron, Nora. *Crazy Salad.* Knopf, 1975.

Fitts, Dudley, ed. and trans. *Poems from the Greek Anthology in English Paraphrase.* New Directions, 1956.

Fleischman, Paul. *Coming-And-Going Men: Four Tales.* Harper & Row, 1985.

————. *Graven Images.* Harper & Row, 1982.

Fletcher, Lucille. *Sorry, Wrong Number.* In *Fifteen American One Act Plays,* edited by Paul Kozelka. Pocket Books, 1971.

Frank, Anne. *The Diary of a Young Girl.* Random House, 1956.

Friedman, Ina. *How My Parents Learned to Eat.* Houghton Mifflin, 1984.

Frost, Robert. *Stopping by Woods on a Snowy Evening.* Dutton, 1978.

Gibson, William. *The Miracle Worker.* Baker (also French), 1959.

Girion, Barbara. *A Very Brief Season.* Macmillan, 1984.

Gold, Robert S, ed. *Point of Departure: Nineteen Stories of Youth & Discovery.* Dell, 1961.

Goldsmith, Oliver. *She Stoops to Conquer.* 1792.

Gould, Jean. *American Women Poets: Pioneers of Modern Poetry.* Dodd, Mead, 1980.

Graham, Harry. *More Ruthless Rhymes for Heartless Homes.* Putnam, 1930.

————. *Ruthless Rhymes for Heartless Homes.* R. H. Russell, 1902.

Haines, John. *Stories We Listened To.* Bench Press, 1986.

Hamilton, Virginia. *The People Could Fly: American Black Folktales.* Knopf, 1987.

Hart, Moss, and George S. Kaufman. *You Can't Take It With You.* Dramatists, 1936.

Hein, Piet. *Grooks.* Doubleday, 1969.

————. *Grooks 2.* Doubleday, 1969.

————. *Grooks 3.* Doubleday, 1970.

————. *Grooks 4.* Doubleday, 1972.

————. *Grooks 5.* Doubleday, 1973.

Heller, Joseph. *Catch-22.* Simon and Schuster, 1961.

————. *God Knows.* Knopf, 1984.

Henson, Jim. *Miss Piggy's Guide to Life.* Knopf, 1981.

Herriot, James. *James Herriot's Dog Stories.* St. Martin's, 1987.

Higman, Perry, translator. *Love Poems from Spain and Spanish America.* City Lights, 1986.

Hopkins, Lee Bennett, ed. *Love and Kisses.* Houghton Mifflin, 1983.

Howker, Janni. *Badger on the Barge and Other Stories.* Greenwillow, 1985.

Janeczko, Paul, ed. *Pocket Poems: Selected for a Journey.* Bradbury, 1985.

————. *Don't Forget to Fly.* Bradbury, 1981.

————. *Going Over to Your Place: Poems for Each Other.* Bradbury, 1987.

————. *Postcard Poems: A Collection of Poetry for Sharing.* Bradbury, 1979.

————. *Strings: A Gathering of Family Poems.* Bradbury, 1984.

Jeffers, Robinson. *Medea.* In *Cawdor & Medea.* New Directions, 1970.

Jones, Diana Wynne. *Warlock at the Wheel & Other Stories.* Greenwillow, 1985.

Joseph, Stephen, ed. *the me nobody knows: children's voices from the ghetto.* Avon, 1969.

Keller, Helen. *The Story of My Life.* Doubleday, 1954.

Kelly, Walt. *Beau Pogo.* Simon & Schuster, 1960.

Kerr, M. E. *Dinky Hocker Shoots Smack.* Harper & Row, 1972.

————. *If I Love You, Am I Trapped Forever?* Harper & Row, 1973.

————. *Night Kites.* Harper & Row, 1986.

Kesey, Ken. *One Flew Over the Cuckoo's Nest.* Viking, 1962.

Koch, Kenneth. *Rose, Where Did You Get That Red?* Random House, 1974.

————. *Wishes, Lies, and Dreams: Teaching Children to Write Poetry.* 2nd ed. Chelsea House, 1980.

Kozelka, Paul, ed. *Fifteen American One-Act Plays.* Pocket Books, 1971.

Lamb, Wendy, ed. *Meeting the Winter Bike Rider and Other Prize Winning Plays.* Dell, 1986.

Larrick, Nancy, ed. *Tambourines! Tambourines to Glory! Prayers and Poems.* Westminster, 1982.

Lee, Benjamin. *It Can't Be Helped.* Farrar, Straus & Giroux, 1979.

Livingston, Myra Cohn, ed. *Speak Roughly to Your Little Boy: A Collection of Parodies and Burlesques.* Harcourt Brace Jovanovich, 1971.

Longfellow, William Wadsworth. *Hiawatha* (illustrated by Susan Jeffers). Dial, 1983.

Marquis, Don. *archy and mehitabel.* Doubleday, 1927.

Mason, Steve. *Johnny's Song: Poetry of a Vietnam Veteran.* Bantam, 1986.

Masters, Edgar Lee. *Spoon River Anthology.* Macmillan, 1915.

McCullough, Frances. *Love Is Like the Lion's Tooth: An Anthology of Love Poems.* Harper & Row, 1984.

McKinley, Robin, ed. *Imaginary Lands.* Greenwillow, 1986.

Merriam, Eve, ed. *If Only I Could Tell You: Poems for Young Lovers and Dreamers.* Knopf, 1983.

———. *Inner City Mother Goose.* Simon and Schuster, 1969.

———. *Out Loud.* Atheneum, 1973.

———, and Nancy Larrick, eds. *Male and Female Under Eighteen.* Avon, 1973.

Millay, Edna St. Vincent. *Poems Selected for Young People.* Harper & Row, 1979.

Miller, Arthur. *Death of a Salesman.* Viking, 1949.

Patrick, John. *The Teahouse of the August Moon.* Dramatists, 1953.

Paulin, Mary Ann, and Susan T. Berlin. *Outstanding Books for the College Bound.* American Library Association, 1984.

Peck, Richard. *The Ghost Belonged to Me.* Viking, 1975.

Perelman, S. J. *The Last Laugh.* Simon & Schuster, 1981.

———. *The Most of S. J. Perelman.* Simon & Schuster, 1958.

Plotz, Helen, ed. *Eye's Delight: Poems of Art and Architecture.* Greenwillow, 1983.

———. *Gladly Learn and Gladly Teach: Poems of the School Experience.* Greenwillow, 1981.

———. *Imagination's Other Place: Poems of Science and Mathematics.* Crowell, 1955.

———. *Saturday's Children: Poems of Work.* Greenwillow, 1982.

Prelutsky, Jack. *Nightmares: Poems to Trouble Your Sleep.* Greenwillow, 1976.

Raffel, Burton, ed. *The Signet Classic Book of American Short Stories.* Penguin, 1986.

Riley, James Whitcomb. *The Gobble-Uns'll Get You If You Don't Watch Out.* Lippincott, 1975.

Rose, Reginald. *Twelve Angry Men.* In *Great Television Plays* selected by William I. Kaufman. Dell, 1969.

Rylant, Cynthia. *Children of Christmas: Stories for the Season.* Orchard Books Watts, 1987.

———. *Every Living Thing.* Bradbury, 1985.

Schwartz, Alvin. *Tomfoolery: Trickery and Foolery with Words.* Lippincott, 1973.

Segel, Elizabeth, ed. *Short Takes: A Collection of Short Stories.* Lothrop, Lee & Shepard, 1986.

Serling, Rod. *A Storm in Summer* in *Great Television Plays, Vol. 2.* Ned E. Hooper and Patricia Neale Gordon, eds. Dell, 1975.

Service, Robert W. *The Shooting of Dan McGrew and the Cremation of Sam McGee.* Young Scott, 1969.

Seuss, Dr. (Theodor Seuss Geisel). *Horton Hatches the Egg.* Random House, 1940.

Shaw, George Bernard. *Pygmalion.* 1913.

Shengold, Nina, ed. *The Actor's Books of Contemporary Stage Monologues.* Penguin, 1987.

Shepherd, Jean. *A Fistful of Fig Newtons.* Doubleday, 1982.

———. *The Ferrari in the Bedroom.* Dodd, Mead, 1973.

———. *In God We Trust, All Others Pay Cash.* Doubleday, 1976.

———. *Wanda Hickey's Night of Golden Memories and Other Disasters.* Doubleday, 1971.

Spiegl, Fritz, ed. *A Small Book of Grave Humor.* Arco, 1973.

Stegner, Wallace, ed. *Great American Short Stories.* Dell, 1985.

Sullivan, Frank. *The Night the Old Nostalgia Burned Down.* Little, Brown, 1953.

Thayer, Ernest L. *Casey at the Bat.* Prentice-Hall, 1964 (written in 1888).

Townsend, John Rowe. *Kate and the Revolution.* Lippincott, 1983.

Twain, Mark. *Adventures of Huckleberry Finn.* 1884.

Vidal, Gore. *Visit to a Small Planet* in *Visit to a Small Planet and Other Television Plays* by Gore Vidal. Little, Brown, 1956.

Walker, Alice. *Good Night Willie Lee, I'll See You in the Morning.* Dial, 1979.

——— . *The Color Purple.* Harcourt Brace Jovanovich, 1982.

Waugh, Evelyn. *The Loved One.* Little, Brown, 1948.

Westall, Robert. *The Haunting of Chas McGill & Other Stories.* Greenwillow, 1983.

——— . *Rachel and the Angel & Other Stories.* Greenwillow, 1987.

White, E. B. *The Second Tree from the Corner.* Harper, 1954.

Wibberley, Leonard. *The Mouse That Roared.* Little, Brown, 1955.

Wodehouse, P. G. *Carry on, Jeeves.* 1925; Penguin, 1975.

——— . *The Inimitable Jeeves.* 1931; Penguin, 1975.

——— . *Jeeves and the Feudal Spirit.* 1954; Penguin, 1975.

——— . *The Mating Season.* 1949; Harper & Row, 1983.

——— . *Meet Mr. Mulliner.* 1927; Penguin, 1981.

——— . *Much Obliged, Jeeves.* 1971; Penguin, 1982.

——— . *Mulliner Nights.* 1933; Penguin, 1975.

——— . *Stiff Upper Lip.* 1963; Harper & Row, 1983.

——— . *Very Good, Jeeves.* 1930; Penguin, 1975.

Zindel, Paul. *Let Me Hear You Whisper.* Harper & Row, 1974.

Zolotow, Charlotte, ed. *An Overpraised Season.* Harper & Row, 1987.

For information on the availability of paperback editions of these titles, please consult the most recent edition of *Paperbound Books in Print,* published annually by R. R. Bowker Company.

ADULTS AND THE LITERATURE OF YOUNG ADULTS

EVALUATING, PROMOTING, AND USING YOUNG ADULT BOOKS

Chances are that you are studying adolescent literature because you expect to work, or are already working, in some situation that calls for you to bring young adults in touch with books. This chapter is centered around five professional roles for adults who work with books and young readers: the librarian, the English teacher, the reading teacher, the social studies teacher, and the counselor or youth worker. These areas were chosen to give focus and organization to the information, but it should be realized that there is considerable overlap. Everyone working with young readers and books needs to be skilled in suggesting the right book for the right student or at least pointing someone in the right direction. When two people are talking about a book they both enjoyed, there is no way to divide the conversation into such discrete categories as literary analysis, personal feelings, sociological implications, and evaluation of potential popularity. Librarians will find themselves discussing books as if they were classroom teachers. Teachers can adopt some of the promotional techniques that librarians use, and librarians can use some book discussion tactics that teachers use. In short, the organization of this chapter may make it appear that the work different professionals do with young readers and books is quite separate. But in reality, nearly all adults who work with young readers and books have much the same goals and share many of the same approaches.

All of us will meet wide-ranging differences in abilities and personalities, which implies great differences in interests. Those interests demand an alert and prepared adult who is aware of them, who can uncover them, and who knows an enormous number of titles to meet them. To an inexperienced person, the knowledge of books a librarian or teacher can call forth seems magical, but developing that repertoire takes time, patience, and hard work. Reading many young adult books comes with the territory for the professional, but so does reading professional books, magazines of all sorts, several newspapers, adult books and much, much more. The professional likes to read (or would not be working with books), so that makes the job easier and more fun, but the professional reads beyond the areas that are personally enjoyable. For example, whether a professional likes science fiction or not, he or she must know titles of new science fiction. When young adults ask a teacher or librarian for another book like *The Martian Chronicles* (or *Forever* or *The Hitchhiker's Guide to the Galaxy* or *Crossings* or *The Color Purple*), they pay that person a sublime compliment. Woe unto the teacher or librarian who says, "I'm sorry, but I don't know anything about science fiction," or "Why don't you read something besides science fiction? Why not broaden your reading background just a bit?" Anything like that kills interest. To do this to someone who is just beginning to try books is almost criminal and may turn someone away from reading. In any given group, a teacher or librarian might find students like these and gradations between: Alice reads nothing at all (she did once but now that she has become a woman she has put away childish things); Brenda reads nothing because her reading skills are so poor she is virtually illiterate; Candy read a book once, her first book all the way through, and she hated it; Del reads magazines and an occasional sports biography if he's in an intellectual mood; Emily reads Sweet Valley High romances; Fred reads all kinds of books as long as they're science fiction; George reads a few books but always classics ("He's going to college," his mother says proudly); Howie reads only religious books and has already warned the teacher about the Satanic powers in *Lord of the Flies* scheduled for class reading in two weeks; Imogene reads anything that is popular—Harold Robbins, best-sellers, novelizations of movies and television specials; Jon reads classics, football stories, mysteries, and everything else and refuses to be pigeonholed; Jean reads from the Great Books list and anything else a college suggests for its prospective students; and Lynn reads all the time, perhaps too much—she's bright but socially immature.

Serving the needs of such a diverse group is far from easy, but when the job is well done, it's a valuable contribution.

EVALUATING BOOKS

No matter which role you will play in relation to books and young people, you will want help in evaluating and selecting the books that are best for your purposes. Because juvenile divisions of publishing houses distribute approximately 2,000 books per year with between one-fourth and one-third targeted for teenagers, it's necessary that book people share the reading responsibilities and pool their information through written evaluations.

Evaluation underlies nearly all writing about books. Even when someone is simply making notes to serve as a reminder of the contents of a book, that person is making an evaluation and concluding that the book is one worth remembering. Three concerns run throughout the evaluation of young adult literature: (1) What different types of writing meet specific needs, and how can they do it best? (2) Should reviews of young adult books be less promotional and more critical? (3) Is the current writing and scholarship in the field aimed too much at the uses of literature rather than at the analysis of the literature itself?

Writing Notecards

The type of writing most often done by teachers and librarians is the making of notecards. College students in young adult and children's literature classes sometimes look on this activity as little more than a teacher-imposed duty that they will be only too glad to leave behind once the class is finished. But in reality, making notes is probably going to be a lifelong activity for anyone who works professionally with books. Notecards form a continuous record of the books someone has read and can personally recommend. Teachers and librarians use the cards to jog their memories when they compile book lists, when students ask for "a good book," and when they plan teaching units and promotional activities.

The comments put on notecards vary according to the needs of the writer. Most people include the publisher and date, a short summary of the story, the characters' names, and the other details that make this book different, and a brief evaluation. The writer might also add a few comments suggesting future uses of the book. For example, if the book were Alice Childress' *A Hero Ain't Nothin' But a Sandwich*, a librarian might write the card in the form of a booktalk including information about the movie. An English teacher might note that it would be a good book for illustrating the literary principle of point of view. A reading teacher might note that it is short and easy reading except that the use of black dialect would probably cause problems for less skilled readers. A youth worker might make a note about the potential of the book as a catalyst to get kids talking about what they think adults should do in situations like Benjie's and whether or not the responsibility belongs to Benjie rather than to those around him. In a community where books are judged as appropriate for school study on the basis of their topic and such things as "perfect" grammar and happy endings, someone might note that it would be desirable to share the book with other professionals and adult friends of the library in order to develop community support for its use. Positive reviews and honors won might also be helpful information. The sample card that follows was prepared by a student in an adolescent literature class who was planning to be an English teacher.

Writing Annotations

Annotations are similar to notecards but they are usually written for someone else to see rather than for the writer's own use. And since they are usually a part of an annotated bibliography or list on which space is at a premium, writers must make efficient use of every word. Communicating the plot and

A Hero Ain't Nothin' But a Sandwich by Alice Childress.
Coward, McCann & Geoghegan, 1973, Avon paperback.

The best part of this drug-related book is that
it shows people really trying. A family rallies
around thirteen-year-old Benjie. The dad is just
living with the family, but he proves himself to be
a real father. The story is told from several
viewpoints—one chapter at a time. This makes it
good for showing that not all people who live in a
ghetto feel and act the same. It's open-ended with
the reader being left to wonder whether or not
Benjie shows up for drug counseling. Realistic,
black dialogue adds to the authenticity. I liked it.
Could be used as a read-aloud introduction to a
unit on drugs.

tone of a book as well as a recommendation in only one or two interesting sentences is challenging, but no one wants to read lists of characters and plot summaries all starting with "This book. . . . " That annotations can be intriguing as well as communicative is shown by the two samples given below for Virginia Hamilton's *Sweet Whispers, Brother Rush*. To save space, the bibliographical information given on the lists is not reprinted here.

Poetic, many-layered novel of 14-year-old Teresa's devotion to her retarded and doomed brother Dab. A strong story of hope and the power of love.

School Library Journal, December, 1982

Fourteen-year-old Tree learns a lot about her family and the interconnections between their past and present tragedies from Brother Rush, her uncle's ghost.

Booklist, March 15, 1983

Notice how both writers communicated the age of the protagonist, the fact that it was a family story, and, through the use of *doomed* and *tragedies* that it was a fairly heavy or serious book. The writers also hinted at mystery and intrigue, the first one through "Poetic, many-layered . . . hope and the power of love" and the second one through the reference to "Brother Rush, her uncle's ghost."

Writing Reviews

Librarians and teachers also commonly write reviews for local and national circulation newspapers, magazines, and journals. Probably fewer than two dozen people in the United States are full-time reviewers of juvenile books, but hundreds of teachers and librarians do it on a part-time basis.

A problem in the reviewing of juvenile books is that more books are published than there is room in the media for reviewing. Major reviewing sources for young adult books include *The ALAN Review, Booklist, Bulletin of the Center for Children's Books, English Journal, Horn Book Magazine, Kirkus Reviews, New York Times Book Review, Publishers Weekly, School Library Journal,* and *VOYA.* Of these sources, only *School Library Journal* attempts to review each book it receives. But in addition to these, dozens of national publications carry occasional review articles, and many library systems sponsor reviewing groups whose work is published either locally or through such nationally distributed publications as *Book Waves* from the Bay Area (Northern California) Young Adult Librarians and *Books for the Teen Age* from the Young Adult Services Office of the New York Public Library. And some teachers of children's and young adult literature work with their students to write regular review columns for local newspapers.

When publishers send out their new books, review editors glance through them and select the ones to forward to reviewers. Because the editor doesn't anticipate reviewing all books, it's likely that the publisher who can afford to send out the most copies will get the most reviews, as will the author whose name is already recognized. The fact that juvenile books are reviewed mostly by librarians and teachers working on a part-time basis slows down the reviewing process, especially if they take time to incorporate the opinions of young readers. With adult books, reviews often come out prior to or simultaneously with the publication of the book, but with juvenile titles it's not uncommon to see reviews appearing a full year or more after the book was released.

Although young adult books get off to a slower start than do adult books, once launched, they stay around longer. Teachers work them into classroom units, librarians promote them, and paperback book clubs keep selling them for years. Children continue to grow older and to advance in their reading skill and taste so that every year there is a whole new set of students ready to read *A Separate Peace, The Catcher in the Rye,* and even *The Outsiders.* As a result, reviews, articles, and papers continue to cover particular titles years after their original publication dates.

The field of juvenile reviewing is sometimes criticized for being too laudatory because the reviews are written by book lovers who are anxious to "sell" literature. Also, those editors who have room for only a limited number of reviews devote their space to the books they think are the best, so of course they are complimentary.

People generally evaluate books on the basis of either literary quality, reader interest, or potential popularity, or on what the book is teaching, i.e., its social and political philosophy. It's important that evaluators make clear their primary emphasis lest readers misunderstand them. For example, a critic may review a book positively because of its literary quality, but a reader will interpret the positive review as a prediction of popularity. The book is purchased and put on the shelf where it is ignored by teenagers. The purchaser feels cheated and loses confidence in the reviewing source.

In an attempt to resolve that kind of conflict, when Mary K. Chelton and Dorothy M. Broderick founded *VOYA (Voice of Youth Advocates),* they devised the evaluation code shown in Table 10.1. Each review is preceded by a *Q* number indicating *quality* and a *P* number indicating *popularity.* They suggest that a fringe benefit to using such a clearly outlined code is that it helps librarians analyze their buying patterns. Those who lean heavily toward either quality or popularity will see their biases and be able to strike a more appropriate balance.

A quite different set of criteria from either popularity or literary quality is that of social or political values. The Council on Interracial Books for children has been very open about its belief that books should "become a tool for the conscious promotion of human values that lead to greater human liberation."[1] The organization provides checklists for reviews to use in examining books for racism, sexism, elitism, materialism, individualism, ageism, conformity, escapism, positive vs. negative images of females and minorities, cultural authenticity, and the level of inspiration toward positive action. It is expected that reviews in the *Interracial Books for Children Bulletin* will focus on such matters.

However, most reviewers—whether or not they realize it—are influenced by their personal feelings toward how a book treats social issues. For example, Sue Ellen Bridgers' *Notes for Another Life* was highly recommended and praised in *Horn Book Magazine,* the *New York Times Book Review,* and the *Bulletin of the Center for Children's Books,* but when Janet French reviewed the book for *School Library Journal* she wrote:

> The blurb suggests that this is "a family chronicle for all ages." It would have been more accurate to describe it as a propaganda vehicle for female domesticity. Good women subordinate their talents and yearnings to the home and their children; all other paths lead to havoc. For a riveting story of four deserted children, lead readers instead to Cynthia Voigt's marvelously upbeat *Homecoming.*[2]

Table 10.1   VOYA EVALUATION CODE

Quality	Popularity
5Q: Hard to imagine it being better written.	5P: Every young adult was dying to read it yesterday.
4Q: Better than most, marred only by occasional lapses.	4P: Broad general young adult interest.
3Q: Readable without serious defects.	3P: Will appeal without pushing.
2Q: A little better editing or work by the author would have made it 3Q.	2P: For the young adult reader with a special interest in the subject.
1Q: Hard to understand how it got published.	1P: No young adult will read unless forced to for assignments.

This review was written in such a way that readers can easily recognize that the reviewer's opinion was shaped by her disagreement with the plot. For a reviewer to use this as the basis for a negative recommendation is perfectly justifiable *if* the situation is made clear. The problem comes when reviewers reject books on the basis of such social issues but don't admit to themselves, much less to their readers, that their feelings have been influenced by whether a story sharpens or dulls whatever personal ax they happen to be grinding at the moment.

There are as many reviewing styles as there are journals and individual reviewers. But nearly all reviews contain complete bibliographical information including number of pages and prices, perhaps a cataloguing number, the intended age level, a summary statement of the contents, and some hint of the quality of the book as evaluated by the reviewer. A few years ago an issue of *Top of the News,* the ALA publication now called *Journal of Youth Services in Libraries,* had as its feature topic "Reviews, Reviewing, and the Review Media." Editor Audrey Eaglen solicited answers to the question, "What Makes a Good Review?"[3] Author-illustrator Rosemary Wells said, "an intelligent review . . . is never obsequious, if it is favorable. It is never flip, if it is unfavorable. It never quotes from the front flap." School librarian Katherine Haylman wanted reviewers to tell her of "any clever device or intriguing aspect of the book which could be used to pique the interest of a group and 'sell' the book." She also wanted reviewers to say whether there was "a potentially controversial issue in the book, be it strong language, explicit sex, violence, or whatever," not so she could avoid buying the book, but so that she could plan and prepare and thereby deal with a conflict should it arise.

Dorothy Broderick, an editor and educator, wanted comments on the attractiveness of the cover illustration: "While we might feel that no one should judge a book by its cover, the truth is that everyone does." Author Walter Dean Myers wanted every review to "contain a clear-cut commitment as to recommendation or nonrecommendation." He doesn't have the time to read every book published, and is hoping that some literate person will help him decide where he should invest his reading hours.

Patty Campbell, author and critic, wanted to know first "if a book has magic for YA's." Then she wanted "to be alerted to format faults: does the size and shape make it look like a baby book? . . . Is the word *children* used anywhere on the dust jacket?" And if there is going to be a film or television tie-in, who are the stars and when will it be released?

The reviewer must decide what information is most important for the particular book being reviewed and for the particular audience for which the review is being written. Writing reviews is a skill that improves with practice and effort. A good way to begin developing this skill is to study several reviews of the same book as they appear in different publications. Note the essentials that seem to be the same in each review and then compare the information that is different. See if you can explain the differences in light of the source's reading audience.

For the person reading reviews, one of the biggest problems is that they all run together and begin sounding the same. To keep this from happening, reviewers need to approach their task with the same creative spirit with which authors write books. They need to think of new ways of putting across the point that a book is highly recommended or that it has some unique quality that readers should watch for as in these two excerpts of reviews which were written by authors reviewing books written by other authors. Granted, authors probably have had more practice in working with words and therefore their skill is greater than that of most reviewers, but they probably also try harder because they know how important it is to do something to make a review stand out, to give the reader something by which to remember the book.

The first excerpt is taken from a review of Alice Childress' *Rainbow Jordan* written by Anne Tyler for the *New York Times Book Review:*

> Rainbow is so appealing that she could carry this book on her own, but she doesn't have to. There's Miss Josie, who gives us her clearer view to balance what Rainbow tells us. . . . And there's the mother herself—short-tempered, inconsistent, sometimes physically abusive, not much of a mother at all, really. Seen through Rainbow's adoring eyes, she's at least someone we can understand ("Life is complicated," Rainbow says, "I love her even now while I'm putting her down.") In fact, Rainbow's story moves us not because of her random beatings or financial hardships, but because Rainbow needs her mother so desperately that she will endlessly rationalize, condone, overlook, forgive. She is a heartbreakingly sturdy character, and *Rainbow Jordan* is a beautiful book.[4]

Katherine Paterson made these comments about Virginia Hamilton's *Sweet Whispers, Brother Rush* as part of an article she wrote for the *New York Times Book Review:*

> There are those who say that Virginia Hamilton is a great writer but that her books are hard to get into. This one is not. It fairly reaches off the first page to grab you, and once it's got you, it sets you spinning deeper and deeper into its story. Needless to say, this is not a conventional ghost story. In fact, the function of the ghost in this book is to provide 14-year-old Tree Pratt with a place from which to view her world. . . . In this book everyone we meet, including the ghost, is wonderfully human. . . . The language too is of Miss Hamilton's own special kind, which uses the speech forms of the young to enhance rather than restrict the music of the book.[5]

Writing Scholarly and Pedagogical Articles

A fourth kind of writing about young adult books is made up of articles or papers that go into more depth than is possible in reviews. Since most reviewers of juvenile books have little hope of coming out with a "scoop" or of being the first one to pass judgment on a new book, they focus on deeper treatments or on tying several books together. Dorothy Matthews analyzed the writing about adolescent literature that appeared in professional journals over a five-year period.[6] She categorized the writing into three types. First were those articles that focus on the subjective responses of readers to particular books, such as reader surveys, lists of popular titles, and reviews written from the point of view of how the book is likely to affect young readers. Articles of this kind are primarily descriptive.

The second type was also descriptive and consisted of pedagogical articles giving teachers lists of books that fit together for teaching units, ideas for book promotion, and techniques for teaching reading, social studies, or English. They may include brief comments on the literary qualities of the novels, but, again, the writer's primary intention is to be informative.

The third kind of writing was that restricted to the books themselves. It is in this group that Matthews thinks hope lies for the development of a body of lasting scholarly knowledge that will be taken seriously by the academic community. These papers include discussions of adolescent literature as a genre, historical background of the field, relationships between authors and their work, patterns that appear in YA novels, and themes and underlying issues. More of this kind of literary analysis is being done as authors write books serious enough to support it. Examples of some of these articles are included in Appendix C, "Some Outstanding Books and Articles about Young Adult Literature" (page 580).

Also, a look into a recent edition of *Dissertation Abstracts International* will show an increasing number of dissertations being written on young adult literature. However, the majority of topics deal more with social or pedagogical issues than with literary ones, for example, *A Study of Changes in the Attitudes of Characters in Novels Written for Adolescents by Four Black Authors* by Janice Mueller Anderson at the University of Iowa (1984); *Adolescents' and Teachers' Views of the Adolescent in Western Society as Portrayed in Selected Popular Novels of Adolescence: An Ethnographic Study* by Tommy R. Harrison at the University of Alabama (1986); *A Study of Common Characteristics Found in Selected Adolescent Novels* by Raymond Eugene Huey at Ball State University (1985); *Images of Mothers in Adolescent Literature* by Rhoda Jean Maxwell at Michigan State University (1986); and *The Young Female Protagonist in Juvenile Fiction: Three Decades of Evolution* by Beverly Burgoyne Young at Washington State University (1985).

Fairly new journals that support the growing body of literary criticism about books for young readers include *Children's Literature in Education: An International Quarterly, Children's Literature, ALAN Review,* and *VOYA (Voice of Youth Advocates).* Within the last fifteen years, these journals have joined the other well-established journals listed in Appendix B (page 574).

In summary, evaluative writing about young adult books falls into four categories: notecards for personal use, annotations, reviews, and scholarly or pedagogical writing. Most of you will be involved in the first kind, that is, making notecards for your own use. But some of you will also be making annotations, writing reviews, and doing scholarly or pedagogical analyses. This latter kind of writing and critiquing can be especially intriguing because significant changes have occurred within recent years and relatively few scholars have worked with young adult literature. This means there is ample opportunity for original research and observation whether from the viewpoint of a teacher, a librarian, or a counselor or youth worker. The field as a whole will grow strong as a result of serious and competent criticism and analysis.

USING YA LITERATURE IN THE LIBRARY

When discussing public libraries, it is often assumed that every library has a young adult librarian and a special section serving teenagers. Although this may be the ideal arrangement, certainly there are many libraries where this has never been the practice and many others where shrinking budgets are making young adult librarians an endangered species. The February 1984 *VOYA (Voice of Youth Advocates)* addressed this problem from several viewpoints. In an editorial, Mary K. Chelton warned YA librarians that they had to document the need for their services to young adults and that they had to develop support groups in the community. She recommended two publications of the American Library Association, *The Planning Process* and *Output Measures for Public Libraries,* warning that if young adult librarians ignore such advice and the work that it entails—even if it's in favor of reading the latest YA novel—they do so at their own peril.[7]

The special issue of *VOYA* was motivated by two actions—the abolishing in 1983 of the position of Coordinator of Young Adult Services in the Los Angeles City Library system and a proposal being considered by the Atlanta and Fulton County Library to integrate Young Adult services into a "Young People's Program" in which the children's librarians would extend their work to include 13- to 15-year-olds. Anyone over 16 would be served as an adult. Dorothy Broderick asked several librarians to respond to the Fulton County proposal. She compiled their statements in an article, "Whose Job Is It Anyway?" from which the following excerpts are taken.[8] Ruth Rausen noted that although teenagers can be persuaded to enter a children's room on a temporary basis, "they go reluctantly and make it clear that they do not belong there." An additional problem is that "their size, voices, and active natures can only be intimidating to children." Julia Losinski pointed out that even though collections are typically quite small, the service is large. "The purpose of young adult services is to provide a transition from the children's collection to the resources of the total library." "Who," she asked, "will be serving the children while the children's librarian accompanies the teenager venturing 'into the larger adult collection.' "

Penelope S. Jeffrey didn't think that the same person who runs programs for preschoolers, prepares story hours for older children, and reviews hundreds of children's books would be able to involve teenagers in decision making and manage to keep up with the fads and continuously changing interests of youth.

The young adult section of the Mesa, Arizona, Public Library offers carousels of records, magazines, and paperback books to entice readers.

"A frequently neglected area is periodicals directed at teens. Take a look at the newsstand. Even so-called 'nonreaders' are purchasing periodicals on media stars, hobbies, sports, music, and other youth interests." Regina Minudri's point was that YA librarians deal not only with "safe" YA books, "but also with adult materials of interest to young adults. These are often, by their very nature, controversial. It is not happenstance that many censorship cases involve books for young adults; books which explore life, sexuality, and conflict." She added that the differences between the way one works with children and with teenagers is "as much in perception as in attitude."

In a companion piece, "And All for the Want of a Horseshoe-Nail: Dilemma of a Writer—And of Us All," author Adrienne Jones expresses her concern over "the plight of the writers whose novels are not written for the large 'popular' audience." The fate of the writers of the "serious," the "quality" books "who know at the outset that their audience is relatively small," is intimately connected with the fate of young adult librarians who purchase and promote such books as *To Kill a Mockingbird, Summer of My German Soldier, The Catcher in the Rye, After the First Death,* and *A Sound of Chariots.* Jones worried that with cutbacks in YA services, only "popular" books, i.e., formula novels, would survive just as "popular taste in TV assures a long run for *The Dukes of Hazzard* and allows *The Paper Chase* to quickly disappear."[9]

As these people point out, it takes more than a shelf of books labeled YA to make up something that can honestly be called YA services. This section will discuss a few of those things as related to literature.

Matching Books with Readers

Most people working with books and young readers have come to accept the idea that there is no such thing as one sacred list of books that every student should read. The best that can be hoped for are agreeable matches between particular books and particular students. To bring about such matches, adults need to be acquainted with a wide range of books and with individual students. A commonly used technique in getting to know students is to ask them what books they have enjoyed previously and then to suggest something similar or something by the same author. An alternative is to ask young readers to describe the book they would most like if an author were going to write a book just for them, and then to suggest three or four books that contain elements they have mentioned.

Other people use written forms of reader interest surveys in which students write down their hobbies, the kinds of classes they are taking, what they want to do for a career, what books they have read, and the kinds of stories they most enjoy. The problem with such forms is that they are usually filled out and then stored in a drawer. No one has time to interpret them. However, one creative librarian designed a reader interest survey that could be answered on a computer card to which she added the students' reading test scores. She programmed the computer with one hundred of the best books she had read. All of the students got individual computer printouts suggesting six books that they would probably like and that would be within their reading level. Her students were intrigued with the idea of getting their own printouts, but what made the program successful was that she had read and personally reacted to each book that she wrote into the program. The individualized printouts were conversation starters from which one-to-one relationships developed. Although the librarian worked hard to initiate the project, she considered it well worth the effort because once the machinery was set in order, it could be done for hundreds of students almost as easily as for thirty.

The key to being able to recommend the right book to the right student is for adults to have such a large and varied reading background that they can personally act as a computer. Skilled teachers and librarians program their minds to draw relationships between what students tell or ask and what they remember about particular books. Experience sharpens this skill, and those librarians who make an effort consistently to read a few new books every month increase their repertoire of books rapidly.

WILLIAM SLEATOR
on Creating Readers

There is a pervasive attitude in the literary community that people who write for young adults are not "real" writers. Naturally I think this is baloney.

In the first place, people who write for young adults are, in a very real sense, *creating* readers. Adults who read have already developed the habit of reading for pleasure. But many teenagers have not. You can't just tell them that reading is the best entertainment there is, and that their lives will be vastly improved if they become addicted to reading. You have to prove it to them, by giving them books that they cannot put down. And that's where I come in.

My primary conscious preoccupation when writing is to tell a good story. Of course, like anyone who aims to be a quality writer, I work hard on style, on character development, on plot. But I'm also trying to write a riveting book. Things happen fast, the book has to be exciting, suspenseful, never a dull moment. There's no room for the padding that fills up so many 1100-page adult books. And that's one reason why it's so much fun to write for adolescents.

You also have to work very hard at establishing credibility—teenagers are often more skeptical than adults. This is especially important when you are writing fantasy or science fiction. I always start my books in the real world, in a mundane situation—and let the weirdness creep in gradually. It's like a challenging puzzle—to trick the readers into believing that this crazy thing could really happen to them.

When I get letters from kids who tell me they usually don't like to read, but couldn't put down one of my books, I feel I have really succeeded. We are all doing a little to help create a new generation of readers, and that will certainly make the world a better place to live in.

The other nice thing about writing young adult books—if I dare to mention it—is that, because of public libraries and school libraries, you can make a living at it. The people I know who write adult books, who consider me to be second rate, all have full-time jobs to support their writing. And so, when they tell me that writing for young people is "good practice," I am laughing all the way to the bank.

William Sleator's books include *The Boy Who Reversed Himself,* Dutton, 1986; *Fingers,* Macmillan, 1983; and *Singularity,* Dutton, 1985.

Booktalks

With all of their other responsibilities, few librarians have as much opportunity as they would like to guide individual reading on a one-to-one basis. The next best thing is giving presentations or booktalks to groups. In her highly recommended *Booktalk! Booktalking and School Visiting for Young Adult Audiences,* Joni Bodart defines a booktalk "in the broadest terms" as "what you say to convince someone to read a book." She goes on to describe the act as:

⬛ Sharing your enjoyment of a book with other people and convincing them that they would enjoy it too. . . . As a dramatic art, booktalking has something in common with storytelling, although in content it more nearly resembles an unfinished murder mystery—it doesn't say "who dunnit," but it makes you want to find out. . . . A good booktalk is enticing. It is a come-on. It is entertaining. And it is fun, for both the listener and the booktalker.[10]

Another advantage that Bodart mentions is that when a librarian comes to a classroom with a cartload of books and a set of interesting booktalks, it lets students know "that somebody (an adult who is not a teacher) thinks that books are important, and is willing to visit their class to say so."

In an article in *School Library Journal,* Mary K. Chelton added her testimony.

⬛ The best young adult librarians I have known, whether they see their book selection role as one of expanding horizons and literary tastes or of just giving kids what they want (and most of us usually fall somewhere in between), have a "hidden agenda" for promoting the love of reading for pleasure, and have found booktalks a superb way of doing that. . . . Once acquired, this skill can be adapted to floor work with individual readers, radio spots, booklist annotations, and class visits in the library or in the classroom. It can be combined with slide-tape, film, or musical presentations, and with outreach skills.[11]

The simplest kind of booktalk may last only sixty seconds. In giving it, the booktalker has the obligation to let listeners know what to expect. For example, it would be unfair to present only the funniest moments in a serious book—a reader might check it out expecting a comedy. If a book is a love story, then some clue should be given, but care needs to be taken because emotional scenes read out loud and out of context can sound silly. The cover of a book often reveals its tone, which is one of the reasons for holding up a book while it is being talked about or of showing slides if a presentation is being given to a large audience.

Booktalks need to be carefully prepared ahead of time. It takes both concentration and skill to select the "heart" of a story. People who try to ad lib have the advantage of sounding spontaneous, but they also run the risk of using up all their time telling about one or two books or of getting bogged down in telling the whole story, which would defeat the purpose. Most young readers do not want to hear a ten- or fifteen-minute talk on one book, unless it is dramatic and used as a change of pace along with several shorter booktalks. This whole procedure works well if the librarian comes to a class with a cart full of books ready to be checked out. Most of the class period can be devoted to the booktalks with the last fifteen minutes saved for questions and answers, browsing, and check-out time.

This kind of group presentation has the advantage of introducing students to the librarian, which is especially important with public librarians. When students go to the library already feeling acquainted, they are more at ease in initiating a one-to-one relationship, a valuable part of reading guidance. It also has the advantage of giving students more freedom in choosing books that really appeal to them. For example, if a student asks a librarian to recommend a good book, the librarian will probably not have time to tell the student about more than two or three books. The student usually feels an obligation to take one of these books whether or not it really sounds appealing. But when the librarian presents twenty or thirty different titles, then students have the advantage of being able to choose from a much larger offering. This also enables students to learn about and to select books that might cause them embarrassment if they were recommended on a personal basis. For example, if a girl is suspected of having lesbian leanings, it may not help the situation for the librarian to hand her Nancy Garden's *Annie on My Mind.* But if this were included among several books introduced to the class and the student chose it herself, then it might fill a real need. And the fact that the librarian had talked about it, showing that she had read it, opens the door for the girl to initiate a conversation if she so desires.

Another advantage to group presentations is that they are obviously more efficient. For example, if a social studies class is beginning a unit on World War II in which everyone in the class is required to read a novel having something to do with the war and also write a small research paper, it makes sense for the librarian to give the basic information in one group presentation. Being efficient in the beginning will enable the librarian to spend time with individual students who have specific questions rather than making an almost identical presentation to thirty individuals.

Table 10.2 gives some suggestions that should increase one's chances for success with booktalks. Mary K. Chelton's article served as a basis for this table.

Displays

Making displays is another effective way to promote books. Most young adults have some common needs though they might not admit them or even be aware of them. The sensitive adult who knows books can quietly alert students to titles and authors that might prove worthwhile. It can be done simply, indeed the simpler and less obvious the better, perhaps nothing more than a sign that says "Love John Wayne Films?—You'll Love These" (books on courage and facing death, though not identified in just that way), or "Did You Cry Over *Gone with the Wind?*" (books about love problems and divorce).

None of these simple gimmicks involves much work, but, more important, they do their job without the librarian seeming pushy or nosy. The point is to alert young adults to many titles on all kinds of themes. No book report is required and no one will know whether John checks out Howard Fast's *April Morning* because his father recently died or because he likes American history.

Table 10.2 **DO'S AND DON'T'S FOR BOOKTALKING**

Do	Don't
1. Do prepare well. Either memorize your talks or practice them so much that you can easily maintain eye contact.	1. Don't introduce books that you haven't read or books that you wouldn't personally recommend to a good friend as interesting.
2. Do organize your books so that you can show them as you talk. To keep from getting confused, you might clip a note card with your talk on it to the back of each book.	2. Don't "gush" over the books. If it's a good book and you have done an adequate job of selecting what to tell, then it will sell itself.
3. When presenting excerpts, do make sure they are representative of the tone and style of the book.	3. Don't tell the whole story. When listeners beg for the ending, hand them the book. Your purpose is to get them to read.
4. Even though you might sometimes like to focus on one or two themes, do be sure, over the months you meet with any group, that you present a wide variety of books. Include informative books that young readers would probably like to know about but might be too embarrassed to ask for.	4. Don't categorize books as to who should read them, for example, "This is a book you girls will like"; or show by the books you have brought to a particular school that you expect only Asian-Americans to read about Asian-Americans and only American Indians to read about American Indians, and so forth.
5. Do experiment with different formats, for example, a short movie, some poetry, or one longer presentation along with your regular book talks.	5. Don't give literary criticisms. You have already evaluated the books for your own purposes and if you did not think they were good, you would not be presenting them.
6. Do keep a record of which books you have introduced to which groups. This can be part of your evaluation when you compare before and after circulation figures on the titles you have talked about. Also, good record keeping will help you not to repeat yourself with a group.	
7. Do be assertive in letting teachers know what you will and will not do. Perhaps distribute a printed policy statement explaining such things as how much lead time you need, the fact that the teacher is to remain with the group, and how willing you are to make the necessary preparation to do booktalks on requested themes or topics.	

When it comes to promoting books, librarians should not be ashamed to borrow ideas from the world of commerce. After all, we are competing directly for students' time and interest and indirectly for a share of the library budget and the taxpayers' dollars. As part of this competition, we should not overlook the benefits of having attractive, professional-looking displays and bulletin boards. They should give evidence that things are happening and they should help patrons develop positive attitudes toward books and reading.

Well-done displays draw attention to selected books and therefore make it more likely that they will be read. Even if there is no artwork connected with a display, it can still promote books simply by showing the front covers. Preparing displays can bring the same kind of personal satisfaction that comes from creatively decorating a room or painting a picture. People with negative feelings toward making displays have probably had bad experiences in which the results did not adequately compensate for the amount of time and effort expended. One way to correct this imbalance is to follow some general principles that help to increase the returns on a display while cutting down on the work.

1. Go window shopping in the best stores—the ones that appeal to the young adults that you are wooing—and when you see a display that you like, adapt its features to your own purposes.
2. Promote more than one book and have multiple copies available. Enthusiasm wanes if people have to put their names on a list and wait.
3. Tie the displays into current happenings and take advantage of television and movie tie-ins with mini-displays including a poster and an advertisement supplemented by copies of whatever book is currently being featured.
4. Use displays to get people into the library. Offer free bibliographies and have announcements of their availability made through local media.
5. Put your displays in high traffic areas where everyone, not just those who already use the young adult collection, will see them.
6. Use interchangeable parts so that it isn't necessary to start from scratch each time. Stained fruit baskets and crates from grocery stores, leaning boards with screwed in hooks for holding books, and boxes covered with drapes are all good ways to get variety and height into a display. Plain backgrounds are better than patterned ones to focus attention on the books.

The changing location of portable displays is in itself an attention getter. A portable display can be as small as a foot-square sandwich board set in the middle of a table or as large as a camper's tent set up in the middle of a room and surrounded by books about camping, hiking, backpacking, ecology, and nature foods. If space is a problem, small bulletin boards can be hung from the ceiling or stood against pillars or walls. They can do double duty, for example, dividing the children's section from the young adult section or separating a reading corner with its casual furniture from the desks and tables set aside for study.

It's a good idea to give students a sense of ownership over the displays by involving them as much as possible. Art teachers are usually happy to work with librarians to have a place where student work can be attractively displayed. Students also might enjoy lending such things as family portraits or baby pictures to add interest to a display of genealogy books. Occasionally students working as library interns or helpers will enjoy the challenge of doing displays all by themselves, bringing in trash for a display on recycling or ecology or bringing in an overstuffed chair and a footstool as the focal point of a display of leisure-time books. Whatever is interesting and different is the key to tying books in with real life. An ordinary object—a kitchen sink, a moped, or a torn

A customer looks over American Library Association posters with YA appeal. They were on display at an ALA convention booth.

and dirty football jersey—is out of the ordinary when it appears on a bulletin board or a display table.

Also, don't overlook the possibility of tying commercial posters in with books. Remember the part that the poster message, "Don't disturb the universe," played in Cormier's *The Chocolate War.* The American Library Association offers attractive posters, and within the last few years The Children's Book Council has begun to offer some promotional material suitable for teenagers.

Programs

Stores have special sales and events to get people into the marketplace where they will be tempted to buy something. In the same way ambitious librarians put on young adult programs to do something special for those who regularly use the library and, at the same time, to bring nonusers into the library. Opinions are divided on whether or not programs should necessarily be designed to promote the use of library materials, and on whether they should be educational rather than recreational. Without getting into a discussion of both viewpoints or a complete description of how to set up young adult programs, we can offer some advice from people whose libraries have been especially active in arranging programs:

1. Take a survey, or better, talk with your teenage clientele to see what their interests and desires are.
2. Avoid duplicating the kinds of activities that students do in school and in conjunction with other community agencies.
3. Include young adults in planning and putting on programs. The library can be a showcase for young adult talent.
4. Work with existing youth service agencies to cosponsor events, or plan them in conjunction with school programs so as to have the beginning of an audience and the nucleus of a support group.
5. Do a good job of publicizing the event. The publicity may influence people unable to come so that they will feel more inclined to visit the library at some other time.
6. Have a casual setting planned for a relatively small group with extra chairs available in case more people come than you expect. Bustling around at the last minute to set up extra chairs gives an aura of success that is more desirable than having row upon row of empty chairs with a few people sitting here and there.

Among the kinds of programs commonly held are film programs, outdoor music concerts featuring local teenage bands, talent shows in a coffeehouse setting, chess tournaments, and contests in such areas as filmmaking and decorating sweat shirts. Workshops are held in computer programming, photography, creative writing, bicycle repair, and all sorts of crafts ranging from macramé and embroidery to the silkscreening of T-shirts and posters. Another kind of program features guest speakers. In public libraries these are often on subjects that school librarians tend to shy away from such as self-defense and rape prevention, drug and birth control information, and an introduction to various hotlines and other agencies that help young adults. Large-scale workshops are sometimes held in libraries to which various schools bring their students. For example, in a town with three high schools, one big day on choosing careers may be planned at the community library. Guest speakers who could not give up three days of time may be willing to make a single appearance and special exhibits and displays can be set up once rather than three times.

Regardless of the topic or format of a program, librarians should view programs as opportunities to encourage library visitors to become regular book users. The following practices will help:

1. Hold the program so that it is in or very near the young adult book section. If this is impractical, try routing traffic past the YA area or past displays of YA books.
2. Distribute miniature bibliographies, perhaps printed on a bookmark or in some other easy-to-carry format.
3. Schedule the program to end at least a half-hour before the library closes so that participants can browse and sign up for library cards.

4. Just as grocery and discount stores crowd the checkout areas with all kinds of tempting little items, place paperback book racks where they are equally tempting.

5. For ten or fifteen minutes at the start of the program while waiting for latecomers to straggle in, do a welcome and warm-up by giving a few booktalks related to the subject of the evening.

Some libraries have had success with book discussion groups in which teenagers serve as readers and critics. This usually works best if their evaluations can be shared perhaps on a bulletin board, in a teen opinion magazine, through a display of books they recommend, in a monthly column in a local newspaper, or through the periodic printing and distribution of annotated lists of favorites.

When an author is invited to speak, it is the host librarian's responsibility to begin several weeks in advance to be sure that people are reading the author's books. English and reading teachers should be notified so that they can devote some class time to the author's work. A panel of students who especially enjoyed the author's work might be set up to interact with the author at the end of the formal presentation. Another way to involve students, and perhaps teachers, would be to invite three or four to have lunch or dinner with the guest author. (Check this out first since some people prefer to be left alone before they are to speak.) If you are setting up an author's visit, it is usually best that you first write the publisher of the author's most recent book. State how much money, if any, you have available. Sometimes publishers will pay for the transportation of an author, but at your end you will usually need to pay at least for food and housing, and if possible, offer an honorarium. If you have no money, say so immediately, and then be patient, flexible, and grateful for whomever you get. What could happen is that an author will be scheduled to speak in or near your area and will come to you as an extra. Also it is highly possible that there are young adult authors living in your own state. The Children's Book Council (67 Irving Place, New York, NY 10003) has a geographical listing of authors. However, it should be considered only a beginning as not all authors are listed with them.

▌ *USING YA LITERATURE IN ENGLISH CLASSES*

Young adult literature has seldom been invited to sit at the head of the table in English classes, but change is in the wind. When Connie Epstein wrote the English departments of the Ivy League and Seven Sister colleges and universities asking what they recommended for precollege reading, responses leaned toward the expected classics. However they also included the following comments:

■ I'd have secondary school teachers weigh books on a scale and award letter grades for reading done by the pound.

> Arthur R. Gold, Chair
> English Department at Wellesley

■ You can never quite be sure what will spark, and what will dull, a young reader's interest. . . . I therefore recommend a great diversity of works for a school library, and a certain eccentricity of taste.

> Richard Johnson, Director
> Freshman English program at Mount Holyoke

■ New directions in curricular thinking and simple proliferation of curricular options for high-school students have tended to erode whatever communal core of literary experience might have existed earlier.

> Peter M. Briggs, Associate Professor
> English Department at Bryn Mawr[12]

In doing research for her Ph.D. dissertation at the University of Houston in 1981, Barbara Samuels found that it was not fear of censorship, lack of funding, nor district or department requirements that kept English teachers from including young adult novels in their curriculum. Instead the following reasons were cited:

1. Teachers were unfamiliar with the genre and had not read many examples. Fewer than half of the 268 respondents to her national survey had taken a college class in young adult literature or even a course that included a unit on such novels.
2. Teachers believed that young adult novels were not sufficiently challenging in structure and style to be taught to average and above average high school students.
3. Teachers felt that as transmitters of culture, they were responsible for exposing students to time-tested classics of world literature.[13]

The solving of problem 1 will indirectly solve problems 2 and 3 because knowledgeable teachers can select those books for teaching that are worthy of class time and they can also use young adult books as bridges to studying respected modern literature as well as the classics of world literature.

Going back to the theory of reading development discussed in Chapter 2, teachers need to keep in mind that lasting progress is necessarily slow and is accomplished in infinitely small steps. None of us want young people to get stuck on a reading level that is beneath their ability or emotional maturity, but it's unrealistic to think that we can prevent this simply by assigning "hard books" or classics. As Robert LeBlanc observed, high school students have to be led to a love of fiction gradually. "Unfortunately, many students are lost as lifelong readers by the abrupt shift from what they choose to read outside of school to what they are assigned to read in school. The jump from Nancy Drew and the Hardy Boys to *Moby Dick* and *Crime and Punishment* leaves out adolescent literature which can serve as a bridge between these two very different kinds of reading experiences."[14]

For large numbers of junior and senior high school students it's already a giant leap to go from watching television or from skimming magazines and record jackets to reading "real books" by such authors as Virginia Hamilton, Mildred Lee, and Cynthia Voigt. The trick is in finding out just where students are and then in helping them to go a little bit further.

Pairing Books

A teaching method which is becoming increasingly popular is the pairing of significant young adult books with respected adult books. The idea isn't totally new. For example, one of Dell's long time best-sellers is a paperback edition of *Romeo and Juliet* along with the script from *West Side Story*. One reason that such pairing is successful is that as educational attitudes have moved away from the free thinking of the late '60s and early '70s into the "back to basics" movement of the late '70s and on into the "push for excellence" philosophy of the '80s and '90s, teachers feel more anxious that young readers make observable progress. The pairing of books helps both students and their teachers feel this sense of progression. In "An English Teacher's Fantasy," Robert LeBlanc suggested pairing Sue Ellen Bridgers' *Home Before Dark* with John Steinbeck's *The Grapes of Wrath;* Mildred Taylor's *Roll of Thunder, Hear My Cry* with Harper Lee's *To Kill a Mockingbird;* and Irene Hunt's *Across Five Aprils* with Ernest Hemingway's *For Whom the Bell Tolls.* LeBlanc gave as his rationale for such pairings:

> These book teams have several advantages over teaching significant literature in isolation. The reader is hooked on the theme by reading the easily manageable adolescent novel first. The more difficult book has the advantage of being based on a familiar theme and is associated with the positive, successful experience of reading the young adult novel. The long term benefit for young readers is that they are more likely to make the connection between adolescent literature and its adult counterpart—the best seller [and then go on to become lifelong readers].[15]

Author Patricia Lee Gauch suggested in an article entitled " 'Good Stuff' in Adolescent Fiction" that teachers pair Mildred Taylor's *Roll of Thunder, Hear My Cry* with Maya Angelou's *I Know Why the Caged Bird Sings;* M. E. Kerr's *Gentlehands* with Elie Wiesel's *Night;* and Robert Cormier's *The Chocolate War* with Walter Van Tilburg Clark's *The Ox-Bow Incident.* She explained, "This isn't 'babying kids into reading decent prose.' It's yoking 'good stuff' with 'good stuff,' to take advantage of the length and teen-centered subject of the younger book."[16]

Susan Nugent recommended Patricia McKillip's *The Night Gift* and Robert C. O'Brien's *Z for Zachariah* as good books for teaching the concept of setting as an integral part of plot before moving on to Nathaniel Hawthorne's *The Scarlet Letter.* Barbara Wersba's *Run Softly, Go Fast* and Maia Wojciechowska's *Don't Play Dead Before You Have To* are easy books (especially the latter one) to use in discussing literary style prior to going on to the more complex *The Catcher in the Rye.*[17] Librarian Judy Druse has compiled a four-page handout of such recommended book pairs which she uses in workshops sponsored by Econo-Clad Books, P.O. Box 1777, Topeka, KS 66601. (At the time of this writing, copies can be requested by mail.)

The idea of pairing could be extended beyond particular books to authors who have similarities in either their writing styles or in the themes they pursue. Units could begin with a significant author for young adults, continue on to a modern author for adults, and then finally to an established author. Table 10.3 illustrates some possible combinations with suggested thematic and literary focal points upon which teaching could be based.

Discussing Books

Nearly everyone agrees that discussing books is valuable. It enables students to exchange ideas, and to practice their persuasive techniques by arguing about and examining various interpretations. Another advantage of discussing a book is that, through verbalization, readers get a handle on their own thoughts. Their ideas and reactions intermingle with those of the author, which is one of the things that reading is all about.

Probably most adults who have worked with books and young readers remember having had some wonderful conversations about books, but they probably also remember having had some distinctly nondescript conversations in

Table 10.3   *TEACHING RELATIONSHIPS BETWEEN YA AND ESTABLISHED LITERATURE*

Significant Author for Young Adults	Significant Modern Author for Adults	Significant Established Author	Thematic Focus	Literary Focus
Katherine Paterson	Anne Tyler	Mark Twain	Personal Growth	Development of Character
Robert Cormier	James Baldwin	Henrik Ibsen	The Individual vs. the System	Development of Plot
Sue Ellen Bridgers	Flannery O'Connor	Jane Austen	Human Relationships	Exploration of Tone
Virginia Hamilton	John Steinbeck	The Brontës	Survival	Settings and Their Effects on Story
M. E. Kerr	Carson McCullers	D. H. Lawrence	Coming of Age	Style

which students recited the plot of the story and then had nothing more to say. With a little planning and a modicum of skill, such negative experiences can be avoided or at least kept to a minimum.

Teachers know that one of their most valuable techniques is that of asking questions and responding carefully to student answers so that a genuine exchange of ideas occurs. If this takes place right after or during the reading of a piece of literature, then new information will be taken in, measured, evaluated, and integrated with the tentative conclusions already reached. To bring about this kind of "enlargement through talk," adults have to walk a middle ground between accepting just any comment that a student makes and having a prepared list of examination-type questions with one and only one acceptable answer. The best discussions resemble the kind of real-life conversations that good friends have when they've both read a new book and are anxious to share opinions and gain insights from each other.

The sense of equality necessary in this kind of discussion may be unsettling to teachers who are accustomed to arriving in class with either a lecture to be given or a set of dittos to be filled out. As Robert C. Small, Jr., wrote in "Teaching the Junior Novel," the generally accepted goal of a high-school literature program is to place the student in a position of incapacity while the teacher is elevated to that of translator. With most adult novels, students are at a tremendous disadvantage when they are asked to evaluate the accuracy with which an author has written about such concerns as marriage and divorce, ambition, greed, and hate. Even though these situations and feelings are related to teenage problems, they are not matters with which students have had experience. In contrast, when the subject of the book is a modern teenager, the balance of knowledge is changed. At least in the area of evaluating the characters, their problems, and the resolution of those problems, Small says "the students can justifiably be said to speak from a greater authority than their teacher."[18] But of course the teacher still has greater knowledge than the students in such matters as the development of plot, setting, characterization, theme, dialogue, and point of view and can use this knowledge to lead the students to worthwhile analysis and evaluation.

When students are at a stage in their intellectual development in which their primary interest is in finding themselves and their peers in the books they read, it stands to reason that an appropriate approach to use in talking about books will be that of subjective response. Suzanne Howell uses the following questions as a "bridge" for those "just finding the way to affective response."

1. What was your immediate (first) response to the story? What was your immediate (first) feeling about the story? What were your immediate (first) associations? (What did the story remind you of?) What were your immediate (first) ideas? (What ideas came to your mind?)
2. Does the story remind you of anything you've seen on TV, anything you've read before, and so forth?
3. Can you relate the story to anything in your own experience?
4. Can you relate any characters in the story to anyone you know?
5. What questions does the story raise in your mind?

It was Howell's experience that students do better in class discussion if they have first taken time to write down their responses. Otherwise, they tend to hide their feelings behind euphemisms or they resort to the objective kinds of analyses that they think most teachers really want. But as students become accustomed to the subjective response approach, they learn to trust their judgments and their feelings. Certainly some responses show more sensitivity than others, but no responses are "right" or "wrong," since each was triggered by something in the story. As classes work, there is a natural progression from subjective response to objective interpretation. As an example, Howell cited a discussion about Virginia Moriconi's short story "Simple Arithmetic," which is told through "letters to and from a boy whose parents give him everything but love." The subjective response of nearly everyone in the class was that they hated Stephen's father. These are the steps through which the class discussion went:

> "I hated Stephen's father."
> "Stephen's father is a cold person."
> "Stephen's father is a cold, detached person, as shown by the fact that he corrects Stephen's spelling instead of dealing directly with his personal problems."
> "The author reveals the character of Stephen's father indirectly through his tone and the style of his letters to Stephen."[19]

Larry Andrews suggested that when students have a superficial "I like it" or "I don't like it" response, their reactions may be based on only one aspect of the material, such as whether or not it had a happy ending or was about a subject that they like. Class discussions encourage students to go beyond this initial response. He recommended breaking reading into preassigned sections. At the end of a section, students express their response to a particular section and, based on these responses, predict what will happen in the next section. By defending their predictions against others', students have to look more deeply at their responses; they have to see if their clues actually appear in the piece or whether they are so familiar with literary techniques and patterns that they are just making good guesses. As students try to agree on what will come next, they look carefully for the clues laid down by the author. Then as they read the rest of the piece to see how their ideas match the author's, they begin to see the difference between a quality piece of literature with its inevitable conclusion and the poorly written one in which an author cheated by relying on an unjustified coincidence or an unbelieveable character to make the plot come out all right.[20]

A practice that is becoming increasingly common in English classes is to concentrate on a theme rather than on a particular book. The teacher selects five to ten titles with a closely related theme and group members read one or more of them. When the group discussion is held, it centers on the common theme with readers of various books telling how the theme was developed in their particular books. Both small and large group discussions can be held.

The smaller the group doing the discussing, obviously the greater the number who get to talk. For example, when a class of thirty students spends a half-hour talking about a story, there will probably be time for a maximum of twenty well-developed comments. But, if for half the time the class were divided into five or six groups, then the number of comments offered by students could be increased to something like sixty or seventy. Worthwhile discussions do not happen automatically. Students must be trained and given guided practice. It's a good idea especially with inexperienced students for the teacher to get a discussion going in the class as a whole and then to offer suggestions or help in the continuation of the talk in the small groups. Students are apt to be more serious and to attend to the task at hand if they must come up with something to be shared with the group as a whole.

For a class to read different but related books there are several advantages. It is easier to get four or five copies of a particular title than to get thirty. Or if purchased with school funds, it seems a better use of money to acquire several different titles that will be available later for students to read individually. The books can also be at different reading levels with students self-selecting the ones with which they feel most comfortable. And books that might cause public relations problems if they were assigned to a large group can be read and studied by a small number of students who make their own decisions on whether or not they want to read a particular title.

In any kind of discussion, there needs to be ample time for thinking. When, for example, teachers ask students to explain the motivation of a character and then give them twelve seconds in which to do it, they force students to oversimplify.[21] Characters in literature are just as complex as those in real life and should be approached with equal respect.

The only questions that can be asked and answered in rapid-fire order are those to which students already know the answers. At the beginning of a discussion these may serve to refresh memories and to ensure that the class is starting from the same factual base, but even simple-sounding questions may have complex answers. It sometimes helps if during a discussion, the teacher's questioning begins at a concrete or factual basis and then moves progressively toward the abstract. One such schema has been developed and recommended by Edward J. Gordon and Dwight L. Burton.[22] It is printed below with examples of questions based on Nadine Gordimer's short story, "A Company of Laughing Faces." Gordimer's story, published in her 1960 collection *Not For Publication and Other Stories* as well as in several anthologies, is set at a beach resort in South Africa. Seventeen-year-old Kathy Hack, the only child of a doting mother has been brought from the semi-retirement village where her parents live, to spend the Christmas Holidays. "Mrs. Hack couldn't be expected to part with Kathy—after all, she *is* the only one," but she did realize that "the child must get out among youngsters once in a while," hence their two-day train trip to the beach. Kathy spends her time in "a company of laughing faces," and learns—not altogether happily—what her mother means by "being young."

1. *Questions requiring students to remember facts:*
   A. Describe the setting of the story.
   B. Describe the protagonist and the other major characters.
   C. What new things had Kathy's mother bought for her?
   D. List the major events in the story.
2. *Questions requiring students to prove or disprove a generalization made by someone else.*
   A. Although the story is set in a South African resort, I think it could have happened at any resort frequented by the upper middle class. Do you agree or disagree? What differences were there between this holiday and American college students going to Florida beaches during spring break? Are these differences crucial to the story?
   B. Some readers have interpreted this story as saying that Kathy was a conformist. Do you agree? In what ways was she a conformist? In what ways was she different?
   C. One interpretation is that the nameless young man in the story represents the anonymous crowds of young people at the resort. Do you agree or disagree? On what evidence?
   D. When Kathy put on her new clothes, the author said that the "disguise worked perfectly." Was Kathy in "disguise" any more than the others? Support your answer with evidence from the story as well as from your own experiences.
3. *Questions requiring students to derive their own generalizations.*
   A. What kind of relationship did Mrs. Hack and Kathy have?
   B. What is Kathy's perception of being young? Who has shaped that perception? Did the events in the story change her perception?
   C. Why doesn't the author give "the young man" a name?
   D. Why does the author contrast the constant activity of the other young people with Kathy's stillness?
4. *Questions requiring students to generalize about the relation of the total work to human experience:*
   A. What did Kathy mean when she said that the sight in the lagoon was "the one truth and the one beauty" in her holiday?
   B. Compare Kathy's relationship with the nameless young man to that of the Bute boy. What is the author saying by showing these two different relationships?
   C. Relate the different parts of the story to Kathy's development in life.
   D. What is the significance of the statement, "The only need she [Kathy] had, these days, it seemed, was to be where the gang was; then the question of what to do and how to feel solved itself." Is Kathy satisfied with the answer the gang provides for her? Why or why not?
5. *Questions requiring students to carry generalizations derived from the work into their own lives:*

    A. Have you been in a situation similar to the one experienced by Kathy? How did it make you feel?

    B. What kinds of security do you get from a group? How hard is it to break away?

    C. Have you seen parents like Kathy's mother? What are some ways that young people defend themselves from well-meaning parents who don't understand the situation?

Probably the most important part of a discussion—and unfortunately the most often ignored—is the summing up. In too many classes, the bell rings in the midst of a discussion and students rush away without gathering their thoughts. Such "fly-away" endings cause students to lose respect for class discussions. If they think the teacher is just filling in time until the bell rings, they won't put forth their best efforts. The successful teacher keeps an eye on the clock and saves at least a couple of minutes to draw things together before students are distracted from the topic at hand. Also, good teachers continually work to develop skill in summarizing throughout a discussion. They draw attention to those points that the class basically agrees upon, they praise insightful comments that help the rest of the class see something they might have missed, they search out reasons for disagreement, and they lead students to see connections between the present discussion and previous ones about similar themes or topics.

Using YA Literature to Develop Oral Communication Skills

As Susan Nugent wrote when she was recommending pairing books to help teach literary concepts:

> Learning difficult concepts (such as point of view, symbolism or internal monologue) while reading difficult and often unfamiliar content prematurely places too many demands upon the student. Instead, adolescent literature allows the student to focus on the new concept, addressing that demand while reading about more familiar content. The point is that a difficult concept plus difficult content often results in frustration.[23]

What she said about learning difficult literary concepts is equally relevant to the development of oral communication skills. Speaking in front of a group is enough of a strain that teachers need to do what they can to provide subject matter with which students feel comfortable. As shown in the descriptions of the half-dozen classroom activities given below, young adult literature can often serve this purpose.

Television Talk Shows   As an alternative to having students get up and "report" on an author, encourage students to do enough research that they will feel comfortable impersonating "their" author participating in a television talk show. One student will serve as the moderator for a panel of four or five authors. The moderator will ask the authors about their families, education, important influences, and the kind of writing they do, etc. Work with the moderators to devise a variety of questions so that the presentation won't bog down with the same questions being asked over and over again. As part of the format, have each author come prepared to read a short excerpt from a favorite piece. Good sources for students to find information include Gale Research's *Something about the Author* and *Something about the Author Autobiography Series* and Twayne Publisher's series on YA authors which includes *Presenting Robert Cormier, Presenting M. E. Kerr, Presenting Norma Fox Mazer,* and *Presenting S. E. Hinton.* Other sources include articles from such periodicals as *English Journal, Voya, School Library Journal,* and *The ALAN Review.*

Group Presentations of Books   Introduce a dozen or more books to your class and then let groups of three or four students choose to read the same title. Allow some time for in-class reading, but also have students read at home so that they can use in-class time for guided group discussion. For the climax of the unit, have students prepare an "original" way to present their book to the class. Valerie Sheppard has described how her ninth-grade English students finished up this kind of a unit focusing on character development. Those reading John Steinbeck's *The Red Pony* did a kind of readers' theatre "because they thought the language used by the characters gave a clearer picture of traits than their actions." A narrator filled in the blank spaces. Those reading Arthur Conan Doyle's *The Hound of the Baskervilles* thought of a fast-paced melodrama and so they made signs and gathered props which they used to make an 8mm movie (a TV video would work just as well). As the movie was shown, they described the plot. Those reading Mary Stewart's *The Hollow Hills* were inspired by the fast-paced second chapter to devise a one-act play. Students with S. E. Hinton's *The Outsiders* created a police file and did a lineup of gang members while reciting their character traits. The group that had Robert Cormier's *I Am the Cheese* tried to duplicate the interweaving effects of the three levels of the story by presenting a kind of three-ring circus. Students in two of the rings would pantomime action while in the third ring, characters were speaking dialogue. This continued until all three rings had shared some dialogue.[24]

Group Analyses   When assigning students to work in groups, it's sometimes a good idea to number off so that participants will be working with students other than those they ordinarily sit with. In this exercise which makes use of semantic differentials, the point is for groups to come to some consensus. Prior to dividing into groups, the teacher prepares a semantic differential form similar to the one shown in Table 10.4 for Robert Lehrman's *Juggling.* The purpose of such a form is to help students see that any one book has many aspects on which readers base their reactions. Students mark the lines showing their reactions. Then when they get in groups of either three or four, they compare to see where they agree and where they disagree. Students whose answers differ considerably from the others will need to explain their reasoning. Perhaps they

Table 10.4 **JUGGLING *BY ROBERT LEHRMAN***

The sports part of this story was:

exciting   +—+—+—+—+   boring

too much   +—+—+—+—+   too little

The love part of this story was:

believable   +—+—+—+—+   unbelievable

touching   +—+—+—+—+   boring

At the end of the story I felt:

confidence in Howie Berger's future   +—+—+—+—+   fear for Howie Berger's future

love for his father   +—+—+—+—+   hate for his father

sympathy for Howie   +—+—+—+—+   disgust for Howie

sympathy for Sandy   +—+—+—+—+   disgust for Sandy

The men on the soccer team were:

unusual   +—+—+—+—+   ordinary

the most interesting part   +—+—+—+—+   the least interesting part

---

will convince the other group members. Give each group a clean form on which they are to record a group opinion which they report to the rest of the class. The exercise could be repeated for other books with different aspects being charted, for example, aspects of literary evaluation as shown in Table 10.5 for Robert Newton Peck's *A Day No Pigs Would Die.* With any one listing, the focus of the semantic differentials should be limited so as not to spread a discussion too thin.

Literary Terminology   At the beginning of an independent reading activity, list a dozen or so of the literary terms that are defined in Chapter Two, for example, *foreshadowing, in media res, denouement, metaphor, personification,* etc. Choose ones that will be at an appropriate level of difficulty for your students. Type the list with brief definitions. Cut three copies of the list into slips of paper each containing one term. Put the slips in a basket and have students draw out a slip. At the end of the unit, the three students who drew out a particular term will be responsible for teaching the concept to the rest of the class. Immediately after the drawing, pass around a copy of the entire list for students to initial so they won't "forget" what they are responsible for. In their reading over the next week or so students

Table 10.5   **A DAY NO PIGS WOULD DIE** *BY ROBERT NEWTON PECK*

Make a mark on the line where your opinion falls. Be ready to explain your reasoning.

AS = Agree Strongly
A = Agree
NA = Neither Agree Nor Disagree
D = Disagree
DS = Disagree Strongly

	AS	A	NA	D	DS
1. The author was skilled at foreshadowing. He made what happened feel "right."					
2. Rob was portrayed as a dynamic character, that is, one who changed and developed in the course of the story.					
3. The changes in Rob were believable.					
4. The author was careful with historical and agricultural details. (Check information about Shakers and about goiters, for example.)					
5. The emotions that Rob felt were presented so as to be believable.					

watch for examples of the literary device they have drawn out. At the end of the unit, the three students who have the same term get together and plan a brief presentation to teach the literary term to the class using the examples they found in their reading.

TV Situation Comedies   For an independent reading project, let students choose from the more lighthearted books written by Paul Zindel, M. E. Kerr, Paula Danziger, and Judie Angell. Richard Peck's *The Ghost Belonged to Me, Ghosts I Have Been,* and *The Dreadful Future of Blossom Culp* as well as Judy Blume's *Blubber, Superfudge,* and *Tales of a Fourth Grade Nothing* would also be good. Three or four students who have read books by the same author work in a group to propose a TV sitcom. They will have between five and ten minutes to sell their "idea" to a production company being played by the class. The students will have to agree on such matters as the setting and theme of the sitcom, which of the author's characters have enough depth to last over several shows, which incidents would make good visual footage, what actors would be good to play the parts, what type of music would make a good theme song, and whether or not it is likely that commercial sponsors could be found. Each presentation should conclude with a synopsis of a sample show.

Pros and Cons of Censorship   In a mature class, students could role-play participants in a school board hearing on whether or not a particular book should be used in an English class or be allowed to remain in a school library. So as not to brand any particular book or raise the ire of past or future censors, it might be wise to base the class exercise on a case history with a made-up example. Prepare students for the discussion by sharing with them some of the information in Chapter Twelve. Many teachers take an "out of sight, out of mind" approach to censorship, never mentioning the word (c.f., people who never talk about cancer) lest they give people ideas. However, some of these same teachers have been surprised to find themselves at censorship hearings facing their former students as opponents. It's much better to discuss censorship issues before people get personally involved in a controversy.

Combining the Teaching of Writing with Literature

As Ted Hipple has pointed out, "In the contemporary secondary school English classroom, writing occupies center stage. It captures the attention of the public, gets the grants, even, in some instances, is tolerated by students." But, he went on to argue that writing has not, nor should not, replace the teaching of literature. "What is needed is a more effective blending of the study of literature and the teaching of writing."[25]

He outlined three kinds of literature writing activities, all of which can be used with young adult books. The first is creative writing using YA literature as a model. He does not recommend assigning students to write the same amount as an adult author would; instead they focus on only a small part, perhaps a monologue or a dialogue. For example, Michelle in *The Bigger Book of Lydia* by Margaret Willey imagines a conversation that she plans to have with her mother. Students can be asked to write a new conversation between Michelle and her mother, one in which the mother does not respond in the way Michelle imagines she will.

Another idea is to assign students to write the beginning of a story, "those opening few sentences or paragraphs that set the scene and mood, introduce the central characters, and suggest the plot." Some students may get caught up in their creativity and go on to finish the story. But whether they write a whole story or only a beginning, they are likely to feel more successful in writing about their own feelings and experiences which is more often the kind of writing found in books by Robert Lipsyte, Paula Danziger, and Judy Blume than in books by Stephen Crane, Nathaniel Hawthorne, or Walt Whitman.

An alternative is to assign students to rewrite a small piece of a story or book. For example, students who didn't like the ending of Katherine Paterson's *Bridge to Terabithia* can try writing a new ending. Students who think that Maureen Daly's *Seventeenth Summer* is outdated can rewrite a section to make it contemporary. Sections from books in which the physical setting is important, such as Wilson Rawls' *Where the Red Fern Grows* and Frank Bonham's *Durango Street,* can be rewritten with different settings, which may lead students to recognize the relationship between setting and plot. A similar exercise is to rewrite a small section changing the sex of a character or the ethnic group to which the character belongs. Additional incidents, conversations, or descriptions might also be written, for example, newspaper accounts of the events in Robert Cormier's *After the First Death* and M. E. Kerr's *Gentlehands;* "Dear

Abby" letters or diary entries for any of the troubled teens in Hila Colman's or Norma Klein's books; and love letters between the characters in such books as Harry Mazer's *I Love You, Stupid!* Judy Blume's *Tiger Eyes,* and Robert Cormier's *The Bumblebee Flies Anyway.*

The second approach to teaching writing in relation to literature is writing about literature. This is the approach most commonly used. Students begin it in fourth grade when they write book reports and continue it throughout their schooling. In Hipple's words, the important thing for the teacher to remember is:

> Students aren't born critics, able to discuss the importance of Hardy's settings or Hemingway's characterizations without help. Teachers can provide students useful critical topics, can suggest criteria appropriate for judging specific pieces of literature, and can aid students in discovering what makes a piece of literature work. . . . Ideally, students should begin this kind of study with something specific to look for, a work's emotional effect and how that is wrought, its reflection of great life, its internal consistency, then examine the work in this light, and finally write about what they see. Their insights may be a bit shallow, but they will be theirs.[26]

The third approach that Hipple suggests is writing in response to literature. The students write about their own feelings using "literature as a stimulus, a springboard, to what are often personal, affective kinds of writing." Since this kind of writing is to reflect students' own unique responses, the teacher needs to allow considerable freedom. A list of options can be presented, but students should always be given the opportunity to ignore the teacher's suggestions and do something different.

Hipple suggested what he calls lit/comp units in which he takes "a small portion of a total work—one stanza from a poem, twenty lines or so from a play, a paragraph from a novel or short story" and uses this excerpt as the stimulus for a variety of writing activities. Table 10.6 is an example of one such exercise. Similar lit/comp units could be created in relation to excerpts from many YA books.

USING YA LITERATURE IN THE READING CLASSROOM

In one sense this section is superfluous because this whole book is devoted to the teaching and promoting of reading, but there are some things about the interests and responsibilities of teachers of reading that differ from those of English teachers or of librarians. One difference is that, except for remedial programs, the teaching of reading as an academic discipline in the high schools is a fairly recent development. The assumption used to be that normal students had received enough formal instruction in reading by the time they completed elementary school. They were then turned over to English teachers who taught

Table 10.6 THE PRINCESS BRIDE *BY WILLIAM GOLDMAN*

William Goldman ended his "good parts version" of S. Morgenstern's "Classic Tale of True Love and High Adventure," *The Princess Bride,* with these two paragraphs:

But that doesn't mean I think they had a happy ending either. Because, in my opinion anyway, they squabbled a lot, and Buttercup lost her looks eventually, and one day Fezzik lost a fight and some hot-shot kid whipped Inigo with a sword and Westley was never able to really sleep sound because of Humperdinck maybe being on the trail.

I'm not trying to make this a downer, understand. I mean, I really do think that love is the best thing in the world, except for cough drops. But I also have to say, for the umpty-umpth time, that life isn't fair. It's just fairer than death, that's all.

Here are some suggestions for writing. Choose to do at least two of them:

1. Goldman says that "Love is the best thing in the world, except for cough drops." Make a list of ten other modern inventions he might have used in this comparison. Why do you think he chose cough drops?
2. For the "umpty-umpth time," Goldman says that "Life isn't fair," but then he adds that it is "fairer than death." Ask ten friends or family members for their opinion on the fairness of life. Try to get them to give you examples supporting their opinion of whether life is usually fair or unfair. Jot down their answers and when you have at least ten, try to organize the thoughts and write a several-paragraph essay discussing life's "fairness."
3. Write a traditional ending to Cinderella and then write a more realistic "downer" ending in Goldman's style. Tell what happens to Cinderella, the Prince, the Prince's parents, Cinderella's parents, and her stepsisters.
4. Choose a book you've read in the last two years and make a list of "the good parts," i.e., the parts you would leave in if you were going to abridge the book for "a good parts version."
5. Look in a current newspaper. Find a news story and then rewrite it as a fairy tale using Goldman's style.
6. Watch *The Princess Bride* movie and compare the visual ending of the movie with the verbal ending of the book.

If none of these ideas appeals to you, then make up a topic of your own or based on your reading of the book do one of the following:

1. Make a list of all the names (characters, creatures, and places) in *The Princess Bride* and then tell how Goldman used the names to do more than help readers keep the characters straight. Which names sound like other words? What are the connotations of some of the names? Where in the book did he explain about the power of a name?
2. Reread the two or three pages near the beginning of the book where Goldman tells about his father reading him *The Princess Bride:* "For the first time in my life, I became actively interested in a *book.* Me the sports fanatic, me the game freak, me the only ten-year-old in Illinois with a hate on for the alphabet wanted to know *what happened next.*" Write about the first time you remember being hooked on a book. What was it? Why did you like it? Was someone reading it to you? Do you still like the same kind of story, etc.?
3. Remember how the giant Fezzik loved rhymes. Make a list of at least ten rhymes for him. Try putting some of them in a little poem about the story.

---

mostly literature, grammar, and composition. Certainly English teachers worked with reading skills, but they were not the primary focus. Today more and more states are passing laws setting minimal reading standards for high school graduation, and this has meant that reading has become almost a regular

KATHERINE PATERSON
on Comfort and Calm

During the period when my youngest was sweating out the wait for college acceptance, I came upon her in the living room reading. Now that was not in itself extraordinary. Mary has been a reader since she was five. But the book my intelligent eighteen-year-old was absorbed in was *Charlotte's Web* which she first met when she was about three. She looked up at me, her eyes shining. "This is a great book," she said.

When adults talk about books for young adults, I wish they'd remember how hard it is to be an adolescent—how many life-shaping decisions must be made at a time when most people are not ready to make them. Parents and teachers may try to encourage and reassure, but I have found that my children often return to the stories they loved when they were young to help them get through rough periods.

Books for young adults should include mind and heart stretchers like the classics. Can I ever forget what *Tale of Two Cities* and *Cry the Beloved Country* meant to me as a teenager? Surely they will include books like those of Sue Ellen Bridgers and Robert Cormier with which young people will more readily identify. But for comfort, for reassembling the identities that seemed to have come unstuck, what about a fresh look at *Charlotte's Web, Where the Wild Things Are,* or *Tuck Everlasting*?

It might be fun, as well as instructive, to have students write about or discuss their favorite childhood book. A lot can be learned about story structure by examining children's books, and a side benefit for the students may be a few hours of calm amidst the general turbulence of their lives.

Katherine Paterson's books include *Bridge to Terabithia,* Crowell, 1977; *Rebels of the Heavenly Kingdom,* Lodestar, 1983; and *Jacob Have I Loved,* Crowell, 1980.

part of the high school curriculum. In some schools, all ninth-graders now take a reading class, while in other schools, it is only for those students who test one or two years below grade level. Depending on how long it takes them to pass the test, students may take basic reading classes for several semesters.

In the teaching profession the reluctant reader is nearly always stereotyped as a boy from the wrong side of town, someone S. E. Hinton would describe as an outsider, a greaser. Actually reluctant readers come in both male and female varieties and from all social and I.Q. levels. Many of them have fairly good reading skills; they simply don't like to read. Others are poor readers partly because they get so little practice. What these students have in common is that they have been disappointed in their past reading. The rewards of reading—what they received either emotionally or intellectually—have not come up to their expectations, which were based on how hard they worked to read the material. They have therefore come away feeling cheated.

The reading profession has recognized this problem and has attempted to solve it by lowering the price the student has to pay, that is, by devising reading materials that are easier, that demand less effort from the student. These are the controlled vocabulary books commonly known as high-low books, meaning high interest, low vocabulary. They are moderately successful. One problem is that there isn't enough variety to appeal to everyone. A disproportionate number of them have been written to the stereotyped target audience of the young male from a motorcycle gang. The authors are rarely creative artists; they are educators who have many priorities that come before telling a good story. An alternative approach to encourage reluctant readers is to make the rewards greater rather than to reduce the effort. This is where the best adolescent literature comes into the picture. The rewards are often high enough to fully recompense supposedly reluctant teenage readers. And once these readers enjoy the satisfaction of receiving what they consider full pay for their work, then they are happy to play the reading game.

Young adult literature has a good chance of succeeding with the reluctant reader for the following reasons:

1. It is written specifically to be interesting to teenagers. It is geared to their age level and their interests.
2. It is usually shorter and more simply written than adult material, yet it has no stigma attached to it. It isn't written down to anyone nor does it look like a reading textbook.
3. There is so much of it—almost 800 new books published every year— that individual readers have a good chance of finding books that appeal to them.
4. As would be expected since they are the creations of some of the best contemporary writers, the stories are more dramatic, better written, and easier to get involved in than are the controlled vocabulary books.
5. The language used in good adolescent literature is much more like the language that students are accustomed to hearing. In this day of mass media communication, a student who does not read widely may still have a fairly high degree of literary and language sophistication gained from watching television and movies.

Taking all of this into account, there are still some types of adolescent literature that will be enjoyed more than others by reluctant readers. In general, reluctant readers want the same things from the books they read that the rest of us want, only they want them faster and in less space. If it's information they are looking for, they want it to be right there. If they are reading a book for thrills and chills, they want it to be really scary. And if it's for humor, they want it to be really funny. And if they're not sure about committing themselves for a large chunk of time, they want books in which they can get a feeling of accomplishment from reading short sections or even paragraphs. This helps explain the continuing popularity of the *Guinness Book of World Records*.

Booklist publishes an annual "High-Interest/Low-Reading Level Booklist" compiled by a YASD committee. (Single copies in leaflet format can be ordered from *Booklist,* American Library Association, 50 E. Huron St., Chicago, IL 60611, for fifty cents and a stamped, self-addressed envelope.) The list is divided into three different reading levels figured on the Fry Readability Scale, none of which are above grade six. The committee considers "titles intended for the young adult that are written using controlled vocabulary, short sentences, short paragraphs, simplicity of plot, and uncomplicated dialogue." Selection criteria included a sense of timeliness, maturity of format, and appeal of content. Fiction must include "believability of character and plot as well as realistic dialogue."

The push for higher reading scores has had the effect of opening the high school curriculum to reading classes for all students, not just those with low reading scores. For example, study skills courses are commonly given in which students are taught principles of skimming, reading for the main idea, and speed reading.

Another class that has been taught since the 1930s, but which enjoyed a new surge of popularity in the 1970s, is individualized reading. In this class, students spend most of their time reading books of their choice. The thinking behind the organization of such classes is that one of the chief reasons that out-of-school reading drops off so dramatically when children leave elementary school is that the social structure of high school leaves students little time for reading. Classes go under such titles as Paperback Power, Paperback Reading, Contemporary Reading, Individualized Reading, and Personalized Reading. The following guidelines have been gleaned from several successful programs, most notably that of the one at Cedar Falls High School in Cedar Falls, Iowa, directed by Barbara Blow.[27]

1. Students can read any books they choose.
2. When students register for the course, a note goes home to parents explaining that the choice of books is up to the student and his or her parents. This is a friendly note, inviting parent participation, and quoting from parents of previous students who have enjoyed recommending books to their children and talking about reactions, and so on.
3. When students finish reading each book, they have a ten to fifteen minute individual conference in which they discuss the book with the teacher. The teacher makes suggestions for other books that the student will probably enjoy.
4. The teacher reads each book (or at least skims it) prior to the discussion. To enable teachers to build up a sufficiently large background of reading so that they can talk knowledgeably about the books, most programs have the same teacher handle several sections over an extended period of time. This contrasts with some unstructured (and usually unsuccessful) programs in which the course is seen more or less as a free reading study hall with little or no preparation required from the teacher.

5. The room is organized and students seated so as to minimize in-class visiting and make it easy to take the roll and locate students for conferences.

6. Teachers' aides handle such clerical tasks as taking the roll, scheduling conferences, recording grades, and checking out books so that the teacher (or teachers, if it is team-taught) can concentrate entirely on student conferences.

7. Conferences are held in nearby offices or screened-off areas so that they will not disturb the students who are reading and so that the teachers' attention will not be divided between the class and the individual student.

8. Nearly all class time is reserved for reading. The exceptions are three or four days in a semester when the librarian gives booktalks.

9. Although students are allowed to select their own books from any source, a special individualized paperback collection is made available to them. This includes multiple copies of popular books so that when enthusiasm about a book spreads from one student to another, copies will be available.

10. Lists of the books most frequently read by class members are distributed at regular intervals to serve as idea sources for further reading.

11. Students sign up a week in advance for conferences so that the teacher has time to read the book and so that the teacher has time to plan an approach. Some schools give students suggestions for organizing their discussion so that the student takes the initiative. Others are teacher-directed.

12. Grading is handled in various ways including credit for promptness and good attendance, numbers of pages read, quality of preparation for conferences, selection of "challenging" books, and so forth. Some teachers reported that it was necessary to be fairly stringent so that students understood that the class was serious and not just a study hall.

13. Some programs emphasize the keeping of a record card marking down the number of pages read each day. Students get a feeling of achievement as their number of pages steadily increase.

The kind of individualized reading program that is described here is not for the dysfunctional or disabled reader. It is for the average or above-average student who simply needs a chance to read and discuss books. In effect, it is one last try on the part of the school to instill in young people the habit of reading for pleasure. The student who lacks the skills for this kind of reading class or for a more standard class in literature needs expert help from a professional reading teacher. Preparing teachers for that kind of role is beyond the scope of this book.

USING YA LITERATURE IN THE SOCIAL STUDIES CLASS

One of the great values and pleasures of literature is that it frees us to travel vicariously to other times and places. Movies, television, and photographs allow people to see other places, but literature has an added dimension. It allows the reader to share the thoughts of another person. It has been said that one never feels like a stranger in a country whose literature one has read. In today's jet age, distances are rapidly shrinking and it is more important than ever that people feel at home in other countries and with other cultures. People then begin to realize that members of the human race, regardless of where or how they live, have more similarities than differences.

Historical fiction, fiction set in other countries, fiction about members of ethnic groups in the United States, and well-written informative books should all be part of high-school social studies classes. When Laurence Yep wrote *Dragonwings,* he fictionalized the true story of a Chinese immigrant in California who made a flying machine in 1909 that flew for twenty minutes. Yep explained in an afterword that very little was actually known about the man because "Like the other Chinese who came to America, he remains a shadowy figure. Of the hundreds of thousands of Chinese who flocked to these shores we know next to nothing." What Yep wanted to do with his story was to change at least a few of these people from "statistical fodder" into real people with "fears and hopes, joys and sorrows like the rest of us."

This is what good literature can do for any mass of social facts, figures, and statistics. Esther Forbes' *Johnny Tremain* breathes life into a study of the American Revolution. Irene Hunt's *Across Five Aprils* does the same thing for the Civil War, and Anne Frank's *The Diary of a Young Girl,* Johanna Reiss' *The Upstairs Room,* and Nathaniel Benchley's *Bright Candles* do it for World War II. In thinking about history, these books come immediately to mind because it is the wars that have been covered in traditional history textbooks. But within recent years, critics have been vociferous in their objection to the glorification of violence and war in histories and the lack of information about the contributions of women and minorities. Such critics are asking for an enlarged view of history that will teach how everybody lived, not just soldiers and statesmen, not just the winners, but ordinary people at home. What was happening in all the years when people were not fighting wars?

It may be in answering these questions that literature can make its biggest contribution to the social studies class. A book with the power of Robert Newton Peck's *A Day No Pigs Would Die* gives readers a feel for rural Vermont life in the 1920s. Anne Stallworth's *This Time Next Year* shows what the Depression did to farm families, and Jessamyn West's *The Massacre at Fall Creek* makes readers think of what it meant in 1824 to have to change one's thinking on something so basic as whether or not it is murder to kill an Indian.

However, it is important for readers to realize that no one book can tell them everything about what every person in a particular group thinks and feels. Many different books need to be read, always keeping in mind the fact that each book presents only one perspective. Stereotypes exist in people's minds for two reasons. One is that the same attitudes are repeated over and over so that they become the predominant image in the reader's mind. Another is that an individual may have had only one exposure to a particular race, group, or country. For example, a young reader who knows nothing about Africa and then reads D. R. Sherman's *The Lion's Paw,* about a young Bushman caught in a conflict between white hunters and his and a lion's needs, can hardly be said to have developed an understanding of a whole continent and its people. Nevertheless, the reader will have learned something and will perhaps have become intrigued enough to continue reading. Similarly, a reader who finishes Chaim Potok's *The Chosen* doesn't know everything about Hasidic Jews, but he or she knows a lot more than before, including the fact that there are groups within groups.

By reading widely and sharing their findings, social studies class members can lead each other to go beyond stereotypes. They will begin to realize that every person is a unique blend of characteristics even though that person may be a member of particular group.

USING YA LITERATURE IN CLARIFYING HUMAN RELATIONS AND VALUES

Workers with church and civic youth groups, teachers of classes in human relations, and professional counselors working with young adults have all found that adolescent literature can be a useful tool in the work they do. When talking about using books for the general purposes of helping students understand their own and other people's feelings and behavior, we sometimes use the term "bibliotheraphy." But it is a word that goes in and out of fashion, at least in reference to the informal kind of work that most teachers and librarians do with young adults. Its technical meaning is the use of books by professionally trained psychologists and psychiatrists in working with people who are mentally ill. It is because of this association with illness that many "book" people reject the term. Their reasoning is that if a young adult is mentally ill and in need of some kind of therapy, then the therapy should be coming from someone trained in that field rather than from someone trained in the book business or in teaching and guiding normal and healthy young adults.

However, most people agree that normal and healthy young adults can benefit psychologically from reading and talking about the problems of fictional characters. They get the kinds of insights that are reflected in the following comments collected from students by Ina Ewing, a teacher at Maryvale High School in Arizona:

The book [Judy Blume's] *Forever* shows a girl making a hard decision. Every girl has to make that decision at one time or other and so Kathy is

CYNTHIA VOIGT
on Learning and Knowing

I have a theory that the real difference between kids and adults is that kids expect themselves to be learning and adults expect themselves to know. This seems to me to be both a central and an essential difference.

If I expect myself to be learning, my attitude towards experiences, people, the whole side show, is characterized by questions and curiosity; probably more important, my understanding of who I am, myself, is that I am changing, growing, adding to myself. If I expect myself to know, then I stand before the world as a completed creature—and I am bound to be a disappointment to everybody concerned in the encounter. If I must know, in order to be a self I recognize and respect, the possibility for change diminishes. If I require the adults around me to know, I diminish them.

This may just be the difference between growing up and grown-up. Kids have it easy because there is no question that they are in process. Adults stand under the danger, or the temptation, of thinking that process ought to have been completed, or has been completed—which is, of course a fool's paradise. I don't know about the rest of the adults out there, but it seems to me I spend my time perpetually growing up, with no end in sight to the arduous and uneasy occupation—which strikes me, on the whole, as a good thing, and a beneficial thing. I don't envy kids, the young, and I don't regret the years I've got on them, but one of the things I cherish about teaching is that constant reminder, unspoken but clear, that learning, not knowing, is what it's about.

Cynthia Voigt's books include *Izzy, Willy-Nilly,* Atheneum, 1986; *Dicey's Song,* Atheneum, 1982; and *The Runner,* 1985.

like a lot of girls I know. My friends don't talk about it though, so it's good to read about someone else's decision. I think it helps.

[In reference to John Neufeld's *Lisa, Bright and Dark*] I never realized that even kids our age have big enough problems to go crazy. I always thought the ones who went nuts were the ones who were taking dope. I would sure try to help a friend of mine though who thought she was going crazy. It must be scary.

[In reference to Paul Zindel's *The Pigman*] When my grandma died my grandpa came to live with us. It was a big bother because I had to move into a room with my brother. Now I'm glad that he has a place to stay so he won't be so lonely.

■ [In reference to Paula Danziger's *The Cat Ate My Gym Suit*] I think that this book says that you should listen to your parents but I also think it says that you should stand up for what you believe in. This book made it seem so easy to stick to a cause. I would be so afraid like Marcy was. She was shy at first. That's me. Well then when she really believed in something it was easy not to be so shy. I could maybe find a cause.

■ [In reference to Ann Head's *Mr. and Mrs. Bo Jo Jones*] I liked the way the book told the side of a couple that makes it when they get married. Most books tell you that if a girl and guy have to get married, it won't last. Even though they had their share of problems, they made their marriage work in the end. It shows that sometimes pregnancy occurs because love is strong in spite of everything else.[28]

All teenagers have problems of one type or another, and simply finding out that other people have them too provides some comfort. We are reassured to know that our fears and doubts have been experienced by others. We feel more confident when we read about people successfully coping with problems that we may have in the future. Notice that of the five student comments given here, only one refers to an actual event. The others are conjectures about things that might happen.

David A. Williams, a communications professor at the University of Arizona, said in a newspaper interview that he would die happy if he could "prove that a positive correlation exists between the rise of anxiety in the country and the decline of pleasure reading." Research done during the 1950s and 1960s has shown that anxiety is directly related to a poor concept of oneself. "It seems to me," he said, "that the human being's major concern in life is to determine what it means to be a human being." The paradox is that before people can see themselves, they have to get outside of themselves and look at the whole spectrum of human experience to see where they fit in. "When we are feeling anxious it is usually because we have a narrow perspective which sees only what it wants to see." Someone who is anxiety-ridden, paranoid, or resentful selects from life's experiences things to validate those feelings. For people like this, reading can put things back into perspective. "When we read about others who have suffered similar anxieties, we don't feel so cut off and, although the world doesn't change, we change the way we look at it."[29]

Books put things into perspective because they talk about the human experience in ways that bring readers back to an awareness of their commonality with other human beings and open up avenues of communication that successful discussion leaders tap into.

However, it is important for adults to be careful in guiding students to read and talk about personal problems. No one should be forced to participate in such a discussion nor should a special effort be made to relate stories to the exact problem that a group member is having. In fact, it would probably be best to avoid matching up particular problems with particular students. When someone is in the midst of a crisis, chances are good that he or she does not want to read and talk about someone else in a similar predicament. As a general rule, one will probably get the most from such a discussion before and/ or after—rather than during—a time of actual crisis.

The kinds of groups in which such discussions are usually held are clubs, church groups, classes on marriage and human relations, counseling sessions, and "rap" sessions at crisis centers and various institutions to which young people are sent. Since these groups are often the kind where membership changes from meeting to meeting and there are no pressures for participants to do outside reading as "homework," a leader will probably be disappointed or frustrated if the discussion is planned around the expectation that everyone will have read the book. A more realistic plan is for the leader to give a summary of the book and a ten- to twenty-minute prepared reading of the part that best delineates the problem or the topic for discussion. Using fairly well-known books, including ones that have been made into movies, will increase the chances of participation. Using popular books will also make it easier for students whose appetites have been whetted to find the book and read it on their own.

In an adult group of professionals, the same purpose would be accomplished by reading a case study that would then be discussed. But case studies are written for trained adults who know how to fill in the missing details and how to interpret the symptoms. Teenagers are not psychologists, nor are they social workers or philosophers. Literature may be as close as they will ever come to discussing the kinds of problems dealt with in these fields. And the oral presentation of a well-written fictional account has the advantage of being entertaining and emotionally moving in ways that factual case studies could not be.

What follows the oral presentation can be extremely varied depending on the nature of the group, the leader's personality, and what the purpose of the goal of the discussion is. The literature provides the group—both teenagers and adults—with a common experience presented through the neutral (as far as the group is concerned) eyes of the author. This common experience can then serve as the focus for discussion. Pressures and tensions are relieved because everyone is talking in the third person about the characters in the book, although in reality many of the comments will be about first-person problems.

The theory developed by Lawrence Kohlberg and his associates at Harvard University during the 1960s about how people solve moral problems is relevant. According to Kohlberg findings, moral judgment is not something that can be taught intellectually. Rather it develops with experience and age, in a predictable sequence. Longitudinal studies conducted in many different cultures have shown that young people between the ages of ten and twenty-five go through six stages of development in their attempts to solve moral problems. People sometimes become fixated at one of these stages, for example, an adult operating at the second stage, that of immediate reciprocity, sort of a you-be-nice-to-me and I'll-be-nice-to-you approach. Typically, however, people continue to progress through the stages, which are grouped into three levels. Table 10.7

shows these levels and stages. The table is taken from one of the few articles that has been written on the relationship between books and the behaviors involved in moral judgment, "Moral Development and Literature for Adolescents" by Peter Scharf.

In Scharf's article he made the point that the way a reader responds to a particular story will depend on the stage of moral judgment that he or she has reached. For example, at age thirteen a reader is apt to respond to Feodor Dostoevsky's *Crime and Punishment* as a mystery, but at age twenty the same reader would be more likely to look at it as a complex study of human morals. Great literature has an impact at almost any age, but naturally students will respond the most to that which fits the particular level at which they are struggling to make sense of the world. At the beginning levels (early teens), readers are reassured to read books in which there are definite rules and clear-cut examples of right and wrong. As readers move into the conventional or middle levels, they are interested in literature that focuses on social expectations. According to Scharf, this literature:

> stimulates a sense of moral conventionality by praising "appropriate" social attitudes. Often protagonists will represent heroic values which are reflected and emulated by young readers. Villains are often portrayed as "unfeeling" or "cruel" in often one-dimensional, somewhat stereotyped ways. Good literature of this type presents a coherent moral universe in which good and evil are polarized and defined. . . . While this type of literature may seem "corny" or "sentimental" to adults, it is a necessary stage toward the learning of more complex personal moral philosophies.[30]

As students become confident at this level and feel that they understand the expectations of society, they begin tentatively to explore and question these expectations. Many young people reject the conventional moral order and seek to set up or to find a more satisfactory social order. Scharf wrote:

Table 10.7   **CLASSIFICATION OF MORAL JUDGMENT INTO LEVELS AND STAGES OF DEVELOPMENT**

Levels	Stages of Development
Level I. Preconventional	Stage 1: Obedience and punishment orientation
	Stage 2: Naively egoistic orientation
Level II. Conventional	Stage 3: Good-boy orientation
	Stage 4: Authority and social-order maintaining orientation
Level III. Postconventional	Stage 5: Contractual legalistic orientation
	Stage 6: Conscience or principle orientation

SOURCE: Adapted from Lawrence Kohlberg, "Stage and Sequence: The Cognitive Developmental Approach to Socialization," from *Handbook of Socialization Theory and Research* edited by David Goslin. Copyright © 1969 by David A. Goslin. Reprinted by permission.

▉   Needless to say, this questioning is disturbing to many adults, including librarians. They fail to see that such a rejection of conventional societal truth is a critical step in the adolescent's defining for himself an autonomous value base.[31]

Because many young adults are in the stage of rebellion and questioning, Holden Caulfield in Salinger's *The Catcher in the Rye* speaks forcefully to them. As people mature, they gradually pass through this stage of rebellion and are not so concerned with society and its expectations. Instead they develop an internal system by which they make moral judgments. This final stage is distinct from both early adolescent conformity and the relativism and nihilism of middle adolescence. Scharf thinks that books and libraries have a unique role in providing readers with the range of material that they need to reflect upon in developing their inner values.

In conclusion, literature can in no way solve someone's problems. But it can serve as a stimulus to thought, and it can open channels of communication. It can serve as a conversation topic while rapport and understanding grow between an adult and a teenager or among the members of a group. And reading widely about all kinds of problems and all kinds of solutions will help to keep young people involved in thinking about moral issues.

Table 10.8 shows what young adult literature can and cannot do when it is used as a tool to teach about human relations and values.

This chapter has shown that evaluating, using, and promoting books with young readers is a shared opportunity and responsibility. It belongs not only to

---

Table 10.8   **THE POWERS AND LIMITATIONS OF YA LITERATURE**

What literature can do:	**What literature cannot do:**
1. It can provide a common experience or a way in which a teenager and an adult can focus their attention on the same subject.	1. It cannot cure someone's emotional illness.
2. It can then serve as a discussion topic and a way to relieve embarrassment by enabling people to talk in the third person about problems with which they are concerned.	2. It cannot guarantee that readers will behave in socially approved ways.
3. It can give young readers confidence that, should they meet particular problems, they will be able to solve them.	3. It cannot directly solve readers' problems.
4. It can increase a young person's understanding of the world and the many ways that individuals find their places in it.	
5. It can comfort and reassure young adult readers by showing them that they are not the only ones who have fears and doubts.	
6. It can give adults as well as teenagers insights into adolescent psychology and values.	

librarians and English and reading teachers but to everyone who works closely with young people and wants to understand them better. It can serve as a medium through which to open communication with young adults about their concerns.

We focused on librarians, teachers, and youth workers or counselors, but we could also have mentioned many others, including parents. Contrary to the impression given by the mass media, many parents serve in the roles described here, that is, teacher, counselor, conversation partner, and reading friend.

NOTES

[1]*Human and Anti-Human Values* (New York: Council on Interracial Books for Children, 1976), p. 4.

[2]Janet French, "Review of *Homecoming*," *School Library Journal* 28 (September 1981): 133.

[3]Audrey Eaglen, "What Makes a Good Review," *Top of the News* 35 (Winter 1979): 146–152.

[4]Anne Tyler, "Looking for Mom," *New York Times Book Review,* April 26, 1981, p. 52.

[5]Katherine Paterson, "Family Visions," *New York Times Book Review,* November 14, 1982, p. 41.

[6]Dorothy Matthews, "Writing about Adolescent Literature: Current Approaches and Future Directions," *Arizona English Bulletin* 18 (April 1976): 216–19.

[7]Mary K. Chelton, "Editorial," *VOYA* 6 (February 1984): 310, 315.

[8]Dorothy M. Broderick, "Whose Job Is It Anyway?" *VOYA* 6 (February 1984): 320–26.

[9]Adrienne Jones, "And All for the Want of a Horseshoe-Nail," *VOYA* 6 (February 1984): 316–18, 327.

[10]Joni Bodart, *Booktalk! Booktalking and School Visiting for Young Adult Audiences* (New York: H. W. Wilson, 1980), pp. 2–3.

[11]Mary K. Chelton, "Booktalking: You Can Do It," *School Library Journal* 22 (April 1976): 39–43.

[12]Connie C. Epstein, "The Well-Read College-Bound Student," *School Library Journal* 30 (February 1984): 32–35.

[13]Barbara G. Samuels, "Young Adult Novels in the Classroom?" *English Journal* 72 (April 1983): 86–88.

[14]Robert LeBlanc, "An English Teacher's Fantasy," *English Journal* 69 (October 1980): 35–36.

[15]LeBlanc, 35–36.

[16]Patricia Lee Gauch, " 'Good Stuff' in Adolescent Fiction," *Top of the News* 40 (Winter 1984): 125–29.

[17]Susan Nugent, "Adolescent Literature: A Transition into a Future of Reading," *English Journal* 73 (November 1984): 35–37.

[18]Robert C. Small, "Teaching the Junior Novel," *English Journal* 61 (February 1972): 222–29.

[19]Suzanne Howell, "Unlocking the Box: An Experiment in Literary Response," *English Journal* 66 (February 1977): 37–42.

[20]Larry Andrews, "Responses to Literature: Enlarging the Range," *English Journal* 66 (February 1977); 60–62.

[21]This is what James Hoetker found in "better" schools with "better" staff. Teachers were asking five questions per minute. "Teacher Questioning Behavior in Nine Junior High School English Classes," *Research in the Teaching of English* 2 (Fall 1968): 99–106.

[22]Edward J. Gordon, "Levels of Teaching and Testing," *English Journal* 44 (September 1955): 330–34; and Dwight L. Burton, "Well, Where Are We in Teaching Literature?" *English Journal* 63 (February 1974): 28–33.

[23]Nugent, 35.

[24]Valerie Sheppard, "A Novel Unit with Several Books," *Arizona English Bulletin* 24 (October 1981): 44–47.

[25]Ted Hipple, "Writing and Literature," *English Journal* 73 (February 1984): 50.

[26]Hipple, 52.

[27]Barbara Blow, "Individualized Reading," *Arizona English Bulletin* 18 (April 1976): 151–53.

[28]Ina Ewing, "The Psychological Benefits of Young Adult Literature," unpublished paper, Arizona State University Department of Educational Technology and Library Science, Spring semester, 1978.

[29]"Feeling Uptight, Anxious? Try Reading, UA Prof Says," *Tempe Daily News,* December 15, 1977.

[30]Peter Scharf, "Moral Development and Literature for Adolescents," *Top of the News* 33 (Winter 1977): 131–36.

[31]Scharf, 131–36.

TITLES MENTIONED IN CHAPTER TEN

Adams, Douglas. *The Hitchhiker's Guide to the Galaxy.* Crown, 1980.

Alter, Eric. *The Dukes of Hazzard: Goin' Racin'.* Warner, 1983.

Angelou, Maya. *I Know Why the Caged Bird Sings.* Random House, 1970.

Benchley, Nathaniel. *Bright Candles.* Harper & Row, 1974.

Blume, Judy. *Blubber.* Bradbury, 1974.

_____ . *Forever.* Bradbury, 1975.

_____ . *Superfudge.* E. P. Dutton, 1980.

_____ . *Tales of a Fourth Grade Nothing.* E. P. Dutton, 1972.

_____ . *Tiger Eyes.* Bradbury, 1981.

Bodart, Joni. *Booktalk! Booktalking and School Visiting for Young Adult Audiences.* H. W. Wilson, 1980.

Bonham, Frank. *Durango Street.* Dutton, 1967.

Bradbury, Ray. *The Martian Chronicles.* Doubleday, 1958.

Bridgers, Sue Ellen. *Home Before Dark.* Knopf, 1976.

Campbell, Patricia J. *Presenting Robert Cormier.* G. K. Hall, 1985.

Childress, Alice. *A Hero Ain't Nothin' But a Sandwich.* Putnam, 1973.

Clark, Walter Van Tilburg. *The Ox-Bow Incident.* Random House, 1940.

Commire, Anne. *Something About the Author* Series. Gale Research, 1972–continuing.

Cormier, Robert. *After the First Death.* Pantheon, 1979.

_____ . *I Am the Cheese.* Knopf, 1977.

_____ . *The Bumblebee Flies Anyway.* Pantheon, 1983.

_____ . *The Chocolate War.* Pantheon, 1974.

Daly, Jay. *Presenting S. E. Hinton.* G. K. Hall, 1987.

Daly, Maureen. *Seventeenth Summer.* Dodd, Mead, 1942.

Danziger, Paula. *The Cat Ate My Gym Suit.* Delacorte, 1974.

Dostoevsky, Feodor. *Crime and Punishment.* 1866.

Doyle, Arthur Conan. *The Hound of the Baskervilles.* 1902.

Fast, Howard. *April Morning.* Crown, 1961.

Forbes, Esther. *Johnny Tremain.* Houghton Mifflin, 1943.

Frank, Anne. *The Diary of a Young Girl.* Random House, 1956.

Garden, Nancy. *Annie on My Mind.* Farrar, Straus & Giroux, 1982.

Golding, William. *Lord of the Flies.* Coward, McCann, 1955.

Goldman, William. *The Princess Bride.* Harcourt Brace Jovanovich, 1973.

Gordimer, Nadine. *Not For Publication and Other Stories.* Viking, 1960.

Greene, Bette. *Summer of My German Soldier.* Dial, 1973.

Hamilton, Virginia. *Sweet Whispers, Brother Rush.* Putnam, 1982.

Hawthorne, Nathaniel. *The Scarlet Letter.* 1850.

Head, Ann. *Mr. and Mrs. Bo Jo Jones.* Putnam, 1967.

Hemingway, Ernest. *For Whom the Bell Tolls.* Scribner, 1940.

Hinton, S. E. *The Outsiders.* Viking, 1967.

Holtze, Sally H. *Presenting Norma Fox Mazer.* G. K. Hall, 1987.

Hunt, Irene. *Across Five Aprils.* Follett, 1964.

Hunter, Mollie. *A Sound of Chariots.* Harper & Row, 1972.

Kerr, M. E. *Gentlehands.* Harper & Row, 1978.

Knowles, John. *A Separate Peace.* Macmillan, 1960.

Lee, Harper. *To Kill a Mockingbird.* Little, Brown, 1951.

Lehrman, Robert. *Juggling.* Harper & Row, 1982.

Mazer, Harry. *I Love You, Stupid!* Crowell, 1981.

McKillip, Patricia. *The Night Gift.* Atheneum, 1976.

Melville, Herman. *Moby Dick.* 1851.

Mitchell, Margaret. *Gone with the Wind.* Macmillan, 1936.

Neufeld, John. *Lisa, Bright and Dark.* Phillips, 1969.

Nilsen, Alleen P. *Presenting M. E. Kerr.* G. K. Hall, 1986.

O'Brien, Robert C. *Z for Zachariah.* Atheneum, 1975.

Palmour, Vernon E. *The Planning Process.* American Library Association, 1980.

Paterson, Katherine. *Bridge to Terabithia.* Crowell, 1977.

Peck, Richard. *Ghosts I Have Been.* Viking 1977.

———— . *The Dreadful Future of Blossom Culp.* Delacorte, 1983.

———— . *The Ghost Belonged to Me.* Viking, 1975.

Peck, Robert Newton. *A Day No Pigs Would Die.* Knopf, 1972.

Porter, Hal. *The Paper Chase.* Angus & Robertson, 1966.

Potok, Chaim. *The Chosen.* Simon & Schuster, 1967.

Rawls, Wilson. *Where the Red Fern Grows.* Doubleday, 1974.

Reiss, Johanna. *The Upstairs Room.* Crowell, 1972.

Russel, Alan, and David A. Boehm, eds. *Guinness Book of World Records.* Sterling, 1988.

Salinger, J. D. *The Catcher in the Rye.* Little, Brown, 1951.

Sarkissian, Adele. *Something about the Author Autobiography Series.* Gale, 1985.

Sherman, D. R. *The Lion's Paw.* Doubleday, 1975.

Stallworth, Anne. *This Time Next Year.* Vanguard, 1972.

Steele, Daniele. *Crossings.* Delacorte, 1982.

Steinbeck, John. *The Grapes of Wrath.* Viking, 1939.

Steinbeck, John. *The Red Pony.* Covici-Friede, 1937.

Stewart, Mary. *The Hollow Hills.* Morrow, 1973.

Taylor, Mildred, *Roll of Thunder, Hear My Cry.* Dial, 1976.

Van House, Nancy A., et al. *Output Measures for Public Libraries.* American Library Association, 1987.

Voigt, Cynthia. *Homecoming.* Atheneum, 1981.

Walker, Alice. *The Color Purple.* Harcourt Brace Jovanovich, 1982.

Wersba, Barbara. *Run Softly, Go Fast.* Atheneum, 1970.

West, Jessamyn. *The Massacre at Fall Creek.* Harcourt Brace Jovanovich, 1975.

Wiesel, Elie. *Night.* Farrar, Straus & Giroux, 1960.

Willey, Margaret. *The Bigger Book of Lydia.* Harper & Row, 1983.

Wojciechowska, Maia. *Don't Play Dead Before You Have To.* Harper & Row, 1970.

Yep, Laurence. *Dragonwings.* Harper & Row, 1976.

Zindel, Paul. *The Pigman.* Harper & Row, 1968.

For information on the availability of paperback editions of these titles, please consult the most recent edition of *Paperbound Books in Print,* published annually by R. R. Bowker Company.

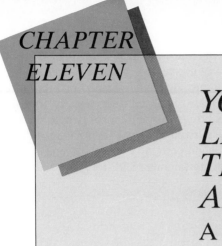

CHAPTER ELEVEN

YOUNG ADULT LITERATURE, THE MASS MEDIA, AND BIG BUSINESS

A Symbiotic Relationship

Too many teachers are guilty of looking upon the mass media as an adversary, thinking that if it weren't for television, movies, Sony Walkmans, and magazines, students would read more books. David Burmester compared this head-in-the-sand approach to Plato's objections to the practice of writing. Plato feared that those who wrote down their thoughts would become mentally lazy; they wouldn't have to think incisively. Of course, Plato was wrong, just as wrong, Burmester says, as are teachers who refuse to bring the study of movies and television into classrooms and "not sandwiched in between sentence structure and *Silas Marner,*" but as an important topic of its own.[1]

Such study is beyond the scope of this text, but there are many aspects of the mass media and big business that relate directly to young adult literature. Only since YA lit became part of big business have substantial numbers of talented authors been able to devote their full attention to writing for young people, and the best publishers use some of their profits from mass-marketed books and magazines to support high quality books judged to have the potential of reaching small numbers of readers over long periods of time.

One "myth" discussed in Chapter 1 was that if kids see a film, they won't read the book. Solid evidence has put this idea to rest, but people still worry that movies and television take the place of books. A more realistic attitude is to view print and nonprint media as symbiotic. Authors Paul Zindel, Glendon Swarthout, and S. E. Hinton have all written screenplays as well as books for young people, and one of the good things that has happened because of the dual visibility given to their work is that many people who knew nothing about books for teenagers now realize that there is such a thing as "YA lit." This knowledge has to be helpful when teachers and librarians seek funds from taxpayers, school boards, and library trustees.

We all know that discussing movies and television with young people can be intellectually stimulating. They get more involved when talking about "their" media than when talking about the same ideas and themes in relation to literature written fifty, one hundred, or two hundred years ago. In its finest moments, the modern mass media has brought to millions of people the best of our plays, poems, stories, and novels. Even at its worst, it has introduced people to literary traditions and has taught certain symbols and conventions while raising people's expectations for entertainment and story.

MOVIES

Of the approximately l00 movies listed in a local TV guide for one week (including cable offerings), at least two dozen were aimed at a teenage audience. Some of these were descendants of the 1968 *Night of the Living Dead* and the more recent *Friday the 13th* (1980) and *A Nightmare on Elm Street* (1985), while others such as *Police Academy* (1984) and *Revenge of the Nerds* (1984) relied on heavy humor. A few others supposedly featuring high school students bordered on soft porn and in theaters were restricted to adult audiences. But the largest portion of the teen films had characteristics similar to those that Maia Mertz and David England identified as belonging to modern adolescent literature.

1. They involve a youthful protagonist.
2. They employ a point of view presenting the adolescent's interpretation of the events of the story.
3. They are characterized by directness of exposition, dialogue, and direct confrontation between principal characters.
4. They take place over a limited period of time and in a limited number of locales, having few major characters, and resulting in a change or growth step for the young protagonist.
5. The main characters are highly independent in thought, action, and conflict resolution.
6. The protagonists reap the consequences of their actions and decisions.
7. The screenwriters drew upon their sense of adolescent development and the concomitant attention to the legitimate concerns of adolescents.
8. The films mirror current societal attitudes and issues.
9. The stories most often include gradual, incremental, and ultimately incomplete "growth to awareness" on the part of the central character.
10. The films are hopeful.[2]

There's nothing particularly new about movies that fit this description. *Rebel Without a Cause* attracted young adults in droves way back in 1955. What is new is the number of films calculatedly put together to attract young people. John Hughes' recent films *Sixteen Candles* (1984), *The Breakfast Club* (1985), *Ferris Bueller's Day Off* (1986), and *She's Having a Baby* (1987) blur into each other, even for their intended audience.

In a different class are popular movies for general audiences such as *Flashdance* (1983), *An Officer and a Gentleman* (1982), *The Color Purple* (1985), *Ordinary People* (1980), and *Terms of Endearment* (1983). Each of these movies had at least one young adult main character who fitted the Mertz and England descriptors. In a visual medium, youthful characters are especially appealing simply because of their physical attractiveness. A second reason for their appeal relates as much to books as to movies. Young people's emotions are especially intense and their lifestyles are undergoing the kinds of changes that form the basis for interesting plots as they make decisions about leaving home, for example, or choosing a mate, or deciding on the values they will live by for the rest of their lives.

Steven Spielberg's 1987 *Empire of the Sun,* which is based on J. G. Ballard's semi-autobiographical book about the young son of wealthy colonialists caught in China at the beginning of World War II, is almost a perfect example of the romantic quest discussed in Chapter Four. The movie opens with scenes proving the boy's specialness. He is shown singing in the choir of his exclusive school and then being chauffeured to his mansion home where he is adored by talented and beautiful parents and obeyed and revered by servants. The first jarring scene of the movie is when the boy, dressed in party clothes, sits in an abandoned airplane pretending he's a fighter pilot, but he is soon brought face-to-face with reality when he encounter's a group of grim Japanese soldiers waiting for a real battle.

Myra Forsberg, writing for the *New York Times,* described this scene as the foreshadowing of the movie's theme, which parallels director Steven Spielberg's own coming-of-age into the making of adult movies. In the movie, the boy is accidentally separated from his parents as they try to flee before the Japanese invasion. He goes through all the nightmares of a dangerous quest, first by himself and then with help from a most unlikely source—a couple of American ne'er-do-wells who at first hope to get ransom money for him. They are all imprisoned with other foreigners until the atom bomb is dropped on Nagasaki and the war ends. During these two years, the boy again proves himself to be a worthy hero. Spielberg told Forsberg that in depicting the dawn of the Atomic Age:

> I wanted to draw a parallel story between the death of this boy's innocence and the death of the innocence of the entire world. When that white light goes off in Nagasaki and the boy witnesses the light—whether he really sees it or his mind sees it doesn't matter. Two innocents have come to an end, and a saddened world has begun.[3]

From the perspective of the romantic quest, the most touching scene is after the liberation of the camp when the boy in his new status and maturity is reunited with his family. From Spielberg's standpoint, the significance is that in this movie he came to terms with the kind of innocence that he had been clinging to for most of his adult life, "which was a celebration of a kind of naivete that has been reconfirmed countless times" by the numbers of people who went to see *E.T., Back to the Future,* and *Goonies.*[4]

This difference that Spielberg cites between his earlier "innocent" movies and the loss of innocence in *Empire of the Sun* might be interpreted as the difference between E. B. White's *Charlotte's Web* and Robert Newton's Peck's *A Day No Pigs Would Die.* In White's children's book, a beloved but useless pig wins a ribbon at the County Fair and is allowed to live a long and happy life, while in Peck's YA book a beloved but useless pig wins a ribbon at the County Fair but must be slaughtered anyway.

In the early 1980s, several books published for teenagers made it to the big-time movies, not just to television specials as M. E. Kerr's *Dinky Hocker Shoots Smack,* Bette Greene's *Summer of My German Soldier,* Richard Peck's *Are You in the House Alone?,* and Judy Blume's *Forever* had done in the 1970s. In the summer of 1982, S. E. Hinton's *Tex* was released as a Walt Disney Studio movie directed by Tim Hunter and starring Matt Dillon as Tex and Jim Metzler as big brother Mason. The following spring, Hinton's *The Outsiders* directed by Francis Ford Coppola was released, to be followed by *Rumble Fish.* Robert Cormier's *I Am the Cheese* came out the following summer, but it must have been a great disappointment to Robert Cormier, as well as to its financial backers. After a very short New York run, it was released to television where, because of the distractions of interruptions for commercials and the generally less concentrated viewing of a home television audience as compared to a darkened theater audience, viewers had an even harder time getting involved in the complex story with its flash-forwards and its repetitious scenes of Adam (Robert McNaughton of *E.T.* fame) riding his bicycle through the Vermont countryside.

Even though kids liked *The Outsiders* (see "A Boy's View of *The Outsiders,*" Todd Camhe, *Los Angeles Times Calendar,* April 3, 1983, pp. 18–19) and the week of its release it grossed five million dollars and was the biggest money-maker in several large cities, adult reviewers competed to see who could be the most cleverly negative about it. Vincent Canby, writing in the *New York Times,* started his review with "It's as if someone had handed Verdi a copy of 'The Hardy Boys Attend a Rumble' and, holding a gun to the poor man's head, forced him to use it as a libretto."[5] David Denby, a reviewer for *New York Magazine,* labeled the movie "the cinematic equivalent of purple prose," while Peter Rainer, a reviewer for the *Los Angeles Herald Examiner,* called it a "gusty, overblown vacuum."[6]

Tex was much more successful. Richard Schickel writing in *Time* magazine praised the new sophistication of Walt Disney studios and called the movie "modest, intelligent, and entirely engaging."[7] When movie critics Gene Siskel and Roger Ebert did a TV program about movies with young male protagonists, which aired September 3, 1983, they cited *Tex* for being what the others only pretend to be—stories of growing up to be a man. They criticized the falseness

Movies with young protagonists and young adult books share some common characteristics and therefore find a wide audience among teenagers.

of the male/female relationships shown in such movies as *Porky's, The Last American Virgin, Going All the Way, Spring Break, Homework, Class,* and *Private School.* In what they described as an epidemic of horny teenage movies, they pointed out how the boys never risk a real relationship. There is always a wall—either real or figurative—between them and the women they lust after. What is missing in these "lust/hate" relationships is affection, friendship, and honesty. They praised the line in *Tex* where big brother Mace confesses to fifteen-year-old Tex that he's never had sexual intercourse. The implication is that probably most of his friends haven't either and that it's generally unwise to believe everything one hears in locker rooms. Siskel and Ebert thought this bit of honesty was worth all of the other movies put together.

Because producing a movie is such a large task, it has to be done by a team of people rather than by one individual. Glendon Swarthout in talking about the movie version of his *Bless the Beasts and Children* spoke resignedly about the great part that luck plays in putting a film together. Writing the book was an individual artistic endeavor that he controlled with his own intellect, but once it got to the movie studios, literally hundreds of creative people had an input.

Joanne Greenberg said much the same thing when she spoke at the 1983 American Library Association convention about her experience with *I Never Promised You a Rose Garden,* which she wrote under the pseudonym Hannah Green. She compared selling the movie rights to her book to selling a well-loved car. You make the people who buy it promise to give it a good home and not to soup it up with headers and rainbow tape. They promise faithfully and even say you'll be invited to come and look it over occasionally. But then the buyer falls on hard times and has to sell the car to someone else. In a half-hearted way he passes on your requests, but of course he doesn't insist because he's anxious for the sale. The same thing happens again and again and eventually everyone forgets that you were the original owner. Years later you see your old car coming down the street. You hardly recognize it because it not only has headers and rainbow tape, it has a hood scoop, mag wheels, and a blower.

But regardless of the disappointment that authors might feel in the movie productions of their books, it is interesting to note that of the books on the Honor List that are still popular after a decade, a surprisingly large number have been made into either television or feature-length movies, for example, *Mr. and Mrs. Bo Jo Jones, The Autobiography of Miss Jane Pittman, Go Ask Alice, Red Sky at Morning, The Andromeda Strain, Sounder, Where the Lilies Bloom, Alive, Watership Down, Dinky Hocker Shoots Smack, A Hero Ain't Nothin' But a Sandwich, Summer of My German Soldier,* and *The Chosen.*

Movies in the Classroom

In 1931, Samuel Rosenkranz reminded English teachers:

> We continue to teach standards of evaluation in the drama and to ignore the cinema, and our pupils continue to patronize the cinema and to ignore the drama. We refuse to recognize the fact that they are going to the picture shows, and that we must adapt our literature and composition courses in such a manner that adequate recognition is given to the fact that there are some genuine needs to be met.[8]

No one would argue that feature films ought to be *the* content of English classes, but films can help in a multitude of ways. Feature films may spark interest in a thematic unit. They may be useful in comparing a novel in print and what happens to it when it becomes a theatrical film or a TV film. And they may clear up meanings of literary terms, for example, flashbacks are almost always clearer in film than in print, while character development in print and film have both similarities and differences—a useful topic for discussion.

In the later 1960s and early 1970s when film was commonplace in many secondary classes, *Media and Methods* was the most exciting and most widely read magazine aimed at high school teachers. Some of the *M & M* articles are still worth reading, both to remind teachers of the excitement of the time and of the ways that film can be handled for the good of teachers, students, literature, film, and English classes.[9] Tony Richardson's film, *The Loneliness of the Long Distance Runner* (1962), from Alan Sillitoe's story, was *the* film to use in class, partly because of Tom Courtenay's electric performance as the Borstal (reform school) boy. *Loneliness* is still very much worth seeing and talking about, but so is Franco Zeffirelli's 1968 *Romeo and Juliet* and Nicholas Ray's 1955 *Rebel Without a Cause,* which starred James Dean.

But those were films, reels in cans, almost certain to be used with l6mm projectors. Few of the *Media and Methods* readers from the '60s and '70s would have believed that a mere twenty years later a VCR, a videocassette, and a TV set could have gone so far in replacing films on reels—no more ripped sprocket holes, no more staples used to splice broken film, no more burned out projector bulbs, no more streamers of film piling up on the floor, and no more rips in screens. Even better, no more ordering of an expensive film and praying that the school's budget would hold up and that the film would arrive in decent shape close to the time you planned to use it.

Today, it's easy to purchase or rent any number of worthwhile films (and many that no one could justify intellectually for use in schools or private homes) from an incredible number of video stores. Some schools have developed their own video libraries of films that are particularly useful. Others rent films or tape sitcoms or soap operas for class use, erasing them, of course, within the legally allowed time. Many first-rate films, including those listed below in chronological order, can be purchased for less than $20.00 to be used over and over.

Intolerance (1916), D. W. Griffith's atonement for the racial sins in *Birth of a Nation. Intolerance* is not merely the greatest silent film; it's one of the greatest films any time, any place.

The General (1927), Buster Keaton's masterpiece about a would-be Confederate soldier who becomes a hero. The "General" is his train.

The Gold Rush (1925), Charlie Chaplin's first great feature film about the little tramp (rivaled only by *Modern Times*).

King Kong (1933), sometimes silly, but always fun and full of adventure.

The 39 Steps (1935), Alfred Hitchcock's finest film, and still the best mystery adventure tale around. Moody and virtually a text on filmmaking.

The Lady Vanishes (1938), a lesser film than *The 39 Steps,* but not by much, and funny and suspenseful to boot.

Citizen Kane (1941), not always appreciated by young people but with careful timing and good preparation, the film still works well. It's been listed several times in polls as the greatest film ever made.

The Magnificent Ambersons (1942), in some ways a more complex and better film than *Kane* but since Welles lost control of the cutting, what we have is a flawed but still fabulous film.

The Third Man, Welles' finest mood piece is a study of evil.

My Darling Clementine (1946), John Ford's finest Western partly because of Henry Fonda's delightful portrait of Wyatt Earp. (The only other Ford Western that rivals this is *The Searchers* with John Wayne's finest job of acting, but it's more expensive.)

I Heard the Owl Call My Name (1973), the only TV film on this list but an honest account of Margaret Craven's novel and a great performance by Tom Courtenay.

Raiders of the Lost Ark (1981), the mysticism gets a bit heavy-handed and sticky by the end, but this is almost certainly the most breathtaking attempt to mimic the old Saturday afternoon serials.

Short Films

As helpful as feature films can be, they have several disadvantages, the chief one being that they are rarely shorter than 75 to 100 minutes long. Allowing time for taking attendance and making a few comments before and after the film, a single showing can take up to three class periods. Short films are much more flexible and can be shown twice or even three times in a single class period. In addition, as David Burmester argues, they are concentrated—much as a short story is—and can stimulate discussion and thought for writing.[10]

But short films aren't merely useful tools. They can be, again like short stories, works of art. Back in the late 1960s and early 1970s most teachers would have had firsthand experience with using short films or seeing them at local or state film workshops and festivals. Today, some teachers are unaware of the riches available in the short films most likely stored in their own school libraries or within easy reach at a university film library. If copies of *Media and Methods* are still available, teachers would be wise to reacquaint themselves with the short films then popular and usually still available.[11]

Just as there is no one feature film that must be seen to appreciate and understand feature films, so there is no one film that represents all short films. But over the years those listed below have become teachers' favorites because they force young adults out of comfortable ruts through cajoling, threatening, provoking, shocking, amusing, or bewildering just as short stories do, just as all good literature does. The bonus is that they achieve their effects in little more than half an hour, sometimes even less.

"Night and Fog" (originally distributed by Contemporary Films out of Mc-Graw-Hill but now so widely available in film libraries that it hardly matters who distributes it; 31 min., black and white and color. Alain Resnais is one of the greatest French New Wave filmmakers, but this film is not experimental. It's a quiet, extremely quiet, film with a French narration that seems at first unemotional. (The English subtitles are rarely needed.) Resnais contrasts black and white footage (taken by German photographers and captured near the end of World War II) of German concentration camps with color shots of the same camps after the war—mounds of hair, operating tables for "medical research," and the like. We can barely tolerate without weeping this most powerful statement about humanity's inhumanity.[12]

"Nahanni" (National Film Board of Canada, 19 min., color). Albert Faille dreams of the legendary gold fields at the headwaters of the Nahanni River in northwest Canada. Even though he's now ancient and has made seven unsuccessful tries to find them, he prepares for his eighth try with incredible optimism.

"Joseph Schulz" (Wombat Films, 13 min., color). A young German soldier is ordered to be part of a firing squad to execute partisans during World War II. He learns that he cannot kill without reason and finally joins the partisans and is killed by his former friends. Students often find this farfetched until they're told the film is based on truth. Then they're puzzled and sometimes even frightened.

"Peege" (Phoenix Films, 28 min., color). A husband and wife and two grandsons visit a mother/grandmother near death in a nursing home, and one grandson stays behind for a few minutes to say goodbye to the person who once meant the world to him. It's beautifully acted and far more than a tearjerker.

"The Ugly Little Boy" (Learning Corporation of America, 19 min., color). Isaac Asimov's tale is about an unemotional nurse hired by a lab to care for a little boy being transported from prehistoric times for study. The creature is ugly but it is human and the nurse, and viewers, fall in love with him.

"The Veldt" (Barr Films, 24 min., color). Ray Bradbury's lovely/nasty little story is about two children in the future who have both a strange playroom and no love for their parents.

"I'm a Fool" (Coronet/MTI, 38 min., color). One of the American Short Story Series, this one is Sherwood Anderson's touching and funny story of a young racetrack worker who falls in love and tells outrageous lies to his beloved. Ronny Howard is fine as is Amy Irving.

"An Occurrence at Owl Creek Bridge" (Films, Inc., 27 min., black and white). Ambrose Bierce's great short story is beautifully recreated by Robert Enrico. The film won a prize at Cannes, was the only outside film ever shown by Rod Serling on "The Twilight Zone," and has been used over and over by teachers grateful for the film's quality and value for young people.

"Neighbors" (National Film Board of Canada, 9 min., color). Norman McLaren was and is the genius of short films, and this may be his finest work. Two men, once friendly neighbors, go to war over a flower—absurd and terrifying. Other McLaren films (from the National Film Board) include "Pas de Deux" and "A Chairy Tale."

"Hardware Wars" (Pyramid Films, 13 min., color). Hardly the greatest entry from a company that still has the most exciting catalogue of short films but a funny spoof of *Star Wars* with that wonderful warrior, Augie Ben Doggie.

A brief list of short films producers and distributors can be found at the end of this chapter, but nothing less than seeing many short films will alert teachers and librarians to the riches that can be found.

◼ *RECORDS AND CASSETTES*

Records have long been a basic part of an English teacher's repertoire of teaching tools and gimmicks, particularly those several recordings of Shakespeare's plays and Robert Frost's recordings of his own poetry. But there's much more out there now that cassettes take care of the problems of dropped or scratched phonograph records.

A headline in the August 27, 1987, *New York Times* announced "Recordings of Books Are a Rising Factor in Cassette Market." Herbert Mitgang wrote the story about "hundreds of small and large companies that are spinning out audiocassettes on every conceivable subject—from self-help to Shakespeare. Every category of book on and off the best-seller lists, in fiction and nonfiction, can now be found if not seen."[13] Among the readings that teachers can use are Toni Morrison's readings from *Tar Baby* or *Song of Solomon* from American Audio Prose Library, stories by Ray Bradbury including "There Will Come Soft Rains" read by Leonard Nimoy on a Caedmon cassette, Joan Hickson's reading of four Agatha Christie stories under the title of *Miss Marple Investigates* on a Listening for Pleasure cassette, a dramatization of Richard Adams' *Watership Down* on a Mind's Eye cassette, Robert Van Gulik's *Murder in Canton* or Voltaire's *Candide* on a Recorded Books cassette, and dramatizations of the "Sweet Valley High" series and Marion Zimmer Bradley's *City of Sorcery* on Warner Audiocassettes.

A brief list of some producers and distributors of cassette tapes (and some records) can be found at the end of this chapter, but nothing will replace teachers and librarians requesting catalogs and glancing through at the riches that can be found—Peter Matthiessen reading from *The Snow Leopard;* Woody Allen reading from *Getting Even;* Ray Bradbury reading all of *The Martian Chronicles;* Linda Ellerbee reading from *And So It Goes;* Anne McCaffrey reading from *The White Dragon;* Virginia Hamilton reading from *Zeely;* Ernest Gaines reading from *A Gathering of Old Men,* and more and more yet.

Perhaps the most useful company for teachers is Random House Media with materials available in three forms. Cassettes alone can be ordered for Esther Forbes' *Johnny Tremain* or Robert Cormier's *The Chocolate War* or Anne Frank's *The Diary of a Young Girl.* Filmstrips and cassettes (or cassettes alone) can be ordered for Joan Blos' *A Gathering of Days* or Bruce Brooks' *The Moves Make the Man* or Edgar Lee Masters' *The Spoon River Anthology.* Cassettes alone or filmstrips with cassettes or VHS videocassettes can be ordered for Virginia Hamilton's *Sweet Whispers, Brother Rush* or Katherine Paterson's *Jacob Have I Loved* or Elizabeth Yates' *Amos Fortune, Free Man.* J. R. R. Tolkien's *The Hobbit* is available on VHS alone. And the American Short Story

JANE LANGTON
on Illustrations

I wish books for older children had pictures. For that matter, I wish fiction for adults had illustrations, as so many novels did in the nineteenth century. Few books now are illustrated except for picture books. And that seems to me a shame, because there is a peculiar connection between pictures, text, and memory. A good text is far more memorable when it has been crystallized in the memory with good pictures.

Without pictures the story vaporizes, vanishes, disappears from the mind much more quickly. When I think of *Alice in Wonderland,* I of course envision Tenniel's *Alice.* What would Milne's stories be without Ernest Shepard's masterful drawings of the Hundred-Acre Wood, without his incomparable pictures of Piglet and Pooh? The importance of the drawings by Garth Williams for E. B. White's *Stuart Little* and *Charlotte's Web* is underscored by the lesser appeal of his *Trumpet of the Swan*—illustrated, yes, but without the perfection of the drawings by Williams.

To make an unforgettable classic there must be a wonderful story and equally wonderful pictures. May they come back soon, books for teenagers thickly sprinkled with pictures!

Jane Langton's books include *The Fledgling,* Harper & Row, 1980; *Paper Chains,* Harper & Row, 1977; and *Emily Dickinson Is Dead,* Penguin, 1986.

Series (available from Coronet Films as films) can be purchased in filmstrip format from Random House Media.

Records or cassettes are not intended to replace books. Teachers and librarians know that recordings can supplement books and may even encourage some young people to read, but there are those who worry that recordings are designed to replace books.

 We will lose something very stirring in the American tradition when we walk upstairs to find our kids listening to Mark Twain on headsets. Tapes are one more disincentive to literacy. In the case of serious works of art, there is something precious about the silence that surrounds reading.[14]

Finally, cassettes of young adult novels that may be ordered for the blind are listed in one of the typically offbeat and helpful Young Adult columns in *Booklist* for November 15, 1985. The address for ordering those books is The Library of Congress National Library Service for the Blind and Physically Handicapped, Washington, DC 20542.

◢ *TELEVISION*

In the previous section, we noted that many movies had characteristics similar to those Maia Mertz and David England identified as belonging to modern adolescent literature. That's equally true of many popular TV shows, but while John Hughes' films are marketed directly to young adults, TV producers are less specific in their advertising. Even though the sponsors of such popular shows as "Facts of Life," "Gimme a Break," "Happy Days," "Three's Company," and "Diff'rent Strokes" may be thinking of a teenage audience, they are happy to get any spillover audiences they can.

TV is unquestionably popular with young people; it always has been, but in quite different ways than movies. Movies are social rituals, bringing people together and providing supposedly safe outlets for young people. And as adults gladly tell the young, movies can be an art form. Fewer adults grant that TV has been, or can be, artistic. Virtually every TV season begins with newspaper headlines or magazine articles questioning whether this year (1968 or 1978 or 1988 or 1998) is not the worst TV season on record. William A. Henry asked, "Is TV Getting Better or Worse?" in the March 12, 1988, *TV Guide* and fearlessly answered his question in the last three lines: "The answer, then, is this. TV has definitely been getting better. Soon, fearfully soon, it may start getting worse."

Some adults seem frighteningly preoccupied—much more than teenagers—with TV's sex and violence. MTV comes in for its share of attacks, but then so do "Dynasty," "The A-Team," "Miami Vice," "Hawaii Five-O," and their depressingly mediocre ilk. But worse yet, TV fare as good as "Cheers," "Hill Street Blues," "Duet," and "L.A. Law" receive almost as much criticism.

Television, for many young people, is a friend, or a substitute for a friend. Racing or trudging home and turning on the TV set brings sound into some homes where no adults are likely to be found for several hours. TV doesn't scold or belittle young people. Instead it makes them feel safe and comfortable. Of course, the sound may be ignored, but it serves its purpose. Loneliness and boredom can be partially, or temporarily, alleviated by noise, almost any kind of noise, and TV noise is generally socially acceptable.

How much TV do young people watch?

◢ By the time the average person graduates from high school, he or she has watched more than 17,000 hours of television, having spent only about 10,800 hours sitting in the classroom.[15]

◢ According to A. C. Nielsen Company, young adult males spend an average of 25.2 hours per week in front of the TV set, while young adult females watch 24.2 hours of TV weekly.[16]

What do young people want from TV, other than company and comfort? No surprises there—entertainment. When getting ready to write this chapter, we took a hopelessly unscientific poll of four classes from a nearby high school, two classes taking honors English and two classes reading at least two grades below grade level. We asked students what programs they most enjoyed watching.

The most frequently watched and enjoyed shows of the honors classes were "news shows" generally followed by "Cheers," "L.A. Law," "Magnum," and "Nova," along with reruns of "Sanford and Son" and "Star Trek." The poorer readers enjoyed "Family Ties," "Head of the Class," "21 Jump Street," and "Wheel of Fortune," along with reruns of "Gimme a Break." Except that the honors group enjoyed "news shows" and "Nova," distinctions are blurred between the kinds of programs enjoyed by the two groups. Shows that were equally popular with both groups were "Alf," "The Cosby Show," "Facts of Life," and reruns of "The Brady Bunch" and "M*A*S*H."

The continued fascination that high school and young college students feel for daytime soap operas—and to a lesser extent nighttime soaps like "Dynasty" and "Dallas"—often amazes teachers, but the reasons for their popularity aren't difficult to fathom. Soap operas provide cheap and easily accessible fantasies day after day after day. Granted, good writing and honest statements about life aren't literary commonplaces in soaps like "The Days of Our Lives" or "The Young and the Restless"or "All My Children" or "General Hospital," but that's something that worries only English teachers, not young people. Soaps allow, or even encourage, viewers to imagine themselves as rich and free, while involved in incredibly complex but fascinating emotional dilemmas as they do all sorts of exciting things. The best part is that it's all vicarious and is available any time that a young person flicks on the TV set, or more and more today, the VCR.

Those of us who worry about young people getting too many "emotional roller coaster rides too early in life," as we heard one adult say, have probably forgotten what it's like to be young and trying to experience all the world has to offer. We've also forgotten how in the early days of TV when radio drama was dying and movies feared TV so much that studios forbade movie stars from appearing on it, TV controlled the social life of adults, and maybe some young people. Shows like "Name That Tune," and "Ed Sullivan" and "The Show of Shows" were so incredibly popular that some viewers developed their social calendar around TV. In New York City, so many people watched the same shows that the city's water pressure was affected when they all took bathroom breaks during the commercials.

That day is over for most people. The ubiquitous VCR allows us to tape a movie broadcast at 4:00 A.M. and replay it after dinner. In the March 19, 1988, *TV Guide,* Neil Hickey commented on the popularity of VCRs and their implications for our future entertainment.

■ Consider: more homes now have VCRs than have cable. By 1995, more than 80% of TV homes will have at least one VCR, according to informed estimates; and folks will be buying 520 million prerecorded cassettes (up from 22 million in 1985) and renting four billion of them (up from 700 million in 1985). In brief, that harmless looking little rectangular box next to your TV set is gradually moving to stage center as the nation's preferred entertainment medium.[17]

Only a few paragraphs further, Hickey notes that television networks who once were horrified by VCRs and the prospect of people copying and keeping network shows now accept the inevitability of VCRs and have begun to consider ways VCRs might help networks.

> The networks are just now beginning to take the VCR into account in their scheduling and promotional strategy. When CBS flung "Tour of Duty" into the breach against the invincible "Cosby Show," for example, the network considered the extraordinary step of recommending to viewers in its ads and promos that, if they must watch "Cosby," they owed it to themselves to at least tape "Tour of Duty." CBS didn't do that but thinks it will in the future.[18]

VCRs are simple to use and virtually every young adult knows how to operate them and to work the fast forward button to cut ads out and do all sorts of tricks that would have seemed magic to previous generations.

Prerecorded tapes used to be mostly movies, but more and more TV shows are available. For example, *The Best of John Belushi* and *The Best of Dan Aykroyd* from the golden days of "Saturday Night Live" have held up well, and young adults find them funny, particularly Belushi's work. A number of sketches from "Monty Python's Flying Circus" seem even funnier and more lunatic than when first broadcast, especially "The Piranha Brothers," "The Semaphore Version of Wuthering Heights," "Killer Sheep," and "The Death of Mary, Queen of Scots." The same comment could apply to two particularly hysterical episodes of "Fawlty Towers," "The Kipper and the Corpse" and "Basil the Rat."

Television and the Classroom

Critics of TV are easy to find, both those who attack TV generally and those who attack teachers who use media in the classroom. But obviously some TV is immediately applicable to education, for example, impeachment proceedings against an elected official in government classes, programs on the Vietnam struggle in history classes, a "Masterpiece Theatre" production of *Northanger Abbey* in English literature classes, or a Metropolitan Opera production of *Turandot* in music classes.

Early in March 1988, the MacArthur Foundation provided 4.5 million dollars to place twenty significant television series on the shelves of 4,000 public libraries, videotapes that could be borrowed by library patrons. And those patrons presumably include high school teachers and librarians. One series, "The Jewel in the Crown," will be available only for private showing, not public performance, but the other nineteen could be used as patrons see fit. Among these are "I, Claudius," David Attenborough's "Life on Earth," Kenneth Clark's "Civilization," Jacob Bronowski's "Ascent of Man," and Bill Moyers' "A Walk Through the Twentieth Century."

These are admittedly exceptionally fine examples of what television offers, but the rest of it is not as bad as some people would have us believe. English teachers need to achieve a balance between being horrified or condescendingly amused by young adults' TV tastes and caving into youthful judgments. If we're to have any chance to affect TV or young people's interests and tastes, then we must consider before we judge. Television isn't going to go away, regardless of the hopes expressed in Jerry Mander's *Four Arguments for the Elimination of Television* or Marie Winn's *The Plug-in Drug* or Neil Postman's *Amusing Ourselves to Death: Public Discourse in the Age of Show Business*. These critics have a point, but what they want us to do—ignore TV and get back to print curriculum—is only part of our job.

An equally important part is to work with students and fellow educators to discover the kind of medium that TV is, existing largely on advertising revenue with material that someone hopes or assumes the public will enjoy. Seeking answers to such questions as the following will be at least a beginning:

Who makes the decisions as to what the "public" will enjoy?

What kinds of people write for TV?

What kinds of material have been popular over the years?

Why were Westerns once a staple of TV but are now rarely seen during prime time?

What goes into the making of a commercial success?

What would a writer do to create a show aimed at young adults?

Why did sit-coms like "The Dick Van Dyke Show" and the "Mary Tyler Moore Show" falter in their early episodes only to become TV comedy classics?

What distinguishes PBS shows from commercial network shows?

What distinguishes cable TV from commercial networks?

Why is *TV Guide* such a successful magazine?

What kinds of audiences watch reruns of "Taxi"? "Nova"? "Gilligan's Island"? "Cheers"? "Barney Miller"? "The Brady Bunch"?

Does a continual diet of TV violence desensitize viewers?

What distinguishes legitimate TV violence from gratuitous violence?

Why do some groups object to the sexism in "Wonder Woman" or "Charlie's Angels" or beauty contests?

Why do some groups object to the sex in "Charlie's Angels" or "Moonlighting" or "L.A. Law"?

Who determines what content can (or cannot) be televised?

What pressure groups successfully exercise some control over TV?

What heroes does TV assume or create?

All these questions, and more, deserve thought in English classes. Most young adults passively accept TV, never considering how all those pictures get onto the air. Television, as critics pro and con are fond of saying, is an educational medium. The question is, of course, what is TV teaching and how is it being taught? We need to examine the values that television espouses and how they are made clear. And we need to recognize that students, and adults as well, are manipulated by TV, sometimes innocently, sometimes not. For example, when young people attend a football game, they're free to watch whatever they wish—the cheerleaders, the quarterback fading back to pass, the split end streaking down the field, the pulling guard making the block that allows the play to succeed, the hot dog vendor, the mountain five miles away, or even the birds rising and falling in the thermals above the stadium.

Not so on TV. When viewers watch a televised football game, the director chooses the several shots available and selects the one viewers across the country will see. No choices. If viewers watch, there's no voting. The director will choose other shots, sooner or later, and viewers are likely to get to see pretty much what they would have seen had they gone to the game, but the order of what they would have wanted to see and what they were forced to look at would rarely approximate each other.

Unless you're a sports fan, this probably sounds trivial, but it nevertheless illustrates the power that TV directors and camera operators have to control what viewers will see. On news broadcasts, whether it's shots from Panama (or wherever America is involved) or shots of a new ballet or a record high jump, viewers are being told precisely how to look at an event, and they are being told, in effect, what is worth looking at.

Just as important, viewers need to remember that the sequence of shots that appear on TV began and ended in time. Something happened before those shots began and after they ended, and we are rarely given a context. And those shots came from a photographer stationed someplace in space. The shots that seem so frightening and so unambiguous might have seemed even more so from another angle and another place. But—might they seem less dramatic, less convincing, somehow less honest from another angle and another space?

MUSIC TELEVISION VIDEOS AND VIDEO GAMES

Two kinds of screen drama belong almost exclusively to teenagers. These are the short dramas of video games and the longer, more symbolic dramas in the rock music videos prepared for television such as the ones on MTV.

Gillian Cross' *Chartbreaker,* which was included on several 1987 best book lists, begins with a one-page "Personal File" on rock singer Janis Mary Finch—known only as Finch—star singer for the British band Kelp. In Chapter 1, she confides to readers that "Oh, sure, you know exactly what happened in the very beginning. *You* and *I* know and the vicarandthepostmanandthewindow-cleaner and the whole WORLD know the story."

The reason everyone knows her story is that they've seen the famous video that shows her as a runaway sipping coffee in a roadside cafe. There's "no sound except the chink of the spoon against the cup." Then she begins singing, her voice "very high and clear and slow, with Dave's harmonica as the only backing." The video is about her leaving home and joining the band. When she looks up from the cup of coffee her face is a blank:

> But down in my coffee cup the black and white reflection of my face stares up, shifting and changing all the time. Sad, happy, tough, leering, bored . . . changing clothes and wigs and make-up. Pentathlete, lion-tamer, karate *sensei,* headmistress . . . clown, mafia boss, geisha, prime minister. . . . That bit of the video took about a week to shoot—I think we produced five different versions in the end—and I got to try all my fantasies on for size.

As soon as Finch finishes the two-page description of the video and the envious letters that she gets from kids, she writes, "Well, kids, sorry to disappoint you, but you can forget all that. Because that's not quite how it was, not in real life," and she goes on to tell how it was in real life.

Chartbreaker was published first in England and its success reflects the important part that popular music plays in the lives of teenagers. Rock music videos prepared for television, such as the ones shown on MTV, are wonderful condensations of dramatic stories. Although many of us would hesitate to call them literature, if we accept a broad definition of literature as all writings in either prose or verse that are of an imaginative nature and reflect a particular culture, then music videos qualify as literature. They can be used to help students gain a broader view of literature and the interrelatedness of popular culture and "literature with a capital L."

As Susan Latta described her initial experience with MTV, "It was terribly annoying at first. Instead of music providing a background to listen to while I was occupied with something else, it had suddenly become a visual experience as well as an aural one. I realized that I was being forced to think about the music, its emotional impact, the lyrics, the imagery—in other words, its poetic qualities."

Latta went on to recommend that English teachers use video music as "stepping stones to develop abilities that will help students in approaching literature and writing." She gave the following reasons for the potential success of rolling a television set into a classroom and for a change of pace looking closely at a music video:

1. Near the top of any list of what teenagers are interested in will be music and television. Video music combines these two media into a new, exciting art form.
2. Music videos are easily available, either on cable television or as part of such syndicated programs as "Solid Gold," "Top Ten," and "Music Magazine." Video stores rent the best ones gathered together in album formats, for example, "MTV Closet Classics."

3. The videos are short, only three or four minutes, yet they are packed with imagery and symbolism which can serve as the basis for such thought-provoking questions as these based on Michael Jackson's "Billy Jean":

Who is Billy Jean? Why do we never see her? Who is the man in the trenchcoat? Is it Jackson himself as some viewers assert, and if it is, what is the meaning of this "alter ego"? Why was a shabby setting chosen, and in this setting, why is Jackson so fashionably dressed? What is the function of the fantasy elements? Why is a hobo's attire changed from rags to a tuxedo when Jackson throws a coin into his cup? What role does the cat, who suddenly changes into a dog at one point in the video, play? Is it symbolic of Billy Jean? How do the images of the video tie in with the song's lyrics which are ostensibly about a paternity suit?[19]

While the music videos are good for studying images and symbolism, video games are good raw material to look at in relation to theme and plot. Because they have to be so pared down, the plots are easily seen. In the first generation of video games, plots were little more than protagonist (the player) vs. another (the machine). The point of the games was to see how long the player could keep a ball in motion. In the second generation of games, plots were extended to protagonist vs. nature as when rocket ships were threatened by asteroids, and protagonist vs. society as when players had to protect themselves from aliens. The makers of video games soon went beyond such basic plots to create a variety of protagonists in a variety of situations. We sent a class of college students to the basement of the Student Union and told them to play a video game and then come back with an analysis of plot and theme. Here are some of their statements:

In most video games, players have to protect themselves. But in *Death Chase* the player is the attacker. You drive around the course searching for unwary pedestrians. When you run one down, a horrible scream is heard and a gravestone appears on the spot accompanied by vaguely funereal music. The moral seems to be "Get them before they get you." I'm ashamed to admit it was fun.

In *Donkey Kong,* a gorilla abducts a fair maiden, climbs to the top of what looks like several floors of a warehouse where he ties the maiden to a post. A man (the player) tries to climb the girders to get to the top and rescue the maiden, but the gorilla is throwing barrels down to crush him. The theme could be that love is a never-ending quest since the man can never get to the woman. I didn't see a donkey. Someone told me the name was supposed to be *Monkey Kong* (after King Kong), but the inventors were Japanese and didn't realize they had made an English spelling error.

Frogger teaches the lesson that "Life is Hell" or that you should learn to get to your goal without getting in the way of others. The poor little frog stands on the curb forlornly gazing at his mission—to cross a busy street with five lanes of cars and trucks and then to cross a river with rows of logs, turtles, alligators, and other foes. He is safe only when he can hop into a home bay on the bank without touching any shrubs. Maybe the theme is that it pays to persevere or that success *is* possible if you try hard enough.

▗ When I played *Pac-Man,* it made me think of my life in school. My professors are Speedy, Shadow, Bashful, and Pokey, and they are out to get me. I try to avoid collisions with these professors as I struggle to get my assignments done, always moving quickly but cautiously. My reward when I turn in an assignment is like when Pac-Man eats an energy dot. I get to turn around and chase my professors for a little while, but it's just so they can spill more work on me. When I receive a good grade it's like when Pac-Man eats the cherry, orange, apple, and strawberry to receive more points. As the game progresses, Pac-Man's opponents move faster and so Pac-Man has to move faster too. This is like toward the end of the semester when we are swamped with a lot of work and pressured to finish.

▗ What I got out of the game *Centipede* is that after all life's challenges, it doesn't get any easier. There will always be obstacles in the way and once you get around one, there are more to overcome.

▗ The most expensive game (50 as compared to 25 cents) is *Dragon's Lair.* It is a computerized romantic quest complete with a sword buried in stone, castles to assault, chasms to cross, mountains to climb, dragons to slay, and a princess to be rescued. A player who is really expert can actually rescue the princess. This is the only game that has the possibility of a happy ending.

These comments about a sampling of video games illustrate both similarities and differences between their storylines and those found in the majority of books that are offered to young readers. Notice how pessimistic most of the games are, how they nearly all end in the defeat of the protagonist. Yet with books, the demand from parents has been that their children be given happy stories, ones in which the young reader is left with hope. Perhaps it's just that most adults, at least most educators, don't play video games and therefore do not know enough to criticize them for their pessimism and glorification of violence as well as the sexism, racism, and general hostility that some of them exhibit. However, teachers wishing to discuss such matters with their students would need to approach the task cautiously. Teenagers are extra sensitive to criticisms of "their culture," especially from outsiders.

In the last couple of years, as people have seen some of their neighborhood video parlors close, they have concluded that the fad has passed and video games are a thing of the past. But just as Mark Twain's explanation that the rumors of his death were greatly exaggerated, video games are far from extinct. As the old machines wear out, they are replaced with new and different games.

(Users will tell you that the main difference is that you can't play as long on a single quarter.) And as with some other teenage fads such as their slang and their fashions, the general culture is adopting them.

During the 1987 Christmas season, the biggest sellers in Arizona toy stores were video games adapted for home use by preteens. And a January, 1988, article in the *New York Times* told about a grown-up interactive video game that had been shown in three museums and was now set up in an experimental arts space in New York City. It is a continuing video collage known as "The Erl King," which "uses electronic computer wizardry to lure the viewer through a mazelike journey of images and sounds that lasts from half-an-hour to 45 minutes or more."[20] When viewers touch the screen, the first thing they see is soprano Elizabeth Arnold singing "Erlkonig," Schubert's interpretation of Goethe's poem. The scene that follows is determined by the viewer and the computer. Possibilities range "from footage of a Chinese chef cutting up a chicken to a lecturer discoursing on the Freudian imagery of the Goethe poem." The poem might reappear later as spray-painted graffiti or as an overlay during a bagpipe concert.

"The Erl King" took four years to build and cost $70,000, plus donated lab time and technical contributions. It consists of three videodisk players controlled by a computer and a touch-sensitive monitor. The computer is programmed with 600 lines of text, several segments of music and imagery, and such literary motifs as a Freudian dream being re-enacted in Anna Freud's Viennese sitting room plus a contemporary analysis of the same dream by psychoanalyst Stuart Schneiderman. The creator, Grahame Weinbren, is a 40-year-old maker of experimental films. He first saw an interactive video at the 1982 World's Fair in Knoxville, and although he has only made the one piece he says it has become his medium:

> I think of "The Erl King" as a model of the conscious mind. You're wandering around someone's mind and go down a little path and see one of his memories. You take another path and see that person's desires. Another path will show you his beliefs, and another what he imagines. The medium is so incredibly rich. It's as different from ordinary video as sound cinema was from silent movies.[21]

Somewhere between the complications of "The Erl King" and the simplicity of a *Pac-Man* game are the interactive computer programs designed to involve kids in either reading or writing stories. As of now, these computer programs are sort of like automated versions of the popular Choose-Your-Own-Adventure stories. But as producer Weinbren has shown, possibilities are unlimited. The programs now available for school use are undoubtedly going to become much more sophisticated and easy to use in the near future.

We suggest bringing the study of rock music, videos, and video games into literature classes because we want students to see that all of literature has common elements which appeal to something deep within the human psyche.

The love of story is one of the things that sets humans apart. And of all the literature discussed in this book, that of the pop culture, mass media, is the most accessible. All one needs to do is to turn on the radio or television set, enter a movie theater, put on a record or tape, or enter a video gameroom. These media put a frame around a bit of life. People who do not have this kind of commercially prepared drama create it for themselves through ceremony, dance, telling or acting out stories, or just plain eavesdropping on their neighbors.

MAGAZINES

Magazines and their place in school and library collections have changed considerably since the days when girls read *Seventeen* and boys read the joke page in *Boy's Life* and looked at the pictures in *National Geographic*. In the Young Adult room of the Mesa, Arizona, Public Library, one side of the large bookshelf commanding front-and-center attention is devoted to new books while the other side features almost three dozen magazines. Noticeably missing are *Dragon, Hot Rod, Mad, Right On,* and *Thrasher*. In the same kind of vinyl cover that protects the magazines is a boldly blocked message:

> PLEASE NOTE: Due to high loss the current issues of the following magazines can only be requested by leaving a library card or some form of I.D. at the Y.A. Service Desk.

Dragon is related to the Dungeons and Dragons game; *Hot Rod* is a hobby book for car enthusiasts; *Mad* is filled with humorous spoofs; *Right On* is aimed at a black audience with an emphasis on motion picture and music entertainment; while *Thrasher* is a skateboarding magazine.

What's on the shelves for readers to pick up and browse through ranges from serious magazines featuring student work, e.g., *Youth '88* and the library's own teenage written publications *The Open Shelf* (general reviews and comments) and *E.T.* (science fiction and fantasy) to general audience magazines focusing on topics of interest to teenagers, for example, *The Rolling Stone, Musician,* and *The Rock Yearbook*. A large number are aimed at special interests, for example, *Bicycling, Outdoor Life, Muscular Development,* and *Rider: Touring, Sport, and Street Motorcycling at Its Best*. Science fiction fans will find *Starlog: The Science Fiction Universe* and *Isaac Asimov's Science Fiction*. The vocabulary in *Omni* restricts it to better readers while the kinds of stories in Scholastic's *Choices* make it more appealing to girls than to boys. Among the relatively few magazines that are read by both sexes are *Freebies: The Magazine with Something for Nothing* and *Career World*. Because of the abundance of advertising money for cosmetics and fashions, numerous magazines are aimed at girls, for example, *Teen, Teenage, YM* (Young Miss), and

TG (Teen Generation). This latter magazine has as its subtitle *The Voice of Young Canadians.* The Arizona librarian reported that it was popular with American teens because they are eager for new fashion ideas.

In some ways, teen magazines in England, Australia, and Canada have received proportionately more attention than they have in the United States, where paperback books have been the primary media. In 1987, Australia's second biggest publisher, Fairfax Ltd., sent editor Sandra Yates to New York to create a teen magazine similar to the popular Australian *Dolly.* The result was *Sassy,* which after three issues had a circulation of 280,000 and was predicted to go to one million by 1993. (*Seventeen's* circulation is 1.86 million while *Teen's* is 1.19). *Time* magazine in its May 16, 1988, issue wrote about big business and "pajama-party journalism," under the heading "From Feminists to Teenyboppers." The story was triggered by the fact that *Sassy* and *MS* magazine are now owned by the same corporation, a pairing that *Time* writer Laurence Zuckerman viewed "about as likely as a business lunch between Author Germaine Greer and Pop Singer Tiffany." In asking whether *Sassy* readers will grow up to become *MS* subscribers, he opined that "Women may want issues, but girls just want to have fun." As his idea of fun, he described the new magazine as having:

> . . . tackled such topics as losing one's virginity ("If you don't feel like you can talk to your partner, then it's probably time to reconsider"), how to kiss (not too wet or too wide, and never with flavored lip-gloss), and the "Truth About Boys' Bodies" ("the average amount of semen per ejaculation is one-quarter of an ounce"). Sandwiched between the glossy but no-nonsense fashion pages and gushing paeans to the latest teen idols is at least one hard-hitting article, like the story of a teen whose best friend died of AIDS.[22]

There are magazines for every taste—even a few that will please teachers—but what's important for educators to realize is that many students who won't pick up books are eager to read the latest magazines in their areas of interest. With many of the teen magazines, poor readers can feel their first success with the printed word because much of the information is communicated through easy-to-read layouts and photographs and the material, which is presented in short digestible chunks, is of prime interest to teens. But just as important is the fact that there's no limit to the challenges that good students can find in magazines. A much higher percentage of adult Americans read magazines rather than books, and yet in school we give people little help in introducing them to magazines or in picking out the ones that they will get the most from. It is almost as if kids find magazines in spite of teachers rather than because of them. We would do well to change our attitudes and look upon magazines as taking up where books leave off in presenting up-to-date information on a wide variety of topics chosen to be especially interesting to young adults.

CHANGES IN MARKETING BROUGHT ABOUT BY BIG BUSINESS

The bottom line for publishers has always been to make a profit. Until recently, the best way to do that with books for young readers was to produce books that teachers would assign for class reading and that librarians would promote. The problem novels of the '60s and '70s owe much of their success to the fact that the best of these books had themes that were interesting and challenging to adults as well as to young readers, and so teachers and librarians joined in promoting them as leisure-time reading. These professionally trained adults acted as buffers between publishers and young readers. But in 1979, the chain of B. Dalton Booksellers separated their children's from their YA books. In the early '80s, the Walden chain followed B. Dalton's example and established its own YA sections. Tom Stanley, Avon's manager of marketing, explained:

> Book people are just beginners who need to take lessons from those who sell clothes, movies, and records. We would never expect teenagers to look for their clothes in the children's departments of stores. They go to the youth boutiques, yet we continue to send them to the children's sections for their books. We've got to realize that the teenage market is an offshoot of adult rather than children's books and treat it accordingly.[23]

Speaking on an editor's panel at the 1987 National Council of Teachers of English conference in Los Angeles, Jean Feiwel, former editor of Avon's Flare line and now Young Adult editor at Scholastic, said that this decision to market directly to teenagers was the single most important event to have happened in YA publishing over the last two decades. Bookstore sales to teenagers tripled between 1980 and 1983,[24] and have continued to climb. The new methods of marketing gave a tremendous boost to the paperback houses because teens prefer not only the lower prices but also the lighter weight and more convenient size of paperbacks. For the first time, many teens began reading books they owned rather than ones they borrowed from a library or were assigned from English classes.

The change in marketing has some similarities to what happened back in the 1950s to books for young children. Parents used to be told not to "interfere" by teaching their children to read. That was the school's business. But then the Russians launched Sputnik, which triggered an education explosion in the United States. Rudolf Flesch wrote his best-selling *Why Johnny Can't Read,* Congress passed the National Defense Education Act providing money for libraries to purchase supplemental reading books, and Random House, with the help of Dr. Seuss, launched its series of easy-to-read books written under strict vocabulary control. Many literary critics compared controlled vocabulary books to rice pudding without any raisins. The idea of taking a list of words and then trying to find a story that could be told with these particular words

ALVIN SCHWARTZ
on Economics

Two or three times a year my publishers send me reviews of my books. In a recent batch, one in particular caught my eye. It was a review of *More Scary Stories to Tell in the Dark* by a member of a library book selection committee in a large midwestern city. The reviewer recommended that they buy the book,

but concluded by saying, "This seems like a short book for the price."

Well, I stopped and thought about that. The book has 128 pages, and the price at that point for a library edition was $10.89. "Is that too much," I wondered, "or does she have a budget problem, or doesn't she understand?"

By then I had gotten a pencil out. I don't write by the yard, but even so. . . . It had taken me about four months to find the tales I used and a lot I didn't use, five months to retell them, and two months to do the notes and sources the reviewer had found so reassuring. It had taken the illustrator three or four months to do the drawings. On top of that there was the editing, the designing, and the rest of it. So quite an investment was involved.

If one assumed that fifty children read the copy that library probably bought, the cost would be about twenty-two cents a child, including royalties to the author and illustrator which are not so royal as some people think.

That didn't seem too burdensome to me. It seemed like quite a bargain, in fact, far less, on a per reader basis, than a can of soda or a candy bar or something else that is here one minute and gone the next.

I will ignore the reviewer's implication that a book with more pages is worth more than a book with fewer pages. But an important question remains. What *is* a good book worth?

Alvin Schwartz's books include *Scary Stories to Tell in the Dark,* Lippincott, 1981; *More Scary Stories to Tell in the Dark,* Lippincott, 1984; and *Telling Fortunes: Love Magic, Dream Signs, and Other Ways to Tell the Future,* Lippincott, 1987.

---

rather than taking a story and then trying to find the best words to tell that story was revolutionary. But just as revolutionary was the way the books were sold. The publishers bypassed schools and libraries and mass marketed the books directly to the parents of the intended readers. The eventual result was good for everyone. More children owned and read books, they went on to read more complex books, and the extra money brought in by these increased sales attracted better writers to the field, resulting in more and better books for both home and school use.

The direct marketing of fiction to teenagers may have some equally happy results, but many people are doubtful and point to the current popularity of books they consider junk food. And the utopian vision of teenagers browsing through shelves and shelves of books to make completely free choices has not materialized. Compared to libraries, bookstores have very little space, and what they set aside for a "Young Adult" section is considerably smaller than the "Children's" section. And there is still a middleman, i.e., the buyer for the company stores. Although this person has a much larger budget than any librarian ever had, he or she also has considerably greater space restrictions as well as personal prejudices and preferences. These buyers have the job of selecting an extremely limited number of titles but in numbers rounded off to the nearest thousand.

One result has been a whole new interest in cover art, which one art director described as "the flaps in pictures," and another described as "a small poster that gives you some information about what's happening in the book." In an article, "The YA Cover Story," Dilys Evans showed the contrasting styles that the same company, sometimes even the same artist, will use for a paperback and a hardback cover. Hardbacks are marketed to librarians who, while wanting appealing covers, also want something that looks "literary." "And they demand that a cover not misrepresent the story; they care deeply about accuracy and attention to detail inside the book, and this holds true for the cover as well." In contrast, the prime goal of those designing paperback covers is that they will reach out and hook a potential reader. The paperback market is built on the concept of impulse buying, and Ellen Krieger, editorial director at Avon, explained:

> A sales rep has only seconds to convince a store buyer that a particular cover will catch the browser's attention. In the YA area, we are competing not only with other books in a very crowded market but with all the other things advertisers are urging kids to spend their recreational dollars on— movies, tapes, videos, the latest fad accessory. Sometimes we have to focus on an aspect of the story that has immediate teen appeal, like a boy-girl relationship, even if it isn't really the central storyline. Of course, we remain true to the book. We wouldn't manufacture a romance that isn't there or play up one that's inconsequential, but realistically, if we don't package a book so kids will pick it up, it's not going to get read no matter how terrific it is.[25]

In general, paperback covers are more likely to be full color paintings based on photographs (paintings are considered softer and more romantic), the colors will be lighter and more upbeat, clothing will be in the latest fashion, and if there is a boy/girl relationship it will be highlighted in the foreground with the other parts of the story serving as background. Artists for the hardcover book are usually given a flat fee between $400 and $1,000 from which they must pay for any props and models. YA paperback artists receive between $1,200 and $3,000, plus help with models and props. Sometimes the paperback company even takes the photographs on which the artist is to base the painting.

In a bookstore, space is money, so the company buyers are looking for the books that will sell the fastest and run the least risk of having to be returned or destroyed. To entice buyers to make large purchases, publishers offer discounts proportioned to the number of copies ordered. The two biggest paperback houses, Dell and Bantam, are now owned by the same parent company. Although their editorial staffs will remain separate, they are under the same financial management and so will be under the same pressures to make the big sales and offer the same discounts to the buyers.

George Nicholson, editor for Delacorte and Dell, speaking at the 1987 NCTE convention, explained that with the buyers there's a tremendous amount of luck involved. The companies purposely rotate their buyers from area to area so that no one has a chance to become the grand doyenne of science fiction, of cookbooks, of YA lit., etc. Nicholson understood the reasons behind this, but he regretted never having the time to educate buyers to the unique aspects of YA literature. In the beginning, B. Dalton was willing to focus on promoting individual authors, but the Walden stores decided from the start to focus on particular series or imprints.

Early in the '80s, knowledgeable people including Nicholson were predicting that because of the new importance of the paperback and its direct marketing, companies would be able to skip the costly and time-consuming process of publishing and distributing hardbacks. Instead, they could go directly to original paperbacks. These predictions were supported by two notable success stories. Norma Fox Mazer's *Taking Terri Mueller* came out as an Avon Flare original paperback in 1981, and when it proved successful, was issued in 1983 as a hardback for libraries by William Morrow. Joyce Carol Thomas' *Marked by Fire,* which also came out as an Avon original paperback in 1982, was chosen by the *New York Times* as one of the best books of the year.

Although publishers market books directly to teenagers in bookstores, they also support school use through distribution of a wide variety of catalogs and teaching guides.

"That couldn't happen in 1988," said Jean Feiwel, editor of both of these books and a strong supporter of the concept of the original paperback. Speaking also at the 1987 NCTE meeting under the title of "The Best of Times/The Worst of Times," she said that to her disappointment, she has been forced to come back to the practice of producing a hardback first, followed by a paperback. "What happened," she said, "is that the teen romance industry killed the original paperback." Publishers who had never considered a YA market jumped on the bandwagon to take advantage of quick sales. The practice of attention being paid to an individual author was lost in the glut of genre and series books. The Sweet Valley High books are one of the smartest concepts to come along since Nancy Drew, but with many of the series books the tail is wagging the dog. They are little more than covers wrapped around ideas, and those ideas aren't very well done. "We have to have the hardbacks to get reviews, and we have to have reviews to establish an author."[26]

Serious publishers are increasingly interested in controlling the destiny of a book from the beginning to the end, said Nicholson, who echoed Feiwel's concerns. For the first time, his company is losing the rights to books they've produced for the past five or ten years. The original hardback publisher is calling the book home, perhaps to get more money from another paperback house, but more likely, the hardback publisher has expanded to print paperbacks and will produce companion volumes.

As publishing houses get bigger and more centralized, we can expect this trend to continue. There will be more companies with dual divisions like Scholastic and Scholastic Hardcover, Dell and Delacorte, and Harper & Row with its Harper Keypoint paperbacks. Earlier, Nicholson explained that in a change from the past, today's publishers make a long-term investment in authors. It is big business from both sides. Fifteen years ago the authors he worked with nearly all had some supplemental means of support, but now he works with authors who earn $100,000 a year from their books. He estimated that there are between 25 and 30 YA writers making considerable sums of money. One of the reasons is that companies work with an author and develop several ideas which result in multibook contracts. "There's never enough money to fully promote single books," so the multi-book contract is more efficient both in terms of publicity and editorial help. Also, when a company develops a writer, then that author isn't going to be ashamed to talk about writing something "to order."

    For example, we saw the television pilot "Square Pegs," and we talked with Marjorie Sharmat about writing a companion set for the TV series. The television show was cancelled, but the books are going strong, 250,000 copies have been sold. Ten years ago we were feisty and literary in a way that was false. Today we aren't so self-conscious. We realize that an author's inspiration can come from lots of different places. After all, Sinclair Lewis wrote plots for Jack London and Theodore Dreiser is known to have bought some of his plots. I would be uncomfortable with a writer who lived only on other people's ideas—that's a hack vs. an author, but I'm glad our people aren't ashamed to talk about the business end of publishing, because even frivolous books need not be badly written.[27]

Few people would argue with the statement that money is power or that the field of young adult literature could use some powerful friends when it comes to such issues as censorship, allocations of school and library funds, and promotion of reading as a worthwhile activity. More money in the business will undoubtedly attract better talent. Increased sales will mean more and perhaps better independent reading (because it will be self-chosen), and when the general public recognizes young adult literature as a field of its own perhaps we won't have so much trouble getting library positions reserved for YA specialists.

On the negative side, critics fear that minorities will be ignored because they aren't the big spenders in shopping mall bookstores. Another fear is that everything will be watered down to suit mass tastes, comparable to most television programming. But there are some crucial differences which are that one person at a time reads a book while television is usually viewed by a group. And even with cable television, the number of channels from which a viewer can choose is limited, while with books there can be thousands of choices. Also, television is paid for by advertisers while readers pay the production costs of books.

In spite of these differences, it will probably be well for those of us who specialize in young adults and their reading to think of ourselves as an advocacy group for teenagers. We will need to keep reminding publishers that there is no such thing as *one* young adult audience. There are dozens of such audiences all needing their own kinds of books. An illustration of the influence that publishers can have on a book is what happened with Lloyd Alexander's *Prydain* series. When Dell first published it in paperback, they commissioned Evaline Ness to do the drawings and they promoted the books as children's literature by using large type and lots of space and by advertising the fact that *The High King* had won the Newbery Award. A few years later, they reissued the books packaged as mythical hero tales for older readers, and then in a later edition they packaged them as fantasy. Each edition was successful, but with an entirely different group of readers.

A special challenge for people in our business is to make sure that each generation of teenagers is offered a balanced array of reading materials. The nature of big business is to follow trends. A good idea by one company is soon imitated by all the companies so that what ends up at the corner drugstore or the shopping mall bookstore is most likely a lopsided collection. In the '70s it was mostly grim problem novels, in the '80s it was the romances followed by occult books, and by now there is probably some other fad. What this means is that librarians and teachers need to work extra hard at providing the kinds of books that aren't the current trendsetters. It would be unfortunate if young people missed out on developing the reading habit simply because the books that happened to be handy during three or four key years weren't a type that appealed to them.

NOTES

[1] David Burmester, "The Case for Video Study," *English Journal* 73 (March 1984): 104–6.

[2] Maia Pank Mertz and David K. England, "The Legitimacy of American Adolescent Fiction," *School Library Journal* 30 (October 1983): 119–23.

[3] Myra Forsberg, "'Sun' Dawns on a New Spielberg," *Arizona Republic,* February 11, 1988, p. C-3.

[4] Forsberg, p. C-3.

[5] Vincent Canby, "Screen: 'Outsiders,' Teen-Age Violence," *New York Times,* March 25, 1983, p. 18.

[6] Quoted in "Calendar Supplement,"*Los Angeles Times,* April 3, 1983, p. 18

[7] Richard Schickel, "Cinema: Antic Storms, Lopsided Charm," *Time* 120 (October 11, 1982): 89.

[8] Samuel Rosenkranz, "English at the Cinema," *English Journal* 20 (December 1931): 824.

[9] Of the many *Media and Methods* articles, we'd especially recommend John M. Culkin, "A Rationale for Film Study in the High School," *Media and Methods* 2 (April 1966): 18–23; John M. Culkin, "I Was a High School Movie Teacher," *Media and Methods* 2 (May 1966): 22–27, and Hugh Gilmore, "What Film Teaching Is Not," *Media and Methods* 7 (September 1970): 40–41. Other articles by Frank McLaughlin, David Sohn, William Kuhn, Richard A. Lacey, Adele Stern, Paul Carrico, Rodney Sheratsky, and Fred Marcus are still readable and perceptive. Few magazines now 15 to 29 years old are much more than museum pieces, but *Media and Methods* still is great fun to read.

[10] David Burmester, "Short Films Revisited," *English Journal* 73 (January 1984): 66–72.

[11] Notably, but not exclusively, in Ron Epple, "A Great Short New List of Short Films." *Media and Methods* 7 (March 1971): 23–38; "Short Films: The Pick of the Flicks," *Media and Methods* 12 (December 1975): 22 ff.; "From Reel to Real: The Best of the Recent Short Films," *Media and Methods* 15 (December 1978): 42–68.

[12] Much has been written about Resnais' film, but one particularly helpful article is Charles Krantz, "Teaching 'Night and Fog': History and Historiography," *Film and History* 15 (February 1985): 2–15.

[13] *New York Times*, August 27, 1987, p. 21 (national edition).

[14] Jonathan Kozol quoted by James Brooke in "Books on Tapes Attract Big Numbers of Readers," *New York Times,* July 2, 1985, p. 24 (national edition).

[15] James D. Kirkman, *Television Production Today!* (Skokie, IL: National Textbook Co., 1987), p. 2.

[16] Kirkman, p. 4.

[17] Neil Hickey, "The Verdict on VCRs (So Far)," *TV Guide* 36 (March 19, 1988): 13.

[18] Hickey, pp. 13–14.

[19] Susan Latta, "MTV and Video Music: A New Tool for the English Teacher," *English Journal* 73 (January 1984): 38-–39.

[20] Stephen Holden, "Grown-Ups' Video Game Is a Mazelike Journey," *New York Times*, January 2, 1988, p. 10.

[21] Holden, p. 10.

[22] Laurence Zuckerman, "From Feminists to Teenyboppers," *Time* (May 16, 1988): 77.

[23] Personal interview with Tom Stanley, November 19, 1982.

[24] Sue Chastain, "Teens Find Love in the Pulp Racks," *Philadelphia Inquirer,* November 22, 1982, D-1, 4.

[25] Dilys Evans, "The YA Cover Story," *Publishers Weekly* 32 (July 24, 1987): 112-–115.

[26] "The Past Twenty Years—Highs and Lows in Publishing Books for Young Adults," panel of publishers' representatives at the ALAN Workshop, NCTE 1987 Annual Convention, November 23, 1987, Los Angeles.

[27] George Nicholson, "The People behind the Books," *Literature for Today's Young Adults,* 2nd ed. (Scott, Foresman, 1985), pp. 438–39.

■ PRODUCERS AND DISTRIBUTORS OF SHORT FILMS (AND VIDEOS OF SHORT FILMS)

Barr Films, 12801 Scharbarum Avenue, P.O. Box 7878, Irwindale, CA 91706-7878

BFA Educational Media, 468 Park Avenue South, New York, NY 10016

Centre Productions (distributed by Barr Films)

Coronet/MTI Film and Video, 108 Wilmot Road, Deerfield, IL 60015

Encyclopaedia Britannica, 425 N. Michigan Avenue, Chicago, IL 60611

Films Incorporated, 5547 N. Ravenswood, Chicago, IL 60640-9979

International Film Bureau, Inc., 332 S. Michigan Avenue, Chicago, IL 60604

Learning Corporation of America, 1350 Avenue of the Americas, New York, NY 10019

Mass Media Ministries, 2116 N. Charles St., Baltimore, MD 21218

National Film Board of Canada, 16th Floor, 1251 Avenue of the Americas, New York, NY 10020-1173

Phoenix Films, 468 Park Avenue South, New York, NY 10016

Pyramid Films, Box 1048, Santa Monica, CA 90406

Texture Films, P.O. Box 1337, Skokie, IL 60076

Wombat Film and Video, 250 W. 57th St., New York, NY 10019

■ PRODUCERS AND DISTRIBUTORS OF CASSETTES (AND SOMETIMES RECORDS)

American Audio Prose Library, Inc., P.O. Box 842, Columbia, MO 65205

Audio Editions, P.O. Box 998, Burlingame, CA 94011

Bantam Audio Publishing, Bantam Books, 666 Fifth Ave., New York, NY 10103

Caedmon, 1995 Broadway, New York, NY 10023

Ingram Spoken Audio, 347 Reedwood Drive, Nashville, TN 37217

Listening for Pleasure, Box 588, Lewiston, NY 14092

The Mind's Eye, Box 6727, San Francisco, CA 94101

Random House Media, Dept. 437, 400 Hahn Road, Westminster, MD 21157

Recorded Books, Inc., P.O. Box 79, Charlotte Hall, MD 20622

Simon and Schuster Audio, 1230 Avenue of the Americas, New York, NY 10020

Spoken Arts, 310 N. Ave., New Rochelle, NY 10801

Warner Audio, P.O. Box 718, New York, NY 10011

■ A STARTER BIBLIOGRAPHY ON MEDIA

Bluestone, George. *Novels into Film.* Baltimore: Johns Hopkins University Press, 1957 (available in an inexpensive University of California Press paperback).

Foster, Harold M. *The New Literacy: The Language of Film and Television.* Urbana, IL:

National Council of Teachers of English, 1979.

Halliwell, Leslie. *The Filmgoer's Companion,* 8th ed. New York: Hill and Wang, 1985. Consistently the most fascinating and helpful guide to almost anything about films.

Johnson, Nicholas. *How To Talk Back to Your Television Set.* Boston: Little, Brown, 1970. Despite its age, this remains the most cogent criticism about television.

Kirkham, James D. *Television Production Today!* Skokie, IL: National Textbook Company, 1987. Despite its title, the book has much to say about TV that is not necessarily concerned with production details.

Knight, Arthur. *The Liveliest Art: A Panoramic History of the Movies,* rev. ed. New York: Macmillan, 1979. Knight packs an incredible amount of information about film history and techniques and personalities into a small space.

Levinson, Richard, and William Link. *Stay Tuned: An Inside Look at the Making of Prime-Time Television.* New York: St. Martin's Press, 1981. The world of TV from two men who've been involved with the medium for years; intimate and honest.

Maltin, Leonard. *Movies and Video Guide.* New York: Bantam, yearly. A handy and inexpensive guide to several thousand movies you're likely to see on TV.

Mander, Jerry. *Four Arguments for the Elimination of Television.* New York: Morrow, 1978.

Morrow, James, and Murray Suid. *Media and Kids: Real-World Learning in the Schools.* Rochelle Park, NJ: Hayden, 1977.

Postman, Neil. *Amusing Ourselves to Death.* New York: Viking, 1986. How to solve America's educational problem simply—get rid of TV.

Scheuer, Steven. *The Complete Guide to Video Cassette Movies.* New York: Henry Holt, 1987.

Schrank, Jeffrey. *Understanding Mass Media.* Skokie, IL: National Textbook Co., 1981. The best introductory compendium of media material for use in schools.

Stein, Benjamin. *The View from Sunset Boulevard: America as Brought to You by the People Who Make Television.* New York: Basic Books, 1979.

Winn, Marie, ed. *The Plug-In Drug.* New York: Viking, 1985.

TITLES MENTIONED IN CHAPTER ELEVEN

Adams, Richard. *Watership Down.* Macmillan, 1974.

Alexander, Lloyd. *The Foundling and other Tales of Prydain.* Dell, 1973.

_____ . *The High King.* Henry Holt, 1968.

Allen, Woody. *Getting Even.* Random House, 1971.

Anonymous. *Go Ask Alice.* Prentice-Hall, 1971.

Armstrong, William. *Sounder.* Harper & Row, 1969.

Austen, Jane. *Northanger Abbey.* (first published in 1817).

Ballard, J. G. *Empire of the Sun.* Simon and Schuster, 1984.

Blos, Joan. *A Gathering of Days.* Scribner, 1979.

Blume, Judy. *Forever.* Bradbury, 1975.

Bradford, Richard. *Red Sky at Morning.* Lippincott, 1968.

Bradbury, Ray. *The Martian Chronicles.* Doubleday, 1958.

Bradley, Marion Zimmer. *City of Sorcery.* DAW Books, New American Library, 1984.

Brooks, Bruce. *The Moves Make the Man.* Harper & Row, 1984.

Childress, Alice. *A Hero Ain't Nothin' But a Sandwich.* Putnam, 1973.

Cleaver, Vera, and Bill Cleaver. *Where the Lilies Bloom.* Harper & Row, 1969.

Cormier, Robert. *I Am the Cheese.* Knopf, 1977.

_____ . *The Chocolate War.* Pantheon, 1974.

Crichton, Michael. *The Andromeda Strain.* Knopf, 1969.

Cross, Gillian. *Chartbreaker.* Holiday, 1987.

Ellerbee, Linda. *And So It Goes.* Putnam, 1986.

Flesch, Rudolf. *Why Johnny Can't Read: And What You Can Do About It.* Harper & Row, 1955.

Forbes, Esther. *Johnny Tremain.* Houghton Mifflin, 1943.

Frank, Anne. *The Diary of a Young Girl.* Norton, 1957.

Gaines, Ernest J. *The Autobiography of Miss Jane Pittman.* Dial, 1971.

_____ . *A Gathering of Old Men.* Knopf, 1983.

Green, Hannah. *I Never Promised You a Rose Garden.* Holt, Rinehart and Winston, 1964.

Greene, Bette. *Summer of My German Soldier.* Dial, 1973.

Hamilton, Virginia. *Sweet Whispers, Brother Rush.* Putnam, 1982.

_____ . *Zeely.* Macmillan, 1967.

Head, Ann. *Mr. and Mrs. Bo Jo Jones.* Putnam, 1967.

Hinton, S. E. *The Outsiders.* Viking, 1967.

_____ . *Rumble Fish.* Delacorte, 1979.

_____ . *Tex.* Delacorte, 1979.

Kerr, M. E. *Dinky Hocker Shoots Smack.* Harper & Row, 1972.

Mander, Jerry. *Four Arguments for the Elimination of Television.* Morrow, 1978.

Masters, Edgar Lee. *The Spoon River Anthology.* Macmillan, 1915.

Mazer, Norma Fox. *Taking Terri Mueller.* Avon, 1984.

Matthiessen, Peter. *The Snow Leopard.* Viking, 1978.

McCaffrey, Anne. *The White Dragon.* Ballantine, 1980.

Morrison, Toni. *Song of Solomon.* New American Library, 1978.

_____ . *Tar Baby.* Knopf, 1981.

Paterson, Katherine. *Jacob Have I Loved.* Harper & Row, 1980.

Peck, Richard. *Are You in the House Alone?* Viking, 1976.

Peck, Robert Newton. *A Day No Pigs Would Die.* Knopf, 1972.

Postman, Neil. *Amusing Ourselves to Death: Public Discourse in the Age of Show Business.* Viking, 1986.

Potok, Chaim. *The Chosen.* Simon and Schuster, 1967.

Sillitoe, Alan. *The Loneliness of the Long Distance Runner.* Knopf, 1960.

Swarthout, Glendon. *Bless the Beasts and Children.* Doubleday, 1970.

Thomas, Joyce Carol. *Marked by Fire.* Avon, 1982.

Tolkien, J. R. R. *The Hobbit: Or There and Back Again.* Houghton Mifflin, 1938.

Van Gulik, Robert. *Murder in Canton.* Scribner, 1967.

Walker, Alice. *The Color Purple.* Harcourt Brace Jovanovich, 1982.

White, E. B. *Charlotte's Web.* Harper & Row, 1952.

Winn, Marie, ed. *The Plug-in Drug.* Viking, 1977.

Yates, Elizabeth. *Amos Fortune, Free Man.* Dutton, 1967.

For information on the availability of paperback editions of these titles, please consult the most recent edition of *Paperbound Books in Print,* published annually by R. R. Bowker Company.

CHAPTER TWELVE

CENSORSHIP
Of Worrying and Wondering

Whether they like it or not, most teachers and librarians know that censorship is part of their professional lives. A few headlines from 1987 and 1988 suggest that news of censorship frequently appears in the daily press. The *Arizona Republic* for April 4, 1987, carried an UPI story about Tipper Gore (wife of Tennessee's senator Albert Gore, Jr.) and her war on porn rock and TV violence in her book, *Raising PG Kids in an X-Rated Society*. The May 26, 1987, *Miami Herald* headlined the front page, "Panhandle Fighting Battle of the Books," and provided details of Bay County (Florida) Superintendent of Schools Leonard Hall and his banning—or attempted banning—of books as disparate as Robert Cormier's *The Chocolate War*, Farley Mowat's *Never Cry Wolf*, Stephen Crane's *The Red Badge of Courage*, Jack London's *The Call of the Wild*, Shakespeare's *Hamlet*, Bernard Malamud's *The Fixer*, and Lillian Hellman's *The Little Foxes*. The *Arizona Republic* for December 10, 1987, contained a story of a Crown King, Arizona, teacher who had started a reading club and unhappily titled it the "666 Reading Club" (the number of pages the teacher wanted students to read each month). Members of a local church who considered the number 666 to be a sign of the devil were frightened and took their case to the school board. The *San Francisco Examiner* for October 10, 1987, summarized a report by People for the American Way on the most widely attacked books of the last year including Cormier's *The Chocolate War*, J. D. Salinger's *The Catcher in the Rye*, John Steinbeck's *Of Mice and Men*, Shel Silverstein's *A Light in the Attic*, Twain's *Adventures of Huckleberry Finn*, the anonymous *Go Ask Alice*, Judy Blume's *Deenie* and *Forever*, and Harper Lee's *To Kill a Mockingbird*. James J. Kilpatrick's syndicated column for December 31, 1987, concerned Canadian author Farley Mowat who had formerly been banned from entering the United States for several impossibly silly reasons and who was now free to enter, thanks to the efforts of bemused New York Senator Daniel Moynihan. And early 1988 brought us a reminder of an old dispute about the indecency of Allen Ginsberg's poem, "Howl," and the beat generation when the Pacifica Radio Network decided not to carry a live reading of the poem because, as a *New York Times* writer on January 6, 1988, noted, "of recent rulings by the Federal Communications Commission concerning indecent language."

English teachers and librarians are painfully aware that book banning has become extremely serious—some would call it epidemic—in the last fifteen or so years. As Colin Campbell wrote:

> A censorial spirit is at work in the United States, and for the past year or so it has focused more and more on books. Efforts to remove certain titles from school and public libraries, from paperback racks and bookstores, from the eyes of adults as well as children, have increased measurably.[1]

The American Library Association has been on record against censorship since the 1920s, but its strongest statement first appeared in 1939 as the Library Bill of Rights. The document has periodically been tightened and strengthened, and the latest version, that of January 23, 1980, can be found in the *Intellectual Freedom Manual,* 2nd ed. The entire *Intellectual Freedom Manual* is filled with provocative ideas and helpful suggestions and should be required reading for librarians and English teachers alike. The National Council of Teachers of English was a bit late entering the battle, but the first edition in 1962 of *The Students' Right to Read* set forth NCTE's position and contained a widely used form for complaints, "Citizen's Request for Reconsideration of a Book." The 1972 edition expanded and updated the earlier edition. In 1982, the complaint form was amended to read "Citizen's Request for Reconsideration of a Work," and a complementary publication, *The Students' Right to Know* by Lee Burress and Edward B. Jenkinson, elaborated on NCTE's position toward education and censorship.

A BRIEF HISTORY OF CENSORSHIP

Some English teachers and librarians apparently believe the censorship of young adult reading began with the publication of J. D. Salinger's *The Catcher in the Rye.* But censorship goes far back in history. Plato believed in censorship. In *The Republic,* he argued that banishing poets and dramatists from his perfect state was essential for the moral good of the young. Writers often told lies about the gods, he maintained, but even when their stories were true, writers sometimes made the gods appear responsible for the evils and misfortunes of mortals. Plato reasoned that fiction was potentially emotionally disturbing to the young. Plato's call for moral censorship to protect the young is echoed by many censors today.

In *The Leviathan* in 1615, Thomas Hobbes justified the other basic case for censorship. Humanity was, in Hobbes' view, inherently selfish, venal, brutish, and contentious. Strife was inevitably humanity's fate unless the state established and enforced order. Hobbes acknowledged the right of subjects to refuse to obey a ruler's orders if he did not protect his people, but in all cases the sovereign had not merely the right but the duty to censor anything for the good of the state.

Between Plato and Hobbes and thereafter, history offers a multitude of examples of censorship for moral or political good—the Emperor Chi Huang Ti burned Confucius' *Analects* in 211 B.C.; Julius Caesar burned much of the Library of Alexandria in 48–47 B.C.; English officials publicly burned copies of William Tyndale's translation of the Bible in 1525; the Catholic Index of Forbidden Works was published in 1555; Prime Minister Walpole forced passage of a Licensing Act in 1737 which required that every English play be examined and approved before production, and on and on and on.

America's premier censor, though hardly its last, appeared in the early 1870s. Anthony Comstock came from a religious family, and before he was eighteen, he had raided a saloon to drive out the devil and the drinkers. In June 1871, Comstock was so outraged by repeated violations of Sunday Closing Laws by saloons in his neighborhood that he reported them to the police. They ignored him which taught him a good lesson about the futility of fighting city hall alone. Armed with the Lord's help and his own determination, Comstock secured the help of three prominent men and founded the Society for the Suppression of Vice in New York in 1872, and he was off and running. The following year he went to Washington, D.C., to urge passage of a federal statute against obscenity and abortion and contraceptive devices. That same year, he was commissioned a Special Agent of the Postmaster General, all without salary until 1906.

With the new law and Comstock's zeal and energy, he confiscated and destroyed "bad" literature and imprisoned evil authors and publishers almost beyond belief. By 1914, he had caused the arraignment of 3,697 people with 2,740 convicted or pleading guilty, total fines of $237,134.30, and prison sentences totaling 565 years, 11 months, and 20 days. In his last year of life, 1915, Comstock added another 176 arrests and 140 convictions. He also caused fifteen suicides.[2]

His most famous book was *Traps for the Young* (1883). By traps, Comstock meant the devil's work for young people—light literature, newspaper advertisements, saloons, literature obtained through the mail, quack medicine, contraceptives, gambling, playing pool, free love and anyone who advocated it, and artistic works (fine arts, classics of literature, photographic reproductions of art). Comstock was convinced that any young person who shot pool or smoked or chewed tobacco or drank or read dime novels or did anything else he disapproved of (and that catalogue was long indeed) was doomed to hell and to a life of crime and degradation.

Librarians, as may be seen in "Fiction and Libraries" in Chapter 13 of this book, were more frequently pro-censorship that anti-censorship. As Arthur E. Bostwick wrote in 1910:

> In the exercise of his duties in book selection it is unavoidable that the librarian should act in some degree as a censor of literature. It has been pointed out that no library can buy every title that is published, and that we should discriminate by picking out what is best instead of by excluding what is bad.[3]

Mark Twain's encounters with late nineteenth-century censors are described in Chapter 13, but he was hardly the only major writer of his time to come under attack. Stephen Crane's *The Red Badge of Courage* was attacked for lacking integrity and being inaccurate. At the sixth session of the American Library Association in 1896, a discussion of *The Red Badge of Courage* and whether it should be included in a list of ALA recommended books brought forth comments that revealed more about the critics than about the book:

> Mr. Larned: "What of Crane's *Red Badge of Courage*?"
>
> A. L. Peck: "It abounds in profanity. I never could see why it should be given into the hands of a boy."
>
> G. M. Jones: "This *Red Badge of Courage* is a very good illustration of the weakness of the criticism of our literary papers. The critics in our literary papers are praising this book as being a true picture of war. The fact is, I imagine, that the criticisms are written by young men who know nothing about war, just as Mr. Crane himself knows nothing about war. Gen. McClurg, of Chicago, and Col. Nourse, of Massachusetts, both say that the story is not true to the life of the soldier. An article in the *Independent,* or perhaps the *Outlook,* says that no such profanity as given in the book was common in the army among the soldiers. Mr. Crane has since published two other books on New York life which are simply vulgar books. I consider the *Red Badge of Courage* a vulgar book, and nothing but vulgar."[4]

It is more difficult to know how much censorship occurred in English classes of the nineteenth century since the major journal for English teachers, the *English Journal,* did not begin until 1912, but a few items may suggest that English teachers endured or perhaps encouraged censorship at the time. Until 1864, Oberlin College would not allow Shakespeare to be studied in mixed classes. That Shakespeare was apparently of questionable value can be seen by an editorial in 1893 lauding students of Oakland High School who objected to using an unexpurgated edition of *Hamlet*:

> All honor to the modest and sensible youths and maidens of the Oakland High School who revolted against studying an unexpurgated edition of

Hamlet! The indecencies of Shakespeare in the complete edition are brutal. They are more than indelicacies, they are indecencies. They are no part of Shakespeare's thought, have no connection with the play, and can be eliminated with as little jar as could the oaths of a modern slugger. Indeed, Shakespeare's vulgarity was, to all intents and purposes, profanity, scattered promiscuously through the lines with no more meaning than so many oaths.[5]

An editorial writer in 1890 quoted from a contemporary account in the *Congregationalist* about books some young people had been reading.

> In this series of papers we purposely avoid all mention of some thoroughly bad books chosen by our young friends. We remember hearing the principal of a young ladies' seminary, in trying to express her strong disapproval of a certain book, say impulsively to the pupils, "I think I should expel a girl if I found her reading such a work." Before the week closed no less than three copies were in surreptitious circulation. There is something in human nature which craves that which is prohibited. Just so surely as we gave the titles of books worthy of condemnation, some youth would thirst instantly for a knowledge of their contents.[6]

Would that present-day censors could recognize what this critic obviously recognized, that merely mentioning an objectionable title creates new readers by the hundreds.

And one last incident a few years later: An English teacher reported on her use of *Treasure Island* with a junior high school class. Of the students who were enthusiastic, one student well on her way to becoming a literary censor wrote:

> *Treasure Island* should be read, firstly, because it is by a famous author, secondly, most people like it and, thirdly, because it is considered a classic.

Two other students objected. A boy wrote:

> I like a cleaner story. In this story there is too much bloodshed, drinking, and swearing.

A girl, however, pointed out the evil nature of the story and the nefarious and inevitable consequences of reading Stevenson's awful book:

> This story full of murder, fighting, and wiping blood off of knives is not suitable for boys and girls to read and if these kinds of books were not written there would not be so many boys go wrong. I don't think there should be any more books written like it, because it don't learn you anything and nowadays we should read books that do us some good.[7]

A modern censor could not have said it better.

AND WHAT IS THE STATE OF CLASSROOM AND LIBRARY CENSORSHIP TODAY?

Censorship was hardly a major concern of English teachers or school librarians (though it certainly was for public librarians) until recently. Before World War II, it rarely surfaced in schools although John Steinbeck's *The Grapes of Wrath* and *Of Mice and Men* caused some furor in newspapers, and when students began to read the books, the furor reached the schools. After World War II, Norman Mailer's *The Naked and the Dead* and J. D. Salinger's *The Catcher in the Rye* and other books "indicative of a permissive, lax, immoral society," as one censor noted, caught the eyes of adults and young adults alike. Granted, most objections were aimed at the writers and bookstores that stocked them. Few high school teachers would use or high school librarians would stock anything objectionable for several years, but teachers were now aware that they needed to be more careful about books they allowed students to read for extra credit or book reports. Two events changed the mild worry into genuine concern.

Paperback books seemed to offer little of intellectual or pedagogical value to teachers before World War II. Even after the war, many teachers blithely assumed paperbacks had not changed, and given the often lurid covers, teachers seemed to have a point, though it was more superficial than real. Administrators and parents continued to object even after the Bible and Plato's *Dialogues* and *Four Tragedies of Shakespeare* proved to teachers and librarians that paperbacks had merit. Students discovered even earlier that paperbacks were handy to stick in a purse or back pocket, and paperback titles were appealing, not stodgy as were most textbooks. So paperbacks came to schools, censors notwithstanding, and these cheap and ubiquitous books created problems galore for teachers.

Perhaps as important, young adult books until about 1967 were generally safe, pure, and simplistic, devoid of the reality that young people daily faced—violence, pregnancy, premarital sex, profanity, drinking, smoking, abortion, runaways, alienation, the generation gap, suicide, death, prejudice, poverty, class distinctions, drugs, divorce, and on and on. Sports and going to the prom and getting the car for the big Friday night date loomed large as the major problems of young adult life in too many of these novels. Young people read them for fun, knowing that they were nothing more than escape reading with little relationship to reality or to anything of significance. Then in 1967, Ann Head's *Mr. and Mrs. Bo Jo Jones* and S. E. Hinton's *The Outsiders* appeared and young adult literature changed and could not go back to the good-old-pure days. Paul Zindel's *The Pigman* followed in 1968, and while all YA books that followed were hardly great or honest, a surprising number were. English teachers and librarians who had accepted the possibility of censorship with adult authors popular with the young—Steinbeck, Fitzgerald, Heller, Hemingway, for example—now learned that the once safe young adult novel was no longer safe, and censorship attacks soon began. Head's and Hinton's and

Zindel's books were denounced, but so were young adult novels as good as Robert Lipsyte's *The Contender* (1967), A. E. Johnson's *A Blues I Can Whistle* (1969), John Donovan's *I'll Get There. It Better Be Worth the Trip* (1969), Jean Renvoize's *A Wild Thing* (1971), and that was merely the beginning.

Surveys of the state of censorship since 1963 indicate that censorship is either getting worse or fewer teachers and librarians are willing to lie quietly while the censor trods over them. Lee Burress' pioneer study, "How Censorship Affects the School," in October 1963 was only the first of these surveys. Nyla H. Ahrens' doctoral study in 1965 was the first national survey. State surveys of Arizona censorship conditions appeared in the February 1969 and February 1975 *Arizona English Bulletin*. National studies appeared ever more often: L. B. Woods' "The Most Censored Materials in the U.S." in the November 1, 1978, *Library Journal,* Burress' "A Brief Report of the 1977 NCTE Survey" in James Davis' *Dealing with Censorship,* and the much anticipated and disappointing *Limiting What Students Shall Read* in 1981. The 1982 survey of high school librarians by Burress found that 34 percent of the librarians reported a challenge to at least one book as compared to 30 percent in his 1977 survey. And a recent survey of censorship in Canada by David Jenkinson in the *Canadian Library Journal* for February 1986 was no more optimistic about censors and censorship.

But surveys often make for dull reading and convey all too little about the individual teacher or librarian besieged by censors. Reports of incidents, taken from newspaper clippings or the *Newsletter on Intellectual Freedom,* at least

Comments about censorship of all kinds appear with almost nauseating regularity in the daily press as is shown by this collection of articles.

hint at the emotional and pedagogical dilemmas faced by real people. Here are just a few such incidents:

1. *April 1971, Phoenix, Arizona. Love Story* was no longer permitted to be sold in the Camelback High School bookstore after a parent complained about the four-letter words. The associate principal was quoted as saying, "We don't wish to have any controversial books in the bookstore or the library. *Love Story* will probably be a classic in five years, but for the time being, it will not be sold in Camelback."[8]

2. *March 1972, Dallas, Texas.* Two school trustees attacked *The Catcher in the Rye.* One said, "I think high school-age people are just too young, not stable enough, to handle this kind of material . . . I think it's kind of silly to teach our youngsters living at home not to use profanity and then have the school encourage them to read books containing such material. To me that is endorsement and I don't think public schools should be endorsing something like that."[9]

3. *May 1972, Old Town, Maine.* Members of the local school committee objected to *Manchild in the Promised Land* in an elective course, "The Nature of Prejudice," because, as they said, there were no blacks in Old Town so prejudice was not that much of a problem. By a 4–3 vote, the committee banned the book from the schoolrooms immediately and from the school library after the close of the term.[10]

4. *1973, Pinellas County, Florida.* The Citizens Commission on Education asked the board of education to remove Eric Partridge's *Dictionary of Slang and Unconventional English* from the library. The chairman of the group linked the book's presence to the 696 suspensions for student profanity during that school year.[11]

5. *November 1973, Drake, North Dakota.* Three dozen copies of *Slaughterhouse-Five* were burned in the school incinerator by order of the school board. A minister called the book "profane" and "obscene" and the "tool of the devil." The school superintendent noted, "That's the way we get rid of all our trash." At a hearing about the book, the board brought in a town policeman who testified that Vonnegut's book was "filthy" although he admitted he didn't know the name of the book and admitted he had not read it. The teacher in question was fired, sued, and won his case (but not restitution for the job) in June 1975.[12]

6. *1974, Wild Rose, Wisconsin.* An administrator banned Dee Brown's *Bury My Heart at Wounded Knee* though he had never read the book, but he had heard a radio review which led him to believe the book was "slanted." He talked the matter over with an English teacher who didn't agree, but the administrator would not relent. "If there's a possibility that something might be controversial, then why not eliminate it," he said.[13]

7. *November 1975, Logan County, Kentucky.* The school board banned *Go Ask Alice.* The superintendent said that the "school system was not censoring any book [but wanted to get this one off the shelves] to keep

it out of the hands of small children who might be affected by its graphic, blunt language." A board member agreed the book was obscene but "did not want to make an issue out of the matter and would keep it quiet" if possible.[14]

8. *March 1976, Island Trees, New York.* In the start of what became in 1982 *the* major court battle about the right of school boards to ban books over student protests, the Island Trees School Board ordered these books removed—*Black Boy, Slaughterhouse-Five, The Naked Ape, Laughing Boy, Go Ask Alice, A Hero Ain't Nothin' But a Sandwich, Down These Mean Streets,* and *The Fixer.* The ban was later lifted on *Laughing Boy* and partially so on *Black Boy.*[15]

9. *April 1977, Eldon, Missouri.* By a 6–0 vote, the school board banned *The American Heritage Dictionary* because it included too many four-letter words. A Missouri Highway Patrol trooper had been offended by "39 objectionable words." According to the trooper, "If people learn words like that, it ought to be where you and I learned them—in the streets and in the gutter." The *St. Louis Post-Dispatch* began its article on the Eldon matter: "I'm rough," admitted a construction worker at Eldon's South Side Bar. "I've used all kinds of language. But not at home, and not in front of my daughter. That's what these damned bars are for."[16]

10. *August 1978, Issaquah, Washington.* The school board voted 3–1 to ban *The Catcher in the Rye* from high school classes after an objector told the board she had counted "785 profanities." The book, she said, "brainwashes students" and "is part of an overall communist plot in which a lot of people are used and may not even be aware of it." In June 1979, the board returned the book to the classroom.[17]

11. *July 1982, Fresno, California.* Three mothers, all members of a group called Family IMPACT (Interested Monitoring Persons Against Contemporary Textbooks), told the State Curriculum Commission that some new elementary reading texts were "primers for rebellion" because the books taught children to lie, cheat, and steal. The books also contained "an overwhelming stress on death, killing, and violence." One of the mothers said, "I cannot communicate with my oldest boy" and blamed textbooks for his dropping out of school. Another of the three found soft-porn in some text illustrations. She found a picture of a rabbit yawning at a crocodile offensive because "the far leg on the bunny starts in the center of his tummy. It appears subliminally to represent a different part of the body." Two months later, the same women objected to a Holt, Rinehart and Winston book, once more because of "subtle subliminal" art, this time a girl wearing what the mother called a "transparent skirt." The mother told the Holt representative that her group studies textbooks with "high-powered magnifying glasses." A new member of the State Curriculum Commission told the Holt representative to remove the material. "Why run the risk of offending some well-intentioned people?" The

Holt representative went along with the suggestion, saying, "I agreed with him completely. I'd rather do that than have a controversy at a public meeting. When you're publishing a book, if there's something that is controversial, it's better to take it out."[18]

12. *January 1983, Montgomery, Alabama.* Four members of the state textbook committee filed a minority report asking for the rejection of approximately one hundred works approved for use in Alabama schools. Among the words objected to were Anne Frank's *The Diary of a Young Girl* ("a real downer"), Maya Angelou's *I Know Why the Caged Bird Sings* ("preached hatred and bitterness against whites"), and Ibsen's *A Doll's House* (feminist propaganda).[19]

13. *December 1983, Howard, Wisconsin.* After one parent objected to Judy Blume's *Forever* in the high school library, a five-person committee was created and the book was removed from the shelves pending a committee report. The parent said, "I just feel that it demoralizes marital sex. If it had pictures, you could put it in the adult bookstore."[20]

14. *November 1985, Lassen County, California.* Parents objected to a performance of Lillian Hellman's *The Children's Hour.* At a school board meeting, one parent announced, "If something isn't fit for my five-year-old to watch, it's not fit for me to watch."[21]

15. *May 1986, Wasco Union High School, California.* The principal of the high school decided that John Gardner's *Grendel* and Gabriel Garcia-Marquez's *One Hundred Years of Solitude* did not meet the standards determined by the school board. The board president added, "It is not our intention to convert public classrooms into Sunday school classes, and students are entitled to a liberal education as much as possible, but we also have a duty to the community and we must guard against the use of garbage being passed off as literature."[22]

16. *February 1987, Sinking Valley, Kentucky.* Parents of a fifteen-year-old student demanded removal of William Faulkner's *As I Lay Dying* and Arthur Miller's *Death of a Salesman* and *The Crucible.* The parents said that Faulkner's novel was "pure filth. The man that wrote it must be a little off his gourd. In my opinion, it's not just my daughter I'm fighting for—I'm fighting for the rights of others. I can't see where it would enrich them. They're filling their heads with this junk."[23]

SOME ASSUMPTIONS ABOUT CENSORSHIP AND CENSORS

Given the censorship attacks of the last sixteen years, we can make the following assumptions about censorship.

First, any work is potentially censorable by someone, someplace, sometime, for some reason. Nothing is permanently safe from censorship, not even books most teachers and librarians would regard as far removed from censorial eyes—

not *Hamlet* or *Julius Caesar* or *Silas Marner* or *Treasure Island,* or anything else.

Second, the newer the work, the more likely it is to come under attack.

Third, censorship is capricious and arbitrary. Two teachers bearing much the same reputation and credentials and years of experience and using the same work will not necessarily be equally free from attack (or equally likely to be attacked). Some schools in conservative areas go free from censorship problems even though teachers may use controversial books. Other schools in relatively liberal areas may come under the censor's gun.

Fourth, censorship spreads a ripple of fear. The closer the censorship, the greater the likelihood of its effect on other teachers. But if the newspaper coverage of the incident has been extensive, the greater the likelihood that schools many miles away may feel the effect. Administrators may gently (or loudly) let their teachers know it is time to be traditional or safe in whatever the teachers choose for the coming year.

Fifth, censorship does not come only from people outside the school. Administrators, other teachers or librarians, or the school board may initiate an incident. That often surprises some English teachers or librarians. It should not.

other teachers won't come to your rescue

Sixth, censorship is, for too many educators, like cancer or a highway accident. It happens only to other people. Most incidents happen to people who know "it couldn't happen to me." It did and it will.

Seventh, schools without clear and established and school board-approved policies and procedures for handling censorship are accidents waiting to happen. Every school should develop a policy and a procedure which helps both educators and objectors when an incident arises. The aim of both policy and procedures should be to ensure that everyone has a fair hearing, not to stall or frustrate anyone.

Eighth, if one book is removed from a classroom or library, no book is safe any longer. If a censor succeeds in getting one book out, every other person in the community who objects to another book should, in courtesy, be granted the same privilege. When everyone has walked out of the library carrying all those objectionable books, nothing of any consequence will be left no matter how many books remain. Some books are certain to offend some people and be ardently defended by others. Indeed, every library will have books offensive to someone, maybe everyone. After all, ideas do offend many people.

Ninth, educators and parents should, ideally, coexist to help each other for the good of the young, but the clash of parents with some educators appears to be sadly inevitable. Some people would prefer to see young adults *educated* which means allowing them to think and wonder about ideas and to consider the consequences of those ideas. Others would prefer to see young people *indoctrinated* into certain community or family values or beliefs or traditions and to eschew anything controversial. With so little in common between these two philosophies of schooling, disagreement is not only natural but certain.

Educators should be aware that not everyone who objects to a book is necessarily a censor. Most parents are sincerely concerned about the welfare of their children, but making a special effort to go to school to make a complaint is likely to make them feel resentful or nervous or angry. If taking time from work were not enough reason to feel irritated, many parents have a built-in ambivalent love-hate feeling about schools. Maybe they had a miserable time with a teacher when they were young. They may worry about being talked down to by a much younger teacher or librarian. They may wonder if anyone will take them or their complaint seriously.

Unfair as it doubtlessly seems, educators will need to be considerate and reasonable and to listen more than talk for the first few minutes. Once objectors calm down and recognize that the teacher or librarian might just possibly be human, then and only then will the educator learn what is really troubling the parents. Everyone may learn, sometimes to the teachers' surprise, that no one wants to ban anything, but parents do wonder *why* the teacher is using the book or *why* the librarian recommended it to their child. They may want their child to read something else but agree that they have no wish to control the reading of anyone else. If that is true, the problem is easier to handle, not always easy but certainly easier.

But sometimes the objectors really are censors, and they have no desire to talk and reason, only to condemn. For these people, we can make the following assumptions.

Censors seem unwilling to accept the fact that the more they attack a book, the greater the publicity and likelihood that more young adults will read the offensive book. In their messianic drive to eliminate a book, censors create a wider and wider circle of readers. In some cases with older or more obscure works, they revive something that has been virtually dead for years. If *Romeo and Juliet* once went largely ignored by young adults before Zeffirelli's film, censors have now replaced the film as a motivation to read the play.

Censors will not believe that in trying desperately to keep young people pure and innocent they often expose those young people to the very thing the censors abhor. Several years ago, a group violently objected to a scholarly dictionary which contained some "offensive" words. Worried that others might not believe all those degrading, evil, pernicious words were so easily found in one work, censors compiled a sort of digest of "The Best Dirty Words in _____," duplicated the list, and disseminated it to anyone curious, including the very students censors claimed to be protecting. More than one censor has read the "offensive" parts of a book aloud at a school board meeting to prove his points while young students raptly listened.

Censors often have a simplistic belief that there is an easily established and absolute relationship between books and deeds. A bad book, however, defined, produces bad actions. What one reads, one immediately imitates. To read profane language automatically leads to young people swearing. Presumably, nonreading youngsters who swear must eagerly await more literate fellows to instruct them in the art of the profane. To read about seduction is to wish to seduce or to be seduced (though it is possible the wish may precede the book). To read about crime is to wish to commit that crime, or at the very least something vaguely anti-social. Anthony Comstock loved to visit boys in jail because when he asked what led them into the world of crime, they told him exactly what he wanted to hear (as they knew full well), that dime novels and drinking and shooting pool were *the* sources of all their present misery. J. Edgar Hoover was also a true believer in the one-to-one relationship between bad material and criminal acts.

Sociologists and psychologists and educators know that only rarely is there a simple explanation for a complex act. What makes young people delinquent? Perhaps bad reading. Perhaps violence on television. Perhaps home life, friends, acquaintances, school experiences, parents, teachers, religion, jobs, or any number of other variables, all interrelated. Perhaps no one cause is individually responsible. Censors like simplistic, easy, satisfying, lazy answers to tough questions. That puts them one up on teachers and librarians. Censors do not need to think to react or to believe.

Censors believe that whatever material the school provides is an index to what the school or the teachers or the librarians believe. If the school library has copies of Heller's *Catch-22* and Plato's *Dialogues,* and one teacher recommends Orwell's *1984* and another teaches the *Adventures of Huckleberry Finn,* the librarian and the teachers and the school must approve of bloodshed and homosexuality and socialism and drugs and slavery and much, much more that is objectionable.

Censors seem to have limited, if any, faith in the ability of young adults to read and think. Censors wonder if young people can handle controversial, suspect books like Huxley's *Brave New World* or Salinger's *The Catcher in the Rye,* the young are so innocent and pure and untainted by contact with reality. That may have been what caused one censor who objected to Ann Head's *Mr. and Mrs. Bo Jo Jones* and Paul Zindel's *The Pigman* to announce to an audience, "Teenagers are too young to learn about pregnancy."

A related act of censorial faith is the assumption that whatever a teacher says is automatically believed and accepted by students. If a teacher assigns something to be read by tomorrow, by tomorrow that something will be read and believed. Young people asked to read a short story will always read carefully, heed precisely whatever point the story or the author seems to be making, and then go and do likewise. Many a teacher would be happy if even 50 percent of the class read anything during a given week, much less everything and that carefully.

Censors seem to have no sense of humor, or at least none is exhibited at times of censorial stress. Having none, they dislike and distrust any literature that is ironic or satiric or humorous, regarding all as time-wasters.

Censors alternately love and hate English teachers and librarians. Censors would appear to hate what educators use, but censors would also appear to approve of great literature, particularly the classics. Being essentially nonreaders, they know little about literature but that it must be uplifting and noble and fine. They may claim to have read the uplifting when they were young, "back when schools knew what they were doing," but they often cannot remember titles; when they do their comments suggest the book was read in an emasculated child's edition. Censors assume that classics have no objectionable words or actions or ideas. So much for *Crime and Punishment, Oedipus Rex, Hamlet, Madame Bovary, Anna Karenina,* and most other classics. For censors, the real virtue of great literature is that it is old, dusty, dull, and hard to read, in other words, good for young people.

Censors care little what others believe. Censors are ordained by God to root out evil, and they are divinely inspired to know the truth. Where teachers and librarians may flounder searching for the truth, censors need not fumble for they *know.* They are sincerely unable to understand that others may regard the censors' arrogance as sacrilegious, but they rarely worry since they represent the side of morality. One censor counts for any number of other parents. When Judy Blume's *Deenie* was removed from an elementary library in the Cotati-Rohnert Park School District, California, in October 1982, a trustee said that a number of parents from a nearby college wanted the book retained, but "the down-to-earth parents who have lived in the district for quite awhile didn't want it,"[24] and that was clearly that. No one counted the votes, but no one needed to. Orwell knew what he was talking about when he wrote, "All animals are equal but some are more equal than others." Censors would agree with Orwell's comment if not his ironic intention.

Finally, censors use language carelessly or sloppily. Sometimes they cannot possibly mean what they say. The administrator who said, "We don't wish to have any controversial books in the bookstore or the library," either did not understand what the word *controversial* meant or he was speaking gibberish (the native tongue of embarrassed administrators talking to reporters who think they may have a juicy story here). Three adjectives are likely to pop up in the censors' description of objectionable works: *filthy, obscene,* or *vulgar* along with favored intensifiers like *unbelievable, unquestionably,* and *hopelessly* though a few censors favor oxymoronic expressions like *pure garbage* or *pure evil.* Not one of the adjectives is likely to be defined operationally by censors who assume that *filth* is *unquestionably filth,* and everyone shares their definition. Talking with censors is, thus, often difficult, which may disturb others while it is often a matter of sublime indifference to the censors. If talking is difficult, communicating with them is usually nigh unto impossible.

ATTACKS ON MATERIALS

Who Are the Censors?

There are three reasonably distinct kinds of censors and pressure groups: (1) those from the right, the conservatives; (2) those from the left, the liberals, and (3) an amorphous band of educators and publishers and editors and distributors who most other educators might assume would be opposed to censorship. The first two groups operate from different guiding principles, or so one would assume. But it is sometimes easy for educators to be confused

CHRIS CRUTCHER
on the Truth As We See It

For me, the worst thing about young adult literature is that it's called that. There seems to be a tendency for us to sometimes think our job with young people is to "model" rather than to "reflect" in literature; that we're supposed to depict the way things should be rather than the way they are so our readers won't get any "funny ideas." Often if we use rough language or gritty situations or include negative adult characters we get heat from so-called young adult experts who believe we have an obligation to turn our backs on the really unseemly aspects of life on this planet.

I believe I have a unique view because I know very little about any kind of literature other than my own, and therefore judge myself by different standards—or no standards—and because I have spent more than fifteen years looking at the extremes of the spectrum of families as an educator and as a child abuse therapist. I think it is incredibly disrespectful and potentially damaging to foster the myths of our society—myths of the unconditional sanctity of the family; myths of the innate good of any particular institutional spirituality; myths of unexamined patriotism, and on and on. In other words, we owe the same thing to young adult readers as we do to adult readers; that is, the honest depiction of our observations—the truth as we see it.

I don't write for young adults. I write about young adults.

Chris Crutcher's books include *Running Loose,* Greenwillow, 1983; *Stotan,* Greenwillow, 1986; and *The Crazy Horse Electric Game,* Greenwillow, 1987.

whether the attack stems from the right or the left, the coercive methods, the censorial rhetoric, and the messianic fervor seem so similar. The third group is unorganized and functions on a personal, ad hoc, case-by-case approach, though people in the group are more likely than not to feel sympathetic to the conservative case for censorship.

There are an incredible number of small censorship or pressure groups on the right who continue to *worry* educators (worry in the sense of alarm *and* harass). Many are better known for their acronyms which often sound folksy or clever, for example, Save Our Schools (SOS); People of America Responding to Educational Needs of Today's Society (PARENTS); Citizens United for Responsible Education (CURE); Let's Improve Today's Education (LITE); American Christians in Education (ACE); and everyone's favorite, Let Our Values Emerge (LOVE). Probably the most powerful, far beyond the state boundary implied by the title, was Parents of New York—United (PONY-U). Chapter 9 in Ed Jenkinson's *Censors in the Classroom: The Mind Benders* summarizes quite well the major groups, big or small.

With few exceptions, these groups seem united in announcing that they want to protect young people from insidious forces that threaten the schools, to remove any vestiges of sex education and secular humanism from classes or libraries, to put God back into public schools, and to restore traditional values to education. Very few announce openly that they favor censorship of books or teaching materials, though individual members of the groups may so proclaim. Indeed, what is particularly heartening about the groups is that many of them maintain that they are anti-censorship, though occasionally a public slip occurs. The president of the Utah chapter of Citizens for Decency was quoted as saying:

> I am opposed to censorship. We are not a censorship organization. But there are limits to the First Amendment. People have the right to see what they want on television, but that has nothing to do with the right to exhibit pornography on television. We're not stopping anyone from buying books and magazines or going to the movies they want. They just can't do it in Utah. Let them go to Nevada. Nobody there cares.[25]

Whether anyone from Nevada with a similar anti-censorial attitude responded with a suggestion that people from Nevada seeking cheap thrills should go to Utah is unknown. Something similar to the above comment came from the Rev. Ricky Pfeil. Wheeler, Texas, apparently has its moral problems with objectionable movies like *Porky's* and *Flashdance* and *E.T.* (Pfeil's argument against the latter film was, "The film's an attempt to show something supernatural and it's not God. There's only one other power that's supernatural and that's Satan.") The good minister also is against censorship, as he said:

> You know, I am not for censorship. People have a right to see what they want or read what they want, but I'd just as soon they go to Los Angeles to get a copy of *Playboy* magazine. I'm responsible for here. Evil left unchecked will go rampant. God tells me what to do.[26]

Given the doublespeak of Ms. Brimhall and the Rev. Pfeil, readers will admire the honest and the original Constitutional interpretation of the Rev. Vincent Strigas, co-leader of the Mesa (Arizona) Decency Coalition. Slashing merrily away at magazines that threatened the "moral fiber" of residents, the Rev. Strigas answered complaints about his approach:

> Some people are saying that we are in violation of First Amendment rights. I do not think that the First Amendment protects people [who sell] pornographic materials. The Constitution protects only the freedom to do what's right.[27]

Surely there is no ambiguity in that message.

Two highly vocal and nationally visible conservative groups have worried educators for several years. If the Eagle Forum and the Moral Majority *seemed* pro-censorship until recently, teachers and librarians can now turn to other that secular humanism implies. Such was the case when secular humanism reared its ugly head at a meeting of the Utah Association of Women.

> One woman says with disgust that two recent school board members didn't know what secular humanism was; thus they weren't qualified to run for office. Lots of "tsks" run through the group until a young woman visitor apologizes for her ignorance and asks, Just what is secular humanism? There is an awkward silence. No one gives a definition, but finally they urge her to attend a UAW workshop on the subject. Later in the meeting, during a discussion of unemployment a vice-president says, "Our young people are only taught to do things that give them pleasure. That's secular humanism."[29]

Fortunately for educators already concerned about the many pressure groups from the right, only one pressure group from the left need concern them, but that one group is worrisome. The Council on Interracial Books for Children was formed in 1965 to change the all-white world of children's books and to promote literature which more accurately portrayed minorities or reflected the goals of a multiracial, multiethnic society. They offer meetings and publications to expedite their goals, but for most teachers, the CIBC is best known for its often excellent *Bulletin.*

No humane person would disagree with the CIBC's goals. And, as it has maintained over the years, the CIBC does not censor teaching or library materials. It has, however, perhaps inadvertently, perhaps arrogantly, been guilty of coercing educators into not purchasing or stocking or using books offensive to the CIBC or its reviewers. Its printed articles have attacked Paula Fox's *The Slave Dancer,* Ouida Sebestyen's *Words by Heart,* and Harper Lee's *To Kill a Mockingbird* and, by implication, have criticized those who stocked or taught these books.

The CIBC has argued that *evaluation* is hardly identical with *censorship,* and no one would dispute an organization or journal's right to criticize or lambast any book with which it disagreed for whatever reason. But the CIBC and the *Bulletin* are unable to see any distinction between *Bulletin* reviews and reviews appearing in the *New York Times Book Review,* the *Horn Book Magazine, School Library Journal,* or *Voice of Youth Advocates,* not a difference in quality but in kind. *Bulletin* reviews are, whether the CIBC accepts it or not, a call for censorship based on social awareness. If book reviewer X reviews a YA book in any national publication except for the CIBC *Bulletin,* readers may disagree with the reviewer's opinion, but in any case readers will decide on their own whether they wish to buy or reject the book. Differences in taste are so commonplace that almost no one would attack someone else for choosing or not choosing to purchase on literary merit or personal taste. And, as anyone knows who reads many reviews of the same book, literary merit is an inexact term used to justify personal judgments.

But literary merit does not loom large in the reviews in CIBC's *Bulletin.* Replacing it are terms like *racist, sexist, handicappist,* and *ageist,* all of them

opponents, for both organizations have announced that they, too, are not
favor of censorship. In the November 1981 issue of the Eagle Forum's *Phyli
Schlafly Report,* the leader of the group castigated librarians for buying
"tremendous quantity of pornographic and trashy fiction" and for not stockir
"conservative, pro-family, and patriotic" books. Judith Krug agreed that be
hind Schlafly's strident rhetoric there lay a valid point, that as the America
Library Association had said for years:

> ■ Books should be readily available to the general public and to student
> on all sides of controversial issues of public importance. But often they ar
> not.[28]

Krug noted that these principles are uncontestably valid and should apply t
all book selection in a library. Readers can only assume that fairness an
balance are the hallmarks of the Eagle Forum's attitude toward both librarie
and education, and the day when individual (or units) of the group attempte
to censor books lies safely in the past.

Best known of all censors in America today are Mel and Norma Gabler wh
operate a small but powerful company out of their Longview, Texas, home
Educational Research Analysts came about when the Gablers found a vas
difference between their son's American history text and ones they remem
bered. Norma Gabler appeared before the State Board of Education in 196:
and went largely ignored. Upset, she came home and did her spadework or
offensive textbooks. (Most texts seem to be offensive to the Gablers until the
help writers and publishers to correct the material and remove secular human
ism and anything that might prove offensive to Christians or any proponents o
traditional values.) Now Educational Research Analysts cranks out thousand
of pages of textbook analyses and reviews to aid any school or school board i
selecting the best, the most proper, and the most accurate texts by the Gablers
standards. Readers who wish to know more about the Gablers or their orga
nization should read William Martin's "The Guardians Who Slumbereth Not,'
a model of fair play reporting by a writer who does not agree with the Gabler
on fundamental points but who clearly likes and admires their openness an
caring.

Whatever else conservative groups may agree or disagree on, they seen
united in opposing secular humanism and the teaching of evolution. Secula
humanism is both too large and too fuzzy to handle adequately in a fev
paragraphs (or even a short chapter). Briefly, if inexactly, conservatives appea
to define secular humanism as any teaching material which denies the existenc
of (or ridicules the worth of) absolute values of right and wrong. Secula
humanism is said to be negative, anti-God, anti-American, anti-phonics, an
anti-afterlife and pro-permissive, pro-sexual freedom, pro-situation ethics, pro
socialism, and pro-one worldism. Conservatives hopelessly intolerant abou
secular humanism often have problems explaining what the term means t
outsiders, or even insiders, usually defining the presumably philosophical tern
operationally and offering little more than additional examples of the horro

personal judgments, none of them objective though doubtless all are used sincerely and, in the case of a favorite author gone awry, sometimes sadly. If librarians purchase or teachers use a book attacked in the *Bulletin,* those educators had better be prepared to defend it against the true believer who will often assume the worst about them, that they are racists or sexists or worse. In most cases, it is less troublesome simply to avoid buying or using any book which has aroused the ire of the CIBC or a CIBC reviewer. The CIBC carries greater weight with librarians and teachers and school officials than it apparently is willing to recognize, and it is hardly a secret—save perhaps to the CIBC—that it is regarded by many as a censor. And supporters of the CIBC are almost certain to assume the worst about anyone who dares to criticize the organization, witness the letters to the editor that followed Lillian Gerhardt's editorial, "The Would-be Censors of the Left" in the November 1976 *School Library Journal* or Nat Hentoff's article, "Any Writer Who Follows Anyone Else's Guidelines Ought to Be in Advertising" a year later in the same magazine.

The case for the racist-free library is carried to its absurd conclusion by Bettye I. Latimer in "Telegraphing Messages to Children about Minorities." After defining censorship as: "the actual destruction of a book through banning, exiling, or burning it, so that no one has access to it," Latimer proclaims that she is "strongly opposed to censorship for adult readers, since adults are responsible for their own values," but that apparently does not hold true for young people:

> I am *not* suggesting censorship for books that are racist-oriented. I *am* suggesting that we remove these books to archives. This will permit scholars and researchers to have access to them. Since old racist books have no use in constructing healthy images for today's children, they need to be put in cold storage. As for contemporary racist books, educational institutions ought to stop purchasing and thereby stop subsidizing publishers for being racist.
>
> Finally, I would like to see librarians, teachers, and reading coordinators reeducate themselves to the social values which books pass on to children. I invite them to learn to use antiracist criteria in evaluating and assessing books.[30]

Amidst all the noble sentiments in these words, some people will sense a hint of liberal censorship or pressure at work. All censors, whatever their religious or sociological biases, *know* what is good and bad in books and are only too willing to *help* the rest of us fumbling mortals learn what to keep and what to exile (or put in the archives).

The third kind of censorship or pressure group comes from within the schools, teachers or librarians or school officials who either censor materials themselves or support others who do. Sometimes these educators do so fearing reprisals if they do not. Sometimes they do so because they fear being noticed, preferring anonymity at all costs. Sometimes they are fearful of dealing with reality in literature. Sometimes they regard themselves as highly moral and opposed to whatever they label immoral in literature. Sometimes they prize (or so claim) literary merit and the classics above all other literature, and refuse to consider teaching or recommending anything recent or second-rate however they define those terms.

Fear permeates many of these people. A survey of late 1960s Arizona censorship conditions among teachers uncovered three such specimens:

   I would not recommend any book any parent might object to.

   The Board of Education knows what parents in our area want their children to read. If teachers don't feel they can teach what the parents approve, they should move on.

   The English teacher is hired by the school board which represents the public. The public, therefore, has the right to ask any English teacher to avoid using any material repugnant to any parent or student.[31]

Lest readers assume that Arizona is unique in certifying these nonprofessionals, note these two Connecticut English Department Chairs quoted in Diane Shugert's "Censorship in Connecticut" in the Spring 1978 *Connecticut English Journal:*

   At this level, I don't feel it's [censorship] a problem. We don't deal with controversial material, at least not in English class.

   We have no problems at all in my department. The teachers order books directly and don't clear them with me or with a committee. But *I* receive the shipments. Copies of books that I think to be inappropriate simply disappear from the book room.[32]

In a letter to the book review editor of the *School Library Journal,* a librarian told how she had been approached by a parent objecting to words in Alice Childress' *A Hero Ain't Nothin' But a Sandwich.* The librarian particularly objected to the book's listing among the "Best Books of the Year for 1973." She wrote:

   Our school strongly recommends you remove this book from your list as profanity at the junior high level is not appropriate in a library book.[33]

More recently, the book was the subject of a school hearing when two Arizona mothers argued, "Most kids don't have the maturity to handle this." A junior high school principal agreed when he said, "I would like to see it banned altogether. That kind of language is not acceptable. I don't want any book on the shelf that would result in a student being disciplined if he used that language. Otherwise, our disciplinary policy will go out the window."

The December 1973 *School Library Journal* carried an article by Mary F. Poole objecting to Johanna Reiss' *The Upstairs Room:*

> ▌ The book proved to be a well-told account of a truly horrible situation. It is peopled with well delineated characters, who are in truth, "people with weaknesses and strengths," an aim of the author which was accomplished quite well: so the more than 50 irreverent expletives and the use of one four-letter word in the book are mere baggage or are used for their shock appeal, their monetary value, out of unconcern for the name of God, or to prove that the author is not a prude. Take your choice.[34]

The question of whether an author can make a valid moral or psychological point with "strong language," a typical euphemism in such cases, raged in letters in the following issues.

Similarly, Patty Campbell's "The YA Perplex" column in the December 1978 *Wilson Library Bulletin* led to increased letters as Campbell noted, "Judging from the letters to the editors in various library publications, obscene language rings alarm bells for most librarians"[35] and proceed to review three possibly controversial novels, Fran Arrick's *Steffie Can't Come Out to Play,* Kin Platt's *The Doomsday Gang,* and Sandra Scoppettone's *Happy Endings Are All Alike.* Sure enough, controversy produced letters, the best or most typical from an admitted self-censoring high school librarian. After announcing that he had played football and coached for eleven years—proving, one can assume, that he was a real man, not a wimp—he added:

> ▌ I have a philosophy of what it should be like within the walls and pages (especially pages) of a library. Two different worlds? You bet.
>
> Do I want our teens to see a sugarcoated world through rose-colored glasses? Why not? Is there anything wrong with reading about the good things that happen? . . . Is it wrong for a character of fiction to say "gosh darn" instead of "damn it"?
>
> In my library censorship lives, and I'm not ashamed or afraid to say it, either. I have books like *The Boy Who Could Make Himself Disappear* on my shelves, but these are few and far between. To all you so-called liberal librarians out there in city or country schools now condemning this letter, I say to you: "The kids of today are great! Do you want to help give them a boost or a bust?"[36]

And at least one book distributor was only too willing to help librarians precensor books. The Follett Library Book Company of Crystal Lake, Illinois (not to be confused with Follett Publishing Company in Chicago), has for several years marked titles with a pink card *if* three or more customers had objected to the vocabulary or illustrations or subject matter of a book. The cards read:

■   Some of our customers have informed us of their opinion that the content or vocabulary of this book is inappropriate for young readers. Before distributing this book, you may wish to examine it to assure yourself that the subject matter and vocabulary meet your standards.[37]

Publishers, too, have been guilty of rewriting texts or asking authors to delete certain words to make books or texts more palatable to highly moral librarians or communities. "Expurgation Practices of School Book Clubs" in the December 1983 *Voice of Youth Advocates* and Gayle Keresey's "School Book Club Expurgation Practices" in the Winter 1984 *Top of the News* uncovered censorship practices in Scholastic Book Club selections, as titles were changed and deletions of offensive words or ideas occurred between the hardback edition and its publication in a paperback club edition.

What Do the Censors Censor?

The answer to that question is easy—almost anything. Books, films, magazines, anything that might be enjoyed by someone is likely to feel some censor's scorn and moral wrath.

Some works, however, are more likely to be attacked. Judging from state and national surveys of censorship conditions, these works are almost certain to be objected to last year, this year, next year, and for years to come.

J. D. Salinger's *The Catcher in the Rye* (seemingly on every censor's hit list and leading every survey but one as the most widely censored book in America)

Go Ask Alice (the only close rival to *Catcher* on hit lists)

Steinbeck's *Of Mice and Men* and *The Grapes of Wrath*

Joseph Heller's *Catch-22*

Aldous Huxley's *Brave New World*

William Golding's *Lord of the Flies*

Harper Lee's *To Kill a Mockingbird*

Kurt Vonnegut's *Slaughterhouse-Five*

Judy Blume's *Forever*

Slightly behind these ten golden favorites come these adult novels widely read by young adults:

Ken Kesey's *One Flew over the Cuckoo's Nest;* Ernest Hemingway's *The Sun Also Rises, For Whom the Bell Tolls,* and *A Farewell to Arms;* F. Scott Fitzgerald's *The Great Gatsby;* Eve Merriam's *The Inner City Mother Goose;* Claude Brown's *Manchild in the Promised Land;* Gordon Parks' *The Learning Tree;* George Orwell's *1984* and *Animal Farm;* Jerzy Kosinski's *The Painted Bird;* Mark Twain's *Adventures of Huckleberry*

Finn; and Alexander Solzhenitsyn's *One Day in the Life of Ivan Denisovich.*

Along with these come young adult novels:

Judy Blume's *Deenie* and *Are You There, God? It's Me, Margaret;* Robert Cormier's *The Chocolate War* and *After the First Death;* Paula Fox's *The Slave Dancer;* Alice Childress' *A Hero Ain't Nothing But a Sandwich;* Johanna Reiss' *The Upstairs Room;* Rosa Guy's *Ruby;* M. E. Kerr's *Dinky Hocker Shoots Smack;* S. E. Hinton's *The Outsiders;* Paul Zindel's *The Pigman* and *My Darling, My Hamburger;* and Norma Klein's *Mom, the Wolfman and Me.*

And who could forget favorites like *The American Heritage Dictionary* and *Romeo and Juliet* and *Othello* and *The Merchant of Venice*? Or short stories (and films) like Shirley Jackson's "The Lottery" or Ambrose Bierce's "An Occurrence at Owl Creek Bridge"? Or modern plays like Thornton Wilder's *Our Town* or Tennessee Williams' *The Glass Menagerie* or *Summer and Smoke* or Arthur Miller's *Death of a Salesman* or *All My Sons*?

Readers surprised to discover an obvious censorial title not on the list above should feel free to add whatever they wish. Anyone who wishes to expand the list (easy and probably necessary for some) should casually read any issue of the *Newsletter on Intellectual Freedom* or skim through James E. Davis' *Dealing with Censorship* or any other book on censorship. The list of objectionable works could go on and on and on and on.

Why Do the Censors Censor What They Do?

That is a far more important and far more complex question than merely asking what do censors censor. Unfortunately for readers who want simple answers and an easy to remember list of reasons, the next paragraphs will certainly be disappointing.

In "Censorship in the 1970s; Some Ways to Handle It When It Comes (and It Will)" in early 1974, Donelson listed eight different kinds of materials which get censored. Those which censors

1. deem offensive because of sex (usually calling it "filth" or "risque" or "indecent")
2. see as an attack on the American dream or the country ("un-Ameri-can" or "pro-commie")
3. label peacenik or pacifistic—remember the Vietnam War had not yet become unpopular with the masses
4. consider irreligious or against religion or, specifically, un-Christian
5. believe promote racial harmony or stress civil rights or the civil rights movement ("biased on social issues" or "do young people have to see all that ugliness?")
6. regard as offensive in language ("profane" or "unfit for human ears")

7. identify as drug books, pro or con ("kids wouldn't hear about or use drugs if it weren't for these books")
8. regard as presenting inappropriate adolescent behavior and therefore likely to cause other young people to act inappropriately.[38]

Then Ed Jenkinson added more in "Dirty Dictionaries, Obscene Nursery Rhymes and Burned Books" in James E. Davis' *Dealing with Censorship;* adding fourteen in all, such as young adult novels, works of "questionable" writers, literature about or by homosexuals, role playing, text lacking proper rules of grammar, sexist stereotypes, and sex education.

Presumably that was that. Not so. Jenkinson added even more—the new list totaled twenty-three reasons for censoring—in *Censors in the Classroom: The Mind Benders.* New to the list were materials that defamed historical personalities, assignments that invaded the privacy of young people, secular humanism, nudity, values clarification, pagan cultures and lifestyles, and behavior modification.

More was to come, by Jenkinson alone. His 1979 *Publishers Weekly* article[39] listed forty targets, new among them being sociology, anthropology, the humanities generally (if secular humanism is bad, so then must be humanism or anything that sounds like humanism, and that easily extends to humanities), ecology, world government, world history if it mentions the United Nations, basal readers lacking phonics, basal readers with many pictures or drawings, situation ethics, violence, and books that do not promote the Protestant ethic or do not promote patriotism.

And in a later effort to expand his list, Jenkinson listed sixty-seven censorial objections in the May 1980 *Missouri English Bulletin*[40] adding these to the list: "Soviet propaganda," citizenship classes, uncaptioned pictures in any text but especially history texts, black dialects, science fiction, concrete poetry, world literature in translation, psychodrama, magazines that have ads for alcohol or contraceptives, songs in basal readers or history texts, cartoons in textbooks, texts that refer to the United States as a democracy rather than a republic, and "depressing thoughts." The last of the objections is truly depressing, apparently for censors and educators alike.

Teachers and librarians should remember that the announced objection may not always be the real objection. Censors have been known to attack Huxley's *Brave New World* or Orwell's *1984* for their sexual references only for others to discover that the real objection was to the frightening political attitudes the author displayed (or was thought to display). An attack on the language in John Howard Griffin's *Black Like Me* was only a subterfuge for one censor's hatred of blacks (and any minority group) as an investigation disclosed.

The underlying reasons for the announced reasons often are more significant than teachers or librarians may suspect. Parents worried about the moral climate facing their children are painfully aware that they apparently cannot change the material on television nor can they successfully fight the movies offered by local theatres nor can they do away with local "adult" bookstores.

Whom then can they fight? What can they change? An easy answer—attack teachers and librarians and local schools to do away with materials that censors do not like.

Inflation, depressions, recessions, rising taxes, threats of nuclear war, gas prices, rising food costs, all these depress most of us most of the time. But there is little we can do to attack the gigantic problems spurred on by who knows what or whom. Either we give up or, in the case of censors, we strike back at the only vulnerable element in most communities, the schools. And why not attack schools, what with the rising militancy of teachers and the massive public criticism of schools' performances on SAT or ACT tests? Why not indeed? And censors attack.

SOME COURT DECISIONS WORTH KNOWING ABOUT

Legal battles and court decisions often seem abstract and dull and irrelevant to practical matters for too many educators, but several court decisions have been significant and have affected thousands of educators who hardly knew the battles had taken place, much less their disposition. A brief run-through of two kinds of decisions, those involving attempts to define obscenity and its supposed influence on readers and viewers and those directly involving schools and school libraries, may be helpful to readers.

Court Decisions About Obscenity and Attempting to Define Obscenity

Since censors frequently bandy the word *obscene* about in attacking books, teachers and librarians should know something about the history of courts vainly attempting to define the term.

While it was hardly the first decision involving obscenity, the first decision announcing a definition of and a test for obscenity came about in an English case in 1868. *The Queen v. Hicklin* (L.R. 3 Q.B. 360) concerned an ironmonger who was also an ardent anti-papist. He sold copies of *The Confessional Unmasked: Showing the Depravity of the Romish Priesthood, the Iniquity of the Confessional and the Questions Put to Females in Confession,* and though the Court agreed that his heart was pure, his publication was not. Judge Cockburn announced a test of obscenity which was to persist in British law for nearly a century and in American law until the 1930s:

> I think the test of obscenity is this, whether the tendency of the matter charged as obscenity is to deprave and corrupt those whose minds are open to such immoral influences, and into whose hands a publication of this sort may fall.

Clearly, but not exclusively, Cockburn was attempting to protect young people.

In 1913 in *United States v. Kennerly* (209 F. 119), Judge Learned Hand ruled against the defendant since his publication clearly fell under the limits of the Hicklin test, but he added:

> I hope it is not improper for me to say that the rule as laid down, however consonant it may be with mid-Victorian morals, does not seem to me to answer to the understanding and morality of the present time, as conveyed by the words, "obscene, lewd, or lascivious." I question whether in the end men will regard that as obscene which is honestly relevant to the adequate expression of innocent ideas, and whether they will not believe that truth and beauty are too precious to society at large to be mutilated in the interest of those most likely to pervert them to base uses.

Then in 1933 and 1934, two decisions (5 F. supp. 182 and 72 F. 2d 705) overturned much of the Hicklin test. James Joyce's *Ulysses* had been regarded as obscene by most legal authorities since its publication, largely for Molly Bloom's soliloquy. The novel was stopped by Customs officials and tried before Judge John M. Woolsey of the Federal District Court for Southern New York. Woolsey found the book "sincere and honest" and "not dirt for dirt's sake" and ruled that in matters determining what is obscene, the work *must* be judged as a whole, not on the basis of its parts. An appeal to the Federal Circuit Court of Appeals in 1934 led to Judge Learned Hand's upholding Woolsey's decision.

In 1957 in *Butler v. Michigan* (352 U.S. 380), Butler challenged a Michigan statute which tested obscenity in terms of its effect on young people, arguing that this restricted adult reading to that fit only for children. Mr. Justice Frankfurter agreed, and wrote:

> The State insists that, by thus quarantining the general reading public against books not too rugged for grown men and women in order to shield juvenile innocence, it is exercising its power to promote the general welfare. Surely, this is to burn the house to roast the pig. . . . The incidence of this enactment [the Michigan statute] is to reduce the adult population of Michigan to reading only what is fit for children.

Frankfurter agreed with Butler and declared the Michigan statute unconstitutional.

Later in 1957 in *Roth v. United States* (354 U.S. 476), the U.S. Supreme Court announced that obscenity was not protected by the Constitution, for "implicit in the history of the First Amendment is the rejection of obscenity as utterly without redeeming social importance." (That phrase, "without redeeming social importance" was to cause problems for several years thereafter.) Reading for the majority, Justice Brennan added a new definition of obscenity:

> Obscene material is material which deals with sex in a manner appealing to prurient interest.

And a new test:

> whether to the average person, applying contemporary community standards, the dominant theme of the material taken as a whole appeals to prurient interest.

Roth rejected the Hicklin test (already in patches) as "unconstitutionally restrictive of the freedoms of speech and press."

Jacobellis v. Ohio (84 S. Ct. 1676) in 1964 further refined the *Roth* test when Justice Brennan announced that the "contemporary community" standard referred to national standards, not local standards though Chief Justice Warren angrily dissented, arguing that community standards meant local and nothing more.

In 1966 in *Memoirs v. Attorney General of Massachusetts* (86 S. Ct. 975) Justice Brennan further elaborated on the *Roth* test:

> Under this definition, as elaborated in subsequent cases, three elements must coalesce: it must be established that (a) the dominant theme of the material taken as a whole appeals to a purient interest in sex; (b) the material is patently offensive because it affronts contemporary community standards relating to the description or representation of sexual matters; and (c) the material is utterly without redeeming social value.

The *Ginsberg v. New York* (390 U.S. 692) decision in 1968 did not develop or alter the definition of obscenity, but it did introduce the concepts of variable obscenity and caused some concern for librarians and English teachers. Ginsberg, who operated a stationery store and luncheonette, had sold "girlie" magazines to a sixteen-year-old boy in violation of a New York statute which declared illegal the sale of anything "which depicts nudity" and "was harmful" to anyone under seventeen years of age. Ginsberg maintained that New York State was without power to draw the line at the age of seventeen. The Court dismissed his argument, sustained the New York statute, and wrote:

> The well-being of its children is of course a subject within the State's constitutional power to regulate.

The Court further noted, in lines that proved worrisome to anyone dealing in literature, classic or modern or what-have-you:

> To be sure, there is no lack of "studies" which purport to demonstrate that obscenity is or is not "a basic factor in impairing the ethical and moral development of . . . youth and a clear and present danger to the people of the state." But the growing consensus of commentators is that "while these studies all agree that a causal link has not been demonstrated, they are equally agreed that a causal link has not been disproved either."

Those words were lovingly quoted by censors across the nation, though few of them bothered to read the citations in the decision which suggested the dangers of assuming too much either way about the matter.

Then in 1973, five decisions were announced by the Court. The most important, *Miller v. California* (413 U.S. 15) and *Paris Adult Theatre II v. Slaton* (413 U.S. 49), enunciated a new (or more refined) test, one designed to remove all ambiguities from the past tests and to endure. That the test proved as ambiguous and as difficult to enforce and understand as previous tests should come as no surprise to readers. After attacking the 1957 *Roth* test, the majority decision read by Chief Justice Burger in *Miller* provided this three-pronged test of obscenity:

> The basic guidelines for the trier of fact must be: (a) whether "the average person, applying contemporary community standards" would find that the work, taken as a whole, appeals to the prurient interest; (b) whether the work depicts or describes in a patently offensive way, sexual conduct specifically defined by the applicable state law; and (c) whether the work taken as a whole lacks serious literary, artistic, political or scientific value.

To guide state legislatures with "a few plain examples of what a state statute could define for regulation under the second part (b) of the standard announced in this opinion," the Court provided these:

> (a) Patently offensive representations or descriptions of ultimate sexual acts, normal or perverted, actual or simulated.
> (b) Patently offensive representations or descriptions of masturbation, excretory functions, and lewd exhibition of the genitals.

After this so-called "Miller catalogue," Burger announced that "contemporary community standards" meant state standards, not national standards.

Paris Adult Theatre II repeated and underscored *Miller* and added more worrisome words about the dangers of obscenity and what it can lead to. Chief Justice Burger, again, for the majority:

> But, it is argued, there is no scientific data which conclusively demonstrates that exposure to obscene material adversely affects men and woman or their society. It is urged on behalf of the petitioner that, absent such a demonstration, any kind of state regulation is "impermissible." We reject this argument. It is not for us to resolve empirical uncertainties underlying state legislation, save in the exceptional case where that legislation plainly impinges upon rights protected by the Constitution itself. . . . Although there is no conclusive proof of any connection between antisocial behavior and obscene material, the legislature of Georgia could quite reasonably determine that such a connection does or might exist.

In other words, no proof exists that obscenity does (or does not) lead to any certain antisocial actions (or nonactions), yet state legislatures can assume or guess that such a relationship may exist and pass legislation to that effect.

Justice Brennan dissented, noting that the dangers to "protected speech are very grave" and added that the decision would not halt further cases before the Court:

> The problem is that one cannot say with certainty that material is obscene until at least five members of this Court, applying inevitably obscure standards, have pronounced it so.

To few observers' surprise, Brennan's prophecy proved correct.

On January 13, 1972, police in Albany, Georgia, seized the film *Carnal Knowledge* (starring Jack Nicholson) and charged the manager with violating a state statute against distributing obscene material. He was convicted in the Superior Court and the decision was affirmed by a divided vote in the Georgia State Supreme Court. In 1974, the U.S. Supreme Court announced its decision in *Jenkins v. the State of Georgia* (94 S. Ct. 2750), Justice Rehnquist reading the unanimous decision to reverse the Georgia Supreme Court opinion. Although *Carnal Knowledge* had been declared obscene by state standards and though it had a scene showing simulated masturbation, Rehnquist stated that "juries do not have unbridled discretion" in determining obscenity and that *Carnal Knowledge* had nothing which fell "within either of the two examples given in *Miller*."

The history of litigation and court decisions about obscenity and its definition are hardly models of clarity or consistency. Anyone interested in more details of this frustrating but fascinating story should read that marvelous book by Felice Flanery Lewis, *Literature, Obscenity and Law*.

Court Decisions About Teaching and School Libraries

If the implications of court decisions about obscenity are a bit vague, decisions about teaching and school libraries are not notably better. Courts are notoriously leery of decisions involving schools and libraries, but a few decisions, not unsurprisingly ambiguous, are worth noting about school libraries.

The U.S. Supreme Court had ruled in *Tinker v. the Des Moines (Iowa) School District* (393 U.S. 503) in 1969:

> First Amendment rights, applied in light of the special characteristics of the school environment, are available to teachers and students. It can hardly be argued that either students or teachers shed their constitutional rights to freedom of speech or expression at the schoolhouse gate.

But the Courts, federal or state, seemed unwilling to extend those rights to the school library in *Presidents Council, District 25 v. Community School Board No. 25* (457 F. 2d 289) in 1972. A New York City school board voted 5–3 in 1971 to remove all copies of Piri Thomas' *Down These Mean Streets* from junior high libraries because of its offensive nature and language. The U.S. Court of Appeals, Second Circuit, held for the school board. The book, so the Court decided, had dubious literary or educational merit, and since the state had delegated the selection of school materials to local school boards and there was no evidence of basic constitutional impingement by the board, the Court saw no merit in the opposing view.

Presidents Council was cited for several years thereafter as the definitive decision, but since it was not a Supreme Court decision, it served as precedent only for judges so inclined. A different decision prevailed in *Minarcini v. Strongsville (Ohio) City School District* (541 F. 2d 577) in 1977. The school board refused to allow a teacher to use Heller's *Catch-22* or Vonnegut's *God Bless You, Mr. Rosewater,* ordered Vonnegut's *Cat's Cradle* and Heller's novel removed from the library, and proclaimed that students and teachers were not to discuss these books in class. The U.S. District Court found for the school board, but on appeal to the U.S. Circuit Court of Appeals, the three-member panel reversed the lower court. Judge Edwards focused on the main issues of the case in eloquent words widely quoted and much admired by school librarians:

> ■ A library is a storehouse of knowledge. When created for a public school it is an important privilege created by the state for the benefit of the students in the school. That privilege is not subject to being withdrawn by succeeding school boards whose members might desire to "winnow" the library for books the content of which occasioned their displeasure or disapproval. Of course, a copy of a book may wear out. Some books may become obsolete. Shelf space alone may at some point require some selection of books to be retained and books to be disposed of. No such rationale is involved in this case.

The opinion of the Court that library books gained a tenure of sorts and could not easily be culled by a school board was at odds with the parallel U.S. Circuit Court in *Presidents Council,* but again, the Ohio decision served as precedent only if judges in other Federal District Courts (or Federal Appeals Courts) so wished to use it.

A year later in *Right to Read Defense Committee of Chelsea (Massachusetts) v. School Committee of the City of Chelsea* (454 F. Supp. 703) in the U.S. District Court for Massachusetts, another decision supported the rights of students and libraries. The librarian of Chelsea High School ordered and made available a paperback anthology, *Male and Female under Eighteen,* containing a poem by a student, "The City to the Young Girl," which had, as the judge wrote, "street language." A parent felt the language was "offensive" and called the board chairman who was also the editor of the local paper. The chairman-

ROBERT LIPSYTE
on Knowing the Questions

Once, YA books could get by as superficial escapist mindwash, but now that television offers junk food for the head, YA books have not only the responsibility (which they always had and often refused to assume) but the desperate need, if they wish to survive, to engage young people on a deeper level, on a searching, helpful, option-expanding level. For example, this current range for "realistic sexuality"—Well, there's too much sexuality, unexplained, teasing sexuality in the culture as is. We don't need to know that boys and girls have sex. If YA literature is to be worthwhile, to be necessary, it must go be-yond to expose more questions (young people often need the right questions more than answers) about relationships between girls and boys, about the possibility of relationships that don't put sexual pressure on boys and girls, about ways of diffusing the terrible pressures of "scoring" for boys, of losing or keeping virginity for girls, about honest ways of looking at sex through characters we can identify with and who entertain us, and perhaps coming to the radical conclusion that sex is at once less important than the deodorant makers would have us believe, yet more intrinsic a part of our lives than books up to now have told us. And abortion and birth control and loving and considerate sexual technique must eventually be dealt with, too, again in a way that is a part of the story being told—rather than the story being the candy-coating for a "problem" book that can move off the shelf. Gay sex must be treated as honestly as hetero-sex. Beyond sex, into sex roles, into job vs. family, into making money, into political involvement, YA books must also be ready to offer a view of the world that is uncompromising in realism, but also hopeful of improvement—and willing to leave unanswered, unpat major questions. The world is going to get more complicated, not less, and young people are going to have more available information and more chances for physical and emotional encounters. If YA literature is going to be in their knapsack as they march up the electronic grid road, then the entire community of interest here—writers, editors, publishers, teachers, and librarians—are going to have to be willing to admit we don't know the answers any better than the readers do, but we might have an idea what the most important questions are.

Robert Lipsyte's books include *Assignment Sports,* Harper & Row, 1970 and 1984; *The Contender,* Harper & Row, 1967; and *One Fat Summer,* Harper & Row, 1982.

editor concluded that the poem was "filthy" and contained "offensive" language and should be removed from the library. He scheduled an emergency meeting of the school committee to consider the subject of "objectionable, salacious and obscene material being made available in books of the High School Library" and wrote an article for his newspaper about the matter concluding with these words:

■ Quite frankly, I want a complete review of how it was possible for such garbage to even get on bookshelves where 14-year-old high school ninth graders could obtain them.

The superintendent urged caution and noted that the book could not be removed from the library without a formal review, but the chair was adamant. When the librarian argued that the poem was not obscene, the chair-editor wrote in his newspaper:

■ [I am] shocked and extremely disappointed to have our high school librarian claim there is nothing lewd, lascivious, filthy, suggestive, licentious, pornographic or obscene about this particular poem in this book of many poems.

The school committee claimed "an unconstrained authority to remove books from the shelves of the school library." While the judge agreed that "local authorities are, and must continue to be, the principal policy makers in the public schools," he was more swayed by the reasoning in *Minarcini* than in *Presidents Council*. He wrote:

■ The Committee was under no obligation to purchase *Male and Female* for the High School Library, but it did. . . . The Committee claims an absolute right to remove *City* from the shelves of the school library. It has no such right, and compelling policy considerations argue against any public authority having such an unreviewable power of censorship. There is more at issue here than the poem *City*. If this work may be removed by a committee hostile to its language and theme, then the precedent is set for removal of any other work. The prospect of successive school committees "sanitizing" the school library of views divergent from its own is alarming, whether they do it book by book or one page at a time.

What is at stake here is the right to read and be exposed to controversial thoughts and language—a valuable right subject to First Amendment protection.

What may prove to be the most significant decision about school libraries began in September 1975 when three members of the Island Trees (New York) School Board attended a conference sponsored by the conservative Parents of New York—United (PONY-U). After examining lists of books deemed "objectionable" by PONY-U, the three returned home, checked their district's school libraries, and found several suspect works—Bernard Malamud's *The Fixer,* Vonnegut's *Slaughterhouse-Five,* Desmond Morris' *The Naked Ape,* Piri Thomas' *Down These Mean Streets,* Langston Hughes' edition of *Best Short*

Stories of Negro Writers, Oliver LaFarge's *Laughing Boy,* Richard Wright's *Black Boy,* Alice Childress' *A Hero Ain't Nothin' But a Sandwich,* Eldridge Cleaver's *Soul on Ice,* and *Go Ask Alice.* In February 1976, the board gave "unofficial direction" that the books be removed from the library and delivered to the board for their reading.

Once the word got out, the board issued a press release attempting to justify its actions, calling the books "anti-American, anti-Christian, anti-Semitic, and just plain filthy" and argued:

> ▌ It is our duty, our moral obligation, to protect the children in our schools from this moral danger as surely as from physical or medical dangers.

When the board appointed a review committee—four members of the school staff and four parents—they politely listened to the report suggesting that five books should be returned to the shelves, two should be removed *(The Naked Ape* and *Down These Mean Streets),* and ignored their own chosen committee. (The board did return one book to the shelves, *Laughing Boy,* and placed *Black Boy* on a restricted shelf available only with parental permission.) Stephen Pico, a student, and others brought suit against the board claiming that their rights under the First Amendment had been denied by the board.

The U.S. District Court heard the case in 1979 and granted a summary judgment to the board. The Court held that the state had vested school boards with broad discretion to formulate educational policy, and the selection or rejection of books was clearly within their power. The Court found no merit in the First Amendment claims of Pico et al. A three-judge panel of the U.S. Court of Appeals for the Second Circuit (638 F. 2d 404) reversed the District Court's decision 2–1 and remanded the case for trial. The case then, though not directly, wended its way to the U.S. Supreme Court, the first such ever to be heard at that level.

In a strange and badly fragmented decision—and for that reason it is unclear just how certainly it will serve as precedent—Justice Brennan delivered the plurality (*not* majority) opinion in *Board of Education, Island Trees Union Free School District v. Pico* (102 S. Ct. 2799). He immediately emphasized the "limited nature" of the question before the court, for "precedents have long recognized certain constitutional limits upon the power of the State to control even the curriculum and classroom," and he further noted that *Island Trees* did not involve textbooks "or indeed any books that Island Trees students would be required to read." The case concerned only the removal, not the acquisition, of library books. He concluded the first section of his opinion by pointing out that the case concerned two questions:

> ▌ First, Does the First Amendment impose *any* limitations upon the discretion of petitioners to remove library books from the Island Trees High

School and Junior High School? Second, If so, do the affidavits and other evidential materials before the District Court, construed most favorably to respondents, raise a genuine issue of fact whether petitioners might have exceeded those limitations?

Brennan proceeded to find for Pico (and ultimately for the library and the books):

> ... we think that the First Amendment rights of students may be directly and sharply implicated by the removal of books from the shelves of a school library.
>
> Petitioners emphasized the inculcative function of secondary education, and argue that they must be allowed *unfettered* discretion "to transmit community values" through the Island Trees schools. But that sweeping claim overlooks the unique role of the school library. ... Petitioners might well defend their claim of absolute discretion in matters of *curriculum* by reliance upon their duty to inculcate community values. But we think that petitioners' reliance upon that duty is misplaced where, as here, they attempt to extend their claim of absolute discretion beyond the compulsory environment of the classroom, into the school library and the regime of voluntary inquiry that there holds sway.
>
> Petitioners rightly possess significant discretion to determine the content of their school libraries. But that discretion may not be exercised in a narrowly partisan or political manner. ... Our Constitution does not permit the official suppression of ideas. Thus whether petitioners' removal of books from their school libraries denied respondents their First Amendment rights depends upon the motivation behind petitioners' actions. If petitioners *intended* by their removal decision to deny respondents access to ideas with which petitioners disagreed, and if this intent was the decisive factor in petitioners' decision, then petitioners have exercised their discretion in violation of the Constitution.

Four pages follow before Justice Blackmun's generally concurring opinion and Justices Burger, Rehnquist, Powell, and O'Connor offered their stinging dissents, but it is clear that school librarians won something, though precisely what and how much will need to be resolved by future court decisions.

It is equally clear that secondary teachers lost something in *Island Trees*. In an understandable ploy, the American Library Association, the New York Library Association, and the Freedom to Read Foundation submitted an *Amicus Curiae* brief which sought to distinguish between the functions of the school classroom and the school library, a distinction that worked to the advantage of the school librarian but certainly not to that of the classroom teacher. Apparently, Brennan bought the argument as readers will see comparing Brennan's words with those from the brief below:

▐   This case, however, is about a library, not a school's curriculum. This is an extremely important distinction for the evaluation of the First Amendment interests at stake here.

The school board below banned books from a library. Thus, this case does not present an issue concerning the board's control of curriculum, i.e., what is taught in the classroom. We freely concede that the school board has the right and duty to supervise the general content of the school's course of study.

Whether these words will cause serious disagreements between teachers and librarians remains to be seen. Certainly, that phrase, "we freely concede," has rankled a number of English teachers who recognized that *Island Trees* was a serious setback for intellectual freedom in the classroom.

Anyone who assumed that *Pico* settled school censorship problems must have been surprised by four court decisions from 1986 through 1988. If these decisions were expected to clear up the censorial waters, instead they made the waters murkier and murkier.

On July 7, 1986, The U.S. Supreme Court announced its decision in *Bethel School District v. Fraser* upholding school officials in Spanaway, Washington, who had suspended a student for using sexual metaphors in describing the political potency of a candidate for student government. Writing the majority opinion in the 7–2 decision, Chief Justice Burger said, "Surely it is a highly appropriate function of public school education to prohibit the use of vulgar and offensive terms in public discourse. . . . schools must teach by example the shared values of a civilized social order." To some people's surprise, Justice Brennan agreed with Justice Burger that the student's speech had been disruptive though Brennan refused to label the speech indecent or obscene.

That decision worried many educators, but a lower court decision on October 24, 1986, frightened more teachers. *Mozert v. Hawkins County (Tennessee) Public Schools* began in September 1983 when the school board of Hawkins County refused a request by parents to remove three books in the Holt, Rinehart and Winston reading series from the sixth, seventh, and eighth grade program. The parents formed Citizens Organized for Better Schools and ultimately brought suit against the school board. U.S. District Judge Thomas Hull dismissed the lawsuit, but on appeal before the Sixth Circuit of the Court of Appeals, a panel of three judges remanded the case back to Judge Hull.

Not all the testimony in the trial during the summer of 1986 concerned humanism, particularly secular humanism, but so it seemed at times. Vicki Frost, one of the parents who initiated the suit, said that the Holt series taught "satanism, feminism, evolution, telepathy, internationalism, and other beliefs that come under the heading of secular humanism."[41] Later she explained why parents objected to any mention of the Renaissance by saying that "a central idea of the Renaissance was a belief in the dignity and worth of human beings," presumably establishing that teaching the Renaissance was little more than teaching secular humanism.

Judge Hull ruled in favor of the parents in October 24, 1986, but the U.S. Sixth Circuit Court of Appeals later overturned Hull's decision. Worse yet for the fundamentalist parents, the U.S. Supreme Court refused to hear an appeal of the Court of Appeals' ruling in February 1988. Beverly LaHaye, leader of the Concerned Women for America, who had filed the original suit in 1983 and whose group had helped finance the legal fees for the parents, said, "School boards now have the authority to trample the religious freedom of all children." Other people, notably educators, were grateful to the court for giving them the right to teach.

While Mozert worked its way through the courts, an even more troublesome and considerably louder suit was heard in Alabama. Judge Brevard W. Hand had earlier helped devise a suit defending the right of Alabama to permit a moment of silence for prayer in the public schools. The U.S. Supreme Court overturned Judge Hand's decision so he devised another suit, *Smith v. School Commissioners of Mobile County, Alabama,* alleging that social studies, history, and home economics textbooks in the Mobile public schools unconstitutionally promoted the "religious belief system" of secular humanism, as Judge Hand wrote in his March 4, 1987, decision maintaining that 44 texts violated the rights of parents.

The decision was both silly and certain, but those who feared the boogeyman of secular humanism celebrated for a few weeks. Then, late in August 1987, the Eleventh U.S. Circuit Court of Appeals reversed Judge Hand's decision. The Court of Appeals did not address the question whether secular humanism was or was not a religion, but it did agree that the 44 texts did not promote secular humanism. Phyllis Schlafly said she was not surprised by the ruling, but it mattered little since the decision would be appealed to the U.S. Supreme Court. Oddly enough for a case that began so loudly, the plaintiffs were mute, the date for the appeal quietly passed, and all was silence.

The fourth case, *Hazelwood School District v. Kuhlmeier,* will trouble many educators, though nominally the case was concerned with school journalism and the publication of a school newspaper. The case began in 1983 when the principal of a high school in Hazelwood, Missouri, objected to two stories in the school newspaper dealing with teenage pregnancy and divorce's effect on young people.

Associate Justice Byron White wrote the majority opinion in the 5–3 decision announcing that educators (i.e., administrators) are entitled to exercise great control over student expression. Nothing in White's pronouncements would stop students from beginning their own independent newspaper outside the campus, but little in his words could encourage young people to want to work on the usual school-supported paper.

The consequences of *Hazelwood* may be more serious than many teachers expect. Kirsten Goldberg's words suggest potential problems to come.

Less than a month after the U.S. Supreme Court's decision expanding the power of school officials to regulate student speech, lower courts in three widely differing cases have cited the ruling in upholding the actions of school administrators.

The court decisions, which came less than a week apart, support a Florida school board's banning of a humanities textbook, a California principal's seizure of an "April Fool's" edition of a school newspaper, and a Nebraska school district's decision not to provide meeting space to a student Bible club.[42]

Extralegal Decisions

Most censorship episodes do not result in legal hearings and court decisions. Teachers or librarians come under attack and unofficial rumor-mongering charges are lodged because someone objects and labels the offending work "obscene" or "filthy" or "pornographic." The case is heard in the court of public opinion, sometimes before the school board, with few legal niceties prevailing. The censors (and too often the school board) almost never operate under any definitions of obscenity that a court would recognize, but their interpretations of the issues are operationally effective for their purposes. The book may not always be judged as a whole book (though individual parts may be juicily analyzed), and the entire procedure may be arbitrary and capricious. With all its inherent sloppiness, the trial is speedier than a court hearing. The decision, once announced, rapidly disposes of the offending book and frequently the teacher or librarian to boot, a variation of old-fashioned Western justice at work. Extralegal trials need not be cluttered with trivia like accuracy or reasoning or fairnerss or justice. Many of the sixteen censorship incidents described earler in this chapter were handled extralegally.

Why would librarians or teachers allow their books and teaching materials to be so treated? Court cases cost money, lots of money, and unless a particular case is likely to create precedent, many lawyers would discourage educators from going to the courts. Court cases, even more important, cause friction among the community and—surprising to many neophyte teachers and librarians—cause almost equal friction among a school's faculty. A teacher or librarian who assumes that all fellow teachers will support a case for academic freedom or intellectual freedom is a fool. Many educators, to misuse the word, will have little sympathy for troublemakers or their causes. Others will be frightened at the prospect of possibly antagonizing their superiors. Others will "know their place" in the universe. Others are morally offended by anything stronger than "darn" and may regard most of modern literature (and old literature) as inherently immoral and therefore objectionable for high school students' use. Others will find additional or different reasons aplenty for staying out of the fray. And that, more likely than not, is the reason most censorship episodes do not turn into court cases.

WHAT TO DO BEFORE AND AFTER THE CENSORS ARRIVE

Certain steps should be taken by librarians and teachers, preferably acting in concert, to prepare for censorship.

Before the Censors Arrive

Teachers and librarians should have some knowledge about the history of censorship and why citizens would wish to censor. They should keep up-to-date with censorship problems and court decisions and what books are coming under attack for what reason. That means they should read the *Newsletter on Intellectual Freedom, School Library Journal, English Journal, Wilson Library Bulletin, Journal of Youth Services in Libraries,* and *Voice of Youth Advocates* along with other articles cited in the bibliography that concludes each issue of the *Newsletter.* A lot of work? Of course, but better than facing a censor totally ignorant of the world of censorship. Laziness and unprofessionalism are always easier than handling any job professionally.

They should develop clear and succinct statements, devoid of any educational or library or literary jargon, on why they teach literature or stock books. These

Some materials are essential for librarians and teachers who want to keep up-to-date on censorship.

statements ought to be made easily available to the public, partly to demonstrate educators' literacy—always an impressive beginning for an argument—and to make parents feel that someone intelligent works in the school, partly because teachers and librarians have a duty to communicate to the public what is going on and why it goes on.

They need to develop and publicize procedures for book selection in the library or the classroom. Most parents have not the foggiest notion how educators go about selecting books, more or less assuming it comes about through sticking pins through a book catalogue. It might be wise to consider asking some parents to assist teachers and librarians in selection, partly to let parents learn how difficult the matter is, partly to use their ideas (which might prove surprisingly helpful).

They need to develop procedures for handling censorship should it occur. The National Council of Teachers of English monographs *The Students' Right to Read* and *The Students' Right to Know* should prove helpful, as should the American Library Association's *Intellectual Freedom Manual,* both for general principles and specific suggestions. Whether adopted from any of these sources or created afresh, the procedure should include a form to be completed by anyone who objects to any teaching material or library book, and a clearly defined way in which the matter will be handled after completion of the form. (Will it go to a committee? How many are on the committee? Are people outside the school on the committee? How many teachers? Administrators?) The procedural rules must be openly available for anyone to consult, the procedures must apply to everyone (no exceptions should be allowed, no matter whether the complainant is the local drunk or the school board president), every complainant must be treated courteously and promptly, and the procedures must be approved by the school board. If the board does not approve the procedures, they have no legal standing. If the school board is not periodically reminded of the procedures—say, every couple of years—it may forget its obligation. Given the fact that many school boards will change membership slightly in three or four years and may change its entire composition within five or six, teachers and librarians should take it upon themselves to remind the board, else an entirely new board may wonder why it should support something it neither created nor particularly approves of.

Teachers who assign long works (other than texts) for common reading should write rationales, statements aimed at parents but open to anyone, explaining why the teacher chose *1984* or *Silas Marner* or *Manchild in the Promised Land* or *Hamlet* for class reading and discussion. Rationales should answer the following though they should be written as informal essays, not answers to essay tests: (1) Why would the teacher use this book with this class at this time? (2) What specific objectives—not couched in behavioral terms unless the teachers are anxious to alienate parents—literary or pedagogical, is the teacher aiming at? (3) How will this book meet those objectives? (4) What problems of style, tone, theme, or subject matter exist and how will the teacher face them? Answering those questions should force teachers to take a fresh look at the book and think more carefully about the possibilities and problems inherent in the book. Rationales are *not* designed to protect the teacher by showing careful advance preparation before teaching, although clearly such rationales would be valuable should censorship strike. Rather, rationales should be written for public information easily available to the public as part of the professional responsibility of teachers. Diane Shugert offers a number of sample rationales in the Fall 1983 *Connecticut English Journal* and in "How to Write a Rationale in Defense of a Book" in James Davis' *Dealing with Censorship*.

Educators should woo the public to gain support for intellectual and academic freedom. Any community will have its readers and former teachers interested in students' freedom to read. Finding them ahead of time is part of teachers and librarians' jobs. Waiting until censorship strikes is too late. Pat Scales' ideas about working with parents in the November 1983 *Calendar* (distributed by the Children's Book Council) are most helpful. Scales was talking to a parent who helped in Scales' school library and who had picked up copies of Maureen Daly's *Seventeenth Summer* and Ann Head's *Mr. and Mrs. Bo Jo Jones* and wondered about students reading books with such provocative covers. Scales asked the mother to read the books before forming an opinion. From that experience came a program called "Communicate Through Literature" with monthly meetings to discuss with parents the reading that young adults do.

Educators should be prepared to take on the usual arguments of censors, for example, that educators are playing word games when we insist that we select and some parents try to censor. There is a distinction between *selection* and *censorship* no matter how many people deliberately or inadvertently misuse or confuse the two. The classic distinction was drawn by Lester Asheim in 1952:

> Selection begins with a presumption in favor of liberty of thought; censorship with a presumption in favor of thought control. Selection's approach to the book is positive, seeking its values in the book as a book, and in the book as a whole. Censorship's approach is negative, seeking for vulnerable characteristics wherever they can be found anywhere in the book, or even outside it. Selection seeks to promote the right of the reader to read; censorship seeks to protect not the right—but the reader himself from the fancied effects of his reading. The selector has faith in the intelligence of the reader; the censor has faith only in his own.
>
> In other words, selection is democratic while censorship is authoritarian, and in our democracy we have traditionally tended to put our trust in the selector rather than in the censor.[43]

Finally, teachers and librarians should know the organizations that may be the most helpful should censorship strike. Diane Shugert's "A Body of Well-Instructed Men and Women: Organizations Active for Intellectual Freedom," in James Davis' *Dealing with Censorship,* has a long list of such groups.

After the Censors Arrive

Teachers and librarians should begin by refusing to panic, easier said than done but essential. Censors always have one advantage. They can determine the time and the place for the attack. No matter how well prepared the teacher or the librarian, only the censor can say *when*.

Educators should not be too surprised or appalled to discover that not all their fellow teachers or librarians will rush in with immediate support. If teachers and librarians will assume they represent the entire cause by themselves, they are far better off and considerably less likely to be instantly disillusioned.

Educators ought to urge the potential censors to talk first to the teacher or librarian in question before completing the complaint form, not to stall the objectors but to assure everyone of fair play all around. Teachers or librarians may discover what others have before, that objectors sometimes simply want to be heard and their complaints treated with dignity and dispatch. Sometimes, teachers and librarians may even be able to talk calmly—once the need to battle has died down—with the objectors and to reason with them, which is not exactly the same as convincing them that the teachers or librarians are necessarily right. The objectors may even see why the offending work was assigned or recommended, sometimes even seeing the difficulty in choosing a book for a class or an individual. Many teachers and librarians, though by no means all, agree that if parents ask that their child not be required to read a certain book, educators must agree to find a substitute book. If a substitute book is to be found and if it is to meet a different fate than the first book, parents must help in selecting the new book. Most objectors are deadly serious about their children's education, and they will understand why the substitute book should not be easier or shorter (thus rewarding the student) or harder and longer (thus unduly punishing the student). Finding another book approximately as long and as difficult as the original choice is no easy matter, but parents who demand substitutes must help, lest the teacher offend once more.

Librarians and teachers must treat objectors with every possible courtesy, though courtesy may not always be what educators first consider. Objectors should be expected to complete the school's forms detailing the objection, but the forms should be easily accessible and politely distributed. The complaint form should *never* be used to stall objectors. If it is so long that objectors get discouraged, the school may win one battle, but it will have produced one disgruntled citizen, and at school bond time, one irritated citizen and friends are quite enough to harm the cause of education.

Last, a committee (spelled out in detail prior to the censorship) meets to look at and discuss the complaint. After considering the problem though before arriving at a decision, the committee must meet with the teacher or librarian in question *and* the objectors to hear their cases. The committee will then make its decision and forward it to the highest administrator in the school who will forward it to the superintendent who will forward it to the school board.

That body, already aware of the policy and procedures much earlier adopted to handle such matters, will consider this objection and make its decision, probably after at least one open meeting.

In no case and at no level should the actions of the educators or administrators or the school board be viewed as pro forma but rather thoughtfully considered actions to resolve a problem, not to create newer and bigger ones. Objectors should feel that they have been listened to and courtesy has been extended them at all levels and all stages.

We believe that the school—classroom or library—must be a center of intellectual ferment in the community. This does not imply that schools should be radical, just that they should be one place where freedom to think and inquire is protected, where ideas of all sorts can be considered, analyzed, investigated, discussed, and their consequences thought through. We believe librarians and English teachers must protect these freedoms, not merely in the abstract but in the practical day-by-day world of the school and library. To protect those freedoms we must fight censorship, for without them no education worthy of the name is possible.

NOTES

[1]Colin Campbell, "Book Banning in America," *New York Times Book Review,* December 20, 1981, p. 1.

[2]Comstock's life and work have been the subject of many books and articles. Heywood Broun and Margaret Leech's *Anthony Comstock: Roundsman of the Lord* (New York: Albert and Charles Boni, 1927) is amusing and nasty and still worth reading. A brief overview of Comstock's life can be found in Robert Bremner's introduction to the reprinting of *Traps for the Young* (Cambridge: Harvard University Press, 1967), pp. vii–xxxi. See also Paul S. Boyer's *Purity in Print: The Vice-Society Movement and Book Censorship in America* (New York: Charles Scribner's Sons, 1968) and Robert W. Haney's *Comstockery in America: Patterns of Censorship and Control* (Boston: Beacon Press, 1960).

[3]Arthur E. Bostwick, *The American Public Library* (New York: Appleton, 1910), pp. 130–31.

[4]*Library Journal* 21 (December 1896): 144.

[5]"Unexpurgated Shakespeare," *Journal of Education* 37 (April 13, 1883): 232.

[6]"What Books Do They Read?" *Common School Education* 4 (April 1890): 146–47.

[7]Evaline Harrington, "Why Treasure Island?" *English Journal* 9 (May 1920): 267–68.

[8]"Book Store Bans *Love Story,*" "Teen Gazette," *Phoenix Gazette* (April 3, 1971), p. 2.

[9]*Newsletter on Intellectual Freedom* 21 (July 1972): 105–106.

[10]*Newsletter on Intellectual Freedom* 21 (July 1972): 116.

[11]*Newsletter on Intellectual Freedom* 23 (May 1974): 32.

[12]Widely reported. For a firsthand account by the teacher attacked, see Bruce Severy, "Scenario of Bookburning," *Arizona English Bulletin* 17 (February 1975): 68–74.

[13]*Newsletter on Intellectual Freedom* 23 (November 1974): 145.

[14]*Logan Leader* (Russellville, Logan County, Kentucky, November 1, 1975): p. 1.

[15]Widely reported. See *Newsletter on Intellectual Freedom* 25 (May 1976): 61–62.

[16]*Newsletter on Intellectual Freedom* 26 (July 1977): 101, and *St. Louis Post-Dispatch* (May 29, 1977), pp. 1, 5.

[17]*Newsletter on Intellectual Freedom* 27 (November 1978): 138, 144.

[18]William Trombley, "School Texts Called 'Primers for Rebellion,'" *Los Angeles Times* (July 30, 1982), pp. 1–3, 22, and William Trombley, "Fresno Group Gets Textbooks Changed," *Los Angeles Times* (September 9, 1982), pp. II–1, 7.

[19]*Newsletter on Intellectual Freedom* 32 (March 1983): 39.

[20]*Newsletter on Intellectual Freedom* 33 (March 1984): 39.

[21]*Newsletter on Intellectual Freedom* 35 (July 1986): 119.

[22]Ibid.

[23]*Newsletter on Intellectual Freedom* 36 (May 1987): 90.

[24]*San Francisco Examiner* (October 8, 1982), p. B–4.

[25]Louise Kingsbury and Lance Gurwell, "The Sin Fighters: Grappling with Gomorrah at the Grass Roots," *Utah Holiday* 12 (April 1983): 46.

[26]Lee Grant, "Shoot-out in Texas," Calendar section, *Los Angeles Times* (December 25, 1983), p. 21.

[27]*Phoenix Gazette,* June 10, 1981, p. SE–6.

[28]"Editorial," *Newsletter on Intellectual Freedom* 31, (January 1982): 4.

[29]Kingsbury and Gurwell, p. 52.

[30]Bettye I. Latimer, "Telegraphing Messages to Children About Minorities," *The Reading Teacher* 30 (November 1976): 155.

[31]*Arizona English Bulletin* 11 (February 1969): 37.

[32]Diane Shugert, "Censorship in Connecticut," *Connecticut English Journal* 9 (Spring 1978): 59–61.

[33]*School Library Journal* 21 (December 1974): 34.

[34]"*The Upstairs Room*: Room for Controversy," *School Library Journal* 20 (December 1973): 67.

[35]*Wilson Library Bulletin* 53 (December 1978): 340.

[36]*Wilson Library Bulletin* 53 (February 1979): 421.

[37]*Publishers Weekly* 215 (April 30, 1979): 24.

[38]Ken Donelson, "Censorship in the 1970s: Some Ways to Handle It When It Comes (and It Will)," *English Journal* 63 (February 1974): 47–51.

[39]"Protest Groups Exert Strong Impact," *Publishers Weekly* 216 (October 29, 1979): 42–44.

[40]"Sixty-Seven Targets of the Textbook Protesters," *Missouri English Bulletin* 38 (May 1980): 27–32.

[41]*Arizona Republic* (July 12, 1986), p. D–3.

[42]Kirsten Goldberg, "Censorship Decision Is Rapidly Coloring Other School Cases," *Education Week* 7 (February 17, 1988): 1.

[43]Lester Asheim, "Not Censorship but Selection," *Wilson Library Bulletin* 28 (September 1953): 67. See also Asheim's later article, "Selection and Censorship: A Reappraisal," *Wilson Library Bulletin* 58 (November 1983): 180–184. Julia Turnquist Bradley's "Censoring the School Library: Do Students Have the Right to Read?" *Connecticut Law Review* 10 (Spring 1978): 747–775 also draws a distinction between *selection* and *censorship*.

A STARTER BIBLIOGRAPHY ON CENSORSHIP

Bibliographical Sources

McCoy, Ralph E. *Freedom of the Press: An Annotated Bibliography.* Southern Illinois University Press, 1968.

_____ . *Freedom of the Press: A Bibliocyclopedia Ten-Year Supplement.* Southern Illinois University Press, 1979.

Newsletter on Intellectual Freedom. A bimonthly edited by Judith F. Krug with a sizable bibliography at the end of each issue. Available from the American Library Association, 50 East Huron Street, Chicago, Illinois 60611.

Books

Ahrens, Nyla H. *Censorship and the Teaching of English: A Questionnaire Survey of a Selected Sample of Secondary Teachers of English.* Dissertation, Teachers College, Columbia University, 1965.

Bosmajian, Haig A., ed. *Censorship: Libraries and the Law.* Neal-Schuman, 1983.

_____ . *The First Amendment in the Classroom,* 5 volumes. New York: Neal-Schuman. No. 1, *The Freedom to Read,* 1987, and No. 2, *Freedom of Religion,* 1987. The others—No. 3, *Freedom of Expression;* No. 4, *Academic Freedom;* and No. 5, *The Freedom to Publish*—are promised soon.

Boyer, Paul S. *Purity in Print: The Vice-Society and Book Censorship in America.* Charles Scribner's Sons, 1968.

Burress, Lee, and Edward B. Jenkinson. *The Students' Right to Know.* National Council of Teachers of English, 1982.

Carrier, Esther Jane. *Fiction in Public Libraries, 1876–1900.* Scarecrow Press, 1965.

Censorship Litigation and the Schools. American Library Association, 1983.

Cline, Victor B., ed. *Where Do You Draw the Line?* Brigham Young University Press, 1974.

Davis, James E., ed. *Dealing with Censorship.* National Council of Teachers of English, 1979.

DeGrazia, Edward, ed. *Censorship Landmarks.* R. R. Bowker, 1969. Censorship cases reprinted from 1663 through 1968. A basic source.

Fiske, Marjorie. *Book Selection and Censorship: A Study of School and Public Libraries in*

California. University of California Press, 1968.

Geller, Evelyn. *Forbidden Books in American Public Libraries, 1876–1939: A Study in Cultural Change.* Greenwood Press, 1984.

Haight, Anne Lyons. *Banned Books,* 4th ed. R. R. Bowker, 1978.

Hefley, James C. *Textbooks on Trial.* Victor Books, 1976. A defense of Mel and Norma Gabler and their work.

Hentoff, Nat. *The First Freedom: The Tumultuous History of Free Speech in America.* Delacorte, 1980.

Intellectual Freedom Manual, 2nd ed. American Library Association, 1983. Basic for all the help it provides.

Jenkinson, Edward B. *Censors in the Classroom: The Mind Benders.* Southern Illinois University Press, 1979.

Lewis, Felice Flanery. *Literature, Obscenity and Law.* Southern Illinois University Press, 1976. *The* book on literature and its battles with various courts.

Moffett, James. *Storm in the Mountains: A Case Study of Censorship, Conflict, and Consciousness.* Southern Illinois University Press, 1988.

Oboler, Eli M., ed. *Censorship and Education.* H. W. Wilson, 1981.

O'Neil, Robert M. *Classrooms in the Crossfire: The Rights and Interests of Students, Parents, Teachers, Administrators, Librarians and the Community.* Indiana University Press, 1981.

The Students' Right to Read. National Council of Teachers of English, 1982.

Articles

"Are Libraries Fair: Pre-Selection Censorship in a Time of Resurgent Conservatism." *Newsletter on Intellectual Freedom* 31 (September 1982): 151, 181–88. Comments by Cal Thomas, Vice-President of the Moral Majority, and Nat Hentoff, Village Voice columnist and author of *The First Freedom.*

Asheim, Lester. "Not Censorship, but Selection." *Wilson Library Bulletin* 28 (September 1953): 63–67.

_____ . "Selection and Censorship: A Reappraisal." *Wilson Library Bulletin* 58 (November 1983) 180–84.

Bjorklun, Eugene C. "Secular Humanism: Implications of Court Decisions." *Educational Forum* 52 (Spring 1988): 211–21.

Booth, Wayne C. "Censorship and the Values of Fiction:" *English Journal* 53 (March 1964): 155–64.

Bradley, Julia Turnquist. "Censoring the School Library: Do Students Have the Right to Read?" *Connecticut Law Review* 10 (Spring 1978): 747–75.

Briley, Dorothy. "Are the Editors Guilty of Precensorship?" *School Library Journal* 29 (October 1982): 114–15.

Broderick, Dorothy. "Censorship—Reevaluated." *School Library Journal* 18 (November 1971): 30–32.

Bryant, Gene. "The New Right and Intellectual Freedom." *Tennessee Librarian* 33 (Summer 1981): 19–24.

Bundy, Mary Lee, and Teresa Stakem. "Librarians and the Intellectual Freedom: Are Opinions Changing?" *Wilson Library Bulletin* 56 (April 1982): 584–89.

Burger, Robert H. "The Kanawha County Textbook Controversies: A Study of Communication and Power." *Library Quarterly* 48 (April 1982): 584–89.

Burress, Lee A. "How Censorship Affects the School." Wisconsin Council of Teachers of English, *Special Bulletin* No. 8 (October 1963): 1–23.

Campbell, Colin. "Book Banning in America," *New York Times Book Review,* December 20, 1981, pp. 1, 16–18.

"Censorship: An American Dilemma." *Publishers Weekly* 230 (July 11, 1986): 30–46.

Donelson, Kenneth L. "Shoddy and Pernicious Books and Youthful Piety: Literary and Moral Censorship, Then and Now." *Library Quarterly* 51 (January 1981): 4–19.

Edwards, June. "The New Right, Humanism, and 'Dirty Books.'" *Virginia English Bulletin* 36 (Spring 1986): 94–99.

Eudy, Lisa L. "The Influence of the Moral Majority on Public Library Censorship." *Southeastern Libraries* 31 (Fall 1981): 97–101.

"Expurgation Practices of School Book Clubs." *Voice of Youth Advocates* 6 (Fall 1981): 97–101.

Faaborg, Karen Kramer. "High School Play Censorship: Are Students' First Amendment Rights Violated When Officials Cancel Theatrical Productions?" *Journal of Law and Education* 14 (October 1985): 575–94.

FitzGerald, Frances. "A Disagreement in Baileyville." *New Yorker* 59 (January 16, 1984): 47–90.

Glatthorn, Allan A. "Censorship and the Classroom Teacher." *English Journal* 66 (February 1977): 12–15.

Goldstein, S. R. "Asserted Constitutional Rights of Public School Teachers to Determine What They Teach." *University of Pennsylvania Law Review* 124 (June 1976): 1293–1357.

Groves, Cy. "Book Censorship: Six Misunderstandings." *Alberta English '71* 11 (Fall 1971): 5–7.

Hentoff, Nat. "Any Writer Who Follows Anyone Else's Guidelines Ought to Be in Advertising." *School Library Journal* 24 (November 1977): 27–29.

_____ . "When Nice People Burn Books." *Progressive* 47 (February 1983): 42–44.

Hillocks, George, Jr. "Books and Bombs: Ideological Conflicts and the School—A Case Study of the Kanawha County Book Protest." *School Review* 86 (August 1978): 632–54.

Hirschoff, Mary-Michelle Upson. "Parents and the Public School Curriculum: Is There a Right to Have One's Child Excused from Objectionable Instruction?" *Southern California Law Review* 50 (1977): 871–959.

Janeczko, Paul. "How Students Can Help Educate the Censors." *Arizona English Bulletin* 17 (February 1975): 78–80.

Jenkinson, David. "Censorship Iceberg: Results of a Survey of Challenges in Public and School Libraries." *Canadian Library Journal* 43 (February 1986): 7–21.

Kamhi, Michelle Marder. "Censorship vs. Selection—Choosing the Books Our Children Shall Read." *Educational Leadership* 39 (December 1981): 211–15.

Keresey, Gayle. "School Book Club Expurgation Practices." *Top of the News* 40 (Winter 1984): 131–38.

Kingsbury, Louise, and Lance Gurwell. "The Sin Fighters: Grappling with Gomorrah at the Grass Roots." *Utah Holiday* 12 (April 1983): 42–61.

Martin, William. "The Guardians Who Slumbereth Not." *Texas Monthly* 10 (November 1982): 145–50.

Merrill, Martha. "Authors Fight Back: One Community's Experience." *Library Journal* 112 (September 1985): 55–56.

Moffett, James. "Hidden Impediments to Improving English Teaching." *Phi Delta Kappan* 67 (September 1985): 50–56.

Nelson, Jack L., and Anna S. Ochoa. "Academic Freedom, Censorship, and the Social Studies." *Social Education* 51 (October 1987): 424–27.

Niccolai, F. R. "Right to Read and School Library Censorship." *Journal of Law and Education* (January 1981): 23–26.

O'Malley, William J. (S. J.) "How to Teach 'Dirty' Books in High School." *Media and Methods* 4 (November 1967): 6–11.

Orleans, Jeffrey H. "What Johnny Can't Read: 'First Amendment Rights' in the Classroom." *Journal of Law and Education* 10 (January 1981): 1–15.

Peck, Richard. "The Genteel Unshelving of a Book." *School Library Journal* 32 (May 1986): 37–39.

"Rationales for Commonly Challenged Taught Books." *Connecticut English Journal* 15 (Fall 1983): entire issue.

Reed, Michael. "What Johnny Can't Read: School Boards and the First Amendment." *University of Pittsburgh Law Review* 42 (Spring 1981): 653–67.

Rossi, John, et al., eds. "The Growing Controversy over Book Censorship." *Social Education* 46 (April 1982): 254–79.

Small, Robert C., Jr. "Censorship and English: Some Things We Don't Seem to Think About Very Often (But Should)." *Focus* 3 (Fall 1976): 18–24.

Stielow, Frederick J. "Censorship in the Early Professionalization of American Libraries, 1876 to 1929." *Journal of Library History* 18 (Winter 1983): 37–54.

Tollefson, Alan M. "Censored and Censured: Racine Unified School District vs. Wisconsin Library Association." *School Library Journal* 33 (March 1987): 108–12.

Watson, Jerry J., and Bill C. Snider. "Educating the Potential Self-Censor." *School Media Quarterly* 9 (Summer 1981): 272–76.

West, Celeste. "The Secret Garden of Censorship: Ourselves." *Library Journal* 108 (September 1, 1983): 1651–53.

Whaley, Elizabeth Gates. "What Happens When You Put the Manchild in the Promised Land? An Experiment with Censorship." *English Journal* 63 (May 1974): 61–65.

Williams, Patrick, and J. T. Pearce. "Common Sense and Censorship: A Call for Revision." *Library Journal* 98 (September 1, 1973): 2401–02.

Woods, L. B. "The Most Censored Materials in the U.S." *Library Journal* 103 (November 1, 1978): 2170–73.

For information on the availability of paperback editions of these titles, please consult the most recent edition of *Paperbound Books in Print,* published annually by R. R. Bowker Company.

LESSONS FROM
THE PAST

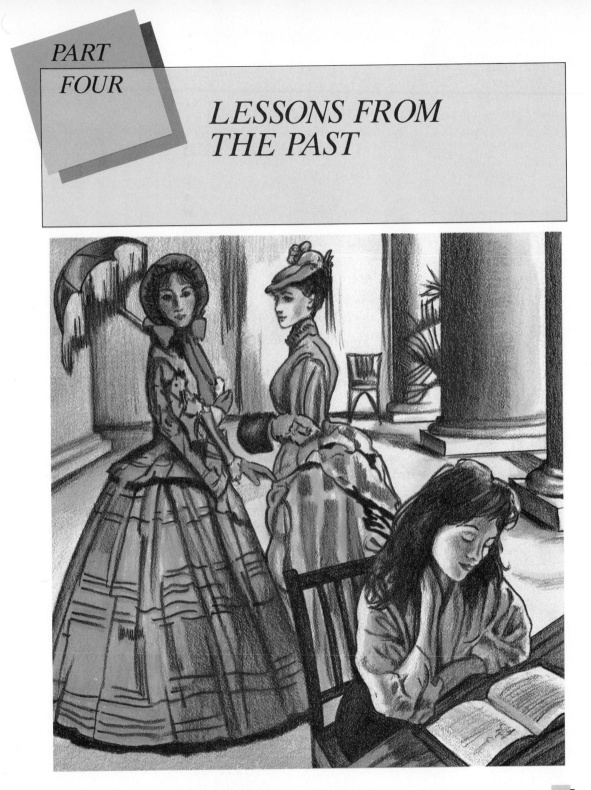

CHAPTER THIRTEEN

1800–1900
A Century of Purity with a Few Passions

Prior to 1800, literature read by children and young adults consisted largely of a few religious novels and many pietistic tracts. They advanced the belief that the young were merely small adults who must, like larger adults, accept the brevity of mortal life and God's judgment soon to come.

By 1800, the United States was no longer a vision but a real and stable country. The attitude toward young people gradually changed during the first half of the nineteenth century for several reasons—our rapid national expansion in territory and population, widespread immigration, and the slow but certain evolution from agrarian to urban society. Developments in medical knowledge led to a decrease in infant mortality and that, along with slowly evolving changes in lifestyle, encouraged a more secular education and reduced the need for children to begin working at the age of thirteen or fourteen. The parental duty to prepare small adults for death slowly became an equally intense parental duty to prepare young people for the role of patriotic and Christian adults.

The newer literature remained pious and somber, but it increasingly hinted at the possibility of humanity's experiencing a satisfying life here on earth. One could participate in responsibilities, work, family life, and even some joy before death. Books continued to reflect adult ideas and fashions, but of this world, not merely the next.

The Protestant ethic rode high. If God put mortals on earth to work hard to suit His purpose, it followed that there was nothing evil but much potential good in working hard for material success. Material success implied wealth to advance God's plan on earth, and that easily led to idealism about and exaltation of successful businessmen. The rise of men not necessarily of the best families but successful in the hard world of business fostered the spirit of democracy.

Literature aimed at young women, and most adult women, emphasized home and family responsibilities, for women were expected to find solace and satisfaction in love, husband, children, and home. In a few books there were subtle hints, some not so subtle, that women had brains and feelings along with responsibilities.

More literature was written for young adults than ever before. An increasingly secularized society produced writers aware that love, adventure, work, and recreation existed in the real world of young people and these could provide useful themes in books. A new kind of novel appeared aimed less obviously at moralizing and instructing.

MORAL WRITERS AND MORAL BOOKS

Hannah More and her tracts, especially *Repository Tracts* (1795–98) with its "The Shepherd of Salisbury Plain," *Moral Sketches* (1819), and *Coelebs in Search of a Wife* (1809), became a necessary and moralistic part of every young person's reading. Almost equally popular was Maria Edgeworth, whose *The Parent's Assistant* (1796), *Moral Tales for Young People* (1801), *Harry and Lucy* (1801), and *Harry and Lucy Concluded* (1825), sold well. Mason Locke Weems, better known as Parson Weems, published his inaccurate *History of the Life and Death, Virtues and Exploits, of General George Washington* (1800), later altered to *The Life of Washington the Great* (1806), and finally altered to *The Life of George Washington* (1808).

John Bunyan's *The Pilgrim's Progress from This World to That Which Is to Come* (Part I, 1678; Part II, also 1678) was predictably popular, a religiously symbolic account of Christian, who flees his doomed city and journeys to the Celestial City. Pleased as adults could be with the pious lessons, Christian's travails through the Slough of Despond, the Valley of Humiliation, the Valley of the Shadow of Death, Vanity Fair, and the Country of Beulah could easily be read by young people as melodrama and adventure.

Daniel Defoe was close behind Bunyan in popularity, not for *Moll Flanders* (1722) or *Roxanna* (1724), but for *The Life and Strange Surprising Adventures of Robinson Crusoe* (1719), based on the true story of Alexander Selkirk, marooned in 1704 at his own request on the uninhabited island of Juan Fernandez until his rescue in 1709. The life was strange, the adventures of Crusoe were exciting, and the book proved a permanent addition to libraries of both young and old, probably because the book was ostentatiously sermonistic and demonstrated that a civilized white person could defeat a hostile environment and ignorant savages.

DOMESTIC NOVELS

In 1855, Nathaniel Hawthorne wrote his publisher bitterly lamenting the state of American literature:

America is now wholly given over to a d—d mob of scribbling women, and I should have no chance of success while the public taste is occupied with their trash—and should be ashamed of myself if I did succeed. What is the mystery of these innumerable editions of *The Lamplighter*, and other books neither better nor worse?—worse they could not be, and better they need not be, when they sell by the 10,000?[1]

The trash was the domestic novel. Born out of a belief that humanity was redeemable, the domestic novel preached morality; woman's submission to man; the value of cultural, social, and political conservatism; a religion of the heart and the Bible; and the glories of suffering.

Most domestic novels concern a young girl, orphaned and placed in the home of a relative or other benefactor, who soon meets a darkly handsome young man with shadows lurking in his past, a man not easily trusted but one eventually worth redeeming and loving. Melodramatic devices were commonplace—illnesses, sobbing women, malevolent men, instinctive benevolence, strange figures, forged letters, disappearing wills, and frightened virgins—each novelist finding it necessary to provide greater thrills than the previous novel or that of any previous novelist. Domestic novels provided moral lessons in the midst of gothic thrills, but they soon created heroines with a love-hate feeling about men, ambivalently frightening, erotic, and attractive to female readers and puzzling if not appalling to male readers.

Heroines differed more in name than in characteristics. Uniformly submissive to—yet distrustful of—their betters and men, they were self-sacrificing and self-denying beyond belief, interested in the primacy of the family unit and a happy marriage as the goal of all decent women. They abhorred sin generally, but particularly tobacco, alcohol, divorce, and adultery.

Domestic novels were a product of the religious sentiment of the time, the espousal of traditional virtues, and the anxieties and frustrations of women trying to find a role in a changing society. These novels became weapons against a male-dominated society and the first American glimmer of feminist literature.

The promise and problems of domestic novels are apparent in the writings of Susan Warner, creator of the genre, and Augusta Jane Evans Wilson, whose *St. Elmo* was one of the all-time best-sellers.

Writing under the pen name of Elizabeth Wetherell, Susan Warner produced more than twenty novels. *The Wide, Wide World* (1850), her best-known novel, was claimed in the 1890s as one of the four most widely read books in England along with the Bible, *Pilgrim's Progress,* and *Uncle Tom's Cabin,* and was still read in the early 1900s. An abridged edition was published in England in 1911, an abridged and illustrated edition was published by the University of London Press in 1950, and the Feminist Press republished the illustrated 1892 edition in 1987.

Her manuscript was at first rejected by several New York publishers. George Putnam was also ready to send it back but decided to ask his mother to read it. The next morning she said, "If you never publish another book, George, publish this." Putnam followed her advice, and the book was out in time to attract the Christmas trade. Sales were slow at first but picked up and the first edition sold out in four months. Translations into French, German, Swedish, and Italian followed. English sales exceeded those of any previous American novel, and, by 1852, *The Wide, Wide World* was in its fourteenth printing.

The author's life paralleled that of her heroine, Ellen Montgomery. Warner's father was pathetically unable to provide, and the household was barren and bitter. Ellen's family life is not so penurious, but her mother dies early and her father is consumed with serious business matters and determines to leave Ellen with Aunt Fortune Emerson. Ellen, to her aunt's displeasure, forms a firm, if platonic, friendship with Mr. Van Brunt, Fortune Emerson's intended, and an even more significant friendship with Miss Alice, daughter of the local minister, who showers Ellen with pity and piety. Unhappily for Alice, but happily for the moral good of the reader, Alice is doomed—she is too good for this world— and in a deathbed scene highly admired by readers old and young, Alice dies. Her brother John, a divinity student, replaced Alice's sermons with his own. Later, Ellen's father dies, and tears flow before and after. In this first of many lachrymose domestic novels, Ellen cries at every turn: she "almost shrieked," "answered with a gush of tears," "burst into tears," "sobbed," "mingled bitter tears with eager prayers," "drew long, sobbing sighs," "watered the rock with tears," and "burst into violent grief." Warner's novel taught morality, the dangers of self-righteousness, and the virtues of submission and religion. Despite its weepy and moralistic nature—perhaps because of it—it was incredibly successful. E. Douglas Branch called it, "The greatest achievement of any of the lady novelists."[2]

Augusta Jane Evans Wilson may well have been the most popular writer of the domestic school for her *St. Elmo* (1867). No other novel so literally touched the American landscape—thirteen towns were named or renamed St. Elmo, as were hotels, railway coaches, steamboats, one kind of punch, and a brand of cigars. Every home seemed to have a copy. Edition after edition appeared, and an indication of the copies sold may be gauged by a notice in a special edition of *St. Elmo* that was "limited to 100,000 copies." Only *Uncle Tom's Cabin* exceeded it in sales, and Wilson was more than once called by her admirers the American Brontë. Men and women publicly testified that their lives had been permanently changed for the better by reading the book.

Edna Earl, heroine of *St. Elmo* and the daughter of a village blacksmith, is orphaned by the death of her father and bereft at the death of her grandfather. Rescued from a train wreck by snobbish and wealthy Mrs. Murray who sets out to raise Edna as her daughter, she finds herself in the same house with St.

Elmo Murray, her benefactor's son, an evil and self-centered man who has not only killed another in a duel but has a well-deserved reputation as a seducer. St Elmo takes one look at Edna and leaves home for four years. Pastor Allan Hammond becomes Edna's friend and teacher. When St. Elmo returns, Edna has Greek, Latin, Sanskrit, Chaldee, Hebrew, and Arabic firmly in hand. Fascinated by Edna, if not by her learning, St. Elmo falls in love, but she despises and rejects him. Edna turns to writing and becomes a successful novelist. The once arrogant and thwarted St. Elmo continues his courtship but is always rejected until he becomes a Christian and finally a minister. They marry, another wicked man reformed by a good woman; another woman proves her innate superiority to man.

DIME NOVELS

Dime novels were as popular as domestic novels (and condemned as strongly) but with a different audience. James Fenimore Cooper's *Leatherstocking Tales* and some adventure writing of the early nineteenth century, tales of Indians, pirates, and mysteries, influenced the subject matter of dime novelists. But it was left to Boston publisher Maturin Murray Ballou to set the physical (and to some degree the emotional) pattern. His sensational novels were usually fifty pages, eight-and-a-half inches by five inches, often illustrated with a lurid woodcut. With wild tales by writers like Edward S. Ellis and Ned Buntline (soon to be staple writers of dime novels), they were a bargain at twenty-five cents.

Beadle and Adams Appear on the Scene

In 1858, Erastus Beadle and his brother Irwin, successful publishers of sheet music in Buffalo, moved to New York City, and with Robert Adams, formed the company of Beadle and Adams, destined for years to be the most successful purveyors of dime novels.

In June 1860, Beadle and Adams published Mrs. Ann S. Stephens' *Malaeska: The Indian Wife of the White Hunter,* probably with the help of Orville J. Victor, the resident editorial genius who guided many dime novels to success. Mrs. Stephens had originally published her novel in 1839 in *The Ladies' Companion,* which she edited, but the reprinting made Beadle and Adams famous and guaranteed her future employment as a dime novelist. Published in a salmon-colored wrapper, *Malaeska* was given the spectacular promotion readers soon associated with Beadle and Adams. On June 7, 1860, an advertisement appeared in the *New York Tribune:*

BOOKS FOR THE MILLIONS

A dollar Book for a dime!
128 pages complete, only ten cents!!!
MALAESKA
The
Indian Wife of the White Hunter
by Mrs. Ann Stephens
Irwin P. Beadle and Co., Publishers

Curious readers buying the six- by four-inch 128-page book may have been unsure about what they were getting, but what they got was apparently good enough, for 65,000 copies were sold.

A bald plot summary makes the first dime novel appear incredibly melodramatic and crude. Malaeska marries a white hunter who, when he is dying, tells his Indian wife to take their child from the wilds of upper New York state to his wealthy parents in New York City. The parents accept the child, and Malaeska remains, for a time, known to him as his nurse. She tries to kidnap the boy to take him home but fails and goes back alone to the woods and her tribe. Her son, not knowing his parents, grows up hating Indians. Later, Malaeska identifies herself to him, he commits suicide, and she dies the next day on her husband's grave. Melodramatic it was, but it was also fast-moving, thrilling, exotic—all for ten cents. Mass literature, priced for the masses, had arrived.

Sales of the eighth dime novel topped all previous efforts after an intriguing promotional campaign. On October 1, 1860, *the New York Tribune* carried this simple ad, sans company, sans price, sans author:

Seth Jones is from New Hampshire.
Seth Jones understands the redskins.
Seth Jones answers a question.
Seth Jones strikes a trail.
Seth Jones makes a good roast.
Seth Jones writes a letter.
Seth Jones objects to sparking.
Seth Jones is in his element.
Seth Jones takes an observation.
Seth Jones can't express himself.

On October 2, 1860, the *New York Tribune* carried another ad:

Seth Jones; or, The Captives of the Frontier.
For sale at all the news depots.

Seth Jones was published that day to 60,000 readers. At least 500,000 copies were sold over the years in the United States alone, and it was translated into ten languages. Contrary to later journals, which damned dime novels often without reading them, contemporary reviews were good, even at times enthusiastic. Four years after the publication of *Seth Jones,* reviewer William Everett wrote:

> Mr. E. S. Ellis' *Seth Jones* and *Trail Hunters* are good, very good. Mr. Ellis' novels are favorites and deserve to be. He shows variety and originality in his characters; and his Indians are human beings, and not fancy pieces.[3]

Seth Jones takes place near the close of the eighteenth century. Seth, a scout in the Revolutionary War, comes to Alfred Haverland's clearing in western New York state to announce that nearby Indians are ready for the warpath. In the attack, Haverland's sixteen-year-old daughter, Ina, is captured, and Seth, along with Ina's sweetheart, goes off on the rescue. At the end of the story Seth is revealed as aristocratic Eugene Morton in search of his lost fiancée. A double wedding, Seth and his love, Ina and hers, concludes the book.

Seth Jones would not have been enough to maintain Beadle and Adams' success by itself, but it served as a prototype, and dime novels numbering about 600 from this publisher alone reaffirmed the success of *Seth Jones.*

Dime Novel Characteristics

For better than ten years, dime novels cost ten cents, ran about 100 pages in small format (about seven by five inches), and were aimed at adults. Then publishers discovered that boys were the most avid readers and concentrated on a younger audience, dropping the price to a nickel (though the public continued to call them dime novels out of habit) and cutting costs. The result was a nickel (or half-dime) novel of sixteen or thirty-two pages, usually part of a series and featuring one fictional hero, Diamond Dick, Fred Fearnot, Buffalo Bill, or some other equally fascinating and impossible character. The cover portrayed in lurid black and white a heroic act of derring-do or a villainous performance of darkest evil.

Action-packed dime novels grabbed the readers with cliff-hanging chapter endings and often farfetched thrills and chills, each surpassing the previous adventure. The vocabulary seemed erudite and the prose was genuinely purple, but boys did not care. Dime novels were superior to anything else on the market.

Daring Davy, The Young Bear Killer; or, The Trail of the Border Wolf by Harry St. George (pen name of the prolific writer of dime novels and later boys' series books, St. George Rathbone), published as number 108 in Beadle's Half Dime Library on August 19, 1879, illustrated the *in medias res* opening common to dime novels, the promised action, the purple prose, and the erudite vocabulary, all in the first brief paragraphs of the first chapter:

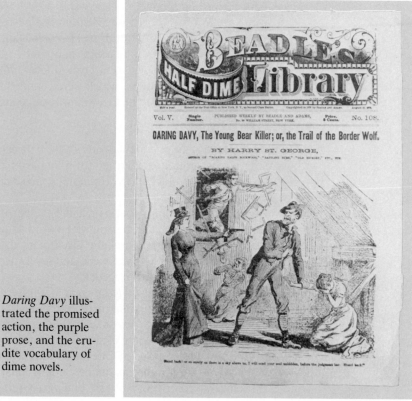

Daring Davy illustrated the promised action, the purple prose, and the erudite vocabulary of dime novels.

"Then Davy Crockett must die!"

The man who gave utterance to this emphatic sentence stood in the middle of a dilapidated old cabin that was almost entirely hidden in the heart of a dense forest. Giant trees grew all around it, their branches drooping so as to almost conceal the log hut from view.

Outside the night breeze swept down the forest aisle, rustling the leaves in the passage and carrying many of them with it to the ground. The fair moon had wheeled up in the eastern heavens, and Jupiter was leading the march of the planets across the firmament. Now and then the melancholy howl of a wolf could be heard, sounding dismally through the silence of the night, and once a panther lent its shrill scream to awaken the echoes of the glen beyond, for the woods of old Tennessee were full of savage game at this early day.

The scene inside the cabin was certainly wild enough to have pleased the most exacting.

Four men stood around a rickety table with drawn knives. The man who had just uttered that sentence of death was a perfect giant in point of size. He was known in the backwoods as Hercules Dan, and had been a hunter and trapper, living on what he could shoot and steal.

Two of the others possessed ill-favored faces, while the last did not condescend to show his features, which were completely hidden under a heavy hat, and rough scarf which he had wound around his neck and the lower half of his face.

Six paragraphs into the tale and already we have threats, implied violence soon to become real, death, poetic writing (or what passed for it), and mystery. The remainder of the roughly 40,000-word novel (three columns of tiny print to the page) was no anticlimax.

Stock characters in dime novels included the hero's closest friend, weaker but almost as decent; an older person who moved about spouting tiresome but supposedly wise sayings; and a comic black man, the butt of all humor, frequently superstitious but always servile and loyal, occasionally surprising the reader by proving wise and courageous.

Dime novels never pretended to be great literature, and their use of standard characters, settings, and situations made readers comfortable. Today's situation comedies, westerns, or mysteries on television do the same as they ease viewers into a relaxed state by providing elements, situations, and plot twists that have become satisfyingly traditional. Dime novels provided what dime novel readers wanted and demanded, rapid beginnings, implied and realized violence, periodic cliffhangers, contrived and fast endings, strained but possible coincidences, good versus evil, vengeance, purity, love, and the sanctity of marriage, all for a nickel.

Beyond the excitement, they provided morality. Virtue victorious and villainy vanquished were the watchwords of dime novels. Thrills, of course, but morality had to be there too, and not just to make them acceptable to parents. Erastus Beadle sincerely believed that books should represent sound moral values, and the strict rules he imposed on his writers insured adventure and morality as this memo to his staff reveals:

So much is said, and justly, against a considerable number of papers and libraries now on the market, that we beg leave to repeat the following announcement and long-standing instructions to all contributors;

Authors who write for our consideration will bear in mind that—

We prohibit all things offensive to good taste in expression and incident—

We prohibit subjects or characters that carry an immoral taint—

We prohibit the repetition of any occurrence which, though true, is yet better untold—

We prohibit what cannot be read with satisfaction by every right-minded person—old and young alike—

We require your best work—

We require unquestioned originality—

We require pronounced strength of plot and high dramatic interest of story—

We require grace and precision of narrative, and correctness in composition.

Authors must be familiar with characters and places which they introduce and not attempt to write in fields of which they have no intimate knowledge.[4]

Some Dime Novel Types and Authors

Many early dime novels were set in the West of the 1840s and 1850s, and some were set in an even earlier "west," for example, upper New York state in *Malaeska*. But with the opening of the West beyond the Mississippi River, the dime novel could use fictional characters like Deadwood Dick, the James Boys, Pawnee Bill, Diamond Dick, and the Young Wild West. Real people like Buffalo Bill, Wild Bill Hickok, and the James Brothers might not have been able to recognize themselves in the fiction written about them since their exploits were mixed only occasionally with something bordering on the truth, but readers cared little.

Rivaling the popularity of the western dime novel was the detective story with such fictional heroes as Nick Carter, Old King Brady, Old Sleuth, Young Sleuth, and Cap Collier. Best known of the writers of detective dime novels was Frederic Van Rensselaer Dey who wrote most of the Nick Carter novels. A dignified man, he was pleased with the success of Nick Carter—he wrote more than a thousand of them—because they were clean: "I never wrote one that could not have been read aloud to a Bible class."[5]

Two other kinds of dime novels that had many fans were sports novels, with heroes like Frank Merriwell and Fred Fearnot, and science fiction novels featuring Frank Reade, Frank Reade, Jr., Jack Wright, and Tom Edison, Jr.

Objections to Dime Novels and Objections to the Objections

By the 1870s, schoolteachers, librarians, writers, and politicians had taken notice of dime novels, first attacking the sensationalism and later attacking the alleged power of dime novels to corrupt morals and to turn the young toward crime. In 1878, William Sumner argued their potential corruptive influence, especially since dime novels were inexpensive and ubiquitous.[6] In 1896 Theodore C. Burgess argued for stronger laws and more vigorous enforcement of laws already on the books to stave off the dime novel menace:

> We have a law against the sale of that which is obscene, and it is worthy of consideration whether a law should not go one step farther—not a long

one—and include such papers as the *Police Gazette* and those other forms of degrading literature known as the dime novel.[7]

A politician tried to get such a bill through the New York Assembly in 1883. Part of the bill read:

> Any person who shall sell, loan, or give to any minor under sixteen years of age any dime novel or book of fiction, without first obtaining the written consent of the parent or guardian of such minor, shall be deemed guilty of a misdemeanor, punishable by imprisonment or by a fine not exceeding $50.[8]

One newspaper noted ironically that the bill would prohibit giving a copy of *Pilgrim's Progress* to a minor without first getting permission, and the length of the sentence, being indeterminant, might range from a few days to life if the judge were of the same persuasion as Goddard.[9]

Both librarians and schoolteachers discovered to their horror that dime novels were widely read by young people, revealing their own naiveté and ignorance about young people. Tales of the horror teachers and librarians felt when they uncovered dime novel addicts among the young were staples of the *Library Journal* and educational journals of the day.[10]

Then critics found startling proof that dime novels created juvenile delinquents. The *Literary News* for May 1884 told of four youngsters in Milwaukee who organized a gang after reading some dime novels. Frustrated in their plan to move west, the gang set fires about the city.[11] The 1883 *New York Herald* warned:

> Pernicious stories of the "dime novel" class continue to do their mischievous work. The latest recorded victim was a New London boy, aged fourteen, who shot himself during a period of mental aberration caused by reading dime novels.[12]

Dime novels also had defenders. William Everett, writing in the prestigious *North American Review* in 1864, found them "unobjectionable morally, whatever fault be found with their literary style and composition. They do not even obscurely pander to vice, or excite the passions."[13] Writing in the *Library Journal* fifteen years later, Thomas Wentworth Higginson hardly overpraised dime novels, but his words were far more perceptive and honest than most other commentators' of the time:

> I have turned over hundreds of dime novels in such places [book stalls] within a year or two, without finding a single word of indecency; they are overly sensational, and, so far as they deal with thieves and house-breakers, demoralizing; but they are not impure.[14]

Other Paperback Books

Dime novels produced one significant offspring: the early paperback novel series costing a dime or less. In 1864 Boston publisher James Redpath announced a series of dime books of high quality, each running from 96 to 124 pages, including Alcott's *On Picket Duty and Other Tales,* Balzac's *The Vendetta,* Swift's *Gulliver's Travels,* and Hugo's *Battle of Waterloo.*

By the 1870s attacks on dime novels were common, and Chicago's Donnelly and Lloyd announced its Lakeside Library containing contemporary and classic books far superior, they argued, to sensational dime novels. Their high moral tone would have been more impressive had not most of their library been books pirated from England or the continent. Beadle and Adams retaliated by starting their Fireside Library, and soon Frank Leslie began his Home Library. Later George Munro published his Seaside Library (the first three titles were Mrs. Wood's *East Lynne,* Mulock's *John Halifax, Gentleman,* and Brontë's *Jane Eyre*), and Harper and Brothers began its Franklin Square Library. Paperback libraries cost little. Publishers needed to develop a stable of writers to create dime novel libraries, but Frank Tousey was able to save money by "borrowing" many stories from his paperback series.

THE POPULAR STORY WEEKLY

American weekly magazines containing large amounts of fiction began in 1837 when depression-hit publishers needed cheaper methods of producing books. They devised a scheme for printing books as newspapers, in many ways like modern Sunday supplements, on which they paid no taxes and which qualified for cheaper postage rates. Newspapers, irritated by what they considered unfair competition, started printing their own fiction supplements, at first for fifty cents, then twenty-five cents, and then six and one-quarter cents. By 1843, the Post Office Department changed the rules charging book rates for supplements as well as for books and newspapers, but by then cheap fiction supplements were well established.

In 1855, Francis S. Street and Francis S. Smith took over the *New York Weekly Dispatch,* and by 1857 they doubled the circulation with Smith's *The Vestmaker's Apprentice; or, The Vampyres of Society,* a tale of villainy and virtue set against a background of greed, filth, and wickedness in New York City. Two years later, Street and Smith bought the *New York Weekly* outright for $40,000 though they had less than $100 between them. Within five years they paid off the debt. Their advertising methods teased the audience with hints of stories to come. To create interest for the forthcoming *Lillian the Wanderer; or The Perils of Beauty,* they announced:

The heroine is a noble-souled and pure, but unfortunate orphan-girl, who is forced by circumstances to leave her home in Europe and come to this country. Upon arriving here, she falls into the clutches of some soulless ruffians, and her sufferings and narrow escapes from a fate worse than death are graphically sketched by the author. In the course of the Story, the reader is introduced both into the miserable hovel of poverty and into the mansion of luxury and wealth, and a clearer insight is had into all classes of society. The Story is written in the Author's best style and cannot fail to create a great sensation.[15]

Street and Smith published sea tales, adventures, and tales of suspense, but the most popular were about love and its tribulations. Mary Kyle Dallas' *Neglected Warnings; or The Trials of A Public School Teacher* was doubtlessly well calculated to keep readers in suspense but was equally calculated to make schoolteachers question Street and Smith's sanity in running the story which they claimed:

. . . will touch a sympathetic chord in the bosom of every reader, male or female. For who is not, either directly or indirectly, interested in those noble institutions, our public schools?[16]

The heroine was perhaps not a typical schoolteacher, for at different times she lay unconscious in the snow dressed only in her nightclothes, was locked in a church, had a friend who was buried alive and rose from his coffin at night, was rescued from a burning ship, and was married only to see her husband arrested for murder during the wedding ceremony.

As with the dime novel, critics found fault with the popular story weekly, especially the sensational stories and the glorification of impossible lives that readers could dream about but never approach. Critics worried that a maid or a working girl in a mill might waste time dreaming about a better life and the perfect man. In truth, popular story weeklies, like dime novels, provided escape literature to cheer up drab people leading drab lives. There was and is nothing wrong with that, critics to the contrary.

TWO MAJORS FOR MINORS: ALCOTT AND ALGER

Louisa May Alcott and Horatio Alger, Jr., were the first writers for young adults to gain national attention, but similarity between the two ends almost as it begins. Alcott wrote about happy families. Alger wrote about broken homes. Alcott's novels were sometimes harsh but always honest. Alger's novels were romantic fantasies. Alcott's novels continue to be read for good reason. Except for the historian or the Alger buff, Alger's novels lie virtually forgotten.

The second daughter of visionary Amos Bronson Alcott, Louisa May Alcott lived her youth near Concord and Boston with a practical mother and a father who was brilliant, generous, improvident, and impractical. After publishing *Hospital Sketches* (1863) based on her work in a Union hospital, she turned to writing thrillers, solely, she maintained, for money. Then, after an abortive effort to create dime novels, she wrote *Little Women,* her most enduring work. The reigning young adults' author of the time was Oliver Optic (the pen name of William T. Adams), and Boston publishers Roberts Brothers were eager to find a story for young adults that might offer competition to Optic's stories published by rival Boston publisher Lee and Shepard. Roberts' representative, Thomas Niles, had once told Alcott, "Stick to your teaching. You can't write," but as a publisher he had requested permission to reprint the successful *Hospital Sketches.* In September 1866 Niles suggested she write a girls' book, and in May 1868 he gently reminded her.

She sent a manuscript off to Niles who thought early parts of it dull, but other readers disagreed, and the first part of *Little Women: Meg, Jo, Beth, and Amy. The Story of Their Lives. A Girl's Book* was published on September 30, 1868, with three illustrations and a frontispiece at $1.50 a copy. *Little Women* was well received by reviewers and sales were good here and in England. By early November 1868, she had begun work on the second part, and *Little Women, or Meg, Jo, Beth, and Amy. Part Second* was published on April 14, 1869.

The book was certainly the Alcott family story, the major difference being that an impractical and therefore unsympathetic father is replaced by an absent and therefore heroic father now on duty with the Union Army. The March family survive happily without him, reminiscent of Alcott's thrillers in which women revenge themselves on men or prove them unnecessary.

The novel has vitality, joy, real life, and love generally devoid of sentimentality, a wistful portrait of a life Alcott wished she could have lived. The Civil War background is subtle, better expressing the loneliness and never ending quality of war than many war novels for all their suffering, death, pain, and horror. Aimed at young adults, *Little Women* has maintained steady popularity with them and with younger children. Adults reread it to gain a sense of where they were when they were young.

Son of an unctuous Unitarian clergyman, Horatio Alger graduated from Harvard at eighteen. Ordained a Unitarian minister in 1864, he served a Brewster, Massachusetts, church only to leave two years later under a cloud of scandal, effectively hushed at the time. Already the author of seven books, Alger moved to New York City and began to write full time.

That same year he sent *Ragged Dick; or, Street Life in New York* to Oliver Optic's *Student and Schoolmate,* a goody-goody magazine. Optic knew salable pap when he saw it, and he bought Alger's work for the January 1867 issue. Published in 1867 or 1868 in hardback, *Ragged Dick* was the first of many successes for Alger and publisher A. K. Loring in Boston and remains Alger's most readable novel, probably because it was the first from the mold that became predictably moldy.

The plot, as in most Alger books, consisted of semiconnected episodes illustrating a boy's first steps toward maturity, respectability, and affluence.

Ragged Dick, a young bootblack, sleeps "in a wooden box half full of straw." Grubby but not dirty, he smokes and gambles occasionally, but the reader immediately recognizes his essential goodness. On his way to work, he meets Mr. Greyson who gives him a quarter for a shine, says he cannot wait for change, and asks Dick to bring the fifteen cents to his office. Dick is the only one surprised, for Greyson sees in Dick what Alger assumes readers see, inherent honesty and nobility. A few minutes later, Dick overhears Mr. Whitney talking to his nephew Frank, who is in need of a guide. Dick volunteers, to no one's surprise (except that of the reader who wonders why anyone would choose a totally unknown bootblack with whom to entrust his nephew). Mr. Whitney accepts, and the boys set out on a nine-chapter tour of the city, a handbook to the sights, sounds, and dangers of New York City.[17]

After Frank and Dick temporarily part, Dick vows a course of self-improvement with Frank as his model. When he returns the fifteen cents change to Mr. Greyson, the much-impressed Greyson asks Dick to attend the church where he teaches Sunday School. That same day, Dick befriends better-educated Henry Fosdick who, in return for sharing Dick's room, agrees to tutor him. He and Fosdick go to church and meet Greyson and his wife and their daughter, Ida, whom Dick clearly likes. Dick and Henry move steadily upward in the world, saving a bit each week and becoming more respectable every day. The novel, although wooden in style and episodically plotted, has touches of reality till this point. Alger, apparently unwilling or unable to move Dick slowly up the ladder of respectability, puts pluck aside and adds the infamous luck that characterized his novels. Dick and Fosdick find themselves on a ferry, a little boy falls overboard, and Dick, ignoring personal danger, follows the child into the water and saves him. A grateful father rewards Dick with new clothing and a job at ten dollars a week, a princely sum for the time.

Some readers inaccurately label Alger's books "rags to riches," but the hero rarely achieves riches though he does find himself at the book's end on the lower rungs of the ladder of success. "Rags to respectability" would be a more accurate statement about Alger's work. Alger wrote at least 119 novels, many of them popular until the early 1900s, selling altogether between sixteen million and seventeen million copies.

▌ *OTHER EARLY SERIES WRITERS*

The Boston publishing firm of Lee and Shepard established the format for young adult series. To the distress of teachers, librarians, and some parents, the series became *the* method of publishing most young adult novels, though it became far more sophisticated in Edward Stratemeyer's hands nearly forty years later. If sales are any index, readers delighted in Lee and Shepard's series just as they delighted in other series from other publishing houses. *Publishers' Trade List* for 1887 contained sixteen pages listing 440 authors and 900 books under the Lee and Shepard logo. Series books clearly sold very well. Four series writers were especially popular: Harry Castlemon, Oliver Optic, Martha Finley, and Susan Coolidge.

Under the pen name of Harry Castlemon, Charles Austin Fosdick wrote his first novel, *Frank the Young Naturalist* (1864), while in the Navy. Admiral David B. Porter agreed to read it and suggested Castlemon submit it to Cincinnati publisher Robert W. Carrol who answered with a $150 check, a letter of praise, and a recommendation that the author follow up with a series of five more books featuring Frank. Castlemon's career was off. He received $200 each for the remainder of the series.

Castlemon's approach was pragmatic. "Boys don't like fine writing. What they want is adventure, and the more of it you can get into 250 pages of manuscript, the better fellow you are."[18]

Oliver Optic, pen name of William Taylor Adams, was a prolific writer, producing more than 100 books for young people under the Lee and Shepard banner. *The Boat Club* (1855), his first book and the first volume of the six book "Boat Club Series" ran through sixty editions and set a pattern for later series.

Kilgour maintains that Optic created mass-production writing for young people which led librarians and teachers to attack Optic as they criticized few other authors.[19] Some irritation may have stemmed from Optic's sales—he was a best-seller during his lifetime and afterwards—but adults never forgave him his fantastic plots and wooden dialogue.

If Optic is remembered today, it is for his quarrel with Louisa May Alcott who attacked his books in her *Eight Cousins* (1875). In Chapter 8, Alcott describes four young men on a rainy Sunday afternoon reading and smoking. Mother appears and has nothing good to say about their choice of reading material, the sensational and unrealistic plots and the language. Optic saw the attack when the episode was first published in the August 1875 *St. Nicholas*. He defended himself in his *Oliver Optic's Magazine* for September 1875 by implying that Alcott may have borrowed the title for *Eight Cousins* from Amanda Douglas' *Seven Daughters,* published in his magazine, and by arguing that she mixed titles and plots and wildy exaggerated the stories. Optic concluded:

> Ah, Louisa, you are very smart, and you have become rich. Your success mocks that of the juvenile heroes you despise. Even the author of "Dick Dauntless" and "Sam Soaker," whoever he may be would not dare to write up a heroine who rose so rapidly from poverty and obscurity to riches and fame as you did; but in view of the wholesale perversion of the truth as we have pointed out, we must ask you to adopt the motto you recommend for others—"Be honest and you will be happy," instead of the one you seem to have chosen: "Be smart and you will be rich."[20]

Attacks by reviewers, teachers, librarians, and even Alcott did not carry the day, for as late as 1900 Lee and Shepard's catalog advertised 123 Oliver Optic novels.

Martha Farquharson Finley wrote the "Elsie Dinsmore" series, probably the most popular series of its time. In twenty-eight volumes, the series carried Elsie through life from childhood to grandmotherhood. A favorite with young women and a girl critics loved to hate, Elsie is persistently and nauseatingly docile, pious, sincere, lachrymose, virtuous, humble, timid, ignorant, and good.

Published in 1867 and running to an amazing number of editions after that, *Elsie Dinsmore* opens with virtuous and Christian Elsie awaiting the return of her beloved but long-absent father. Elsie has continual problems with her cold and indifferent father, Finley's way of demonstrating that children must love parents, no matter how blind the love must be, and that girls must love God and Jesus above all, no matter what the pressures. And if Elsie needs her love or faith tried, her father is unquestionably trying.

The most widely quoted episode, by those who loved or hated the book, occurs one Sunday when father asks Elsie to perform at the piano for guests. Elsie pleads, always in a pious and respectful tone, that the Sabbath forbids secular music, but father demands she remain at the piano until she is willing to play. Several hours pass while Elsie sits playing the martyr but never the piano. Then Elsie feels a pain and suddenly falls. A guest rushes to Elsie:

> "A light! quick, quick, a light!" he cried, raising Elsie's insensible form in his arms; "the child has fainted."
>
> One of the others, instantly snatching a lamp from a distant table, brought it near, and the increased light showed Elsie's little face, ghastly as that of a corpse, while a stream of blood was flowing from a wound in the temple, made by striking against some sharp corner of the furniture as she fell.

Seconds later, her soft eyes open and her first words are:

> "Dear papa, are you angry with me?"

Next morning, a temporarily remorseful father visits Elsie:

> "Elsie, do you know that you were very near being killed last night?"
> "No, papa, was I?" she asked with an awestruck countenance.
> "Yes, the doctor says if that wound had been made half an inch nearer your eye—I should have been childless."
>
> His voice trembled almost too much for utterance as he finished his sentence, and he strained her to his heart with a deep sigh of thankfulness for her escape.

Piety reigns equally in *Elsie's Girlhood* (1872), in which Elsie incessantly cries, faints, loves, and prays; *Elsie's Widowhood* (1880)—Elsie's husband was probably killed because he was an obstacle in plots; *Christmas with Grandma Elsie* (1888); and *Elsie in the South* (1899). Elsie moves from childhood to marriage to widowhood affirming the joys of fainting and crying, the American Dream fulfilled through piety, morality, and prayer.[21]

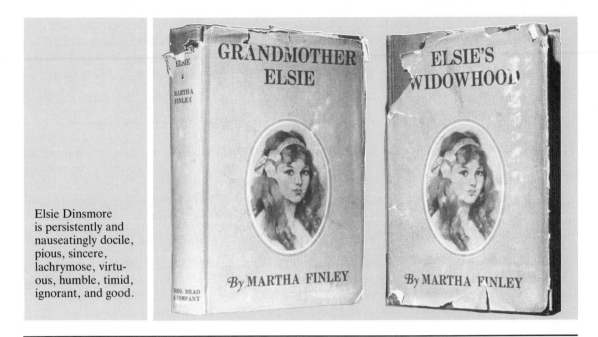

Elsie Dinsmore
is persistently and
nauseatingly docile,
pious, sincere,
lachrymose, virtu-
ous, humble, timid,
ignorant, and good.

Susan Coolidge, pen name of Sarah Chauncey Woolsey, wrote fewer books than other series writers, but one series found wide favor and once rivaled Alcott's books. *What Katy Did* (1872) features tomboy Katy Carr, her widowed doctor-father, and three sisters and two brothers. *What Katy Did at School* (1873) carries sixteen-year-old Katy on to boarding school where her escapades keep her in trouble. *What Katy Did Next (1886)* takes Katy off to Europe and a young naval officer. *Clover* (1888) and *In the Valley* (1891) conclude the series.

Coolidge's heroine resembles Alcott's Jo March in several ways. She is stubborn and sometimes willful but essentially good, loving, and caring. Katy is almost as attractive as Jo and sometimes more believable in her pranks. In 1978, the Public Broadcasting System produced six episodes of Katy's life, condensing too much too fast but proving that Coolidge's books deserve reading today, perhaps even a revival.

THE LITERATURE OF THE BAD BOY

Beginning with Thomas Bailey Aldrich's *The Story of a Bad Boy* in 1870, a literature developed around bad boys, flesh and blood, imperfect boys, tough on the outside and able to survive troubles in a brutal world.

The books were, except for Twain's, nostalgic books about old times, harking back to a golden age that had never been. Sometimes cruel and frequently confusing boyishness with barbarism, they were ultimately patronizing and backward-looking.

Thomas Bailey Aldrich's reputation today rests on *The Story of a Bad Boy.* Serialized in *Our Young Folks,* January to December 1869, and published as a book a year later, Aldrich's part-novel, part-autobiography became an immediate success with critics and readers. William Dean Howells began his review in the *Atlantic*:

> ▮ Mr. Aldrich has done a new thing in—we use the phrase with some gasps of reluctance, it is so threadbare and so near meaning nothing—American literature. We might go much farther without overpraising his pleasant book, and call it an absolute novelty, on the whole. No one else seems to have thought of telling the story of a boy's life, with so great desire to show what a boy's life is, and so little purpose of teaching what it should be; certainly no one else has thought of doing this for the life of an American boy.[22]

Aldrich's book was a novelty, but more important, it told the story of a boy as he was, or might be, not as he should have been. The book marked the beginning of realistic literature about boys, just as Alcott's *Little Women* had served the cause of young women only two years before.

Newspaperman, writer, humorist, and later Governor of Wisconsin, George Wilbur Peck began writing about "Peck's Bad Boy" in *Peck's Sun,* his Milwaukee newspaper-family humor magazine, in 1882 and published *Peck's Bad Boy and His Pa* a year later. The crude jokes go beyond cruelty and the dialect becomes outlandish in later sequels.

Peck's Bad Boy and His Pa devotes separate chapters to the Bad Boy's pranks, often played on his father though the Boy does not discriminate. Two episodes convey the book's spirit. In Chapter 11, the Boy douses his father's handkerchief with rum and wraps it around playing cards. Pa attends a prayer meeting where the preacher asks him to tell about his recent reformation. When Pa speaks, breaking into tears and taking out his handkerchief, cards fly and fumes spread. In Chapter 30, Pa comes home drunk. The Boy pretends to take him to a dissecting room where the Boy and his friends act as if they will cut him up as Pa wakes up and is horrified. Peck had no subtlety, but his humor brought him readers far beyond any other writer of bad boy literature except Twain.

Mark Twain was the capstone of both bad boys' literature and nineteenth-century literature generally. *The Adventures of Tom Sawyer* (1876) and *Adventures of Huckleberry Finn* (1884) took the bad boy theme far beyond Aldrich or Peck. Humor, sometimes savage adventure, and other conventions of the bad boy books can be found in Twain, but compassion is mixed with cynicism, and there is none of the condescension or simplistic nostalgia of earlier bad boy books. As many critics have noted, *Huck Finn,* and to a lesser degree *Tom Sawyer,* are books young and old can read over and over on quite different levels, young adults for adventure and perhaps more, adults for insight and perhaps more.

Twain's problems with the censor are well known. Before *Huck Finn* was published in hardback, the February 1885 *Century Magazine* published extracts but not all that Twain submitted. *Century* editor Richard Watson Gilder apparently found some material too harsh or too coarse and left out the preacher's harangue at the camp meeting and the lynching of Colonel Sherburn.[23]

After the publication of *Huck Finn,* the Concord (Massachusetts) Library banned the book as trashy, vicious, and unfit to be placed next to books by Emerson or Thoreau. Louisa May Alcott said, "If Mr. Clemens cannot think of something better to tell our pure-minded lads and lasses, he had best stop writing for them," a comment Twain felt would sell an additional 25,000 copies. The Concord Library was not alone in damning the book. *The Springfield Republican* wrote in 1885, "They [*Tom Sawyer* and *Huck Finn*] are no better in tone than the dime novels which flood the blood-and-thunder reading population. . . . Their moral tone is low, and their perusal cannot be anything less than harmful."[24]

The Brooklyn Public Library excluded both books from their children's room as "bad examples for ingenuous youth" in 1905. Asa Don Dickinson, Librarian of Brooklyn College, pleaded that Twain's books be put back on the shelves, but "It was no use. The good ladies assured me in effect that Huck was a deceitful boy."[25] Dickinson sent an apologetic letter to Twain and received this reply:

Dear Sir:

I am greatly troubled by what you say. I wrote *Tom Sawyer* and *Huck Finn* for adults exclusively, and it always distresses me when I find that boys and girls have been allowed access to them. The mind that becomes soiled in youth can never again be washed clean; I know this by my own experience and to this day I cherish an unappeasable bitterness against the unfaithful guardians of my young life, who not only permitted but compelled me to read an unexpurgated Bible through before I was 15 years old. None can do that and ever draw a clean sweet breath again this side of the grave. Ask that young lady—she will tell you so.

Most honestly do I wish I could say a softening word or two in defence of Huck's character, since you wish it, but really in my opinion it is no better than God's (in the Ahab chapter and 97 others) and those of Solomon, David, Satan, and the rest of the sacred brotherhood.

If there is an unexpurgated in the Children's Department, won't you please help that young woman remove Huck and Tom from that questionable companionship?[26]

ADVENTURE TALES

The past was a continual source of adventure. George Alfred Henty acquired a fascination for and knowledge of foreign countries and their history as a newspaper reporter, and his eighty or so historical-adventure tales read well even today once readers overcome some dated nineteenth-century diction. Of special worth are *Beric, The Briton: A Story of the Roman Invasion* (1893),

When London Burned: A Story of the Plague and the Fire (1895), and *Winning His Spurs: A Tale of the Crusades* (1892), but Henty is readable in most of his books. John Bennett is best remembered for *Master Skylark: A Story of Shakespeare's Time* (1897), a delightful account of young Nick Attwood, a golden-voiced boy singer involved in more than his share of adventure. Howard Pyle was known as an illustrator of young people's books as well as a writer, and *The Merry Adventures of Robin Hood* (1883) is still read. Even better were *Otto of the Silver Hand* (1888), set in medieval Germany, and *Men of Iron* (1892), a marvelously effective and exciting story of villainy and feudal rights in fifteenth-century England.

Piracy and smuggling have always appealed to our sense of adventure. John Meade Falkner's *Moonfleet* (1898) captivated readers with its story of smuggling in Dorset, England, buried vaults, and a diamond with a curse. Only Robert Louis Stevenson, master of the genre, surpassed Falkner. Stevenson's *Kidnapped* (1886) is a thriller with few faults, but *Treasure Island* (1883) is a jewel among adventure stories, popular then and no less popular now.

Adventures among boys was the theme of three once-popular, now badly underrated writers. Robert Michael Ballantyne is probably best known for *The Coral Island* (1858) since William Golding's *Lord of the Flies* (1955) parallels the earlier book and mentions it. Noah Brooks wrote biographies of Lincoln and a superb story of boys going west across the plains, *The Boy Emigrants* (1876). Best of the three was Kirk Munroe. Two of his excellent novels are *The Flamingo Feather* (1887), about early days in Florida, and *Derrick Sterling* (1888), about a young miner working his way up in life, Alger-like in theme but Dickensian in flavor.

Boys' tales of adventure, many of them first-rate, were easy to find.

The new adventure tales of mystery and detection were handled by the master, Arthur Conan Doyle, whose *Adventures of Sherlock Holmes* (1891) were first published for a delighted *Strand Magazine* audience. Later tales proved equally popular.

Even more exotic adventure was the province of Jules Verne, whose science fiction and adventure tales *Twenty Thousand Leagues Under the Sea* (1872), *From the Earth to the Moon* (1873), and *Around the World in Eighty Days* (1874) delighted and confounded adult and young adult readers for many years.

THE DEVELOPMENT OF THE AMERICAN PUBLIC LIBRARY

Today, we too easily assume that the public library has always played an important role in American educational and cultural life. In fact, its development from colonial time to the founding of the American Library Association in 1876 was as rocky and slow as it was inevitable.

In 1731, Benjamin Franklin suggested to the Junto, a middle-class social and literary club in Philadelphia, that members bring their books to the club so other members might enjoy them. Franklin's suggestion led to the forming of the Philadelphia Library Company, America's first subscription library. Other such libraries soon followed.

These libraries were hardly free public libraries, but they made more books accessible to more people than ever before. They also made clear in their founding statements the moral purpose of a library. The constitution of the Salisbury, Connecticut, Social Library announced its purpose as "The promotion of Virtue, Education, and Learning, and . . . the discouragement of Vice and Immorality."[27]

In 1826, New York Governor DeWitt Clinton urged that school district libraries be established, in effect using school buildings for libraries for people nearby. By 1838, $55,000 was annually appropriated for these libraries. Horace Mann advocated similar libraries for Massachussetts, and similar legislation passed in Connecticut in 1839, Rhode Island and Iowa in 1840, Indiana in 1841, and other states soon followed. Proponents of school district libraries recognized that schools and the availability of many books for school use were mutually beneficial, but the concept failed for several practical reasons:

> They usually consisted of text books, general works, and a smattering of inspirational literature, with little attention paid to their selection. The majority were above the reading level and beyond the interests of all but the most advanced students, and though they were theoretically available to the adults of the community, they were not widely used.[28]

A much more promising approach came in October 1847 when Boston Mayor Josiah Quincy, Jr., suggested that the state legislature be petitioned for permission to levy a tax so that the city could establish a free public library open to all citizens. The petition was granted the following year, and thereafter Boston was to spend $5,000 annually to support its library. On March 20, 1854, the Boston Public Library opened its doors to readers and six weeks later to borrowers.

Other states followed. In 1849, New Hampshire passed the first general library law, and in 1851, the Massachusetts legislature made the 1848 Boston act applicable to all cities and towns in the state. Maine followed in 1854, followed by a deluge of states after the Civil War. By 1863, there were a thousand public libraries in the country and by 1875, two thousand public libraries with at least a thousand books each in their collections.

The first major report on the developing public library came in an 1876 document from the U.S. Bureau of Education. Part I, "Public Libraries in the United States of America, their History, Condition, and Management" contained 1,187 pages with reports and comments and analyses from various prominent librarians plus statistics on 3,649 public libraries with holdings of 300 volumes or more.

That same year marks the beginning of the modern library movement. Melvil Dewey, then assistant librarian in the Amherst College library, was largely responsible for the October 4, 1876, conference of librarians which formed the American Library Association the third day of the meeting. The first issue of the *American Library Journal* appeared that same year (it became the *Library Journal* the following year), the world's first professional journal for librarians— England's *The Library Chronicle* began in 1884 and Germany's *Centralblatt für Bibliothekswesen* in 1889. While there had been an abortive conference in 1853, the 1876 meeting promised continuity the earlier meeting lacked.[29]

In 1884, Columbia College furthered the public library movement when it established the first school of Library Economy (later to be Library Science) under the leadership of Melvil Dewey. The school opened January 5, 1887, offering a three-month course, and soon the course was extended to two years.

Excellent as the public libraries were then, they grew immeasurably in number of libraries and individual holdings through the impetus of Andrew Carnegie's philanthropy. A Scottish immigrant to the United States, Carnegie left millions of dollars for the creation of public libraries across America. He began in 1881 with a gift to Pittsburgh where his steelworkers lived, and by 1920, his money had provided funds to build more than 2,500 other public libraries.[30]

Problems and Lamentations of the Public Librarian

Some common problems then still remain problems for librarians today. At the 1876 meeting, a Mr. Walters asked if there were any way to prevent people from stealing books. A Mr. Vickers replied that he knew of only one effective method, "which was to keep a man standing over each book with a club (laughter)."[31] Four years later, the *Library Journal* devoted three and a half columns to the "Capture of a Notorious Book-Thief"[32] with enough details to make the case sound like something out of Sherlock Holmes.

Proof that the library contained what some readers considered dangerous or immoral material came in 1894 when a Los Angeles librarian brought suit for libel against a local minister. Apparently the library had earlier purchased some French books, a local newspaper had attacked the books, and the minister followed up with a sermon in which he prayed for the soul of the librarian in these words:

> O Lord, vouchsafe thy saving grace to the librarian of the Los Angeles City Library, and cleanse her of all sin, and make her a woman worthy of her office.

The librarian, understandably, was unhappy with the publicity and filed suit.[33]

Fiction and Libraries

The growth of public libraries presented opportunities for pleasure and education of the masses, but arguments about the purposes of the libraries arose almost as fast as the buildings themselves. William Poole listed three common objections to the public library in the October 1876 *American Library Journal:* the normal dread of taxes; the more philosophical belief that government had no rights except to protect people and property, that is no right to tax anyone to build and stock a public library; and concern over the kinds of books libraries might buy and circulate.[34] In this third class of objection, Poole touched upon a controversy that would rage for years, that is, whether a public library is established to provide assistance for scholars or pleasure for the masses. Poole believed that a library existed for the entire community or else there was no justification for a general tax.

Poole's words did not quiet critics who argued that the library's sole *raison d'être* was educational. Waving the banner of American purity in his hands, W. M. Stevenson maintained:

> If the public library is not first and foremost an education institution, it has no right to exist. If it exists for mere entertainment, and for a low order of entertainment at that, it is simply a socialistic institution.[35]

Many librarians agreed.

The problem lay almost exclusively with fiction. Librarians, appalled by what they considered cheap, sensational, *pernicious* (a favorite word, much overused to describe the horror they felt) trash, anointed themselves to bring the unwashed masses to literary, if not personal, salvation.

But the debate over fiction and its propriety had begun much earlier.

Early Attacks on Fiction

The English novel originated by Samuel Richardson in his supposedly moral *Pamela* (1740) and continued by the more realistic, honest, and moral novels of Fielding led to some opposition in England but considerably more in America. Moral qualms became even stronger following the Revolutionary War, partly because of chauvinism but mostly from pietistic reasons, as novel reading became widespread and approached a national craze. Minor American authors warned youth of the dangers of the novel-reading habit. The Rev. Enos Hitchcock, a novelist now forgotten for good reason, wrote to young women in his *Memoirs of the Bloomsgrove Family* (1790):

> Nothing can have a worse effect on our sex, than a free use of these writings which are the offspring of our modern novelists. Their only tendency is to excite romantic notions, while they keep the mind void of ideas, and the heart destitute of sentiment.[36]

Later novelists, perhaps to please moralists and defend themselves from potential attack and perhaps because they themselves wondered about the propriety and inherent decency of novels and novel reading, found occasion, paradoxically, to attack novel reading in their own novels. In the first domestic novel, Susan Warner's *The Wide, Wide World*, lachrymose heroine Ellen Montgomery is forbidden to read *Blackwood's Magazine* since it contains fiction.

Fiction Can Be Dangerous If Taken Internally

The second session of the 1876 American Library Association meeting in Philadelphia was devoted to "Novel-Reading." Controversy rose immediately, symptomatic of an argument to rage for years. A librarian announced that his rules permitted no novels in the library. His factory-worker patrons might ask for them, but he recommended other books and was able to keep patrons without supplying novels. To laughter, he said he never read novels so he "could not say what their effect really was."[37]

His sublimely ridiculous and condescending attitude toward library patrons was echoed by others. Librarians worried that catering to popular taste was dangerous, for "by supplying such books, a library fosters the taste that craves them, and it increases the demand."[38]

Fiction and Young Adults

Librarians particularly worried about fiction's effect on young adults. No doubt they envied the plan devised by the Massachusetts Board of Education in 1840 providing leisure reading for young people but carefully excluding all fiction from its lists. Librarians, generally, had no easy way out, for most of their libraries had fiction. The problem was how to control it and restrict its use among young adults.

Poole argued in 1876 that the problem lay with parents who must regulate the reading of young people. But in the same volume of the *American Library Journal,* William Kite lamented the dangers novels presented to young adults, and library literature did not relinquish the theme for some time.

Teachers worried almost as much as librarians. A principal of a large endowed academy was approvingly quoted by a librarian for having said:

> The voracious devouring of fiction commonly indulged in by patrons of the public library, especially the young, is extremely pernicious and mentally unwholesome.[39]

Similar complaints led some librarians to limit the number of books young adults could take out at one time. When Caroline M. Hewins surveyed library conditions in 1893, she found:

> 90 libraries allow them [young people] to charge a book every day; one (subscription) gives them a dozen a day if they wish. 15 limit them to 2, and 3 to 3 a week, and 15 to only 1. Several librarians in libraries where children are allowed a book a day express their disapproval of the custom and one has entered into an engagement with her young readers to take 1 book in every 4 from some other class than fiction.[40]

A gradual change from piety to morality led to literature that was more subtly if still surely didactic by 1900. Literature read by young adults, whether adult works or those written specifically for young adults—and the latter made great strides in quantity and quality—reflected the increasing freedom of writers. The development of inexpensive and ubiquitous dime novels, the popular story weeklies, and paperback libraries, along with more expensive but equally ubiquitous domestic novels, created a mass market of readers and led to an expanded national literacy. The rise of the public library permitted easier access to a greater quantity of literature just as it raised problems about the purpose of the library, especially for young adults. Series books, for better or worse, began. Expansion of literature written for young adults, and especially series books, lay only a few years away.

◼ NOTES

[1]Caroline Ticknor, *Hawthorne and His Publisher* (Boston: Houghton Mifflin, 1913), p. 141.

[2]E. Douglas Branch, *The Sentimental Years, 1836–1860* (New York: Appleton, 1934), p. 131.

[3]William Everett, "Beadle's Dime Novels," *North American Review* 9 (July 1864): 308.

[4]Quentin Reynolds, *The Fiction Factory, or From Pulp Row to Quality Street* (New York: Random House, 1955), pp. 74–75.

[5]Frederic Van Rensselaer Dey, "How I Wrote a Thousand 'Nick Carter' Novels," *American Magazine* 89 (February 1920): 19.

[6]William Sumner, "What Our Boys Are Reading," *Scribner's Monthly* 15 (March 1878): 681–85.

[7]Theodore C. Burgess, "Means of Leading Boys from the Dime Novel to Better Literature," *Library Journal* 21 (April 1896): 147.

[8]*Publisher's Weekly* 23 (April 28, 1883): 500.

[9]*Ibid.*

[10]See especially Burgess; Clement C. Young, "The Public Library and the Public School," *Library Journal* 21 (March 1896): 140–44; Arthur P. Irving, "Home Reading of School Children," *Pedagogical Seminary* 7 (April 1900): 138–40; "The Pawtucket Free Library and the Dime Novel," *Library Journal* 10 (May 1885): 105; and Ellen M. Cox, "What Can Be Done to Help a Boy to Like Good Books After He Has Fallen into the 'Dime Novel Habit'?" *Library Journal* 20 (April 1895): 118–19.

[11]Quoted in Esther Jane Carrier, *Fiction in Public Libraries, 1876–1900* (Metuchen, NJ: Scarecrow Press, 1965), p. 186.

[12]Quoted in *Library Journal* 8 (March–April 1883): 57.

[13]Everett, p. 308.

[14]T. W. Higginson, "Address," *Library Journal* 4 (September–October 1879): 359.

[15]Mary Noel, *Villains Galore . . . The Heyday of the Popular Story Weekly* (New York: Macmillan, 1954), p. 111.

[16]Noel, pp. 112–13.

[17]See Eric Monkkonen, "Socializing the New Urbanites: Horatio Alger, Jr.'s Guidebooks," *Journal of Popular Culture* 11 (Summer 1977): 77–87, for a fine discussion of *Ragged Dick* as a guidebook and handbook.

[18]Jacob Blanck, *Harry Castlemon, Boy's Own Author* (New York: R. R. Bowker, 1941), pp. 5–6.

[19]Raymond L. Kilgour, *Lee and Shepard: Publishers for the People* (Hamden, Connecticut: Shoe String Press, 1965), p. 270.

[20]Oliver Optic, "Sensational Books," *Oliver Optic's Magazine* 18 (September 1875): 718. For an account of the quarrel, see Gene Gleason, "What Ever Happened to Oliver Optic?" *Wilson Library Bulletin* 49 (May 1975): 647–50; see also an anti-Alcott version in John T. Dizer, "Armed with Pen and Ink: The Oliver Optic–Louisa May Alcott Feud," *Dime Novel Roundup* 56 (August 1987): 50–59.

[21]For a somewhat different point of view, see Jacqueline Jackson and Philip Kendall, "What Makes a Bad Book Good: Elsie Dinsmore" in Francelia Butler, ed., *Children's Literature: Annual of the Modern Language Association Group on Children's Literature and the Children's Literature Association* 7 (1978): 45–67.

[22]*Atlantic* 25 (January 1870): 124.

[23]Robert Berkelman, "Mrs. Grundy and Richard Watson Gilder," *American Quarterly* 4 (Spring 1952): 66–72.

[24]Quoted in *Critic* 3 (March 28, 1885): 155.

[25]Asa Don Dickinson, "Huckleberry Finn Is Fifty Years Old—Yes; But Is He Respectable?" *Wilson Bulletin* 10 (November 1935): 183.

[26]Dickinson, 183.

[27]Jesse H. Shera, *Foundations of the Public Library: The Origins of the Public Library Movement in New England, 1629–1885* (Chicago: The University of Chicago Press, 1949), p. 238.

[28]Elmer D. Johnson, *History of Libraries in the Western World,* 2nd ed. (Metuchen, NJ: Scarecrow Press, 1970), p. 358.

[29]A brief summary of the 1853 and 1876 library conventions can be found in Sister Gabriella Margeath, "Library Conventions of 1853, 1876, and 1877," *Journal of Library History* 8 (April 1973): 52–69.

[30]See George Bobinski, *Carnegie Libraries: Their History and Impact on American Library Development* (Chicago: American Library Association, 1967).

[31]*American Library Journal* 1 (November 30, 1876): 109.

[32]S. S. Green, "Capture of a Notorious Book-Thief," *Library Journal* 5 (February 1880): 48–49.

[33]"The Los Angeles Library Libel Suit," *Library Journal* 19 (October 1894): 340.

[34]William F. Poole, "Some Popular Objections to Public Libraries," *American Library Journal* 1 (October 1876): 48–49.

[35]W. M. Stevenson, "Weeding Out Fiction in the Carnegie Free Library of Allegheny, Pa.," *Library Journal* 22 (March 1897): 135.

[36]Quoted in Tremaine McDowell, "Sensibility in the Eighteenth-Century American Novel," *Studies in Philology* 24 (July 1927): 395.

[37]"Novel Reading," *American Library Journal* 1 (October 1876): 98.

[38]George T. Clark, "Improper Books," *Library Journal* 20 (December 1895): 34.

[39]"Monthly Reports from Public Librarians upon the Reading of Minors: A Suggestion," *Library Journal* 24 (August 1899): 479.

[40]Caroline M. Hewins, "Report on the Reading of the Young," *Library Journal* 18 (July 1893): 252.

◼ TITLES MENTIONED IN CHAPTER THIRTEEN

Alcott, Louisa May. *Eight Cousins.* 1875.

————— . *Hospital Sketches.* 1863.

————— . *Little Women: Meg, Jo, Beth, and Amy. The Story of Their Lives. A Girl's Book.* 1868.

————— . *Little Women, or Meg, Jo, Beth, and Amy. Part Second.* 1869.

Aldrich, Thomas Bailey. *The Story of a Bad Boy.* 1870.

Alger, Horatio. *Ragged Dick; or, Street Life in New York.* 1867.

Ballantyne, Robert Michael. *The Coral Island.* 1858.

Bennett, John. *Master Skylark; A Story of Shakespeare's Time.* 1897.

Brontë, Charlotte. *Jane Eyre.* 1847.

Brooks, Noah. *The Boy Emigrants.* 1876.

Bunyan, John. *The Pilgrim's Progress from This World to That Which Is to Come.* 1678.

Castlemon, Harry (real name: Charles Austin Fosdick). *Frank the Young Naturalist.* 1864.

Coolidge, Susan (real name: Sarah Chauncey Woolsey). *Clover.* 1888.

————— . *In the Valley.* 1891.

————— . *What Katy Did.* 1872.

————— . *What Katy Did at School.* 1873.

————— . *What Katy Did Next.* 1886.

Dallas, Mary Kyle. *Neglected Warnings; or, The Trials of a Public School Teacher.* n.d.

Defoe, Daniel. *The Life and Strange Surprising Adventures of Robinson Crusoe.* 1719.

————— . *Moll Flanders.* 1722.

————— . *Roxanna.* 1724.

Dey, Frederic Van Rensselaer. "Nick Carter" Series.

Doyle, Arthur Conan. *The Adventures of Sherlock Homes.* 1891.

Edgeworth, Maria. *Harry and Lucy.* 1801.

————— . *Harry and Lucy Concluded.* 1825.

————— . *Moral Tales for Young People.* 1801.

————— . *The Parent's Assistant.* 1796.

Ellis, Edward S. *Seth Jones.* 1860.

————— . *Trail Hunters.* 1862.

Falkner, John Meade. *Moonfleet.* 1898.

Finley, Martha (real name: Martha Farquharson). *Christmas with Grandma Elsie.* 1888.

_____ . *Elsie Dinsmore.* 1867.

_____ . *Elsie in the South.* 1899.

_____ . *Elsie's Girlhood.* 1872.

_____ . *Elsie's Widowhood.* 1880.

Golding, William. *Lord of the Flies.* Putnam, 1955.

Henty, George Alfred. *Beric, The Briton: A Story of the Roman Invasion.* 1893.

_____ . *When London Burned: A Story of the Plague and the Fire.* 1895.

_____ . *Winning His Spurs: A Tale of the Crusades.* 1892.

More, Hannah. *Coelebs in Search of a Wife.* 1809.

_____ . *Moral Sketches.* 1819.

_____ . *Repository Tracts.* 1795–1798.

Mulock, Dinah Maria. *John Halifax, Gentleman.* 1857.

Munroe, Kirk. *Derrick Sterling.* 1888.

_____ . *The Flamingo Feather.* 1887.

Optic, Oliver (real name: William Taylor Adams). *The Boat Club.* 1855.

Pyle, Howard. *Men of Iron.* 1892.

_____ . *The Merry Adventures of Robin Hood.* 1883.

_____ . *Otto of the Silver Hand.* 1888.

St. George, Harry (real name: St. George Rathbone). *Daring Davy, The Young Bear Killer; or, The Trail of the Border Wolf.* 1879.

Smith, Francis S. *The Vestmaker's Apprentice; or, The Vampyres of Society.* 1857.

Stephens, Ann S. *Malaeska: The Indian Wife of the White Hunter.* 1860.

Stevenson, Robert Louis. *Kidnapped.* 1886.

_____ . *Treasure Island.* 1883.

Stowe, Harriet Beecher. *Uncle Tom's Cabin.* 1852.

Swift, Jonathan. *Gulliver's Travels.* 1726.

Twain, Mark (real name: Samuel Clemens). *Adventures of Huckleberry Finn.* 1884.

_____ . *The Adventures of Tom Sawyer.* 1876.

Verne, Jules. *Around the World in Eighty Days.* 1874.

_____ . *From the Earth to the Moon.* 1873.

_____ . *Twenty Thousand Leagues Under the Sea.* 1872.

Weems, Mason Locke. *A History of the Life and Death, Virtues and Exploits, of General George Washington.* 1800.

_____ . *The Life of George Washington.* 1808.

_____ . *The Life of Washington the Great.* 1806.

Wetherell, Elizabeth (real name: Susan Warner). *The Wide, Wide World.* 1850.

Wilson, Augusta Jane Evans. *St. Elmo.* 1867.

Wood, Mrs. Henry. *East Lynne.* 1861.

▮ SOME SUGGESTED READINGS

General Comments on Literature 1800–1900

Blanck, Jacob. *Peter Parley to Penrod: A Bibliographical Description of the Best Loved American Juvenile Books.* New York: R. R. Bowker, 1938.

_____ . "A Twentieth-Century Look at Nineteenth-Century Children's Books" in *Bibliophile in the Nursery,* ed. William Targ. Cleveland: World, 1957, pp. 427–51.

Crandall, John C. "Patriotism and Humanitarian Reform in Children's Literature, 1825–1860." *American Quarterly* 21 (Spring 1969); 3–22.

Gorham, Deborah. *The Victorian Girl and the Feminine Ideal.* Bloomington: Indiana University Press, 1982.

Kiefer, Monica. *American Children through Their Books, 1700–1835.* Philadelphia: University of Pennsylvania Press, 1948.

MacLeod, Anne Scott. *A Moral Tale: Children's Fiction and American Culture, 1820–1860.* Hamden, Connecticut: Archon Books, 1975.

Sloane, William. *Children's Books in England and America in the Seventeenth Century.* New York: Columbia University Press, 1955.

Wishy, Bernard. *The Child and the Republic: The Dawn of Modern American Child Nur-

ture. Philadelphia: University of Pennsylvania Press, 1968.

General Comments on Literature 1850–1900

Avery, Gillian. *Childhood's Pattern: A Study of the Heroes and Heroines of Children's Fiction, 1770–1950.* London: Hodder and Stoughton, 1975.

Branch, E. Douglas. *The Sentimental Years, 1836–1860.* New York: Appleton, 1934.

Cadogan, Mary, and Patricia Craig. *You're a Brick, Angela! A New Look at Girls' Fiction from 1839 to 1975.* London: Victor Gollancz, 1976.

Campbell, Patricia J. *Sex Education Books for Young Adults, 1892–1979.* New York: R. R. Bowker, 1979.

Cowie, Alexander. *The Rise of the American Novel.* New York: American, 1948.

Cruse, Amy. *The Victorians and Their Reading.* Boston: Houghton Mifflin, 1935. First published in England as *The Victorians and Their Books.*

Darling, Richard. *The Rise of Children's Book Reviewing in America, 1865–1881.* R. R. Bowker, 1968.

Ellis, Alec. *A History of Children's Reading and Literature.* Oxford: Pergamon Press, 1968.

Van Doren, Carl. *The American Novel.* New York: Macmillan, 1929.

The Domestic Novel

Brown, Herbert Ross. *The Sentimental Novel in America, 1789–1860.* Durham: North Carolina University Press, 1940.

Hofstadter, Beatrice K. "Popular Culture and the Romantic Heroine." *American Scholar* 30 (Winter 1960–61): 98.

Papashvily, Helen Waite. *All the Happy Endings: A Study of the Domestic Novel in America, The Women Who Wrote It, The Women Who Read It, in the Nineteenth Century.* New York: Harper & Row, 1956.

Pattee, Fred Lewis. *The Feminist Fifties.* New York: Appleton, 1940.

Susan Warner

Jordan, Alice M. "Susan Warner and Her *Wide Wide World.*" *Horn Book Magazine* 10 (September 1934): 287–93.

Warner, Anna B. *Susan Warner.* New York: G. P. Putnam's Sons, 1904.

Augusta Jane Wilson

Calkins, Ernest Elmo. "St. Elmo, or, Names for a Best Seller." *Saturday Review of Literature* 21 (December 16, 1939): 3.

Fidler, William Perry. *Augusta Evans Wilson 1835–1900.* University, Alabama: University of Alabama Press, 1951.

Dime Novels (General)

Admari, Ralph. "Ballou: The Father of the Dime Novel." *American Book Collector* 4 (September–October 1933): 121–29.

Curti, Merle. "Dime Novels and the American Tradition." *Yale Review* 26 (June 1937): 761–68.

Hoppenstad, Gary, ed. *The Dime Novel Detectives.* Bowling Green, Ohio: Bowling Green University Popular Press, 1982.

Johannsen, Albert. *The House of Beadle and Adams and Its Dime and Nickel Novels: The Story of a Vanished Literature.* 3 Volumes. Norman: University of Oklahoma Press, 1950, 1962. A basic work.

Jones, Daryl. *The Dime Novel Western.* Bowling Green, Ohio: Bowling Green University Popular Press, 1978.

Leithead, J. Edward. "The Anatomy of Dime Novels: No. 1—Nick Carter." *Dime Novel Roundup* 33 (September 15, 1964): 76–79; and 33 (October 15, 1964): 84–89. From his vast reading and collecting, Leithead wrote prolifically about dime novels in *Dime Novel Roundup,* the best source of information about the subject, and *American Book Collector* until his death in 1970.

Pearson, Edmund. *Dime Novels, or Following an Old Trail in Popular Literature.* Port Washington, New York: Kennikat Press, 1968. First published in 1929.

Reynolds, Quentin. *The Fiction Factory, or From Pulp Row to Quality Street.* New York: Random House, 1955. On Street and Smith.

Smith, Henry Nash. *Virgin Land: The American West as Symbol and Myth.* Cambridge: Harvard University Press, 1950.

Turner, E. S. *Boys Will Be Boys,* 3rd ed. London: Michael Joseph, 1978. Primarily on English Penny Dreadfuls, but Chapter 10 is excellent on the American Frank Reade series.

Dime Novels (Objections to and Objections to the Objections)

Bishop, W. H. "Story-Paper Literature." *Atlantic* 44 (September 1879): 383–93.

Burgess, Theodore C. "Means of Leading Boys from the Dime Novel to Better Literature." *Library Journal* 21 (April 1896): 144–47.

Comstock, Anthony. *Traps for the Young,* ed. Robert Bremner. Cambridge: Harvard University Press, 1967. First published in 1883.

Cox, Ellen M. "What Can Be Done to Help a Boy to Like Good Books after He Has Fallen into the 'Dime Novel Habit'?" *Library Journal* 20 (April 1895): 118–19.

Harvey, Charles M. "The Dime Novel in American Life." *Atlantic* 100 (July 1907): 37–45.

Sumner, William. "What Our Boys Are Reading." *Scribner's Monthly* 15 (March 1878): 681–85.

Popular Story Weeklies

Bishop, W. H. "Story-Paper Literature." *Atlantic* 44 (September 1879): 383–93.

Burgess, Theodore C. "Means of Leading Boys from the Dime Novel to Better Literature." *Library Journal* 21 (April 1896): 144–47.

Louisa May Alcott

Cheney, Ednah D., ed. *Louisa May Alcott: Her Life, Letters and Journals.* Boston: Little, Brown, 1901.

Elbert, Sarah. *A Hunger for Home: Louisa May Alcott and Little Women.* Philadelphia: Temple University Press, 1984.

Myerson, Joel, and Daniel Sheahy, eds. *The Selected Letters of Louisa May Alcott.* Boston: Little, Brown, 1987.

Payne, Alma J. "Louisa May Alcott (1832–1888)." *American Literary Realism, 1870–1910* (Winter 1973): 23–43. Excellent bibliographical material.

Salyer, Sandford. *Marmee: The Mother of Little Women.* Norman: University of Oklahoma Press, 1949.

Saxton, Martha. *Louisa May: A Modern Biography of Louisa May Alcott.* Boston: Houghton Mifflin, 1977.

Stern, Madeleine. *Louisa May Alcott.* Norman: University of Oklahoma Press, 1950. The most readable and satisfying of all the Alcott biographies.

Horatio Alger, Jr.

Alger, Horatio, Jr. "Writing Stories for Boys." *Writer* 9 (March 1896): 36–37.

Falk, Robert. "Notes on the 'Higher Criticism' of Horatio Alger, Jr." *Arizona Quarterly* 19 (Summer 1963): 151–67.

Holland, Norman. "Hobbling with Horatio, or the Uses of Literature." *Hudson Review* 12 (Winter 1959–60): 549–57.

Scharnhorst, Gary. *Horatio Alger, Jr.* Boston: G. K. Hall, 1980.

_____ . *The Lost Life of Horatio Alger, Jr.* Bloomington: Indiana University Press, 1985.

_____ , and Jack Bales. *An Annotated Bibliography of Comments and Criticism.* Metuchen, NJ: Scarecrow Press, 1981.

Seelye, John. "Who Was Horatio? The Alger Myth and American Scholarship." *American Quarterly* 17 (Winter 1965): 749–56.

Early Series Writers

Harry Castlemon

Blanck, Jacob. *Harry Castlemon, Boys' Own Author: An Appreciation and Bibliography.* New York: R. R. Bowker, 1941.

Castlemon, Harry. "How to Write Stories for Boys." *Writer* 9 (January 1896): 4–5.

Martha Finley

Brown, Janet. *The Saga of Elsie Dinsmore*. Buffalo: University of Buffalo Press, 1945.

Jackson, Jacqueline and Philip Kendall. "What Makes a Bad Book Good: Elsie Dinsmore" in Francelia Butler, ed., *Children's Literature: Annual of the Modern Language Association Group on Children's Literature and the Children's Literature Association* 7 (1978): 45–67.

Literature of the Bad Boy

Geller, Evelyn. "Tom Sawyer, Tom Bailey, and the Bad-Boy Genre." *Wilson Library Bulletin* 51 (November 1976): 245–50.

Hunter, Jim. "Mark Twain and the Boy-Book in 19th-Century America." *College English* 24 (March 1963): 430–38.

Trensky, Anne. "The Bad Boy in Nineteenth-Century American Fiction." *Georgia Review* 27 (Winter 1973): 503–17.

Libraries

Development of Libraries in America

Ditzion, Sidney. *Arsenals of a Democratic Culture: A Social History of the American Public Library Movement in New England and the Middle States from 1850 to 1900*. Chicago: American Library Association, 1947.

Harris, Michael H., and Donald G. Davis, Jr. *American Library History: A Bibliography*. Austin: University of Texas Press, 1978.

Margeath, Sister Gabriella. "Library Conventions of 1853, 1876, and 1877." *Journal of Library History* 8 (April 1973): 52–69.

Shera, Jesse H. *Foundations of the Public Library: The Origins of the Public Library Movement in New England, 1629–1885*. Chicago: The University of Chicago Press, 1949.

_____ . "The Literature of American Library History" in Jesse H. Shera, ed., *Knowing Books and Men. Knowing Computers, Too*. Littleton, Colorado: Libraries Unlimited, 1973, pp. 124–61.

Thompson, C. Seymour. *Evolution of the American Public Library, 1653–1876*. Washington, D.C.: Scarecrow Press, 1952.

The Problem of Fiction

Carrier, Esther Jane. *Fiction in Public Libraries, 1876–1900*. New York: Scarecrow Press, 1965.

Crane, the Rev. J. T. *Popular Amusements*. Cincinnati: Cranston and Stowe, 1869. See esp. 121–52 on "Novels and Novel-Reading."

Garrison, Dee. *Apostles of Culture: The Public Librarian and American Society, 1876–1920*. New York: The Free Press, 1979, Chapters 4 and 5.

Orians, G. Harrison. "Censure of Fiction in American Romances and Magazines 1789–1810." *PMLA* 52 (March 1937): 195–214.

Poole, William F. "Some Popular Objections to Public Libraries." *American Library Journal* 1 (October 1876): 45–51.

Taylor, John Tinnon. *Early Opposition to the English Novel: The Popular Reaction from 1760 to 1830*. New York: King's Crown Press, 1943.

Restricting Fiction from Young Adults

Cohen, Max. "The Librarian as Educator, and Not a Cheap-John." *Library Journal* 13 (December 1888): 366–67.

Jones, Richard. "The Moral and Literary Responsibilities of Librarians in Selecting Books for a Public Library." *NEA Journal of Proceedings and Addresses, 1897*. Chicago: The University of Chicago Press, 1897, pp. 1025–28.

Kite, William. "Fiction in Public Libraries." *American Library Journal* 1 (February 1877): 277–79.

Stevenson, W. M. "Weeding Out Fiction in the Carnegie Free Library of Allegheny, Pa." *Library Journal* 22 (March 1897): 133–35.

Young, Clement C. "The Public Library and the Public School." *Library Journal* 21 (April 1896): 140–44.

Loosening Restrictions on Young Adults

Cole, George Watson. "Fiction in Libraries: A Plea for the Masses." *Library Journal* 19 (December 1894): 18–21.

Geller, Evelyn. *Forbidden Books in American Public Libraries, 1876–1939: A Study in Cultural Change.* Westport, Connecticut: Greenwood Press, 1984.

For information on the availability of paperback editions of these titles, please consult the most recent edition of *Paperbound Books in Print,* published annually by R. R. Bowker Company.

Green, S. S. "Sensational Fiction in Public Libraries." *Library Journal* 4 (September–October 1879): 345–55.

Hardy, George E. "The School Library a Factor in Education." *Library Journal* 14 (August 1889): 343–47.

Higginson, T. W. "Address." *Library Journal* 4 (September–October 1879): 357–59.

1900–1940
From the Safety of Romance to the Beginning of Realism

The first forty years of the twentieth century were times of change and challenge, aspiration mixed with frustration. The western frontier disappeared, and the country changed from an agrarian society to an urban one. World War I brought the certainty that it would end all wars. The labor movement grew along with Ford's production lines and cars, cars, cars. President Hoover came along, then the Wall Street crash of 1929 and the Great Depression. By 1938, three million young people from sixteen through twenty-five were out of school and unemployed, and a quarter of a million boys were on the road. Franklin Delano Roosevelt introduced the "New Deal," and Nazi Germany rose in the east. When the end of the Depression seemed almost in sight, the New York World's Fair of 1939 became our optimistic metaphor for the coming of a newer, better, happier, and more secure world. World War II lay just over the horizon, apparent to some, ignored by most.

These forty years saw literary and pedagogical changes, among them new ways of assessing reading interests of young adults and the rise of English teaching as a discipline. There were further developments in series books, "junior" or "juvenile" divisions were started in publishing houses, and pulps and comics began.

READING INTEREST STUDIES

Before 1900, librarians and English teachers published little about reading interests of young people. Many adults, intent on telling the young what to read, had scant interest in finding out what young adults cared to read. English teaching was a relatively new discipline—English was not given the time and attention accorded Latin and other school subjects until late in the nineteenth century—and teachers faced pressure from colleges to prepare the young for study. Recreational reading seemed vaguely time wasting, if not downright wicked. With the exception of a few articles like True's "What My Pupils Read,"[1] reading interests went largely unexplored. But after publication of the Vostrovsky study,[2] the first significant reading interest investigation, came the deluge. From brief two- or three-page articles to books of several hundred pages, reading interest studies ranged from simple, direct status quo reports to complex analyses of what young adults liked and why.

Findings of Reading Interest Studies

Generally, studies revealed that young adults read far more fiction than any other genre. They read books written specifically for them, series books from Stratemeyer's Literary Syndicate such as Tom Swift, Nancy Drew, Hardy Boys, Baseball Joe, and Ruth Fielding, and non-Stratemeyer series like Boys of Bob's Hill, Frank Merriwell, Roy Blakely, and Campfire Girls. They read adolescent books by Barbour, Heyliger, Pease, Terhune, Montgomery, Alcott, O'Brien, Seaman, and Altsheler. They read classics, and they read modern best-sellers.

In effect, they read many of the same writers and books reported in Irving Harlow Hart's "The Most Popular Authors of Fiction between 1900 and 1925,"[3] and they read best sellers selected by the Book-of-the-Month Club when it began in 1926 and the Literary Guild when it began a year later.

Some Reactions

Some investigators and readers reacted predictably and emotionally to reading interest studies. English teacher Alfred M. Hitchcock voiced fears that education and the reading public were hurtling steadily downward:

> Books, magazines, and journals are written to catch the multitudes— the multitudes who are not very keenly intellectual, not gifted with imagination, nor trained to appreciate artistic form—the easy-going, pleasure-seeking, not over-ambitious, somewhat unmoral multitudes. There are notable exceptions, it is true; yet one cannot avoid the suspicion that many writers are content to give the public what the public wants, not what it needs. Reading the truly popular literature of the hour, in the manner in which it is commonly read by the young, can hardly be called an intellectual exercise. It does not challenge the mind; it does not invite the imagination. Too often it feeds the passions rather than the higher emotions. The youth who reads gets little; his moral and intellectual fiber is not strengthened.[4]

The argument over the possible harm that might come from series books, or popular literature sometimes labeled "subliterature," has raged for years, and the end is unlikely to precede the millennium. In the lengthy *Winnetka Graded Book List,* partly concerned with the reading of junior-high students, Washburne and Vogel did not list all books reported; "Books that were definitely trashy or unsuitable for children, even though widely read, have not been included in this list."[5] Enough people were apparently curious about the trashy or unsuitable books to lead the authors to add two supplements.[6] Predictably, *Elsie Dinsmore* was among the damned, and so were Edgar Rice Burroughs' *Tarzan of the Apes,* Eleanor Porter's *Pollyanna,* Zane Grey's westerns, and books from the Ruth Fielding and Tom Swift series. No surprises there, but surprises did pop up. Strangely, Mark Twain's *Tom Sawyer Abroad* was among the unwashed and disapproved. So was Mary Roberts Rinehart's *The Circular Staircase.* Arthur Conan Doyle's *The Adventures of Sherlock Holmes* was recommended, but *The Hound of the Baskervilles* was not acceptable. Such puzzlements must have disturbed readers looking for that most impossible of tools, a list applicable to all teachers, schools, libraries, and students.

Other critics seemed less concerned about the souls of the young even if trash were part of the diet. Critic and English professor William Lyon Phelps argued that reading some relatively poor literature was not only not harmful but almost inevitable for most young readers:

> ▄ I do not believe the majority of these very school teachers and other cultivated mature readers began in early youth by reading great books exclusively; I think they read *Jack Harkaway, an Old Sleuth,* and the works of Oliver Optic and Horatio Alger. From these enchanters they learned a thing of tremendous importance—the delight of reading. Once a taste for reading is formed, it can be improved. But it is improbable that boys and girls who have never cared to read a good story will later enjoy stories by good artists.[7]

Girls' Books and Boys' Books

Teachers and librarians frequently commented that girls' books, particularly up to the middle 1930s, were inferior to boys' books. Franklin T. Baker wrote that girls' books of 1908 were "numerous and . . . often painfully weak" lacking "invention, action, humor"[8] with the obvious exception of Alcott. Two years later Clara Whitehill Hunt agreed that many girls' books were empty, insipid, and mediocre.[9] As late as 1935, a writer could still object to the dearth of good fiction for girls. Reviewing some interesting nonfiction for boys, Julia Carter broke in with what appeared to be an exasperated obiter dictum:

> ▄ Will someone please tell me why we expect the *boys* to know these things and still plan for the girls to be mid-Victorian, and consider them hoydens beyond reclaiming, when instead of shrieking and running like true daughters of Eve, they are interested in snakes and can light a fire with two matches?[10]

Yet only two years later, writers like Caroline Dale Snedeker, Cornelia Meigs, Jeanette Eaton, Mabel Robinson, and Elizabeth Forman Lewis were producing enough quality girls' literature to encourage Alice M. Jordan to write:

> There was a time not long ago when the boys had the lion's share in the yearly production of books intended for young people. So writers were urged to give us more stories in which girls could see themselves in recognizable relationship to the world of their own time, forgetting perhaps that human nature does not change and the vital things are universal. Yet, none the less, the girls had a real cause to plead and right valiantly the writers have responded.[11]

Critics believed then, as they continued to insist for years, that girls would read boys' books but boys would never read girls' books. At least part of the problem of stereotyping girls' and boys' books lay with stereotypes of boys' and girls' roles as expressed by two writers. Clara Vostrovsky, author of the first significant reading interest study, went back to ancient times for her stereotypes suggesting that it was "probable" that the differences in reading interests between boys and girls lay "in the history of the race."[12] Psychologist G. Stanley Hall predicated reading interests of girls and boys on psychological differences:

> Boys love adventure, girls sentiment. . . . Girls love to read stories about girls which boys eschew, girls, however, caring much more to read about boys than boys to read about girls. Books dealing with domestic life and with young children in them girls have almost entirely to themselves. Boys, on the other hand, excel in love of humor, rollicking fun, abandon, rough horse-play, and tales of wild escapades. Girls are less averse to reading what boys like than boys are to reading what girls like. A book popular with boys would attract some girls, while one read by most girls would repel a boy in the middle teens. The reading interests of high-school girls are far more humanistic, cultural and general, and that of boys is more practical, vocational, and even special.[13]

The simple truth, perhaps too obvious and discomforting to be palatable to some parents, English teachers, and librarians, was that boys' books were generally far superior to girls' books. That had nothing to do with the sexual or psychological nature of boys or girls but rather with the way authors treated their audience. Many authors insisted on making their girls good and domestic and dull (if a heroine were allowed some freedom to roam outside the house, she soon regretted it or grew up, whichever came first), perhaps because they thought parents and librarians wanted books that way. Boys were allowed outside the house to find work and responsibilities, of course, but also to find adventure and excitement in their books.

Motion Pictures and Books

From the time motion pictures became a popular medium, librarians and teachers worried that films would lead young adults away from books. As early as 1918, one writer argued that motion pictures were more powerful and created more vivid impressions on the young than books, but he also felt movies would lead to "an increased demand for fiction dealing with the stories exhibited.[14] Eleven years later, Cleveland librarian Marilla Waite Freeman pointed out the number of potential library tie-ins with current movies like *The Covered Wagon, Ben-Hur, Scaramouche, Show Boat,* and *Seventh Heaven.*[15] By 1940, Hollywood's influence on young adults' reading interests and tastes was acknowledged, accepted, and often praised for the good it could do for books, libraries, and classrooms:

Hollywood has a tremendous influence on reading tastes of youth today. Comprehensive surveys made in all libraries indicate that good movies made from books definitely stimulate reading of the book. Release of motion pictures made from books will often have an immediate effect in the school library. Dust is blown off some of the older volumes, or books classified as "too dry," or "not interesting," and they are removed from the shelf for reading and re-reading. There is often renewed interest in the classics.[16]

THE CHANGING ENGLISH CLASSROOM

By 1900, the library played a significant role in helping young adults find reading materials. Although many librarians reflected the traditional belief that classics should be the major reading of youth, other librarians helped young adults to find a variety of materials they liked, not trash, but certainly popular books.

That would have rarely been true of English teachers, saddled as they were with responsibility for preparing young adults for college. College entrance examinations virtually forced secondary school English teachers to feed their students a steady diet of great literature, not because great books were necessarily enjoyable or satisfying but because college exams were predicated on a study of the classics. High schools then hardly touched the masses of young adults, enrolling a mere one of twenty-five young people. They were regarded by most college teachers and many secondary teachers as preparatory schools.

The attention paid to poetry and nonfiction prose was hardly surprising, but some teachers argued for the use of the often ignored novel in the classroom. An Illinois committee surveying English teachers found novels all too rarely used, recommended their use, and then added a warning:

The novel is conspicuous by its absence. The literary history of the Nineteenth Century shows no names more remarkable than those of Scott, Dickens, Thackeray, and Eliot, to say nothing of Hawthorne, Cooper, and

Cable. These men are celebrated for fiction. The novel has become a factor in our life. It is instructive and propagandist; it teaches psychology; preaches a new religion, or attacks the old; gives lessons in sociology; reforms old abuses; satirizes new follies; and continually retells the old but never new story of human life. It forms the greater part of our reading, if library statistics are to be trusted, and certainly is most potent in its influence on human conduct. It therefore belongs in the English course of the high school. Perhaps one is enough; certainly five seems too large a number.[17]

Unhappily, the study of literature was often reserved for the senior year, as William E. Mead lamented in *The Academy* (a journal that is far and away the best source of information about English teaching prior to the *English Journal*).[18]

College Entrance Examinations Ride High

Early entrance exams for college simply required some proof of writing proficiency, but in 1869 and 1870, Harvard began using Milton's *Comus* and Shakespeare's *Julius Caesar* as alternative books for the examination. Four years later Harvard required a short composition based on a question about one of the following: Shakespeare's *The Tempest, Julius Caesar,* and *The Merchant of Venice,* Goldsmith's *The Vicar of Wakefield,* or Scott's *Ivanhoe* and *The Lay of the Last Minstrel.*

In 1894, the prestigious Committee of Ten on Secondary School Studies presented its report, and English became an accepted discipline in the schools, if not yet as respectable as Latin. Chaired by controversial Harvard president Charles W. Eliot, the Committee was appointed by the National Education Association in July 1892 and met later that year to determine the nature, limits, and methods appropriate to many subject matters in secondary school.[19] Samuel Thurber of The Boston Girls' High School was unable to promote his belief that a high school curriculum should consist almost entirely of elective courses, but as chairman of the English Conference, his report liberalized and dignified the study of English. Thurber wrote that one of the chief objectives of English teaching was to "cultivate a taste for reading, to give the pupil some acquaintance with good literature, and to furnish him with the means of extending that acquaintance."[20] Thurber and his committee urged that English be studied five hours a week for four years. Further, the English Conference urged uniform college entrance examinations be established throughout the country.

The result was the publication of book lists, mainly classics, as the basis of entrance examinations. Plays and books such as Shakespeare's *Twelfth Night* and *As You Like It,* Milton's Books I and II from *Paradise Lost,* Scott's *The Abbott* and *Marmion* or Irving's *Bracebridge Hall* virtually became the English curriculum as teachers, inevitably concerned with their students' entry into college, increasingly adapted the English curriculum to fit the list. Not all teachers believed that the enjoyment of reading had anything to do with teaching English, and those who did were given little leeway in their choice of classroom books. Thurber worried about teaching literature too mature for young adults and the inevitable dichotomy between school reading and voluntary reading or real reading, that "dismal gulf" between the study of literature and reading outside the school:

> Not a month ago I saw a boy of fourteen pass through a similar experience. I had just taken from a class *The Lady of the Lake* and put into their hands Stevenson's *Treasure Island.* At the close of the hour an astonished, excited voice said to me: "I—I've read this book!" "Well, and what of that?" "Why, I didn't know we studied *this kind of a book* in school."[21]

Thurber's point was well taken. Teachers labored under the responsibility for preparing students to pass college entrance exams. Their responsibility did not extend to encouraging students to enjoy reading or to extend reading beyond the required text.

The National Council of Teachers of English (NCTE) Begins

Out of the growing protest about college entrance exams, a group of English teachers attending a national Education Association English Table formed a Committee on College Entrance Requirements in English to assess the problem through a national survey of English teachers. The Committee uncovered hostility to colleges presumptuous enough to try to control the secondary English curriculum through the guise of entrance examinations. John M. Coulter, a professor at the University of Chicago, tried to sound that alarm to college professors, without much success:

> The high school exists primarily for its own sake; and secondarily as a preparatory school for college. This means that when the high school interest and the college interest comes into conflict, the college interest must yield. It also means that the function of a preparatory school must be performed only in so far as it does not interfere with the more fundamental purpose of the high school itself. It also means that independent dictation by colleges, either directly or indirectly, must be changed to adaptation to what the high school can do or ought to do, as determined by the high schools themselves. The high school must be regarded as an autonomous, not subordinate, institution.[22]

Some irate teachers recognized that the problem of college control would hardly be the last issue to face English teachers and formed the nucleus of the National Council of Teachers of English. The First Annual Meeting in Chicago on December 1 and 2, 1911, was largely devoted to resentment about actions of the National Conference on Uniform Entrance Requirements, particularly because that body had representatives from twelve colleges, two academies, and only two public high schools (principals, not English teachers). Wilbur W. Hatfield, soon to edit the *English Journal* and then at Farragut High School in Chicago, relayed instructions from the Illinois Association of Teachers of English on two responsibilities NCTE should recommend:

> 1. To include in its list for class reading, study, or whatever you choose to call it, some books of the last ten years. Our present custom of using only old books in the classroom leaves the pupil with no acquaintance with the literature of the present day, from which he is sure to choose his reading after graduation.
> 2. To appoint a committee to compile a list of comparatively recent books suitable for home reading by the pupils.[23]

Later Actions of English Teachers

James Fleming Hosic's 1917 report on the *Reorganization of English in Secondary Schools,* part of a larger report on reorganization of all subject matter fields and all published under the aegis of the U.S. Bureau of Education, looked at books and teaching in ways that must have seemed muddle-headed or perverse to traditionalists. Looking at literature for the tenth, eleventh, and twelfth grades, Hosic chose works that pleased many, puzzled others, and alienated some:

> The literature lesson should broaden, deepen, and enrich the imaginative and emotional life of the student. Literature is primarily a revelation and an interpretation of life; it pictures from century to century the growth of the human spirit. It should be the constant aim of the English teacher to lead pupils so to read that they find their own lives imaged in this larger life, and attain slowly, from a clearer appreciation of human nature, a deeper and truer understanding of human nature. . . . It should be the aim of the English teacher to make [reading] an unfailing resource and joy in the lives of all.[24]

To encourage this, Hosic listed books for study and general reading. Classics were included but so were modern works such as Jackson's *Ramona* and Wister's *The Virginian* for the tenth grade; Kipling's *The Light That Failed* and Johnston's *To Have and To Hold* for the eleventh grade; and Synge's *Riders to the Sea* and Deland's *The Awakening of Helena Richie* for the twelfth grade. Teachers terrified by the contemporary reality reflected in these books—and perhaps equally terrified by the possibility of throwing out age-old lesson plans and tests on classics—had little to fear. In many schools, nothing changed.

Dora V. Smith reported in 1933 that the most widely studied full-length works in secondary schools were classics. *Silas Marner* led the list followed by *Julius Caesar, Idylls of the King, A Tale of Two Cities,* and *Lady of the Lake.*[25] Most such required books were taught at interminable length, teachers seemingly smitten by what came to be known as the "intensive" method, four to six weeks—sometimes even more—of detailed examination per work while horrified or bored students vowed never to read anything once they escaped high school. Another study offered proof that the "intensive" method produced no better test results and considerably more apathy toward literature than the "extensive" method in which students read assigned works faster.[26] This research had a negligible effect on most classroom teachers as did most other significant research.

However, the work of two college professors in the 1930s influenced some English teachers. A 1936 study by Lou LaBrant on the value of free reading at the Ohio State University Laboratory School revealed that students with easy access to different kinds of books and some guidance read more, enjoyed what they read, and moved upward in literary sophistication and taste.[27] Earlier, Dora V. Smith found English teachers knew next to nothing about books written for adolescents. She corrected the situation at the University of Minnesota, establishing the first course in adolescent literature.[28] Later, she wrote:

> We must provide teachers who know books first-hand and recognize their place in the lives of boys and girls. It is fair neither to young people nor to their teachers to send out from our colleges and universities men and women trained alone in Chaucer and Milton and Browning to compete with Zane Grey, Robert W. Chambers, and Ethel M. Dell. At the University of Minnesota we have instituted a course in adolescent literature which aims to supplement the necessary training in the classics given by the English department with this broader knowledge of good books, old and new, for boys and girls and for intelligent, cultured men and women—books not commonly judged worthy of academic consideration.[29]

THE SCHOOL LIBRARY

The development of the school library was almost as slow and convoluted as the development of the public library. In 1823, Brooklyn's Apprentice Library Association established a Youth Library where "Boys over twelve were allowed . . . as were girls whose access to the library was limited to one hour an afternoon, once a week."[30] And in 1853, Milwaukee School Commissioner Increase A. Lapham provided for a library open Saturday afternoons and recommended that schools spend $10 a year for books. Rules for the Milwaukee library were clear and more than a bit reminiscent of rules in some school and public libraries until the 1940s.

> (1) Only children over ten years old, their parents, teachers, and school commissioner could withdraw books; (2) books might be withdrawn between 2:00 p.m. and sunset on Saturdays and kept for one week; (3) withdrawals were limited to one book per person; and (4) fines were to be assessed for overdue or damaged books.[31]

Writers in the early years of the *Library Journal* paid considerable attention to working out good relations between the public library and the schools. Samuel Swett Green of the Worcester, Massachusetts, Free Public Library wrote:

> Teachers and librarians are co-educators.
>
> Librarians should cultivate friendly relations with teachers and let them understand that they are ready to afford them any available facilities for using books and getting them information, and to join them in endeavors to make the books of the library serviceable to their scholars.[32]

Writers in the late 1890s National Education Association's *Journal of Proceedings and Addresses* were equally concerned and a Committee on Relations of Public Libraries to Public Schools Report in 1899 announced:

> The library must be regarded as an important and necessary part of the system of public education.
>
> The teachers of a town should know the public library, what it contains, and what use the pupils can make of it. The librarian must know the school, its work, its needs, and what he can do to meet them.[33]

One question persisted for some time. Should the school depend on the public library or should the school establish its own library within the confines of the school? In 1986, Melvil Dewey recommended to the NEA that it form a library department (as it had for other subject disciplines) since the library was as much a part of the educational system as the classroom. The previous year, a branch of the Cleveland, Ohio, Public Library was established within Central High School, and in 1899, a branch of the Newark, New Jersey, Public Library was placed in a local high school.

In 1900, Mary Kingston became the first library school graduate appointed to a high school library (Erasmus Hall High School, Brooklyn). Mary E. Hall, librarian at Girls' High School in Brooklyn, argued in 1912 the need for many more professionally trained librarians in high school libraries:

> (1) The aims and ideals of the new high school mean we must stop pretending that high school is entirely college preparatory. "It realizes that for the great majority of pupils it must be a preparation for life." (2) Modern methods of teaching demand that a textbook is not enough. "The efficient teacher to-day uses books, magazines, daily paper, pictures, and lantern slides to supplement the textbook." (3) Reading guidance is easier for the school librarian than the public librarian. "The school librarian has the teacher always close at hand and can know the problems of these teachers in their work with pupils."[34]

In 1916, C. C. Certain began standardizing high school libraries across the country as head of an NEA committee. He discovered conditions so mixed, from deplorable (mostly) to good (rarely) that his committee decided to establish a list of minimum essentials for high schools of various sizes. The report divided schools into four different classes (high schools with 500–3,000 enrollment; high schools with 200–500 enrollment; high schools enrolling fewer than 100; and junior high schools) and specified the housing and equipment, the librarians' qualifications, the educational work of the library, the selection and care of books, and the annual appropriations for each of the four classes.[35]

The report, adopted by the NEA in 1918, for the first time allowed high schools to compare their libraries with comparable high school libraries and to determine what was needed to bring them up to standard. How that was to be accomplished was, of course, left up to local personnel and administrators.

Two reports by the U.S. Office of Education, in 1923 and 1929, indicate the growth of high school libraries. The 1923 report found only 947 school libraries with more than 3,000 volumes, and they were largely in the northeastern part of the country. Six years later, the report found 1982 school libraries with holdings of more than 3,000 volumes, and the libraries were more equally spread over the country, New York having 211 such libraries and California having 191.[36]

The unspectacular, if steady, growth of high school libraries slowed down drastically during the Depression. In 1934, Charlotte H. Clark and Louise P. Latimer argued that the high school library was incredibly costly and unnecessarily duplicated the work of the public library in an article that answered the title, "The Taxpayer and Reading for Young People: Would a 'Library in Every School' Justify the Cost?"[37]

And five years before the 1945 American Library Association's publication of *School Libraries for Today and Tomorrow,* which established modern guidelines for developing school libraries, a letter from a school principal made clear that no matter what the ALA or NCTE or NEA or any group wished, school librarians and school libraries remained low on the list of priorities of too many schools. The principal wrote:

> The Southern Association requires that we have a librarian next year. I should like to have a person who can teach one class in algebra, one in English, one in American history, and one in French, coach basketball, direct the glee club, take care of the library, and type my letters. Salary, $75.00 a month.[38]

EDWARD STRATEMEYER'S LITERARY SYNDICATE

Whatever disagreements librarians and English teachers may have had over the years about books suitable for young adults, they ineffectively bonded together and opposed the books produced by Edward Stratemeyer and his numerous writers. Stratemeyer founded the most successful industry ever built around adolescent reading. Sometime in 1886, he took time off from working for his stepbrother and wrote an 18,000-word serial, *Victor Horton's Idea,* on brown wrapping paper and mailed it to *Golden Days,* a Philadelphia weekly boys' magazine. A check for seventy-five dollars arrived shortly, and Stratemeyer's success story was underway. By 1893 Stratemeyer was editing *Good News,* Street and Smith's boys' weekly, building circulation to more than 200,000. In addition to editing a few other boys' magazines, his work at Street and Smith made his name known to the public, particularly young adults. Even more important, he came to know staff writers such as William T. Adams, Edward S. Ellis, and Horatio Alger, Jr. When Optic and Alger died leaving some uncompleted manuscripts, Stratemeyer was asked to finish the last three Optic novels, and he completed (or possibly wrote from scratch) at least eleven and possibly as many as eighteen Alger novels.

His first hardback book published under his own name was *Richard Dare's Venture; or, Striking Out for Himself* (1894), first in a series he titled "Bound to Succeed." By the close of 1897, Stratemeyer had six series and sixteen hardcover books in print.

A major breakthrough came in 1898. After Stratemeyer sent a manuscript about two boys on a battleship to Lothrop and Shepard, one of the most successful publishers of young adult fiction, Admiral Dewey won his great victory in Manila Bay, and a Lothrop reader asked Stratemeyer to place the boys at the scene of Dewey's victory. He rewrote and returned the book shortly, and *Under Dewey at Manila; or, The War Fortunes of a Castaway* hit the streets in time to capitalize on all the publicity. Not one to miss an opportunity, Stratemeyer used the same characters in his next books, all published from 1898 to 1901 under the series title "Old Glory." Using the same characters in

English teachers and librarians loudly opposed the books by Edward Stratemeyer, but his Literary Syndicate was the most successful industry ever built around adolescent reading.

contemporary battles in the Orient, Stratemeyer created another series called "Soldiers of Fortune," published from 1900 through 1906.

By this time Stratemeyer had turned to full-time writing and was being wooed by the major publishers of his day, notably Grossett & Dunlap and Cupples & Leon. For a time he turned to stories of school life and sports, the "Lakeport" series (1904–1912), the "Dave Porter" series (1905–1919), and the most successful of his early series, the "Rover Boys" (thirty books from 1899 to 1926), books so popular they sold in Canada, Australia, and England, were translated into German and Czechoslovakian, and somewhere between five or six million copies were sold across the world.

But Stratemeyer aspired to greater things. Between 1906 and 1910, he approached both his publishers suggesting they reduce the price of his books to fifty cents. The publishers may have been shocked to find an author willing to sell his books for less money, but, as they soon realized, mass production of fifty-centers increased their revenue and Stratemeyer's royalties almost geometrically.

But an even greater breakthrough came, at roughly the same time, when he evolved the idea of his Literary Syndicate, perhaps modeled loosely after Alexandre Dumas' fiction factory in which Dumas and sixty or more anonymous assistants produced 277 books. Stratemeyer was aware that he could create plots and series faster than he could possibly write them. Details of the Stratemeyer Syndicate are fuzzy, but the general outline is clear. Stratemeyer advertised for writers who needed money and sent them sketches of settings and characters along with a chapter-by-chapter outline of the plot. Writers had a few weeks to fill in the outlines, and when the copy arrived, Stratemeyer tightened the prose and checked for discrepancies with earlier volumes of the series. Then the manuscript was off to the printer and checks went out to the writers, from fifty to one hundred dollars depending upon the writer and the importance of the series.

Possibly we may never know all the Syndicate authors. Stratemeyer wrote the books appearing under his own name and presumably those under the pen names Arthur M. Winfield or Captain Ralph Bonehill. Leslie McFarlane wrote the first twenty-six Hardy Boys and three of the Dana Girls, Howard Garis (better known for his "Uncle Wiggily" stories) wrote the first thirty-five Tom Swift books, and Harriet Adams, Stratemeyer's daughter, may have written the Dana Girls and the Nancy Drew books, though that common assumption has been challenged.[39]

Stratemeyer books had common formulaic elements that held readers through book after book. The first lines promised adventure, and the rest of the chapters delivered thrills page after page. Andrew Svenson, Harriet Adams' partner in the Syndicate until his death, summarized both the technique and the power of the Stratemeyer Syndicate books:

The trick in writing children's books is to set up danger, mystery and excitement on page one. Force the kid to turn the page. I've written page one as many as 20 times. Then in the middle of each chapter there's a dramatic point of excitement and, at the chapter's end, a cliffhanger.[40]

Readers of books featuring Baseball Joe, Tom Swift, the Hardy Boys, or Nancy Drew will remember that heart-stopping, chapter-ending sentence, "Watch out, Joe!" (or Tom, or Frank, or Nancy). Heroes and heroines were trustworthy, resilient, strong, courageous, and likable. Perhaps most important, they proved the equal, if not the superior, of adults. It is no accident that Nancy Drew, the most successful of all the many Stratemeyer Syndicate protagonists, represents a catalog of characteristics her young readers most admired, the most significant being her love of mysteries, her independence, her popularity, and her ability to solve puzzles totally befuddling adult characters.

The use of hooks typified most series books. Early in the opening chapters in any but the initial volumes of a series, a hook to the previous volume or volumes would appear. In the last paragraph or two of the last chapter, another hook would be thrown out to attract readers to the next volume:

> As Helen relaxed from her recent adventures, she thought of herself, "How peaceful it will be to spend a few weeks at the farm just enjoying myself." Helen could not forsee that in only a few weeks she would find a mysterious bracelet and be caught up again in a mystery that would puzzle her and amaze her friends.

Finally, roughly halfway through the second chapter of many series books, action was suspended to summarize the preceding volumes, no greater problem in the second or third volume, but as series ran to many volumes, summaries became highly compressed and almost frantic.

Attacks on Stratemeyer were soon in coming. Librarian Caroline M. Hewins criticized both Stratemeyer's books and the journals that praised his output:

> Stratemeyer is an author who mixes "would" and "should," has the phraseology of a country newspaper, as when he calls a supper "an elegant affair" and a girl "a fashionable miss," and follows Oliver Optic closely in his plots and conversations.[41]

Most librarians supported Hewins, but the effect of librarians' attacks hardly affected Stratemeyer's sales. A far more stinging and effective attack came in 1913. Chief Boy Scout executive James E. West was disturbed by the deluge of what he thought inferior books and urged the Library Commission of the Boy Scouts of America to establish a carefully selected and recommended library to protect young men. Not long afterward, Chief Scout Librarian Franklin K. Mathiews urged Grosset & Dunlap to make better books available in fifty-cent editions—to compete with Stratemeyer—and on November 1, 1913, the first list appeared in a Boy Scout publication, "Safety First Week."

But that was not enough to satisfy Mathiews. In 1914, Mathiews wrote his most famous article under the sensational title, "Blowing Out the Boy's

Brains," a loud and vituperative attack, sometimes accurate but often unfair. Mathiews' most famous sentence was widely quoted: "I wish I could label each one of these books: 'Explosives! Guaranteed to Blow Your Boy's Brains Out.' "[42] The attack was mildly successful for the moment though how much harm it did to Stratemeyer's sales is open to question. Stratemeyer went on to sell more millions of books. When he died in 1930, his two daughters ran the Syndicate and daughter Harriet Adams continued it until her death in 1982. But the Syndicate persists, presumably forever.

Series covered everything young adults care about from adventure to scouting, the circus, Indians, mysteries, prehistoric times, science fiction, and every war in which we have been involved.

Series books were inevitably moral. Whatever parents, teachers, or librarians might have objected to about the unrealistic elements of the books or the poor literary quality, they would have agreed that the books were clearly on the side of good and right, if simplistically so. Series books—and many adult books as well—repeatedly underlined the same themes. Sports produced truly manly men. Foreigners were not to be trusted. School, education, and life should be taken seriously. The outdoor life was healthy, physically and psychologically. Good manners and courtesy were essential for moving ahead. Work in and of itself was a positive good and would advance one in life. Anyone could defeat adversity, any adversity, *if* that person had a good heart and soul. The good side (ours and God's) always won in war. Evil and good were clearly and easily distinguishable. And good always triumphed over evil (at least by the final chapter).

THE COMING OF THE "JUNIOR" OR "JUVENILE" NOVEL

Though countless books had been published and widely read by young adults for years, the term "junior" or "juvenile" was first applied to young adult literature during the early 1930s.

Rose Wilder Lane's novel *Let the Hurricane Roar* had been marketed by Longmans, Green, and Company as an adult novel. A full-page blurb on the front cover of the February 11, 1933, *Publishers Weekly* bannered THE BOOK THAT MAKES YOU PROUD TO BE AN AMERICAN! and quoted an unnamed reader, presumably an adult, saying, "Honestly, it makes me ashamed of cussing about hard times and taxes." The tenor of the ad and ones to follow suggest an adult novel likely to be popular with young adults as well. It had been the same with the earlier serialization of the novel in the *Saturday Evening Post,* and also with the many favorable reviews. But, sometime later in 1933, Longmans, Green began to push the novel as the first of their series of "Junior Books," as they termed them.

That the company wanted to attract young adults to Lane's novel is not difficult to understand. Lane wrote of a threatening frontier world she had known in a compelling manner certain to win readers and admirers among young adults. *Let the Hurricane Roar* tells of newly married David and Molly and their life on the hard Dakota plains. David works as a railroad hand for a time, Molly waits for her baby to arrive, and both strive for independence and the security of owning their own fifty-acre homestead. When they reach that dream and the baby is born, all looks well, but David overextends his credit, grasshoppers destroy the wheat crop, and no employment can be found nearby. David heads East to find work and later breaks his leg, leaving Molly isolated on the Dakota plains for a winter. Neighbors flee the area, and Molly battles loneliness, blizzards, and wolves before David returns. In summary, *Let the Hurricane Roar* sounds melodramatic, but it is not. In a short, quiet, and loving work, Lane made readers care about two likable young adults living a tough life in a hostile environment. The book's popularity is attested to by its twenty-six printings between 1933 and 1958 and a recent reissue in paperback under the title *Young Pioneers*.

The development of publishing house divisions to handle books lying in limbo between children's and adults' books grew after *Let the Hurricane Roar,* though authors of the time were sometimes unaware of the "junior" or "juvenile" branches as John R. Tunis was when he tried to market *Iron Duke* in 1934 and 1935. After sending the manuscript to Harcourt, Tunis was invited into the president's office. Mr. Harcourt clearly did not want to talk about the book, but instead took the startled author directly to the head of the Juvenile Department. He explained that Harcourt wanted to publish the book as a juvenile, much to Tunis' bewilderment and dismay, since he had no idea what a "juvenile" book was. Thirty years later he still had no respect for the term. "That odious term juvenile is the product of a merchandising age."[43]

PULPS AND COMICS AND STUFF

Hardcover books had four rivals for young adult readership during the first forty years of the twentieth century: pulp magazines, comic strips, comic books, and Big-Little Books. All four were disliked and attacked by many teachers, librarians, and parents, and all were widely read by young adults.

Pulp Magazines

Frank Munsey began his magazine *Argosy* in 1891 for adults, but it proved popular with young and old alike. By 1903, Street and Smith had begun publishing *Popular Magazine* aimed at rivaling *Argosy* but rapidly developed a stable of pulp magazines (so-called because of the high fiber content used in the cheap paper) for specialized interests—*Detective Story, Western Story, Love*

Story, Sports Story and *Sea Stories.* Other pulps followed: *Top-Notch, Flying Aces, Real Love, Battle Stories, Spy Stories, Ranch Romances,* and *Lariat,* producing popular heroes like Clarence E. Mulford's Hopalong Cassidy, Walter Gibson's The Shadow, Richard Wormser's Nick Carter, and Lester Dent's Doc Savage. Long after the death of pulp fiction, writer Jack Smalley explained the two basics of all pulp stories, "All you needed to sell a story to the pulps was a good title and an arresting lead paragraph."[44]

Comic Strips

When James Swinnerton began his "Little Bears" in 1892 in the *San Francisco Examiner,* he surely was unaware that he had created an art form soon to be emulated by other artists and read by people of all ages. A year later, bitter rivals Joseph Pulitzer of the *New York World* and William Randolph Hearst of the *New York Journal* were feuding, as usual. Pulitzer purchased a four-color rotary press to reprint artworks in his Sunday supplement. The rotary press did not work well, but the Sunday editor suggested it would work for comic art, so Pulitzer went to Richard F. Outcault who created a comic strip, "Down in Hogan's Alley." One character stood out in all the slum scenes, a strange-looking boy with an oriental face, a bald head, and only one tooth. Due to a freakish printing accident, the boy appeared in bright yellow and thus was born on February 16, 1896, the best remembered early comic strip, "The Yellow Kid." A year later, Rudolph Dirks began "The Katzenjammer Kids," and comic strips were here to stay.

By 1900, the comic strip formula was established—dialogue was contained in balloons, strips had sequential narratives, from one drawing to the next, but generally developed only one joke, and they presented a continuity from day to day or week to week that readers could depend on.

Winsor McCay's "Little Nemo in Slumberland," the most innovative of the early strips, pictured surrealistic but magnificently drawn dreams of the six-year-old boy. In 1911, the greatest of all comic strips began, George Herriman's "Krazy Kat." Herriman's work set an imposing and almost impossible to surpass standard of creativity, whimsy, and humor for other writers. Krazy was a strange, androgynous creature hated by Ignatz Mouse who threw brick after brick at Krazy only to be caught by Offisser B. Pupp.

George McManus' "Bringing Up Father" in 1913 brought Maggie and Jiggs to the nation as the first domestic comic strip. Later popular comic strips were Frank King's "Gasoline Alley" (1919)—the first comic strip to advance characters chronologically and still one of the great comic strips—Harold Gray's "Little Orphan Annie" (1924), Chester Gould's "Dick Tracy" (1931), Alex Raymond's magnificently drawn "Flash Gordon" (1934), Bill Holman's wacky "Smokey Stover" (1935), Jerry Siegel and Joe Shuster's "Superman" (1938), and Walt Kelly's loving contribution to American folklore and culture, "Pogo" (1949).

Comic Books

Comic books began as an offshoot of comic strips. A collection of "The Yellow Kid" strips was published in March 1897, and reprints of other comic strips were offered at least through the early 1920s. In 1922, a reprint magazine, *Comic Monthly,* began, each month given to reprints of a different comic strip, and in 1929, George Delacorte published thirteen issues of *The Funnies,* the first four-color comic books.

In 1933, 10,000 copies of *Funnies on Parade* were published by Eastern Color Printing Company in New York and distributed as a premium by Procter & Gamble. Later that same year, M. C. Gaines convinced Eastern that other companies could use the gimmick for premiums, and Eastern printed *Famous Funnies: A Carnival of Comics,* reprints of Sunday color comics, in quantities of more than 100,000. Sure of success, Gaines asked Eastern to print 35,000 copies of *Famous Funnies, Series 1,* a sixty-four page book that sold for ten cents in chain stores.

National Periodical Publications' *New Fun* (after the first issue, entitled *More Fun*) in 1935 was the first comic book to publish original material, not merely reprints. Later that year Walt Disney began his *Mickey Mouse Magazine* (in 1940 to become *Walt Disney's Comics and Stories*), a combination of reprinted and original material.

Detective Comics in 1937 was the first themed nonreprint comic book. Published by National Periodical Publications, the company soon became known in the trade as DC Comics. DC's *Action Comics* opened in June 1938 with a character soon to become part of American mythology, "Superman," who began as one of several strips but was soon given his own separate publication. Later comic heroes included Batman, who appeared first in DC's *Detective Comics #27* in 1939. The Sub-Mariner and the Human Torch debuted in Marvel Comics that same year, Captain Marvel started in Fawcett's *Whiz Comics* in 1940, and Wonder Woman first appeared in DC's *All-Star Comics #8* a year later.

By the close of 1941, over 160 comic book titles were distributed monthly, selling more than twelve million copies. A year later *Crime Does Not Pay* brought realistic crime stories to readers. In 1950 William M. Gaines, son of M. C. Gaines, began realistic crime horror comics, *Crypt of Terror, The Vault of Horror, Weird Science,* and *Two-Fisted Tales.*

The suspicion of parents, teachers, librarians, and other critics that comic books had a potentially evil influence on the young led to formation of a U.S. Senate Subcommittee, chaired by Estes Kefauver, to investigate detrimental effects of comic books. It also led to an investigation by psychologist Frederic Wertham resulting in a bitter attack on crime, horror, and hero comics.[45]

After a Senate Subcommittee Report and the furor surrounding Wertham's impassioned book, publishers, fearful of pressures to come, staved off some of the fury by creating a Comics Code Authority banning profanity, nudity, excessive violence and horror, portrayal of crime as attractive, and disrespect for established authority. The Code also recommended less slang and better grammar in comics. Presumably, critics, teachers, librarians, and parents were pacified. Few young people probably noticed anything very different in the comics, and things soon were back to normal.

Big-Little Books

Less significant than pulps, comic strips, or comic books, Big-Little Books still were widely read (and today bring a nice sum for sound copies). Published originally by Whitman in cardboard covers, they normally had one page of text facing a full-page illustration. Sizes varied from approximately three inches by three inches to those slightly larger. Selling for ten cents and usually featuring a new adventure of a popular comic strip or movie hero, they appealed both to those who liked comic books and those presumably a little more literate. The first Big-Little Book, *The Adventures of Dick Tracy,* was printed in 1932, and hundreds followed based on comic strips such as "Flash Gordon," "Skippy," "Terry and the Pirates," "Moon Mullins," or "Apple Mary"; on movies, movie characters or actors such as "Our Gang," "Donald Duck," Gene Autry, Jackie Cooper, or Johnny Mack Brown; and other sources such as *The Three Musketeers, Tom Swift and His Magnetic Silencer,* or Edgar Bergen and Charlie McCarthy.

THE LITTLE BLUE BOOKS

All too little has been written about the work of Emanuel Haldeman-Julius and his incredible and influential library of Little Blue Books. Basing his operation in Girard, Kansas, Haldeman-Julius sold roughly five hundred million copies from his library of about two thousand titles, many purchased by young adults with—or without—parental permission. Although he lived in the heart of the Bible belt and was always controversial, he gained the respect of many midwesterners earnestly—sometimes desperately—seeking education. A rationalist and an atheist, he had an ingrained belief in the educational perfectibility of humanity if people had inexpensive good books readily available. Haldeman-Julius began by publishing small, paperbound books at twenty-five cents each. He soon discovered enough interested readers to drop the price to fifteen cents, then ten cents, and finally five cents, selling them in bulk by mail. Two-page ads in newspapers and magazines such as *Saturday Evening Post, Popular Mechanics, Ladies Home Journal,* and the *New York Times Book Review* brought him first orders and repeat business. The blue-covered books dealt with an incredible variety of subjects. The scope of these five-cent books was without parallel in American publishing. Using that amazing nickel, one could purchase titles as different as Poe's *The Fall of the House of Usher,*

Darrow's *Debate on Capital Punishment, The Diary of Samuel Pepys,* Doyle's *Sherlock Holmes Problem Stories,* Verne's *Five Weeks in a Balloon, Nature Poems of Wordsworth, An Encyclopedia of Sex, Famous $12,000 Prize-Winning Tongue-Twisters,* and Haldeman-Julius' own *The Art of Reading.* He even published Will Durant's *The Story of Philosophy* (1926) in a dozen or so booklets.

A FEW BOOKS YOUNG ADULTS LIKED

Books popular with young adults fall into six reasonably discrete categories, each a mixture of good (or adequate) and bad (or dismal) books. Some deserve reading today; others deserve the interment already decently provided.

And a Little Child Shall Lead Them (Though God Knows Where)

Among the most popular books prior to World War I were those featuring a small child, usually a girl, who significantly changed people around her. At their best, they showed an intriguing youngster humanizing sterile or cold people. At their worst (and they often were) they featured a rapturously happy and miraculously even-dispositioned child who infected an entire household— perhaps a community—with her messianic drive to improve the world through cheer and gladness.

The type began promisingly with Kate Douglas Wiggin's *Rebecca of Sunnybrook Farm* (1904). Nothing Wiggin wrote surpassed Rebecca, which sold more than a million and a quarter copies between 1904 and 1975. Living in a small town during the 1870s, the optimistic heroine is handed over to two maiden aunts while her parents cope with a large family. She is educated despite her imperfections, high spirits, and rebelliousness, and at the close of the book seems cheerfully on her way upward to a better life. Wiggin's book preaches acceptance of the status quo, not surprising for the time, but the heroine gets herself into believable scrapes, the book does not overly sentimentalize either itself or the world, and humor is more common than sadness or preaching. The book deserved its success, just as it deserves reading today.

Anne of Green Gables (1908) by Lucy Maud Montgomery was a worthy successor. As in Wiggin's book, Anne travels to an alien society. Here, a childless couple who wants to adopt a boy gets Anne by mistake. Anne changes the couple for the better, but they also change her, and Anne's delightfully developed character goes far to remedy any defects in the book. Docile as she tries to be (and occasionally succeeds), she is alive, charming, and impulsive. When the book ends, Anne is believably ready to take on responsibilities.

Wiggin and Montgomery generally managed to skirt the sea of sentimentalism, that fatal syrupy deep beloved by bad writers. Occasionally, Rebecca and Anne waded out dangerously far, but their common sense, their impulsiveness, their love of laughter, and their ability to laugh at themselves saved them and brought them back to shore. After them came the disaster: authors and characters so enamored of humanity, so convinced that all people were redeemable, so stickily and uncomplainingly sweet and good that they drowned in goodness while many readers gagged.

Jean Webster's *Daddy-Long-Legs* (1912) was sticky enough in its picture of a college girl who falls in love with her benefactor. Gene Stratton Porter was worse in her *Freckles* (1904), *A Girl of the Limberlost* (1909), *Laddie* (1913), and *Michael O'Halloran* (1915) where sentiment is all and coincidence and a good heart solve every problem.

But it was Eleanor Porter who wrote the genre's magnum opus and destroyed it with *Pollyanna* (1913). *Pollyanna* is usually remembered as a children's book, but it began as a popular adult novel, eighth among best-sellers in 1913 and second in 1914. So sickeningly sweet is the heroine that countless adults and young people could rightfully credit her with their diabetes. Orphaned Pollyanna comes to the house of rich Aunt Polly, who scorns her. Lovely but wholesome Pollyanna plays her "Glad Game," befuddling Nancy, the maid. Nancy asks Pollyanna to explain the game:

> "Why, it's a game. Father taught it to me, and it's lovely," rejoined Pollyanna. "We've played it always, ever since I was a little, little girl. I told the Ladies' Aid, and they played it—some of them."
>
> "What is it? I ain't much on games, though."
>
> Pollyanna laughed again, but she sighed, too: and in the gathering twilight her face looked thin and wistful.
>
> "Why, we began it on some crutches that came in a missionary barrel."
>
> *"Crutches!"*
>
> "Yes. You see I'd wanted a doll, and father had written them so; but when the barrel came the lady wrote that there hadn't any dolls come in, but the little crutches had. So she sent 'em along as they might come in handy for some child, sometime. And that's when we began it."
>
> "Well, I must say I can't see any game about that," declared Nancy, almost irritably.
>
> "Oh, yes; the game was to find something about everything to be glad about—no matter what 'twas," rejoined Pollyanna, earnestly, "And we began right then—on the crutches."
>
> "Well, goodness me! I can't see anythin' ter be glad about—gettin' a pair of crutches when you wanted a doll!"
>
> Pollyanna clapped her hands.
>
> "There is—there is," she crowed. "But I couldn't see it either, Nancy, at first," she added, with quick honesty. "Father had to tell it to me."
>
> "Well, then, suppose *you* tell *me*," almost snapped Nancy.
>
> "Goosey! Why, just be glad because you *don't—need—'em!*" exulted Pollyanna, triumphantly. "You see it's just as easy—when you know how!"

To the loathing of sensible people, the "Glad Game" raged across the country. But Pollyanna does more than laugh at personal misfortunes. She reunites once-happy and now miserable lovers and friends, saves Aunt Polly from a loveless life, eliminates gloom for miles around, rescues the miserable, and gladdens everybody, just everybody.

Hearth, Home, and Responsibility (with Bits of Sin)

Studies of motherhood and true love were popular with young adults and adults. At times, little hints (and sometimes broad brushstrokes) of sin, redeemed or otherwise, made the stories more palatable.

Alice Hegan Rice could easily have created an ocean of treacle in *Mrs. Wiggs of the Cabbage Patch* (1901), but instead she portrayed an optimistic family led by an indomitable mother in the midst of a Louisville slum without making either seem unbelievable. Her publisher doubted the book would sell and printed only 2,000 copies for the first edition. Once they were rapidly picked up, he admitted his guess was wrong and began turning out 40,000 copies a month. The book was a best-seller and remains in print today.

Several writers were unable to keep large doses of sentimentalism and goodness from their books, though no rival for sweetness arose to challenge Gene Stratton Porter or Eleanor Porter. John Fox, Jr., wrote of his beloved Cumberland Mountains and the coming of civilization and machines in *The Little Shepherd of Kingdom Come* (1903) and *The Trail of the Lonesome Pine* (1908). Harold Bell Wright moved to the Ozarks in search of better health and found interesting people, God, and a deep belief in muscular Christianity. He began preaching in a schoolhouse and spent the next twelve years moving from pastorate to pastorate. *The Shepherd of the Hills* (1907) and *The Calling of Dan Matthews* (1909) made money by attacking the hypocrisy of formalized religion, especially in big cities. By then Wright had left the pulpit for full-time writing, and later books were consistent best-sellers endorsed by ministers and attacked by literary critics. The first printing of *The Winning of Barbara Worth* (1911) ran to 175,000 copies and the printing of *Their Yesterdays* (1912) was even larger. *When a Man's a Man* (1916) and *The Re-creation of Brian Keith* (1919) are typically Wright, strong on theme and sermonistic to a fault. Brief bits of plot and stereotyped characters are manipulated to ensure that readers understand Wright's point about home and God and church.

If the sanctity of the home and the love of God sold well, sin was equally attractive. In 1907, Elinor Glynn published *Three Weeks,* portraying the queen of a mythical European country who forgets her husband and duties for a glorious three weeks' sex romp with a handsome Englishman. Readers realized that it was nothing more than romanticized pornography, the love scenes on the tigerskin rug justified their feelings, the sales and libidos rose. What the book lacked in psychological probing, it compensated by pages of physical probing. Just as sin-laden and equally popular was *The Sheik* (1921) by Edith Maude Hull. The abduction of self-centered Diana Mayo by the sensual Sheik and his rough treatment of her excited millions. The film version starring

Rudolph Valentino was superior to the book. For many readers, young and old, these books broke conventions long overdue for destruction, and they were widely if covertly read.

Moving Westward

The closing of the West heightened interest in an exciting, almost magical, era. A few writers, aiming specifically at young adults, knew the West so well that they became touchstones for authenticity in other writers. George Bird Grinnell wrote *Pawnee Hero Stories and Folk Tales* (1889) and *By Cheyenne Campfires* (1926) and established an honest and generally unsentimentalized portrait of Indian life. Both he and Charles A. Eastman often appeared on reading interest studies as boys' favorites. Eastman's autobiography, *Indian Boyhood* (1902), was justifiably praised for its sense of time and place. Joseph Altsheler wrote more conventional adventure tales of the West, often lapsing into melodrama, but he was for some time a favorite for *The Last of the Chiefs* (1909) and *The Horsemen of the Plains* (1910).

Far more sentimental but much more popular was Will James' *Smoky, The Cowhorse* (1926), originally published as an adult novel, soon read by thousands of young adults, and twice filmed to appreciative audiences. The story of a colt befriended by a cowboy, the horse's kidnapping and mistreatment, and the eventual reuniting of horse and man is still a tearjerker of the highest order.

The best written and most sensitive western of the time for young people was Laura Adams Armer's *Waterless Mountain* (1931). Unfortunately, the slow-moving, almost nonexistent plot about a young Navajo boy training to become a Medicine Priest was too mystical and mythical for young readers, and enthusiastic librarians and teachers had little success getting teenagers to read the novel.

The first great writer to focus on the West and its mystique of violence and danger mixed with open spaces and freedom was Owen Wister, whose *The Virginian: A Horseman of the Plains* (1902) provided a model of colloquial speech and romantic and melodramatic adventure for novels to follow. "When you call me that, *smile!*" was endlessly quoted by boys for years thereafter. Andy Adams was a far more trustworthy guide to the West in *The Log of a Cowboy: A Narrative of the Old Trail Days* (1903), but the public was clearly more interested in thrills and spills than it was in accuracy. Zane Grey fulfilled whatever need the public had with his incredibly romantic pictures of life in the older days of the West in *The Spirit of the Border* (1906), and *The Wanderer of the Wasteland* (1923). The best of his books—certainly the most-remembered and probably the epitome of the overly romanticized western—was *Riders of the Purple Sage* (1912) filled with classic elements: the mysterious hero, the innocent heroine, evil villains, and the open land. Criticized as Grey has been by librarians and teachers—who seem in general to have read little or nothing of his work—he was and is read, and his books stay in print. Anyone who wishes to know what the western dream was must read Grey.

Rah Rah for the School and Fair Play

With more young adults attending school and with the steadily rising popularity of sports—especially college football and professional baseball—more school-sports stories appeared. For many teachers and professors then and now, academic excellence and sports are mutually exclusive terms. Some people worried that football was too rough; many that it would distract from studies. We associate the term "football fever" with modern times, but it was used near the turn of the century when one educator fretted about sports:

> I noticed two years ago, when the football fever was raging, that it was generally believed that a college's success in football drew students to it, and that some schools thought it necessary to make football a leading feature in their "fit for college."[46]

William Gilbert Patten was not the first writer of sports novels, but he was the first to introduce a regular, almost mythic, sports character soon recognized throughout America—Frank Merriwell. In 1895, Ormond Smith (of Street and Smith) urged Patten, one of his stable of dime novelists, to write a school and sports series with lots of adventure. Under the pen name of Burt L. Standish, Patten created heroic Frank Merriwell and in two weeks wrote a story that appeared as "Frank Makes a Foe" in *Tip Top Weekly* in 1896. Circulation boomed and Patten and Frank Merriwell were hits. Several hundred stories about Frank followed, and Patten later combined a number of them into hardback books. A natural leader, incredible boxer, expert duelist, exemplary baseball player, and all-round great guy, Frank is decent, heroic, modest, and everything a mother could wish for.

Although they did not create heroes as well known as Frank Merriwell, three better writers stand out for their more realistic sports books.

Owen Johnson wrote for adults, but *The Varmint* (1910) and *The Tennessee Shad* (1911), about sports and pranks at Lawrenceville School, were widely read by boys. *Stover at Yale* (1911) is about sports, but more significant to Johnson was his attack on Yale's problems—snobbery, social clubs, fraternities, senior societies, and anti-intellectualism.

Ralph Henry Barbour wrote an incredible number of fine books, beginning with *The Half-Back* (1899), presenting believable boys in believable situations at school playing the sports of different seasons. Dated as his books are by rule changes, they are still readable. Rarest of all for the time, Barbour presented few villains. His books became repetitious over the years as he used the same formula—a boy attending school and learning who and what he might become through sports—but the formula was Barbour's invention. His theme was stated in the dedication to *The Half-Back:* "To Every American Boy Who Loves Honest, Manly Sports." He sincerely believed that sports presented opportunities and challenges for every boy, a belief predicated on three acts of faith: schools must have school spirit, school spirit comes from sports, and sports must be amateur and free of any taint of commercialism or professionalism.

Barbour's best book is *The Crimson Sweater* (1907), first of a four-volume "Ferry Hill" series. While the plot is not unlike his other books, there is more humor and it introduces his most delightful girl, Harry (or Harriet), sprightly and alive and fun and highly competitive with boys.

William Heyliger followed in the same pattern with *Bartley: Freshman Pitcher* (1911). But Barbour's concerns were sports and school, whereas Heyliger wrote more varied books: school and sports stories in his "St. Mary's" series, "Fairview High" series, and "Lansing" series; and ground-breaking vocational stories in *High Benton* (1919) and *High Benton, Worker* (1921).

School stories for girls never had a similar number of readers, but some had loyal readers, and a few deserve reading even today. Laura Elizabeth Richards was best known for *Peggy* (1899) in which a poor girl goes to school and becomes a hero in basketball. Marjorie Hill Allee deserved praise for *Jane's Island* (1931) with its portrait of the biological laboratories and scientists at Woods Hole and its sense of place and its delight in scientific exploration. Even better was *The Great Tradition* (1937), set at the University of Chicago, which successfully mixed romances, college life, and the spirit of scientific adventure.

Best of them all was Mabel Louise Robinson's *Bright Island* (1937) for spunky Thankful Curtis who was raised on a small island off the coast of Maine and later attends school on the mainland. *Bright Island* maintains a charm and warmth rare among books and deserves readers today.

Strange Deeds and Far Lands

Young adults, then and now, read tales of adventures as avidly as adults. No other literary genre has been so persistently successful with readers.

The public's fancy near the turn of the century was taken by a craze for adventure-romance set in imaginary countries: Anthony Hope, pen name of Anthony Hope Hawkins, created the passion for never-never lands in *The Prisoner of Zenda* (1894) loosely modeled after Robert Louis Stevenson's *Prince Otto* (1885). Englishman Rudolph Rassendyl, hunting in Rurtania at a crucial time, learns that he closely resembles King Rupert. Rassendyl agrees to foil the machinations of evil plotters, falls in love with the lovely Princess Flavia, but does his duty and nobly leaves the country alone having done his all. Twenty-six printings within the year established his popularity with Americans.

American author George McCutcheon pushed the tale of the mythical kingdom to its limits. In *Graustark: The Story of a Love Behind a Throne* (1901) romance is all, adventures are thrilling beyond real life, and Americans cannot be defeated by anyone. Twenty-nine-year-old American Grenfell Lorry falls in love with lovely Miss Guggenslocker, despite her name. He finds she is, in reality, Princess Yetive of Graustark, and learns that plots against her are brewing. Graustark's debt must be paid by her marriage to the prince of a neighboring country. Lorry foils plots, battles enemies, and wins the princess. Told he cannot marry Yetive since he is only a commoner, he says:

Bright Island is a charming and warm story which deserves readers even today.

I am not a prince, as you are saying over and over again to yourself. Every born American may become the ruler of the greatest nation in the world—the United States. His home is his kingdom; his wife, his mothers, his sisters are his queens and his princesses; his fellow citizens are his admiring subjects if he is wise and good. In my land you will find the poor man climbing to the highest pinnacle, side by side with the rich man. . . . We recognize little as impossible. Until death destroys this power to love and to hope I must say to you that I shall not consider the Princess Yetive beyond my reach.

As the day of adventure fantasy waned, other authors turned to more conventional themes of adventure, notably survival against great odds. John Buchan produced his most enduring work in *The Thirty-Nine Steps* (1915), the tale of an innocent, naive, and not especially bright young man caught in a world of spying and intrigue. Alfred Hitchcock's 1935 film (and two later ones by other directors) helped to maintain the popularity of a book solidly entrenched as a classic of adventure literature.

Survival at sea against nature and fellow man was the theme of Charles Nordhoff and James Norman Hall in several books, notably the Mutiny trilogy about Captain William Bligh, Fletcher Christian, the mutineers, and those loyal to their king in *Mutiny on the Bounty* (1932), *Men Against the Sea* (1934), and *Pitcairn's Island* (1934).

Rarest of all adventure writers is one who creates myth as Edgar Rice Burroughs did in *Tarzan of the Apes* (1914). Tarzan was rarely treated with any courtesy by teachers or librarians, but the ape-man attracted readers in vast numbers. *Tarzan* sold more than thirty-five million copies in the 1920s and 1930s. The sequels added more sales, and the many movies starring several different Tarzans made the character and its author household names.

Reality Can Sell

Although other types of books usually outsold realistic portrayals of the state of humanity, some books critical of society sold well. Margaret Deland broke new ground in her appraisal of a young minister seeking truth and struggling against his Calvinist background in *John Ward, Preacher* (1888). Slightly more sentimental, but even more popular, was her study of a woman living in sin yet seeking salvation for a young orphan in *The Awakening of Helena Richie* (1906).

Booth Tarkington, best known to young adults for *Penrod* (1914) and the condescending *Seventeen* (1902), produced a number of best-selling portraits of humanity, warts and all. His most enduring (and oddly endearing) books of middle-America have proved to be *The Magnificent Ambersons* (1918), a picture of the fall of the young man, and *Alice Adams* (1921), the tale of a dangerous dreamer.

Later iconoclastic writers proved equally popular with young adults. Sinclair Lewis destroyed the myth of the purity of small towns in *Main Street* (1921), the myths about small-town businessmen in *Babbitt* (1922), and the myths about small-minded evangelists in *Elmer Gantry* (1927), but he did not destroy his readers' faith in the process. He did challenge readers to think and convince them that an unexamined idea or belief was seductive and potentially dangerous.

What Lewis began, John Steinbeck carried forward. Lewis attacked people and ideas while Steinbeck attacked institutions and society; Lewis despised people, but Steinbeck loved his fellows. Steinbeck may be, as it has been claimed, less a writer than a social propagandist, but given the social conditions of the 1930s, Steinbeck brought—and continues to bring—a needed voice to social issues. The number of his books that remain popular because of parallel social conditions today (it is difficult for young adults to read Steinbeck purely as a critical social historian) is impressive. *In Dubious Battle* (1936), surely his best book, and *The Red Pony* (1937) are sympathetic depictions of loneliness and the importance of family loyalty just as much as they are studies of social ills, past and present.

Few writers of the time turned to racial issues. Du Bose Heyward's *Porgy* (1925) is probably better known in the George Gershwin opera, *Porgy and Bess,* but both that book and *Mamba's Daughters* (1929) portrayed blacks pushed about by whites and poverty, yet able to keep their dignity. Joseph Gollomb, unfortunately largely forgotten today, wrote four books about a large racially troubled city high school, *That Year at Lincoln High* (1918), *Working Through at Lincoln High* (1923), *Up at City High* (1945), and *Tiger at City High* (1946).

Elizabeth Foreman Lewis deserves to be remembered for her honest and compassionate portraits of life in China, which she knew at first hand as a missionary. She won the Newbery Award for her 1932 *Young Fu of the Upper Yangtze* and its picture of an ambitious young apprentice to a coppersmith, but readers who care about integrity and good writing will find almost equal rewards in *Ho-Ming: Girl of New China* (1934) and *To Beat a Tiger* (1956).

Young adult literature and books read by young adults underwent many changes from 1900 to 1940. Teachers and librarians took more interest in assessing types and titles of books read by young adults. The Stratemeyer Syndicate turned the creation of series stories from a small-scale operation into a major industry. If teachers and librarians heartily disapproved of Stratemeyer's series and other series, young adults read them avidly, though by 1940 most series books were dead except for the lively Hardy Boys and the even healthier Nancy Drew. Publishers added "Junior" or "Juvenile" divisions. Fiction of the time moved slowly and sometimes clumsily from the innocence of *Pollyanna* and *Graustark* to serious and nonromanticized books. Life seemed relatively sure, easy, simple, and safe in 1900; the First World War and the Depression dispelled that myth. When the Depression of the 1930s was ending, World War II and a very different world were just over the horizon, and a different kind of literature was soon to appear for young adults.

NOTES

[1] M. P. True, "What My Pupils Read," *Education* 14 (October 1893): 99–102.

[2] Clara Vostrovsky, "A Study of Children's Reading Tastes," *Pedagogical Seminary* 6 (December 1899): 523–35.

[3] *Publishers Weekly* 107 (February 21, 1925): 619–22.

[4] Alfred M. Hitchcock, "The Relation of the Picture Play to Literature," *English Journal* 4 (May 1915): 296.

[5] Carleton Washburne and Mabel Vogel, *Winnetka Graded Book List* (Chicago: American Library Association, 1926), p. 5.

[6] Carleton Washburne and Mabel Vogel, "Supplement to the Winnetka Graded Book List," *Elementary English Review* 4 (February 1927): 47–52; and 4 (March 1927): 66–73.

[7] William Lyon Phelps, "The Virtues of the Second-Rate," *English Journal* 16 (January 1927): 13–14.

[8] Franklin T. Baker, *A Bibliography of Children's Reading* (New York: Teachers College, Columbia University, 1908), pp. 6–7.

[9] Clara Whitehill Hunt, "Good and Bad Taste in Girls' Reading," *Ladies' Home Journal* 27 (April 1910): 52.

[10] Julia Carter, "Let's Talk about Boys and Books," *Wilson Bulletin for Librarians* 9 (April 1935): 418.

[11] Alice M. Jordan, "A Gallery of Girls," *Horn Book Magazine* 13 (September 1937): 276.

[12] Vostrovsky, p. 535.

[13] G. Stanley Hall, "Children's Reading: As a Factor in Their Education," *Library Journal* 33 (April 1908): 124–25.

[14] Orrin C. Cocker, "Motion Pictures and Reading Habits," *Library Journal* 43 (February 1918): 68.

[15] Marilla Waite Freeman, "Tying Up with the Movies: Why? When? How?" *Library Journal* 54 (June 15, 1929): 519–24.

[16] Louise Dinwiddie, "Best Sellers and Modern Youth," *Library Journal* 65 (November 15, 1940): 958–59.

[17] W. H. Ray et al., "English in the High School," *Academy* 4 (May 1889): 187.

[18] William E. Mead, "A Ten Years' Course in Literature," *Academy* 2 (March 1887): 55.

[19] *Report of the Committee of Ten on Secondary School Studies* (New York: American, 1894). For details about conditions leading to the Committee of Ten's formation, the committee's deliberations, and its influence, see two excellent studies, Edward A. Krug, *The Shaping of the American High School* (New York: Harper & Row, 1964) and Theodore R. Sizer, *Secondary Schools at the Turn of the Century* (New Haven: Yale University Press, 1964).

[20] Samuel Thurber, "Report of English Conference" in *Report of the Committee of Ten on Secondary School Studies* (New York: Appleton, 1894), p. 86. Thurber was both a brilliant teacher and writer whose comments, especially in *School Review* and *Academy,* deserve attention today.

[21] Samuel Thurber, "Voluntary Reading in the Classical High School from the Pupil's Point of View," *School Review* 13 (February 1905): 170.

[22] J. M. Coulter, "What the University Expects of the Secondary School," *School Review* 17 (February 1909): 73.

[23] Wilbur W. Hatfield, "Modern Literature for High School Use," *English Journal* 1 (January 1912): 52.

[24] *Reorganization of English in Secondary Schools,* Department of the Interior, Bureau of Education, Bulletin 1917, No. 2 (Washington: Government Printing Office, 1917), p. 63.

[25] Dora V. Smith, *Instruction in English,* Bulletin, 1932, no. 17. National Survey of Secondary Education Monograph No. 20 (Washington: Government Printing Office, 1933).

[26] Nancy Gillmore Coryell, *An Evaluation of Extensive and Intensive Teaching of Literature: A Year's Experiment in the Eleventh Grade,*

Teachers College, Columbia University, Contributions to Education, No. 275 (New York: Teachers College, Columbia University, 1927).

[27]Lou LaBrant, *An Evaluation of the Free Reading Program in Grades Ten, Eleven, and Twelve for the Class of 1935.* The Ohio State University School, Contributions to Education No. 2 (Columbus: Ohio State University, 1936). See also Lou LaBrant, "The Content of a Free Reading Program," *Educational Research Bulletin* 16 (February 17, 1937): 29–34.

[28]Dora V. Smith, "Extensive Reading in Junior High School: A Survey of Teacher Preparation," *English Journal* 19 (June 1930): 449–62.

[29]Dora V. Smith, "American Youth and English," *English Journal* 26 (February 1937): 111.

[30]Manuel D. Lopez, "Children's Libraries: Nineteenth Century American Origins," *Journal of Library History* 11 (October 1976): 317.

[31]Graham P. Hawks, "A Nineteenth-Century School Library: Early Years in Milwaukee," *Journal of Library History* 12 (Fall 1977): 361.

[32]S. Swett Green, "Libraries and School," *Library Journal* 16 (December 1891): 22. Other representative articles concerned with the relationship include Mellen Chamberlain, "Public Libraries and Public School," *Library Journal* 5 (November–December 1880): 299–302; W. E. Foster, "The School and the Library: Their Mutual Relations," *Library Journal* 4 (September–October 1879): 319–41; and Mrs. J. H. Resor, "The Boy and the Book, or The Public Library a Necessity," *Public Libraries* 2 (June 1897): 282–85.

[33]"The Report of the Committee on Relations of Public Libraries to Public Schools," *NEA Journal of Proceedings and Addresses of the 38th Annual Meeting* (Chicago: The University of Chicago Press, 1899), p. 455.

[34]Mary E. Hall, "The Possibilities of the High School Library," *ALA Bulletin* 6 (July 1912): 261–63.

[35]"A Standard High-School Library Organization for Accredited Secondary Schools of Different Sizes," *Educational Administration and Supervision* 3 (June 1917): 317–38.

[36]Elmer D. Johnson, *History of Libraries in the Western World,* 2nd ed. (Metuchen, New Jersey: Scarecrow Press, 1970), p. 389.

[37]*Library Journal* 59 (January 1, 1934): 9–15.

[38]Louis Shores, "The Public School Library," *Educational Forum* 4 (May 1940): 373.

[39]Geoffrey S. Lapin in "Carolyn Keene, Pseud.," *Yellowback Library* 3 (July/August 1983): 3–5. This article argues that Mildred Wirt wrote numbers 1–7, 11–25, and 30 of the Nancy Drew series while Walter Karig (best known for his 1947 satire *Zotz*) wrote numbers 8–10.

[40]Quoted by Ed Zuckerman, "The Great Hardy Boys' Whodunit," *Rolling Stone,* September 9, 1976, p. 39.

[41]Caroline M. Hewins, "Book Reviews, Book Lists, and Articles on Children's Reading: Are They of Practical Value to the Children's Librarians?" *Library Journal* 26 (August 1901): 58. Attacks on series books, especially Stratemeyer's books, persisted thereafter in library literature. Mary E. S. Root prepared a list of series books not to be circulated by public librarians, "Not to Be Circulated," *Wilson Bulletin for Librarians* 3 (January 1929): 446, including books by Alger, Finley, Castlemon, Ellis, Optic, and others, the others being heavily Stratemeyer. Two months later, Ernest F. Ayers responded, "Not to Be Circulated?" *Wilson Bulletin for Librarians* 3 (March 1929): 528–29, objecting to the cavalier treatment accorded old favorites and sarcastically adding, "Why worry about censorship so long as we have librarians?" Attacks continue today. Some librarians and English teachers to the contrary, the Syndicate clearly is winning, and students seem to be pleased.

[42]Franklin K. Mathiews, "Blowing Out the Boy's Brains," *Outlook* 108 (November 18, 1914): 653.

[43]John Tunis, "What Is a Juvenile Book?" *Horn Book Magazine* 44 (June 1968): 307.

[44]Jack Smalley, "Amazing Confessions of a Pulpeteer," *Westways* (June 1974): 20.

[45]Frederic Wertham, *Seduction of the Innocent* (New York: Holt, Rinehart and Winston, 1954).

[46]E. L. Godkin, "The Illiteracy of American Boys," *Educational Review* 13 (January 1897): 6.

TITLES MENTIONED IN CHAPTER FOURTEEN

Adams, Andy. *The Log of a Cowboy: A Narrative of the Old Trail Days.* 1903.

Allee, Marjorie Hill. *The Great Tradition.* 1937.

_____ . *Jane's Island.* 1931.

Altsheler, Joseph. *The Horsemen of the Plains.* 1910.

_____ . *The Last of the Chiefs.* 1909.

Appleton, Victor (Stratemeyer Syndicate pseudonym). Tom Swift series 1910–1935.

Armer, Laura Adams. *Waterless Mountain.* 1931.

Barbour, Ralph Henry. *The Crimson Sweater.* 1906.

_____ . *The Half-Back.* 1899.

Buchan, John. *The Thirty-Nine Steps.* 1915.

Burroughs, Edgar Rice. *Tarzan of the Apes.* 1914.

Burton, Charles Pierce. Boys of Bob's Hill series. 1905–1939.

Chadwick, Lester (Stratemeyer Syndicate pseudonym). Baseball Joe series. 1912–1928.

Deland, Margaret. *The Awakening of Helena Richie.* 1906.

_____ . *John Ward, Preacher.* 1888.

Dixon, Franklin W. (Stratemeyer Syndicate pseudonym). The Hardy Boys series. 1927–.

Doyle, Arthur Conan. *The Adventures of Sherlock Holmes.* 1891.

_____ . *The Hound of the Baskervilles.* 1902.

Durant, Will. *The Story of Philosophy.* 1926.

Eastman, Charles A. *Indian Boyhood.* 1902.

Finley, Martha Farquharson. Elsie Dinsmore series. 1867–1905.

Fitzhugh, Percy Kees. Roy Blakely series. 1920–1931.

Fox, John. *The Calling of Dan Matthews.* 1909.

_____ . *The Little Shepherd of Kingdom Come.* 1903.

_____ . *The Trail of the Lonesome Pine.* 1908.

Frey, Hildegarde G. Campfire Girl series. 1916–1920.

Glynn, Elinor. *Three Weeks.* 1907.

Gollomb, Joseph. *That Year at Lincoln High.* 1918.

_____ . *Tiger at City High.* 1946.

_____ . *Up at City High.* 1945.

_____ . *Working Through at Lincoln High.* 1923.

Grey, Zane. *Riders of the Purple Sage.* 1912.

_____ . *The Spirit of the Border.* 1906.

_____ . *The Wanderer of the Wasteland.* 1923.

Grinnell, George Bird. *By Cheyenne Campfires.* 1926.

_____ . *Pawnee Hero Stories and Folk Tales.* 1889.

Heyliger, William. *Bartley: Freshman Pitcher.* 1911.

_____ . Fairview High School Series. 1916–1918.

_____ . *High Benton.* 1919.

_____ . *High Benton, Worker.* 1921.

_____ . Lansing series. 1912–1927.

_____ . St. Mary's series. 1911–1915.

Heyward, Du Bose. *Mamba's Daughters.* 1929.

_____ . *Porgy.* 1925.

Hope, Anthony (real name Anthony Hope Hawkins). *The Prisoner of Zenda*. 1894.

Hull, Edith Maude. *The Sheik*. 1921.

Jackson, Helen Hunt. *Ramona*. 1884.

James, Will. *Smoky, the Cowhorse*. 1926.

Johnson, Owen. *Stover at Yale*. 1911.

_____ . *The Tennessee Shad*. 1911.

_____ . *The Varmint*. 1910.

Johnston, Mary. *To Have and To Hold*. 1900.

Keene, Carolyn (Stratemeyer Syndicate pseudonym). Dana Girls series. 1934–.

_____ . Nancy Drew series. 1930–.

Kipling, Rudyard. *Captains Courageous*. 1897.

_____ . *The Light That Failed*. 1890.

Lane, Rose Wilder. *Let the Hurricane Roar*. 1933.

_____ . *The Young Pioneers* (reissue of *Let the Hurricane Roar*). 1976.

Lewis, Elizabeth Foreman. *Ho-Ming: Girl of New China*, 1934.

_____ . *To Beat a Tiger*. 1956.

_____ . *Young Fu of the Upper Yangtze*. 1932.

Lewis, Sinclair. *Babbitt*. 1922.

_____ . *Elmer Gantry*. 1927.

_____ . *Main Street*. 1921.

McCutcheon, George. *Graustark: The Story of a Love Behind a Throne*. 1901.

Montgomery, Lucy Maud. *Anne of Green Gables*. 1908.

Nordhoff, Charles, and James Norman Hall. *Men Against the Sea*. 1934.

_____ . *The Mutiny on the Bounty*. 1932.

_____ . *Pitcairn's Island*. 1934.

Porter, Eleanor. *Pollyanna*. 1913.

Porter, Gene Stratton. *Freckles*. 1904.

_____ . *A Girl of the Limberlost*. 1909.

_____ . *Laddie*. 1913.

_____ . *Michael O'Halloran*. 1915.

Rice, Alice Hegan. *Mrs. Wiggs of the Cabbage Patch*. 1901.

Richards, Laura Elizabeth. *Peggy*. 1899.

Rinehart, Mary Roberts. *The Circular Staircase*. 1908.

Robinson, Mabel Louise. *Bright Island*. 1937.

Scott, Sir Walter. *The Abbott*. 1820.

_____ . *Ivanhoe*. 1819.

_____ . *The Lay of the Last Minstrel*. 1805.

_____ . *Marmion*. 1808.

Standish, Burt L. (real name: William Gilbert Patten). Frank Merriwell series. 1901–1911.

Steinbeck, John. *In Dubious Battle*. 1936.

_____ . *The Red Pony*. 1937.

Stevenson, Robert Louis. *Prince Otto*. 1885.

_____ . *Treasure Island*. 1883.

Stratemeyer, Edward. Bound to Succeed series. 1895–1899.

_____ . Dave Porter series. 1905–1919.

_____ . Lakeport series. 1904–1912.

_____ . Old Glory series. 1898–1901.

_____ . *Richard Dare's Venture; or, Striking Out for Himself*. 1894.

_____ . Rover Boys series. 1899–1926.

_____ . Soldiers of Fortune series. 1900–1906.

_____ . *Under Dewey at Manila; or, The War Fortunes of a Castaway*. 1898.

_____ . *Victor Horton's Idea*. 1886.

Synge, John Millington. *Riders to the Sea*. 1904.

Tarkington, Booth. *Alice Adams*. 1921.

_____ . *The Magnificent Ambersons*. 1918.

_____ . *Penrod*. 1914.

_____ . *Seventeen*. 1902.

Tunis, John R. *Iron Duke*. 1938.

Twain, Mark (real name: Samuel Clemens). *Tom Sawyer Abroad*. 1894.

Webster, Jean. *Daddy-Long-Legs*. 1912.

Wiggin, Kate Douglas. *Rebecca of Sunnybrook Farm*. 1904.

Wister, Owen. *The Virginian: A Horseman of the Plains*. 1902.

Wright, Harold Bell. *The Calling of Dan Matthews*. 1909.

_____ . *The Re-Creation of Brian Keith*. 1919.

_____ . *The Shepherd of the Hills*. 1907.

_____ . *The Winning of Barbara Worth*. 1911.

_____ . *Their Yesterdays*. 1912.

_____ . *When a Man's a Man*. 1916.

SOME SUGGESTED READINGS

General Comments on Literature 1900–1940

Hackett, Alice Payne, and James Henry Burke. *80 Years of Best Sellers, 1895–1975.* New York: R. R. Bowker, 1977.

Hart, James D. *The Popular Book: A History of America's Literary Taste.* Berkeley: University of California Press, 1950.

Mott, Frank Luther. *Golden Multitudes: The Story of the Best Seller in the United States.* New York: Macmillan, 1950.

Sample, Hazel. *Pitfalls for Readers of Fiction.* Chicago: National Council of Teachers of English, 1940.

Reading Interest Studies

Anderson, Roxanna E. "A Preliminary Study of the Reading Tastes of High School Pupils." *Pedogogical Seminary* 19 (December 1912): 438–60.

Belson, Danylu, chairman. "The Reading Interests of Boys." *Elementary English Review* 3 (November 1926): 292–96.

"Books Boys Like Best." *Publishers Weekly* 88 (October 23, 1915): 1315–45.

Brink, William G. "Reading Interests of High School Pupils." *School Review* 47 (October 1939): 613–21.

Charters, W. W. "What's Happened to Boys' Favorites?" *Library Journal* 74 (October 15, 1949): 1577. An especially intriguing article as it sums up five surveys, all in *Library Journal,* in 1907, 1917, 1927, 1937, and finally, 1949.

Jordan, Arthur Melville. *Children's Interests in Reading.* 2nd ed. Chapel Hill: University of North Carolina Press, 1926.

Popkin, Zelda. "The Finer Things in Life." *Harper's Magazine* 164 (April 1932): 602–11.

Scoggin, Margaret C. "Do Young People Want Books?" *Wilson Bulletin for Librarians* 11 (September 1936): 17.

Smith, Franklin Orin. "Pupils Voluntary Reading." *Pedagogical Seminary* 14 (June 1907): 209–22.

Terman, Lewis M., and Margaret Lima. *Children's Reading: A Guide for Parents and Teachers.* New York: Appleton, 1927.

Vostrovsky, Clara. "A Study of Children's Reading Tastes." *Pedagogical Seminary* 6 (December 1899): 523–35.

Waples, Douglas, and Ralph D. Tyler. *What People Want to Read About: A Study of Group Interests and a Survey of Problems in Adult Reading.* Chicago: American Library Association, 1931.

Washburne, Carleton, and Mabel Vogel. *Winnetka Graded Book List.* Chicago: American Library Association, 1926.

_____ . "Supplement to the Winnetka Graded Book List." *Elementary English Review* 4 (February 1927): 47–52; and 4 (March 1927): 66–73.

Young Adult Literature

Cadogan, Mary, and Patricia Craig. *You're a Brick, Angela! A New Look at Girls' Fiction from 1839 to 1975.* London: Gollancz, 1976.

Coryell, Hubert V. "Boys, Books and Bait." *Wilson Bulletin* 2 (April-May-June 1926): 539–46.

Lerman, Leo. "An Industry within an Industry." *Saturday Review of Literature* 24 (November 8, 1941): 3–7.

Smith, Dora V. "American Youth and English." *English Journal* 26 (February 1937): 99–113.

_____ . "Extensive Reading in Junior High School: A Survey of Teacher Preparation." *English Journal* 19 (June 1930): 449–62.

English Teaching

Hatfield, Wilbur W., ed. *An Experience Curriculum in English.* New York: Appleton, 1935.

Hosic, James Fleming, chairman. *Reorganization of English in Secondary Schools.* Department of the Interior, Bureau of Education, Bulletin 1917, No. 2. Washington: Government Printing Office, 1917.

Smith, Dora V. *Evaluating Instruction in Secondary School English.* Chicago: National Council of Teachers of English, 1941.

Thurber, Samuel. "Report of the English Conference" in *Report of the Committee of Ten on Secondary School Studies*. New York: American, 1894, pp. 86–95.

——— . "Voluntary Reading in the Classical High School." *School Review* 13 (February 1905): 168–79.

American Education

Burstall, Sara A. *Impressions of American Education in 1908*. London: Longmans, Green, 1909. A comparison of American and English educational systems by a head mistress of a girls' school in England.

Cremin, Lawrence A. *American Education: The Colonial Experience, 1607–1783*. New York: Harper & Row, 1970.

——— . *American Education: The National Experience, 1783–1876*. New York: Harper & Row, 1980.

——— . *The Transformation of the School: Progressivism in American Education, 1876–1957*. New York: Alfred A. Knopf, 1961. All three are basic sources.

Inglis, Alexander James. *The Rise of the High School in Massachusetts*. Columbia University Contributions to Education, No. 45. New York: Teachers College, Columbia University, 1911. Excellent source material.

Krug, Edward A. *The Shaping of the American High School, 1880–1920*. Madison: University of Wisconsin Press, 1964.

——— . *The Shaping of the American High School, 1920–1941*. Madison: University of Wisconsin Press, 1972.

College-Entrance Requirements

Applebee, Arthur N. *Tradition and Reform in the Teaching of English: A History*. Urbana, IL: National Council of Teachers of English, 1974.

Crowe, John M., Mrs. E. K. Broadus, and James Fleming Hosic. "Report of the Conference Committee on High-School English." *School Review* 17 (February 1909): 85–88.

Eaton, the Reverend Arthur Wentworth. *College Requirements in English, Entrance Examinations (Examination Papers for 1893 and 1894)*. Boston: Ginn, 1894.

Hays, Edna. *College Entrance Requirements in English: Their Effects on the High Schools—An Historical Survey*. New York: Teachers College, Columbia University, 1936.

Hosic, James Fleming. "A Brief Chapter of Educational History Together with a Summary of the Facts So Far Obtained by a Committee on the National Education Association and a List of References." *English Journal* 1 (February 1912): 95–121.

Scott, Fred Newton. "College-Entrance Requirements in English." *School Review* 9 (June 1901): 365–78.

Stout, John Elbert. *The Development of High-School Curriculum in the North Central States from 1860 to 1918*. Chicago: The University of Chicago Press, 1921.

Thomas, Charles Swain, ed. *Examining the Examination in English: A Report on the College Entrance Requirements*. Harvard Studies in Education, No. 17. Cambridge: Harvard University Press, 1931, pp. 1–15.

Free Reading

LaBrant, Lou. "The Content of a Free Reading Program." *Educational Research Bulletin* 16 (February 17, 1937): 29–34.

——— . *An Evaluation of the Free Reading Program in Grades Ten, Eleven, and Twelve for the Class of 1935, the Ohio State University School*. Contributions to Education No. 2. Columbus: Ohio State University Press, 1936.

The School Library.

Cecil, Henry L., and Willard A. Heaps. *School Library Services in the United States: An Interpretive Survey*. New York: H. W. Wilson, 1940.

Fargo, Lucille. *The Library in the School*. Chicago: American Library Association, 1930 (revised several times).

Heller, Frieda M., and Lou LaBrant. *The Librarian and the Teacher of English.* Chicago: American Library Association, 1938.

Logasa, Hannah. *The High School Library: Its Function in Education.* New York: Appleton, 1928.

School Libraries for Today and Tomorrow, Functions and Standards. Chicago: American Library Association, 1945.

The Stratemeyer Literary Syndicate

Billman, Carol. *The Secret of the Stratemeyer Syndicate: Nancy Drew, the Hardy Boys, and the Million Dollar Fiction Factory.* New York: Ungar, 1986.

Dizer, John T., Jr. "Fortune and the Syndicate." *Boys' Book Collector* 2 (Fall 1970): 146–53; and 2 (Winter 1970): 78–86.

_____ . *Tom Swift and Company: Boys' Books by Stratemeyer and Others.* Jefferson, North Carolina: McFarland, 1982.

"For It Was Indeed He." *Fortune* 9 (April 1934): 86.

Johnson, Deidre. *Stratemeyer Pseudonyms and Series Books: An Annotated Checklist of Stratemeyer and Stratemeyer Syndicate Publications.* Westport, CT: Greenwood Press, 1980.

Kuskin, Karla. "Nancy Drew and Friends." *New York Times Book Review.* May 4, 1975, pp. 20–21.

Mason, Bobbie Ann. *The Girl Sleuth: A Feminist Guide.* Old Westbury, NY: Feminist Press, 1975.

McFarlane, Leslie. *Ghost of the Hardy Boys: An Autobiography of Leslie McFarlane.* New York: Two Continents Publishing Group, 1976.

Prager, Arthur. "Edward Stratemeyer and His Book Machine." *Saturday Review* 54 (July 10, 1971): 15.

_____ . "The Secret of Nancy Drew— Pushing Forty and Going Strong." *Saturday Review* 52 (January 25, 1969): 18.

Zukerman, Ed. "The Great Hardy Boys' Whodunit." *Rolling Stone,* September 9, 1976, pp. 37–40.

Series Books

Dizer, John T., Jr. "Boys' Books and the American Dream." *Dime Novel Roundup* 37 (February 15, 1968): 12–17; and 37 (March 15, 1968): 29–31.

Follett, Wilson. "Junior Model." *Bookman* 70 (September 1929): 11–14. An attack on boys' series books.

Garis, Roger. *My Father Was Uncle Wiggily.* New York: McGraw-Hill, 1966.

Girls' Series Books: A Checklist of Hardback Books Published 1900–1975. Minneapolis: Children's Literature Research Collections, University of Minnesota Library, 1978. A most handy research help.

Hudson, Harry K. *A Bibliography of Hard-Cover Boys' Books.* Rev. ed. Tampa, Florida: Data Print, 1977. The prototype for the *Girls' Series Books* listed above and *the basic book* in studying series books.

Kilgour, Raymond L. *Lee and Shepard: Publishers for the People.* Hamden, CT: Shoe String Press, 1965.

Prager, Arthur. *Rascals at Large, or The Clue in the Old Nostalgia.* New York: Doubleday, 1971.

Root, Mary E. "Not to Be Circulated." *Wilson Bulletin for Librarians* 3 (January 1929): 446. See the response by Ernest F. Ayres, "Not to Be Circulated?" *Wilson Bulletin for Librarians* 3 (March 1929): 528–29.

Soderbergh, Peter A. "Bibliographical Essay: The Negro in Juvenile Series Books, 1899–1930." *Journal of Negro History* 58 (April 1973): 179–82.

Yost, Edna. "The Fifty-Cent Juveniles." *Publishers Weekly* 121 (June 18, 1932): 2405–8.

_____ . "Who Wrote the Fifty-Cent Juveniles?" *Publishers Weekly* 123 (May 20, 1933): 1595–98.

Pulps

Goulart, Ron. *An Informal History of the Pulp Magazine.* New Rochelle, NY: Arlington House, 1972.

Wilkinson, Richard Hill. "Whatever Happened to the Pulps?" *Saturday Review* 45 (February 10, 1962): 60.

Comics and Comic Books
Couperie, Pierre. *A History of the Comic Strip.* New York: Crown, 1968.
Daniels, Les. *Comix: A History of Comic Books in America.* New York: Outerbridge and Dienstfrey, 1971.
Daviss, Bennett. "World of Funnies Is 'Warped with Fancy, Woofed with Dreams.' " *Smithsonian* 18 (November 1987): 180–95.
McDonnell, Patrick, Karen O'Connell, and Georgia Riley de Havenon. *Krazy Kat: The Comic Art of George Herriman.* New York: Abrams, 1986.
Robinson, Jerry. *The Comics: An Illustrated History of Comic Strip Art.* New York: G. P. Putnam's Sons, 1974.

For information on the availability of paperback editions of these titles, please consult the most recent edition of *Paperbound Books in Print,* published annually by R. R. Bowker Company.

Wertham, Frederic. *Seduction of the Innocent.* New York: Holt, Rinehart and Winston, 1954.

Haldeman-Julius and His Little Blue Books
Herder, Dale M. "Haldeman-Julius, the Little Blue Books, and the Theory of Popular Culture." *Journal of Popular Culture* 4 (Spring 1971): 881–91.
————— . "The Little Blue Books as Popular Culture: E. Haldeman-Julius' Methodology" in Russell B. Nye (ed.), *New Dimensions in Popular Culture.* Bowling Green, Ohio: Bowling Green University Popular Press, 1972, pp. 31–42.
Mordell, Albert. *The World Of Haldeman-Julius.* New York: Twayne, 1960.

1940–1966
From Certainty to Uncertainty in Life and Literature Courtesy of Future Shock

Nineteen-forty began uncertainly as we moved from the Depression into a prewar economy and employment market. Our involvement in World War II began with heavy losses in the Pacific and proceeded to victory at Iwo Jima, North Africa, and Omaha Beach. From a hatred of Communism before 1941 we moved to a temporary brotherhood during World War II. Then came Yalta, the Iron Curtain, blacklisting, and Senator McCarthy. We went from "Li'l Abner" to "Pogo," and from Bob Hope to Mort Sahl. Problems of the time included school integration, racial unrest, the civil rights movement, riots in the streets, and women's rights. We went from violence to more violence and the assassinations of John Kennedy and Malcolm X. The economy swung from inflation to recession and back again. We started World War II with the nation united; then we went to the Korean War with the nation unsure; we ended with the Vietnam War and an increasingly divided nation. The twenty-five years between 1940 and 1965 revealed a country separated by gaps of all kinds: generational, racial, technological, cultural, and economic.

MORE READING INTEREST STUDIES

By 1940, reading interest studies were fixtures in educational journals, and increasingly they did not merely report findings but interpreted results and questioned the literature used in schools. In 1946, George W. Norvell reported, "Our data shows clearly that much literary material being used in our schools is too mature, too subtle, too erudite to permit its enjoyment by the majority of secondary-school pupils."[1] Norvell arrived at six implications for secondary schools: (1) Assigned material should be enjoyable to young adults; (2) "In addition to the study in common, there [should] be much wide reading through which young people may enjoy the materials which appeal to them individually"; (3) Teachers should refrain from choosing materials to please themselves and place the students' interests first; (4) Three-fourths of the selections currently used should be replaced by more interesting materials; (5) New programs should find materials to interest boys usually bored by the present curricula; and (6) "To increase reading skill, promote the reading habit, and produce a generation of book-lovers, there is no factor so powerful as interest."[2]

Others supported Novell's contention that young adults' choices of voluntary reading rarely overlapped books widely respected by more traditional English teachers. In 1947 Marie Rankin surveyed eight public libraries in Illinois, Ohio, and New York to discover the most consistently popular books with adolescents. Helen Boylston's *Sue Barton, Senior Nurse,* led the list.[3] Twelve years later, Stephen Dunning surveyed fourteen school and public librarians on junior novels popular with students. Librarians listed the top ten as Maureen Daly's *Seventeenth Summer,* Henry Gregor Felsen's *Hot Rod*, Betty Cavanna's *Going On Sixteen,* Rosamund Du Jardin's *Double Date,* Walter Farley's *Black Stallion,* Sally Benson's *Junior Miss,* Mary Stolz's *The Sea Gulls Woke Me,* Rosamund Du Jardin's *Wait for Marcy,* James Summers' *Prom Trouble,* and John Tunis' *All-American.*[4]

Near the height of the outpouring of published studies, Jacob W. Getzels assessed the value of reading interest surveys and found most of them wanting in "precision of *definition,* rigor of *theory,* and depth of *analysis.*"[5] He was, of course, right. Most reports were limited to a small sample from a few schools—often only one school—and little was done except to ask students what they liked to read. From a scientific point of view, most were hopelessly deficient.

But the studies had value. They gave librarians and teachers insight into books young adults liked and books they might like. They suggested which tastes were current and which were changing, which books were being read and which were losing popularity. More important, they gave insights into young adults and their interests, not just in reading but in other areas as well, and that suggested all sorts of activities in schools and libraries to attract recalcitrant readers. They brought hope to librarians and teachers that no matter how reluctant readers were in school, somewhere out there somebody was reading, a hope that—as any librarian or teacher knows—needs constant rekindling.

G. Robert Carlsen summarized the reading interests discovered up to 1954 and argued that books could help to fulfill three broad areas of young adult needs:

■ Young people need assurance of the status of human beings. With the end of childhood, children are painfully stirred by a desire to find that they as individuals are important creations of God, capable of infinite development.

A second area of need in the developing adolescent is for assurance of his own normality. Young people need to test their reactions, to experiment with them to find out whether or not they are normal human beings; but they do not want to reveal their own abnormality to others—if abnormality it is—by asking direct questions.

A third need of young people that seems to govern their reading choices, particularly in the later period, is a need for role-playing. With the developing of their personality through adolescence, they come to a semi-integrated picture of themselves as human beings. They want to test this picture of themselves in the many kinds of roles that it is possible for a human being to play and through testing to see what roles they may fit into and what roles are uncongenial.[6]

■ HAVIGHURST'S DEVELOPMENTAL TASKS

The work of Robert J. Havighurst at the University of Chicago was helpful to teachers and librarians in both reading interests and bibliotherapy. Havighurst maintained that at various stages in life (infancy and early childhood, middle childhood, adolescence, adulthood, and old age) certain tasks were imposed by society upon each of us.

He first listed five adolescent tasks and later expanded them to ten:

1. Achieving new and more mature relations with age-mates of both sexes.
2. Achieving a masculine or feminine social role.
3. Accepting one's physique and using the body effectively.
4. Achieving emotional independence of parents and other adults.
5. Achieving assurance of economic independence.
6. Selecting and preparing for an occupation.
7. Preparing for marriage and family life.
8. Developing intellectual skills and concepts necessary for civic competence.
9. Desiring and achieving socially responsible behavior.
10. Acquiring a set of values and an ethical system as a guide to behavior.[7]

Implications for helping young adults find books illustrating or illuminating the ten developmental tasks were obvious.

■ BIBLIOTHERAPY COMES TO THE SCHOOLS

In writing his account of the use of books as part of his treatment for psychiatric patients in 1929, Dr. G. O. Ireland used the term *bibliotherapy,*[8] a new term for librarians and English teachers. By the late 1930s and early 1940s articles dealing with bibliotherapy became almost commonplace. A 1939 author asked, "Can There Be a Science of Bibliotherapy?"[9] and was answered a year later:

> The science of bibliotherapy is still in its infancy, yet public libraries are featuring readers' advisory services, and hospital libraries are on the increase. All school librarians who practice individual reading guidance are participating, perhaps unconsciously, in a program of bibliotherapy.[10]

By the 1950s, bibliotherapy was firmly entrenched in the schools. Philosophically, it was justified by Aristotle's *Poetics* and the theory of emotional release through catharsis, a theory with little support except for unverifiable personal testimonials.

One clear and easy application of bibliotherapy was the free reading program (sometimes too clear and too easy for the inept amateur psychologist/English teacher who, finding a new book in which the protagonist had acne, sought out the acne-ridden kid in class saying, "You must read this—it's about you." Not incidentally, an apocryphal story). Lou LaBrant, popularizer of free reading, sounded both a recommendation and a warning when she wrote:

> Certainly I can make a much wiser selection of offerings if I understand the potential reader. . . . The first step has been taken when we have some assurance that the book or short selection which we recommend or teach will have a hearing; that it will come within the understanding of the young reader because it deals with problems with which he is conversant and that it will hold some appeal to him because he, like the author of the piece, is concerned with a certain aspect of living.
>
> This does not mean, as some have interpreted, that a young reader will enjoy only literature which answers his questions, tells him what is to be done. It is true, however, that young and old tend to choose literature, whether they seek solutions or escape, which offers characters or situations with which they can find a degree of identification.[11]

THE RISE OF PAPERBACKS

Young adult readers might assume paperbound books have always been with us. But, despite the success of dime novels and libraries of paperbacks in the late 1800s, paperbacks as we know them entered the mass market in 1938 when Pocket Books offered Pearl Buck's *The Good Earth* as a sample volume in mail-order tests. In the spring of 1939, a staff artist created the first sketch of Gertrude the Kangaroo with a book in her paws and another in her pouch. It became Pocket Books' trademark. A few months later, the company issued ten titles in 10,000-copy editions, most of them remaining best-sellers for years. By the close of 1939, Pocket Books had published twenty-four other titles that sold more than one and a half million copies. In 1940, the company published fifty-three more titles selling more than 4.5 million copies.

Avon began publishing in 1941, Penguin (in the United States) entered in 1942, and Bantam, New American Library, Ballantine, Dell, and Popular Library began publishing in 1943. By 1951, sales had reached 230 million paperbacks annually.

Phenomenal as the growth was, paperbacks were slow to appear in schools although a look at an early edition of Bowker's *Paperbound Books in Print* reveals an incredible number of titles available in areas from philosophy to adolescent books. That did not prevent some librarians from complaining that paperbacks did not belong in libraries because they were difficult to catalog and attractive to steal. It did not prevent some teachers and principals from maintaining that paperback covers were lurid and the contents little more than pornography. In 1969 (and later in some schools) paperbacks were as serious a disciplinary matter as pornography:

> "I'd rather be caught with Lady Chatterley in hardcover than *Hot Rod* in paperback," a precocious high school junior in New York City told me earlier this year. "Hard covers get you one detention, but paperbacks get you two or three," he explained.
>
> Curriculum change is painfully slow in inner city schools where change is most needed. But even in the ghetto, changing perceptions of paperback books are making this high school junior's report a rare phenomenon. It seems that paperbacks are beginning to make the education scene. Having served its fifty years in educational purgatory, the paperback is becoming an acceptable "innovation" which, I suppose, means that it is no longer a true innovation.[12]

The innovation was overdue. Paperbacks were ubiquitous, comfortably sized, and inexpensive, and students bought their own libraries while some teachers and librarians wondered where all their customers had gone. Part of the early enthusiasm for paperbacks and acceptance in the schools came from the creation of the Scholastic Book Clubs and the many editions of the Readers' Choice Catalogs. Later, Dell's Yearling and Mayflower books would become the major suppliers of books written specifically for young adults, but by 1966 paperbacks were very much a part of young adults' lives.

CHANGES AND GROWTH IN YOUNG ADULT LITERATURE

In 1941, Leo Lerman surveyed the growth of juvenile literature defined as "books upon every conceivable subject for boys and girls ranging in age from six months to eighteen years," from 1920 to 1940. Noting that during that twenty-year span, 14,536 juvenile books had been printed, Lerman concluded, "Children's books have become big business—an industry within an industry."[13] Lerman might have been surprised by the growth of young adult literature in the years that followed, particularly with the development of paperback books.

More important than mere quantity, the quality of young adult literature rose steadily, if at times hesitatingly and uncertainly, from 1941 to 1965. Series books, so popular from 1900 to 1940, died out—except for Stratemeyer Syndicate stalwarts Nancy Drew, the Hardy Boys, and one new series, Tom Swift, Jr.—killed by increasing reader sophistication and the wartime scarcity of paper.

Much young adult literature of the 1940s and 1950s celebrated those wonderful high school years. Books seemed at times to concentrate on concerns with dating, parties, class rings, preparing for the school prom, senior year, the popular crowd (or learning to avoid it), and teen romance devoid of realities like sex. Books often sounded alike, looked alike, and read alike, but they were unquestionably popular.

Plots were usually simple, simplistic, and too often simple-minded. One or two characters might be slightly developed, but other characters were merely sketched or tossed in as stock figures or stereotypes. Major characters faced a dilemma (joining a school sorority, playing football unfairly, joining the popular crowd, going to an all-night dance), adult figures stood by hoping the protagonists would come through morally unscathed, and after a bit of hesitation or uncertainty, the morals of the community and the goodness of young adults were reaffirmed. Books dealt almost exclusively with white, middle-class values and morality. Endings were almost uniformly happy and bright, and readers could be certain that neither their morality nor their intelligence would be challenged.

Taboos may never have been written down, but they were clear to readers and writers. Certain things were not to be mentioned—obscenity, profanity, suicide, sexuality, sensuality, homosexuality, protests against anything significant, social or racial injustice, or the ambivalent feelings of cruelty and compassion inherent in young adults and all real people. Some things could be mentioned, but rarely, and introduced by implication rather than direct statement and only then as bad examples for thoughtful, decent young adults: pregnancy, early marriage, drugs, smoking, alcohol, school dropouts, divorce, alienation of young adults. Consequently, YA books were often innocuous and pervaded by a saccharine didacticism. They taught good, adult-determined attitudes: life is rewarding for the diligent worker and difficult for the slacker; a virtuous life is not merely its own reward but leads to a richer life here on earth; serious dilemmas deserve serious attention by adults who would then tell young adults how to handle the problems but not to think for themselves till later; fast driving kills, fast marriages do not last, fast money is evil money, fast actions will surely be regretted, and fast dates are dangerous. Good boys and girls must accept adult and societal rules as good and just without question; young people would survive all those funny preoccupations and worries of adolescence and emerge as thoughtful, serious adults.

Despite all those unwritten rules, some writers transcended the taboos and qualifications even in the 1940s and 1950s. Reviewing young adult literature in 1960, Stanley B. Kegler and Stephen Dunning could write: "Books written for adolescents are improving in quality. Books of acceptable quality have largely replaced poorly written and mediocre books."[14] Three years later, they queried editors of young adult books and found taboos still operating if lessening: "There are few house rules regarding taboos—other than those dictated by 'good taste and common sense.' " One editor responded:

> I see very little change in taboos in the past ten years. There are franker discussions of the problems of sex in nonfiction.

Another wrote:

> I think the number of narrow-minded taboos—smoking, drinking, swearing, etc.—have diminished. A creative author works best in "responsible" freedom. If an author is serious and responsible, and if we are, and if we together work within the areas of honest good taste, it is difficult to see how we can offend.[15]

By the end of the 1960s many, though hardly all, taboos had disappeared as unwritten restrictions. Most authors learned that in young adult literature, as in all literature, good books do not set out deliberately to break taboos although some bad books seem to try to do so. Good books take up life and real problems and follow characters and emotions as they wend their way through reality, touching on or breaking their taboos where necessary. A few authors seemed deliberately to court taboo subjects, notably Jeanette Eyerly with *Drop-Out* (1963), her dropout and early marriage novel; *A Girl Like Me* (1966), her pregnancy novel; *Radigan Cares* (1970), her political novel; and *Bonnie Jo, Go Home* (1972), her abortion novel. Indeed that led to legitimate criticism of some writers for writing a "drug" novel or a "suicide" novel or a "pregnancy" novel. What William Rose Benét wrote about children's books in 1941 remains a persistent problem for writers of young adult books today. "You don't write for children anymore. You consult Gallup polls as to what they like, and compile statistics as to how they react."[16] Similarly, some adolescent novels have fixed on an apparently popular theme, a social or emotional ill for example, and are not novels about people but about things. That may increase sales, but it diminishes their chances of survival. Good books focus on people with problems. Bad books focus on problems that seem incidentally to involve people.

NINE OUTSTANDING WRITERS FOR YOUNG ADULTS

Nine authors stand out for their psychological perception and exceptional writing talent. They are profiled below.

Florence Crannell Means' books such as *Shuttered Windows* and *The Moved-Outers* hold mirrors up to prejudice.

Florence Crannell Means

Means was popular in the 1930s, and her popularity held up well into the 1940s and later. *A Candle in the Mist* (1931), about a young orphan boy who traveled with a family to Minnesota in 1871, mixed history with suspense and revealed a talented writer, but later books revealed even more talent. *Tangled Waters* (1936), the story of a fifteen-year-old Navajo girl on her Arizona reservation, was her first successful effort at characterizing a minority. Her first black adolescent appears in *Shuttered Windows* (1938). Sixteen-year-old Harriet Freeman grows up in Minneapolis and then chooses to live for a year with her great-grandmother on an island off the South Carolina coast. Formulaic as the plot is and paternalistic as the tone is by today's standards, the book conveyed a sense of worth and dignity about black people rare in young adult or adult literature for that time. *The Moved-Outers* (1945), a story of Japanese-Americans forced into relocation camps during World War II, may appear dated and mild by today's standards, but it still has power. Means was unable to avoid drawing the too obvious moral about the danger of an increasingly totalitarian America, but her heart was in the right place. Her message was more powerful at the time than we now can realize, given the rabid anti-Japanese climate persisting even after World War II.

Later books, *Tolliver* (1963), *It Takes All Kinds* (1964), and *Our Cup Is Broken* (1969), are worth reading and establish Means as an important writer, one worth reading and even studying for the mirror she holds up to prejudice.

John Tunis

Newspaperman John Tunis published his first young adult novel, *Iron Duke,* in 1938. After four years of athletics at a small high school, Jim Wellington (the Iron Duke) wants desperately to enter the athletic big time at Harvard. His efforts are, at first, realistically unsuccessful, but the book is a character study involving athletics, not just another sports story. What his first book promises, *All-American* (1942) delivers. The novel may be dated by changes that have taken place in football and in society, but it is a remarkable work for its time. Ronald Perry plays football for the Academy team and is partially responsible for injuring a local high school opponent in a crucial game. His Academy friends don't worry about the incident, but Perry cannot live with his guilt at the Academy. He leaves to go where he finds he is even less wanted, the local high school. There he learns some important lessons about racism and reality. The football team slowly accepts him, but after a successful season, an invitation to a postseason game in the South requires that a black athlete stay home. Perry leads a quiet and tentative revolt, joined by a few of his teammates. To his surprise, he finds that things can change when people care. *All-American* seems somewhat paternalistic now, but for the time and the society then, it was a remarkable, even radical novel for young adults.

Yea! Wildcats (1944) eloquently mixes basketball with incipient totalitarianism in a small town. Its sequel, *A City for Lincoln* (1945), is also nominally a basketball story, but Tunis' liberal inclinations and didacticism led to a study of American politics, one of his least successful novels for young adults and one of his most intriguing for adults. Another successful account of basketball mania, *Go, Team, Go!,* is a fine novel about public pressure on a coach who cares about more than merely winning. *Silence Over Dunkerque* (1962) contains nothing remotely athletic, but it is a good straightforward picture of the horrors and cruelty of war. Tunis' greatest book appeared in 1967. *His Enemy, His Friend* is a brilliant fusion of war and its aftermath and sports. A German soldier during World War II is forced to order the execution of some townspeople. Years later, the son of one of those executed opposes the soldier's team in a soccer match.

Tunis occasionally let his moral outrage and sensitivity carry him away, but at his best he wrote the finest sports stories since Ralph Henry Barbour. Tunis knew the power of athletic glory for good and for evil, and he knew what locker rooms smell like.

Maureen Daly

Daly published only one novel for young adults before 1980, but it endures. *Seventeenth Summer* (1942) is about shy, unnoticed Angie Morrow and her love for Jack Duluth in the summer before she is to set off for college. Very little happens in the novel, but very little happens during any one summer in most of our lives. Angie falls in love, she dates, and her relationship with Jack leads to misunderstandings and frustrations, mostly sexual. And at the close of the book, she and Jack part, sadly, as most first lovers do.

But it is not the plot so much as certain aspects of the story that make *Seventeenth Summer* different. In addition to portraying a young boy and girl sensitively and honestly, Daly shows a society in which drinking beer and even smoking will not inevitably lead to damnation, not only for young adults. At one point, Jack takes Angie to a roadhouse where they see a male pianist with painted fingernails. Angie innocently asks Jack to explain, and Jack stutters, looks embarrassed, and offers no satisfactory answer, but the reader recognizes what Angie does not.

Some critics, librarians, and English teachers are deeply, personally offended by Angie's innocence. They maintain that she could never have been *that* innocent, *that* naive, gullible, and unsuspecting. Innocence and sophistication are difficult to define at best. Some sophisticated young adults even today, more than forty years after Angie, wear a veneer of worldliness that, if penetrated even the tiniest bit, reveals a frightened innocent.

Possibly, say the accusers, but even so, Angie certainly wasn't typical of her time, not even of that 1942 world where good was good and bad was bad and never the twain could meet. Other girls of the time, so the reasoning goes, weren't all that innocent. They would have been aware of the physical implications (and consequences) of love, even first love.

But Daly never claimed Angie was typical. Angie was an individual, not a representative of seventeen-year-old girls in 1942. Writers, at least serious writers, create individuals out of the masses, not to represent the masses. And Angie is an individual.

Esther Forbes

Primarily a historian, in fact winner of the Pulitzer Prize for history in 1942 for *Paul Revere and the World He Lived In,* Forbes wrote one still-popular novel for young adults. *Johnny Tremain* (1943) sets fourteen-year-old Johnny in pre-Revolutionary War times. A cocky apprentice to a silversmith and clearly a young genius in the making, Johnny cripples his hand. Partly because of that and partly because of the fervor of the time, he becomes involved with patriots Sam Adams, John Hancock, and Paul Revere. The spirit of the time is well captured by historian Forbes, but readers who care little about history can still find an engrossing and exciting tale about Johnny, his injury, his friends, and war.

Forbes did not write again for young adults, but the number of readers who continue to enjoy *Johnny Tremain* is wide indeed.

Henry Gregor Felsen

Felsen began writing for young adults during World War II, but his first three major books concern short, fat Bertie in *Bertie Comes Through* (1947), *Bertie Takes Care* (1948), and *Bertie Makes a Break* (1949). Probably read by young adults because Bertie's troubles have hilarious results, the books are still a fascinating study of adolescent failure.

After a singularly dull stab at a vocational novel, Felsen wrote *Two and the Town* (1952) about a young couple forced to marry because the girl is pregnant. Old-hat today but fifteen years ahead of its time, the book could safely have been placed in the hands of any young adult by any parent as a sure warning of the consequences of "doing it," for Felsen preached endlessly and was mercilessly moral to the boy and girl. Still, *Two and the Town* broke ground in young adult literature by treating pregnancy honestly and seriously. What the reactions of young adults or parents might have been is largely conjectural, for many librarians skirted the issue of censorship by not buying the book. Contemporary reviewers recognized that the book might cause trouble. One began:

> Many libraries will not buy this, and others will treat it with kid gloves, but we need it. Factual pamphlets and books treating sex miss the emotions of error and repair that this book, written for and about youth, presents.[17]

Felsen's fame came with publication of *Hot Rod* (1950), and two other similar books, *Street Rod* (1953) and *Crash Club* (1958). *Hot Rod* is still occasionally read, though its didacticism is strong, particularly in the scene near the end in which accident victims are buried.

Paul Annixter

Under the Annixter pen name, Howard A. Sturtzel wrote many novels, often with his wife Jane Sturtzel, but his exceptional book is *Swiftwater* (1950), a tale of excitement, symbolism, and ecology mixed with some stereotyped characters. Cam Calloway feels a kinship with the wild geese near his Maine farm, and his feelings and his love are emulated by his son Bucky. Something of a footloose wanderer, Cam dreams more than he acts. Bucky is both dreamer and actor, and his drive to find roots for himself and his mother and to establish a wild game preserve for his beloved geese becomes the heart of the novel. Much has been made of the early scenes between Bucky and the wolverine, with the animal symbolizing evil, perhaps too much so. However, individual chapters of the novel are excellent short stories in their own right, and the whole novel is a most convincing, honest, and well-written novel for young adults.

Jack Bennett

South African journalist Bennett wrote three novels for young adults, two of them among the best of the time. In *Jamie* (1963), set on a large South African farm, Jamie wants to be like his father. The opportunity to become a man comes early when Jamie's father is killed by a maddened water buffalo. Jamie's vow to kill the animal becomes almost a mania.

Mister Fisherman (1965) may remind readers of Theodore Taylor's *The Cay*, but Bennett's story of a young white boy helped by an old black fisherman to survive at sea is a better book.

Bennett's third novel, *The Hawk Alone* (1965), is an excellent study of white hunter Gord Vance. Vance had done everything and had shot everything. When he discovers he has outlived his time, that he is no longer a man, only a myth and a legend, Vance realizes that his hunting days are over. He knows he serves no valuable function, not even for himself, and he decides that suicide is the answer. Realistic, insightful, and extraordinarily well written, *The Hawk Alone* deserves far more readers than it ever attracted.

James Summers

Popular as Summers' books were at the time they were written, Summers is now almost forgotten. Capable of writing charming fluff, he could also write sensitive novels. *Operation ABC* (1955) is almost a case study of a football hero, apparently successful in everything, who literally cannot read and fears college because he would be unmasked as a fraud. *The Wonderful Time* (1957) shows a nineteen-year-old returning to high school after a stretch in the Army, trying desperately to fit into a world that is no longer his. *The Shelter Trap* (1962) is about some gifted students who decide to live for a short time in a fallout shelter.

Summers has a wonderful ability to capture American youth, but his chief asset as a writer is also his major liability: his incredible ear for young adult jargon. Unhappily, by the time any of his books was published, the jargon was not merely dated but dead.

His two best books are *Ring Around Her Finger* (1957), a study of a young marriage told from the boy's point of view, and *The Limit of Love* (1959), a remarkable delineation of a sexual love affair. Ronnie Jordan knows she has missed two periods, and boyfriend Lee Hansen worries and blames Ronnie for ruining his life. In the weeks that follow the mess leaves them emotionally bankrupt and no longer in love, but Lee remains a boy while Ronnie emerges as a real woman ready to face problems and her own responsibilities. *The Limit of Love* is now dated, but it was a book far ahead of its time.

Mary Stolz

Stolz is, simply put, our most consistently artistic writer for young adults. Richard S. Alm spoke for teachers and librarians when he wrote that Stolz is "versatile and most skilled . . . [and] writes not for the masses who worship Sue Barton but for the rarer adolescent."[18] She joined the literary scene with her first novel, *To Tell Your Love* (1950), an introspective and moving portrait of a young girl waiting vainly all summer for a phone call from the boy she loves.

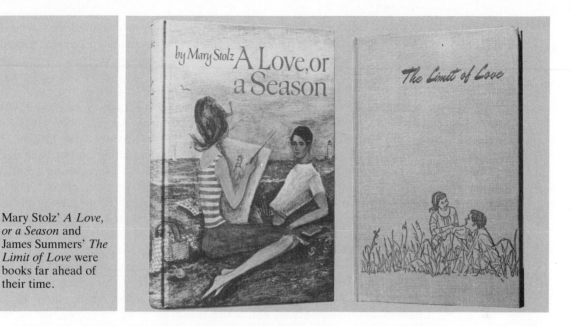

Mary Stolz' *A Love, or a Season* and James Summers' *The Limit of Love* were books far ahead of their time.

Her two finest works are *Pray Love, Remember* (1954), a remarkable story of popular, lovely, and cold Dody Jenks who does not like her family or herself, and *A Love, or a Season* (1964) in which love between Harry and Nan threatens to get out of hand and become too passionate before they can handle it or themselves. Readers today may find *A Love, or a Season* a bit naive, but some girls presumably still have serious doubts about capriciously hopping into bed, no matter how intense the love may seem.

BOOKS POPULAR WITH YOUNG ADULTS

Reading of young adults fell loosely into six areas, some containing many popular titles, some only a few.

Career Books March On

Emma Bugbee was not the first to write career novels, but her five books about young newspaper reporter Peggy Foster begin the deluge in the 1930s which carried on until the 1950s. Bugbee was a reporter for 55 years, first with the *New York Tribune,* and *Peggy Covers the News* (1936) and its four sequels realistically conveyed the ambivalent excitement and boredom of getting and writing the news. Events do seem telescoped and thrills and success come too easily to Peggy—problems that increased as career novels multiplied—but the picture of a young woman breaking into a male-dominated profession served a purpose for its time.

Almost every job was covered by vocational books sugar-coated with fiction—librarianship by Lucile Fargo's *Marian Martha* (1936), and fashion designing by Christie Harris' *You Have to Draw the Line Somewhere* (1964), secretarial work by Blanche Gibbs and Georgiana Adams' *Shirley Clayton, Secretary* (1941), television work by Dorothy McFadden's *Lynn Decker: TV Apprentice* (1953), and on and on. Hardly an occupation escaped the eagle eyes of publishers and writers eager to ensure that every young adult, of whatever vocational persuasion, should have at least one novel about his or her field. Presumably no author penned any book-length fiction about garbage collectors or hangmen, but had any youngster expressed an interest in those fields, some author prompted by a publisher would have churned out *Robert Gimstock: Sanitation Expert* or *Hanging Them High with Harold*.

Without question, books about nursing led popularity polls with girls, and Helen Dore Boylston was the most popular of the writers. Her Sue Barton series ran to seven volumes from *Sue Barton, Student Nurse* (1936) to *Sue Barton, Staff Nurse* (1952) and is still readable, albeit dated. Curiously, Sue Barton seems more popular today in Great Britain. Boylston's chief rival, in a field where authors' names generally meant little and changed as publishers sought another vocational interest, was Helen Wells, whose Cherry Ames nursing series ran to twenty volumes and whose Vicki Barr flight stewardess series ran to thirteen books.

Lucille G. Rosenheim's *Kathie, The New Teacher* (1949), mediocre as it is, suggests both the strengths and weaknesses of vocational novels. Kathie Kerber, new seventh-grade teacher at Hillcrest, meets in one year all the problems and prejudices that a teacher with bad luck would perhaps meet in the first ten years of teaching. She encounters romance, intolerant students, a sneak thief, the town skinflint, sentimental parents, and much more. Everything comes too fast and easily and impossible problems are rapidly disposed of because Kathie cares and has a good heart.

Whatever freshness the vocational novel may once have had, by the late 1940s it was a formula and little more. Four or five characters were certain to appear: a decent and attractive, if sometimes shy, hero/heroine just graduating from high school or college and needing a job desperately; one or two friends of different temperaments—two men if the book was directed at girls since romance was doomed to raise its head; a villain or at the very least a crotchety older person who puts temporary obstacles in the professional path of the protagonist; and an older and wiser person who helps the protagonist to advance. Early in the book the insecure hero/heroine suffers a mixture of major and minor setbacks, but, undaunted, the protagonist wins the final battle and a place in her or his profession. The novel passes rapidly and lightly over the job's daily grind, focusing instead on the high points, the excitement and events that make any job potentially, if rarely, dramatic.

Adventure and Suspense

There was no diminution of interest in adventure or suspense though the interest was largely fulfilled by various kinds of war books until the late 1940s.

Young adult war literature at first tended to be nonfiction such as Carl Mann's *He's in the Signal Corps Now* (1943), or it consisted of military-vocational novels such as Elizabeth Lansing's *Nancy Naylor, Flight Nurse* (1944).

True stories about battles and survivors were ultimately more popular. Richard Tregaskis was widely popular for the blood, death, and heroism of *Guadalcanal Diary* (1943), but by far the most respected and beloved of war reporters was Ernie Pyle for *Here Is Your War* (1943) and *Brave Men* (1944). Two accounts of heroism are still read today, not as museum pieces, but as exciting and effectively told accounts of men caught in war who find depths of courage and personal values within themselves that they might not otherwise have believed. They are Robert Trumbull's *The Raft* (1942) about three Navy fliers forced down in the Pacific, and Quentin Reynolds' *70,000 to One* (1946) about an American airman on a small Pacific island with 70,000 Japanese troops.

Of the many novels published about World War II, something more than mere bravado and jingoism could be found in John Hersey's *A Bell for Adano* (1944), John Horne Burns' sadly neglected but masterful *The Gallery* (1947), Norman Mailer's *The Naked and the Dead* (1948), and James Jones' *From Here to Eternity* (1951), though his *The Pistol* (1959) and *The Thin Red Line* (1962) are better novels.

Perhaps as a reaction to the realities of war, the most popular series of books for both adults and young adults during the 1950s and 1960s centered about the fascinating James Bond, Agent 007. Ian Fleming caught the mood of the time, eager for escapist excitement tinged with what appeared to be realities.

Three historical novels full of adventure and growing up appealed to some young adults. Elizabeth Janet Gray's *Adam of the Road* (1942) revealed the color and music of the Middle Ages, as young Adam Quartermain became a minstrel. Marchette Chute's *The Innocent Wayfaring* (1943) covered only four days in June 1370 as Anne runs away from her convent school to join a band of strolling players. Chute's *The Wonderful Winter* (1954) was equally successful in conveying a sense of time. Young Sir Robert Wakefield, treated like a child at home, runs off to London to become an actor in Shakespeare's company.

Love, Romance, Passion, and Sex

Writers for young adults contributed several fine romances. Margaret E. Bell wrote of an earlier, more innocent, time in Alaska in *Love Is Forever* (1954) about a young and often troubled marriage. Vivian Breck, pen name of Vivian Breckenfield, wrote a superior study of young marriage in *Maggie* (1954). One of the most popular books, and one still read and most readable, is Benedict and Nancy Freeman's *Mrs. Mike* (1947), the story of Mike Flannigan and Kate O'Fallen who marry and move to the dangers of the northern Canadian wilderness. Mary Medearis' *Big Doc's Girl* (1942) is an authentic picture of love and a young girl forced by her father's death to change her life.

Perhaps the ideal romance of the time was *Green Dolphin Street* (1944) by Elizabeth Goudge, a writer who had long produced sensitive studies of small-town life in England but nothing approaching a best seller in America. *Green Dolphin Street* had everything working for it—a young and handsome man in love with one of a pair of sisters. He leaves and writes home his wishes, but the wrong sister accepts. The true love, apparently thwarted by his unfaithfulness, becomes a nun. Passion, love, and adventure are all handled well by a first-rate writer.

Kathleen Winsor was also one of a kind, though what one and what kind was widely debated. When her *Forever Amber* (1944) appeared, parents worried, censors paled, and young adults smiled. Winsor's book was hardly the first to be banned in Boston, but her publisher was adept at turning what appeared to be a defeat into a major victory, gloriously announcing in papers far and wide that the contents were indeed too shocking for Bostonians but not too strong for other cities. City fathers in many towns urged that it be banned, but most readers were only curious, not salacious, and *Forever Amber* sold more than a million and a half copies in three years. Generally, young adults ignored the fuss and read the book.

Society's Problems

Young adults, especially in the last year or two of high school, have often been receptive to books about human dilemmas about the ways society functions or malfunctions. Society changed rapidly and drastically from 1940 through 1966, and malfunctions seemed almost the norm and the human consequences deeply disturbing.

Of increasing concern to many young adults was their growing awareness that the democracy announced in our Constitution was more preached than practiced. As the censorship applied to John Steinbeck's *The Grapes of Wrath* (1939) and *Of Mice and Men* (1937) lessened—though it never entirely disappeared—young readers read of the plight of migrant workers and learned that all was not well with our country.

Many were deeply bothered by Alan Paton's stories of racial struggles in South Africa, *Cry the Beloved Country* (1948), and Paton's most mature study of love in the midst of injustice, *Too Late the Phalarope* (1953). Still more were touched by the sentiment and passion of Harper Lee's *To Kill a Mockingbird* (1960). Viewed as dated and patronizing by some critics today, *Mockingbird* was for many young adults the first book they had read about racial problems in the South, a book that gave them a hero in the gentle but strong Atticus Finch and some understanding of the American dream gone sour.

Richard Wright and his books served as bitter prototypes for much black literature. *Native Son* (1940) shocked some blacks and many whites with the stored-up anger of Bigger Thomas, and *Black Boy* (1945) was both Wright's autobiography and his denouncement of America.

The greatest black novel, and one of the greatest novels of any kind of the last fifty years, is *Invisible Man* (1952) by Ralph Ellison. Existential in tone, *Invisible Man* is at different times bawdy (the incest scenes remind readers of Faulkner without being derivative), moving, frightening, but always stunning and breathtaking.

Several white writers were popular with young adults for their statements about racial dilemmas. Lillian Smith was attacked for her novel *Strange Fruit* (1944), the story of a marriage of a black and a white. A court decision banning the book temporarily made a few reactionaries happy, but the book's national reception and sales were good enough to distress racists. John Howard Griffin suffered some censorship for his novel *The Devil Rides Outside* (1952) though less than he experienced with his popular and sometimes reviled *Black Like Me* (1961), his account of temporarily becoming black, traveling through much of the South, and suffering indignities common to blacks. Griffin's books may have become dated, though not so much as some think, but accusations of some blacks that *Black Like Me* was paternalistic seem ill-advised and revisionist.

Three black nonfiction writers are still read. Claude Brown painted a stark picture of black ghetto life in *Manchild in the Promised Land* (1965), and, despite anguished cries from many parents about the "filth" in the book, Brown's book appears to have a permanent place in the literature of oppression and freedom. Malcolm X and Alex Haley, the latter better known for *Roots,* painted a no more attractive picture in *The Autobiography of Malcolm X* (1965). The most enduring work may prove to be Eldridge Cleaver's *Soul on Ice* (1968), an impassioned plea by a black man in prison who wrote to save himself.

Writings about blacks aimed at young adults were not long in coming. Lorenz Graham brought realistic black characters to young adult literature. If *South Town* (1958) with its characters seeking a better life in the North seems dated today, *North Town* (1965) is still believable as it moves the Williams family and son David, the major character, into conflict with both whites and blacks. *Whose Town?* (1969) brings David more problems as he sees his best friend shot by a white man. Graham's books probed for answers but did not provide any easy ones.

Nat Hentoff has written good topical books that quickly become dated, for example, his story of Vietnam and draft resistance, *I'm Really Dragged but Nothing Gets Me Down* (1968), and his somewhat lesser study of radical teachers and high school revolutions, *In the Country of Ourselves* (1971). His first novel for young adults was a superb story of a white boy trying to break into the black world of jazz, *Jazz Country* (1965). It is an unusual topic, and perhaps neither blacks nor whites are comfortable with the themes or the characters, which is sad because Hentoff is a remarkable, compassionate, and honest writer. *Jazz Country* is a major work.

Of the nonfiction writings for young adults about blacks, Shirley Graham has provided several good biographies: *There Was Once a Slave: The Heroic Story of Frederick Douglass* (1947), probably her best book; *Your Most Humble Servant: The Story of Benjamin Banneker* (1949), her most intriguingly different story; *The Story of Phillis Wheatley: Poetess of the American Revolution* (1949); and *Booker T. Washington: Educator of Hand, Head, and Heart* (1955). Elizabeth Yates won applause for *Amos Fortune, Free Man* (1950) and the Newbery Award a year later, but her account of a slave who gained freedom in 1801 and fought the rest of his life for freedom for other blacks has been attacked by some black groups as paternalistic, a word much overused by black critics who assume that any white writer is inherently incapable of writing about blacks.

Personal Problems and Initiation Novels

Intrigued and concerned as many young adults were about social issues and dilemmas, something far more immediate constantly pressed in upon them— their own personal need to survive in an often unfriendly world. As one youngster said, "What do they mean, 'What am I going to do when I grow up?' First I have to survive and that's a problem with school and parents and my girl friend."

Superior to earlier authors like Betty Cavanna and Rosamund du Jardin, Anne Emery preached acceptance of the status quo, especially acceptance of parental rules, but she wrote books that were popular with young adult women. With an exception here and there, her books avoided controversy yet they appeared to focus on social concerns. *Going Steady* (1950) and *Sorority Girl* (1952) were typical of Emery, but her best book was *Married on Wednesday* (1957).

Mina Lewiton dealt with far more suspect, even controversial, topics. *The Divided Heart* (1947) was an early study of the effect of divorce on a young woman, and *A Cup of Courage* (1948) was an honest and groundbreaking account of alcoholism and its destruction of a family. Later, Zoa Sherburne proved more enduring with her portrait of alcohol's effect in *Jennifer* (1959), though her best and most likely to last book is *Too Bad About the Haines Girl* (1967), a superb novel about pregnancy, honest and straightforward without being unduly preachy.

But something far more significant appeared during the same years that the personal problem novel seemed supreme. The *bildungsroman,* a novel about the initiation, maturation, and education of a young adult, grew in appeal. The number of such books, most of them originally published for adults but soon read by young adults, appearing from 1940 onward was prodigious.

One of the first, now nearly forgotten, was Dan Wickenden's *Walk Like a Mortal* (1940). Seventeen-year-old Gabe McKenzie learns that he will never achieve his longed-for excellence in athletics, and he accepts his excellence in journalism as a substitute. His neurotic mother and dull father are verging on separation and Gabe must accept the fact of his own conflicting loyalties. Girls found an equally appealing and honest book in Betty Smith's *A Tree Grows in Brooklyn* (1943).

But no book won the young adult favor or the adult opposition that J. D. Salinger's *The Catcher in the Rye* (1951) did. Still the most widely censored book in American schools and still hated by people who assume that a disliked word (*that* word) corrupts an entire book, *Catcher* has been read ever since it became a selection of the Book-of-the-Month Club. Holden Caulfield may indeed be what so many have accused him of being, vulgar and cynical and capable of seeing only the phonies around him, but he is also loyal and loving to those he sees as good or innocent. His struggle to preserve innocence leads him to the brink of a mental breakdown. *Catcher* is many things, literary, profane, sensitive, cynical. For many young adults it is the most honest and human story they know about someone they recognize—even in themselves— a young man caught between childhood and maturity and unsure which way to go. Whether *Catcher* is a masterpiece like James Joyce's *Portrait of the Artist as a Young Man* depends on subjective judgment, but there is no question that Salinger's book captured—and continues to capture—the hearts and minds of countless young adults as no other book has.

Most teachers and librarians would have predicted just as long a life for John Knowles' *A Separate Peace* (1961) and William Golding's *Lord of the Flies* (1955), but fame and longevity are sometime things, and despite many articles in *English Journal* about the literary and pedagogical worth of both books, they seem to be in a state of decline.

Sports and Cars

Sports stories continued to be popular with some young adults, though aside from John Tunis no writer of any great talent appeared between 1940 and 1966.

Nonfiction was not yet as popular as it would later become, but one of the best books of the time was the autobiography of Boston Red Sox outfielder Jim Piersall, *Fear Strikes Out* (1955), telling about his life as an athlete and his mental breakdown. Almost equally worthwhile was Roy Campanella's *It's Good to Be Alive* (1959) dealing with his life as a catcher and his adjustment to a tragic and almost fatal car accident.

Occasionally, a good sports novel appeared. Two authors were the best of the crop. John F. Carson's basketball novels convey a love of the game and an understanding of the power of athletics for good or evil. They are *Floorburns* (1957), *The Coach Nobody Liked* (1960), and *Hotshot* (1961). C. H. Frick, pen name of Constance Frick Irwin, used clever plot twists to make her sports novels different. *Five Against the Odds* (1955) features a basketball player stricken with polio, *Patch* (1957) is about a runner who loves running for its own sake, not because it may lead to winning anything, and *The Comeback Guy* (1961) focuses on a too-popular, too-successful young man who gets his comeuppance and works his way back to self-respect through sports.

THE RISE OF CRITICISM OF YOUNG ADULT LITERATURE

Today, we take criticism of young adult literature for granted in journals such as the *ALAN Review, Top of the News, School Library Journal, English Journal, Wilson Library Bulletin, Horn Book Magazine, Children's Literature in Education, The Lion and the Unicorn,* and *Interracial Books for Children Bulletin,* but it developed slowly. In the 1940s, journals provided little information and less criticism of young adult literature, excepting book lists, book reviews, and occasional references to a few authors or titles in articles on reading interests or raising young peoples' literary tastes. A teacher and author as gifted as Dwight L. Burton could devote considerable space in 1947 to the worth of Daly's *Seventeenth Summer* or Wickenden's *Walk Like a Mortal,* but Burton's perceptive comments were more appreciative than critical.[19] Given the times and the attitude of many teachers and librarians, appreciation or even recognition may have been more important than criticism.

Four years later, Burton wrote the first criticism of young adult novels, again concerned with Daly and Wickenden, but this time injecting criticism along with appreciation and commenting on more titles, among them Paul Annixter's *Swiftwater,* Betty Cavanna's *Going on Sixteen,* and Madeleine L'Engle's *The Small Rain.* Concluding his article, Burton identified the qualities of the good young adult novel and prophesied its potential and future:

> The good novel for the adolescent reader has attributes no different from any good novel. It must be technically masterful, and it must present a significant synthesis of human experience. Because of the nature of adolescence itself, the good novel for the adolescent should be full in true invention and imagination. It must free itself of Pollyannaism or the Tarkington-Henry Aldrich-Corliss Archer tradition and maintain a clear vision of the adolescent as a person of complexity, individuality, and dignity. The novel for the adolescent presents a ready field for the mature artist.[20]

In 1955 Richard S. Alm provided greater critical coverage of the young adult novel.[21] He agreed with critics that many writers presented "a sugar-puff story of what adolescents should do and should believe rather than what adolescents may or will do and believe," but he argued that if writers like Janet Lambert and Helen Boylston wrote airy exercises in superficialism, other writers provided young adults with books of greater psychological accuracy and literary merit. Not only did Alm cite specific authors and titles he found good, he painted their strengths and weaknesses in clear strokes and concluded by offering teachers some questions that might be useful in analyzing the merit of young adult novels.

A year later, Emma L. Patterson began her fine study of the origin of young adult novels, "The junior novel has become an established institution."[22] Her command of history, her knowledge of trends in young adult novels, her awareness of shortcomings and virtues of the novels, and her understanding of the place of young adult novels in schools and libraries made her article essential reading for librarians and teachers.

Despite the leadership of Burton, Alm, and Patterson, helpful criticism of young adult literature was slow in coming, but biting criticism was soon forthcoming. Only a few months after Patterson's article, Frank G. Jennings' "Literature for Adolescents—Pap or Protein?"[23] appeared. The title was unambiguous, but if any reader had doubts about where Jennings stood, the doubt was removed with the first sentence, "The stuff of adolescent literature, for the most part, is mealy-mouthed, gutless, and pointless." The remainder of the article added little to that point, and if Jennings did overstate his case, Burton, Alm, Patterson, and other sensible supporters would have agreed that much young adult literature, like much adult literature, was second-rate or worse. Jennings' article was not the first broadside attack, and it certainly would not be the last.[24]

Much of the literature written for young adults from 1940 through 1966 goes largely and legitimately ignored today. But some writers for young adults between 1940 and 1966 are still read, perhaps by an audience younger than originally intended, but often by readers as old as their first ones. Maureen Daly and Esther Forbes are still widely read.

More important than mere longevity is the effect these authors had on books appearing after 1966. Readers before then could not have anticipated S. E. Hinton's *The Outsiders* or Paul Zindel's *The Pigman,* which were to appear in only a year or two, much less Isabelle Holland's *The Man Without a Face,* Norma Klein's *Mom, The Wolfman and Me,* Rosa Guy's *Ruby,* or Robert Cormier's *The Chocolate War,* all to be published soon afterward. But the iconoclastic, taboo-breaking novels today would not have been possible had it not been for earlier novels that broke ground and prepared readers, teachers, and librarians (and even some parents) for contemporary novels. Society's changes, of course, inevitably lead to changes in literature, but changes in young adult literature can be attributed in large part to authors like Tunis, Means, Annixter, Daly, and Stolz.

◼ NOTES

[1]George W. Norvell, "Some Results of a Twelve-Year Study of Children's Reading Interests," *English Journal* 35 (December 1946): 532.

[2]Norvell, "Some Results . . . ," p. 536.

[3]Marie Rankin, *Children's Interests in Library Books of Fiction,* Teachers College, Columbia University, Contributions to Education, No. 906 (New York: Teachers College, Columbia Univ., l947).

[4]Stephen Dunning, "The Most Popular Junior Novels," *Junior Libraries* 5 (December 15, 1959): 7–9.

[5]Jacob W. Getzels, "The Nature of Reading Interests: Psychological Aspects" in *Developing Permanent Interests in Reading,* ed. Helen M. Robinson, Supplementary Education Monographs, No. 84, December 1956 (Chicago: University of Chicago Press, 1956), p. 5.

[6]Robert Carlsen, "Behind Reading Interests," *English Journal* 43 (January 1954): 7–10.

[7]Robert J. Havighurst, *Human Development and Education* (New York: Longmans, Green, 1953), pp. 111–56.

[8]G. O. Ireland, "Bibliotherapy: The Use of Books as a Form of Treatment in a Neuropsychiatric Hospital," *Library Journal* 54 (December 1, 1929): 972–74.

[9]Alice I. Bryan, "Can There Be a Science of Bibliotherapy?" *Library Journal* 64 (October 15, 1939): 773–76.

[10]William A. Heaps, "Bibliotherapy and the School Librarian," *Library Journal* 65 (October 1, 1940): 789.

[11]Lou LaBrant, "Diversifying the Matter," *English Journal* 40 (March 1951): 135.

[12]S. Alan Cohen, "Paperbacks in the Classroom," *Journal of Reading* 12 (January 1969): 295.

[13]Leo Lerman, "An Industry Within an Industry," *Saturday Review of Literature* 24 (November 8, 1941): 3.

[14]Stanley B. Kegler and Stephen Dunning, "Junior Book Roundup—Literature for the Adolescent, 1960," *English Journal* 50 (May 1961): 369.

[15]Stanley B. Kegler and Stephen Dunning, "Junior Book Roundup," *English Journal* 53 (May 1964): 392.

[16]"Children's Books," *Saturday Review of Literature* 24 (November 8, 1941): 12.

[17]*Library Journal* 77 (July 1952), 1216.

[18]Richard S. Alm, "The Glitter and the Gold," *English Journal* 44 (September 1955): 320.

[19]Dwight L. Burton, "Books to Meet Students' Personal Needs," *English Journal* 36 (November 1947): 469–73. See also G. Robert Carlsen, "Literature and Emotional Maturity," *English Journal* 38 (March 1949): 130–38; and Isabel V. Eno, "Books for Children from Broken Homes," *English Journal* 38 (October 1949): 457–58 for similar articles.

[20]Dwight L. Burton, "The Novel for the Adolescent," *English Journal* 40 (September 1951): 363–69.

[21]Richard S. Alm, "The Glitter and the Gold," *English Journal* 44 (September 1955): 315.

[22]Emma L. Patterson, "The Junior Novels and How They Grew," *English Journal* 45 (October 1956): 381.

[23]*English Journal* 45 (December 1956): 226–31.

[24]See, for example, Alice Krahn, "Case Against the Junior Novel," *Top of the News* 17 (May 1961): 19–22; Esther Millett, "We Don't Even Call Those Books!" *Top of the News* 20 (October 1963): 45—47; and Harvey R. Granite, "The Uses and Abuses of Junior Literature," *Clearing House* 42 (February 1968): 337–40.

◼ TITLES MENTIONED IN CHAPTER FIFTEEN

Annixter, Paul. *Swiftwater.* A. A. Wyn, 1950.

Bell, Margaret Elizabeth. *Love Is Forever.* Morrow, 1954.

Bennett, Jack. *The Hawk Alone.* Little, Brown, 1965.

—————. *Jamie.* Little, Brown, 1963.

—————. *Mister Fisherman.* Little, Brown, 1965.

Benson, Sally. *Junior Miss.* Doubleday, 1947.

Boylston, Helen Dore. *Sue Barton, Senior Nurse.* John Lane, 1950.

—————. *Sue Barton, Staff Nurse.* Little, Brown, 1952.

—————. *Sue Barton, Student Nurse.* Little, Brown, 1936.

Breck, Vivian. *Maggie,* Doubleday, 1954.

Brown, Claude. *Manchild in the Promised Land.* Macmillan, 1965.

Buck, Pearl S. *The Good Earth.* John Day, 1931.

Bugbee, Emma. *Peggy Covers the News.* Dodd, Mead, 1936.

Burns, John Horne. *The Gallery.* Harper & Row, 1947.

Campanella, Roy. *It's Good to Be Alive.* Little, Brown, 1959.

Carson, John F. *The Coach Nobody Liked.* Farrar, Straus, Giroux, 1960.

—————. *Floorburns.* Farrar, Straus, Giroux, 1957.

—————. *Hotshot.* Farrar, Straus, Giroux, 1961

Cavanna, Betty. *Going on Sixteen.* Ryerson, 1946.

Chute, Marchette. *The Innocent Wayfaring.* Scribner's, 1943.

—————. *The Wonderful Winter.* E. P. Dutton, 1954.

Cleaver, Eldridge. *Soul on Ice.* McGraw-Hill, 1968.

Daly, Maureen. *Seventeenth Summer.* Dodd, Mead, 1942.

Du Jardin, Rosamund. *Double Date.* Longmans, 1953.

—————. *Wait for Marcy.* Longmans, 1950.

Ellison, Ralph. *Invisible Man.* Random House, 1952.

Emery, Anne. *Going Steady.* Westminster, 1950.

—————. *Married on Wednesday.* Ryerson, 1957.

—————. *Sorority Girl.* Westminster, 1952.

Eyerly, Jeanette. *Bonnie Jo, Go Home.* Lippincott, 1972.

—————. *Drop-Out.* Lippincott, 1963.

—————. *A Girl Like Me.* Lippincott, 1966.

—————. *Radigan Cares.* Lippincott, 1970.

Fargo, Lucile Foster. *Marian Martha.* Dodd, Mead, 1936.

Farley, Walter. *Black Stallion.* Random House, 1944.

Felsen, Henry Gregor. *Bertie Comes Through.* E. P. Dutton, 1947.

—————. *Bertie Makes a Break.* E. P. Dutton, 1949.

—————. *Bertie Takes Care.* E. P. Dutton, 1948.

—————. *Crash Club.* Random House, 1958.

—————. *Hot Rod.* E. P. Dutton, 1950.

—————. *Street Rod.* Random House, 1953.

—————. *Two and the Town.* Scribner's, 1952.

Forbes, Esther. *Johnny Tremain.* Houghton Mifflin, 1943.

—————. *Paul Revere and the World He Lived In.* Houghton Mifflin, 1942.

Freedman, Benedict and Nancy. *Mrs. Mike.* Coward, McCann & Geoghegan, 1947.

Frick, Constance H. *The Comeback Guy.* Harcourt Brace Jovanovich, 1961.

—————. *Five Against the Odds.* Harcourt Brace Jovanovich, 1955.

—————. *Patch.* Harcourt Brace Jovanovich, 1957.

Gibbs, Blanche L., and Georgiana Adams. *Shirley Clayton, Secretary.* Dodd, Mead, 1941.

Golding, William. *Lord of the Flies*. Coward, McCann & Geoghegan, 1955.

Goudge, Elizabeth. *Green Dolphin Street*. Coward, McCann &Geoghegan, 1944.

Graham, Lorenz. *North Town*. Crowell, 1965.

_____ . *South Town*. Follet, 1958.

_____ . *Whose Town?* Crowell, 1969.

Graham, Shirley. *Booker T. Washington: Educator of Hand, Head, and Heart*. Julian Messner, 1955.

_____ . *The Story of Phillis Wheatley: Poetess of the American Revolution*. Julian Messner, 1949.

_____ . *There Was Once a Slave: The Heroic Story of Frederick Douglass*. Julian Messner, 1947.

_____ . *Your Most Humble Servant: The Story of Benjamin Banneker*. Julian Messner, 1949.

Gray, Elizabeth Janet. *Adam of the Road*. Viking, 1942.

Griffin, John Howard. *Black Like Me*. Houghton Mifflin, 1961.

_____ . *The Devil Rides Outside,* William Collins Sons, 1952.

Harris, Christie. *You Have to Draw the Line Somewhere*. Atheneum, 1964.

Hentoff, Nat. *I'm Really Dragged but Nothing Gets Me Down*. Simon and Schuster, 1968.

_____ . *In the Country of Ourselves*. Simon and Schuster, 1971.

_____ . *Jazz Country*. Harper & Row, 1965.

Hersey, John Richard. *A Bell for Adano*. Knopf, 1944.

Jones, James. *From Here to Eternity*. Scribner's, 1951.

_____ . *The Pistol*. Scribner's, 1959.

_____ . *The Thin Red Line*. Scribner's, 1962.

Knowles, John. *A Separate Peace*. Macmillan, 1960.

Lansing, Elizabeth. *Nancy Naylor, Flight Nurse*. Crowell, 1944.

Lee, Harper. *To Kill a Mockingbird*. Lippincott, 1960.

L'Engle, Madeleine. *The Small Rain*. Vanguard, 1945.

Lewiton, Mina. *A Cup of Courage*. McKay, 1948.

_____ . *The Divided Heart*. McKay, 1947.

Mailer, Norman. *The Naked and the Dead*. Clarke, Irwin, 1948.

Malcolm X. and Alex Haley. *The Autobiography of Malcolm X*. Grove, 1965.

Mann, Carl. *He's in the Signal Corps Now*. McBride, 1943.

McFadden, Dorothy. *Lynn Decker: TV Apprentice*. Dodd, Mead, 1953.

Means, Florence Crannell. *A Candle in the Mist*. Houghton Mifflin, 1931.

_____ . *It Takes All Kinds*. Houghton Mifflin, 1964.

_____ . *The Moved-Outers*. Houghton Mifflin, 1945.

_____ . *Our Cup Is Broken*. Houghton Mifflin, 1969.

_____ . *Shuttered Windows*. Houghton Mifflin, 1938.

_____ . *Tangled Waters: A Navajo Story*. Houghton Mifflin, 1936.

_____ . *Tolliver*. Houghton Mifflin, 1963.

Medearis, Mary. *Big Doc's Girl*. Lippincott, 1942.

Paton, Alan. *Cry the Beloved Country*. Scribner's, 1948.

_____ . *Too Late the Phalarope*. Scribner's, 1953.

Piersall, James Anthony, and Albert Hirshberg. *Fear Strikes Out*. Little, Brown, 1955.

Pyle, Ernie. *Brave Men*. Holt, Rinehart and Winston, 1944.

_____ . *Here Is Your War*. Holt, Rinehart and Winston, 1943.

Reynolds, Quentin James. *70,000 to One*. Random House, 1946.

Rosenheim, Lucille G. *Kathie, the New Teacher*. Julian Messner, 1949.

Salinger, J. D. *The Catcher in the Rye*. Little, Brown, 1951.

Sherburne, Zoa. *Jennifer*. Morrow, 1959.

_____ . *Too Bad about the Haines Girl.* Morrow, 1967.

Smith, Betty. *A Tree Grows in Brooklyn.* Harper & Row, 1943.

Smith, Lillian. *Strange Fruit.* Reynal, 1944.

Steinbeck, John. *The Grapes of Wrath.* Viking, 1939.

_____ . *Of Mice and Men.* Viking, 1937.

Stolz, Mary Slattery. *A Love, or a Season.* Harper & Row, 1964.

_____ . *Pray Love, Remember.* Harper & Row, 1954.

_____ . *The Sea Gulls Woke Me.* Harper & Row, 1951.

_____ . *To Tell Your Love.* Harper & Row, 1950.

Summers, James. *The Limit of Love.* Ryerson, 1959.

_____ . *Operation ABC.* Westminster, 1955.

_____ . *Prom Trouble.* Ryerson, 1954.

_____ . *Ring Around Her Finger.* Westminster, 1957.

_____ . *The Shelter Trap.* Westminster, 1962.

_____ . *The Wonderful Times.* Ryerson, 1957.

Tregaskis, Richard William. *Guadalcanal Diary.* Random House, 1943.

Trumbull, Robert. *The Raft.* Holt, Rinehart and Winston, 1942.

Tunis, John R. *All-American.* Harcourt Brace, 1942.

_____ . *A City for Lincoln.* Harcourt Brace, 1945.

_____ . *Go, Team, Go!* Morrow, 1954.

_____ . *His Enemy, His Friend.* Morrow, 1967.

_____ . *Iron Duke.* Harcourt Brace, 1938.

_____ . *Silence over Dunkerque.* Morrow, 1962.

_____ . *Yea! Wildcats.* Harcourt Brace, 1944.

Wickenden, Dan. *Walk Like a Mortal.* Morrow, 1940.

Winsor, Kathleen. *Forever Amber.* Macmillan, 1944.

Wright, Richard. *Black Boy.* Harper & Row, 1940.

_____ . *Native Son.* Harper & Row, 1940.

Yates, Elizabeth. *Amos Fortune, Free Man.* Aladdin, 1950.

▪ SOME SUGGESTED READINGS

General Comments on Literature, 1940-1966

Alm, Richard. "The Glitter and the Gold." *English Journal* 44 (September 1955): 315–22.

Burton, Dwight. *Literature Study in the High Schools.* 3rd ed. New York: Holt, Rinehart and Winston, 1970.

_____ . "The Novel for the Adolescent." *English Journal* 40 (September 1951): 363–69.

Carlsen, G. Robert. "Forty Years with Books and Teen-Age Readers." *Arizona English Bulletin* 18 (April 1976): 1–5.

Davis, James E. "Recent Trends in Fiction for Adolescents." *English Journal* 56 (May 1967): 702–24.

Edwards, Margaret A. "The Rise of Teen-Age Reading." *Saturday Review* 37 (November 13, 1954): 88.

Epstein, Jason. "Good Bunnies Always Obey: Books for American Children." *Commentary* 35 (February 1963): 112–22.

Hackett, Alice Payne, and James Henry Burke. *80 Years of Best Sellers, 1895–1975.* New York: R. R. Bowker, 1977.

Hart, James D. *The Popular Book: A History of America's Literary Taste.* Berkeley: University of California Press, 1950.

Hentoff, Nat. "Getting Inside Jazz Country." *Horn Book Magazine* 42 (October 1966): 528–32.

Jennings, Frank G. "Literature for Adolescents—Pap or Protein?" *English Journal* 45 (December 1951): 526–31.

Nordstrom, Ursula. "Honesty in Teenage Novels." *Top of the News* 21 (November 1964): 35–38.

Rosenblatt, Louise M. *Literature as Exploration.* 3rd ed. New York: Noble and Noble, 1977.

Rosenheim, Edward W., Jr. "Children's Reading and Adults' Values" in *A Critical Approach to Children's Literature.* Sara Innis Fenwick, ed. Chicago: University of Chicago Press, 1967, pp. 3–14.

Sample, Hazel. *Pitfalls for Readers of Fiction.* Chicago: National Council of Teachers of English, 1940.

Reading Interest Studies

Anderson, Esther M. "A Study of Leisure-Time Reading of Pupils in Junior High School." *Elementary School Journal* 48 (January 1948): 258–67.

Anderson, Scarvia B. *Between the Grimms and "The Group": Literature in American High Schools.* Princeton: Educational Testing Service, 1964.

Barbe, Walter. "A Study of the Reading of Gifted High-School Students." *Educational Administration and Supervision* 38 (March 1952): 148–54.

Carlsen, G. Robert. "Behind Reading Interests." *English Journal* 43 (January 1954): 7–12.

_____ . "For Everything There Is a Season." *Top of the News* 21 (January 1967): 103–10.

Dunning, Stephen. "The Most Popular Junior Novels." *Junior Libraries* 5 (December 1959): 7–9.

Edwards, Margaret A. "A Time When It's Best to Read and Let Read." *Wilson Library Bulletin* 35 (September 1960): 43–45.

Getzels, Jacob W. "The Nature of Reading Interests: Psychological Aspects." *In Developing Permanent Interest in Reading.* Helen M. Robinson, ed. Supplementary Education Monographs, No. 84. Chicago: University of Chicago Press, 1956, pp. 5–9.

Lapides, Linda P. "Unassigned Reading: Teen-Age Testimonies I and II: A Decade of Teen-Age Reading in Baltimore, 1960–1970." *Top of the News* 27 (April 1971): 278–91.

Nelms, Ben F. "Reading for Pleasure in Junior High School" *English Journal* 55 (September 1966): 676–81.

Norvell, George W. *The Reading Interests of Young People.* Boston: D. C. Heath, 1950.

_____ . "Some Results of a Twelve-Year Study of Children's Reading Interests." *English Journal* 35 (December 1946): 531–36.

Petitt, Dorothy. "A Search for Self-Definition: The Picture of Life in the Novel for the Adolescent." *English Journal* 49 (December 1960): 616–26.

Plotz, Helen. "The Rising Generation of Readers." *New York Times Magazine,* August 5, 1956, p. 44.

Rankin, Marie. *Children's Interests in Library Books of Fiction.* Teachers College, Columbia University Contributions to Education, No. 906. New York: Teachers College Press, 1947.

Scanlan, William J. "One Hundred Most Popular Books of Children's Fiction Selected by Children." *Elementary English* 25 (February 1948): 83–97.

Scoggin, Margaret C. "Young People's Reading Interests Not Materially Changed in Wartime." *Library Journal* 68 (September 15, 1943): 703–6.

Soares, Anthony T. "Salient Elements of Recreational Reading of Junior High School Students." *Elementary English* 40 (December 1963): 843–45.

Havighurst's Developmental Tasks

Brooks, Alice. "Integrating Books and Reading with Havighurst's Developmental Tasks." *School Review* 58 (April 1950): 211–19.

Havighurst, Robert J. *Developmental Tasks and Education.* New York: Longmans, Green, 1948.
—————— . *Human Development and Education.* New York: Longmans, Green, 1953.
Johnson, Gladys B. "Books and the Five Adolescent Tasks." *Library Journal* 68 (May 1, 1943): 350–52

Bibliotherapy
Beatty, William K. "A Historical Review of Bibliotherapy." *Library Trends* 11 (October 1962): 106–17.
Bryan, Alice I. "Can There Be a Science of Bibliotherapy?" *Library Journal* 64 (October 15, 1939): 773–76.
Darling, Richard L. "Mental Hygiene and Books: Bibliotherapy as Used with Children and Adolescents." *Wilson Library Bulletin* 32 (December 1957): 293–96.
Dreyer, Sharon Spredemann. *The Bookfinder: A Guide to Children's Literature about the Needs and Problems of Youth Aged 12–15.* Circle Pines, Minnesota: American Guidance Service, 1977.
Elser, Helen. "Bibliotherapy in Practice." *Library Trends* 30 (Spring 1982): 647–59.
Heaps, Willard A. "Bibliotherapy and the School Librarian." *Library Journal* 65 (October 1, 1940): 789–92.
Hynes, Arleen McCarthy. "Bibliotherapy—The Interactive Process." *Catholic Library World* 58 (January–February 1987): 167–70.
Jackson, Evalene P. "Bibliotherapy and Reading Guidance: A Tentative Approach to Theory." *Library Trends* 11 (October 1962): 118–26.
Lindeman, Barbara, and M. Kling. "Bibliotherapy: Definitions, Uses, and Studies." *Journal of School Psychology* 7 (1968–69): 34–41.
Newton, Eunice S. "Bibliotherapy in the Development of Minority Group Self-Concept." *Journal of Negro Education* 38 (Summer 1969): 257–65.
Riggs, Corinne W., ed. *Bibliotherapy: An Annotated Bibliography.* Newark, Delaware: International Reading Association, 1971.

Russell, David H. and Caroline Shrodes. "Contributions of Research in Bibliotherapy to the Langauge Arts Program." *School Review* 58 (September 1950); 335–42; and 58 (October 1950): 411–20.
Warner, Lucy. "The Myth of Bibliotherapy." *School Library Journal* 27 (October 1980): 107–11.

Paperbacks
Butman, Alexander, Donald Reis, and David Sohn, eds. *Paperbacks in the Schools.* New York: Bantam, 1963.
Davis, Kenneth C. *Two-Bit Culture: The Paperbacking of America.* Boston: Houghton Mifflin, 1984.
Enoch, Kurt. "The Paper-Bound Book: Twentieth-Century Publishing Phenomenon." *Library Quarterly* 24 (July 1954): 211–25.
Lewis, Freeman. "The Future of Paper-Bound Books." *Bulletin of the New York Public Library* 57 (October 1953): 506–15.
—————— . "Paper-Bound Books in America." *Bulletin of the New York Public Library* 57 (February 1953): 55–75.
Schick, Frank L. *The Paperbound Book in America: The History of Paperbacks and Their European Background.* New York: R. R. Bowker, 1958.

Career Books
Edwards, Anne. "Teen-Age Career Girls." *English Journal* 42 (November 1953): 437–42.
Forrester, Gertrude. *Occupational Literature: An Annotated Bibliography.* New York: H. W. Wilson, 1971.
Haebich, Kathryn A., ed. *Vocations in Biography and Fiction.* Chicago: American Library Association, 1962.
Ives, Vernon. "Careers for Sale: $2.00 List." *Horn Book Magazine* 19 (March–April 1943): 107–12.
Splaver, Sarah. "The Career Novel." *Personnel and Guidance Journal* 31 (March 1953): 371–72.

APPENDIX A
HONOR SAMPLING

Title and Author	Hardbound Publisher	Publishing Division	Paperback Publisher	Genre	Protagonist Sex	Age	Number of Pages	Media Edition TV	Movie	Ethnic Group or Unusual Setting
1987										
After the Rain Norma Fox Mazer	Morrow	J	Avon	Realistic Fiction	F	mid teens	290			
The Crazy Horse Electric Game Chris Crutcher	Greenwillow	J		Realistic Fiction	M	late teens	224			Black secondary characters
The Goats Brock Cole	Farrar, Straus, Giroux	J		Realistic Fiction	M/F	early teens	184			
Permanent Connections Sue Ellen Bridgers	Harper & Row	J	Harper	Realistic Fiction	M/F	17	264			
Princess Ashley Richard Peck	Delacorte	J	Dell	Realistic Fiction	F	15	208			
Sons from Afar Cynthia Voigt	Atheneum	J		Realistic Fiction	M	mid teens	224			
The Tricksters Margaret Mahy	Macmillan	J	Macmillan	Fantasy	F	17	266			New Zealand

1986

Title / Author	Publisher	Level	Genre	Sex	Age	Pages			Setting / Notes
All God's Children Need Traveling Shoes — Maya Angelou	Random House	A	Autobiography	F	adult	210			Black
A Band of Angels — Julian Thompson	Scholastic	J	Realistic Suspense	M/F	mid teens	294			Some black characters
Cat, Herself — Mollie Hunter	Harper & Row	J	Realistic Fiction	F	mid teens	279			British nomads
The Catalogue of the Universe — Margaret Mahy	Macmillan	J	Realistic Fiction	F	17	185			New Zealand
Izzy, Willy-Nilly — Cynthia Voigt	Atheneum	J	Realistic Fiction	F	15	288			
Midnight Hour Encores — Bruce Brooks	Harper & Row	J	Realistic Fiction	F	16	288			

1985

Title / Author	Publisher	Level	Genre	Sex	Age	Pages			Setting / Notes
Betsey Brown — Ntozake Shange	St. Martin	A	Realistic Fiction	F	13	207	Musical Play		Black
Beyond the Chocolate War — Robert Cormier	Knopf	J	Realistic Fiction	M	17	234			
Dogsong — Gary Paulsen	Bradbury	J	Realistic Fiction	M	13	177			Eskimo
In Country — Bobbie Ann Mason	Harper & Row	A	Realistic Fiction	F	17	247		•	
The Moonlight Man — Paula Fox	Bradbury	J	Realistic Fiction	F	15	192			Nova Scotia
Pocket Poems: Selected for a Journey — Paul Janeczko, ed.	Bradbury	J	Poetry	M/F	teens	138			
Remembering the Good Times — Richard Peck	Delacorte	J	Realistic Fiction	M/F	mid teens	192			
Wolf of Shadows — Whitley Strieber	Knopf	J	Science Fiction	F	mixed	105			Postnuclear wilderness

Title and Author	Hardbound Publisher	Publishing Division	Paperback Publisher	Genre	Protagonist Sex	Age	Number of Pages	Media Edition TV	Movie	Ethnic Group or Unusual Setting
1984										
The Changeover: A Supernatural Romance Margaret Mahy	Macmillan	J	Scholastic	Fantasy	M/F	mid teens	214			New Zealand
Cold Sassy Tree Olive Ann Burns	Ticknor & Fields	A	Dell	Historical Fiction	M/F	mixed	391			1906 rural Georgia
Downtown Norma Fox Mazer	Morrow	J	Avon	Realistic Fiction	M/F	early teens	216			
Interstellar Pig William Sleator	Dutton	J	Bantam	Science Fiction	M	16	197			
A Little Love Virginia Hamilton	Putnam	J	Berkley	Realistic Fiction	F	mid teens	207			Black
The Moves Make the Man Bruce Brooks	Harper & Row	J	Harper	Realistic Fiction	M	early teens	280			Black and white
One-Eyed Cat Paula Fox	Bradbury	J	Dell	Realistic Fiction	M	11	216			1934 upstate New York
Sixteen: Short Stories by Outstanding Writers for Young Adults Donald R. Gallo, ed.	Delacorte	J	Dell	Short Stories	M/F	mixed	179			

1983

Title / Author	Audience	Publisher	Genre	Sex	Age	Pages		Setting
Beyond the Divide, Kathryn Lasky	J	Macmillan	Historical Fiction	F	teens	254		1800s West
The Bumblebee Flies Anyway, Robert Cormier	J	Pantheon	Realistic Fiction	M/F	teens	211		
A Gathering of Old Men, Ernest J. Gaines	A	Knopf	Realistic Fiction	M	elderly	214		Depression South, Black
Poetspeak: In Their Work, About Their Work, Paul Janeczko, ed.	J	Bradbury	Poetry			224		
A Solitary Blue, Cynthia Voigt	J	Atheneum	Realistic Fiction	M	7–18	182		

1982

Title / Author	Audience	Publisher	Genre	Sex	Age	Pages		Setting
The Blue Sword, Robin McKinley	J	Greenwillow	Fantasy	F	late teens	272		Middle Ages
Class Dismissed! High School Poems, Mel Glenn	J	Clarion	Poetry	M/F	teens	96		
The Darkangel, Meredith Ann Pierce	J	Atlantic	Fantasy	F	early teens	223		
A Formal Feeling, Zibby Oneal	J	Viking	Realistic Fiction	F	16	162		
Homesick: My Own Story, Jean Fritz	J	Putnam	Autobiography Fiction	F	10–12	163		Pre-War China
A Midnight Clear, William Wharton	A	Knopf	Realistic Fiction	M	early 20s	241	●	World War II
Sweet Whispers, Brother Rush, Virginia Hamilton	J	Philomel	Occult	F	14	224		Black

Title and Author	Hardbound Publisher	Publishing Division	Paperback Publisher	Genre	Protagonist Sex	Age	Number of Pages	Media Edition TV	Movie	Ethnic Group or Unusual Setting
1981										
Let the Circle Be Unbroken Mildred D. Taylor	Dial	J	Bantam	Realistic Historical Fiction	F	16	394			Depression South, Black
Little Little M. E. Kerr	Harper & Row	J	Bantam	Humor Realistic Fiction	F	18	183			
Notes for Another Life Sue Ellen Bridgers	Knopf	J	Bantam	Realistic Fiction	M/F	13–16	252			
Rainbow Jordan Alice Childress	Coward McCann	J	Avon	Realistic Fiction	F	14	142			Black
Stranger with My Face Lois Duncan	Little, Brown	J	Dell	Occult	F	17	250			
Tiger Eyes Judy Blume	Bradbury	J	Dell	Realistic Fiction	F	15	206			Mexican-American, New Mexico
Westmark Lloyd Alexander	Dutton	J	Dell	Historical Fiction	M	16	184			England
1980										
The Beginning Place Ursula K. Le Guin	Harper & Row	J	Bantam	Fantasy	M/F	early 20s	183			
Jacob Have I Loved Katherine Paterson	Crowell	J	Avon	Realistic Historical Fiction	F	teens	216			island in Chesapeake Bay
A Matter of Feeling Janine Boissard	Little, Brown	A	Fawcett	Realistic Fiction	F	17	214			Translated from French
The Quartzsite Trip William Hogan	Atheneum	A	Avon	Realistic Fiction	M/F	17–18	307			

1979

Title / Author	Publisher		Paperback	Genre		Age	Pages		Theme
√ After the First Death / Robert Cormier	Pantheon	J	Avon	Suspense	M	13	233		
√ All Together Now / Sue Ellen Bridgers	Knopf	J	Bantam	Realistic Fiction	F	12	238		
√ Birdy / William Wharton	Knopf	A	Avon	Realistic Fiction	M	teens & early 20s	310	•	
√ The Disappearance / Rosa Guy	Delacorte	J	Dell	Realistic Fiction	M	16	246		Black
√ The Last Mission / Harry Mazer	Delacorte	J	Dell	Suspense	M	16	182		World War II
√ Tex / S. E. Hinton	Delacorte	J	Dell	Realistic Fiction	M	15	194	•	
√ Words by Heart / Ouida Sebestyen	Little, Brown	J	Bantam	Historical Fiction	F	12	162		1920s Western U.S.

1978

Title / Author	Publisher		Paperback	Genre		Age	Pages		Theme
✗ Beauty: A Retelling of the Story of Beauty and the Beast / Robin McKinley	Harper & Row	J		Fantasy •	F	15	247		Medieval
√ The Book of the Dun Cow / Walter Wangerin, Jr.	Harper & Row	J	Pocket Books	Fantasy	M	—	255		
√ Dreamsnake / Vonda N. McIntyre	Houghton Mifflin	A	Dell	Science Fiction	F	teens	313		
√ Father Figure / Richard Peck	Viking	J	NAL	Realistic Fiction	M	17	192	•	
√ Gentlehands / M. E. Kerr	Harper & Row	J	Bantam	Realistic Fiction	M	16	183		German, Jewish

Title and Author	Hardbound Publisher	Publishing Division	Paperback Publisher	Genre	Protagonist Sex	Age	Number of Pages	Media Edition TV	Movie	Ethnic Group or Unusual Setting
1977										
Hard Feelings Don Bredes	Atheneum	A	Bantam	Realistic Fiction	M	16	377			
I Am the Cheese Robert Cormier	Knopf	J	Dell	Realistic Fiction	M	14	233		●	
I'll Love You When You're More Like Me M. E. Kerr	Harper & Row	J	Dell	Realistic Fiction	M/F	17	183			
Ludell & Willie Brenda Wilkinson	Harper & Row	J	Bantam	Realistic Fiction	F	16	181			Black
One Fat Summer Robert Lipsyte	Harper & Row	J	Bantam	Realistic Fiction	M	16	150			
Trial Valley Vera and Bill Cleaver	Lippincot	J	Bantam	Realistic Fiction	F	17	158			Rural Isolated
Winning Robin Brancato	Knopf	J	Bantam	Realistic Fiction	M	17	211			

1976

Title / Author	Publisher		Publisher	Genre	Sex	Age	Pages			Setting / Subject
Are You in the House Alone? Richard Peck	Viking	J	Dell	Realistic Fiction	F	16	156	•		
Dear Bill, Remember Me? Norma Fox Mazer	Delacorte	J	Dell	Realistic Short Stories	F	teenage	195			
The Distant Summer Sarah Patterson	Simon & Schuster	A	Archway	Historical Fiction Romance	F	16	153			World War II
Home Before Dark Sue Ellen Bridgers	Knopf	J	Bantam	Realistic Fiction	F	14	176			Migrant Workers
Never to Forget Milton Meltzer	Harper & Row	J	Dell	New Journalism			217			Jewish
Ordinary People Judith Guest	Viking	A	Ballantine	Realistic Fiction	M	17	263		•	

1975

Title / Author	Publisher		Publisher	Genre	Sex	Age	Pages			Setting / Subject
Dragonwings Laurence Yep	Harper & Row	J	Harper & Row	Historical Fiction	M	12	248			Chinese American
...eral Berton Roueche	Harper & Row	A	Avon	Horror Fiction	M/F	20s	137			
Is That You Miss Blue? M. E. Kerr	Harper & Row	J	Harper & Row	Realistic Fiction	F	14	170			
The Lion's Paw D. R. Sherman	Doubleday	A		Realistic Fiction	M	16	233			African Native
The Massacre at Fall Creek Jessamyn West	Harper & Row	A	Fawcett	Historical Fiction	M/F	adult, teen	373			1800s, Native American
Rumble Fish S. E. Hinton	Delacorte	J	Dell	Realistic Fiction	M	14	122			
Z for Zachariah Robert C. O'Brien	Atheneum	J	Macmillan	Science Fiction	F	16	249			Postnuclear

Title and Author	Hardbound Publisher	Publishing Division	Paperback Publisher	Genre	Protagonist Sex	Age	Number of Pages	Media Edition TV	Movie	Ethnic Group or Unusual Setting
1974										
The Chocolate War Robert Cormier	Pantheon	J	Dell	Realistic Fiction	M	14	253			
House of Stairs William Sleator	Dutton	J	Scholastic	Science Fiction	M/F	teens	166			
If Beale Street Could Talk James Baldwin	Dial	A	Dell	Realistic Fiction	F	19	197			Black
M. C. Higgins, the Great Virginia Hamilton	Macmillan	J	Macmillan	Realistic Fiction	M	13	278			Black
1973										
A Day No Pigs Would Die Robert Newton Peck	Knopf	J	Dell	Historical Fiction	M	13	159			1920s rural Vermont
The Friends Rosa Guy	Holt	J	Bantam	Realistic Fiction	F	14	203			West Indian, Black
A Hero Ain't Nothin' But a Sandwich Alice Childress	Coward, McCann	J	Avon	Realistic Fiction	M	13	126			Black
The Slave Dancer Paula Fox	Bradbury	J	Dell	Historical Fiction	M	13	176			1800s, Black
Summer of My German Soldier Bette Greene	Dial	J	Bantam	Historical Fiction	F	14	199	●		Southern U.S., Jewish

1972

Title / Author	Publisher		Imprint	Genre		Age	Pages			Topic
Deathwatch Robb White	Doubleday	J	Dell	Suspense Fiction	M	early 20s	228	•		
Dinky Hocker Shoots Smack! M. E. Kerr	Harper & Row	J	Dell	Humor Realistic Fiction	F	16	198	•		
Dove Robin L. Graham	Harper & Row	A	Bantam	Nonfiction	M	16	199			Ocean voyage
The Man Without a Face Isabelle Holland	Lippincott	J	Harper & Row	Realistic Fiction	M	16	248			
My Name is Asher Lev Chaim Potok	Knopf	A	Fawcett	Realistic Fiction	M	early 20s	369			Jewish
Soul Catcher Frank Herbert	Putnam	A	Berkley	Suspense Fiction	M	early 20s	250			Native American
Sticks and Stones Lynn Hall	Follett	J	Dell	Realistic Fiction	M	16	220			
Teacup Full of Roses Sharon Bell Mathis	Viking	J	Avon	Realistic Fiction	M	17	125			Black

1971

Title / Author	Publisher		Imprint	Genre		Age	Pages			Topic
The Autobiography of Miss Jane Pittman Ernest Gaines	Dial	A	Bantam	Historical Fiction	F	lifetime	245	•		Black
The Bell Jar Sylvia Plath	Harper & Row	A	Bantam	Realistic Fiction	F	19	296		•	
Go Ask Alice Anonymous	Prentice-Hall	J	Avon	Nonfiction	F	16	159	•		
His Own Where June Jordan	Crowell	J	Dell	Realistic Fiction	M/F	15	89			Black
Wild in the World John Donovan	Harper & Row	J	Avon	Realistic Fiction	M	17	94			Rural isolated

Title and Author	Hardbound Publisher	Publishing Division	Paperback Publisher	Genre	Sex Protagonist	Age	Number of Pages	Media Edition TV	Movie	Ethnic Group or Unusual Setting
1970										
Bless the Beasts and Children Glendon Swarthout	Doubleday	A	Pocket Books	Realistic Fiction	M	young teens	205		•	
I Know Why the Caged Bird Sings Maya Angelou	Random House	A	Bantam	Biography	F	childhood	281			Black
Love Story Erich Segal	Harper & Row	A	Avon	Realistic Fiction	M/F	early 20s	131		•	
Run Softly, Go Fast Barbara Wersba	Atheneum	J	Bantam	Realistic Fiction	M	19	169			
1969										
I'll Get There. It Better Be Worth the Trip John Donovan	Harper & Row	J		Realistic Fiction	M	13	189			
My Darling, My Hamburger Paul Zindel	Harper & Row	J	Bantam	Realistic Fiction	M/F	17/18	168			
Sounder William H. Armstrong	Harper & Row	J	Harper & Row	Historical Fiction	M	14	116		•	Rural black, 1930s
Where the Lilies Bloom Vera and Bill Cleaver	Lippincott	J	NAL	Realistic Fiction	F	14	174		•	Rural isolated

1968

Title / Author	Publisher	J/A		Genre	M/F	Age	Pages			Subject
The Pigman Paul Zindel	Harper & Row	J	Bantam	Realistic Fiction	M/F	16	182			
Red Sky at Morning Richard Bradford	Lippincott	A	WSP	Realistic Fiction	M	17	256	•		Mexican-American
Soul on Ice Eldridge Cleaver	McGraw-Hill	A	Dell	New Journalism	M	20s	210			Black

1967

Title / Author	Publisher	J/A		Genre	M/F	Age	Pages			Subject
The Chosen Chaim Potok	Simon & Schuster	A	Fawcett	Realistic Fiction	M	teen	284	•		Jewish
The Contender Robert Lipsyte	Harper & Row	J	Harper & Row	Realistic Fiction	M	17	167			Black
Mr. and Mrs. Bo Jo Jones Ann Head	Putnam	A	NAL Signet	Realistic Fiction	F	18	253		•	
The Outsiders S. E. Hinton	Viking	J	Dell	Realistic Fiction	M	14	156	•		
Reflections on a Gift of Watermelon Pickle Stephen Dunning and others	Scott, Foresman	J		Poetry	M/F	mixed	160			

APPENDIX B BOOK SELECTION
GUIDES

The sources listed below are designed to aid professionals in the selection and evaluation of books and other materials for young adults. An attempt was made to include sources with widely varying emphases. However, in addition to these sources—most of which appear at regular intervals—many specialized lists are prepared by committees and individuals in response to current and/or local needs. Readers are advised to check on the availability of such lists with librarians and teachers. For purposes of comparison, the 1988 prices are included, but readers should expect that many of them will have risen because of inflation.

The ALAN Review. Assembly on Literature for Adolescents, National Council of Teachers of English. Order from William Subick, NCTE, 1111 Kenyon Rd., Urbana, Il 61801. $15.00 for three issues.

This publication has appeared three times a year since 1973. It is currently edited by Arthea (Charlie) Reed of the University of North Carolina and is unique in being devoted entirely to adolescent literature. Each issue contains "Clip and File" reviews of approximately twenty new hardbacks or paperbacks and includes several feature articles, news announcements, and occasional reviews of professional books.

Book Bait: Detailed Notes on Adult Books Popular with Young People. Ed. Eleanor Walker. 4th ed., 1988. $12.95. American Library Association, 50 E. Huron Street, Chicago, IL 60611.

A useful bibliography for bridging the gap between young adult and adult novels, this listing contains one hundred books with extensive annotations that include plot summaries, discussions of appeal to teenagers, hints for booktalks, and suggested titles for use as follow-ups. Arrangement is alphabetical by author; subject and title indexes are appended.

Booklist. American Library Association, 50 E. Huron Street, Chicago, IL 60611. $51.00 for twenty-two issues.

The size of the reviews varies from twenty-word annotations to three hundred-word essays. "Books for Young Adults" (ages fourteen through eighteen) is a regular feature. Occasionally, books in both the children's and adult sections are also marked YA. A review constitutes a recommendation for library purchase. Stars are given to books of high literary quality. Multimedia materials are also reviewed and a special section highlights books that have both a high interest potential for teenagers and a lower-than-average reading level. An early spring issue includes the annual "Best Books for Young Adults" list drawn up by the ALA Young Adult Services Division.

Books for the Teen Age. Annual. Ed. Office of Young Adult Services. New York Public Library, Fifth Avenue and 42nd St., Room 58, New York, NY 10018. $5.00 per copy in person, $6.00 by mail.

This sixty-four-page guide with minimal annotations is updated yearly and is thus an outstanding source of current titles which have been "tested and tried with teenage readers." Grouping is by subject; titles and author indexes are included.

Books for You: A Booklist for Senior High School Students. Eds. Richard Abrahamson and Betty Carter, 1988. National Council of Teachers of English, 1111 Kenyon Rd., Urbana, IL 61801. $12.95 nonmembers, $9.95 members.

Nearly 1400 books are listed and described in this bibliography intended to help students find "pleasurable reading." Annotations consist of one- or two-sentence summaries. Titles are grouped by subject or theme; title and author indexes are appended. The book is prepared by an ongoing committee in NCTE with a new edition appearing every five years. Since all books in this edition appeared between the beginning of 1982 and 1985, the 1982 and 1976 editions of *Books for You* are worth holding onto for the information they have on earlier books.

Bulletin of the Center for Children's Books. Eds. Betsy Hearne, Roger Sutton, and Zena Sutherland. The University of Chicago Graduate Library School, University of Chicago Press, 5801 S. Ellis Ave., Chicago, IL 60637. $27.00 institutions, $24.00 individuals.

This monthly (except August) journal reviews approximately sixty new books for children and young adults each issue. Though there is a time lag between the publication date and the appearance of a review, the *Bulletin* includes both recommended and not recommended titles. The consistency of the reviews can be depended upon. An added feature is the inclusion of developmental values and curricular uses. The back cover lists books, articles, and bibliographies of current interest to teachers, parents, and librarians.

Children's Literature in Education: An International Quarterly. Agathon Press, Inc., 111 Eighth Ave., New York, NY 10011. Individuals, $18.00 per year, institutions, $35.00.

Directed by a United Kingdom Editorial Committee and a United States Editor (currently Anita Moss from the University of North Carolina at Charlotte) and Editorial Board, this quarterly journal is one of the best sources for scholarly criticism. The editors show a preference for substantive analysis rather than pedagogical advice or quick once-overs. A goodly proportion of the articles are about YA authors and their works.

English Journal. National Council of Teachers Of English, 1111 Kenyon Rd., Urbana, IL 61801. $35.00 for eight issues, which includes membership in NCTE.

Aimed at high school English teachers, nearly every issue contains something about new books of interest to teenage readers. Reviews, articles about young adult literature in the classroom, interviews with successful authors, and a yearly "Young Adult Book Poll" are among the regular features.

High Interest—Easy Reading: For Junior and Senior High School Students. Ed. Dorothy Matthews. Fifth Edition, 1988. National Council of Teachers of English, 1111 Kenyon Rd., Urbana, IL 61801. $6.25 nonmembers, $5.00 members.

Grouped by subject, this listing is aimed at reluctant young adult readers rather than at parents or teachers. Criteria for inclusion are high interest, easy reading, and literary quality. The annotations are written in the form of miniature book talks; author and title indexes are appended.

Horn Book Magazine. The Horn Book, Inc., Park Square Building, 31 St. James Avenue, Boston, MA 02116. $32.00 for six issues, $26.00 introductory offer for new subscribers.

This magazine has been devoted to the critical analysis of children's literature since 1924. Reviews are approximately two-hundred words long and in a typical issue seven or eight adolescent novels will be reviewed under the heading of "Stories for Older Readers." Popular appeal takes a back seat to literary quality in the selection of titles for review. Feature articles are frequently of interest to teachers and librarians working with young adults.

Interracial Books for Children Bulletin. Council on Interracial Books for Children, 1841 Broadway, Room 500, New York, NY 10023. Institutions $24.00, individuals $16.00 for eight issues.

Nearly all reviews and articles in this twenty-five page bulletin are written for the purpose of examining the relationship between social issues and how these are treated or reflected in current fiction, nonfiction, and curriculum materials.

Journal of Reading. International Reading Association, 800 Barksdale Rd., Box 8139, Newark, DE 19711-8139. $33.00 for eight issues, which includes membership in The International Reading Association.

The audience for this journal is high school reading teachers. Although most of the articles are reports on research in the teaching of reading, some articles focus on reading interests and literature. Also included are reviews of new young adult books.

Journal of Youth Services in Libraries (formerly *Top of the News*). Joint publication of the Association for Library Service to Children and the Young Adult Services Division of the American Library Association, 50 E. Huron Street,

Chicago, IL 60611. Included in the dues of ALSC and YASD members; non-members pay $30.00 for four issues.

Although the journal does not have room to review juvenile books on a regular basis, feature articles are often of interest to young adult librarians. Also of interest is the "Added Entries" column in which professional publications are reviewed.

Junior High School Library Catalog. Eds. Richard H. Isaacson and Gary L. Bogart. 5th ed. H. W. Wilson Company, 950 University Ave., Bronx, NY 10452. $80.00.

Designed as a suggested basic book collection for junior high school libraries, this volume is divided into two major parts. The first includes an annotated listing by Dewey Decimal Number for nonfiction, author's last name for fiction, and author's/editor's last name for story collections. The second part relists all books alphabetically by author, title, and subject. Cumulated every five years with yearly supplements, this is an outstanding reference tool for junior high school librarians.

Kirkus Reviews. Kirkus Service, Inc., 200 Park Avenue South, New York, NY 10003. $255.00.

Although this is one of the most expensive sources, it is also one of the most complete and up-to-date. Reviews are approximately two hundred words long, and a section is devoted to young adult books.

Kliatt Young Adult Paperback Book Guide. 425 Watertown St., Newton, MA 02158. $27.00 for three issues with five interim supplements.

Because teenagers prefer to read paperbacks, this source serves a real need. It attempts to review all paperbacks (originals, reprints, and reissues) recommended for readers ages twelve through nineteen. A code identifies books as appropriate for advanced students, general young adult readers, junior high students, students with low reading abilities, and emotionally mature readers who can handle "explicit sex, excessive violence and/or obscenity." Reviews are arranged by subject. A titles index and a directory of cooperating publishers are included.

New York Times Book Review. New York Times Company, 229 W. 43rd St., New York, NY 10036. 52 issues, $22.00.

The currency of the reviews makes this an especially valuable source. Most weeks there is a section featuring children's books, many of which are suitable for teenagers. Of special interest are a fall and spring issue devoted almost exclusively to children's books—the fall issue usually includes a roundup of the "best books" of the year.

School Library Journal. R. R. Bowker Company. 249 W. Seventeenth Street, New York, NY 10011. $56.00; subscriptions, P.O. Box 1978, Marion, OH 43305-1978.

The most comprehensive of the review media, SLJ reviews both recommended and not recommended books. Reviews are written by a panel of four hundred librarians who are sent books particularly appropriate to their interests and backgrounds. Starred reviews signify exceptionally good books. Books of interest to teenagers will appear in the children's listing identified by grade levels (5–up, 6–8, 9–12, etc.) if they come from the juvenile division of a publisher or in a special young adult listing if they come from the adult division of the publisher.

Senior High School Library Catalog. Eds. Ferne Hillegas and Juliette Yakkov, 13th ed. H. W. Wilson Company. 950 University Ave., Bronx, NY 10452. $96.00.

Using the same format as the *Junior High School Library Catalog* (see above), this lists some books appropriate for both junior and senior high school collections as well as those aimed specifically at readers in grades ten through twelve. Like its companion volume, it is cumulated every five years with yearly supplements and is an invaluable aid for anyone involved in the building of a high-school library collection.

Voice of Youth Advocates (VOYA). Scarecrow Press. P.O. Box 4167, Metuchen, NJ 08840. Editorial correspondence to Dorothy M. Broderick, 1226 Cresthaven Drive, Silver Spring, MD 20903. $27.00 for six issues.

One of the aims of this publication, founded in 1978, is "to change the traditional linking of young adult services with children's librarianship and shift the focus to its connection with adult services." Feature articles are especially good because they present viewpoints not commonly considered. About one-fourth of the journal is devoted to reviews in the following categories: pamphlets, mysteries, science fiction, audiovisual, adult and teenage fiction and nonfiction, and professional books.

Wilson Library Bulletin. H. W. Wilson Co. 950 University Avenue, Bronx, NY 19452. $38.00 for ten issues, expanding to eleven issues in 1989.

Although the focus of the *Wilson Library Bulletin* is much broader than young adult librarianship, "The Young Adult Perplex," edited by Cathi Edgerton, is a regular feature that reviews current books. Other columns of interest to YA teachers and librarians include "Front Row Center" edited by Judith Trojan, "SF Universe," edited by Don Sakers, and "Video Shopper" edited by Brad Carty.

Your Reading: A Booklist for Junior High and Middle School Students. Eds. James E. and Hazel K. Davis. 1989. National Council of Teachers of English, 1111 Kenyon Rd., Urbana, IL 61810. Price not set.

Approximately 2,000 books published since 1982 are described in this new edition compiled by the Committee on the Junior High and Middle School Booklist. The book is designed for student use, and the annotations are written to capture student interest. Categories of books range from adventure stories to the supernatural and include books about youngsters dealing with physical handicaps, emotional problems, and the death of a parent or friend. Nonfiction books include biography, fine arts, history, hobbies and crafts, sciences, and sports. Author and title indexes and a directory of publishers are provided.

APPENDIX C SOME OUTSTANDING BOOKS AND ARTICLES ABOUT YOUNG ADULT LITERATURE

Brief annotations are given for works where titles are not self-explanatory.

The list below represents our personal choices. We followed the ground rules of the first edition, and that may explain, if not justify, why some works were included or excluded.

1. Books or articles were primarily on young adult literature, not on the psychology of the young, cultural milieu, literary history, or literary criticism. If we had wanted to include the last, we'd have chosen Eudora Welty's *The Eye of the Story* and left it at that. Since we didn't, we won't.

2. Books or articles had to cover more than just one author. No matter how good the articles were on Virginia Hamilton or Alan Garner or Judy Blume (and some were very good indeed), we ignored them in favor of articles with wider implications.

3. Books or articles had to excite us. No doubt some readers will find us culpable for our tastes in including this or ignoring that. So be it.

4. No books or articles were included to fit into some category otherwise ignored. We make no claims that the list below is balanced to have the proper number of this or that kind of book or article, whether it would be on censorship or minority literature or feminist literature. We chose what we did because we believed in them.

5. No books or articles by Nilsen or Donelson appear below. Readers may continue to assume either that we believe none of our work belongs under the rubric "outstanding" or that we are modest to a fault.

BOOKS

Histories of Young Adult Literature

Avery, Gillian. *Childhood's Pattern: A Study of the Heroes and Heroines of Children's Fiction 1770–1950*. London: Hodder and Stoughton, 1975.

Bingham, Jane, and Grayce Scholt. *Fifteen Centuries of Children's Literature: An Annotated Chronology of British and American Works in Historical Context*. Westport, CT: Greenwood Press, 1980.

Cadogan, Mary, and Patricia Craig. *You're a Brick, Angela! A New Look at Girls' Fiction from 1839 to 1975*. London: Victor Gollancz, 1976. A delightful and witty view of girls' books and social history.

Campbell, Patricia J. *Sex Education Books for Young Adults, 1892–1979*. New York: R. R. Bowker, 1979. Accurate, critical, and often very funny.

Carter, Humphrey, and Mari Pritchard. *The Oxford Companion to Children's Literature*. New York: Oxford University Press, 1984.

Crouch, Marcus. *The Nesbit Tradition: The Children's Novel in England 1945–1970*. London: Ernest Benn, 1972.

_____ . *Treasure Seekers and Borrowers: Children's Books in Britain 1900–1960.* London: Library Association, 1962.

Darling, Richard. *The Rise of Children's Book Reviewing in America, 1965–1881.* New York: R. R. Bowker, 1968. Impressive and scholarly study of early children's and YA books, book reviewing, and reviewers.

Darton, F. J. Harvey. *Children's Books in England: Five Centuries of Social Use,* 2nd ed. Cambridge: Cambridge University Press, 1958. First published in 1932 and still a basic source.

Fraser, James H., ed. *Society and Children's Literature* (papers from the 1976 Simmons College School of Library Science Symposium). Boston: David R. Godine, 1978. Especially good are papers by Anne Scott MacLeod, R. Gordon Kelly, and Fred Erisman.

Girls' Series Books: A Checklist of Hardback Books Published 1900–1975. Minneapolis: Children's Literature Research Collections, University of Minnesota Library, 1978. Not as thorough as Hudson (see below) but most helpful in working with series books.

Hudson, Harry K. *A Bibliography of Hard-Cover Boys' Books,* rev. ed. Tampa, FL: Data Print, 1977. An outstanding checklist of boys' series books, mostly of this century.

Kensinger, Faye Riter. *Children of the Series and How They Grew, or A Century of Heroines and Heroes, Romantic, Comic, Moral.* Bowling Green, OH: Bowling Green State University Popular Press, 1987. Nothing profound but fun to browse through.

Kiefer, Monica. *American Children Through Their Books, 1700–1835.* Philadelphia: University of Pennsylvania Press, 1948.

MacLeod, Anne Scott. *A Moral Tale: Children's Fiction and American Culture, 1820–1860.* Hamden, CT: Archon Books, 1975.

Mason, Bobbie Ann. *The Girl Sleuth: A Feminist Guide.* Old Westbury, NY: Feminist Press, 1975. Perceptive and witty comments about girls' series books, especially Nancy Drew.

Meigs, Cornelia, et al. *A Critical History of Children's Literature,* rev. ed. New York: Macmillan, 1969. An encyclopedic study of children's literature, often including YA books, from ancient times onward.

Musgrave, P. W. *From Brown to Bunter: The Life and Death of the School Story.* London: Routledge & Kegan Paul, 1985.

Quigly, Isabel. *The Heirs of Tom Brown: The English School Story.* London: Chattot & Windus, 1982.

Sloane, William. *Children's Books in England and America in the Seventeenth Century.* New York: Columbia University Press, 1955.

Townsend, John Rowe. *Written for Children: An Outline of English-Language Children's Literature,* 3rd ed. Philadelphia: Lippincott, 1988. The most readable history, albeit more English than American.

Criticism of Young Adult Literature

Broderick, Dorothy M. *Images of the Black in Children's Fiction.* New York: R. R. Bowker, 1973. Racism and YA literature.

Chambers, Aidan. *Reluctant Reader.* London: Pergamon Press, 1969. One of the great books about YA literature. Sympathetic and helpful ideas about bringing books to the hard-to-get-to reader.

Children's Literature Review. Detroit: Gale Research Company, 1976. A continuing series and a basic source of material.

Contemporary Literary Criticism. Detroit: Gale Research Company, 1973. A continuing series with essential source material.

Dixon, Bob. *Catching Them Young: Political Ideas in Children's Fiction.* London: Pluto Press, 1977.

_____ . *Catching Them Young: Sex, Race and Class in Children's Fiction.* London: Pluto Press, 1977.

Egoff, Sheila A. *Thursday's Child: Trends and Patterns in Contemporary Children's Literature.* Chicago: American Library Association, 1981. The most important book in the field in the last fifteen years.

Harrison, Barbara, and Gregory Maguire, eds. *Innocence and Experience: Essays and Conversations on Children's Literature.* New York: Lothrop, Lee and Shepard, 1987. Materials from Simmons College Center programs.

Hazard, Paul. *Books, Children and Men.* Trans. Marguerite Mitchell. Boston: Horn Book, 1944. Nominally about children and literature but really about readers of any kind at any age with clear implications for young adults.

Hearne, Betsy, and Marilyn Kaye, eds. *Celebrating Children's Books: Essays on Children's Literature in Honor of Zena Sutherland.* New York: Lothrop, Lee and Shepard, 1981. Papers by Lloyd Alexander, Robert Cormier, Virginia Hamilton, John Donovan, John Rowe Townsend, David Macaulay, and others.

Inglis, Fred. *The Promise of Happiness: Value and Meaning in Children's Fiction.* Cambridge: Cambridge University Press, 1981.

Kohn, Rita, compiler. *Once Upon . . . a Time for Young People and Their Books: An Annotated Resource Guide.* Metuchen, NJ: Scarecrow Press, 1986.

Lukens, Rebecca. *A Critical Handbook of Children's Literature,* 3rd ed. Glenview, IL: Scott, Foresman, 1986. Criteria and aspects of children's literature easily applicable to YA literature.

MacCann, Donnarae, and Gloria Woodward, eds. *The Black American in Books for Children: Readings on Racism.* Metuchen, NJ: Scarecrow Press, 1972.

Salmon, Edward. *Juvenile Literature As It Is.* London: Henry J. Drane, 1888. Sympathetic and forward-looking views on the values of children's and YA literature. Undeservedly neglected.

Sloan, Glenna Davis. *The Child as Critic.* New York: Teachers College Press, 1975. Application of Northrop Frye's critical theories to children's and YA literature.

Stanford, Barbara Dodds, and Karima Amin, eds. *Black Literature for High School Students.* Urbana, IL: National Council of Teachers of English, 1978.

Stensland, Anna Lee. *Literature by and about the American Indian: An Annotated Bibliography,* 2nd ed. Urbana, IL: National Council of Teachers of English, 1979.

Sutherland, Zena, ed. *The Arbuthnot Lectures, 1970–1979.* Chicago: American Library Association, 1980. Talks by John Rowe Townsend, Ivan Southall, Jean Fritz, and Sheila Egoff, among others.

Tarbert, Gary C., and Barbara Beach, eds. *Children's Book Review Index: Master Cumulation 1965–1984,* five volumes. Detroit: Gale Research Company, 1985.

Libraries and Young Adult Literature

Bodart, Joni. *Booktalking and School Visiting for Young Adult Audiences.* New York: H. W. Wilson, 1980.

Edwards, Margaret A. *The Fair Garden and the Swarm of Beasts: The Library and the Young Adult,* rev. ed. New York: Hawthorn, 1974. The problems and joys of being a YA librarian.

Marshall, Margaret R. *Libraries and Literature for Teenagers.* London: Andre Deutsch, 1975.

Rochman, Hazel. *Tales of Love and Terror: Booktalking the Classics, Old and New.* Chicago: American Library Association, 1987.

English Classrooms and Young Adult Literature

Burton, Dwight L. *Literature Study in the High Schools,* 3rd ed. New York: Holt, 1970. For many teachers, the book that introduced them to YA literature.

Carlsen, G. Robert. *Books and the Teen-Age Reader,* 2nd ed. New York: Harper & Row, 1980.

Corcoran, Bill, and Emrys Evans, eds. *Readers, Texts, Teachers.* Upper Montclair, NJ: Boynton/Cook, 1987. A fine collection of pedagogical material on literature.

Fader, Daniel. *The New Hooked on Books.* New York: Berkley, 1976. First published in 1966 as *Hooked on Books* and revised in 1968, Fader's book probably led more English teachers to take YA books seriously than any other source.

Probst, Robert E. *Response and Analysis: Teaching Literature in Junior and Senior High School.* Portsmouth, NH: Boynton/Cook, Heinemann, 1988. Far and away, the best book in its field.

Sample, Hazel. *Pitfalls for Readers of Fiction.* Chicago: National Council of Teachers of English, 1940. Too little known, unfortunately, since it has many insights into reading popular fiction and the dangers thereof.

"Young Adult Literature," entire issue of the November 1984 *English Journal.* Especially good for articles by G. Robert Carlsen, Don Gallo, Ellen Kolba, and Janice Hartwick Dressel.

Authors of Young Adult Literature

Cech, John, ed. *American Writers for Children, 1900–1960. Dictionary of Literary Biography,* Volume Twenty-Two. Detroit: Gale Research Company, 1933.

Commire, Anne, ed. *Something About the Author.* Detroit: Gale Research Company, 1971. A continuing series about many authors, their lives and their books. An indispensable source of help.

——— . *Yesterday's Authors of Books for Children.* Detroit: Gale Research Company, 1977. Authors who died prior to 1961. Extremely useful.

Estes, Glenn E., ed. *American Writers for Children before 1900. Dictionary of Literature Biography,* Volume Forty-Two. Detroit: Gale Research Company, 1985.

——— . *American Writers for Children since 1960: Fiction. Dictionary of Literary Biography,* Volume Fifty-Two. Detroit: Gale Research Company, 1986.

Haviland, Virginia, ed. *The Openhearted Audience: Ten Authors Talk About Writing for Children.* Washington, DC: Library of Congress, 1980. Talks by Joan Aiken, Ivan Southall, Virginia Hamilton, and others.

Helbig, Alethea K., and Agnes Regan Perkins. *Dictionary of American Children's Fiction, 1859–1959.* Westport, CT: Greenwood Press, 1985.

——— . *Dictionary of American Children's Fiction, 1960–1984.* Westport, CT: Greenwood Press, 1986.

Jones, Cornelia, and Olivia R. Way. *British Children's Authors: Interviews at Home.* Chicago: American Library Association, 1976. Interviews with Nina Bawden, Alan Garner, Allan Campbell McLean, K. M. Peyton, Rosemary Sutcliff, Barbara Willard, and others.

Kirkpatrick, D. L. ed. *Twentieth-Century Children's Writers,* 2nd ed. New York: St. Martin's Press, 1983. A mammoth (1507-page) index of authors listing biographical and bibliographical details along with critical assessments.

Rees, David. *The Marble in the Water: Essays on Contemporary Writers of Fiction for Children and Young Adults.* Boston: Horn Book, 1980. Essays on Penelope Farmer, Alan Garner, Ursula Le Guin, Mildred Taylor, and others.

Robinski, Jim. *Behind the Covers: Interviews with Authors and Illustrators of Books for Children and Young Adults.* Littleton, CO: Libraries Unlimited, 1980. Interviews with Avi, Patricia Lee Gauch, William Sleator, Todd Strasser, and others.

Sarkissian, Adele, ed. *Writers for Young Adults: Biographies Master Index.* Detroit: Gale Research Company, 1984. A handy help in locating information about YA authors.

Townsend, John Rowe. *A Sense of Story: Essays on Contemporary Writers for Children.* Philadelphia: Lippincott, 1971. Essays on John Christopher, Paula Fox, Leon Garfield, Scott O'Dell, K. M. Peyton, Patricia Wrightson, and others.

Weiss, M. Jerry, ed. *From Writers to Students: The Pleasures and Pains of Writing.* Newark,

DE: International Reading Association, 1979. Interviews with Judy Blume, Vera and Bill Cleaver, Mollie Hunter, M. E. Kerr, Norma and Harry Mazer, Laurence Yep, and others.

Wintle, Justin, and Emma Fisher, eds. *The Pied Pipers: Interviews with the Influential Creators of Children's Literature.* New York: Paddington Press, 1974. Interviews with Scott O'Dell, Leon Garfield, Judy Blume, Lloyd Alexander, Alan Garner, K. M. Peyton, and others.

Books of Readings About Young Adult Literature

Egoff, Sheila, G. T. Stubbs, and L. F. Ashley, eds. *Only Connect: Readings in Children's Literature,* 2nd ed. New York: Oxford University Press, 1980. Significant articles by Edward W. Rosenheim, John Rowe Townsend, Donnarae MacCann, C. S. Lewis, Rosemary Sutcliff, and others.

Fox, Geoff, et al., eds. *Writers, Critics, and Children: Articles from Children's Literature in Education.* New York: Agathon Press, 1976. Articles from an important journal by Nina Bawden, Peter Dickinson, Myles McDowell, Edward Blishen, and others.

Haviland, Virginia, ed. *Children and Literature: Views and Reviews.* Glenview, IL: Scott, Foresman, 1973. Articles by Hester Burton, Frank Eyre, Peter Dickinson, Sylvia Engdahl, and others.

Salway, Lance, ed. *A Peculiar Gift: Nineteenth Century Writings on Books for Children.* London: Kestrel, 1976. Articles and excerpts from books about children's and YA British literature from authors such as Edward Salmon and Joseph Conrad.

Varlejs, Jana, ed. *Young Adult Literature in the Seventies: A Selection of Readings.* Metuchen, NJ: Scarecrow Press, 1978. Articles by G. Robert Carlsen, Dorothy Broderick, Mary Chelton, Linda Lapides, Lou Willett Stanek, and others.

▌ PERIODICALS

History and Young Adult Literature

Ashford, Richard K. "Tomboys and Saints: Girls' Stories of the late Nineteenth Century." *School Library Journal* 26 (January 1980): 23–38.

Cantwell, Robert. "A Sneering Laugh with the Bases Loaded." *Sports Illustrated* 16 (April 23, 1962): 67–70, 73–76. Baseball novels for boys—especially novels by Barbour and Heyliger.

Carlsen, G. Robert. "Forty Years with Books and Teen-Age Readers." *Arizona English Bulletin* 18 (April 1976): 1–5. From 1939 to 1976 in YA literature.

Crandall, John C. "Patriotism and Humanitarian Reform in Children's Literature, 1825–1860." *American Quarterly* 21 (Spring 1969): 3–22. An excellent overview of children's and YA books and periodicals before Alcott.

Edwards, Margaret A. "The Rise of Teen-Age Reading." *Saturday Review of Literature* 37 (November 13, 1954): 88–89, 95. The state of YA literature in the 1930s and 1940s and what it led to.

Evans, Walter. "The All-American Boys: A Study of Boys' Sports Fiction." *Journal of Popular Culture* 6 (Summer 1972): 104–21. Formulas underlying boys' school sports books, notably Barbour and series books.

"For It Was Indeed He." *Fortune* 9 (April 1934): 86–89, 193–94, 204, 206, 208–9. An important, influential, and biased article on Stratemeyer's Literary Syndicate.

Geller, Evelyn. "The Librarian as Censor." *Library Journal* 101 (June 1, 1976): 1255–58. Social control as censorship in late nineteenth-century library selection.

_____ . "Tom Sawyer, Tom Bailey, and the Bad-Boy Genre." *Wilson Library Bulletin* 52 (November 1976): 245–50.

Hutchinson, Margaret. "Fifty Years of Young Adult Reading, 1921–1971." *Top of the News* 29 (November 1973): 24–53. A "survey (of) the field of young adult reading for the last fifty years by examining articles indexed in *Library Literature* from its inception in 1921." Admirable.

Kelly, R. Gordon. "American Children's Literature: An Historiographical Review." *American Literary Realism, 1870–1910* 6 (Spring 1973): 89–107.

Lapides, Linda F. "A Decade of Teen-Age Reading in Baltimore, 1960–1970." *Top of the News* 27 (April 1971): 278–91. YA favorites over ten years.

Morrison, Lillian, "Fifty Years of 'Books for the Teen Age.' " *School Library Journal* 26 (December 1979): 44–50.

Radner, Rebecca. "You're Being Paged Loudly in the Kitchen: Teen-Age Literature of the Forties and Fifties." *Journal of Popular Culture* 11 (Spring 1978): 789–99. Ways in which Maureen Daly and other YA novelists of the 1940s influenced young women, not always for the best.

Repplier, Agnes. "Little Pharisees in Fiction." *Scribner's Magazine* 20 (December 1896): 718–24. Assessment of the didactic and joyless tone of the "goody-goody" school of fiction.

Trensky, Anne. "The Bad Boy in Nineteenth-Century American Fiction." *Georgia Review* 27 (Winter 1973): 503–17.

Vostrovsky, Clara. "A Study of Children's Reading Tastes." *Pedagogical Seminary* 6 (December 1899): 523–35. A pioneer effort at a statistical account of the kinds of books young people read.

Criticism and Young Adult Literature

Abrahamson, Jane. "Still Playing It Safe: Restricted Realism in Teen Novels." *School Library Journal* 22 (May 1976): 38–39.

Brewbaker, James M. "Are You There, Margaret? It's Me, God—Religious Contexts in Recent Adolescent Fiction." *English Journal* 72 (September 1983): 82–86.

Campbell, Patty. "Perplexing Young Adult Books: A Retrospective." *Wilson Library Bulletin* 62 (April 1988): 20, 22, 24, 26. Campbell looks back on ten years of her column on YA books.

Carlsen, G. Robert. "For Everything There Is a Season." *Top of the News* 21 (January 1965): 103–10. Stages in reading growth and reading tastes.

_____ . "The Interest Rate Is Rising." *English Journal* 59 (May 1970): 655–59. YA literature, the nature of literature, and the reality of YA readers.

Early, Margaret J. "Stages of Growth in Literary Appreciaiton." *English Journal* 49 (March 1960): 161–67. A seminal article.

Edwards, Margaret A. "A Time When It's Best to Read and Let Read." *Wilson Library Bulletin* 35 (September 1960): 43–47. Myths of buying books for young adults demolished.

Engdahl, Sylvia. "Do Teenage Novels Fill a Need?" *English Journal* 64, (February 1975): 48–52. Justification and criteria for the best YA novels.

Evans, Dilys. "The YA Cover Story." *Publishers Weekly* 232 (July 24, 1987): 112–15. Differences between hardcover and paperback covers.

Gauch, Patricia Lee. " 'Good Stuff' in Adolescent Fiction." *Top of the News* 40 (Winter 1984): 125–29.

Green, Samuel S. "Sensational Fiction in Public Libraries." *Library Journal* 4 (September-October 1879): 345–55. All the usual warnings about dime novels and other sensational fiction coupled with some extraordinary forward-looking and intelligent comments about young adults and books. The entire issue for September-October is worth reading, especially for T. W. Higginson's "Address," pp. 357–59, William P. Atkinson's "Address," pp. 359–62, and Mellen Chamberlain's "Address," pp. 362–66.

Hanckel, Frances, and John Cunningham. "Can Young Gays Find Happiness in YA Books?" *Wilson Library Bulletin* 50 (March 1976): 528–34. An argument for more authenticity and less preachiness in YA books about gays.

Hentoff, Nat. "Fiction for Teen-Agers." *Wilson Library Bulletin* 43 (November 1968): 261–64. Worries about the shortcomings of YA fiction.

_____ . "Tell It as Is." *New York Times Book Review,* May 7, 1967, pp. 3, 51.

Hinton, Susan. "Teen-Agers Are for Real." *New York Times Book Review,* August 27, 1967, pp. 26–29. Brief and excellent.

Hipps, G. Melvin. "Adolescent Literature: Once More to the Defense." *Virginia English Bulletin* 23 (Spring 1973): 44–50. One of the most intelligent arguments for YA books.

Janeczko, Paul B. "Seven Myths About Adolescent Literature." *Arizona English Bulletin* 18 (April 1976): 11–12.

Kraus, W. Keith. "Cinderella in Trouble: Still Dreaming and Losing." *School Library Journal* 21 (January 1975): 18–22. Pregnancy in YA novels from Felsen's *Two and the Town* (1952) to Neufeld's *For All the Wrong Reasons* (1973).

_____ . "From Steppin' Stebbins to Soul Brothers: Racial Strife in Adolescent Literature." *Arizona English Bulletin* 18 (April 1976): 154–60.

Martinec, Barbara. "Popular—But Not Just a Part of the Crowd: Implications of Formula Fiction for Teenagers." *English Journal* 60 (March 1971): 339–44. Formulaic elements in six YA novelists. Provocative.

Matthews, Dorothy. "An Adolescent's Glimpse of the Faces of Eve: A Study of the Images of Women in Selected Popular Junior Novels." *Illinois English Bulletin* 60 (May 1973): 1–14.

_____ . "Writing About Adolescent Literature: Current Approaches and Future Directions." *Arizona English Bulletin* 18 (April 1976): 216–19.

McDowell, Myles. "Fiction for Children and Adults: Some Essential Differences." *Children's Literature in Education* 4 (March 1973): 48–63.

Meltzer, Milton. "Where Do All the Prizes Go? The Case for Nonfiction." *Horn Book Magazine* 52 (February 1976): 17–23.

Merla, Patrick. " 'What Is Real?' Asked the Rabbit One Day." *Saturday Review* 55 (November 4, 1972): 43–49. The rise of YA realism and adult fantasy.

Mertz, Maia Pank, and David A. England. "The Legitimacy of American Adolescent Fiction." *School Library Journal* 30 (October 1983): 119–23.

Neufeld, John. "The Thought, Not Necessarily the Deed: Sex in Some of Today's Juvenile Novels." *Wilson Library Bulletin* 46 (October 1971): 147–52. Urges that YA novels need the "whole kid," sex, warts, and dirty jokes as well as naivete and freedom.

Peck, Richard. "In the Country of Teenage Fiction." *American Libraries* 4 (April 1973): 204–7. Concerns about YA needs and YA books.

_____ . "Some Thoughts on Adolescent Literature." *News from ALAN* 3 (September-October 1975): 4–7. The "discernible traits" of YA novels.

Peck, Richard, and Patsy H. Perritt. "British Publishers Enter the Young Adult Age." *Journal of Youth Services in Libraries* 1 (Spring 1988): 292–304. A helpful survey of British publishers' use of YA books, particularly those from American authors.

Pollack, Pamela D. "The Business of Popularity: The Surge of Teenage Paperbacks." *School Library Journal* 28 (November 1981): 25–28. Changes in paperback practices, especially the development of YA romances.

Popkin, Zelda F. "The Finer Things in Life." *Harpers* 164 (April 1932): 602–11. The contrast between what young adults like to read and what parents and other adults want them to read.

"Romance Series for Young Readers: A Report to Educators and Parents in Concert with the National Education Association." *Interracial Books for Children Bulletin* 12 (Nos. 4 & 5, 1981): 4–31. Hard-sell comments that teenage romances are sexist trash.

Root, Sheldon L. "The New Realism—Some Personal Reflections." *Language Arts* 54 (January 1977): 19–24. What the new realism brought to children's and YA books and the criteria by which it needs to be evaluated.

Ross, Catherine Sheldrick. "Young Adult Realism: Conventions, Narrators, and Readers." *Library Quarterly* 55 (April 1985): 174–191.

Silver, Linda R. "Criticism, Reviewing, and the Library Review Media." *Top of the News* 35 (Winter 1979): 123–30. On reviewing YA books. The entire issue is excellent, especially Rosemary Weber's "The Reviewing of Children's and Young Adult Books in 1977," pp. 121–27; Melvin H. Rosenberg's "Thinking Poor: The Nonlibrary Review Media," pp. 138–42; "What Makes a Good Review? Ten Experts Speak," pp. 146–52; and Patty Campbell's "Only Puddings Like the Kiss of Death: Reviewing the YA Book," pp. 161–62.

Stanek, Lou Willett. "Adults and Adolescents: Ambivalence and Ambiguity." *School Library Journal* 20 (February 1974): 21–25. Comments on the "innocent youth" myth; analyzes several YA novels.

_____ . "The Junior Novel: A Stylistic Study." *Elementary English* 51 (October 1974): 947–53. A pioneer study of YA novels.

_____ . "The Maturation of the Junior Novel: From Gestation to the Pill." *School Library Journal* 19 (December 1972): 34–39. Fiction formulas and the YA novel on pregnancy.

Sutton, Roger. "The Critical Myth: Realistic YA novels." *School Library Journal* 29 (November 1982): 33–35.

Townsend, John Rowe. "Didacticism in Modern Dress." *Horn Book Magazine* 43 (April 1967): 159–64. Argues that nineteenth-century didacticism is remarkably like the didacticism in modern YA novels. A fine article.

_____ . "Standards of Criticism for Children's Literature." *Top of the News* 27 (June 1971): 373–87.

Unsworth, Robert. "Holden Caulfield, Where Are You?" *School Library Journal* 23 (January 1977): 40–41. A plea for more books about males by males.

Wigutoff, Sharon. "Junior Fiction: A Feminist Critique." *The Lion and the Unicorn* 5 (1981): 4–18.

Using Young Adult Literature in Classrooms and Libraries

Chelton, Mary K. "Booktalking: You Can Do It." *School Library Journal* 22 (April 1976): 39–43. A rationale for and some ways to give booktalks.

Hipps, G. Melvin. "Adolescent Literature and Values Clarification: A Warning." *Wisconsin English Journal* 20 (January 1978): 5–9.

Mearns, Hughes. "Bo Peep, Old Woman, and Slow Mandy: Being Three Theories of Reading." *New Republic* 48 (November 10, 1926): 344–46. Witty and profound.

Nelms, Ben F. "Reading for Pleasure in Junior High School." *English Journal* 55 (September 1966): 676–81.

Peck, Richard. "Ten Questions to Ask about a Novel." *ALAN Newsletter* 5 (Spring 1978): 1, 7.

Probst, Robert E. "Adolescent Literature and the English Curriculum." *English Journal* 76 (March 1987): 26–30.

_____ . "Three Relationships in the Teaching of Literature." *English Journal* 75 (January 1986): 60–68.

Scharf, Peter. "Moral Development and Literature for Adolescents." *Top of the News* 33 (Winter 1977): 131–36. Application of Lawrence Kohlberg's six stages of moral judgment to YA books.

Scoggin, Margaret C. "Do Young People Want Books?" *Wilson Bulletin for Librarians* 11 (September 1936): 17–20, 24.

Shontz, Marilyn Louise. "Selected Research Related to Children's and Young Adult Services in Public Libraries." *Top of the News* 38 (Winter 1982): 125–42. Contains an excellent list of sources.

Small, Robert C., Jr. "The Junior Novel and the Art of Literature." *English Journal* 66 (October 1977): 56–59. Using YA novels to teach aspects of the art of the novel.

————. "Teaching the Junior Novel." *English Journal* 61 (February 1972): 222–29.

Thurber, Samuel. "Voluntary Reading in the Classical High School from the Pupil's Point of View." *School Review* 13 (February 1905): 168–79. A marvelous modern article, no matter what the date, from the best writer and thinker of the time on teaching English. Anything by Thurber is worth reading.

ACKNOWLEDGMENTS

(p. 24) From an interview with Leon Garfield by Justin Wintle from *The Pied Pipers: Interviews with the Influential Creators of Children's Literature* by Justin Wintle and Emma Fisher. Copyright © 1973 and 1974 by Justin Wintle. Reprinted by permission of Paddington Press Ltd.

(p. 43) From "Finally Only the Love of the Art" by Donald Hall, *The New York Times Book Review,* January 16, 1983. Copyright © 1983 by the New York Times Company. Reprinted by permission.

(p. 57) From "Newbery Award Speech" by Katherine Paterson, *Horn Book Magazine,* August 1981. Reprinted by permission of the author.

(p. 65) From an introduction to *Lord of the Flies* by E. M. Forster. Copyright © 1962 by Coward-McCann, Inc. Reprinted by permission of the Putnam Publishing Group.

(p. 73) From "Sentimental Education" by Harold Brodkey. Reprinted by permission of International Creative Management. First published in *The New Yorker.* Copyright © 1958 by Harold Brodkey.

(p. 82) From "Bait/Rebait: Literature Isn't Supposed to Be Realistic" by G. Robert Carlsen from *English Journal,* January 1981, Vol. 70. Copyright © 1981 by National Council of Teachers of English.

(p. 92) Reprinted by permission of the American Library Association from Sheila Egoff, "Beyond the Garden Wall" (May Hill Arbuthnot Honor Lecture) *Top of the News* 35(3): 264 (Spring 1979); Copyright © 1979 by the American Library Association.

(p. 110) "Some Thoughts on the Black YA Novel," by Al Muller from ALAN Newsletter, Assembly on Literature for Adolescents— NCTE, Vol. 5, No. 2, Winter 1978. Reprinted by permission.

(p. 117) From review by Jean Fritz of "Up in Seth's Room" by Norma Fox Mazer from *The New York Times Book Review,* January 20, 1980. Copyright © 1980 by The New York Times Company. Reprinted by permission.

(pp. 136, 137) From "Bait" by Dean Hughes; from "Rebait" by Kathy Piehl from *English Journal,* December 1981, Vol. 70, No. 8. Copyright © 1981 by National Council of Teachers of English. Reprinted by permission of National Council of Teachers of English.

(p. 137) Abridgment of excerpt from "The Young Adult Perplex" by Patty Campbell, *Wilson Library Bulletin,* April 1982, Vol. 56, No. 8, p. 612. Copyright © 1982 by the H. W. Wilson Company. Reprinted by permission.

(p. 139) From "Holden Caulfield, Where Are You?" by Robert Unsworth. Reprinted with permission from *School Library Journal,* January 1977. Copyright © 1977 by R. R. Bowker Co./A Xerox Corporation.

(p. 139) From "Bringing Boys' Books Home" by Hazel Rochman. Reprinted with permission from *School Library Journal,* August 1983. Copyright © 1983 R. R. Bowker Co./A Xerox Corporation.

(p. 142) From "The Business of Popularity: The Surge of Teenage Paperbacks" by Pamela D. Pollack. Reprinted with permission from *School Library Journal,* November 1981. Copyright © 1981 by R. R. Bowker Co./A Xerox Corporation.

(p. 201) From introduction to *Profiles of the Future* by Arthur C. Clarke. Copyright © 1984 by Arthur C. Clarke. Reprinted by permission of Henry Holt and Co., Inc. and Scott Meredith Literary Agency, Inc.

(p. 203) From "Ray Guns and Rocket Ships" by Robert A. Heinlein, *The Library Journal,* July 1953, Vol. 78, No. 13. Copyright 1953 by Cahners Publishing Company. Reprinted by permission.

(p. 205) From "Runaround" by Isaac Asimov. Copyright 1942 by Street & Smith Publications, Inc. Copyright © 1970 by Isaac Asimov. Reprinted by permission of the author.

(p. 258) From "Where Do All the Prizes Go?" by Milton Meltzer, *The Horn Book Magazine,* February 1976, pp. 17, 19. Reprinted by permission of The Horn Book, Inc., Boston, MA.

(p. 273) "Turning Off: The Abuse of Drug Information" by Peter G. Hammond. Reprinted with permission from *School Library Journal,* April 1973. R. R. Bowker Co./A Xerox Corporation.

(p. 292) "Separation" from *The Moving Target* by W. S. Merwin. Copyright © 1963 by W. S. Merwin. Reprinted with permission of Atheneum Publishers, an imprint of Macmillan Publishing Company.

(p. 294) "The Portrait" from *The Poems of Stanley Kunitz* by Stanley Kunitz. Copyright © 1971 by Stanley Kunitz. Reprinted by permission of Little, Brown and Company.

(p. 294) From Comments by Stanley Kunitz on his poem "The Portrait." Reprinted by permission of Stanley Kunitz.

(p. 295) From "Among Iron Fragments" by Tuvia Ruebner, translated from the Hebrew by Robert Friend. Reprinted by permission of Robert Friend.

(p. 299) From "Ouchless Poetry" by Don Mainprize from *English Journal,* February 1982, Vol. 71, No. 2. Reprinted by permission of the National Council of Teachers of English.

(p. 299–300) From "Teaching Poetry Writing in Secondary School" by Alberta Turner from *English Journal,* September 1982, Vol. 71. Reprinted by permission of the National Council of Teachers of English.

PHOTO AND ILLUSTRATION CREDITS

The authors and publisher would like to thank Harper & Row, Publishers, Inc., for the use of their illustrative material.

(p. 12)   William Bond

(p. 25)   Pamela Older

(p. 42)   © Tom Victor

(p. 67)   From *El Bronx Remembered* by Nicholasa Mohr. Jacket art by Nicholasa Mohr. Reprinted by permission of Harper & Row, Publishers. From *In Nueva York* by Nicholasa Mohr. Copyright © 1977 by Nicholasa Mohr. Jacket art by Leo and Diane Dillon. Reprinted by permission of The Dial Press.

(p. 74)   Wendy Gavin Gregg

(p. 140)   Sarah Krauskopf

(p. 171)   Cover from *The Strange Affair of Adelaide Harris* by Leon Garfield. Copyright © 1971 by Leon Garfield. Illustrated by Fritz Wegner; illustrations copyright © 1971 by Longman Young Books. Reprinted by permission of Pantheon Books, a division of Random House, Inc.   Cover of *The Eagle of the Ninth* by Rosemary Sutcliff. Copyright 1954 by Oxford University Press, London. Reprinted by permission of Oxford University Press, London.

(p. 190)   David Stemple

(p. 194)   Map from *The Stone and the Flute* by Hans Bemmann, translated by Anthea Bell. First published in German under the title *Stein und Floete* by K. Thienemanns Verlag. Translation copyright © 1986 by Anthea Bell. Reprinted by permission of Penguin Books Ltd.

(p. 221)   From *Roll of Thunder, Hear My Cry* by Mildred D. Taylor. Copyright © 1976 by Mildred D. Taylor. Jacket art and design by Jerry Pinkney.   From *Let the Circle Be Unbroken* by Mildred D. Taylor. Copyright © 1981 by Mildred D. Taylor. Jacket painting and design by Wendell Minor. Reprinted by permission of The Dial Press.

(p. 259)   Catherine Noren

(p. 277)   Cover from *Changing Bodies, Changing Lives* by Ruth Bell et al. Copyright © 1980 by Ruth Bell. Photographs by John Launois/Black Star, Peter Vadnai/Editorial Photocolor Archives, and Dan Nelkin. Jacket design by Richard Adelson. Reprinted by permission of Random House, Inc.

(p. 291)   Jacket cover from *Postcard Poems* edited by Paul B. Janeczko (cover photo by Robert Verrone) used by permission of Bradbury Press, an affiliate of Macmillan, Inc. (Bradbury Press, 1979).

(p. 323)   From *Motel of the Mysteries* by David Macaulay. Copyright © 1979 by David Macaulay. Reprinted by permission of Houghton Mifflin Company.

(p. 346)   Courtesy of Mesa, Arizona, Public Library

(p. 370)   Jill Paton Walsh

(p. 389)   David S. Strickler/The Picture Cube

(p. 395)   Jay McManus

(p. 408)   Pryde Brown

(p. 447)   Anon Rupo

(p. 454)   Cover from *The First Freedom* by Nat Hentoff. Copyright © 1980 by Namar Productions, Ltd. Jacket design copyright © 1980 by Mike Stromberg. Reprinted by permission of Delacorte Press, a division of Bantam, Doubleday, Dell Publishing Group, Inc.   Cover from *Dealing with Censorship* edited by James E. David. Reprinted by permission of the National Council of Teachers of English.   Cover from *The Students' Right to Read*. Reprinted by permission of the National Council of Teachers of English.   Cover from *The Students' Right to Know* by Lee Burress and Edward B. Jenkinson. Reprinted by permission of the National Council of Teachers of English.   Cover from *Censors in the Classroom* by Edward B. Jenkinson. Copyright © 1979 by Southern Illinois University Press. Reprinted by permission of Southern Illinois University Press.

(p. 473)   ASU Media Production. All Rights Reserved.

(p. 483)   Cover from *Grandmother Elsie* and *Elsie's Widowhood* by Martha Finley. Copyright 1910 by Charles Finley.

(p. 486)   ASU Media Production. All Rights Reserved.

(p. 510)   Cover from *Ruth Fielding: Clearing Her Name* by Alice B. Emerson, 1928. Reprinted by permission of Simon & Schuster, Inc.   Cover from *Tom Swift and His Motorcycle* by Victor Appleton, 1910. Reprinted by permission of Simon & Schuster, Inc.   Cover illustration by Russell H. Tandy reprinted by permission of Grosset & Dunlap, Inc., from *The Clue in the Diary*, A Nancy Drew Mystery by Carolyn Keene, copyright 1932 by Grosset & Dunlap, Inc., copyright renewed © 1960 by Harriet S. Adams and Edna C. Squier.

(p. 524)   Cover from *Bright Island* by Mabel L. Robinson. Reprinted by permission of Random House, Inc.

(p. 542)   From *Shuttered Windows* by Florence Crannell Means. Copyright 1938 by Florence Crannell Means. Copyright © renewed 1966 by Florence Crannell Means. Reprinted by permission of Houghton Mifflin Company.   From *The Moved-Outers* by Florence Crannell Means. Copyright 1945 by Florence Crannell Means. Copyright © renewed 1972 by Florence Crannell Means. Reprinted by permission of Houghton Mifflin Company.

(p. 547)   From *A Love, or a Season* by Mary Stolz. Copyright © 1954, 1964 by Mary Stolz. Reprinted by permission of Harper & Row, Publishers.   From *The Limit of Love* by James L. Summers. Copyright © 1959 by James L. Summers. Reprinted by permission of The Westminster Press.

SUBJECT INDEX

CRITICS AND COMMENTATORS

AUTHOR AND TITLE INDEX